Marriage and Family Development

MARRIAGE AND FAMILY DEVELOPMENT

Sixth Edition

EVELYN MILLIS DUVALL

BRENT C. MILLER

1817

HARPER & ROW, PUBLISHERS, New York

Cambridge, Philadelphia, San Francisco

London, Mexico City, São Paulo, Singapore, Sydney

Sponsoring Editor: Alan McClare
Project Editor: Nora Helfgott
Cover Photo: Dunn, DPI
Text Art: Vantage Art, Inc.
Illustrations: Noel Malsberg
Production: Jeanie Berke
Compositor: ComCom Division of Haddon Craftsmen, Inc.
Printer and Binder: R. R. Donnelley & Sons Company

Marriage and Family Development, Sixth Edition
Copyright © 1985 by Harper & Row, Publishers, Inc.

Library of Congress Cataloging in Publication Data

Duvall, Evelyn Ruth Millis, 1906–
  Marriage and family development.

  Includes bibliographies and index.
  1. Family. 2. Family—United States. I. Miller,
Brent C. II. Title.
HQ734.D9593 1985   306.8   84-4528
ISBN 0-06-041826-5

89 9 8 7 6 5 4

Contents

Illustrations

Tables

Preface

Because so much has happened in marriage and family life since the fifth edition appeared in 1977, this edition is new from beginning to end. In this edition current census data, some of them as yet unpublished, bring demographic profiles of American marriages and families into sharp focus. For these otherwise unattainable figures and many other kindnesses, we are grateful to a friend of many years, Dr. Paul C. Glick, who was with the Population Division of the U.S. Bureau of the Census until his retirement in mid-1981. In addition to recent census data, our revision is based on family studies reported in professional journals; academic, popular, and governmental publications; national polls of college students and adults; changing marriage and family laws and policies affecting families; and occasional case study excerpts.

The conceptual framework of earlier editions is fine-focused to present developmental tasks of individual family members and to examine basic family developmental tasks stage by stage throughout the entire family life cycle. This conceptual framework is enriched with the addition of two new chapters—one dealing with individual growth in the ability to love and the other exploring the development of heterosexual relationships that lead to marital commitment.

Transitions throughout the family life cycle are considered anew: couples marry; most become parents; their children grow through infancy, through preschool and school ages, and through adolescence and are launched into lives of their own as they leave home for college, for work, for military service, or for households of their own; middle-aged parents become grandparents, then aging couples as they live out their lives as family members until death separates them in the final transition.

New are fresh insights into pregnancy and childbearing; early infant- and child-parent interaction; contemporary adolescent life-styles, pressures, and challenges; living together before marriage; the many interlocking facets of divorce, remarriage, stepparenthood, and co-parenthood; research-based descriptions of America's minority families; the cultures of poverty and of affluence; and death in the family context.

Numerous tables bring together findings of many studies on a particular topic, sometimes contradictory and sometimes consistent, for easy access by teachers and students to relevant data. In a given area of study, bases for understanding both convergence and divergence of research findings are suggested. Figures highlight textual material, often putting trends into sharp focus, and graphically present pertinent information. All sources are keyed in the text to specific references for each chapter.

As coauthor of this edition, the senior author chose Brent C. Miller, chairman of the Research and Theory Section of the National Council on Family Relations and active teacher of family relations at the university level. His many commitments made it impossible for him to write as much of the text as we had hoped, but he reorganized the first six chapters and carefully reviewed Chapters 7 through 17 for which Evelyn Duvall assumes major responsibility.

The coauthors acknowledge their common debt to Dr. Reuben Hill, who for years has guided their professional growth and continues to stimulate their thinking in family development theory, its research potentials, and its many unsolved problems that challenge us, our colleagues, and—we hope—our students.

Evelyn Millis Duvall
Brent C. Miller

PART ONE

FAMILY DEVELOPMENT: BASIC CONCEPTS

Chapter 1

Understanding Marriages and Families Today

MAJOR CONCEPTS

Value and importance of marriage and
    family life
Reasons for formal marriage and family
    study
Marriage
Family
Family of orientation
Family of procreation
Nuclear family
Extended family

Functions of families
Family life in the past
Family household
Nonfamily household
Conceptual frameworks or perspectives
    Structure-functional
    Symbolic-interactional
    Systems
    Exchange
    Family developmental

In recent years marriage and family life have received both harsh and favorable commentary. Some have emphasized the decline, decay, and demise of the kind of marriages and families familiar to most of us. However, there is also a resurgence of the point of view that the family is a *Haven in a Heartless World* (Lasch 1977) and that it is *Here to Stay* (Bane 1976). There is no question that marriage and family patterns have changed dramatically, but their persistence, adaptability, and importance to individuals are perhaps all the more remarkable.

THE IMPORTANCE OF MARRIAGE AND FAMILY LIFE

Regardless of how marriage and the family are considered institutionally as elements of society, the issues and experiences they encompass are personal, private concerns for most people. Virtually all of us know marriages and families firsthand. The large majority of us grew up in families, and over 90 percent of adults in the United States marry at some time in their lives. These are not incidental or trivial experiences—they are highly salient. When asked about various aspects of their lives, Americans say that family life brings them greater feelings of satisfaction than any other dimension of life (Andrews & Withey 1976; Campbell, Converse, & Rodgers 1976). Based on a nationally representative sample, one author wrote: "The evidence is consistent and substantial: married people see their lives more positively than unmarried people. Despite the fact that attitudes toward marriage are changing in this country, especially among young people, the marriage pattern continues to contribute something uniquely important to the feelings of well-being of the average man and woman" (Campbell 1981, 226–227).

Marriage and family experiences will continue to be important in the future, judging from nationwide interviews of high school seniors. These surveys, conducted annually since 1976 by scientists at the University of Michigan, find large majorities of young men and women looking forward to marriage and parenthood. "When it comes to plans or expectations about marriage and family, most seniors are squarely in the mainstream of traditional values" (ISR Newsletter, 1981).

Several of the most highly acclaimed recent Hollywood movies—perhaps reflecting national sentiments—focus powerfully on marriage and family issues such as finding closeness and love *(Goodbye Girl),* experiencing divorce and single parenthood *(Kramer vs.*

Kramer), coping with tragedy and stresses in family life *(Ordinary People),* and dealing with aging partners and parents *(On Golden Pond).*

WHY STUDY MARRIAGE AND FAMILY LIFE?

Some people believe that they have, almost intuitively, an accurate grasp of what marriage and family life are all about. If so, is there any need for studying these issues? We obviously think so. Personal marriage and family experiences are not likely to provide one with a very representative viewpoint. Although our own experiences may be extremely important to us, they form a mental set that influences our view of what marriage and family life are like for others. In the previous edition of this text, 10 reasons were listed in response to the question of why marriage and family study are needed:

1. To provide a broader view of family life than that afforded by experience in any one family;
2. To correct the fallacies and distortions that persist about marriages and families;
3. To focus on the normal aspects of family life rather than the unusual or atypical often sensationalized by the news media;
4. To scrutinize objectively what "everyone knows," which is sometimes inaccurate;
5. To recognize the family as the hub of society around which other institutions and groups revolve;
6. To learn more about the contribution of family life to human development;
7. To update the changes in marriage and families resulting from their adaptation to changing social conditions;
8. To foresee predictable problems and potentials in families as they change in form and function over the years;
9. To establish reliable bases for making individual and family decisions about matters that occur and recur throughout the life span; and
10. To adopt valid plans and policies for future family situations in a given home, community, or nation.

These 10 specific reasons for family study remain valid today. In a somewhat more general sense, though, it seems appropriate to summarize that objective studies of marriage and family life can have both personal and professional payoffs. After a systematic study of marriage and family patterns, students should have an enhanced understanding of their own life experiences. For those who work with families professionally, knowing about marriages and families in a scientific sense provides the basis for assisting them more intelligently.

This then is a book about marriages and families. It is especially focused on families in North America, but within this context it is not limited to any particular family or type of family. It is a book about understanding marriages and families, about how they are similar and different, and especially about how they change, predictably, with the passage of time.

DEFINITIONS OF MARRIAGE AND FAMILY

Although laypersons often do not distinguish between marriage and family life, it is important to make marriage and family concepts as clear as possible. In most cases that you are familiar with, marriage is *monogamous,* the dyadic or pair relationship between one man and one woman. There are, however, cultures in which *polygamy* is acceptable or preferred; a man may have more than one wife *(polygyny),* or in a few cultures a woman can have more than one husband *(polyandry).* Given these variations, perhaps *marriage* can be most accurately defined as the socially recognized relationship between a man and woman that provides for sexual relations, legitimizes childbearing, and establishes a division of labor between spouses. Each of these defining elements is briefly elaborated below.

Marriage is *social* in the sense that it is publicly recognized and regulated by civil or religious authorities in virtually every culture. In order to be married in the United States, for example, a license must be obtained, an authorized officiator and witnesses need to be present, and so on. By definition, marriage is not something that couples do by themselves. Marriage is also *heterosexual;* although same-sex couples have had wedding ceremonies performed, as yet they have not been legally recognized. Many couples have sexual relations before or outside of marriage, but marriage is still the relationship in which *sexual relations* are normative—both accepted and expected to occur. Marriage *legitimates childbearing* in the sense that societies attempt to identify both parents of a child and usually hold them responsible for the child's welfare. Although illegitimacy, or nonmarital fertility, is increasingly common and appears to be losing some of its stigma, some couples still feel the pressure to marry because of pregnancy. Marriage establishes a *division of labor* most obviously in cultures where the roles of husbands and wives are clearly delineated and differentiated. In these societies, spouses simply enter into and perform previously established traditional roles. In more contemporary societies, spouses still establish some division of labor within and outside of the home, even though how tasks will be divided might not be as apparent for them ahead of time.

Whereas *marriage* refers to the relationship between spouses, families arise, in a sense, out of marriage. The term *family* usually connotes children and blood relations in contrast to the marital or conjugal ties formed legally through marriage.

Everyone "knows" what a family is, but few can define the term in ways acceptable to others. Social scientists study families from many angles and define them by describing the many forms, functions, and conditions of family life in contemporary society. We agree that "the family" is an elusive concept, defying definition, because it encompasses so many variant forms and meanings. Because of the astonishing variety of families there are, scholars hesitate to define a "typical" family. In spite of these cautions and caveats, there are many important concepts that define aspects of family life that are useful to understand.

Among the most basic conceptions of family is the distinction made between the *family of orientation,* in which one was a child, and the *family of procreation,* in which one becomes a parent. Most people have experiences with both of these overlapping families, and a major part of life, especially affective and intimate relations, occurs in these contexts. Figure 1.1 illustrates these basic types of families.

It is common to hear people speak casually of nuclear or extended families. A *nuclear family* consists of parent(s) and child(ren). This most elemental or nuclear family unit includes members of two (parent and child) generations. A married couple with several children, a single mother with dependent children, or a couple with one child would all be considered nuclear families. Some people would argue that both parents must be present in order to constitute a nuclear family, but this seems to be more an aspect of the concept of the *traditional* nuclear family rather than the elemental or nuclear parent-child unit.

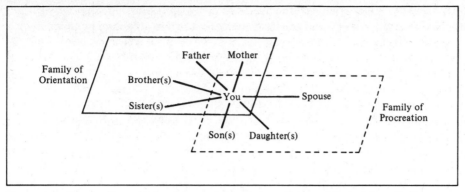

Figure 1.1 The families of orientation and procreation. *Source:* Adapted from G. R. Leslie, *The Family in Social Context,* 5th ed. (New York: Oxford University Press, 1982).

By contrast, *extended families* include relatives in addition to the nuclear unit of parent(s) and child(ren), such as grandparents or grandchildren (vertical extensions to three or more generations) or adult siblings (lateral extensions including uncles and aunts or nieces and nephews within the same two generations). Individual families can be identified as nuclear or extended according to these definitions, but families sometimes change from one to the other, particularly in times of ill health or economic difficulties when families are more likely to move in together or to help care for extended family members. At a different level the concepts of nuclear and extended families are useful in comparing societal or subcultural variations. For example, Chinese or Japanese families living in the United States are two to three times as likely to be vertically extended (having aged parents living with them) as are those of Irish or German descent.

But how do we define just a *regular family?* A dated but frequently quoted definition is:

> The family is a group of persons united by ties of marriage, blood, or adoption; constituting a single household; interacting and communicating with each other in their respective social roles of husband and wife, mother and father, son and daughter, brother and sister; and creating and maintaining a common culture. (Burgess & Locke 1953, 7–8)

These authors were obviously describing the nuclear family because they did not attempt to include extended kinfolk in their definition. And, as was common at the time, their definition focused on families including two parents and children of both sexes.

A more recent definition, written by 17-year-old Future Family Leaders, is much broader. They defined *family* as

> a unit of people, usually related, usually living together at least part of their lives, working together to satisfy their necessities and relating to each other to fulfill their wants. A family does not have to exist within the confines of the traditional legal concepts of marriage and parenthood, but every family has one or two adults who accept the responsibilities of parenthood and children who receive the guidance of the parents. The family is a small social unit consisting usually of husband, wife, and children, but sometimes excluding one of these members, or including other relatives,

even nonrelated friends. The only real qualification for belonging to a family is a willingness to love and to try to understand its other members, to stand by them in times of stress and also in times of happiness. The family is the unit which gives the individual his strongest sense of community, and which, more than any other institution, lends stability and security to his life. (McCormack 1974)

This definition might be faulted for being too inclusive. For example, the assertion that "the only real qualification for belonging to a family is a willingness to love and to try to understand its other members" applies equally well (and sometimes better) to close friends who are not family members. There are also, unfortunately, families in which family members would not pass the "only real qualification" to love, understand, and stand by one another.

Perhaps the simplest and most straightforward definition is provided by the U.S. Census Bureau. According to their definition, a family is a group of two or more persons who are related by blood, marriage, or adoption and residing together. The last defining element here, that they "reside together" is important for purposes of census enumeration and reporting, but there are many situations and times in life when family members do not live in the same household. Reduced to its barest essentials, a family is a group of people who are related to each other by blood or legal ties. Almost always they live together for at least part of their lives, and they usually perform the functions for which families are so highly valued. But what families do—the functions they perform—is another issue to which we next direct our attention.

FUNCTIONS OF MODERN FAMILIES

Many functions formerly performed within or by families are now shared with or provided by others. The production, preparation, and preservation of food are now Big Business. The education and religious training of children are now, to a large extent, entrusted to schools and churches. Protective services are provided by police and fire departments. Medical care is provided by doctors, nurses, and teams of technicians. What functions are left for the family to perform? What, indeed, but the most important of all—those that contribute to producing human beings capable of living competently in a world that their ancestors never knew. Contemporary families fulfill at least six important functions:

1. *Generating affection* between husband and wife, between parents and children, and among members of the generations. Love is a product of family living. Men and women in Western societies usually marry for love and usually have children as an expression of their love for one another. Their children need to have love in an emotional climate of ongoing affection in order to thrive. The family in North America stays together through the years not because it has to, but because the members want to, out of enduring affection for one another. Ideally, both parents and children grow in a climate of mutual affection that contributes to their healthy development.

2. *Providing personal security and acceptance.* Most people look to the family for the security and acceptance they need to live lives of dignity and worth. Within the family, individuals can make mistakes and learn from them in an atmosphere of protective security. The family is one of the few remaining places where complemen-

tary rather than competitive relationships can be fostered and enjoyed. Thus the family provides a home base with stability that allows its members to develop naturally—in their own way, at their own pace.

3. *Giving satisfaction and a sense of purpose.* The family gives human beings a sense of basic satisfaction and worth that the world of work only occasionally provides. An unskilled laborer may derive only minimal satisfaction from a job, and the person in more challenging work may find it fraught with anxiety, conflict, and struggle. It is in the family setting that adults and children enjoy life and each other —in family gatherings and celebrations, around the family table, in family rituals, on family trips, and in many other activities that family members find satisfying. Parents often feel that they live for one another and for the children for whom they are responsible.

4. *Ensuring continuity of companionship.* Perhaps only within the family group can this need be met today. Friends, neighbors, colleagues, and others may or may not remain close by for more than a few years. Jobs change, neighborhoods shift, and people move on. In most cases family associations alone can be expected to endure. In ways not expected outside the family, the continuing presence of sympathetic companions encourages family members to relate the happenings of the day and to share the disappointments and satisfactions of life as they occur. Who but members of one's own family can delight so fully in the flush of success or share so completely the burden of failure?

5. *Providing social placement and socialization.* In every society individuals learn what is expected of them and where they fit in the social hierarchy through their families. At birth a child automatically acquires his family's status by virtue of the genetic, physical, ethnic, national, religious, cultural, economic, political, and educational heritage unique to his parents and their kin. The family acts as the transmitter of the cultural heritage from one generation to the next. It performs the task of interpreting to its members the meaning of the many situations of which they are a part. Older family members serve as role models for the younger ones.

> It is also generally recognized that lifelong patterns of behavior, values, goals, and attitudes of children are strongly associated with the characteristics of their parents, especially as these are expressed in childbearing and family life styles. Although later experiences outside the home also have important influences on the developing child, the availability of these experiences to him and the ways in which he uses them are strongly affected by what he has learned in his home. (Chilman 1966, 2)

6. *Inculcating controls and a sense of what is right.* Within the family individual members first learn the rules, rights, obligations, and responsibilities characteristic of human societies. Family members feel free to criticize, to correct and to order, to praise or to blame, to reward or to punish, to entice or to threaten each other in ways that would be unthinkable elsewhere. "In all these ways, the family is an instrument or agent of the larger society; its failure to perform adequately means that the goals of the larger society may not be attained effectively" (Goode 1964, 5). The kinds of praise and punishment experienced by children in their earliest years instill in them the sense of right and wrong that they will carry into adulthood in their moral values and in their definitions of the good, the right, and the worthy.

The family, functioning as a "choosing agency," evaluates and selects from among many ways of life—and so is a primary source of human values that spread outward into society as a whole.

THE PAST: FICTION AND FACT

It is helpful to have an understanding of the past in order to understand contemporary marriage and family patterns. Americans tend to hold a cherished but erroneous view of marriage and family life in earlier times, what Goode (1956) has called the "classical family of western nostalgia." The popular conception holds that in the same house lived mom and dad, their six or seven children, an aging grandparent, and maybe a cousin, uncle, or aunt. The lives of these extended family members supposedly were intertwined in duties and relationships close to hearth and home, embodying a fond memory of what family life was like in the good old days before life became so hectic and complex. Even contemporary authors (e.g., Toffler & Toffler 1981) who write about families often boldly describe historical changes from extended to nuclear families, and from nuclear families to diverse life-styles.

Only in recent years have scholars refined the conceptual and methodological tools to gather hard evidence about families in former times. Computer technology and increasing interest in the lives of common people have helped to bring about a clearer understanding of the family in history. Some of the most notable findings have come from the work of French demographers, led by Louis Henry, who have systematized a method of community-wide *family reconstitution,* the linking together of vital family events (births, marriages, deaths) through parish registers and other documents (Wrigley & Schofield 1981). Other influential writings have come from England in the Cambridge group's studies of household and family composition (Laslett 1971). Coupled with the work of American family historians (Hareven 1977; Seward 1978), these developments have resulted in the rapid growth of the new field of family history, the emergence in 1976 of the *Journal of Family History,* and marriage and family textbooks with a historical perspective (Gordon 1978).

Not surprisingly, historical evidence does document that families were once considerably larger than they are now. In 1700 the average mother had borne 7.4 children by age 45. By 1910 the number had shrunk to 4.7; by 1940, to 2.9; and by 1960, to 2.7. Through the 1970s and into the 1980s women are bearing children at somewhat less than replacement levels (Westoff 1978). Lodgers, servants, and other nonfamily members were also more common in earlier households, which averaged about six persons in 1790 as compared with just under three per household currently (Kobrin 1976).

Contrary to popular opinion, however, contemporary scholars are quite certain that the majority of European (Laslett 1971) and American (Seward 1978) families were rarely extended to include nonnuclear relatives. In most countries studied, the incidence of extended families has remained almost constant over the last several centuries. It is difficult, if not impossible, to determine what differences in family sentiments there might have been then as compared with now. But it is accurate to say that before the twentieth-century families were larger, although not substantially more extended, than they are today. Although extended family kin usually did not live in the same residence, they probably did live physically nearer and might have been more closely involved in everyday associations. Given the convenience of modern telephones, mail service, and ease of travel, we really do not know if contemporary families are "in touch" with extended relatives more or less often now than in the past.

BRIEF DEMOGRAPHIC PROFILE OF THE UNITED STATES

The U.S. Census Bureau enumerates the occupants of each household at the beginning of each decade. Although people usually think of families as the residential living units that are contacted by census takers, single individuals and unrelated people living together are also counted as nonfamily households. Families make up a majority of households in the United States, but nonfamily households are increasing.

Between the years 1970 and 1981 the population of the United States grew from about 205 million to 229 million, an increase of about 12 percent (Population Reference Bureau 1982). During these same years, however, the total number of households increased 30 percent, from 63.4 million to 82.4 million. In other words, the number of households grew more rapidly than the population did during the 1970s. This more rapid increase in the number of households is partly attributed to young people leaving their parents' homes at earlier ages; to more divorces, which usually result in additional households; and to increased longevity of the elderly who maintain their own homes.

Figure 1.2 shows that in 1970, 51.4 million of the total 63.4 million households in the United States were family types (81 percent); of these, 44.7 million were maintained by married couples, and 6.7 million were maintained by a man or woman with no spouse present. By 1981, 60.3 million of the United States' total 82.4 million households were families (73 percent). Female-headed family households increased from 5.5 million to 9.3 million between 1970 and 1981. The bottom of Figure 1.2 also shows that the number of nonfamily households increased by 10.1 million between 1970 and 1981.

The demographic data just reviewed show a decline in the proportion of all households that are family households. They also reveal a decline in the proportion of family households headed by married couples who live together. Unmarried couples living together made up 3.5 percent of all couple households in 1981, and the actual number of such couples tripled between 1970 and 1981 (Population Reference Bureau 1982). In spite of these changes and dire predictions about the demise of family life, the great majority of all children under 18 still live with two parents. The proportion of dependent children who live with both parents was 77 percent in 1980 (down from 88 percent in 1960), whereas the proportion of children living in single-parent homes rose from 9 to 20 percent between 1960 and 1980. Although approximately three-quarters of young children currently live with two parents, Norton and Glick (1979) have predicted that 45 percent of children born in recent years are likely to spend some time in a single-parent home if current trends continue.

FAMILY DEVELOPMENT AND ALTERNATIVE PERSPECTIVES

Family study, as presented in this book, is an ongoing activity of the several behavioral and social sciences. Table 1.1 lists 15 of the sciences and disciplines conducting research on one or more aspects of family life. The illustrative studies listed are a sampling of the kinds of studies undertaken in these areas (see pp. 13–14).

Families can be studied from many points of view, and, obviously, each provides or emphasizes a somewhat different aspect of the reality to be found in family contexts. Each of these vantage points has its own basic assumptions, concepts, and methods of study. The specialized concepts of the different disciplines and perspectives provide, as it were, a variety of lenses through which marriage and family phenomena can be viewed. Each group of related concepts, or conceptual framework, focuses attention on a particular facet of family

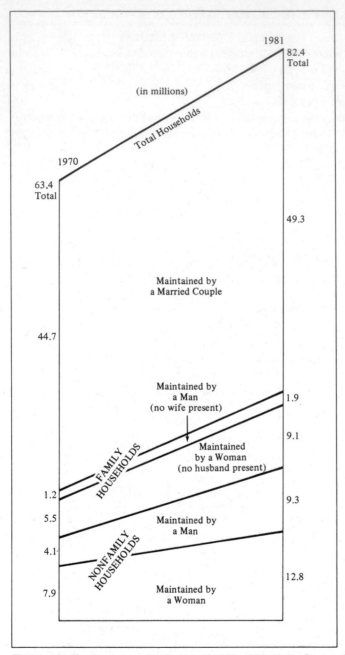

Figure 1.2 Family and nonfamily households, 1970–1981. *Source:* Population Reference Bureau, "U.S. Population: Where We Are and Where We're Going," *Population Bulletin* 37, no. 2 (1982).

Table 1.1 BEHAVIORAL SCIENCES AND DISCIPLINES INVOLVED IN FAMILY STUDY

Disciplines	Illustrative studies
Anthropology Cultural anthropology Social anthropology Ethnology	Cultural and subcultural family forms and functions Ethnic, racial, and social status family differences Families in primitive, developing, and industrial societies
Counseling and therapy Counseling theory Clinical practice Evaluation	Dynamics of interpersonal relationships in marriage and family Methods and results of individual, marriage, and family counseling
Demography	Census and vital statistics on many facets of family life Cross-sectional, longitudinal, and record-linkage surveys Fertility, family planning, and population control
Economics	Consumer behavior, marketing, and motivation research Insurance, pensions, and welfare needs Standards of living, wage scales, socioeconomic status Mate selection and children as market decisions
Education Early childhood Early elementary Secondary College Parent Professional	Child-rearing methods Developmental patterns Family life education Motivation and learning Preparation for marriage Sex education
History	Origins of family patterns Family reconstitution Social influences on the family Social trends and adaptations
Home economics Family relationships Home economics education Home management Nutrition	Evaluation of family practices Family food habits and nutrition Home management practices Relationships between family members
Human development Child development Adolescent development Middle age and aging	Child growth and development Developmental norms and differences Nature of cognitive learning Cross-cultural variations Personality development Social roles of aging
Law	Adoption and child protection Child care and welfare Marriage and family law Divorce and marital dissolution Sexual controls and behavior Parental rights and responsibilities

Table 1.1   *(Continued)*

Disciplines	Illustrative studies
Psychoanalysis	Abnormal and normal behavior
	Clinical diagnosis and therapy
	Foundations of personality
	Stages of development
	Treatment of mental illness

Psychology
    Clinical
    Developmental
    Social
	Aspirations and self-concepts
	Drives, needs, and hungers
	Dynamics of interpersonal interaction
	Learning theory
	Mental health
	Therapeutic intervention

Public health	Epidemiology and immunization
	Family health and preventive medicine
	Maternal and infant health
	Pediatric health education
	Venereal disease
Religion	Church policies on marriage and family
	Families of various religions
	Interfaith marriage
	Love, sex, marriage, divorce, and family in religious contexts

Social work
    Family casework
    Group work
    Social welfare
	Appraising family need
	Devising constructive programs for family assistance
	Measuring family functioning

Sociology	Courtship and mate selection
	Family formation and functioning
	Effects of social change on families
	Family crises and dissolution
	Prediction of family success
	Social class influence on families

life. Over the years various conceptual frameworks have been highlighted in family studies.

Hill and Hansen (1960) authored an influential article that highlighted the following as the five major conceptual approaches in family studies: (1) symbolic-interactional, (2) structure-functional, (3) situational, (4) institutional, and (5) developmental. Although Nye and Berardo's (1966) monograph included any perspective that might be remotely useful to family studies, literature surveys in the late 1960s and early 1970s (Cerny, Dahl, Kamiko, & Aldous 1974; Klein, Calvert, Garland, & Poloma 1969) found that the symbolic-interactional, structure-functional, and developmental frameworks stood out as the most utilized by American family scholars. In reviewing the previous decade, Broderick (1971) suggested that the symbolic-interactional framework had been most productive of research and that the structure-functional approach had most stimulated theory papers, whereas the developmental approach had contributed some of both.

With these findings as background, Klein, Schvaneveldt, and Miller (1977) surveyed over 100 family theorists to find out which conceptual frameworks would be acknowledged as guiding them in their work. When asked if they thought in terms of conceptual frameworks, 82 of the respondents said yes, 4 said sometimes, and 10 said no. As found in the literature reviews, the symbolic-interactional, structure-functional, and developmental frameworks stood out as being most identified with and used by the family theorists surveyed. However, the systems and exchange perspectives were frequently written in by the family theorists as approaches that they thought were increasingly important in their own work and to the field as a whole. In the most recent analyses of conceptual frameworks in the field, symbolic-interactional, exchange, and systems perspectives appear to be the most highly used (Burr, Hill, Nye, & Reiss 1979; Holman & Burr 1980; Klein, Schvaneveldt, & Miller 1977), although the family developmental perspective continues to attract the attention of theorists (Hill & Mattessich 1979) and researchers (Nock 1981). Two of the older and two of the newer conceptual approaches, respectively, used in family studies are contrasted with family development below.

1. The *structure-functional* approach, deriving from anthropology and sociology, has long been used in family studies. It views the family as a social system within society, interacting with other social systems like the school or functioning in small groups such as the husband-wife dyad. This approach copes especially well with the relationship of the family with other institutions in society and with what the family contributes to the larger society as a whole. It does not deal, however, with changes over time.

2. The *symbolic-interactional* approach to family studies has also been around for a long time. It has been used at the microlevel of interaction between individuals. The central theme of symbolic-interaction is that the best way to understand people and their relations is to deal with the meanings and values that they hold in their minds, because these motivate their behavior most directly. Actions, behaviors, objects, and so on become symbols or acquire shared meaning in the interaction between individuals, and family interaction is best understood in this context.

3. The *exchange approach* has not been widely employed in family studies until recently (Nye 1978, 1979), but it is currently popular among family scholars. The most important concepts in this approach are rewards, costs, and profits and a normative context of reciprocity and equity. Some authors see the exchange perspective as being essentially a theory about choices: people make choices so as to reduce their costs and maximize rewards and profits. Although Nye (1979) indicates that in a more generic sense the exchange approach is useful at both individual and institutional levels, its primary use in family studies so far seems to have been at interpersonal levels of analysis.

4. *Systems perspectives* are widely used across various disciplines in engineering and the natural and social sciences. Systems emphasize sets of objects, their relations, and their boundaries. The elements in a system are interdependent, and the system as a whole experiences inputs and outputs and responds to feedback with control

regulation. Family systems have been studied by Kantor and Lehr (1975) and overviewed by Broderick and Smith (1979).

5. The *family development approach* combines the concepts, insights, and methods of a number of disciplines. From rural sociology comes the generational sweep of the family life cycle. From human development study comes awareness of developmental tasks, of critical periods of development, and of the teachable moment. From sociology come the ideas of social change, social class, and the cultural influences that shape and are shaped by families. From psychology are borrowed the contributions of learning theory and interaction processes. From home economics are taken the themes of child development and family relationships, home management, housing, and family practices.

QUALITIES OF FAMILY DEVELOPMENT STUDY

Family development follows the orderly sequential changes in growth, development, and dissolution or decline throughout the entire family life cycle. Family development sees family life cycles overlapping one another in intergenerational interaction in predictable ways throughout the full life span. Simply summarized, family development study:

1. Keeps the family in focus throughout its history,
2. Sees each family member in interaction with all other members,
3. Observes the ways in which individuals and the family unit influence one another,
4. Recognizes what a given family is going through at any particular time,
5. Highlights critical periods of personal and family growth and development,
6. Views both the universals and the variations among families,
7. Appreciates the ways in which the culture and families influence each other, and
8. Provides a basis for forecasting what a given family will be going through at any period in its life span.

Ways of anticipating what to expect are inherent in family development. Of course, one can never be certain because each family differs in many ways from every other. But, generally, you can predict some important things about the overall pattern of a family's activities if you know these three things: (1) where the family is in time (in history, year, season, day, and hour) and in its life cycle; (2) the number, age, and relatedness of the family members in the household; and (3) how the family is viewed in the community, as seen in its ethnic, religious, and social class status. When you know these three things before you meet a given family, you know what significant elements to look for and what forces you may expect to find in action within the family and its members.

Growing Edges of Family Development

Family development study has not yet achieved a full theoretical base thoroughly tested by research. Functioning best in longitudinal research (Hill 1964), it encounters a number of problems that smaller, shorter-term, cross-sectional studies do not have. Data from families over their entire life spans are hard to gather, largely because families outlive the research team, as well as its commitment, its financing, and its authority to continue. Keeping in touch with the same families over many months and years is made difficult by changes in their residence, configurations, and interest in the project over a considerable period of time. Ingenious ways to circumvent these research problems are being devised as the family development approach is explored. Still lacking to date, however, are adequate cross-cultural and subcultural studies in family development.

While studying normal, intact families, the family development approach may lose track of families with problems such as premature dissolution, divorce, remarriage, single parenthood, stepparents, and the many combinations of "his children, her children, and their children," herein discussed explicitly in Chapters 7 through 15 inclusive.

No one knows better than those who use the family development approach the many problems it presents. Nevertheless, interest in this way of seeing and studying families has been growing ever since it was first designed in preparation for the first National Conference on Family Life in Washington, D.C., in 1948 (Duvall and Hill 1948). Its scope and content are increased through accretions of research data coming out of child development centers, human development programs, and family study centers in major universities across the United States.

SUMMARY

In spite of earlier doomsday predictions to the contrary, marriage and family life are popular, important, and valued in contemporary society. Nationwide surveys of adults in the United States find that a good marriage and family are considered to be among the most important aspects of life. Interviews about the future with high school students suggest that this will continue to be the case.

Marriage refers to the socially recognized heterosexual relationship that legitimizes childbearing and establishes a division of labor. *Family* means a group of two or more individuals who are related to each other by blood, marriage, or adoption and usually live together. Almost universally children grow up in families of orientation and form families of procreation when they become adults. Nuclear families include parent(s) and child (ren); families can be extended vertically to include three or more generations or laterally to include additional relatives within the same two generations. Contemporary families serve many functions, but their primary roles are affective and interpersonal. Although conceptions of large extended families in the past are highly romanticized and often inaccurate, the evidence suggests that nuclear families have almost always been the predominant form.

There are alternative ways of viewing marriage and family life. Conceptual frameworks or perspectives focus on and accentuate different aspects of marriage and family experiences. Structure-functional and symbolic-interactional frameworks are older but still popular ways of viewing marriage and family behavior. Structure-function focuses on what families do (their functions) in societies and how families are affected by their structural characteristics. Symbolic-interaction, at a more microinterpersonal level, stresses the importance of shared symbols to convey meaning between individuals. Systems and exchange perspectives are both newer to family studies. The systems approach stresses the boundaries of family relationship and the interdependence of family members. The exchange perspective emphasizes reciprocity and equity in exchanges between family members. The family developmental approach, which is used throughout this text, highlights normative changes in families over time. Some of the important concepts that will be included are the family life cycle, stages and sequences of development, developmental tasks, and critical role transitions.

There are both personal and professional gains to be expected from studying marriage and family life. Gaining a better understanding of one's own life as well as obtaining practical knowledge about changes in marriages and families over time are likely benefits.

So this is a text about family development—how families typically change over time. In the next two chapters foundations are laid for the family developmental approach by explaining the central concepts of the family life cycle and developmental tasks.

REFERENCES

Andrews, F. M., & Withey, S. B. 1976. *Social indicators of well-being.* New York: Plenum.

Bane, M. J. 1976. *Here to stay: American families in the twentieth century.* New York: Basic.

Broderick, C. B. 1971. Beyond the five conceptual frameworks: A decade of development in family theory. *Journal of Marriage and the Family* 33:139–159.

Broderick, C. B., & Smith, J. 1979. The general systems approach to the family. In *Contemporary theories about the family,* ed. W. R. Burr, et al. Vol. 2. New York: Free Press.

Burgess, E. W., & Locke, H. J. 1953. *The family: From institution to companionship.* New York: American Book.

Burr, W. R., Hill, R., Nye, F. I., & Reiss, I. L., eds. 1979. *Contemporary theories about the family.* Vols. 1–2. New York: Free Press.

Campbell, A. 1981. *The sense of well-being in America.* New York: McGraw-Hill.

Campbell, A., Converse, P., & Rodgers, W. 1976. *The quality of American life.* New York: Russell Sage.

Cerny, V., Dahl, N., Kamiko, T., & Aldous, J. 1974. International developments in family theory: A continuation of the initial "Pilgrim Progress." *Journal of Marriage and the Family* 36:169–173.

Chilman, C. S. 1966. *Growing up poor.* Washington, D.C.: Welfare Administration Publication no. 13.

Duvall, E. M., & Hill, R. 1948. *Dynamics of family interaction: Working papers. National Conference on Family Life.* Mimeographed, out of print.

Goode, W. 1956. *After divorce.* New York: Free Press.

———. 1964. *The family.* Englewood Cliffs, N.J.: Prentice-Hall.

Gordon, M. 1978. *The American family: Past, present, and future.* New York: Random House.

Hareven, T. K. 1977. *Family and kin in urban communities, 1700–1930.* New York: New Viewpoints.

Hill, R. 1964. Methodological issues in family development research. *Family Process* 3:186–206.

Hill, R., & Hansen, D. A. 1960. The identification of conceptual frameworks utilized in family study. *Marriage and Family Living* 22:308.

Hill, R., & Mattessich, P. 1979. Family development theory and life span development. In *Life span development and behavior,* ed. P. B. Baltes & O. G. Brim, Jr. Vol. 2. New York: Academic.

Holman, T., & Burr, W. R. 1980. Beyond the beyond: The growth of family theories in the 1970's. *Journal of Marriage and the Family* 42:729–741.

ISR Newsletter. 1981. *Marriage and parenthood continue to be important goals for young people.* Ann Arbor, MI: Institute for Social Research.

Kantor, D. H., & Lehr, W. 1975. *Inside the family: Toward a theory of family process.* New York: Harper & Row.

Klein, D. M., Schvaneveldt, J. D., & Miller, B. C. 1977. The attitudes and activities of contemporary family theorists. *Journal of Comparative Family Studies* 8:5–27.

Klein, J. F., Calvert, G. P., Garland, N., & Poloma, M. M. 1969. Pilgrims Progress I: Recent developments in family theory. *Journal of Marriage and the Family* 31:677–687.

Kobrin, F. E. 1976. The fall in household size and the rise of the primary individual in the United States. *Demography* 13:127–138.

Lasch, C. 1977. *Haven in a heartless world: The family besieged.* New York: Basic Books.

Laslett, P., ed. 1971. *Household and family in past time.* Cambridge, MA: Cambridge University Press.

Leslie, G. R. 1982. *The family in social context.* 5th ed. New York: Oxford University Press.

McCormack, P. 1974. New family definitions from future leaders. UPI release. Sarasota *Herald-Tribune,* August 4, 1974, p. 6-E.

Nock, S. L. 1981. Family life cycle transitions: Longitudinal effects on family members. *Journal of Marriage and the Family* 43:703–714.

Norton, A. J., & Glick, P. C. 1979. What's happening to households? *American Demographics* 1:19–23.

Nye, F. I. 1978. Is choice and exchange theory the key? *Journal of Marriage and the Family* 40:219–233.

———. 1979. Choice, exchange, and the family. In *Contemporary theories about the family,* ed. W. R. Burr, R. Hill, F. I. Nye, & I. L. Reiss. Vol. 2. New York: Free Press.

Nye, F. I., & Berardo, F. 1966. *Emerging conceptual frameworks in family analysis.* New York: Macmillan.

Population Reference Bureau. 1982. U.S. population: Where we are and where we're going. *Population Bulletin* 37, no. 2. Washington, D.C.: Population Reference Bureau, Inc.

Seward, R. R. 1978. *The American family: A demographic history.* Beverly Hills, CA: Sage.

Toffler, A., & Toffler, H. 1981. The changing American family: Welcome to the "electronic cottage." *Family Weekly,* March 22, pp. 8–13.

U.S. Bureau of the Census. 1975. Household and family characteristics: March 1974. *Current Population Reports,* Series P-20, no. 276. Washington, D.C.: U.S. Department of Commerce, p. 6.

Westoff, C. F. 1978. Marriage and fertility in the developed countries. *Scientific American* 239:51–57.

Wrigley, E. A., & Schofield, R. S. 1981. *The population history of England, 1541–1871.* Cambridge, MA: Harvard University Press.

Chapter 2

The Family Life Cycle: Developmental Perspective on Families

MAJOR CONCEPTS

Family life cycle
Stages of the family life cycle
Family career
Alternative stage categories
Length of life cycle stages
Historical changes in
    the family life cycle

Plurality patterns
The lineage bridge
Variations from the typical
    family life cycle

The family life cycle is the fundamental concept in understanding how families change over time. The family life cycle can be divided into stages that are conceptually distinct and that typically occur in a given sequence. The timing, sequence, and occurrence of family structural changes over time has been called the "family career" (Aldous 1978).

THE FAMILY LIFE CYCLE CONCEPT

There is a predictability about family development that helps us know what to expect of any given family at any given stage. Much as each individual who grows, develops, matures, and ages undergoes the same successive changes and readjustments from conception to senescence as every other individual, the life cycles of individual families follow a common sequence of family development (Hill & Mattessich 1979).

The family life cycle, used as a frame of reference, affords a longitudinal view of family life. It is based on the recognition of successive phases and patterns as they occur within the continuity of family living over the years. It opens the way for study of the particular problems and potentials, rewards and hazards, vulnerabilities and strengths of each phase of family experience from beginning to end.

Families mature as their children grow through childhood into adolescence and finally into marriages and families of their own. Families that once expanded to accommodate the requirements of growing children later contract as they release these same children as young adults. The bustling years when family life runs at a hectic pace eventually give way to the slower-moving years of the empty nest period when the middle-aged and aging parents face the latter half of their marriage together. With the prolongation of life, these later years present new opportunities and problems.

Families, like individual persons, progress from birth to death in the steps and patterns inherent in the human condition. And, like their separate members, families express their individuality in the distinctive ways in which they proceed through the universal life cycle. Each family history has its own unique design.

FAMILY MEMBERS' LIFE SPANS

The stages through which a family may be expected to pass can be generalized from statistical profiles of family experience in much the same way that life expectancy can be predicted from the actuarial tables compiled by life insurance companies. Data for an individual family member may deviate from the schema at any point without invalidating the predictions, which hold true at a given time for the population as a whole.

Woman's Life Today

Using official figures from the U.S. Bureau of the Census and projections through the 1980s, the life of the typical woman living in the United States today may be outlined as follows. She comes into her family of orientation at birth; she starts school at 6, enters her teens at 13, and marries when she is 23, more or less. At this point she leaves her family of orientation and enters her family of procreation. Her first child is born about two years later, and her last child arrives before she is 30. By the time she is about 31 her first child is in school. The child becomes a teenager when she is in her late thirties and marries when she is 51 or so (earlier for daughters, later for sons). She shares her middle age in the empty nest with her husband until his death, which comes when she is in her late sixties. Then she has a decade, more or less, of widowhood until her own death (Table 2.1).

College-educated women marry later, have the first baby at a later age, and enter the next stage of the family life cycle somewhat later than women with less education (Spanier & Glick 1980). However, the smaller number of children borne by college-educated women offsets their later age at marriage to some extent. Thus the life cycle profiles for the college woman and the typical American woman in the United States tend to parallel each other in the latter half of life, from the launching stage onward.

The typical American woman, with or without a career, spends the first two decades of her life growing up as a child and adolescent, preparing herself for adulthood. She spends the next 25 to 30 years bearing and rearing children, and the last 25 to 30 years with her husband or alone after their children have grown and left home. More than half of her married life remains after her children have gone.

Such a view of life through the years raises many questions about the kind of education a woman needs, not only for the immediate future but also for the years ahead. The successive roles of a woman are played out not only in the quick-moving years of young womanhood but through the ever-changing tempos of the entire family life cycle.

Modern Man's Life

The profile of the life of the American man, using parallel statistical data, differs slightly from that of the American woman. Like her, the male typically enters his family of orientation at birth, goes to school at 6, and becomes a teenager at 13. He marries two years later than the woman, when he is 25, more or less. At this point he begins his family of procreation. His first child is born when he is about 27, and his last child is born when he is about 32. He becomes a father of teenagers when he is about 40, and by the time he is in his mid-fifties he becomes the father of the bride (or groom) when his first child marries. After the children leave, he and his wife live in an empty nest, their day-to-day parenting roles over. The chances

Table 2.1 LIFE SPAN OF A MODERN AMERICAN WIFE AND MOTHER

		Death	78±	
75				
70	Widow	Husband dies	67±	
65				
60				
55	Middle-aged wife (empty nest)	Last child marries	53±	Family of procreation
50	Launching stage mother	First child marries	51±	
45				
40	Mother of teenager(s)	First child a teenager	38±	
35				
	Mother of school-ager(s)	First child in school	31±	
30	Mother of preschooler(s)	Last baby born	29±	
25	Childbearing mother	First baby born	25±	
	Wife	Marries	23±	
20				
15		Enters teens	13	Family of orientation
10				
		Goes to school	6	
5				
0		Born	0	

Note: U.S. Bureau of the Census data are used throughout this text. Students may want to refer to Norton (1983) in which June 1980 survey data differ somewhat from census figures, which we use since they include projections and expected lifetime experience of today's young women.

Source: Current unpublished census data with projections for the 1980s by Paul C. Glick, personal communication, 1981.

are that he retires in his mid-sixties. Characteristically, he is the first spouse to die, but if he survives longer than average, he may or may not be widowed through his final years.

Each man attains the successive stages in his life cycle at his own particular pace. Usually, however, his second decade of life is spent in becoming a young man, his third in becoming a husband and father. He and his wife will spend the first two years or so as a couple before their first child arrives. His forties and fifties will be characterized by the launching of teenagers and young adults into lives of their own. Then, after his last child has married and left home, he may expect to spend another 14 years (plus or minus) as a member of a couple again. A twosome once again, he and his wife will share the experience of grandparent-hood. The chances are that he will leave his wife a widow, so that life insurance, retirement plans, housing requirements, and related concerns must be considered as they plan for their later years (Table 2.2).

FAMILY LIFE CYCLE STAGES

The family life cycle may be divided into few or many stages on the basis of several factors. It is possible to think of a two-stage family life cycle: (1) the expanding family stage, in which the family is taken from its inception to the time when its children are grown; and (2) the contracting family stage, in which children are being launched by the family into lives of their own and in which the family continues to contract through the later years until only one or both of the original pair still remain at home. Such a two-stage cycle delineation is usually too simple for research purposes, but the factor of shifting plurality patterns in the family was one of the first used to identify stages in the family life cycle.

Years ago, Sorokin, Zimmerman, and Galpin (1931) discussed a four-stage family life cycle based on the changing family member constellation within the family: (1) married couples just starting their independent economic existence, (2) couples with one or more children, (3) couples with one or more adult self-supporting children, and (4) couples growing old.

Kirkpatrick and others (1934) saw a four-stage cycle of the family life cycle in terms of the place of the children in the educational system: (1) preschool family, (2) grade school family, (3) high school family, and (4) all-adult family.

In plotting the changing financial income and outgo patterns throughout the family life cycle, Bigelow (1942) elaborated on the school placement factor in a cycle he divided into seven periods: (1) establishment period, (2) childbearing and preschool period, (3) elementary school period, (4) high school period, (5) college period, (6) period of recovery, and (7) period of retirement.

The most complex breakdown of the family life cycle into stages elaborates the 8-stage cycle of this text into 24 stages (Rodgers 1962). Following not only the predictable develop-ment of a family as the oldest child grows, Rodgers' proposal also keeps the youngest child in focus. His delineation calls for two preschool family stages, three school-age, four teenage, five young adult, and five launching stages, plus the stages before children arrive and after they are gone. The first of these is the beginning family stage. The next 20 make provision in each family life cycle stage for a possible youngest child who theoretically plunges the family back into an earlier age group interest as younger children arrive. Rodgers explains, "The solution follows Duvall quite closely. Birth, entry into school, departure from the family system, retirement, and dissolution of the system are easily identifiable. We can do

Table 2.2 LIFE SPAN OF A MODERN AMERICAN HUSBAND AND FATHER

75		Death of other spouse	78±
70			
	Widower?	Death of one spouse	69±
65	Retiree?	Retires?	65
60			
55	Middle-aged husband (empty nest)	Last child marries	55±
	Launching stage father	First child marries	53±
50			
45			
40	Father of teenager(s)	First child a teenager	40±
35			
	Father of school-ager(s)	First child in school	33±
	Father of preschooler(s)	Last child born	31±
30			
	Childbearing father	First baby born	27±
25	Husband	Marries	25±
20			
15			
		Enters teens	13
10			
		Goes to school	6
5			
0		Born	0

Family of procreation (25± to 69±)

Family of orientation (0 to 20)

Source: Current unpublished census data with projections for the 1980s by Paul C. Glick, personal communication, 1981.

this, however, for the additional position of last child, as well as first-born, which is a modification of the Duvall approach" (Rodgers 1962, 62).

The 24-stage family life cycle proposed by Rodgers has not been used much in research, and there is little evidence that the youngest child's age and school placement critically affect a family's development (Aldous 1978). Furthermore, the elaboration is too detailed for practical use. Therefore, we continue to depict the family life cycle as consisting of eight stages (Table 2.3).

The Eight-Stage Family Life Cycle

The Duvall eight-stage family life cycle is a refinement of the seven-stage formulation developed for the first National Conference on Family Life (Duvall & Hill 1948). It represents a combination of four factors used in determining family life cycle stages: (1) plurality patterns, (2) age of the oldest child, (3) school placement of the oldest child, and (4) functions and statuses of families before children come and after they leave. This combination has proved to be workable in the study of American families as well as of those in other countries. It parallels reliable data available from government sources and from basic research studies. The age and school placement of the oldest child are used as criteria of family life cycle stage intervals from the arrival of the first child in the family to the launching-center stage, when the focus shifts to those remaining in the original family. Stage 6 (families as launching centers) begins with the first child's leaving home and concludes with the departure of the last child.

Overlap of Family Life Cycle Stages

A clear-cut sequence of stages in the family life cycle occurs only in a family with one child. In families with more than one child, there are several years of overlap at various stages. Our thesis is that families grow and develop as their children do. Our answer to the question of overlapping of stages is that a family grows through a given stage with its oldest child and in a sense "repeats" as subsequent children come along. We see a family being pushed into coping with new unknowns as its oldest child becomes a preschooler, goes to school, enters the teens, and finally leaves home for a life of his or her own.

As younger children come along, they arrive in a family already familiar with the normal sequence of children's growth because of their experience with the eldest. Thus a younger sibling who is born at the time when a family is seeing its firstborn into preschool

Table 2.3   DUVALL'S EIGHT-STAGE FAMILY LIFE CYCLE

	Designation and descriptive qualities
Stage	
1	Married couples (without children)
2	Childbearing families (oldest child birth–30 months)
3	Families with preschool children (oldest child 2½–6 years)
4	Families with schoolchildren (oldest child 6–13 years)
5	Families with teenagers (oldest child 13–20 years)
6	Families launching young adults (first child gone to last child's leaving home)
7	Middle-aged parents (empty nest to retirement)
8	Aging family members (retirement to death of both spouses)

arrives in a preschool family because of the family's involvement with the oldest child. The oldest child is always taking the family with him or with her out into the growing edges of family experience. Younger children necessarily arrive in a different family than that into which the firstborn came—a significant difference being the degree of the family's experience with children of various ages.

Duration of Family Life Cycle Stages

Remembering that not all families move through the family life cycle in the same way, it is possible nevertheless to plot the time usually taken by American families to progress through each of the eight stages of the cycle. This is done by utilizing census data that provide profiles of families as well as of individuals according to designated markers in their life histories.

Americans usually think of a family as a unit consisting of a father, a mother, and two or three young children. Advertisements and educational materials often portray this stage of the family life cycle as though it were the only one that mattered. Commercials commonly assume that the family with young children is *the family.* Holiday sentiments and everyday assumptions put this stage of the family life cycle so much in the forefront that others are relatively ignored. Such a stereotype is understandable. The childbearing and child-rearing stages are important in family relationships, in the family's contact with school, church, and community, in the development of the personalities of the children, and for the family as a consumer, with its bulging appetites for more and more goods. Yet this period in the family life cycle is but a small fraction of the whole. It represents only a few years—an average of a dozen or so—out of the total of 50 to 60 years of the average family life span.

In schools and colleges, it is common in courses about marriage and family life to spend the greater part of the time on the processes leading to marriage, the adjustments of the newly married pair, and their functions as expectant and actual parents. This, of course, is justifiable in that it reflects the readiness of the student, as well as the significance of the husband-wife relationship, for the stability of the family. Yet such an emphasis gives an inaccurate portrayal of the time the married pair will spend together as a couple in the family they have established. Young adults about to finish their education, establish themselves vocationally, and take the marriage step can better make the decisions necessary for these immediate goals by keeping their probable entire family life cycle in mind.

If the man and woman contemplating marriage are of the average ages reported by the U.S. Bureau of the Census as typical at first marriage, birth of children, marriage of last child, and death of spouse, the family cycle they may envision for themselves is largely ignored in courses that focus solely on the young married couple. Figure 2.1 shows nearly one-half of the marriage is typically spent after the couple's children have grown and gone.

The significance of the duration of the various stages—for education, budgeting, housing, health, recreation, home management, and a host of other family resources and services —will be dealt with in part in Part Three where separate chapters are devoted to each stage of the family life cycle.

MARRIED COUPLES AS FAMILIES

Three stages of the family life cycle, as we define it, deal with the husband and wife as a couple only: stage 1 as a married couple before children come and stages 7 and 8 as a married couple

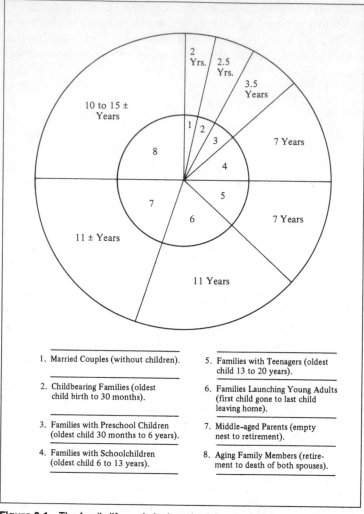

1. Married Couples (without children).

2. Childbearing Families (oldest child birth to 30 months).

3. Families with Preschool Children (oldest child 30 months to 6 years).

4. Families with Schoolchildren (oldest child 6 to 13 years).

5. Families with Teenagers (oldest child 13 to 20 years).

6. Families Launching Young Adults (first child gone to last child leaving home).

7. Middle-aged Parents (empty nest to retirement).

8. Aging Family Members (retirement to death of both spouses).

Figure 2.1   The family life cycle by length of time in each of eight stages. *Source:* Based upon data reported in Tables 2.1 and 2.2 from the U.S. Bureau of the Census and from the National Center for Health Statistics, Washington, D.C.

after their children have grown and left home. It can be argued that a couple without children is not a family but, more accurately, a married couple.

However, when the whole family is viewed in perspective over the years, the newly married couple appear as the "beginning family," which develops quickly in the majority of cases into the childbearing family. The norm is for the young married couple to be a family-in-the-making not only because their children eventually make a family of them, but because they think of themselves as potential parents long before children actually arrive. In terms of the time factor alone, many couples spend as much time (or more) during the early married stage as expectant parents as they do before pregnancy occurs.

The middle-aged or aging couple who have already been through the childbearing,

-rearing, and launching stages of the family cycle are parents of grown children. They quite probably have grandchildren. More often than not, they maintain a home to which children return. They make a home for varying lengths of time for their married children and grandchildren and, in some cases, for their own aging parents and older relatives. They continue to think of themselves as "family" and to function as family members long after their own children are grown and involved in lives of their own. Therefore, we describe them as being in the later stages of the family life cycle.

TWENTIETH-CENTURY CHANGES IN THE FAMILY LIFE CYCLE

Now more than in the past, children survive the early years of life; more mothers come through childbearing safely; and a larger percentage of men and women live out their full life span. Both husband and wife can now anticipate more years of marriage and family living than was typical at the beginning of this century.

Twentieth-century changes in the number and spacing of children and in the life expectancy of men and women have affected the life cycle of the typical American family in ways shown in Figure 2.2. Mothers who have married in the 1970s are younger by several years at the time of their last child's birth than were mothers who married in earlier decades of this century. Today's mothers are younger when their last child marries and thus have more years with their husbands after their children have grown and gone than earlier generations had. For couples who survive together until their last child marries, the length of their empty nest period is increased to 16.3 years (median age of death of one spouse [68.6 years] minus median age at marriage of last child [52.3 years]), for young adults who entered their first marriage during the 1970s (Glick 1977).

Census studies in both the United States (Glick 1977; Norton 1980; Spanier & Glick 1980) and Canada (Rodgers & Whitney 1981) have recently highlighted family life cycle changes in this century. The reports by Norton and by Spanier and Glick are unique in several respects: they break down life cycle changes by race, education, and number of times married. The tables are too complex and detailed to reproduce, but their results can be summarized as follows:

1. Most of the critical family life cycle events have varied within fairly narrow ranges over successive decades during the last half century for women of all socioeconomic groups combined. The lower the level of educational attainment, however, the earlier a woman begins her family life cycle trajectory—and vice versa.
2. Long-standing differences between blacks and whites with regard to life course events tend to be minimized when educational level is controlled. A significant exception to the higher fertility of black women than of white women, however, is found among those with college degrees. Black women college graduates have lower completed fertility than white women of any birth cohort or educational level.
3. There is a consistent tendency for remarried women in all cohorts and at all educational levels to be about two years younger at first marriage than women married only once.
4. The ages at which events associated with marital disruption occur among mothers of young children have decreased dramatically during the century. An important fact of relevance is that the younger a woman is at the termination of her first marriage, the more likely she is to remarry.

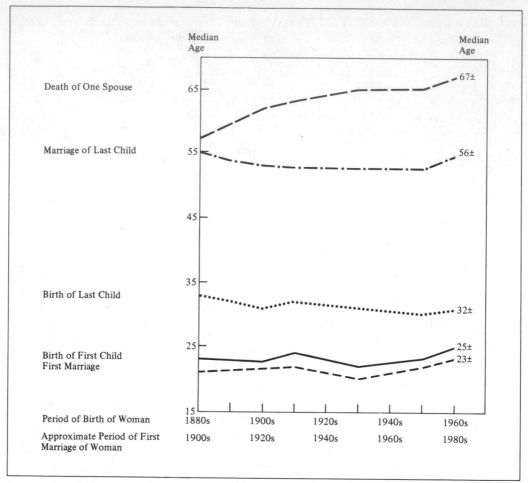

Figure 2.2 Twentieth-century changes in selected family life cycle events. *Sources:* Paul C. Glick, "Updating the Life Cycle of the Family," *Journal of Marriage and the Family* 39 (1977):7; projections to 1980s by Paul C. Glick based upon current unpublished census data and reliable projection methods, personal communications; age at birth and marriage of last child increased by about three years upon advice of Arthur J. Norton, Bureau of the Census, personal communication, July 1983.

5. Black women display greater variation in life cycle trajectories than do white women. This generalization applies even when education and marital history are controlled and would be consistent with the hypothesis that black women tend to have fewer options than white women in choosing the most desirable times for the several events to occur.

6. The higher the educational attainment, the less the variation in the timing of life cycle events, probably for some of the same reasons that tend to influence the patterns of white women. An exception occurs among highly educated women.

7. Women who have been married only once vary considerably less than remarried women in ages at birth of first and last child, partly because of the interruption in childbearing which may occur in conjunction with divorce and remarriage. (Spanier & Glick 1980, 109–110)

Rodgers and Whitney (1981, 735) made specific comparisons between the average ages of major life cycle events in Canada and the United States as follows:

1. Canadians continue to delay childbearing an average of over a year longer than Americans;
2. Canadians have their last child an average of 2.7 years younger than Americans, thereby maintaining their childbearing level at nearly as many or more children per woman;
3. Canadians' last child departs from home an average of 2 years younger and 3.5 years earlier in their marriages;
4. Canadians couples live together about 3 years longer than Americans born in the same decade;
5. Canadians continue to average nearly 2 years more of marriage; and
6. Canadian couples survive together after the departure of their last child about 5 years longer than couples in the United States.

FAMILY LIFE CYCLE CHANGES TO COME

Any forecasting of changes in the American family life cycle for the years ahead must rest on the assumptions that trends already under way will continue and that no great catastrophic upheavals in the form of external threats or internal disintegration will occur. The children and young people of today will be attaining marriageable ages between now and the year 2000. Adults will continue to marry, possibly at later ages than in recent decades. Both sexes and members of minority families will attain higher levels of education than did their parents. Husbands and wives will work for more years of their lives—and at better-paying jobs than was possible before. Most married couples will live by themselves, as practically all of them do now. Divorce and remarriage will continue as an acceptable response to unsatisfactory marriage. Average life expectancy at birth will increase "from 67.9 for males and 75.7 for females in 1972 to 69.9 for males and 78.0 for females in 2020" (U.S. Bureau of the Census 1975, 5; also Parke & Glick 1967, 256).

FROM GENERATION TO GENERATION

Before one family unit has completed its cycle, its grown children have embarked on theirs. Most twentieth-century American family members see a second, third, and perhaps even a fourth family life cycle spun off, as children marry and rear their children, who grow up, marry, and have children, who in turn marry and repeat the family life cycle pattern while older members of the family are still living.

A young couple know not only their own newly established family but that of their parents, grandparents, and possibly their great-grandparents as well. They can look forward to seeing their children and grandchildren and possibly their great-grandchildren launched and married. As they relate intimately to the two or three older generations, and the two or three younger generations, they go around the family life cycle again and again and again with these other close kinfolk. Thus the term *cycle* is appropriate because it means any complete round or series of occurrences that repeats itself. Other terms such as *lifetime family career* and *lineage family cycle* (Feldman & Feldman 1975; Rodgers 1973) are sometimes substituted for the more common *family life cycle* phrase.

Hill (1970) sees parents of married children forming the *lineage bridge* between the older and younger generations in the same family. Three-generational sharing of activities, visiting, and help exchanges are common. Each generation turns to relatives for help from time to time—the grandparents for help in illness and with household management, the parents for emotional gratification, and the married children for material assistance and child care.

The many ways in which families rely on one another have been noted in studies through the years (Duvall 1954; Sussman and Burchinal 1962). The popular notion of the modern family as a vulnerable little nuclear unit of husband, wife, and their children, unsupported by other caring relatives, is not borne out by research. Empirical evidence points rather to a modified extended family within a network of frequent generational interaction (Hill 1970; Lee 1980; Litwak 1959–1960; Sussman 1965).

INTERPERSONAL RELATIONSHIPS INCREASE AS FAMILIES GROW

The size of the family increases by an arithmetical progression. It starts with two persons, as husband and wife marry. Then the first baby arrives, followed by the second, and perhaps others as the family grows in size. According to a law of family interaction, with the addition of each new person to a family the number of persons increases in the simplest arithmetical progression in whole numbers, while the number of personal interrelationships within the group increases in the order of triangular numbers (Bossard 1945, 292).

To find the number of interpersonal relationships within a family, the following formula is used, in which x equals the number of interpersonal relationships, and y equals the number of persons:

$$x = \frac{y^2 - y}{2}$$

Applying this formula to a specific family, the following series emerges: number of persons in the family—2, 3, 4, 5, 6, 7, 8, 9, and so forth; number of relationships in the family— 1, 3, 6, 10, 15, 21, 28, 36, and so forth.

Thus we see that a family consisting of a mother, a father, and three children has a total of five individuals with a total of 10 interpersonal relationships: father with mother, father with first child, father with second child, father with third child; mother with first child, mother with second child, mother with third child; first child with second child, first child with third child, and second child with third child.

Assuming that all four grandparents are living, the family with three children consists of nine persons within the three generations (four grandparents, two parents, and three children), within which a total of 36 interpersonal relationships is possible. As the three children marry, their three spouses swell the number of family members to 12 and their interrelationships to 66, not counting any of the new in-laws. When each of the married children's families has its second child, there now is a probable number of interpersonal relationships totaling 153. As the great-grandparents die, they are replaced by new births in the youngest generation. The last remaining great-grandparent in the final stage of his or her life cycle is quite possibly part of an 18-person family, including more than 150 interpersonal relationships. Figure 2.3 graphically shows how rapidly family relationships increase through the family life cycle, merely within the family lineage—not counting any of the relatives by marriage or the aunts, uncles, cousins, and other kin who are considered part of the family.

USES OF THE FAMILY LIFE CYCLE CONCEPT

The Thirteenth International Seminar on Family Research brought together 70 social scientists from Eastern and Western Europe, Japan, and North America to review the relevance of the family life cycle concept in the study of family life. A variety of approaches to the use

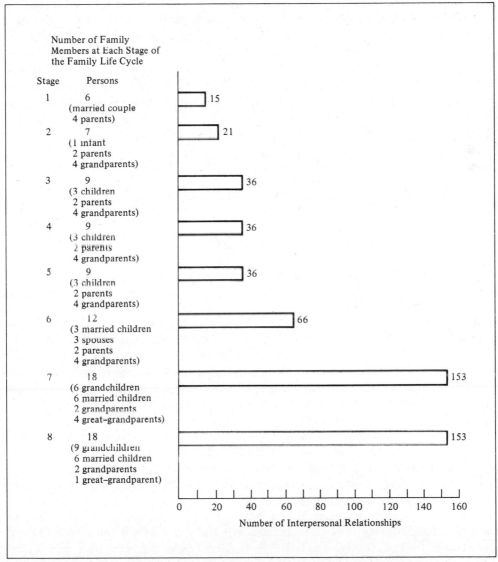

Figure 2.3 Number of interpersonal relationships in a three-child family, by stage in the family life cycle.

of the family life cycle were reported. Among these were (1) a descriptive use that follows life from the cradle to the grave, (2) a dynamic aspect that links functional relationships at one point in time with phenomena at another time, and (3) causal analysis that anticipates from earlier stages what will happen at later stages in family life (Segalen 1974, 817). Goode concluded that "we are once more able to understand how potentially fruitful a family cycle approach might be, even if we cannot neatly put all families into a precise, concrete typology or taxonomy of family cycles" (Goode in Sussman 1974, 60).

The family life cycle is a useful tool in training paraprofessionals (Ogren 1971) and doctors, nurses, home economists, teachers, social workers, and other professionals who work with families; and for educating family members (present and future) for whom life cycle management is relevant (Duvall 1972). Knowing where a family is in its life cycle makes it possible to anticipate a number of vital factors—its relative income level, its consumer practices, whether the wife works, the couple's probable marital satisfaction, areas of possible family conflict, and the nature of its parent-child relationships, for example. "Thus, the family life cycle stage concept has proven to have systematic qualities, because the families its stages group together share a number of other important properties" (Aldous 1978, 115).

VARIATIONS IN THE TYPICAL FAMILY LIFE CYCLE

The life experiences of some individuals do not follow the family life cycle described above. Those who never marry usually leave their families of orientation but do not form families of procreation. Couples who never bear, adopt, or rear children are, technically, married couples rather than families. Such alternatives as homosexual pairs, group marriages, communes, and other familylike households tend to remain outside the typical family life cycle.

Some married couples do not follow the family life cycle timetable. They marry earlier or later than the national norms or bear their children earlier, later, or over a longer period of years than is typical. They, or their children, might have exceptional abilities or disabilities that markedly affect their family life.

Especially difficult to take into account are the many forms of dissolved and reconstituted families—with all that is involved in divorce, remarriage, and the establishment of families in which "your children," "my children," and "our children" are all part of the same family. With the current high divorce rates, there are more parents without partners and more remarriages, each with its own life cycle to complete in its own way. Should increasing rates of divorce, delayed marriage, or alternatives to marriage become long-term trends, a decline in the proportion of adults experiencing "typical" family life cycles may be expected. The problems of delineating family life cycle stages that hold for all families are complex because families themselves are so varied.

In spite of these important variations, through the twentieth century there has been increasing uniformity in the family life cycle owing to two trends: (1) the increasing percentage of persons in marriages and (2) the longer life spans of both males and females (in the past more families ended earlier by death). One computation using birth cohorts of women born between 1890 and 1934 shows a steady increase in the proportion of women who have had a typical family life cycle or one modified by a stable remarriage (Table 2.4). Thus a woman born in the early 1930s, who would be in her fifties in the 1980s, is more likely to have had a typical family life cycle than her mother 20 years before or her grandmother 40 years earlier.

Table 2.4 INCREASING INCIDENCE OF FAMILY LIFE CYCLE EXPERIENCE

Birth cohort	Number out of 1000 women with typical or modified family life cycle experience
1890–1894	575
1900–1904	635
1910–1914	670
1920–1924	740
1930–1934	780

Source: P. Uhlenberg, "Cohort Variations in Family Life Cycle Experiences of U.S. Females," *Journal of Marriage and the Family* 36 (1974): 284–292.

The issue of how family life cycle concepts can be applied to those who divorce and remarry has been recently receiving greater attention. The issues were raised by Aldous (1978) and Boss (1980) and analyzed with census data by Norton (1980).

Boss (1980) devised Table 2.5 as a way of illustrating family boundary changes over the life span. The boundary changes are essentially additions and departures of family members, including the loss of a spouse through divorce, the formation of a new family through remarriage, and so on.

Norton's (1980) census analyses were conducted specifically to compare life cycle measures of women whose marriages had dissolved by divorce and women who had never divorced. The data show that women married twice entered first marriage and bore their first child at earlier ages than women married only once. In addition to the marital status differences in life cycle events, differences by education, race, and cohort or historical effects are clearly apparent. Norton's analysis is a beginning empirical step in applying life cycle concepts to those who divorce, remarry, and resume family careers.

DEBATES ABOUT THE FAMILY LIFE CYCLE

Although the family life cycle concept has been widely used in research and services for families, its utility is still the subject of debate. The most critical questions currently being raised are about how well the stage categories work empirically (Nock 1979). Some investigators (Spanier, Sauer, & Larzelere 1979) report that duration of marriage functions as effectively as stage of the life cycle in explaining some family characteristics. Others have reported that presence or absence of children and length of marriage are the most powerful aspects of the multidimensional family life cycle variable in predicting marital and parental attitudes and characteristics (Nock 1981).

In reply, Aldous and Klein (1979) contend that using cross-sectional data to evaluate the inherently longitudinal nature of changes over the life cycle is misleading. And because the focus of the family life cycle approach points to places in a family's development where changes in status and role occur, the empirical focus should be on the critical transitions themselves rather than on rough categorical stage comparisons using questionable outcome measures. Some scholars have recently undertaken the study of critical transition processes

Table 2.5 ILLUSTRATIVE NORMATIVE LIFE SPAN BOUNDARY CHANGES

Type of life span family boundary changes	Boundary stressors related to physical and psychological membership in the system
Formation of the dyad Rapoport, 1963	Acquisition of a mate. Acquisition of in-laws. Realignment with family of orientation. Incorporating or rejecting former friendships.
Birth of the first child LeMasters, 1957 Russell, 1974 Pridham & Hansen, 1977	Acquisition of a new member. Possible separation from extrafamilial work world. If so, loss of working colleagues, and so on.
Children first going to school Anderson, 1976 Klein & Ross, 1958	Separation of child from the family system to the world of school. Acquisition of child's teacher, friends, and peers, that is, acceptance of them as part of the child's world.
Job-related parent/spouse absence or presence Hill, 1949 Boulding, 1950 Boss, 1975, 1980 McCubbin et al., 1976 Boss, McCubbin, Lester, 1979 Hooper, 1979	Fluctuating acquisition *and* separation due to extrafamilial role, that is, military service, routine absence of the corporate executive, and so on. Stress results from repeated exit and reentry of the member. Also includes job changes such as return of mother to college or work after she has been a full-time homemaker or retirement of father from work back into the home.
Adolescent children leaving home Stierlin, 1974 Boss & Whitaker, 1979	Separation of adolescent from the family system to his peers, school, or job system. Acquisition of the adolescent's peers and intimates—same and opposite sex.
Taking in child(ren) not your own or blending children from different dyads Duberman, 1975 Visher & Visher, 1978, 1979	Acquisition of another's offspring into the family system, that is, stepchildren, grandchildren, other nonrelated children.
Loss of a spouse (through death, divorce, etc.) Parkes, 1972 Lopata, 1973, 1979 Bohannan, 1970 Wallerstein & Kelly, studies 1974–1977 Weiss, 1975 Hetherington, 1971, 1976 Boss & Whitaker, 1979	Separation of mate from the dyad; therefore, dissolution of the marital dyad. Note that in case of divorce, the dyad may continue and function on other levels, such as co-parenting, and so on.
Loss of parent(s) Sheey, 1976 Silverstone & Hyman, 1976 Levinson, 1978	Separation of child from parent(s) (child may likely be an adult).
Formation of a new dyad: remarriage Bernard, 1956 Messinger, 1976 Westoff, 1977 Whiteside, 1978 Roosevelt & Lofas, 1976	Acquisition of a new mate. Acquisition of a new set of in-laws. Realignment with family of orientation and former in-laws, children of former marriage, and so on. Incorporating or rejecting former friendships, former spouses, and so on. Former spouse may still be in partnership with a member of the new dyad regarding parenting.

36

Table 2.5 *(Continued)*

Type of life span family boundary changes	Boundary stressors related to physical and psychological membership in the system
Remaining single Stein, 1976	Realignment with family of orientation. If previously married, realignment with former in-laws. Acquisition of friends, intimates, colleagues, and so on.

Source: P. G. Boss, "Normative Family Stress: Family Boundary Changes Across the Life Span," *Family Relations* 29 (1980): 445–450. Copyrighted 1980 by the National Council on Family Relations, 1219 University Avenue Southeast, Minneapolis, Minnesota 55414. Reprinted by permission.

in family development (Mederer, Hill, & Joy 1981). Other investigators continue to find life cycle stages extremely useful in empirical research. Waite (1980, 291) for example, reported that wives' labor force participation is strongly affected by their stage of the family life cycle. She writes:

> This paper provides evidence of the importance of the familial context in which women make decisions about labor force participation. Wives tend to weigh factors differently in the first three stages of the life cycle. It is not sufficient to divide women into those with and without young children. Mothers who expect future births do not respond to forces which influence market activity in the same way as women who consider childbearing finished.

The heuristic, conceptual, and empirical utility of the family life cycle continues to be widespread. Undoubtedly, many scholars will be involved in assessing its empirical value in studies aimed at understanding marriage and family life. This task seems likely to become increasingly challenging and complex as larger proportions of families dissolve prematurely through divorce and family members embark on new family careers through remarriage.

SUMMARY

Whatever schema for defining family life cycle stages is used, it is merely a convenient division for the study of something that in real life flows from one stage to another without pause or break. Part of the genius of the concept is its explicit awareness that each stage has its beginnings in stages past and its fruition in those yet to come. Being cyclical by definition, the family life cycle has no beginning and no end. No matter where one starts to study a family by means of its family life cycle, there are roots in the near and distant past to be considered. The present stage of the family has grown out of the one just before, and the family is heading toward the stage ahead.

The family life cycle concept provides a perspective basic to family development study. It is the long view, penetrating longitudinally through the life history of a family, that keeps in perspective each of its members in relation to all of the others—past, present, and future. This may be why the family life cycle has proved to be important and useful in anticipating many facets of family behavior (Aldous 1978, Blood & Wolfe 1960; Campbell, Converse, & Rogers 1976; Hill 1970; Lansing & Kish 1957; Waite 1980).

REFERENCES

Aldous, J. 1978. *Family careers: Developmental change in families.* New York: Wiley.

Aldous, J., & Klein, D. M. 1979. Three blind mice: Misleading criticisms of the family life cycle "concept." *Journal of Marriage and the Family* 41:689–691.

Anderson, L. S. 1976. When a child begins school. *Children Today* (August): 16–19.

Bernard, J. 1956. *Remarriage.* New York: Holt, Rinehart, and Winston.

Bigelow, H. F. 1942. In *Marriage and the family,* ed. H. Becker & R. Hill, pp. 382–386. Boston: D.C. Heath.

Blood, R. O., Jr., & Wolfe, D. M. 1960. *Husbands and wives: The dynamics of married living.* New York: Free Press.

Bohannan, P. 1970. *Divorce and after.* New York: Doubleday.

Boss, P. G. 1980. Normative family stress: Family boundary changes across the life span. *Family Relations* 29:445–450. (a)

———. 1980. The relationship of psychological father presence, wife's personal qualities and wife/family dysfunction in families of missing fathers. *Journal of Marriage and the Family* 42:541–549. (b)

Boss, P. G., McCubbin, H. I., & Lester G. 1979. The corporate executive wife's coping patterns in response to routine husband-father absence. *Family Process* 18 (March): 79–86.

Boss, P. G., & Whitaker, C. 1979. Dialogue on separation. *The Family Coordinator* 28:391–398.

Bossard, J. H. S. 1945. The law of family interaction. *American Journal of Sociology* 292.

Boulding, E. 1950. Family adjustment to war separation and reunion. *Annals of the American Academy of Political and Social Science* 272:59–68.

Campbell, A., Converse, P., & Rogers, W. 1976. *The quality of American life.* New York: Russell Sage.

Duberman, L. 1975. *The reconstituted family: A study of remarried couples and their children.* Chicago: Nelson-Hall.

Duvall, E. M. 1954. *In-laws: Pro and con.* New York: Association Press.

———. 1972. Family development applications: An essay review. *Family Coordinator* 21:331–333.

Duvall, E. M., & Hill, R., cochairmen. 1948. Report of the Committee on the Dynamics of Family Interaction. Prepared at the request of the National Conference on Family Life, Washington, D.C. Mimeographed.

Feldman, H., & Feldman, M. 1975. The family life cycle: Some suggestions for recycling. *Journal of Marriage and the Family* 37:277–284.

Glick, P. 1977. Updating the life cycle of the family. *Journal of Marriage and the Family* 39:5–13.

Hetherington, E. M., & Deur, J. 1971. The effects of father absence on child development. *Young Children* 26:233–248.

Hetherington, E. M., Cox, M., & Cox, R. 1976. Divorced fathers. *The Family Coordinator* 25:417–428.

Hill, R. 1949. *Families under stress.* Connecticut: Greenwood Press.

———. 1970. *Family development in three generations.* Cambridge, MA: Schenkman.

Hill, R., & Mattessich, P. 1979. Family development theory and life span development. In *Life span development and behavior,* ed. Paul B. Baltes & Orville G. Brim, Jr. Vol. 2. New York: Academic Press.

Hooper, J. O. 1979. My wife, the student. *The Family Coordinator* 28:459–464.

Kirkpatrick, E. L., et al. 1934. The life cycle of the farm family in relation to its standard of living. Agricultural Experiment Station Research Bulletin no. 121. Madison: University of Wisconsin.

Klein, D. C., & Ross, A. 1958. Kindergarten entry: A study of role transition. In *Orthopsychiatry and the school,* ed. M. Krugman. New York: American Orthopsychiatric Association.

Lansing, J. B., & Kish, L. 1957. Family life cycle as an independent variable. *American Sociological Review* 22:512–519.

Lee, G. 1980. Kinship in the seventies: A decade review of research and theory. *Journal of Marriage and the Family* 42:923–934.

LeMasters, E. E. 1957. Parenthood as crisis. *Marriage and Family Living* 29:352–355.

Levinson, D. J. 1978. *The seasons of a man's life*. New York: Ballantine Books.

Litwak, E. 1959–1960. The use of extended family groups in the achievement of social goals: Some policy implications. *Social Problems* 7:177–187.

Lopata, H. I. 1973. *Widowhood in an American City*. Cambridge, MA: Schenkman.

———. 1979. *Women as widows*. New York: Elsevier.

McCubbin, H., Dahl, B., & Hunter, E. 1976. Research in the military family: A review. In *Families in the military system,* ed. H. McCubbin, B. Dahl, & E. Hunter. Beverly Hills, CA: Sage.

Mederer, H., Hill, R., & Joy, C. 1981. Bridging theory via multimethods: Questionnaire and interview design for capturing critical transition processes in family development. Paper presented at National Council on Family Relations, Milwaukee, WI, 1981.

Messinger, L. 1976. Remarriage between divorced people with children from previous marriages. *Journal of Marriage and Family Counseling* 2:193–200.

Nock, S. L. 1979. The family life cycle: Empirical or conceptual tool? *Journal of Marriage and the Family* 41:15–26.

———. 1981. Family life cycle transitions: Longitudinal effects on family numbers. *Journal of Marriage and the Family* 43:703–713.

Norton, A. 1980. The influence of divorce on traditional life cycle measures. *Journal of Marriage and the Family* 42:63–69.

———. 1983. Family life cycle: 1980. *Journal of Marriage and the Family* 45:267–275.

Ogren, E. H. 1971. Family dynamics for paraprofessional workers. *Family Coordinator* 20:11–16.

Parkes, C. M. 1972. *Bereavement: Studies of grief in adult life*. New York: International Universities Press, Inc.

Parke, R., Jr., & Glick, P. C. 1967. Prospective changes in marriage and the family. *Journal of Marriage and the Family* 29:249–256.

Pridham, K. F., Hansen, M., & Conrad, H. H. 1977. Anticipatory care as problem-solving in family medicine and nursing. *Journal of Family Practice* 4:1077–1081.

Rapoport, R. 1963. Normal crises, family structure, and mental health. *Family Process* 2.

The Rockefeller Foundation. 1975. World population increase, 1750 to 2000. *RF* 2 (March): 1.

Rodgers, R. H. 1962. *Improvements in the construction and analysis of family life cycle categories*. Ph.D. dissertation, Western Michigan University, Kalamazoo.

———. 1973. *Family interaction and transaction: The developmental approach*. Englewood Cliffs, N.J.: Prentice-Hall.

Rodgers, R. H., & Whitney, G. 1981. The family life cycle in twentieth century Canada. *Journal of Marriage and the Family* 43:727–740.

Roosevelt, R., & Lofas, J. 1976. *Living in step: A remarriage manual for parents and children*. New York: McGraw-Hill.

Russell, C. 1974. Transition to parenthood: Problems and gratifications. *Journal of Marriage and the Family* 294–301.

Segalen, M. 1974. Research and discussion around family life cycle: An account of the 13th seminar on family research. *Journal of Marriage and the Family* 36:814–818.

Sheehy, G. 1976. *Passages: Predictable crises of adult life*. New York: Dutton.

Silverstone, B., & Hyman, H. 1976. *You and your aging parents*. New York: Pantheon.

Sorokin, P., Zimmerman, C. C., & Galpin, C. J. 1931. *A systematic source book in rural sociology*. Vol. 2. Minneapolis: University of Minnesota Press.

Spanier, G. B., & Glick, P. C. 1980. The life cycle of American families: An expanded analyses. *Journal of Family History* 5:97–111.

Spanier, G. B., Sauer, W., & Larzelere, R. 1979. An empirical evaluation of the family life cycle. *Journal of Marriage and the Family* 41:15–26.

Stein, P. 1976. *Single.* Englewood Cliffs, NJ: Prentice-Hall.

Stierlin, H. 1974. *Separating parents and adolescents.* New York: Quadrangle.

Sussman, M. B. 1965. Relations of adult children with their parents. In *Social structure and the family: Generational relations,* ed. E. Shanas & G. F. Streib, pp. 62–92. Englewood Cliffs, N.J.: Prentice-Hall.

———. 1974. Family sociology. In *Current research in sociology,* ed. M. S. Archer. Paris: Mouton.

Sussman, M. B., & Burchinal, L. 1962. Kin family network: Unheralded structure in current conceptualizations of family functioning. *Marriage and Family Living* 24:231–240.

Uhlenberg, P. 1974. Cohort variations in family life cycle experiences of U.S. females. *Journal of Marriage and the Family* 36:284–292.

United Nations. 1981. Third world development: A U.S. perspective. *The Interdependent* 7 (July-August): 2.

U.S. Bureau of the Census. 1975. Projections of the population of the United States, by age and sex, 1975 to 2000, with extensions of total population to 2025. *Current Population Reports,* Series P-25, no. 541. Washington, D.C.: Government Printing Office.

Visher, E., & Visher, J. 1978. Common problems of step parents and their spouses. *American Journal of Orthopsychiatry* 48:252–262.

Visher, E., & Visher, J. 1979. *Stepfamilies: A guide to working with step-parents and step-children.* New York: Brunner-Mazel.

Waite, L. J. 1980. Working wives and the family life cycle. *American Journal of Sociology* 86:273–294.

Wallerstein, J. S., & Kelly, J. B. 1974. The effects of parental divorce: The adolescent experience. In *The child and his family: Children at psychiatric risk III,* eds. E. J. Anthony & C. Koupernik. New York: Wiley.

Wallerstein, J. S., & Kelly J. B. 1975. The effects of parental divorce: Experiences of the preschool child. *American Academy of Child Psychiatry* 14:600–616.

Wallerstein, J. S., & Kelly, J. B. 1976. The effects of parental divorce: Experiences of the child in early latency. *American Journal of Orthopsychiatry* 46:20–32. (a)

Wallerstein, J. S., & Kelly, J. B. 1976. The effects of parental divorce: Experiences of the child in later latency. *American Journal of Orthopsychiatry* 46:256–269. (b)

Wallerstein, J. S., & Kelly, J. B. 1977. Divorce counseling: A community service for families in the midst of divorce. *American Journal of Orthopsychiatry* 47:4–22. (a)

Wallerstein, J. S., & Kelly, J. B. 1977. Brief intervention with children in divorcing families. *American Journal of Orthopsychiatry* 47:23–37. (b)

Weiss, R. 1975. *Marital separation.* New York: Basic Books.

Westoff, L. A. 1977. *The second time around: Remarriage in America.* New York: Viking.

Whiteside, M., & Auerbach, L. 1978. Can the daughter of my father's new wife be my sister? Families of remarriage in family therapy. *Journal of Divorce* 1:271–283.

Chapter 3

Developmental Tasks: Individual and Family

MAJOR CONCEPTS

Critical periods
Sensitive periods
Freud's stages of psychosexual
    development
Erikson's stages of psychosexual
    development
Piaget's stages of cognitive
    development

Individual developmental tasks
Teachable moments (readiness)
Interaction of family members'
    developmental tasks
Family developmental tasks

Human development proceeds according to principles that apply to everyone. Persons grow in their own ways and at their own rates—yet in conformity with the developmental process followed by every human being. Knowledge of the universal patterns and principles of human development is basic to an understanding of the ways in which families and their members undertake their developmental tasks.

CRITICAL PERIODS IN HUMAN DEVELOPMENT

Critical periods in physical development occur at the times when specific organs or other aspects of an individual's growth are undergoing their most rapid change. It is during a period of accelerated growth that a given characteristic is most vulnerable to environmental factors. For instance, it is known that some pregnant women who took thalidomide or who contracted German measles during the first three months of pregnancy bore infants whose observable defects were in those parts of the body developing most rapidly at the time when the drug was ingested or the viral attack occurred.

Physical organs of embryos emerge according to a precise schedule that is important for their full, normal development and for their articulation into the rest of the organism. In this sequence of development each organ has its time of origin. The time factor is as important as the place of origin. If the eye, for example, does not arise at the appointed time, it may never be able to develop normally, since the time for the rapid growth of some other part will have arrived, dominating the less-active region and suppressing the belated tendency for eye development.

The organ that misses its time of ascendancy is not only doomed as an entity; its timing malfunctions also endanger a whole hierarchy of organs. The result of normal development is proper relationship of size and function among the body organs—the liver adjusted in size to the stomach and intestine, the heart and lungs properly balanced, and the capacity of the vascular system accurately proportioned to the body as a whole. Through developmental arrest, one or more organs may become disproportionately small, which upsets functional harmony and produces abnormalities.

SENSITIVE PERIODS IN PERSONAL DEVELOPMENT

The concept of *critical period* most accurately applies to physiological and especially embryological development. It means that there is a specific and limited time period during which certain tissues emerge or are formed in a phase of accelerated development. If the tissues do not form or differentiate during this critical period, they never will—the timing and sequencing in the overall developmental scheme is fixed and irreversible. In addition to understanding physical development and maturation, human development is also concerned with the emergence and development of abilities, behaviors, and social relations. In the area of human behaviors and social relations, the evidence is not as clear-cut and unequivocal that their timing is irreversibly critical.

Clearly, however, there are *sensitive periods* during which given behaviors or relations are typically acquired, and missing these experiences might make their future acquisition more difficult or even impossible. For example, Money and Ehrhardt (1972) have cautioned against sex reassignment in hermaphroditic children after around age 2 years when gender identity has become relatively fixed. Relatedly, there has been much speculation about the nature of parent-child attachments during infancy or during latency and the implications of what happens during these sensitive periods for later adult sexual preferences and adjustment. Given the lack of clear and convincing evidence, Bowlby's (1969, 166) comment seems especially appropriate:

> That there are sensitive periods in human development seems more than likely. Until far more is known about them it is wise to be cautious and to assume that the more the social environment in which a human child is reared deviates from the environment of evolutionary adaptedness (which is probably father, mother, and siblings in a social environment comprising grandparents and a limited number of other known families), the greater will be the risk of developing maladaptive patterns of social behavior.

Hypotheses and research findings concerning many facets of human development identify critical and sensitive periods at which a given characteristic or ability emerges. New development arises out of foundations already present. Growth is sequential, each new aspect of development proceeding from previously established structure or skills.

THE STUDY OF HUMAN DEVELOPMENT

Studies of childhood, of adolescence, and of young, middle-aged, and aging adults have recorded and outlined the process of human development throughout the life span. Professional observation and statistical evidence provide a remarkably consistent profile of human development from conception to the end of life.

Freud's Schema of Development

Sigmund Freud was one of the first and most prolific systematic observers of human behavior. His observations were based primarily on clinical interviews and therapy with troubled patients, and some of his writing concerned issues that have been difficult to study empirically (e.g., dreams and the unconscious). In spite of some limitations of representativeness and testability, Freud's observations of human behavior, social relations, and stages of psychosexual development have had an immense impact on our understanding and practice in these areas. His ideas about developmental stages are featured first here not because they are considered most important or most accurate, but because they came early chronologically and because they possess inestimable heuristic importance.

Freud identified the first six stages of human development as:

1. An *oral stage,* dominant during the first year, when infants depend on feeding for physical survival and emotional well-being;
2. An *anal stage,* during which toddlers are expected to conform to adult expectations that center in bowel and bladder training;
3. A *phallic stage,* when preschoolers become impressed with their bodies and with their growing sense of power and ability;
4. An *oedipal stage,* when—during the early school years—boys renounce earlier ties to their mothers and identify with their fathers, whereas girls become more feminine through identification with mothers;
5. A *latency stage,* during which reality orientation is in progress (following resolution of the oedipal conflict); and
6. *Adolescence,* the period beginning with genital maturation and ending when heterosexual maturity and the ability to give and to receive love are attained.

Erikson's Eight Stages in the Life Cycle[1]

Erikson has identified eight stages of life as critical in human psychosocial development. He points to the struggle between the negatives and positives in each stage that must be resolved if the next developmental stage is to be reached. He emphasizes that no victory is completely or forever won as an individual goes from stage to stage in psychosocial development.

1. *Infancy: trust versus mistrust.* The first "task" of infancy is to develop the "cornerstone of a healthy personality," a basic sense of trust—in self and environment. This comes from a feeling of inner goodness derived from "the mutual regulation of receptive capacities with the maternal techniques of provision"—a quality of care that transmits a sense of trustworthiness and meaning. The danger, most acute in the second half of the first year, is that discontinuities in care may cause children's natural sense of loss (as they gradually recognize their separateness from parents) to grow into a basic sense of mistrust that may last through life.
2. *Early childhood: autonomy versus shame and doubt.* With muscular maturation children experiment with holding on and letting go and begin to attach enormous value to their autonomous will. The danger here is that children may acquire a deep sense of shame and doubt if deprived of the opportunity to develop their will while learning their "duty" and, therefore, may come to expect defeat in any battle of wills with those who are bigger and stronger.
3. *Play age: initiative versus guilt.* In this stage children's imaginations are greatly

[1]See Close (1960) and Erikson (1950).

expanded because of their increased ability to move around freely and to communicate. It is an age of intrusive activity, avid curiosity, and consuming fantasies that lead to feelings of guilt and anxiety. It is also the stage of the establishment of conscience. If the tendency to feel guilty is "overburdened by all-too-eager adults," children may develop the belief that they are essentially bad, with a resultant stifling of initiative or a conversion of moralism to vindictiveness.

4. *School age: industry versus inferiority.* The long period of sexual latency before puberty is the age when children want to learn how to do and make things with others. In the process of learning to accept instructions and to win recognition by producing "things," children are also developing the capacity to enjoy work. The danger in this period is the development of a sense of inadequacy and inferiority in children who do not receive recognition for their efforts.

5. *Adolescence: identity versus identity diffusion.* The dramatic physiological changes that come with puberty—rapid body growth and sexual maturity—force young people to question all sameness and continuities relied on earlier and to refight many of the earlier battles. The developmental task is to integrate childhood identifications with the basic biological drives, native endowment, and the opportunities offered in social roles. The danger is that identity diffusion, temporarily unavoidable in this period of physical and psychological upheaval, may result in a permanent inability to "take hold" or, because of youth's tendency to total commitment, in the fixation of a negative identity, a devoted attempt to become what parents, class, or community oppose.

6. *Young adulthood: intimacy versus isolation.* Only as young people begin to feel more secure in their identities are they able to establish intimacy with themselves (with one's inner life) and with others, both in friendships and eventually in a love-based mutually satisfying sexual relationship. A person who cannot enter wholly into an intimate relationship because of the fear of losing identity may develop a sense of isolation.

7. *Adulthood: generativity versus self-absorption.* Out of the intimacies of adulthood grows generativity—the mature person's interest in establishing and guiding the next generation. Lack of this results in self-absorption and frequently in a pervading sense of stagnation and interpersonal impoverishment.

8. *Senescence: integrity versus disgust.* Those who have achieved a satisfying intimacy with other human beings and who have adapted to the triumphs and disappointments of their generative activities as parents and coworkers reach the end of life with a certain ego integrity—an acceptance of their own responsibility for what life is and was and of its place in the flow of history. Without this "accrued ego integration" there is despair, usually marked by a display of displeasure and disgust.

Piaget's Conception of Cognitive Development[2]

Piaget's work on the foundations of cognition puts renewed emphasis on early human development and experience. He sees a definite order in which behavior and thought make their appearance as a result of a child's interaction with the environment. Infants are born

²See Hunt (1961), Piaget and Inhelder (1969), and White (1969).

with reflexes and built-in complexes of the senses, nerves, and muscles that they exercise and learn to use during the *sensorimotor stage* in the first years of life. Piaget sees this as exercising ready-made sensorimotor schemata. Sometime after the first month, babies vary and combine their nursing behavior—looking while sucking or turning the head toward moving objects in what Piaget calls primary circular reactions. Infants' secondary circular reactions, which come next, include initiating and anticipating the behavior of others and reaching out to them. This is close to what Erikson refers to as the basis of trust. Near the end of the first year, infants imitate, play games, and become social beings who recognize that what they do brings about some expected consequence, in what Piaget calls coordination of secondary schemata. Between the first and second years of life, toddlers are curious, "into everything," craving more and more environmental stimulation in tertiary circular reactions. Between 18 and 24 months vocabulary spirals, and infants change into children who operate more by symbols, who remember where things are and look for them, and who delight in problem solving. Piaget calls this stage the internalization of sensorimotor schemata.

Between 18 months and 4 years, during children's *preconceptual* or *preoperational stage,* they accumulate images and form "intuitions." By 9 or 10, children are able to order objects serially by length, later by weight, and at 11 or 12 by volume, in *concrete operations.* The final period, beginning at 11 or 12, is a landmark in that the individual can now understand abstract concepts and propositions as well as concrete objects. This leads to the *formal operations* that provide the intellectual ability for the scientific method.

Bloom's Review of Longitudinal Studies

Bloom (1964) analyzed 1000 longitudinal studies of individuals who were repeatedly measured and observed at different points in their development. By synthesizing the results of numerous studies, he was able to describe development quantitatively for 30 human characteristics. Using the data, he predicted the ages at which 7 of these characteristics have reached a level of development representing 50 percent of their full potentiality (as expected at maturity). The 7 (listed in Table 3.1, pp. 48–49) are height by age 2½, general intelligence by age 4, aggressiveness in males by age 3, dependency in females by age 4, general school achievement by the third grade, and reading comprehension and vocabulary by age 9.

Thurstone's work (1955), reviewed by Bloom, found 80 percent of adult performance levels in children and adolescents in a number of characteristics: perceptual speed by age 12, space and reasoning factors by age 14, number and memory factors by age 16, verbal comprehension by age 18, and verbal fluency that reaches the 80 percent level by age 20. Longitudinal studies of college students show ego development reaching 80 percent levels by age 18 and flattening out in a plateau by age 25 (Sanford 1962).

Research findings underline the Freudian and Eriksonian statements on the crucial importance of the earliest months of life as the infant learns to nurse and develops a sense of trust—in self, in parent(s), and in the world as the infant knows it. Piaget stresses the critical significance of the first weeks and months in the development of intelligence and the ability to learn. Hundreds of studies tracing the development of many human characteristics have pinpointed the timing and significance of critical or sensitive periods for the successful emergence of physical, intellectual, and personality factors. Some of these are indicated in Table 3.1 at ages approximated by Freud, Erikson, Piaget, Bloom, and Thurstone and others.

PATTERNS AND PRINCIPLES OF DEVELOPMENT

Human growth, development, and decline involve a number of types of change, 12 of which are listed in Table 3.2, p. 50.

Each individual is unique in terms of both inherited and environmentally learned aspects, but there is a universally recognized pattern of development throughout the life span. Human growth and development progress according to a number of principles, which are listed in Table 3.3, p. 51.

DEVELOPMENTAL TASKS OF INDIVIDUALS

Developmental tasks are defined as tasks that arise at or near a certain time in the life of an individual, the successful achievement of which leads to happiness and success with later tasks—whereas failure leads to unhappiness in the individual, disapproval by society, and difficulty with later tasks (Havighurst 1972, 2). As physical growth proceeds from one stage of development to the next, the individual must learn to use newfound powers; that is, infants learn progressively to suck, to drink, to swallow soft food, to chew, and eventually to eat at the family table. Teething occurs automatically over time; learning to eat solid foods and to hold a spoon are developmental tasks of early childhood.

Developmental tasks arise at sensitive periods in individuals' growth, when others expect a specific kind of performance from them. Children are expected to learn to read when they go to school; when children are successful, both they and others (teachers, parents, and other kinfolk) are happy about this progress, and children then go on to more complex accomplishments in school and elsewhere. Should reading be difficult to the point of failure (for any of a number of reasons), school progress is slowed, children are unhappy about themselves, and they face the disapproval of others.

Origins of Developmental Tasks

Developmental tasks have two primary origins: (1) physical maturation and (2) cultural pressures and privileges. A secondary origin derived from the first two is found in the aspirations and values of the individual.

As individuals grow, they mature. Growth represents much more than added stature and bulk. It involves the elaboration and maturation of the muscle, organ, bone, and neural systems of the organism according to a predictable sequence. Certain developmental tasks come primarily from the maturation of one or more aspects of the organism. For example, as infants' leg and back muscles develop enough strength, and as the neural connections mature to the point where children have conscious control over movement, they face the developmental task of learning to walk. When the adolescent girl's body develops into one resembling that of a woman, and as she begins to menstruate, she must come to terms with her femaleness and develop a wholesome acceptance of herself as a woman. Later, when she reaches middle age, menopause represents yet another developmental task—that of accepting the termination of her reproductive life and facing the challenge of aging. Many comparable developmental tasks present themselves throughout the lives of both men and women.

Cultural pressures may be recognized in the many rewards and penalties the individual receives (and anticipates) for various behaviors. Society (in the form of peers, associates,

Table 3.1 SENSITIVE PERIODS IN HUMAN DEVELOPMENT (THEORY AND RESEARCH)

Age	Period	Freud	Erikson	Piaget	Bloom (50 percent full potential)	Thurstone and others (80 percent full potential)
23	Parenthood		Generativity			
22	Marriage		Intimacy			
21	Adulthood					
20						Word fluency
19						
18						Verbal comprehension Ego development
17						
16						Number and memory factors
15	Adolescence		Identity	Formal operations		
14						Space and reasoning factors
13	Teenage					
12						Perceptual speed

Age	Period	Freud	Erikson	Piaget		
11						
10					Reading comprehension	
9			Industry		Vocabulary	
8				Concrete operations	General school achievement	Intelligence
7		Latency				
6	School-age	Oedipal				
5			Initiative	Preoperational: intuitive	Dependency	
4		Phallic	Imagination	Preconceptual	General intelligence	
3	Preschool	Anal		Sensorimotor: means-end behavior	Aggression in boys	
2			Autonomy	Internalization	Height	
1	Infancy	Oral	Trust	Circular reactions		
0	Birth			Reflexes		

Sources with approximate ages from Freud, Erikson, Piaget, Bloom, Thurstone, Sanford works cited in "References."

parents, teachers, and all the "significant others" in life) expects and often exerts pressure on the person to conform to the prescribed ways of behaving within a given culture. These expectations and pressures emerge at the times believed appropriate in the culture for individuals to function in the roles and statuses appropriate to their age and sex. Unfortunately, they may be too soon or too late for a particular individual.

When children reach certain ages, they are expected to eat solid foods, to be toilet trained, to walk, to talk, to respect property rights, to mingle socially with members of the other sex, to marry and "settle down," and so on through the entire life span. Regardless of what they are and when they come into effect, these expectancies impel the individuals of the culture to behave in certain ways; thus they are an important origin of their developmental tasks. Examples in our society are learning to read, learning to handle money responsibly, learning how to gain a place for oneself with one's age-mates, and establishing oneself as an acceptable member of the dating crowd as a teenager and among the young married set as a husband or wife.

Developmental tasks differ from culture to culture. Each cultural group has its own developmental definitions and expectations. The fact that these tasks also vary from region to region in our country—even from class to class in the same area—accounts for many persistent problems among children of different ethnic and cultural backgrounds.

Encouragement and support by family and friends are often essential in achieving developmental tasks that the individual alone might find too difficult. As cultural pressures work upon a maturing young person, the emergent personality is formed, with all of its idiosyncratic values and aspirations. These in turn significantly influence the direction and form of future developmental tasks. Two examples of developmental tasks derived primarily

Table 3.2 TWELVE TYPES OF CHANGE IN HUMAN GROWTH, DEVELOPMENT, AND DECLINE

1. Changes in specificity (embryonic growth and development proceeds from simple cells to specific, functioning organ systems).

2. Changes in efficiency (the digestive system is more efficient in childhood than in either infancy or aging).

3. Changes in kind (adult hair differs from baby down and also from thin, drying, aging hair).

4. Changes in color (skin and hair darkens through childhood; hair loses color, and skin darkens in later years).

5. Changes in number (teeth change from none visible at birth to 20, more or less, in the preschooler; then schoolchild gets permanent teeth, which may be lost over the years).

6. Changes in size (organs and stature become larger through the first 20 years; some shrinking of body size is common in later years).

7. Changes in shape (the profile of the body differs in infancy, childhood, adolescence, and adulthood in ways that are predictable).

8. Changes in texture (bones are soft in infancy, harden in childhood, and become brittle in aging).

9. Changes in flexibility (the infant and child's body is elastic and flexible; adult muscles and joints stiffen through the years).

10. Changes in control (the infant has little control; an adult enjoys full control; the aged lose some ability to control physical processes).

11. Changes in teachability (a child learns many skills readily; adults learn with more difficulty).

12. Changes in physical satisfaction (the infant, child, and adolescent enjoy physical activities; the older adult finds less satisfaction in declining powers).

Source: Model freely adapted and expanded from Boyd R. McCandless, *Children: Behavior and Development* (New York: Holt, Rinehart and Winston, 1967), p. 412.

Table 3.3 PRINCIPLES INHERENT IN DEVELOPMENT

1. Development results from both biological maturation and individual learning.

2. Development of human characteristics tends to be orderly, regular, and predictable.

3. Growth rates vary within the different stages of individual development.

4. Individuals grow at a pace appropriate for them, at their stage of development, in their environment.

5. Development tends to be sequential, with each added increment built on earlier ones.

6. Development of specific characteristics is based on previous progress in similar or associated forms.

7. Growth and development are most rapid during the early stages of life.

8. The first months and years are crucial foundations for later development.

9. Early verbal learning is essential for the development of later complex human skills.

10. Socially prescribed expectations order the major events of a lifetime in a given society.

11. Norms for given ages and stages function as social prods or brakes on behavior.

12. Development proceeds in a specific direction, from a known beginning to an expected end.

13. Anticipated end points in development serve as personal goals for individuals.

14. Personal goals are both individually and socially determined.

15. Attainment of personal goals brings a sense of fulfillment and success.

16. Developing individuals face certain responsibilities for maturing and achieving at every stage of life.

17. Individuals may be expected to be at work on developmental tasks appropriate to their stage of development.

18. Developmental tasks successfully accomplished lead to further developmental levels.

19. No one else can accomplish the developmental tasks an individual faces.

20. Few developmental tasks are completed in isolation; most depend on social interaction.

21. Helping persons (parents, teachers, etc.) can be of great help to a child at work on one or more of his developmental tasks.

22. Modification of environment has least effect on characteristics at their periods of least development.

23. Rates of growth and development may be modified most at times of most rapid change.

24. Assistance in development is most effective at times of fastest growth and readiness.

from the personal aspirations and values of the individual are choosing a vocation and achieving a personal philosophy of life, both of which reflect the life around the person.

Basically, a developmental task is a thrust from within the individual to develop in such a way (by modifying present behavior) as to attain a desired goal. The push to change usually comes from within the person but may be evoked by the demands and expectations of others. It receives its direction from the cultural definition of what is expected of an individual at the present stage of development. A developmental task, although culturally defined, is neither a chore nor a duty, in the sense that it is externally imposed. It is rather a growth responsibility that individuals assume for their own development as they adapt to life situations.

Assumption of a given developmental task consists of at least four interrelated operations: (1) perceiving new possibilities for behavior in what seems to be expected or in what more mature others are seen accomplishing, (2) forming new conceptions of self (identity formation), (3) coping effectively with conflicting demands, and (4) wanting to achieve the next step in development enough to work toward it (motivation). To illustrate: A small boy sees somewhat bigger boys riding their bicycles (operation 1—perception); he conceives of himself as a potential bicycle rider (operation 2—identity formation); he resolves the conflicts between his mother's protests that he might get hurt and his own fears of failure with the expectancies of his peers and the demands of his father that he become a "big boy" (operation 3—coping with conflicting demands); and finally, he wants to learn to ride a bike enough to practice what it takes to become proficient at it (operation 4—motivation).

Most of the growth responsibilities individuals confront result from the combined impact of biologic maturing, the environmental forces that work upon them, and individuals' own personal drives, ambitions, and value orientations. Thus the task of being weaned results from a baby boy's physiological maturation (teething, etc.), as well as from cultural pressures in the form of maternal insistence that he take solid foods and his own desire to be a "big boy" and eat as the others in the family do. Teenage dating emerges partly from the biologic maturing of puberty, partly from the cultural pressures of friends and family to have a girl- or boyfriend and go out to young people's activities in the community, and partly from the person's own aspirations to belong, to be accepted, to be recognized.

The Teachable Moment

When the time comes that the body is ready for, that culture is pressing for, and that the individual is striving for some achievement, the teachable moment has arrived. It is at this very moment—at the convergence of its several origins—that the accomplishment of the developmental task is most highly motivated; at that time the individual is most truly ready for the next step in development. Before that, the person is not mature enough for the desired outcome, so that efforts to push the individual through a premature accomplishment may be largely wasted. Readiness also implies that the person has lived fully at the present stage and thus is not being hurried into the next stage.

An illustration is found in the early efforts to toilet train an infant. In the 1920s and 1930s, toilet training was often attempted while the baby was only a few weeks old. At that age the baby's sphincter muscles were not ready for such control; neural connections had not matured enough to make the baby's cooperation possible; and the baby's own aspirations were in quite another direction. It is not surprising that the premature demands of the parent upon the child met with failure and often created persistent conflict. Knowledge of child development has modified these expectancies, and today good practice is to wait for signs that the baby is ready before parents begin assisting and insisting on achievement of toilet-training tasks. This concept of "readiness" is well established in the field of human development.

The concept of the teachable moment goes a bit deeper, since it indicates specifically the three dimensions in which readiness emerges—in the physical organism, in the social pressures, and in the personal values of the individual. It is a useful guide for anyone responsible for the growth, development, and guidance of others: teachers, supervisors, parents—indeed anyone who works with, or cares about, other people. It provides a gauge of what may be expected of given persons and an approximate timetable for anticipating change. This ability to predict what persons at various stages of development are, or soon will be, ready for is of paramount importance to curriculum formulators and educators in general. If we assume that the general purpose of both family life and education is to assist persons in attaining their best potential, we see that some knowledge of developmental tasks —and especially of the teachable moments at which these tasks arise—is highly relevant.

There is a tide in the affairs of men
Which, taken at the flood, leads on to fortune;
Omitted, all the voyage of their life
Is bound in shallows and in miseries.
Shakespeare, Julius Caesar, act 4, sc. 3

Developmental Tasks of the Individual Throughout Life

The developmental tasks faced by individuals as they progress through the years from birth to death are innumerable. It would be impossible to list completely all of the growth responsibilities to be achieved by any one person. Yet there are certain general categories of tasks that allow us to catalog the more common developmental tasks within our culture. A formulation of this type is found in Table 3.4.

Such a listing of the individual's developmental tasks is not all-inclusive, nor is it universally applicable. Different cultures and subcultures make different demands on their members. In most of the cultures of the world today, the general expectancies change from time to time, so that the developmental tasks of one generation differ somewhat from those of the preceding or of the succeeding one.

Whichever society in which individuals mature, they face the developmental tasks peculiar to it at every stage of the life span. The successful achievement of one's developmental tasks brings the individual from a state of helpless dependence as an infant, through varying dimensions of independence as an adolescent, to a mature level of interdependence with others that lasts through the greater part of adulthood.

INTERACTING DEVELOPMENTAL TASKS OF FAMILY MEMBERS

At any given moment children are striving to meet their growth needs, parents are working to reconcile conflicting demands, while children, and parents individually, are struggling to find themselves in the midst of the security and threats of their particular world.

There are times when members of a family find it easy to mutually support and sustain one another, when the various developmental tasks of family members call for the channeling of energies in the same general direction. At such times the family moves as a unit to meet the developmental requirements of each member. Just as naturally, on occasion, the goals, needs, striving, and developmental tasks of family members are in conflict. If we hold the entire family in focus, we see that much of the normal friction between members during the family life cycle is due to incompatibility of the diverse developmental strivings of family members at critical points of growth.

From time to time the developmental tasks of the husband may conflict with those of his wife. A simple illustration can be found in a young husband's developmental task of developing competency in household maintenance. His do-it-yourself projects might clutter up the house at the time when his wife is trying to maintain a pleasant, attractive home amid the already heavy demands of her work projects and small children.

Developmental tasks of children conflict with those of their parents at several stages in the family life cycle. In adolescence the young person is struggling to become emancipated from the authority of the parents, whose own developmental tasks as parents call for sustained guidance and supervision of the not-yet-adult child. At such a time, storms brew and

Table 3.4 DEVELOPMENTAL TASKS IN 10 CATEGORIES OF BEHAVIOR OF THE INDIVIDUAL FROM BIRTH TO DEATH

	Infancy (birth to 1 or 2)	Early childhood (2–3 to 5–6–7)	Late childhood (5–6–7 to pubescence)
I Achieving an appropriate dependence-independence pattern	1. Establishing oneself as a very dependent being 2. Beginning the establishment of self-awareness	1. Adjusting to less private attention; becoming independent physically (while remaining strongly dependent emotionally)	1. Freeing oneself from primary identification with adults
II Achieving an appropriate giving-receiving pattern of affection	1. Developing a feeling for affection	1. Developing the ability to give affection 2. Learning to share affection	1. Learning to give as much love as one receives; forming friendships with peers
III Relating to changing social groups	1. Becoming aware of the alive as against the inanimate, and the familiar as against the unfamiliar 2. Developing rudimentary social interaction	1. Beginning to develop the ability to interact with age-mates 2. Adjusting in the family to expectations it has for the child as a member of the social unit	1. Clarifying the adult world as over against the child's world 2. Establishing peer groupness and learning to belong

Source: An elaboration of Caroline Tryon and Jesse W. Lilienthal III, "Guideposts in Child Growth and Development," *NEA Journal* (March 1950): 189.

Early adolescence (pubescence to puberty)	Late adolescence (puberty to early maturity)	Maturity (early to late active adulthood)	Aging (beyond full powers of adulthood through senility)
1. Establishing one's independence from adults in all areas of behavior	1. Establishing oneself as an independent individual in an adult manner	1. Learning to be interdependent— now leaning, now succoring others, as need arises 2. Assisting one's children to become gradually independent and autonomous beings	1. Accepting graciously and comfortably the help needed from others as powers fail and dependence becomes necessary
1. Accepting oneself as a worthwhile person really worthy of love	1. Building a strong mutual affectional bond with a (possible) marriage partner	1. Building and maintaining a strong and mutually satisfying marriage relationship 2. Establishing wholesome affectional bonds with one's children and grandchildren 3. Meeting wisely the new needs for affection of one's own aging parents 4. Cultivating meaningfully warm friendships with members of one's own generation	1. Facing loss of one's spouse, and finding some satisfactory sources of affection previously received from mate 2. Learning new affectional roles with own children, now mature adults 3. Establishing ongoing, satisfying affectional patterns with grandchildren and other members of the extended family 4. Finding and preserving mutually satisfying friendships outside the family circle
1. Behaving according to a shifting peer code	1. Adopting an adult-patterned set of social values by learning a new peer code	1. Keeping in reasonable balance activities in the various social, service, political, and community groups and causes that make demands on adults 2. Establishing and maintaining mutually satisfactory relationships with the in-law families of spouse and married children	1. Choosing and maintaining ongoing social activities and functions appropriate to health, energy, and interests

Table 3.4 *(Continued)*

	Infancy (birth to 1 or 2)	Early childhood (2–3 to 5–6–7)	Late childhood (5–6–7 to pubescence)
IV Developing a conscience	1. Beginning to adjust to the expectations of others	1. Developing the ability to take directions and to be obedient in the presence of authority 2. Developing the ability to be obedient in the absence of authority where conscience substitutes for authority	1. Learning more rules and developing true morality
V Learning one's psycho-socio-biological sex role		1. Learning to identify with male adult and female adult roles	1. Beginning to identify with one's social contemporaries of the same sex
VI Accepting and adjusting to a changing body	1. Adjusting to adult feeding demands 2. Adjusting to adult cleanliness demands 3. Adjusting to adult attitudes toward genital manipulation	1. Adjusting to expectations resulting from one's improving muscular abilities 2. Developing sexual, clothing, and elimination modesty appropriate to the culture	

Early adolescence (pubescence to puberty)	Late adolescence (puberty to early maturity)	Maturity (early to late active adulthood)	Aging (beyond full powers of adulthood through senility)
	1. Learning to understand contradictions in moral codes, as well as discrepancies between principle and practice, and resolving these problems in a responsible manner	1. Coming to terms with the violations of moral codes in the larger as well as in the more intimate social scene, and developing some constructive philosophy and method of operation 2. Helping children to adjust to the expectations of others and to conform to the moral demands of the culture	1. Maintaining a sense of moral integrity in the face of disappointments and disillusionments in life's hopes and dreams
1. Strong identification with one's own sex mates 2. Learning one's role in heterosexual relationships	1. Exploring possibilities for a future mate and acquiring "desirability" 2. Choosing an occupation 3. Preparing to accept one's future role in manhood or womanhood as a responsible citizen of the larger community	1. Learning to be a competent husband or wife, and building a good marriage 2. Carrying a socially adequate role as citizen and worker in the community 3. Becoming a good parent and grandparent as children arrive and develop	1. Learning to live on a retirement income 2. Being a good companion to an aging spouse 3. Meeting bereavement of spouse adequately
1. Reorganizing one's thoughts and feelings about oneself in the face of significant bodily changes and their concomitants 2. Accepting the reality of one's appearance	1. Learning appropriate outlets for sexual drives	1. Making a good sex adjustment within marriage 2. Establishing healthful routines of eating, resting, working, playing within the pressures of the adult world	1. Making a good adjustment to failing powers as aging diminishes strengths and abilities

Table 3.4 *(Continued)*

		Infancy (birth to 1 or 2)	Early childhood (2–3 to 5–6–7)	Late childhood (5–6–7 to pubescence)
VII	Managing a changing body and learning new motor patterns	1. Developing physiological equilibrium 2. Developing eye-hand coordination 3. Establishing satisfactory rhythms of rest and activity	1. Developing large muscle control 2. Learning to coordinate large muscles and small muscles	1. Refining and elaborating skill in the use of small muscles
VIII	Learning to understand and control the physical world	1. Exploring the physical world	1. Meeting adult expectations for restrictive exploration and manipulation of an expanding environment	1. Learning more realistic ways of studying and controlling the physical world
IX	Developing an appropriate symbol system and conceptual abilities	1. Developing preverbal communication 2. Developing verbal communication 3. Developing rudimentary concept formation	1. Improving one's use of the symbol system 2. Undergoing an enormous elaboration of the concept pattern	1. Learning to use language to actually exchange ideas or to influence one's hearers 2. Beginning understanding of real causal relations 3. Making finer conceptual distinctions and thinking reflectively
X	Relating oneself to the cosmos		1. Developing a genuine, though uncritical, notion about one's place in the cosmos	1. Developing a scientific approach

Early adolescence (pubescence to puberty)	Late adolescence (puberty to early maturity)	Maturity (early to late active adulthood)	Aging (beyond full powers of adulthood through senility)
1. Controlling and using a "new" body		1. Learning new skills and activities expected of adults in the community	1. Adapting interests and activities to reserves of vitality and energy of the aging body
		1. Gaining intelligent understanding of new horizons of medicine and science sufficient for personal well-being and social competence	1. Mastering new awareness and methods of dealing with physical surroundings as an individual with occasional or permanent disabilities
1. Using language to express and to clarify more complex concepts 2. Moving from the concrete to the abstract and applying general principles to the particular	1. Achieving the level of reasoning of which one is capable	1. Mastering technical symbol systems involved in income tax, social security, complex financial dealings, and other contexts familiar in Western society	1. Keeping mentally alert and effective as long as is possible through the later years
	1. Formulating a workable belief and value system	1. Formulating and implementing a rational philosophy of life on the basis of adult experience 2. Cultivating a satisfactory religious climate in the home as the spiritual soil for development of family members	1. Preparing for eventual and inevitable cessation of life by building a set of beliefs that one can live and die with in peace

break within the family as normally as they do in the weather, when two or more energy systems moving in opposite directions collide.

Now unified, now atomized, each family lives out its own unique history. Each family is an arena where interacting personalities try to achieve their own developmental tasks within the pattern of family life—which in turn is evolving in interaction with the larger society of which it is a part.

BASIC FAMILY TASKS

A family must perform certain basic tasks that are essential for its survival and continuity. Basic required or expected tasks of American families are:

1. Providing shelter, food, clothing, health care, and the like for family members;
2. Meeting family costs and allocating such resources as time, space, facilities, and so on, according to each member's needs;
3. Determining who does what in the support, management, and care of the home and its members;
4. Ensuring each member's socialization through the internalization of increasingly mature roles in the family and beyond;
5. Establishing ways of interacting, communicating, expressing affection, aggression, sexuality, and so on, within limits acceptable to society;
6. Bearing (or adopting) and rearing children and incorporating and releasing family members appropriately;
7. Relating to school, church, work, and community life and establishing policies for including in-laws, relatives, guests, friends, mass media, and so forth; and
8. Maintaining morale and motivation, rewarding achievement, meeting personal and family crises, setting attainable goals, and developing family loyalties and values.

Families have these basic tasks as long as they exist. Each family performs its essential functions in its own ways, which may differ from those of others. Families in various ethnic, racial, and social class groupings operate within the freedoms and constraints of their subcultures as well as those of the larger society. As long as families function adequately, their right to live as they wish is not challenged. However, when its norms are not met, society intervenes to protect its members. When family tasks are not being accomplished, welfare, police, fire, education, and health departments, other agency representatives, relatives, and friends invade the family's privacy to monitor, correct, supplement, or take over the basic tasks not being discharged at least minimally within that family. Basic family tasks are so essential that if the family does not perform them, others will.

FAMILY DEVELOPMENTAL TASKS

Family developmental tasks are specific to a given stage of development in the family life cycle. Family developmental tasks are directed toward meeting the requisites for family well-being and continuation at any particular period in the life of the family. Family developmental tasks may be seen as those growth responsibilities that must be accomplished by a family at a given stage of its development in a way that satisfies (1) its members' biological requirements, (2) society's cultural imperatives, and (3) its members' aspirations and values —if the family is to continue as a unit. In much the same way that individual developmental tasks change over the years, so family developmental tasks shift with each stage of the family life cycle.

Family developmental tasks parallel the developmental tasks of individual family members and can be similarly defined. Thus a family developmental task is a growth responsibility that arises at a certain stage in the life of a family, the successful achievement of which leads to present satisfaction, approval, and success with later tasks—whereas failure leads to unhappiness in the family, disapproval by society, and difficulty with later family developmental tasks.

Sources of a Family Developmental Task

A family developmental task arises at any point in a family's life when the needs of one or more family members converge with societal expectations of family performance. As individuals develop, and as they respond to their associates' expectations with new aspirations, they make demands on their families to support their new individual developmental tasks. Such demands exert internal pressure on the family to change. Simultaneously, pressures constraining the family to conform to society's standards of conduct at that time are applied from outside the family. These community pressures vary according to the family's social status, age, and sex composition. The family's sense of identity, its reputation in the community, and its own aspirations are mobilized to meet the new challenges as a family unit, and the new family developmental task is undertaken (Aldous 1978).

Stage-Sensitive Family Developmental Tasks

Stage-sensitive family developmental tasks occur as the family enters each new stage of its development. Critical events such as getting married, bearing children, releasing them as teenagers and young adults, and continuing as a couple through the empty nest and aging years (Table 3.5) propel a family into and through each new stage in its history. Each new developmental crisis necessitates new adaptations and imposes new responsibilities at the same time that it opens up new opportunities and poses new challenges. For instance, as the members of the newly married couple leave their parents' homes, their families are engaged in the family developmental tasks of launching young adults. The young couple enter their own marriage at its establishment phase and must deal with all the critical changes and developmental tasks involved in building a marriage and establishing a family.

FAMILY ASPIRATIONS AND GOALS

Family aspirations are the short-term, tension-reducing objectives that family members view as important at the moment. One family is building a new home; another is saving for a vacation; a third is trying to get out of debt; another is attempting to get its eldest child into college, to nurse an ill member back to health, or to release a young adult into marriage.

Family aspirations are specific to the particular family in its social group at a particular time. Such immediate objectives tend to shift as soon as one step has been reached. Thus once

Table 3.5 STAGE-SENSITIVE FAMILY DEVELOPMENTAL TASKS THROUGH THE FAMILY LIFE CYCLE

Stage of the family life cycle	Positions in the family	Stage-sensitive family developmental tasks
1. Married couple	Wife Husband	Establishing a mutually satisfying marriage Adjusting to pregnancy and the promise of parenthood Fitting into the kin network
2. Childbearing	Wife-mother Husband-father Infant daughter or son or both	Having, adjusting to, and encouraging the development of infants Establishing a satisfying home for both parents and infant(s)
3. Preschool-age	Wife-mother Husband-father Daughter-sister Son-brother	Adapting to the critical needs and interests of preschool children in stimulating, growth-promoting ways Coping with energy depletion and lack of privacy as parents
4. School-age	Wife-mother Husband-father Daughter-sister Son-brother	Fitting into the community of school-age families in constructive ways Encouraging children's educational achievement
5. Teenage	Wife-mother Husband-father Daughter-sister Son-brother	Balancing freedom with responsibility as teenagers mature and emancipate themselves Establishing postparental interests and careers as growing parents
6. Launching center	Wife-mother-grandmother Husband-father-grandfather Daughter-sister-aunt Son-brother-uncle	Releasing young adults into work, military service, college, marriage, and so on with appropriate rituals and assistance Maintaining a supportive home base
7. Middle-aged parents	Wife-mother-grandmother Husband-father-grandfather	Refocusing on the marriage relationship Maintaining kin ties with older and younger generations
8. Aging family members	Widow or widower Wife-mother-grandmother Husband-father-grandfather	Coping with bereavement and living alone Closing the family home or adapting it to aging Adjusting to retirement

the home has been built, other goals appear—for example, the new house must be furnished or the yard must be landscaped.

Beyond the specific and temporary aspirations of a given family are the objectives that society as a whole has for its families. National goals are concerned with family health, safety, stability, standards of living, and levels of education; they are also concerned with the competence of families to develop citizens capable of functioning effectively in a free society. Some national goals for families are designed to protect the country as a whole. In times of national emergency, such as war, families are expected to do their part for the war effort by contributing on the home front and by sending eligible members into service. During the continuing energy crisis, it is important for families to cooperate in conserving the various forms of energy; so too when other shortages appear, families are urged to conserve, recycle, and make do for the welfare of the nation. Many government programs that enlist family support have as their ultimate goal the common good.

Family goals can be seen as falling between the short-term aspirations of a given family at a particular time and the long-term national goals for all families in the society. Ideally, a family's goals have a positive effect on the lives of family members—motivating and supporting them at every step in their psychosocial development (Table 3.5). The modes and course of action followed by a family as it carries out its developmental tasks at any stage in its life cycle reflect the family's goals. Thus family goals at the establishment phase of family life center on adjusting to living as a married couple. When children come, family goals involve providing for their care, nurture, and development. As children mature, family goals are focused on loosening family ties and releasing young adults into families of their own. Family goals profoundly influence family functioning and developmental tasks at every stage of the family life cycle.

Families, as families, have responsibilities, goals, and developmental tasks that are specifically related to the development of their members. All of these developmental tasks —those of family members and of the family as a unit—shift as the family changes and are constantly being modified by the interplay of forces both within and outside of the family in every society, in every age.

SUMMARY

Human development proceeds in stages and sequences that are universal or very nearly so. Three major conceptualizations by Freud, Erikson, and Piaget suggest key stages and their ordering in the predictable development of human beings. Freud's stages of psychosexual development are especially focused on the development of sexual behavior, culminating in late adolescence and early adulthood with heterosexual maturity. Erikson's theory of psychosocial development is more inclusive than Freud's schema, both in terms of the length of time considered (infancy to senescence) and its content (social relations as opposed to sexual relations). Piaget's theory centers on the emergence and development of cognitive abilities originating in sensorimotor experiences and culminating in abstract reasoning.

Many abilities and characteristics typically present in adulthood are largely developed at surprisingly early ages. The concepts of *critical* and *sensitive periods* both refer to specific times when development is "scheduled" to occur, when development is accelerated, and when the individual is particularly susceptible to environmental stimuli. They differ in how set, invariant, and irreversible they are in the process of development.

Individual developmental tasks are those issues or growth responsibilities that confront an individual and that need to be mastered for the person to be happy, to have the approval of others, and to move on to further developmental challenges. They emerge partly as a result of physical maturation and partly from social expectations or cultural norms. In the process of human development, physical abilities, social expectations, and the personal motivation of the individual sometimes converge in unique periods of "readiness" or *teachable moments* that are ripe for the accomplishment of developmental tasks. Many developmental tasks are faced throughout life, and the intersection of the very different, sometimes complementary and sometimes competing, tasks of family members gives family interaction its uniquely effervescent quality.

Families as social units in society also face identifiable tasks, the successful accomplishment of which maintains and increases morale among family members and makes it possible for them to face further challenges in their family life cycle.

REFERENCES

Aldous, J. 1978. *Family careers: Developmental change in families.* New York: Wiley.

Bloom, B. S. 1964. *Stability and change in human characteristics.* New York: Wiley.

Bowlby, J. 1969. *Attachment.* New York: Basic Books.

Close, K. 1960. Youth and the life cycle. (Interview with Erik H. Erikson.) *Children,* March-April, 1960.

Erikson, E. H. 1950. *Childhood and society.* New York: Norton.

Freud, S. 1965. *New introductory lectures on psychoanalysis.* Edited by James Stachey. New York: Norton.

Havighurst, R. J. 1972. *Developmental tasks and education.* 3d ed. New York: David McKay.

Hunt, J. M. 1961. *Intelligence and experience.* New York: Ronald Press.

McCandless, B. R. 1967. *Children: behavior and development.* New York: Holt, Rinehart and Winston, p. 412.

Magrabi, F. M., & Marshall, W. H. 1965. Family developmental tasks: A research model. *Journal of Marriage and the Family* 27:454–461.

Money, J., & Ehrhardt, A. 1972. *Man and woman: Boy and girl.* Baltimore, MD: Johns Hopkins University Press.

Piaget, J., & Inhelder, B. 1969. *The psychology of the child.* New York: Basic Books.

Sanford, N., ed. 1962. *The American college.* New York: Wiley.

Thurstone, L. I. 1955. *The differential growth of mental abilities.* Chapel Hill: University of North Carolina Psychometric Laboratory.

Tryon, C., & Lilienthal, J. W. III. 1950. Guideposts in child growth and development. *NEA Journal* (March): 189.

White, B. L. 1969. The initial coordination of sensorimotor schemas in human infants—Piaget's ideas and the role of experience. In *Studies in cognitive development,* ed. D. Elkind & J. H. Flavell, pp. 237–256. New York: Oxford University Press.

PART TWO

INDIVIDUAL AND RELATIONSHIP DEVELOPMENT

Chapter 4

Sex Differences, Gender Identity, and Gender Roles

MAJOR CONCEPTS

Biological sex
X and Y chromosomes
Androgens and estrogens
Secondary sex characteristics
Hermaphrodite
Masculinity
Femininity
Gender identity
Identification

Gender role
Conventional sex roles
Gender polarization
Sexism
Androgyny
Sex-role transcendence
Role models
Stereotyping

Try and imagine what the world would be like if there were not differences between men and women. No wonder the French say, "Vive la différence." In this chapter we will explore how each human being develops toward sexual maturity as either a male or a female and how much of what we do in life depends on gender distinctions. Major concepts in this chapter include *biological sex characteristics,* which form the foundation of maleness and femaleness, *gender identity,* and *gender roles.* Individuals are born with biological sex characteristics, but they acquire a gender identity and learn "appropriate" gender roles through interactions with family members and others in the larger culture.

BIOLOGICAL DIFFERENCES BETWEEN THE SEXES

Males and females differ in every cell of their bodies. Their chromosomes differ as well as the kinds and amounts of hormones they produce. There are essential differences in both anatomy and physiology. Members of each sex have capacities and limitations that correspond to their basic form and function. These biological differences are a fundamental way of life, and each person must come to terms with them in his or her own way.

Sex Determination

The sex of each individual is determined at the moment of conception. If an X-bearing sperm unites with the X-bearing ovum, a female is conceived. When a Y-bearing sperm fertilizes the X-bearing ovum, a male begins to develop. From that moment on, the miracle of growth and development is under way. The basic genetic differences between a girl (XX) and a boy (XY) influence the balance of female and male hormones present. Hormone production is initiated in the body in both sexes months before birth.

Sex Differentiation

Male and female embryos look very much alike during the first three months of development in the uterus (see Figure 4.1). Both have a tiny genital tubercle in the area of the external genitalia, which is the precursor of the penis in the male and the clitoris in the female. Rolling back from this small protuberance is a double fold of tissue that surrounds the central cleft,

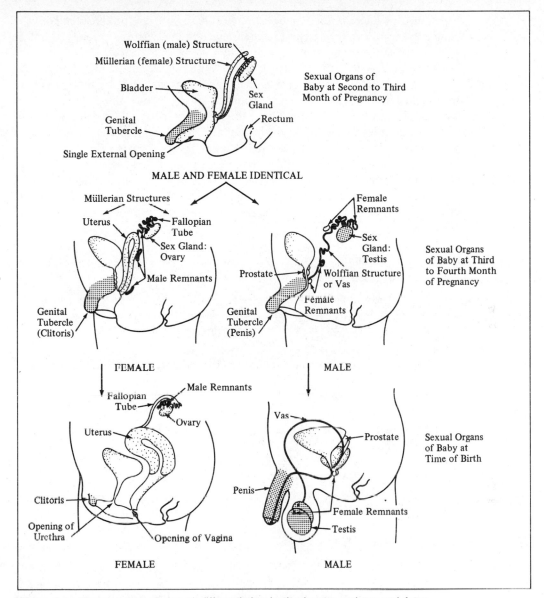

Figure 4.1 Three stages of sexual differentiation in the human embryo and fetus. *Source:* J. Money and A. Erhardt, *Man and Woman, Boy and Girl* (Baltimore, MD: Johns Hopkins University Press, 1972, p. 41).

or slit. By the third or fourth prenatal month, the genital areas of the two sexes show different patterns of development. In the female fetus, tiny labial swellings sweep back from the clitoris to the anus on either side of the slit that is to become the opening to the vagina. In the male the genital tubercle is now seen as the head of the penis at the end of the shaft being formed by the urethral folds that unite behind the penis, while the swelling on either side is enlarging to become the scrotum.

Male hormones *(androgens)* and female hormones *(estrogens)* are produced in both the male and the female early in the course of prenatal development. Male hormones stimulate the growth and maintenance of the male reproductive systems, whereas estrogens influence the development of female structures and functions. Without an adequate supply of the androgen *testosterone,* the male fetus becomes feminized. Estrogens in the mother's body normally supplement any estrogen deficiency occurring during the female's fetal development. Studies at Johns Hopkins University have found that androgens predispose boys to compete for dominance and to be more active than girls. Females tend to expend less energy and to be more nurturant, even as little children (Money & Ehrhardt 1972).

At birth the external genitals distinguish the male; the penis lies over the scrotum, in which hang the testes of the boy baby. In the girl child the outer and inner labia surround the opening to the vagina, with the clitoris at their forepoint. At birth the female's ovaries contain all of the half million or so ova she will ever have. The male testes will become capable of producing millions of sperm daily from puberty on.

Puberal Development of Male and Female

Between birth and puberty, male and female hormones are at low levels in both boys and girls. The puberal growth spurt is triggered by *pituitary hormones* that stimulate the sex glands (testes and ovaries) to increase greatly the levels of androgens in the boy and estrogens in the girl.

Maturing girls rapidly increase in height and weight, breasts develop, hips broaden, and dark, curly hair appears in a triangle in the pubic area as well as under the arms. At about 12 years of age, on the average, the girl begins to menstruate in the monthly cycle of menstruation and ovulation that continues in mature females until menopause.

Boys begin to mature a year or more later than girls. They become taller and gradually stronger as their bones and muscles develop. Male voices become deeper during puberty. Hair gradually appears in the typical male pattern in the pubic region, under the arms, and on the face, chest, arms, and legs. Spontaneous release of semen occurs by ejaculation at intervals from pubescence on, throughout most of the life of the male.

BIOLOGICAL DIFFERENCES BETWEEN MEN AND WOMEN

The mature male is generally taller and heavier than the grown woman. His shoulders and chest are broader, and his hips are narrower than the female's. His muscles are larger, stronger, and more pronounced than those of the woman, whose body is rounded with a subcutaneous fatty layer. Both sexes have pubic and underarm hair, but only the male normally has hair on face and body. Male breasts are rudimentary; female breasts are rounded and potentially capable of lactation. The man's hands and feet are larger, and his fingers and toes are heavier than the woman's.

Male sex cells *(sperm)* are produced in the testes and ejaculated through the penis at frequent intervals throughout the life of the man. Female sex cells *(ova)* mature at the rate of one each month or so in the process of ovulation, which alternates with menstruation in the maturing girl and woman. The female's paired ovaries release one ripe ovum monthly into one of the paired Fallopian tubes that connect with the uterus *(womb).* The cervical (lower) end of the uterus hangs into the upper portion of the vagina, which extends to the opening between the labia. Only the male sex cell can impregnate the female and fertilize the egg. Only the female can ovulate, gestate, give birth, and breast-feed the human infant. Each sex has its own essential biological role in the miracle of creation. A summary of biological sex differences in the male and female is found in Table 4.1.

Table 4.1 NORMAL BIOLOGICAL SEX DIFFERENCES

Male	Female	Characteristic
XY sex chromosomes	XX sex chromosomes	Sex determined by X-bearing sperm to form female (XX) or by Y-bearing sperm to form male (XY) chromosome
Androgens (testosterone)	Estrogens	Male and female sex hormones
Penis	Clitoris	Erectile external genitals
Scrotum, in which hang paired testes	Vulva (major and minor labia)	Sensitive, soft external genitalia
Testes (testicles, paired gonads)	Ovaries (paired gonads in the pelvis)	Male and female sex cells from puberty (or before) through adulthood
Sperm (spermatazoa): millions at frequent intervals from puberty on	Ovum (egg cell): one each 28 $\pm$ days puberty through menopause	Sex cells containing DNA and RNA molecules, determine genetic makeup of each new individual
Vas deferens	Fallopian tubes	Paired tubes in which sperm and ova travel
Prostate (gland surrounding upper urethra)	Glands of Bartholin lubricating glands of vulva and vagina	Moisture-producing glands of genital tracts of male and female
Ejaculation	Menstruation (menses) Ovulation Labor and delivery (birth) Lactation	Release of products of reproductive organs of each sex
Facial and body hair	Underarm and pubic hair	Characteristic adult skin and hair patterns of each sex
Narrow hips, broad shoulders	Broad hips, sloping shoulders	Distinctive body shape of each sex from puberty on
Strong, heavy muscles relative to female	Fatty layer beneath skin over smaller muscles	Distinctive body shape of each sex from puberty on
Rudimentary breasts and nipples	Well-developed breasts and nipples from puberty on	Distinctive body shape of each sex from puberty on
Larynx that enlarges at puberty	Larynx smaller relative to male	Male voice deepens at puberty; female voice remains relatively higher
Taller, heavier, stronger on the average than the female	Shorter, lighter, not as powerful, usually, as the male	Great variations within each sex in height, weight, and muscular strength

DNA = deoxyribonucleic acid
RNA = ribonucleic acid

Individual Differences

Differences among individuals of the same sex are quite as remarkable as those between members of the two sexes. There are women who are taller and stronger than many men. There are men who are smaller and more graceful than many women. A wide range of characteristics usually associated with one sex can be found in members of the other, all within normal ranges. Any of these can be accentuated or downplayed in the way they are expressed by an individual.

MASCULINITY AND FEMININITY

Masculinity and *femininity* are those behavioral characteristics that are usually associated with males and females, respectively. Concepts of masculinity and femininity vary widely from society to society and from time to time. Traditionally, masculinity in the Western world meant strength, bravery, and ambition, whereas femininity was thought of in terms of gentleness and dependence. A man was expected to be strong, silent, and capable, while a woman was considered feminine when she was weak and dependent. Although these definitions of what it means to be masculine and feminine have undergone significant changes, they are still changing rapidly.

BEHAVIORAL DIFFERENCES BETWEEN THE SEXES

Psychological studies over many years have revealed the existence of a multitude of myths concerning differences between the sexes. Unfounded beliefs are (1) that girls are more social than boys; (2) that girls are more suggestible than boys; (3) that girls have lower self-esteem; (4) that girls are better at rote-learning and simple repetitive tasks, whereas boys excel in the higher cognitive processes; (5) that boys are more analytic; (6) that girls are more affected by heredity and boys are more affected by environment; (7) that girls lack achievement motivation; and (8) that girls are auditory and boys are visual.

Four differences between boys and girls are fairly well established according to research (Maccoby & Jacklin 1975):

1. Girls have greater verbal ability than boys.
2. Boys excel in visual-spatial ability.
3. Boys excel in mathematical ability.
4. Boys are more aggressive.

Still to be confirmed are such possible differences between the sexes as tactile sensitivity; fear, timidity, and anxiety; activity level; competitiveness; dominance; compliance; and nurturance and "maternal behavior" (Maccoby & Jacklin 1975). There are athletically active and competitive women, just as there are sensitive boys and nurturing, gentle men. Wide variations are found in intellectual, emotional, social, and behavioral expression in members of both sexes.

Maleness and femaleness are innate, genetically determined "givens" operating within each individual. Masculinity and femininity are learned through action and interaction with others in a given culture from birth onward throughout life. A boy is born male—he becomes masculine; a girl is born female—she learns to be feminine. Males and females are biologically the same across cultures, but the meanings of masculinity and femininity vary greatly.

THEORIES OF SEXUAL DIFFERENTIATION

Scholars of many disciplines are working on the question, How different are the two sexes —and why? Five theories of the nature of masculinity and femininity are often cited.

1. *Anthropological.* There are great cultural differences reflected in the ways in which the roles of the two sexes are defined in various societies around the world (Mead 1949).
2. *Biogenetic.* Recent research points out the importance of hormonal influence on genetic males and females in utero (Money & Erhardt 1972; Money & Tucker 1975).
3. *Psychoanalytic.* Followers of Sigmund Freud talk of oral, anal, and oedipal stages of psychosexual development in which the little boy competes with his father for his mother's love, and the little girl, feeling incomplete because of penis envy, adapts by being subserviently "feminine."
4. *Sociological.* Many scholars consider the main differentiating factor to be socialization through direct interaction with others in the environment who serve as models of masculinity and femininity.
5. *Cognitive-developmental.* Erik Erikson, Jean Piaget, and Jerome Kagan identify stages in children's development over the years in which boys and girls gradually perceive and internalize patterns of masculinity and femininity within a particular society.

Theories and research in the several disciplines have focused so intently on significant differences between the sexes that even greater similarities may have been obscured. A University of Michigan research team reports:

> One result of this obsession is an overemphasis on differences and a corresponding underemphasis on similarities between groups. For example, if one studies the reactions of men and women to 100 words, and they react very similarly to 80 of them, and significantly differently to 20, then it is likely that only the differences will get published—often without even a mention that the similarity of 80 responses existed. (Hefner, Meda, & Oleshansky 1975, 7)

ACQUIRING GENDER IDENTITY

Gender identity is a person's persistent awareness and conception of his or her individuality as a male or female. In some rare cases, a person's gender identity is confused or ambivalent. Almost universally, the announcement "It's a boy!" or "It's a girl!" literally starts each new individual down the road to life. Those around the baby will display gender-appropriate responses, beginning with the choice of a name, pink or blue colors, and so on. A growing awareness of gender will be an essential part of the baby's life from then on. Smart and Smart (1972, 329) share this personal illustration:

Once we gave a pink sweater before a baby was born. When the baby turned out to be a boy, the mother expressed her regrets that she would have to save the sweater until she had a girl. That little boy's color scheme was to leave no doubt in him or anybody else as to what sex he was! He soon received a wealth of trucks, cars, and erector sets but no dolls. His father played boisterously with him, stimulating vigorous motor play, being casual about bumps, discouraging tears. And what happened when someone came along to occupy our pink sweater? She received dolls and homemaking toys. She was held tenderly. Her father stroked her curls, and tickled her chin, and taught her to bat her long eyelashes at him. Big Brother stroked her curls, tickled her chin, and elicited eye-batting also. The mother applauded when Brother was aggressive, active, and courageous, and when Sister was nurturant, beguiling, and sensitive. Often the parents' techniques of influence were subtle—a pat, a shove, a smile, a frown, a tight voice, a song. At other times they were direct—"Don't do that, Brother. Be a big man, like Daddy" or "I was so proud of my girl, acting like a regular little lady."

Long before children are old enough to talk or walk or go to nursery school, their education in what it means to be a boy or a girl is already well begun.

Boy and girl babies are, however, remarkably similar in their early behaviors. Kagan (1975, 2) observes:

In the first two years of life there is a dramatic similarity in the activities of boys and girls. There are sex differences, but they're subtle, they're not overwhelming. There's an enormous overlap. Boys play with tea cups and doll houses. Girls play with bicycles and guns. And the differences are quite trivial in the first two years of life. It's after that that you begin to see boys and girls go off, following different pipers.

Throughout the preschool years, little girls are usually allowed more flexibility than are boys. Both boys and girls may wear jeans, but only girls may wear dresses and hair ribbons. While they are still preschoolers, boys are pressured to avoid anything that smacks of femininity and to limit their behavior to what is clearly masculine. Even in nursery school, it is more acceptable for a girl to be a "tomboy" than for a boy to be a "sissy" (Fling & Manosevitz 1972). Girls of kindergarten age are allowed to "amble gradually in the direction of 'feminine' patterns for five more years" (Hartley 1959). Udry (1974, 52–53) writes:

Any contemporary four-year-old boy who was allowed to wear female clothing would be a neighborhood curiosity, and it is likely that both he and his parents would be considered in need of psychiatric attention. On the other hand, American culture is not nearly so restrictive in eliminating masculine items from the behavioral repertoire of the young girl.

A summary of research (Biller 1967) measuring degree of masculinity in boys reports remarkably stable levels from childhood through adulthood. Warm, supportive fathers, encouraging mothers, older brothers, and peers to grow up with—all are positively related to the adoption of masculine roles by boys. The girl who grows up in a loving family that encourages her development as a person enters adolescence with a secure sense of her femininity. Differential treatment of boys and girls throughout childhood is to be expected, although it is less extreme now than it used to be.

At a relatively early age, children normally come to realize that there are two sexes and that each person belongs to either one sex or the other. Gender identity is being established as a tiny tot begins to understand when called "a boy" or "a girl" and resists being called the other. Each discovers his or her own genitals and those of members of the same and of the other sex. In time the child comes to associate these differences with boyness and girlness. It takes a while for a boy to find out that someday he will be a man and for the girl to learn that she will one day be a woman. Two basic concepts are being acquired: (1) maleness and femaleness and (2) young and mature forms of boy/man and girl/woman. Once children recognize that they belong to one gender and not to the other, they try to become masculine or feminine as they see those attributes modeled for them and expected of them by the persons around them. Children find models of masculinity and femininity in their parents, in other adults in the family, in their brothers, sisters, and playmates of both sexes, and—from very early ages—in the programs and commercials they see on television. The establishment of identity is a creative process in which

> the child synthesizes these three sources of information (parents, children and television) and creates what some psychologists call an ego-ideal, an ideal standard which will be remarkably similar in members of one particular culture. Once he has crystallized that, he starts to mold his behavior, his thoughts, his attitudes, his beliefs so that they will come as close as possible to that ideal. . . . It's important to appreciate that these sex differences pertain to behavior within a particular society. (Kagan 1975, 2–3)

A child's first and most lasting impression of society is found within his or her own family, which mirrors and personifies the larger society of which it is a part.

FAMILY-LEARNED GENDER IDENTITY

It is in the family that the young child has intimate day-to-day associations with members of both sexes and two or more generations. Parents consciously or unconsciously teach their children by such everyday comments as, "That's a good girl," or "What a big, brave boy you are," or "Girls don't do that," or "Don't be a sissy." By a much subtler process, children learn what is expected of them through a multitude of often-repeated rituals, customs, and situations. They are exposed daily to masculine and feminine conduct appropriate to the neighborhood, social class, and racial and ethnic group to which their families belong. They pick up the speech inflections, body stance and posturing, emotional expressions (or repressions), clothing and grooming, likes and dislikes, and other attributes of both sexes expected of their own and older ages. All this takes place as "naturally" as learning how to hold a spoon or how to drink from a cup—by observation, imitation, identification, and practice.

Families shape the gender identities of their members. Hill (1975, 2) reflects the views of social scientists when he says:

> In virtually all societies, the family is the institutional structure for the protection, physical maintenance, socialization and social placement of the young, involving a division of labor by gender among family members.
>
> Moreover, in fulfilling these functions, the family has tended to monopolize the shaping of the basic personality make-up of junior members including the development of the important component, gender identity.

Imitation and Identification

Three-year-old Jane mirrors her mother's every move as the two "women" prepare a meal. A casual observer might think that Jane is imitating her mother. Actually, Jane is working hard at being her mother—in her food preparation roles and in all of her other activities and behaviors. Jane's twin brother, Jim, meantime, lights his imaginary pipe and sits with one leg across the other, perusing the papers before him, just as his father does. Both children are identifying with the parent of the same sex by internalizing what they see their parents doing. They talk over toy telephones with the same inflections and with the same words they hear their parents use. They play house and go through the same dialogues and routines their mother and father have modeled for them only hours before.

Gender identification is thought to be more difficult for boys than for girls. Same-sex identification is easier for the girl because she does not have to shift from mother to father as her role model, as does the boy. The mother's activities are more visible in the typical family than are the father's, whose work tends to be out of the home and beyond the comprehension of little children.

Older brothers and sisters in the family serve as *role models,* as the younger children in the family identify with them. Brim (1973, 43–46), following Koch's (1955, 1956) extensive research, concludes that cross-sex siblings tend to adopt traits of the other sex, with the greater effect for the younger child. These studies are of two-child families. In families with many children, older sisters tend to serve as "little mothers" in helping to rear the younger ones. Their influence might then be expected to be not only that of an older sibling but of a substitute mother as well.

Kindergarten and first-grade children often identify with their teachers, and in playing school they vie to "be the teacher." In early adolescence, boys identify with some local hero or national figure, whereas adolescent girls try out hairstyles, grooming aids, and poses of the glamorous women they see in the mass media. These identifications are relatively short-lived compared with the long-standing identifications with more influential family members.

STAGES IN GENDER IDENTITY DEVELOPMENT

Children progress from one stage to another in the development of their gender identity. First comes the undifferentiated stage of infancy, discussed earlier in this chapter. The second stage is one of active sex-role differentiation in which children of both sexes accept conventional sex roles for themselves and for members of the other sex. Boys may then vigorously reject feminine associations and attributes as they conform to what is expected of them as "big guys." This stage is one of polarization, in which femininity and masculinity are at opposite poles in the eyes of youngsters.

By adolescence, boys are urged to do well in school and to plan for their careers, whereas achievement by girls is often discouraged (Horner 1972; Shaw & McCuen 1971). During the teen years, girls try to become attractive to boys (Laws 1976) and downplay the intellectual and academic excellence that might threaten the teenage boys' egos. These are the years when young adolescent males tend to be especially restrictive in what they expect of girls (Meixel 1976). Young women tend to lower their career aspirations as they approach womanhood (Schwenn 1970). Gagnon and Simon (1973) state that both males and females follow their own sexual scripts that label, elicit, and form human sexuality and that this general consciousness of sexuality in turn gives meaning to gender roles and sexual behavior. Only after the individual develops a sense of his or her own *sexual identity* as a person is a third stage of *sex-role transcendence* possible.

Learning About Gender Roles

As children acquire their gender identity, they are learning about gender roles—what society expects of males and females. *Roles* are expectations of behavior, obligations, and rights that are associated with a given position in a family or social group. *Sex roles* (gender roles) are behavioral expectations specific to members of either sex. Christensen (1975, 3) defines the terms in this way:

> Usually the term *sex* is used to designate biological differences (male or female), *gender* to designate personality differences (with respect to identity and the accompanying attributes of masculinity and femininity), and *role* to designate differences in behavioral expectations lodged within the social structure. To me, the sex role/gender role labels are synonymous and equally acceptable. The important thing to keep in mind is that we are talking about a role that is differentiated according to sex and/or gender.

Hill makes the point that roles are plural—not "the woman's role" but "the many roles of women"; not even "the mother's role" but the many roles built into the mother's position. He sees all gender-role changes within the family context as paired role changes. "If there are changes in the roles of wife, there follow changes in the counter roles of husband; just as changes in father roles bring changes in child roles and coordinately changes in mother roles" (Hill 1975, 2).

SOCIALIZATION

Gender-role learning is an important facet of the socialization of the members of both sexes. Children must be socialized in order to become truly human. *Socialization* is the process by which individuals acquire the knowledge and develop the skills, attitudes, and competence that enable them to function in society (in family, in the community, in the world at large). Socialization continues throughout life as new roles are played in each new situation or group that the individual enters. Socialization always takes place in interaction with others. Social pressures mold newcomers so that they conform to the expectations and the customs of the particular culture they are entering. Socialization is the process by which individuals are helped to:

1. Become acceptable members of the group;
2. Develop a sense of themselves as social beings;
3. Interact with other persons in various roles, positions, and statuses;
4. Anticipate the expectations and reactions of other persons; and
5. Prepare for future roles that they will be expected to fill.

CONVENTIONAL SEX-ROLE STEREOTYPING

Conventional sex roles are the usual behaviors traditionally expected of males and females in most societies. Lee and Groper (1974) list such areas of sex-typed differences as:

1. Communication—different patterns of speech and emotional expression
2. Physical gestures—sitting, walking, stance styles of the two sexes
3. Naming—last names patronymic, first names male or female
4. Group affiliations—sex-segregated children's and adult organizations
5. Dress and grooming—lipstick, earrings, long dresses (female only)
6. Cultural artifacts—sex-typed toys, needlework (female), woodworking
7. Occupations and tasks—many jobs in home and community sex-typed
8. Games and avocations—team sports (more male than female)

Stereotyping rigidly fixes sex roles at opposite extremes, without regard for individual talents and interests. The slender young man with an artistic bent is made to feel somewhat less a "real man" because he falls short of the masculine ideal. The athletically active girl finds herself at a disadvantage in the male-dominated sports world. Since both sexes are limited in the full range of behavior of which they are capable, society is deprived of their maximum contribution, and the individuals are limited in their personality development and fulfillment.

Problems in Gender Polarization

Polarization of gender roles poses particular problems in marriage and family life. Sometimes wives feel limited to expressing themselves through the achievements of their children and husbands. Husbands are often limited in their emotional expressiveness in the family because they were brought up to be "strong, silent" men (Baliswick & Peek 1971). Adults of both sexes should be able to relate sensitively to others, to care for the dependent members of the family, and to receive affection easily from their loved ones. These are the very traits that men find difficult if they have been taught that these traits are feminine. Fathers able to develop warm, intimate relationships with their wives and children know how much some of their colleagues miss by standing on their dignity as males. So too, the "helpless little woman" who must await her husband's homecoming to make some simple repair of an essential piece of household equipment is not only delayed by the breakdown but misses the opportunity of finding personal satisfaction in doing things herself.

In the modern world an adult of either sex has to be self-reliant, independent, and assertive at times. However, the restrictions traditionally associated with femininity make it difficult for women to learn and express such attitudes. Competent wives and mothers are passed over in the world of work and are straitjacketed into housewifery at home. With such stereotyping, everyone loses—the wife-mother, the husband-father, the children, the family, and society as a whole. Using census figures, Bernard (1975, 211–221) estimates that if sexism were eliminated, women's earnings would be increased by 74.5 percent and their unemployment substantially decreased.

Avoiding Sexism

Sexism is prejudicial restriction of individual behavior by gender. This bias often has the general effect of casting girls and women in inferior, submissive roles and of discouraging their participation in the more prestigious areas of life while assigning dominant roles in family and society to males (regardless of competence, in many cases). Except for reproductive functions, both males and females of all ages are capable of a wide diversity of roles and accomplishments that remain unrecognized and underdeveloped because of sexist thinking and practices. During the 1970s there was a mass movement in the direction of affirming equal rights to members of both sexes.

Title IX of the National Education Act focused on equal opportunities for women on the payrolls of schools receiving federal funds and prohibited sexism in textbooks. Major textbook publishers instructed their editors and writers to avoid allusions, statements, and illustrations that perpetuate sex-role stereotyping. One such publisher's guide says:

> Many people today share a determination to create a world in which all young people shall be *free to choose* patterns of life, work, study, and recreation consistent with their innermost aspirations, interests, talents, resources, and energies, and to do so unhampered either by overt discrimination or by an equally limiting tyranny of the norm. Such a tyranny seeks to enforce upon individuals previously unchallenged but often irrelevant, inaccurate, and outdated stereotypes about what it means to be: male or female, black or white, young or old, rich or poor. (Macmillan Guidelines for Creating Positive Sexual and Racial Images in Educational Materials 1975, v)

Androgyny

The word *androgyny* comes from the Greek *andro* "male" and *gyn* "female" and means, literally, "male-female." The term is used in biology to refer to individuals with both male and female genitalia *(hermaphrodites).* In recent years the term *androgyny* has been used to refer to persons with both male and female psychological characteristics. It represents the capacity of a person of either sex to embody the full range of human character traits, despite the fact that some traits may be considered "feminine" and others "masculine" (Heilbrun 1973; Secor 1974).

The concept of androgyny implies that a person may be gentle or tough, yielding or assertive, weak or strong, as occasion demands, and enjoy thereby a greatly expanded range of behavior. Thus individuals of both sexes could potentially cope more effectively with a wide range of situations, with a greater degree of emotional and psychological health (Bem 1975).

Summarizing the literature on the subject, a University of Michigan team sees androgyny as "a combination of male and female qualities in all people, and clearly for some people it means a uniform, unisexual integration of society" (Hefner, Meda, & Oleshansky 1975, 10). Unisex trends in clothing, grooming, and behavior suggest that young people are moving away from rigid male-female polarization and toward a life-style that is less rigidly determined by gender.

Sex-Role Transcendence

Instead of masking the differences between the sexes, sex-role transcendence encourages the expression of differences in all human beings.

> Thus sex-role transcendence implies flexibility (over time, over situation, and over personal moods), plurality, personal choice, and the development of new or emergent possibilities once we move away from the present oppressor-oppressed sex-roles. In essence, we would all be human beings first and males and females second. (Hefner, Meda, & Oleshansky 1975, 10)

Sex-role transcendence offers a pluralistic view of human society in which genuine options are available to everyone in any situation that may arise. The transcendent person is free to do what is appropriate at the time without regard for masculine-feminine labeling. The young father is free to comfort the crying baby tenderly while his wife tackles a competitive examination for a fellowship, because this is their mutual choice at the time. Somewhere along the line, the same couple may redefine their notion of success and realign their roles accordingly. "The neo-macho male is strong enough to reveal his vulnerabilities, confident enough to be sensitive, successful enough to be proud of his mate's career, virile enough to wash dishes, fearless enough to take care of the children" (Mariani 1975, 5).

A person who transcends stereotyped sex roles and traditional demands for conventional gender conformity becomes a self-actualized person according to Maslow, a productive person according to Fromm, a fully functioning person according to Rogers, and a productive personality according to Gilmore. "None of these theories focuses on sex differences or on a different potential growth dependent on the sex of the person. They state that the human being has certain potentials for becoming fulfilled and that if this goal is not realized then one must look to the restraints placed by the culture on the person" (Feldman & Feldman 1975, 6).

Many American Council on Education surveys of freshmen entering colleges and universities over the years provide evidence that some young women have achieved a degree of sex-role transcendence in that they

1. Have argued with teachers,
2. Want administrative responsibility,
3. Want to become authorities in their fields,
4. Do not want to be obligated to anyone, and
5. Believe that large families should be discouraged.

"They are aggressive, ambitious, achievement-oriented, independent, and not interested in full-time domesticity. . . . they actually did transcend polarity in the values they viewed as very important or essential; they were more 'feminine' than other women and also more 'masculine' than were the men" (Bernard 1975, 49–50).

Christensen (1975) proposes that women be given equal access to the more prestigious roles within society, that traditional female tasks be made more prestigious, and that both men and women be given a choice in what they do and in how and where they do it. He sees sex roles as necessary, because of biological differences, to avoid ambiguity and to increase efficiency. "But it is not necessary that these roles cover everything, nor that they be arbitrarily imposed, nor that they give either sex an overall advantage. I do not believe that equality requires the elimination of the sex-role structure, only its alteration" (Christensen 1975, 13).

As gender roles become more flexible, girls may be less likely to have to prove themselves by rushing into early marriage. More of them can be expected to continue their education, to develop their talents, to pursue their interests, and to enter careers of import to them as persons. Meanwhile, boys and men may become more interested in homemaking and child rearing—areas in which they can freely express the gentler, less competitive aspects of their personalities without censure. It is possible, then, that as rigid gender distinctions diminish, the two sexes may more fully appreciate one another in more flexible patterns of intimate association. This holds the promise of greater companionship within marriage and family life.

SUMMARY

Our entire lives are differentiated by sex—being born male or female. In some ways biology is an inescapable destiny; there are primary and secondary biological differences between the sexes, including chromosomes, hormones, anatomy, and physiology. Except for rare cases of hermaphroditic children who are born with incomplete or mixed biological sex characteristics, all of us begin life as either a male or a female.

Gender identity is the awareness or perception of oneself as a male or a female. It is acquired gradually from biological cues but especially from interactions with others. Gender identity consistent with one's biological sex is usually well in progress by age 2 and becomes relatively fixed during the preschool years.

Masculinity and *femininity* are the ways of behaving usually associated with males and females. The behaviors that are considered masculine or feminine, however, vary tremendously over historical time and across cultures. Whereas *male* and *female* mean the same thing around the world, *masculine* and *feminine* do not. Research findings suggest that females are more verbally capable than males and that males are more aggressive and more spatially and mathematically capable than females.

Gender roles are the expectations of behavior for boys and girls, men and women. Gender roles are learned through socialization processes in families, peer groups, and the larger society. *Conventional sex-role stereotypes* define what men and women "should do," or are expected to do, in a given culture. Sex roles provide a pattern and continuity for life, but accepted uncritically they limit the activities and experiences of both sexes.

Androgyny and *sex-role transcendence* are contemporary ideas for reducing the restrictions of rigid sex-role stereotyping. A person who is androgynous can simultaneously express the traits or characteristics that are usually associated with each sex separately. Sex-role transcendence is a societal level idea that implies changes in institutions and organizations to make options more freely available to everyone, regardless of their biological sex.

REFERENCES

Baliswick, J. O., & Peek, C. W. 1971. The inexpressive male: A tragedy of American society. *Family Coordinator* 20:363–368.

Bem, S. 1975. Sex-role adaptability: One consequence of psychological androgyny. *Journal of Personality and Social Psychology* 31:634–643.

Bernard, J. 1975. *Women, wives, mothers: Values and options.* Chicago: Aldine.

Biller, H. B. 1967. Masculine development: An integrative review. The *Merrill-Palmer Quarterly of Behavior and Development* 13 (October).

Brim, O. G., Jr. 1973. Family structure and sex role learning by children. In *Love—marriage—family: A developmental approach,* ed. M. E. Lasswell & T. E. Lasswell, pp. 43–47. Glenview, IL: Scott, Foresman.

Christensen, H. T. 1975. Are sex roles necessary? Paper read at Purdue University, Layfayette, Indiana, April 4, 1975.

Feldman, H., & Feldman, M. 1975. Beyond sex role differentiation. Paper read at International Seminar on Changing Sex Roles in Family and Society, Dubrovnik, Yugoslavia, June 18, 1975.

Fling, S., & Manosevitz, M. 1972. Sex typing in nursery school children's play interests. *Developmental Psychology* 7:146–152.

Gagnon, J. H., & Simon, W. 1973. *Sexual conduct: The social sources of human sexuality.* Chicago: Aldine.

Hartley, R. E. 1959. Sex-role pressures and the socialization of the male child. *Psychological Reports* 5.

Hefner, R., Meda, R., & Oleshansky, B. 1975. The development of sex-role transcendence. Preprint.

Heilbrun, C. G. 1973. Toward a recognition of androgyny. New York: Knopf.

Hill, R. 1975. Family implications of changing sex roles. Paper read at Purdue University, Lafayette, Indiana, April 4, 1975.

Horner, M. 1972. Toward an understanding of achievement-related conflicts in women. *Journal of Social Issues* 28:157–175.

Kagan, J. 1975. Quoted in *Sexuality,* booklet prepared in cooperation with the National Association for Mental Health. New York: p. 2.

Koch, H. L. 1955. Some personality correlates of sex, sibling position, and sex of sibling among five- and six-year-old children. *Genetic Psychology Monographs* 52:3–50.

———. 1956. Sissiness and tomboyishness in relation to sibling characteristics. *Journal of Genetic Psychology* 88:231–244.

Laws, J. 1976. Work motivation and work behavior of women: Future perspectives, signs. In *Psychology of Women: Future Direction in Research,* ed. J. Sherman & F. Denmark. New York: Psychological Dimensions.

Lee, P., & Groper, N. 1974. Sex-role culture and educational practice. *Harvard Educational Review* 44 (August).

Maccoby, E. E., & Jacklin, C. N. 1975. *The psychology of sex differences.* Stanford, CA: Stanford University Press.

Macmillan guidelines for creating positive sexual and racial images in educational materials. 1975. New York: Macmillan.

Mariani, J. 1975. The enlightened stud. *Harper's Magazine* (July): 5.

Mead, M. 1949. *Male and female: A study of the sexes in a changing world.* New York: Morrow.

Meixel, C. 1976. Female adolescents' sex role stereotypes and competence motivation. Ph.D. dissertation, Cornell University.

Money, J., & Ehrhardt, A. 1972. *Man and woman, boy and girl.* Baltimore, MD: Johns Hopkins University Press.

Money, J., & Tucker, P. 1975. *Sexual signatures: On being a man or a woman.* Boston: Little, Brown.

Schwenn, M. 1970. Arousal of the motive to avoid success. Unpublished paper, Harvard University.

Secor, C. 1974. The androgyny papers. *Women's Studies* 2.

Shaw, M., & McCuen, C. 1971. The onset of academic underachievement and sex-role preference on three determinants of achievement motivation. *Developmental Psychology* 4:219–231.

Smart, M. S., & Smart, R. C. 1972. *Children: Development and relationships.* 2d ed. New York: Macmillan.

Udry, J. R. 1974. *The social context of marriage.* 3d ed. Philadelphia: Lippincott.

Chapter 5

Attraction, Dating, and Mate Selection

MAJOR CONCEPTS

Courtship system
  Arranged
  Formally free
Emergence of dating
Reasons and purposes of dating
Dating stages
  Casual
  Regular
  Steady
  Engaged
Turning points in relationships
Relationship trajectories
Breaking up

Endogamy and exogamy
Homogamy and heterogamy
Random versus assortative mating
Endogamous date and mate selection
    filters
  Race
  Religion
  Social class
  Age
  Propinquity
The mating gradient
Hypergamy

From the time children are toddlers, and perhaps even before, they learn about the opposite sex from siblings, playmates, and parents. Interactions between opposite-sex teenagers and young adults are, however, qualitatively different from those of preteen boys and girls. During puberty there is a change in the way that males and females perceive and relate to each other. They become increasingly conscious of their own developing sexual maturity and of the increasingly obvious expectations that they will one day form a partnership with someone of the opposite sex.

In the United States there is, on the average, a period of more than 10 years between the onset of puberty (ages 11–13) and the age of first marriage (ages 23–25). During this decade or so, young people form relationships known as dating, going out, going steady, being pinned, being engaged, and so on. This is a time of forming and testing partnerships before marriage. As a precursor to marriage and family development, this period of life centers around the establishment and development of heterosexual pairs.

COURTSHIP SYSTEMS OVERVIEW

In every society there is an organized or patterned way of pairing up young people, sometimes referred to as the *courtship system. Courtship* sounds old-fashioned, and young people in the United States do not use this term much anymore. To most people the process does not seem all that deliberate, but there is a courtship system in the United States. Young adolescents associate freely together, usually beginning at school-sponsored activities. Over a period of months or years, they pair off in increasingly intimate and exclusive dyads. These relationships are entered into by choice, often breaking up before becoming very serious. Eventually though, young people develop relationships that are publically acknowledged and lead toward greater permanence.

The "free choice" courtship system in the United States stands in contrast to many other countries of the world. In many Eastern societies the system for bringing young people together (or for keeping them apart) is more controlled by parents and other elders in the community.

In most societies throughout the world, marital choice is made by the parents and dating is relatively unknown. For example, dating is virtually unknown in China (one-fourth of the world's population). Although its incidence is slowly increasing in industrialized Japan, it is less known in South America, and the Mediterranean countries of Greece, Spain, Sicily, and is usually prohibited in the Arab states. It is also uncommon in Russia. Most areas of Western Europe now accept dating, but not to the extent that it is accepted in the United States, Great Britain, and other English speaking countries. (Saxton 1980, 232)

Years ago, in a worldwide perspective, Goode (1959) identified five ways that heterosexual relationships are formed:

1. *Child marriage* is arranged in some societies before adolescents have had any opportunity to form heterosexual attachments on their own.
2. Determination of marital partners by *kin relationships* has often been noted in combination with child marriage. Elders in the community might specify that the father's sister's child will marry the mother's brother's child.
3. *Social isolation* from members of the opposite sex is sometimes practiced so that no intimate contact can occur before elders arrange marriages. The association of boys and girls is simply not allowed, or it is very strictly regulated.
4. *Close supervision* of marriageable females allows relationships to develop between young men and women, but they are closely supervised or chaperoned by adults.
5. In *formally free* systems, like the United States, young people have relatively greater autonomy in choosing partners and in continuing the relationship as they wish.

In summary, it can be said that courtship systems range from "free choice," "love match," or "participant-run" systems—where the young people are formally free to select their partners—to "arranged" systems—where parents or other elders choose their marriage partners. In actual practice, however, most patterns of courtship lie between the extremes of young people having complete control and young people being entirely excluded.

Although the U.S. system of selecting partners is formally free, this does not mean that parents do not influence the process. Nearly everyone knows someone whose parents' disapproval caused a relationship to break up or someone whose parents' approval and manuevering pushed them along. In one study nearly one-fourth of mothers and daughters said that mothers should not assist their daughters in the choice of a husband (Bruce 1974). However, the further along the daughters were in the courtship process (dating around, going steady, or engaged), the more involved the mothers actually were in their daughter's relationship. Mothers were also more likely to be involved if they were not employed outside the home (Bruce 1974). In a more recent study, 60 percent of college-age women reported that their mothers were involved in their dating choices as compared with 40 percent of males who indicated parental involvement (Knox & Wilson 1981).

BACKGROUND OF DATING

Many young people today are surprised to find that dating is a recent innovation as courtship systems go. Before the turn of the century, schools in the United States were less likely to be coeducational, and there were other barriers to dating:

> An introduction of the young man to the young woman's parents had to be arranged. This was not always easy. If the parents approved of the young man, there was little leisure time that the couple could spend together, as most young people worked hard in addition to their studies. What little time they had together was usually doing things with other family members. (Cox 1981, 113)

Dating in the United States is thought to have begun among college students after World War I (Gordon 1978), to have become widespread during the 1920s and 1930s, and to have become commonplace among high school students and younger teenagers during the 1940s and 1950s.

There are many interesting speculations about the factors that encouraged dating to emerge in the United States in the early twentieth century. Some of the underlying factors had been changing for many years, including *urbanization*—the movement from rural farms to towns and cities—and *industrialization*. These trends brought greater numbers of young people together in closer association in neighborhoods and coeducational schools, increased their leisure time as compared with time-consuming farm chores, reduced their parents' supervision, and accelerated female involvement in activities outside the home. This was particularly true when World War I shifted women into many jobs that had previously been occupied by men. Before this time, unacquainted young people of the opposite sex rarely met or mingled, and a young woman was carefully supervised by her parents. It was not considered appropriate for a young girl to meet boys casually on her own.

During the same era many *inventions* of the technological age also stimulated dating. The automobile is frequently credited with a central role in making it easier for young people to literally leave parental supervision behind. As the car made parental observation of a young couple much more difficult, the telephone made their conversations easier and probably more frequent. After the invention of the telephone, youth could communicate without the formal introductions that were previously required. The movement from farms to cities also witnessed the development of moving picture shows, soda fountains, dance halls, and various other entertainments that drew young couples into dating and into more informal and unsupervised activities than their parents had known.

Sometimes these changes seemed shocking to the older generations. Often, changes in the behavior of young women were viewed as bordering on the scandalous. Young women began riding bicycles, raising hemlines above the ankles and knees, and going out with young men whom their parents hardly knew. Saxton (1982, 167) summarized five ways that the new practices of dating differed from previous ways American young people started couple relationships:

1. An introduction of a young man to a young woman through a family member was no longer considered necessary, but it became appropriate for a young couple to meet casually without formal introductions.
2. There was no commitment on the part of either the young man or the young woman to continue the relationship beyond the date itself.
3. The activities of dating were planned by the couple themselves, rather than arranged by parents or someone else.
4. Physical intimacies were not as strictly prohibited.
5. There was little supervision from parents or other elders.

ELEMENTS OF DATING

The basic elements of a contemporary date include: (1) some event or activity (2) that is shared or experienced together (3) by two or more persons of the opposite sex. Traditionally, dating roles were clearly formalized: the male would ask the female out, and he was responsible for costs incurred on the date and for bringing her safely home. Murstein (1980, 780) has written: "There is little doubt that the traditional 'date' in which the male picked up the female at her house at an arranged time, wined and dined her at his expense, and returned her to her residence at an arranged time is rapidly disappearing." In recent years dating as a formal event seems to have been giving way to a more casual attitude about going out together. Many people still date in the traditional way, of course, but dating seems generally to have become much more relaxed.

> It may be planned many months or just minutes in advance. It may involve only one couple, or another couple as well, or it may take place in a group you are in. An event becomes a date only when one person, but not necessarily the male, asks the other to share in the activity. They then form a paired relation, publicly recognizable, for the duration of the event. The pairing may be loose, casual, and tentative, or it may be highly tenacious and exclusive. (Saxton 1982, 145)

REASONS, PURPOSES, AND FUNCTIONS OF DATING

When asked why they date, young people give various reasons. A date coming up this weekend would probably be viewed as fun or recreation. Younger teens are especially likely to view dating as fun.

Some date because it is what everyone else does. You date because it is expected; if you do not, people will think something is wrong with you. Social pressure and avoidance of social criticism are reasons for dating. Still others might not know why they date. They may have no particular reason or purpose in mind. It is just a way of passing the time between puberty and adulthood.

Dating is more likely to have a recognized purpose for older adolescents and young adults who sometimes tire of the dating scene. Their purposeful dating is more likely to be directed toward finding and getting to know someone of the opposite sex whom they really like, with whom they feel comfortable, and whom they could marry. Their purpose is to find a partner.

In addition to the reasons and purposes given above, dating has several functions of which young people may not even be aware. As an element in the American courtship system, dating functions to introduce and familiarize young people with others of the opposite sex. Dating provides ways for them to interact with and learn about each other. It is a mechanism of heterosexual socialization. Dating experiences help young people learn what is acceptable and preferable to members of the opposite sex. In short, it is a major way of learning how to act. Dating various partners helps clarify what characteristics are desirable in a mate and teaches one about oneself. Whether or not an individual can name any reason for dating, or recognize its purposes, dating functions as a key element of American courtship by moving individuals into heterosexual relations and, eventually, into marriage.

RELATIONSHIP DEVELOPMENT: STAGES OF DATING

Young people in North America today generally begin dating in their early teens. First dates are usually prompted by school or community activities, especially dances, sports, or parties. College students are most likely to have met their current dating partner through friends or at a party (see Table 5.1), although there are many other ways of becoming dating partners (Knox and Wilson 1981). Early dating experiences are likely to focus on group activities, whereas older teens tend to become more exclusive and intimate in their couple relationships.

Dating relationships tend to follow a sequence or pattern. Although some couples only date once or twice, individuals eventually date someone with whom they have a longer-lasting relationship. Most people have several serious dating relationships that break up before marriage.

Casual dating usually begins with young people "dating around" or "playing the field." A person in this stage is usually dating a number of individuals at the same time (sometimes even more than one in the same night). This stage of dating has also been referred to as a *random dating stage,* but partners do not really date each other randomly.

When someone, for a variety of reasons, is singled out as the preferred partner, the relationship is likely to become more regular. *Regular dating* partners go out with each other frequently and decrease or stop dating others altogether. This is a stage of relationship development when one or both partners come to expect that they will see each other more often and others less. If the relationship ceases to be viewed favorably by one or both parties, partners are likely to go back to casual dating and playing the field again. If the relationship fills the needs of the partners, it becomes increasingly exclusive or steady.

Steady dating is a period of serious dyadic exclusiveness more intense than just dating regularly. Steady dating relationships seem to be entered into much more quickly in contemporary dating, after a shorter casual or dating around experience, than was the case even a few decades ago. One study found that the average age of first going steady dropped from 17 in 1958 to 16.7 in 1968 to 15.9 in 1978 (Bell & Coughey 1980). Especially among younger teens it sometimes seems that virtually everyone is in a steady relationship, and interludes of casual dating around between steadies are very short if not nonexistent. Expectations that the steady relationship should be exclusive are clear: if a person who is supposed to be going steady dates someone else, friends might say that the partner was stepping out on their steady

Table 5.1 HOW 334 UNIVERSITY STUDENTS MET THEIR DATING PARTNER (IN PERCENT)

Ways of meeting	Female (n = 227)	Male (n = 107)
Through a friend	33	32
Party	22	13
At work	12	5
Class	6	9
Other	27	41

Source: D. Knox, and K. Wilson, "Dating Behaviors of University Students," *Family Relations* 30 (1981): 256. Copyrighted 1981 by the National Council on Family Relations, 1219 University Avenue Southeast, Minneapolis, Minnesota 55414. Reprinted by permission.

or cheating. In steady relationships it is common for partners to give some tangible symbol of their commitment to each other. Younger teens frequently exchange school rings. A college-age male might give his steady partner a school ring, fraternity pin, necklace, or lavalier, which in different parts of the country is known as being "pinned" or "lavaliered." Whatever item is given or exchanged to signify the seriousness, its purpose is to signal to others that the partners are "taken" (they are not available) and that the relationship is serious (they are not just another dating couple). Of course, even at this stage of commitment, many couples eventually separate and start a new relationship with someone else. If their relationship continues, probably the next stage for most couples in North America is engagement.

Engagement is a public acknowledgment that the couple is planning or intending to get married. This period differs from going steady because it is explicitly marriage oriented, like being betrothed in some cultures. Traditionally, a diamond engagement ring, or some substitute, has been included as a symbol of the partners' engagement and future marriage. During engagement, relationship exclusiveness is surrounded by norms that are almost as strong as fidelity in marriage. Nowadays, the marriage date may be decided when couples become engaged, but just a few decades ago the engagement was likely to have lasted several years with an indefinite future marriage date. It seems, in fact, that the meaning of engagement has changed considerably from long engagements, during which couples decided whether or not they should get married, to very short contemporary engagements of a few months, during which preparations are made for the approaching wedding date.

The stages of casual dating, regular dating, steady dating, and engagement should not be taken as an invariant sequence through which all premarital relationships must pass. The stages do, however, suggest a pattern that seems to be the most common way for relationships to develop in the United States. There are, of course, variations and departures, including dating only a single partner before marriage, living together temporarily or indefinitely, running away to get married (eloping), and so on. In some geographical areas there is often a stage preceding engagement referred to as *promised*. Being promised includes an expectation of marriage and usually a diamond promise ring, but being promised is not regarded as quite as committed as being engaged. In other parts of North America a sequence of patterned dating activities is a less accurate characterization because young people just hang around in groups and do things together very informally. Regardless of the specific dating stages, almost without exception heterosexual relationships develop a long continua of exclusivity and commitment, and the partners can identify markers or turning points in their relationships.

Turning Points in Relationship Development

One of the novel recent approaches to studying relationship development is based on retrospective interviews (Huston, Surra, Fitzgerald, & Cate 1981). In one series of studies young married people were asked to depict along a time line how the probability of marriage changed from the time their relationship first began until their marriage. The descriptive graphs that resulted suggest a trajectory of development, and sometimes setbacks, in relationships that led to marriage. Figure 5.1 shows one example of the turning points in a premarital relationship.

One of the most interesting aspects about the development of relationships is their

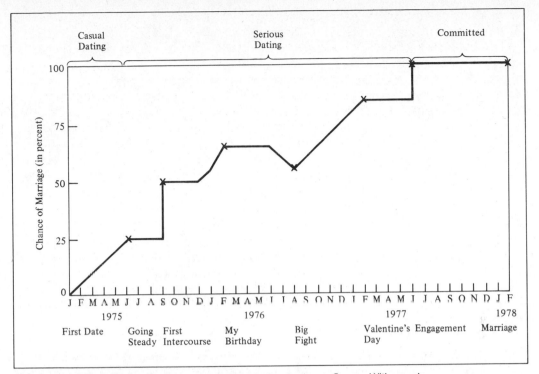

Figure 5.1 Example of turning points in relationship development. *Source:* With permission from T. L. Huston, C. A. Surra, N. M. Fitzgerald, and R. M. Cate, "From Courtship to Marriage: Mate Selection as an Interpersonal Process," in *Personal Relationships 2: Developing Personal Relationships,* ed. S. Duck and R. Gilmour (London: Academic Press, 1981). Copyright Academic Press Inc. (London) Ltd.

variation from the initial meeting to marriage. The turning points data, when graphed, depict these variations visually. Some couples move very rapidly through dating and marry in a matter of months. At the other extreme, a relationship may develop very slowly over a period of several years, often with frequent plateaus and downturns. Huston et al. (1981) grouped the couples they studied into the four patterns or types of relationship development depicted in Figure 5.2 and described them as follows:

Type I: Accelerated-Arrested Courtship, a type which began, on the average and relative to other relationship types, at the highest initial probability of marriage moved rapidly to higher probabilities of marriage, but slowed down in its final progression to marital commitment.

Type II: Accelerated Courtship, a category of relationships escalated more slowly than Type I at first, but then proceeded directly and smoothly to marriage.

Type III: Intermediate Courtship, a type that evolved to marriage at a pace that was slower than the first two types, but more rapid than the fourth; turbulence is most evident, on the average, in the final shift from 80% to 100% probability of marriage.

Type IV: Prolonged Courtship, a group consisting of relationships that took a relatively retarded and rocky path to marriage. (Huston et al. 1981, 76)

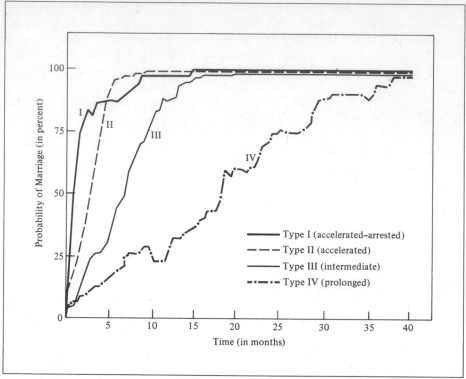

Figure 5.2   Average trajectories to marriage in four relationship types. *Source:* With permission from T. L. Huston, C. A. Surra, N. M. Fitzgerald, and R. M. Cate, "From Courtship to Marriage: Mate Selection as an Interpersonal Process," in *Personal Relationships 2: Developing Personal Relationships,* ed. S. Duck and R. Gilmour (London: Academic Press, 1981). Copyright Academic Press Inc. (London) Ltd.

BREAKING UP

People rarely marry the first person that they date seriously (Landis & Landis 1977), so these earlier relationships must somehow come to an end. There are thousands of studies and many available statistics about the dissolution of marriage that make it possible to describe quite accurately the ending of marriages through death, divorce, annulment, and desertion. By contrast, relatively little is known about the ending of relationships before marriage, and it is difficult to determine the extent of breaking up of less committed relationships. In spite of this lack of information, it would probably be accurate to say that a large majority of adults in the United States have experienced the breaking up of a valued-couple relationship before marriage. And judging from the very high divorce rates in the first few years of marriage, perhaps more couples should have ended their relationships before establishing the legal ties and obligations that marriage entails.

Reasons for breaking up are suggested in a study of 231 college couples who were "going together" (Hill, Rubin, & Peplau 1976). After two years, approximately 40 percent of the couples had broken up, giving a gradual loss of interest in their partner as the main reason. Comparing characteristics of couples who remained together to those who had broken up, the researchers also found that couples who broke up had less equal involvement in the relationship, had been dating for a shorter time, were not dating as exclusively or as much in love, and were less likely to have visualized their relationship as culminating in marriage. Another intriguing finding was that relationship breakups were likely to coincide with semester breaks, graduation, and the end of summer; relationships were much more likely to end at these times than during the day-to-day routine of college activities (Hill, Rubin, & Peplau 1976). Apparently, partners who had been staying together rather passively found such transition points to be appropriate times for ending their couple relationships.

The ending of relationships usually involves some degree of pain and sorrow for at least one of the partners. Although there does not appear to be much research on the subject, it seems logical to expect that the more exclusive and committed the relationship has been, the greater the pain and difficulty experienced in separation. Another factor that probably plays a role in the pain of breaking up is the mutuality or one-sidedness of the partners' desires to see the relationship come to an end. Feelings are likely to be less painful if the decision to break up is a mutual one and more painful if one partner "dumps" the other.

PRINCIPLES OF DATING AND MATE SELECTION

Dating and mate selection are far from chance and random events. There are systematic principles governing who is considered to be within one's "pool of eligibles." Consider, for example, your own thoughts about how the following pairings might seem unlikely, odd, or wrong:

A female high school teacher, age 27, begins dating and marries one of her 17-year-old students;

A fundamentalist Christian meets, dates, and falls in love with a devout Jew;

A young woman from a wealthy New England family falls in love with and wants to marry the mechanic who worked on her car;

A 70-year-old widower marries a beautiful 22-year-old woman; or

A recently married young couple discovers that they are biologically brother and sister who were separated as infants and whose identities have remained unknown.

Romantic novels and the mass media seem to relish plots that include "true love" conquering barriers that tend to keep such relationships from forming. Each of the pairings suggested above is more than plausible; they are based on factual accounts from recent years. But are such relationships common, encouraged, fully accepted? What are the patterns and principles that influence dating and mate selection?

Two central concepts in understanding selectivity in relationship formation and marriage are *exogamy* and *endogamy*. *Exogamous norms* require or exert pressure toward marrying someone *outside* a particular group. Perhaps the two clearest exogamous rules pertain to sex and kinship; strong pressures and even legal restrictions require marriage to be with someone outside the immediate family and of the opposite sex. These exogamous norms are obvious and usually not given any consideration in making dating and marriage choices. Occasionally, however, strong social and legal sanctions are brought to bear when individuals ignore exogamous rules. *Endogamous norms* require or exert pressure toward marriage *within* certain groups. People are expected to marry endogamously or within their own age group, but there are no firm restrictions about this endogamous norm. Much stronger endogamous norms apply to marrying within one's own race, religion, and social class.

Two other important concepts in understanding relationship formation and development are *heterogamy* and *homogamy,* which denote differences and similarities, respectively, in marriage partners. The difference between endogamy and homogamy (or exogamy and heterogamy) as Eshleman (1981, 254) points out, is that endogamous norms *require* or exert pressure in the choice of partners, whereas homogamy and heterogamy simply *denote* that similarities or differences exist. If a couple violated endogamous norms by marrying interracially, it could be said that their marriage was heterogamous with respect to race.

There is a great deal of research showing that persons marry others who are like themselves in many physical, social, and psychological ways (Murstein 1976; Vandenberg 1972). This tendency toward marrying persons with similar characteristics is sometimes called *assortative mating,* meaning that there is a systematic departure from random selection of mates. In his review of mate selection in the 1970s, Murstein (1980, 778). wrote: "In sum, assortativeness for marriage continues to be strongly evident, with no variable having been shown to be completely independent of it." Table 5.2 provides a listing of many of the ways in which marriage tends to be homogamous.

Racial Endogamy

All endogamous norms exert pressure toward marrying within groups, but race is the only characteristic around which laws have actually been written in the United States. Laws preventing interracial intermarriage still existed in 16 states when the U.S. Supreme Court struck down these statutes in 1967. Although racial intermarriage is no longer legally prohibited, norms are observed more strongly with respect to race than to any other endogamous factor.

**Table 5.2 HOMOGAMOUS FACTORS IN
              MATE SELECTION**

Age
Religious affiliation and activity
Residential origins and propinquity
Socioeconomic status
Education
Race
Ethnic background
Physical characteristics (height, weight, etc.)
Psychological traits
   Intelligence
   Interests and hobbies
   Attitudes and values
   Personality

Note: See Vandenberg (1972) for a review of research on these dimensions of homogamy.
Source: S. Vandenberg, "Assortative Mating, or Who Marries Whom?" *Behavior Genetics* 2 (1972): 127–157.

Black and white racial groups in the United States continue to be highly endogamous; fewer than 1 percent of persons in these racial groups marry someone not of their own race. When blacks and whites do intermarry, the most common pairing is black husband and white wife. Between 1960 and 1970 there was a 62 percent increase in marriages of black husbands and white wives and only a 9 percent increase in the marriage of white men to black women (Heer 1974). These increases, however, are based on fewer than 1 percent of all marriages.

Rates of intermarriage vary greatly, depending upon the racial composition of specific geographic areas. For example, in one study it was shown that the District of Columbia had much higher rates of black-white marriages than the country as a whole (Monahan 1976). In states where there are several fairly large minority populations, there are also much higher rates of racial intermarriage. For example, about 1 in 10 marriages is racially mixed in Alaska, and about 1 in 3 marriages in Hawaii involves partners of different races (Monahan 1976). In general, intermarriage rates of smaller racial minorities tend to be higher, presumably owing to limited opportunities to find a partner of their own race.

There is a general trend in the United States toward a more tolerant view of interracial marriages (see Table 5.3). In answer to the question, "Do you approve of marriage between whites and nonwhites?" a Gallup poll found that disapproval had declined from almost three-fourths in 1968 to slightly over one-half in 1978 (Gallup 1978). On the other hand, "approval" increased from about one in five of the respondents to one in three. The higher the respondents' educational level, the more likely they were to approve of interracial marriage. Over half of the college educated "approved" compared with one-third of adults with a high school education and one-fifth with a grade school education. In spite of this greater acceptance of racial intermarriage in the abstract, endogamous norms continue to exert very strong pressure to marry within one's own race.

Religious Endogamy

The difference in acceptance of interracial and interfaith marriages is apparent in both attitude and practice. In the Gallup poll referred to above, a question was also asked about approval of marriage between those of different religions. In 1978 almost three-quarters (73 percent) approved of marriage between Catholics and Protestants, and over two-thirds (69 percent) approved of marriage between Jews and non-Jews as compared with the one-third (36 percent) who approved of marriage between whites and nonwhites. In spite of the acceptance of religious intermarriage in principle, religious endogamy is still an important factor in mate selection; the majority of persons still marry someone with a similar religious background.

Table 5.3 AMERICAN ADULTS' RESPONSES TO THE
QUESTION: "DO YOU APPROVE OF
MARRIAGE BETWEEN WHITES
AND NONWHITES?" (IN PERCENT)

	Approve	Disapprove	No opinion
1968	20	72	8
1972	29	60	11
1978	36	54	10

Source: G. Gallup, "A Question of Race," Report no. 160, *The Gallup Opinion Index* (Princeton, N.J.: The Gallup Poll, 1978).

The norms about religious endogamy depend greatly on the particular religious group being considered. All three major religions in the United States—Protestants, Catholics, and Jews—have at least discouraged, and in some cases forbidden, marrying outside their religion. Saxton (1982) has suggested that this opposition is based on two fears: (1) that the family life of the couple might be disrupted if husband and wife do not belong to the same faith and (2) that religious affiliation might weaken or dissolve as a result of interfaith marriage. Historically, Jews have regarded marriage to Gentiles as a sin, and today a Jew is not considered properly married unless a rabbi has officiated. Until 1970 Roman Catholics could not marry non-Catholics unless a prenuptial agreement was signed by the non-Catholic, who promised to rear the children in Catholicism and not to hinder the Catholic partner's faith. Some Protestant denominations have also taken strong stands against interfaith marriages, but, generally speaking, Protestants have exerted less pressure toward religious endogamy.

Rates of interfaith marriage have increased over time. In one study of Jewish-Gentile marriages, rates were shown to have increased from about 6 percent in the 1950s, to 17 percent in the 1960s, to 32 percent in the early 1970s (Massarik & Chenkin 1973). Over a decade ago intermarriage in the general population was estimated at around 10 percent by Monahan (1971), but this estimate considered marriages between Protestant denominations to be religiously endogamous. Other estimates suggest that about one-third of all marriages are religiously mixed (Barlow 1977). Decreasing religious homogamy is partly due to greater tolerance and acceptance among religious groups. Another element may be increasing geographic mobility and dispersion, which has moved those affiliated with minority religions into more diverse population centers. As stated by Golanty and Harris (1982, 93): "Because Judaism and Catholicism are minority religions in the United States, young people of both faiths are overexposed, statistically speaking, to the larger Protestant group. In certain regions of the country the proportion of Jews or Catholics is so small that religious exogamy (marrying outside the group) is almost inevitable." This generalization has been found to be true for groups such as Catholics and Mormons in largely Protestant areas (Barlow 1977).

Social Class

Social classes are not as discrete and identifiable as races or religions, but there is considerable evidence to suggest that marriages tend to be homogamous with regard to class. A *social class* can be defined as a group of people who share similarities in educational, occupational, and financial backgrounds, life experiences, and opportunities. Those within the same social class tend to associate with each other, possess similar views and experiences, and share access to similar standards of living. Consequently, it should not be surprising that they tend to marry homogamously.

Studies have found that there is a decided tendency toward father's occupational similarity among those who date and marry (Eshleman & Hunt 1965). Similarly, approximately three-fourths of those who married during the 1960s had attained the same or next adjacent level of education (U.S., Bureau of the Census 1972). Educational homogamy has declined somewhat in recent years (Rockwell 1976), but it is still apparent that people tend to marry within their own social class.

The strongest norms about social class endogamy undoubtedly exist among upper-class families. They do, after all, have the most to lose. Upper-class parents exercise far more control over the dating activities of their children than either middle- or lower-class parents (Goode 1973, 258–259). Upper-class youths are most likely to attend private schools with children from other upper-class families and to have closer parental supervision of their parties, dances, and vacations. They usually attend exclusive private colleges or universities, where they are further culturally isolated from youth of the middle and lower classes. The overall effect of social class endogamy is that people usually do not marry someone from a lower social class, and they are unable or unlikely to date and marry someone from a higher social class.

Age Endogamy

Age affects relationship formation and marital choice in two ways. The first arises out of customs and expectations that husbands will be older than their wives. The second age effect in mate selection is *age endogamy,* or the social pressure exerted toward individuals to marry someone of approximately the same age.

For several decades now in the United States, men have averaged about 2½ years older than their wives (Glick & Norton 1977). This age differential has narrowed from the turn of the century when men were about four years older than their wives, on the average. The male-older pattern becomes established in dating relationships: older boys date younger girls in junior and senior high schools; male college students date freshmen and sophomore girls. On the other hand, it is rare for senior women to date freshmen. The result of this male-older dating pattern is that about 80 percent of American men marry younger women. Approximately 10 percent of marriages are between partners of the same age, and in about 1 in 10 marriages the wife is older than her husband.

The second major effect of age is that partners are expected to date and marry someone of approximately the same age. It is most common for partners to be within two or three years of the same age, although there are many couples with somewhat larger age differences. However, the greater the discrepancy in their ages, the more unusual and socially suspect the relationship is likely to be. If a person in their twenties marries someone in their sixties or seventies, people are likely to wonder what influenced the couple to marry in spite of the age difference. Motives such as money and sex might be prominently considered. The principle of age endogamy is more strongly imposed on younger couples than older couples. An older couple of ages 50 and 65 is less likely to experience social pressure toward age endogamy than a couple of 20 and 35, even though partners in both couples have age differences of 15 years or more.

DEVELOPMENTAL MATE SELECTION PROCESSES

There have been several attempts to develop more complete explanations of mate selection choices by describing the combined elements involved in a sequential or developmental fashion (Murstein 1980). Relationship development models are partial theories that build on, but go further than, the individual mate selection characteristics that have been described above. Developmental descriptions of mate selection processes that are featured below include the "filter theory" (Kerkoff & Davis 1962), the "stimulus-value-role theory" (Murstein 1970, 1976), and the "premarital dyadic formation theory" (Lewis 1973) of pair dissolution or continuance.

Kerkoff and Davis (1962) were among the first to combine separate mate selection elements into a more general developmental model. They suggested that the various social attributes and personality characteristics that are considered in mate selection probably operate or come into play at different stages as the relationship develops. If the relationship continues, potential partners are screened or pass through a series of filters—hence the name the *filter theory* of mate selection. After longitudinally studying college couples at various stages of relationship development, they concluded that early in the relationship social attributes such as race, religion, age, and social class act as an initial filter. After the relationship is established, value consensus becomes an increasingly significant screen. Finally, in the longer and most serious relationships, complementary needs appear to play an important role.

The *initial attraction* of partners is one aspect of relationship formation that does not seem to have been fully appreciated until recently. Over and above the status characteristics already discussed, social psychologists have suggested that two basic factors are centrally important in the initial attraction of partners (Huston & Levinger 1978). The first is *physical appearance*. Physical beauty is desired and sought after partly because people appreciate beauty, partly because attractive people are assumed to have other favorable characteristics, and partly because people want to associate with attractive others to enhance their own worth. It should come as no surprise that attractive women have more pressures and opportunities to date, to go steady, and to engage in sexual activities (Kaats & Davis 1970). The second major factor that affects initial attraction between partners is *observation of the other's actions* and inferring from them something about that person's desirability. Both of these initial clues about a person as a potential partner can be assessed from a distance. In order for the relationship to develop further, however, more direct interaction is usually required.

Murstein's (1970, 1976, 1980) stimulus-value-role (SVR) theory takes into account both the interpersonal attraction ideas described in the preceding paragraph and the filter analogy suggested by Kerkoff and Davis (1962) (see Figure 5.3). The SVR theory begins with a stimulus stage during which partners either are or are not chosen because of their interpersonal attraction, based on physical, social, and other "stimulus" factors. The stimulus stage of relationship formation is a first filter or screen that includes perceived status characteristics as well as perceived physical and personality attributes as elements in the initial decision to pair up. As partners become better acquainted, they begin to learn about and compare their attitudes and values. Value comparisons in such important areas as sex, religion, marriage, work, children, and so on are likely to be made. If partners' values are compatible or similar, their relationship will probably pass through the "value filter" and continue. Finally, the role filter is encountered. During this third stage of couple choice, partners consider expected behaviors (self and other) in their present and future relationship. Murstein's theory predicts that couples whose role expectations fit are likely to continue their relationship, whereas couples whose roles fit less well are more likely to break up.

Lewis (1973) suggested the existence and ordering of six pair processes that Americans progressively experience through their dating and courtship careers. His model of *premarital dyadic formation* (PDF) included the process of (1) perceiving similarities, (2) achieving pair rapport, (3) inducing self-disclosure, (4) exploring role taking, (5) achieving interpersonal role fit, and (6) achieving dyadic crystallization. The data from studying a sample of college couples over time were generally supportive of the general thesis that couples who best

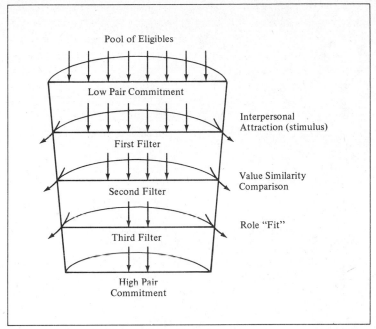

Figure 5.3 Murstein's SVR theory of mate choice. *Source:* Adapted from B. I. Murstein, "Stimulus-Value-Role: A Theory of Marital Choice," *Journal of Marriage and the Family* 32 (1970): 465–481.

achieved these pair processes were more likely to continue their relationships, whereas couples who scored lower on achieving these processes were more likely to dissolve their relationships (see Figure 5.4).

    Murstein's SVR theory of marital choice and Lewis's PDF theory of pair continuance have both been criticized for conceptual and methodological weaknesses (Rubin & Levinger 1974). Lewis's more detailed subprocesses were particularly criticized for positing a sequence for which there has, as yet, been no verification. "Why should the achievement of pair rapport precede the development of role taking accuracy, rather than vice-versa?" (Rubin & Levinger 1974, 229). It is clear, however, that our understanding of these experiences has moved ". . . away from monolithic, single principle approaches, such as those of homogamy and complementary needs, to a belief in multidetermined factors in marital choice" (Murstein 1980, 788).

SUMMARY

In every society there is a regular or patterned way of forming heterosexual partnerships. In some courtship systems male and female pairings are arranged by parents or other adults, but in the United States and many other Western societies partner choices are "formally free." In the United States the development of couple relationships is usually a gradual developmental experience that begins with dating.

    Contemporary dating customs have emerged during the present century and are evolving continually. Vast social changes from rural to city life, cultural changes in leisure time

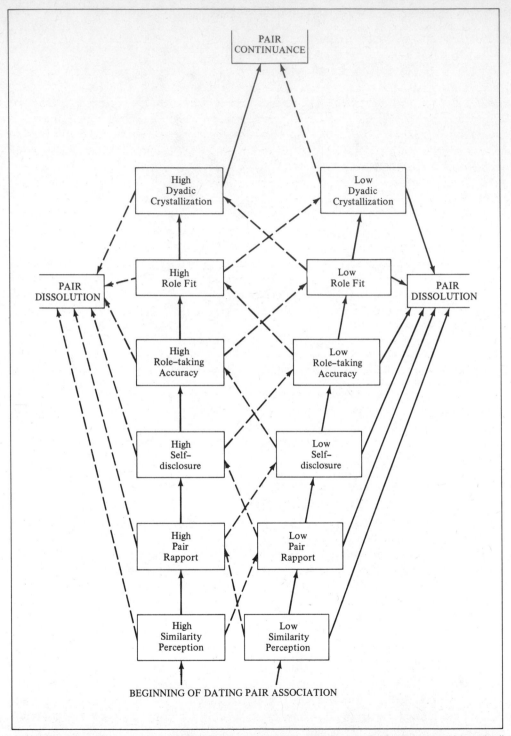

Figure 5.4 Game tree model of couple involvement or dissolution. *Source:* Robert A. Lewis, "A Longitudinal Test of a Developmental Framework for Premarital Dyadic Formation," *Journal of Marriage and the Family* 35 (1973): 19. Copyrighted 1973 by the National Council on Family Relations, 1219 University Avenue Southeast, Minneapolis, Minnesota 55414. Reprinted by permission.

and standards of appropriate conduct, and technological changes in travel and communications have all contributed to the growth of dating.

Today's young people date to have fun, to comply with social pressures, to make friends, to learn about the opposite sex, and to choose a partner. Dating activities usually proceed along continua of exclusivity and commitment through stages of casual, regular, and steady dating to engagement. Studies of turning points in relationships highlight various routes that relationships follow before marriage. Most people do not, however, marry the first person with whom they have a serious relationship, and premarital relationship breakups are a common experience.

Although the establishment of couple relationships in the United States is considered formally free, many factors constrain and shape dating and marital choice. Relationships tend to be homogamous, with partners having many characteristics in common. Strong exogamous norms make it extremely unlikely that relationships will be formed with relatives or persons of the same sex. Endogamous norms exert pressure toward choosing partners within one's own racial, religious, social class, and age groups. Along with residential propinquity, these factors filter out the least likely partners and leave a pool of eligibles among whom marital choices are usually made. Partner choices within the pool of eligibles are not well understood, but values, role expectations, and personality characteristics are all thought to be important.

REFERENCES

Barlow, B. A. 1977. Notes on Mormon interfaith marriages. *Family Coordinator* 26:143–150.

Bell, R. R., & Coughey, K. 1980. Premarital sexual experience among college females, 1958, 1968, and 1978. *Family Relations* 29:353–356.

Bruce, J. A. 1974. The role of mothers in the social placement of daughters: Marriage or work. *Journal of Marriage and the Family* 36:492–497.

Cox, F. D. 1981. *Human intimacy: Marriage, the family, and it's meaning.* St. Paul, MN: West.

Eshleman, J. R. 1981. *The family: An introduction.* 3d ed. Boston: Allyn & Bacon.

Eshleman, J. R., & Hunt, C. L. 1965. *Social class factors in the adjustment of married students.* Kalamazoo: Western Michigan University.

Gallup, G. 1978. A question of race. Report no. 160. *The Gallup Opinion Index.* Princeton, N.J.: American Institute of Public Opinion.

Glick, P. C., & Norton, A. J. 1977. Marrying, divorcing, and living together in the United States today. *Population Bulletin* 32. Washington D.C.: Population Reference Bureau.

Golanty, E., & Harris, B. B. 1982. *Marriage and family life.* Boston: Houghton Mifflin.

Goode, W. J. 1959. The theoretical importance of love. *American Sociological Review* 24:38–47.

———. 1973. *Explorations in social theory.* New York: Oxford University Press.

Gordon, M. 1978. *The American family: Past, present, and future.* New York: Random House.

Heer, D. M. 1974. The prevalence of black-white marriage in the United States, 1960 and 1970. *Journal of Marriage and the Family* 36:246–259.

Hill, C. T., Rubin, Z., & Peplau, L. A. 1976. Breakups before marriage: The end of 103 affairs. *Journal of Social Issues* 32:147–168.

Huston, T. L., & Levinger, G. 1978. Interpersonal attraction and relationships. In *Annual review of psychology,* ed. M. R. Rosenzweig & L. W. Porter. Vol. 29. Palo Alto, CA: Annual Reviews.

Huston, T. L., Surra, C. A., Fitzgerald, N. M., & Cate, R. M. 1981. From courtship to marriage: Mate selection as an interpersonal process. In *Personal relationships 2: Developing personal relationships,* ed. S. Duck & R. Gilmour. London: Academic Press.

Kaats, G. R., & Davis, K. E. 1970. The dynamics of sexual behavior in college students. *Journal of Marriage and the Family* 32:390–399.

Kerkoff, A., & Davis, K. 1962. Value consensus and need complementarity in mate selection. *American Sociological Review* 27:295–303.

Knox, D., & Wilson, K. 1981. Dating behaviors of university students. *Family Relations* 30:255–258.

Landis, J. T., & Landis, M. G. 1977. *Building a successful marriage.* 7th ed. Englewood Cliffs, N.J.: Prentice-Hall.

Lewis, R. A. 1973. A longitudinal test of a developmental framework for premarital dyadic formation. *Journal of Marriage and the Family* 35:16–25.

Massarik, F., & Chenkin, A. 1973. United States national Jewish population study: A first report. *American Jewish Yearbook 74.* Philadelphia, PA: Jewish Publication Society of America.

Monahan, T. P. 1971. Interracial marriage in the United States: Some data on Upstate New York. *International Journal of Sociology of the Family* 1:94–106.

———. 1976. An overview of statistics on interracial marriage in the United States, with data on its extent from 1963–1970. *Journal of Marriage and the Family* 3:223–231.

Murstein, B. I. 1970. Stimulus-value-role: A theory of marital choice. *Journal of Marriage and the Family* 32:465–481.

———. 1976. *Who will marry whom?* New York: Springer.

———. 1980. Mate selection in the 1970s. *Journal of Marriage and the Family* 42:777–792.

Rockwell, R. C. 1976. Historical trends and variations in educational homogamy. *Journal of Marriage and the Family* 38:83–95.

Rubin, Z., & Levinger, G. 1974. Theory and data badly mated: A critique of Murstein's SVR and Lewis' PDF models of mate selection. *Journal of Marriage and the Family* 36:226–231.

Saxton, L. 1980. *The individual, marriage, and the family.* 4th ed. Belmont, CA: Wadsworth.

———. 1982. *The individual, marriage, and the family.* 5th ed. Belmont, CA: Wadsworth.

U.S. Bureau of the Census. 1972. *Census of Population, 1970.* PC (2)-4C. Washington D.C.: Government Printing Office.

Vandenberg, S. 1972. Assortative mating, or who marries whom? *Behavior Genetics* 2:127–157.

Chapter 6

Intimacy, Love, and Sexual Attitudes and Behavior

MAJOR CONCEPTS

Self-love
Romantic love complex
Agape
Philos
Eros
Vulnerability
Liking versus loving
FILO and LIFO
Limerance
Styles of loving
  Best friends
  Game playing
  Logical
  Possessive
  Romantic
  Unselfish
Attraction

Appearance and actions
Wheel theory of love
  Rapport
  Self-revelation
  Mutual dependency
  Fulfillment of basic personality needs
  Clockspring alternative model
Intimacy, patchwork intimacy
Contexts of sexual development
Stages of heterosexual relations
Standards of premarital sexual
  intercourse
  Abstinence
  Double standard
  Permissiveness with affection
  Permissiveness without affection

The preceeding chapter described the development of couple relationships from first date to engagement, emphasizing the *structure* of dating and mate selection in the American courtship system. This chapter focuses on the *content* of couple relationships. What happens to partners, and between them, as their relationships unfold over time? How are we to understand the experiences of love, intimacy, and sexual relations? Although it is possible—and in a sense desirable—to love oneself, most of us think of love and sex as relational experiences that are at the very heart of partnerships.

If the courtship system in the United States is formally free and young people choose their own partners, on what basis do they make these choices? At first glance the answer is so obvious that it seems unnecessary to write about it or study it. Love is the basis of relationship formation in the United States. In a national poll, approximately 80 percent of adults named love as the primary reason that people get married (Roper Organization 1974), and the percentages might be higher among young people. Long before the poll, the lyrics of time-honored ballads assured romantic youth that love and marriage are so intertwined that once two people find they are in love they get married. Although such sentiments express common beliefs in our culture, they provide little help in understanding the development of couple relations. Do love and marriage always go together? Does love lead to marriage? Does marriage lead to love? How is "making" love related to "being" in love? Do people "fall" in love or "grow" in love? What is love anyway, and how does it motivate individuals to become partners and make marital choices?

LEARNING ABOUT LOVE

Human beings are born with the potential to love and be loved. Infants are remarkably helpless and dependent little creatures for an unusually long time. Initially at least, infants are in a most favorable position to receive love. Many influential scholars—including Freud, Maslow, and Harlow—have thought that early experiences in receiving love are very important in the development of love. These scholars have asserted that our later adult capacity to be loving and our ways of receiving love are affected by our love experiences while growing up. Love experiences in infancy and early childhood do not irreversibly determine our ability to give and receive love, but they have an effect on how we feel about ourselves and others and on our relationships with them. Fromm (1956, 59) wrote in his classic *The Art of Loving* that love of oneself is part of being able to love others: "Love of others and love of ourselves are not alternatives. On the contrary, an attitude of love toward themselves will be found in all those who are capable of loving others." From our early years then, perhaps the most important aspect of love development is accepting and loving ourselves.

In addition to the lesson that they can love themselves and love and be loved by others, children also learn at an early age that love is the basis for relationships between men and women. The emphasis on love in our society rapidly changes from the unconditional and selfless love given from parents to children to the *romantic love complex.* It does not take very sophisticated youngsters to get the romantic love message from a variety of sources that bombard them. Television programming and commercials, children's literature, peers and older siblings all convey the same message: "girl and boy meet, fall in love, overcome their differences, and ride off into the proverbial sunset" (Orthner 1981, 158).

These notions about eventual love relations between boys and girls are likely to be thoroughly internalized by the end of grade school years. As adolescence arrives, pressures toward romantic couple relationships intensify. Many girls have barely begun to mature and many boys have scarcely started having racy dreams when their parents and peers begin nudging them toward couple relationships. There are also the not-so-subtle pairings at school dances, parties, and other activities. Perhaps even more powerful, and certainly more pervasive, is the early teen subculture with its idols and their plaintive songs about love. During this time most young people begin, often tentatively and uncertainly, their first dating experiences. Some young people, for a variety of reasons, are not immediately caught up in the romantic love complex, or perhaps they are not as involved as they would like to be. For them, romance writers are busy at work; there are hundreds of thousands of vicarious love stories in paperback, at the box office, and on television. As Orthner (1981, 159) suggests, if all else fails, "they are assured that by using the appropriate cologne, toothpaste, or skin lotion, love will eventually come their way."

The preceding scenario is somewhat overplayed, admittedly, to make the point that young people in the United States are thoroughly indoctrinated to expect love as the basis of their couple relationships. More specifically though, our culture emphasizes *romantic* love as opposed to other elements or dimensions of loving partnerships.

DEFINITIONS AND ELEMENTS OF LOVE

Although there are many definitions of *love,* not all are helpful in understanding couple relations. Orthner (1981, 146) lamented the inadequacy of our love vocabulary by noting that "we can love our boyfriend, girlfriend, husband, or wife, but we can also love fishing, milk, the theater, our country, dogs, and children." Many analyses of love draw from the Greek concepts of agape, philos, and eros. *Agape,* or "spiritual love," is the giving, self-sacrificing, nondemanding dimension of loving another. *Philos,* sometimes called "brotherly love," is characterized by deep and enduring friendship. *Eros,* "erotic or physical love," refers to sexual attraction and desire. Couple relationships usually include all three of these dimensions, but some couple relationships are clearly dominated by one kind more than the others. Most of us grow up expecting and wanting to give or express each of these elements of love and hoping and needing to receive these expressions in return.

A fundamental element in forming close relationships is love vulnerability. In order to love, partners must discard their masks. Jourard (1971, vii) expresses it this way: "We conceal and camouflage our true being before others to foster a sense of safety, to protect ourselves against unwanted but expected criticism, hurt, or rejection." Love is a risky venture because in the process of self-disclosure we expose our innermost personal thoughts and feelings. Cox (1981, 191) writes: "Thus to love is always an adventure because there is danger involved. Indifference is the opposite of love. A lover cares, a lover reveals more of himself or herself, and a lover is vulnerable to being hurt." Nearly everyone takes the risk, according to Fromm (1956), because each individual senses his or her isolation and separateness. Loving and being loved is the way of overcoming aloneness and experiencing human union.

Another important contribution to our understanding of love has been made by Rubin. His early research on this topic was concerned with investigating the nature of love—specifically, how it differed from, or perhaps grew out of, liking (Rubin 1973). Fundamentally, Rubin found that loving is not just an extension of liking but that they are considerably different. People often like others whom they do not love, and occasionally people love others whom they do not particularly like. According to Rubin, *liking* is usually associated with respect or affection for someone; *loving* is characterized by feelings of comfort, ease, warmth, and security in the presence of the other person. Dating partners in Rubin's study were rated much higher on the love scale than best friends were, although both received high liking scores. High love, but not high liking, scores were related to the desire to marry someone. Rubin also found that correlations between loving and liking scales were moderate for men and low among women who are, apparently, better able to distinguish between loving someone and liking them. Another important aspect of Rubin's research was the finding that love and liking have emotional and cognitive elements. People use both their hearts and their minds in forming and appraising their intimate relationships.

Other studies of romantic love have turned up unexpected differences between men and women. Stereotypically, women have been thought to be more vulnerable in love than men, to fall first and fall hardest. But, Kanin, Davidson, and Scheck (1970) reported just the opposite; men were more likely to say that they were in love or to say that they had fallen in love sooner. By the twentieth date, 45 percent of women were still not sure they were in love as compared with only 30 percent of men. Another surprise is that men tend to cling to a dying relationship longer than women do and that they are likely to be more emotionally distraught when it breaks up. Women are more likely to accept the fact that the relationship has ended and to take steps to start over again (Hill, Rubin, & Peplau 1976). These unexpected findings about men and love have been given acronymns: Men are FILO (first in, last out) and women are LIFO (last in, first out). Walster and Walster (1978) even reported that three times more men than women commit suicide after disastrous love affairs. Because mens' attempts at suicide are more successful than womens', it would be interesting to know if women are less or more likely to make suicide *attempts* after breaking up.

A familiar idea about love is that people helplessly fall victim to some mysterious force that strikes them with overwhelming power. This idea has a long history in art and literature but little support from contemporary research. However, recently an interesting analysis of this idea has been published entitled *Love and Limerance* (Tennov 1979). Tennov defines *limerance* as a sudden, overwhelming attraction and attachment to another person, which includes obsessive preoccupation with the other. Limerance is supposed to occur, according to Tennov, in two stages of crystallization. At the first stage the person is preoccupied with thoughts about the other perhaps 30 percent of the time, and at the second stage his or her consciousness is entirely consumed by thinking about and being with the other. In her study of 2000 couples, Tennov found that the majority indicated having had at least one such limerant experience. Needless to say, those whose love experiences are so totally overwhelming are not well understood by those whose love experiences are more temperate. Although Tennov's work provides a more systematic treatment of "rockets, bells, and poetry," some of the supposed characteristics of limerance seem rather dubious (an aching in the center of the chest, just below the sternum?).

STYLES OF LOVING

With the work of Canadian John Lee (1973, 1974), social scientists began to understand more clearly that the ways we experience love are immensely variable. Based on Lee's ideas, Lasswell and several colleagues developed a "Love Scale Questionnaire," which has been widely used in assessing the meanings and manifestations of love (Lasswell & Lasswell 1976). After analyzing thousands of responses, these social scientists have identified six styles of loving. The descriptions of these six styles that appear below are taken from Chapter 5 of the book *Styles of Loving* (Lasswell & Lobsenz 1980).

1. Best-Friends Love

For persons in whom the best-friends style predominates, love grows through companionship, rapport, mutual sharing and dependency, and gradual self-revelation over a long period of time. There is seldom any assumption at the outset of the relationship that it will flower into love or marriage. Friendly lovers find it hard to conceive of becoming emotionally involved with someone they do not know well. Such persons tend to speak of their love as "mature" compared with some of the other styles, which they are likely to see as infatuation.

Typically, a person with this love style is the product of an emotionally secure and close-knit family. He or she has usually been able to count on parents and siblings for companionship, warmth, and support. The divorce rate is low for best-friends couples, but if such a relationship does break up, the lover will most likely want to remain close to the former partner.

2. Game-Playing Love

To the game-playing lover an emotional relationship is a challenge to be enjoyed, a contest to be won. The more experienced one grows at the game, the more skilled one's moves can be, and often a wide range of strategies are developed to keep the game interesting. Commitment is foreign to this style lover. The object of the game is to play amiably at love, to encourage intimacy, yet to hold it at arm's length. The partner is usually kept emotionally off balance, and the game player's affections are never to be taken for granted.

Game-playing lovers have many artifices. For example, they avoid making long-range plans with partners. They usually arrange dates on a spur-of-the-moment basis. They are careful not to go out with the same person too often; that might lead him or her to believe there was some prospect of stability. Much of this kind of love style is found prior to marriage when a one-to-one commitment is not required or expected.

Obviously, men and women who play at love have both charming and infuriating qualities. They are usually self-sufficient, making few demands on the other person and preferring not to have demands made on them. They tend to be amusing, quick-witted, and self-confident. On the other hand, they tend to be self-centered. The charge is often made that game-playing love is not truly love at all, that it is hedonism at best and promiscuity at worst.

3. Logical Love

The logical lover concentrates on the practical virtues found in a relationship. This style has been called "love with a shopping list." "I could never love anyone who didn't meet my requirements for a husband and father [or wife and mother]." Moreover, logical lovers are quite realistic. They usually know exactly what kind of partner they want and are willing to wait for the person who comes closest to meeting their specifications.

It is not uncommon for a lover of this pragmatic bent to avoid any relationship that he or she does not think has a good chance of becoming permanent. "Why should I waste my time?" The modern logical lover may believe that romance does have some place in love, but he or she feels more strongly that love should be an outgrowth of a couple's practical compatibility.

Pragmatic lovers consider themselves in love so long as the relationship is perceived as a fair exchange. If matters turn out not to be what they seemed, logical love calls for an effort to help the partner fulfill his or her original potential. If such efforts fail, the relationship is ended. Not surprisingly, logical love requires patience: patience to find the proper partner; patience to work out problems; and if the relationship should break up, patience to wait to end it until a reasonable and logical time.

4. Possessive Love

The possessive lover has perhaps the most unfulfilling and disturbing love style. Alternating between peaks of excitement and depths of despair, capable of shifting in an eyeblink from intense devotion to intense jealousy, he or she is consumed by the need to possess the partner totally and, simultaneously, to be possessed by the other person. The fear of loss or rejection is always uppermost. Despite this bleak picture, the pattern is usually considered one of the most common definitions of being in love.

At the root of possessive love are two seemingly contradictory emotional factors. On the one hand, such lovers are enormously dependent. At the outset of the love affair they may be too excited to sleep, eat, or think clearly. Unable to control their intense reactions, they often feel helplessly at the mercy of the beloved. Yet at the same time, such lovers are demanding, often placing great emotional burdens on the other person. Supersensitive, the possessive lover is constantly on the alert for the slightest sign that the partner's affection may be slackening. If such a sign is detected, or even imagined, the anxiety-ridden lover demands immediate reassurance.

When affairs of possessive lovers break up, the ending is usually bitter and angry. The possessive lover finds it almost impossible to see his or her former partner again or to retain any concern or affection for him or her. Nevertheless, many perfectly adequate and emotionally healthy people exhibit this style of love to some degree. They prefer intense togetherness. They see jealousy as a natural part of being in love.

5. Romantic Love

Cupid's arrow piercing the heart and instantaneously awakening passionate devotion—no other image so accurately delineates romantic love. The romantic lover is often as much in love with love itself as with the beloved. Love at first sight is not only possible but almost a necessity. The typical romantic lover seeks a total emotional relationship with the partner. Moreover, he or she expects it to provide a constant series of emotional peaks. The fires of this love style are fueled in large part by a powerful sense of physical attraction.

Once they have found each other, two romantic lovers are likely to be quickly in each other's arms. There is a great urgency to merge physically as well as emotionally. Obviously, the intensity of this initial attraction and passion cannot be maintained indefinitely at the same high level. When it begins to taper off, the romantic lover must either substitute fantasies for realities or confront the growing evidence that the other person is not perfect.

One must be willing and able to reveal oneself completely, to commit oneself totally, to risk emotional lows as well as emotional highs, and, finally, to survive without despair if one's love is rejected. A romantic does not demand love but is confidently ready to grasp it when it appears.

6. Unselfish Love

Unselfish love is unconditionally caring and nurturing, giving and forgiving, and, at its highest level, self-sacrificing. It is a characteristic of this love style that one has no sense of martyrdom, no feeling of being put upon. Rather, it rests upon the genuine belief that true love is better expressed in giving than receiving—agape. In a sense, men and women with this style of love never actually "fall in love." Rather, they seem to have a reservoir of loving kindness that is always available. They are ruled less by their own needs than by the needs of others. Unselfish love occurs less often in real life than imagined. Not many people have the emotional fortitude to be so giving. Even if they have, their altruism is not necessarily devoid of all personal rewards. An unselfish lover experiences in return feelings of satisfaction, recognition, even gratitude.

PROCESSES OF FORMING LOVE RELATIONSHIPS

Now that love definitions and examples have been given, our attention turns to the formation of love relationships. The principles of homogamy and endogamy presented in the previous chapter help in understanding how a partner comes to be selected. But how is a love relationship formed with this person?

One of the most widely quoted explanations of how love relationships develop was formulated by Reiss in 1960. In his *wheel theory of love development,* Reiss proposed that (1) the initial rapport between two people leads to (2) their revealing themselves to one another, whereupon they become (3) mutually dependent and (4) fulfill their personality needs (see Figure 6.1). These four processes turn one into the next, constantly wheeling in a clockwise fashion, carrying partners deeper into love. Love development can stop or move backward, as the double arrow in Figure 6.1 indicates: less rapport decreases self-revelation, which decreases mutual dependency, which decreases need fulfillment.

Rapport refers to the partners' abilities to relate easily to one another. A comfortable,

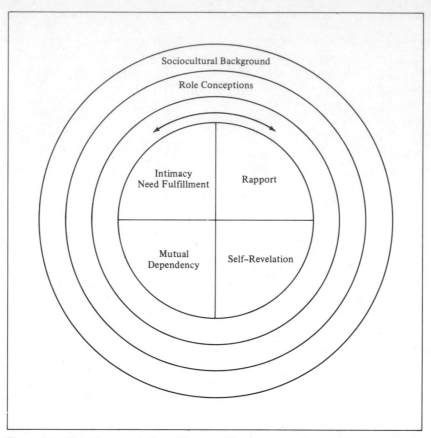

Figure 6.1 Graphic presentation of the wheel theory of love. *Source:* I. L. Reiss, *Family Systems in America,* 3d ed. (New York: Holt, Rinehart and Winston, 1980, p. 129). Copyright © 1980 by Holt, Rinehart and Winston. Reprinted by permission of Holt, Rinehart and Winston, CBS College Publishing.

nonthreatened feeling must be present between partners before there is much chance that love will develop any further, which includes being able to communicate easily with the other person. Homogamy in social and cultural background makes the establishment of rapport more likely because homogamous partners share similar experiences and perceptions. They are more likely to know about similar things and to be able to understand each other.

Reiss (1980) states that *self-revelation* will follow naturally, almost inevitably, if good rapport is established and partners feel relaxed. Self-revelation has to do with personal disclosure, with telling or sharing one's personal views, feelings, and experiences. This kind of personal communication usually occurs after rapport is established because of the vulnerability or risk involved in disclosing oneself to a stranger.

Couples are likely to establish *mutual dependency* through doing things together after they have a comfortable rapport and know one another. Reiss states that mutual experiences that require cooperation build up interdependent habit patterns. Partners come to count on each other and like to share experiences together; in short, they become mutually dependent.

Fulfillment of basic personality needs and intimacy is the final stage of Reiss's wheel theory of love. These deep and basic needs are most likely to be met for adults in couple relationships that include trust, knowledge of one another, and shared experiences. The fulfillment—or, more accurately, the *partial* fulfillment—of basic personality needs is based on rapport, self-revelation, and mutual dependency.

Borland (1975) proposed a *clockspring alternative model* to Reiss's wheel theory of love, with one's real self at the center of the spring (see Figure 6.2). The four processes (rapport, self-revelation, mutual dependency, and need fulfillment) wind the partners into closer and more intimate understanding of each other's real inner selves. The more tightly the relationship winds around the partners' real selves, the more difficult it is to unwind. A love relationship can become closer (wound tighter like a clockspring) or looser, depending on the constantly dynamic interplay of rapport, disclosure, mutual dependency, and need fulfillment.

Usually in the later stages of love development, a special quality emerges that is referred to as *intimacy.* Intimacy implies an unusual depth of mutuality, of sharing one's own and receiving the partner's innermost personal thoughts and feelings. Perhaps the most distinguishing characteristic of intimacy is its depth—one does not form an intimate relationship in a shallow or superficial acquaintance. This depth of intimacy is described by Oden (1974, 4) as "knowledge of the core of something, an understanding of the inmost parts, that which is indicative of one's deepest nature and marked by close physical, mental, or social association."

We tend to think of a single intimate partnership, but individuals often have several persons with whom they are intimate in different ways. Olson (1977) has suggested that there are at least seven types of intimacy: (1) emotional—loving another person; (2) sexual—sharing physical and sexual activities; (3) social—having the same friends and being involved in the same groups; (4) intellectual—sharing and communicating thoughts and ideas; (5)

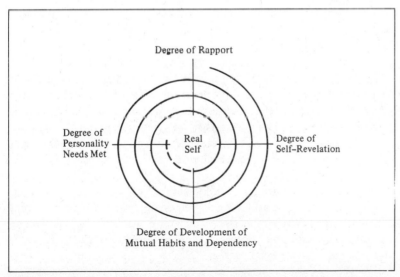

Figure 6.2 The clockspring alternative model for the wheel theory of love development. *Source:* D. M. Borland, "An Alternative Model of the Wheel Theory," *Family Coordinator* 24 (1975): 289–292. Copyrighted 1975 by the National Council on Family Relations, 1219 University Avenue Southeast, Minneapolis, Minnesota. Reprinted by permission.

recreational—sharing a keen interest in a sport or hobby; (6) aesthetic—sharing experiences and ideas of what is beautiful; and (7) spiritual—sharing religious beliefs or a similar sense of life's meaning and purpose. Almost everyone has shared experiences with another person that were unusually mutual, deep, and usually hidden from public knowledge; this kind of intimacy might have been purely emotional or social, as in a special friendship. Kieffer (1977) has referred to the fact that most of us are involved in a variety of intimate relationships with both family and nonfamily members as *patchwork intimacy*. It is particularly in the area of physical intimacy, including sexuality, that heterosexual partnerships have such remarkably pleasurable and painful expressions.

THE CONTEXT OF SEXUAL DEVELOPMENT

Much of what we bring to sexual relations is in our minds. Sexual values, attitudes, and behaviors are acquired gradually over the years, just as we learn about other aspects of our culture. In this respect, human sexuality is immensely complex and vastly different from the mating of animals. The females of other mammalian species have fixed estrous cycles during which they are sexually receptive to males and capable of conceiving. Copulation occurs during these limited periods but not during the longer part of the cycle when females are not receptive. The sex relations of animals, with the exception of man, are set by biological drives.

Human sexual relations are infused with a great many motivations, meanings, and emotions in addition to biological urges. After sexual maturity, human adults remain interested in sex throughout their lives, and most sexual behavior has little to do with reproduction. Perhaps the central meaning of sex in our society is intimate communication, a way of expressing intimacy with one's partner, of sharing emotional and physical closeness. Even this is probably debatable; sex relations are often the pursuit of personal pleasure or just a routine.

In understanding sexual development in the context of our society, it is helpful to recognize the influence of the Judeo-Christian tradition in conveying messages about the meaning and place of sex. In mainstream American society, sex has historically been treated with moderately strong restrictions, compared at least with more sexually permissive cultures (such as Polynesia) and extremely restrictive ones (Islamic societies). Christensen and Gregg (1970) have reported large differences in sexual attitudes and behavior in comparisons of Danish, Midwest U.S., and Intermountain U.S. college students. In addition, at the turn of the century the United States was just emerging from the Victorian period, and during that remarkably closed era sex was not even a topic of conversation. Even today, when sex is used publicly to sell virtually everything in the United States, many adult Americans remain personally reluctant to talk openly about sex.

It is within this broad historical, cultural, and biological background that the development of individual sexuality and sexual relations must be considered. Most people think about sex as a very specific kind of behavior between men and women—namely, sexual intercourse—but the variations around this central act are so vast that they cannot be included fully in this text. Instead, our approach will be to trace briefly the development of individual sexuality and the beginnings of heterosexual interaction within the social and cultural context of North America.

A child's understanding and knowledge of sexuality is greatly influenced by the family environment and microculture in which he or she grows up. The microculture includes friends in the peer group, school and neighborhood norms, church influences, and so on. In the United States today there is immense diversity in the degree to which children are raised under sexually permissive or restrictive values, told as little as possible or given accurate sexual information, and encouraged in or prevented from participation in individual and interpersonal sexual acts. In spite of this diversity, the data are quite clear that virtually all adolescent boys, and probably half the girls, experiment with masturbation.

As far as heterosexual relations are concerned, there is much greater variability. There is a very clear progression of physical intimacy in male-female relations even though partners might not define all these behaviors as overtly sexual. Typically, heterosexual intimacy proceeds as follows:

1. Touching—holding hands, embracing;
2. Kissing—ranging from kisses that are short and tentative to longer and more intimate "deep kissing";
3. Petting—caressing and fondling the erotic areas of the partner's body, usually progressing from light caressing to heavy genital petting; and
4. Sexual intercourse.

Although this pattern of progressive sexual intimacy is very clear, great variability enters the timing of participation in heterosexual acts. The first stage of touching, holding, and embracing is almost universally accepted as appropriate on a first date. A date legitimizes these expressions, which is also true for kissing among the majority of contemporary youth. Petting, however, is another matter. One recent study found interesting gender differences in the acceptability of petting (hands anywhere). Over three-fourths of the female college students said that petting should be delayed beyond the fourth date, whereas only one-third of the men felt that way. By contrast, 31 percent of the men felt that petting should occur on or before the first date, but only 7 percent of the women felt that way (Knox & Wilson 1981). These differences in expectations or acceptance of physical intimacy by degree of involvement were no secret to the college students. "Less than 15% of both sexes said that their dates always shared their understanding of how long people should wait before engaging in kissing, petting, and intercourse" (Knox & Wilson 1981, 257).

In actual practice, continuous involvement in a relationship where affection is present dramatically alters the behavior of female college students. Spanier (1976) found that dating relationships and experiences were more strongly related to sexual activity than sex education sources and knowledge. College students who dated the most and who were most emotionally involved with dates had the most active sex lives. Table 6.1 shows data over a 15-year period from a southern state university at which no petting, light petting, and medium petting all have declined and heavy petting shows considerable increases (Robinson & Jedlicka 1982). Although most male students have usually reported some involvement in heavy petting behavior, the most marked changes shown in the table are in the percentages of college women who report heavy petting behavior.

In American society the expression of sexuality through sexual intercourse is given universal social approval only in marriage. Sexual intercourse is the behavior before or outside of marriage about which there continues to be the greatest social concern. The following section describes changes in premarital intercourse standards and behavior over time and by degree of relationship involvement.

Table 6.1 PETTING BEHAVIOR OF COLLEGE STUDENTS, 1965–1980

Year and degree of petting	Males		Females	
	Percentage	Number	Percentage	Number
None				
1965	1.6	3	8.7	10
1970	2.2	3	1.3	2
1975	2.6	3	3.4	9
1980	3.0	5	1.8	4
Light				
1965	11.6	15	32.3	37
1970	8.9	12	19.5	30
1975	6.9	8	12.7	34
1980	6.6	11	12.9	29
Medium				
1965	14.7	19	24.3	28
1970	9.6	3	19.5	30
1975	10.3	12	16.6	31
1980	5.4	9	12.4	28
Heavy				
1965	71.3	92	34.3	40
1970	79.3	107	59.7	92
1975	80.2	93	72.7	195
1980	84.9	141	72.9	164

Source: I. E. Robinson and D. Jedlicka, "Changes in Sexual Attitudes of College Students from 1965 to 1980: A Research Note," *Journal of Marriage and the Family* 44 (1982): 237–240. Copyrighted 1982 by the National Council on Family Relations, 1219 University Avenue Southeast, Minneapolis, Minnesota 55414. Reprinted by permission.

STANDARDS OF PREMARITAL SEXUAL INTERCOURSE

There has never been a single standard of premarital sexual behavior in the United States. Although there probably is more variation in attitudes about premarital intercourse now than ever before, there have always been pockets of great cultural diversity. Imagine, for example, premarital sexual norms and behaviors in large urban minority ghettos versus rural Amish, Mennonite, or Hutterite colonies. Or, contrast heterogeneous liberal communities with homogeneous communities of fundamentalist Christians or Muslims. Some years ago, Reiss (1960) identified four standards of premarital sexual permissiveness that have been influential in research and writing on this topic:

1. *Abstinence.* Premarital intercourse is considered wrong for both men and women, regardless of circumstances.
2. *Double standard.* Premarital intercourse is more acceptable for men than for women.
3. *Permissiveness with affection.* Premarital intercourse is considered right for both men and women when a stable relationship with love or strong affection is present.
4. *Permissiveness without affection.* Premarital intercourse is considered right for both men and women if they are so inclined, regardless of the amount or stability of affection present.

Abstinence

Since the beginning of the Christian era, abstinence has been the *formal* standard of premarital sexual behavior in the United States and most Western societies. In fact, many states still have laws against premarital intercourse (fornication), although such laws are now very rarely enforced (unless those involved are related or very young and prosecution is for incest or statutory rape). The proportion of those who agree with an abstinent standard has ranged in the United States from about 20 to 80 percent, depending on the age and other characteristics of the sample being studied (Reiss 1980, 78). Generally, older people endorse abstinence most strongly, and presumably at some time in the past the proportion of individuals who endorsed abstinence was much higher than it is today. In relatively recent years the National Opinion Research Center (NORC) has asked representative samples of adults in the United States what they think about premarital sex. Table 6.2 shows that there is a clear downward trend in respondents saying that premarital sex is always wrong. Even so, if the rate of change remains about the same, one in four adult Americans in 1990 will still think that premarital sex is always wrong (Glenn & Weaver 1979).

It has long been known that younger and older adults have quite different attitudes about abstinence (Reiss 1960, 1967). When respondents' age was analyzed in the study referred to above, premarital sex was considered "always" or "almost always wrong" by three out of five respondents who were older than age 50, two out of five respondents aged 30 to 49, and only one in five aged 18 and 19 (Glenn & Weaver 1979). Several factors are thought to contribute to these age differences in premarital sexual standards. Perhaps most obviously, older people grew up and formed their basic values when premarital sex was less acceptable than it is now. Many elements of contemporary society (e.g., movies, songs, literature, television) are conducive to permissive premarital sexual views. In part, then, the generation gap in acceptance of the abstinent standard reflects real changes in what was and is socially and culturally accepted. There is also evidence to suggest that becoming a parent and assuming responsibilities for children makes one become more conservative about premarital sexual behavior (Reiss 1967; Reiss & Miller 1979).

Double Standard

In contrast to the formal standard of abstinence for both sexes, males in most cultures usually have been allowed greater sexual rights than females, and the majority of males have become

Table 6.2 ATTITUDES OF ADULT AMERICANS TOWARD PREMARITAL SEX, 1972–1978 (IN PERCENT)

| | Year | | | | |
Opinion	1972	1974	1975	1977	1978
Not wrong at all	27.3	30.7	32.8	36.5	38.7
Wrong only sometimes	24.3	23.6	24.0	23.0	20.3
Almost always wrong	11.8	12.7	12.3	9.5	11.7
Always wrong	36.6	33.0	30.9	31.0	29.3

Source: Adapted from Norval D. Glenn and Charles N. Weaver, "Attitudes toward Premarital, Extramarital, and Homosexual Relations in the U.S. in the 1970s," *Journal of Sex Research,* 15 (1979): 111.

sexually active before marriage. This *double standard,* which tolerates nonmarital sex for men but restricts and disapproves of it for women, has been observed across many societies. Perhaps the double standard has been so prevalent because of pervasive power differentials between men and women. Historically, men regarded women as property, and their virginity was considered especially important. This is still true in many traditional cultures today. As norms of equality have become more widespread, the double standard has been declining in Western societies. Surveys of male college students in the United States over the past 40 years have shown sharply decreasing concern about whether the bride is a virgin at marriage. Presumably, the bride's virginity would have been very important in earlier times, but in 1939 when college men were first asked to rank the importance of their partner's virginity among 17 other characteristics, it was placed in about the middle of the list. Marital partner's virginity was less important to college men in 1956, it was even less important in 1967, and it was ranked seventeenth out of 18 characteristics in a 1977 survey, just ahead of "similar political background" (Hudson 1980).

Although the double standard regarding premarital sexual behavior has declined sharply in the United States, it has not disappeared. Males are still somewhat more likely than females to want their marital partners to be virgins. Also, more females than males say that premarital sexual activities of all kinds are wrong or immoral, and both males and females think that women's premarital sexual behavior is more immoral than the same behavior in men. In spite of remnants of the double standard, the two most general trends apparent in Table 6.3 are the declining percentages of college students (especially females) who view premarital intercourse as immoral (declining abstinent standard) and the convergence over time in male and female responses (decline in the double standard).

In addition to the attitudes about premarital sexual intercourse described above, reports of sexual behavior also show declining abstinence and decreases in the double standard. Some of the most interesting data of this type were collected in 1965, 1970, 1975, and 1980 at the University of Georgia. In this 15-year period ending in 1980, reports of sexual intercourse among male college students rose from 65 to 77 percent. During the same time, reported sexual intercourse by female students rose from 28 to 63 percent. These findings of larger percentages of males having had sexual intercourse, increasing proportions of nonvirgins of both sexes, and much larger increases in the premarital sexual behavior of young women characterize virtually all of the trend data gathered from various sources (Hunt 1974; Zelnick & Kantner 1980). Based on the most recent representative national data, Zelnick and Kantner (1980) reported that increasing percentages of teens were sexually active at each older age and that 77 percent of males and 69 percent of females had become sexually active by age 19 (see Table 6.4, p. 118).

Permissiveness with Affection

Permissiveness with affection has become increasingly endorsed in the United States at the same time that abstinence and the double standard have been declining (Reiss 1960, 1967, 1980). Apparently, the majority of people now think that it is appropriate for partners who feel strong affection for each other to have sex, especially if the couple are in a stable relationship with a commitment such as engagement. In one study, Knox and Wilson (1981, 257) reported that "the more emotionally involved a person was in a relationship the more likely increasing levels of intimacy were regarded as appropriate." This finding, and the fact

Table 6.3 PERCENTAGE OF 1965, 1970, 1975, AND 1980 COLLEGE STUDENTS STRONGLY AGREEING WITH STATEMENTS ABOUT THE MORALITY OF PREMARITAL SEXUAL RELATIONSHIPS

Statement	Males		Females	
	Percent	Number	Percent	Number
1. I feel that premarital sexual intercourse is immoral.				
1965	33.0	129	70.0	115
1970	14.0	137	34.0	158
1975	19.5	133	20.7	295
1980	17.4	167	25.3	237
2. A man who has had sexual intercourse with a great many women is immoral.				
1965	35.0	127	56.0	114
1970	15.0	137	22.0	157
1975	19.5	138	30.1	296
1980	26.5	166	38.9	234
3. A woman who has had sexual intercourse with a great many men is immoral.				
1965	42.0	118	91.0	114
1970	33.0	137	54.0	157
1975	28.5	130	41.0	295
1980	41.8	165	49.6	236
4. A man who has had sexual intercourse with a great many women is sinful.				
1965	41.0	128	50.0	114
1970	24.0	136	26.0	156
1975	30.5	131	33.6	298
1980	37.1	167	40.4	235
5. A woman who has had sexual intercourse with a great many men is sinful.				
1965	58.0	137	70.0	113
1970	32.0	136	47.0	157
1975	33.6	131	37.2	298
1980	38.9	167	44.5	236

Source: I. E. Robinson and D. Jedlicka, "Changes in Sexual Attitudes and Behavior of College Students from 1965–1980: A Research Note, *Journal of Marriage and the Family* 44 (1982): 239. Copyrighted 1982 by the National Council on Family Relations, 1219 University Avenue Southeast, Minneapolis, Minnesota 55414. Reprinted by permission.

that it is more true for women than for men, has been reported in many studies (Ehrman 1959; King, Balswick, & Robinson 1977; Reiss 1967). In terms of the four premarital sexual standards, Reiss (1980, 187) has stated that "permissiveness with affection has become the dominant standard."

The trend toward more similar liberal sexual attitudes of men and women should not be interpreted to mean that *all* young people think premarital sex is okay. A nationwide survey (Astin, King, & Richardson 1981) of 192,248 entering freshmen in the fall of 1981 found many students who disagreed with living together before marriage and who did not agree with the statement "Sex is OK if people like each other." Table 6.5 shows that roughly one-half to two-thirds of freshmen men—and only one-fifth to one-third of freshmen women—agree with the proposition that premarital sex is all right if two persons like each other.

Table 6.4 PERCENTAGE OF NEVER-MARRIED TEENAGERS WHO HAVE HAD SEXUAL INTERCOURSE, UNITED STATES, 1971, 1976, AND 1979

Age	Females			Males[a]
	1971	1976	1979	1979
15	14	18	22	—
16	20	28	37	—
17	26	42	48	55
18	39	51	56	66
19	46	59	69	77
Average total	27	39	46	

[a]Data for males in earlier years and younger ages are not reported.

Source: Adapted from tables 1 and 2 in M. Zelnick and J. F. Kantner, "Sexual Activity, Contraceptive Use and Pregnancy among Metropolitan-Area Teenagers: 1971–1979," *Family Planning Perspectives* 12 (1980): 230–231, 233–237.

In other words, one-third to one-half of male freshmen and two-thirds to four-fifths of female freshmen do not agree that premarital sex is okay even if partners like each other. There are significant differences in these responses by sex, race, and type of college, as shown in Table 6.5. Men attending black colleges are the most liberal and women at church colleges are the most conservative in this national survey.

As permissiveness with affection has become more generally accepted over the years, the amount of commitment required for sex seems to have declined. Attitudes about premarital sex have historically been quite permissive for engaged couples who are, after all, formally committed to each other and about to be married. Figure 6.3 shows that in 1958 reported intercourse experience was more than twice as high among engaged couples as among couples who were just going steady and more than three times higher than couples who were just dating. By 1978 these differences in premarital sexual intercourse by dating category and commitment had almost disappeared. In the 20 years between 1958 and 1978 the percentage of engaged couples who had sexual intercourse more than doubled, but during the same period sexual intercourse increased over four times among couples who were going steady and increased some five times among those who were just dating on one university campus.

Table 6.5 PERCENTAGES OF MALE AND FEMALE FRESHMEN AGREEING "SEX IS OK IF PEOPLE LIKE EACH OTHER," BY TYPE OF COLLEGE ATTENDED, 1981

Type of college	Men	Women
All two-year colleges	65.6	36.0
All four-year colleges	59.1	28.7
All universities	63.7	32.1
Predominantly black colleges	68.3	36.2
Protestant four-year colleges	42.5	18.1
Catholic four-year colleges	52.5	19.5

Source: Alexander W. Astin, Margo R. King, and Gerald T. Richardson, *The American Freshman: National Norms for Fall 1981* (Los Angeles: Cooperative Institutional Research Program, University of California, 1981), pp. 24, 40.

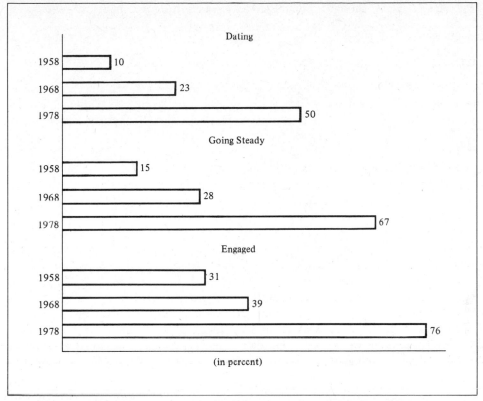

Figure 6.3 Trends in premarital intercourse among college women by dating category, 1958, 1968, and 1978. *Source:* Figure based on data from R. R. Bell and K. Coughey, "Premarital Sexual Experience Among College Females, 1958, 1968, 1978," *Family Relations* 29 (1980):355.

Apparently, a strong relational commitment like engagement has become a less important precondition for sexual relations between partners who feel some degree of affection for each other.

Permissiveness Without Affection

Premarital intercourse without affection has never been endorsed by a very large group of adults in the United States (Reiss 1980). Permissiveness without affection was viewed as acceptable by about 1 in 10 adults in 1963 (Reiss 1967). Male college students have traditionally been more likely than females or older adults have been to endorse permissiveness without affection.

In recent studies there is some suggestion that sexual intercourse without affection is coming to be viewed as even less acceptable. The data reported in Table 6.3 by Robinson and Jedlicka (1982) show increases between 1975 and 1980 in percentages of male and female college students who say that it is "immoral" and "sinful" to have sexual intercourse with "a great many partners." In another recent college sample, only 1 percent of college women said that intercourse "with no particular affection" was appropriate, whereas 10 percent of the male college students thought intercourse without affection was permissible (Knox & Wilson 1981).

REFLECTIONS ON SEXUAL ATTITUDES AND BEHAVIOR

Trends toward more liberal premarital sexual attitudes and behavior have been extensively documented in local-regional (Bell & Coughey 1980; Robinson & Jedlicka 1982) and national samples (Zelnick & Kantner 1980). Recent data from one southern university, however, hint that since 1975 there has been a "movement towards a return to the older attitudes, those which existed prior to the so-called sexual revolution" (Robinson & Jedlicka 1982, 240). There is an apparent contradiction here: sexual behavior with more partners for both males and females is at the highest levels ever reported, but at the same time there appears to be an increasing tendency to consider sexual intercourse with many partners "sinful and immoral." The latter part of this discrepancy has yet to be confirmed in larger, more representative samples, but Robinson and Jedlicka (1982) have tentatively termed the phenomenon a "sexual contradiction." Actually, the discrepancy between attitudes and behavior is not a new issue. Reiss (1980) described many findings that suggest to him that individuals' behavior tends to move ahead of, and be more liberal than, their attitudes. The discrepancy between attitudes and behavior is most often resolved by liberalizing attitudes to "catch up" with behaviors. Although it is less common, people sometimes resolve this dilemma by bringing their sex behavior in line with their attitudes and values. In the midst of often conflicting messages that bombard young people, we would hope that their choices about sexual behavior are made as consciously, freely, and intelligently as possible, with regard for both themselves and others.

SUMMARY

Love is a primary basis for mate selection in North America and in most Western societies. This is not to deny the powerful effects of variables that limit the pool of eligibles (e.g., age, race, religion); rather love operates within or in conjunction with these factors that constrain marital choice. The capacity to give and receive love appears to be inborn but is subject to environmental shaping. The experiences of being loved and coming to accept and love oneself are theorized to be important prerequisites to forming loving relationships. In addition to biological urges, pervasive social norms guide boys and girls into heterosexual interest and the romantic love complex.

Definitions of love often draw from Greek terms and interpretations of the various meanings of love. *Agape* is the selfless, nondemanding dimension of loving another. *Philos* is the deep friendship or brotherly kind of love. *Eros* refers to erotic, physical, or sexual love. Liking and loving have been found to share some similarities but to be quite distinct experiences. In studies of romantic love, men were found to describe themselves as being in love sooner and to hold onto an eroding relationship longer than women did (FILO and LIFO). *Limerance* refers to the overwhelming attraction, attachment to, and preoccupation with another person. All of these love concepts have been considered in describing and studying styles of loving in recent years.

Research in styles of loving suggest that there are empirically distinct patterns of couple love relationships. Best-friends lovers base their relationship on companionship, gradual sharing, and through knowledge of each other. Game-playing lovers view the relationship as a contest or challenge to be enjoyed with little commitment. Logical lovers base their relationship on practical considerations such as compatibility and interlocking interests. Possessive lovers are highly jealous, fearful of rejection, emotional, and sensitive. Romantic lovers expect to "fall" in love rapidly and intensely. Unselfish lovers are self-sacrificing, unconditional, and caring for the other(s) in their life. It is hypothesized that partners are initially attracted to each other based on physical appearance, perceived behaviors, and characteristics. In the wheel theory of love, the steps toward forming love relationships are rapport, self-revelation, mutual dependence, and the fulfillment of basic personality needs. Intimacy develops progressively as partners know each other more deeply through personal disclosure.

Sexual attitudes and behaviors develop within cultural, biological, and historical contexts. Regardless of these contexts, however, sexual behaviors tend to follow a regular pattern of development from touching, to kissing, to petting, to intercourse.

In North America standards of premarital sexual permissiveness have changed over time. Abstinence for both sexes had been the formal standard in the past, but historically most males actually have been sexually active before marriage. Permissiveness with affection, the acceptance of sexual intercourse between partners who feel affection for each other, is the most common standard today. Permissiveness without affection is a small minority point of view, although some persons always have endorsed having premarital sexual intercourse whether or not affection is present.

REFERENCES

Astin, A. W., King, M. R., & Richardson, G. T. 1981. *The American freshman: National norms for fall 1981.* Los Angeles: Cooperative Institutional Research Program, University of California.

Bell, R. R., & Coughey, K. 1980. Premarital sexual experience among college females, 1958, 1968, 1978. *Family Relations* 29:355.

Borland, D. M. 1975. An alternative model of the wheel theory. *Family Coordinator* 24:289–292.

Christensen, H. T., & Gregg, C. F. 1970. Changing sex norms in America and Scandanavia. *Journal of Marriage and the Family* 32:616–627.

Cox, F. D. 1981. *Human intimacy: Marriage, the family and its meaning.* 2d ed. St. Paul, MN: West.

Ehrman, W. 1959. *Premarital dating behavior.* New York: Holt, Rinehart and Winston.

Fromm, E. 1956. *The art of loving.* New York: Harper & Row.

Glenn, N. D., & Weaver, C. N. 1979. Attitudes toward premarital, extramarital, and homosexual relations in the U.S. in the 1970s. *Journal of Sex Research* 15:108–118.

Hill, C. T., Rubin, Z., & Peplau, L. 1976. Breakups before marriage: The end of 103 affairs. *Journal of Social Issues* 32:147–168.

Hudson, J. W. 1980. Men's changing attitudes regarding female chastity. *Medical Aspects of Human Sexuality* 14:137.

Hunt, M. M. 1974. *Sexual behavior in the 1970's.* Chicago: Playboy Press.

Huston, T., & Levinger, G. 1978. Interpersonal attraction and relationships. *Annual Review of Psychology* 29.

Jourard, S. M. 1971. *The transparent self.* New York: Van Nostrand.

Kaats, G., & Davis, K. 1970. The dynamics of sexual behavior of college students. *Journal of Marriage and the Family* 32:390–399.

Kanin, E. J., Davidson, K., & Scheck, S. 1970. A research note on male-female differentials in the experience of heterosexual love. *Journal of Sex Research* 6:64–72.

Kieffer, C. 1977. New depths in intimacy. In *Marriage and alternatives: Exploring intimate relationships,* ed. R. Libby & R. Whitehurst. Glenview, IL: Scott, Foresman.

King, K., Balswick, J. O., & Robinson, I. E. 1977. The continuing premarital sexual revolution among college females. *Journal of Marriage and the Family* 39:455–459.

Knox, D., & Wilson, K. 1981. Dating behavior of university students. *Family Relations* 30:255–258.

Lasswell, M., & Lobsenz, N. M. 1980. *Styles of loving.* New York: Ballantine.

Lasswell, T., & Lasswell, M. 1976. I love you but I'm not in love with you. *Journal of Marriage and Family Counseling* 2:211–224.

Lee, J. A. 1973. *The colours of love.* Toronto, Canada: New Press.

———. 1974. Styles of loving. *Psychology Today* 8:44–51.

Oden, T. C. 1974. *Game free: A guide to the meaning of intimacy.* New York: Harper & Row.

Olson, D. H. 1977. Communication and intimacy. Unpublished manuscript. Department of Family Social Science, University of Minnesota, St. Paul.

Orthner, D. 1981. *Intimate relationships: An introduction to marriage and the family.* Reading, MA: Addison-Wesley.

Reiss, I. L. 1960. *Premarital sexual standards in America.* New York: Free Press.

———. 1967. *The social context of premarital sexual permissiveness.* New York: Holt, Rinehart and Winston.

———. 1980. *Family systems in America.* 3d ed. New York: Holt, Rinehart and Winston.

Reiss, I. L., & Miller, B. C. 1979. Heterosexual permissiveness: A theoretical analysis. In *Contemporary theories about the family,* ed. I. Nye & I. Reiss. Vol. 1. New York: Free Press.

Robinson, I. E., & Jedlicka, D. 1982. Change in sexual attitudes and behavior of college students from 1965 to 1980: A research note. *Journal of Marriage and the Family* 44:237–240.

Roper Organization. 1974. *The Virginia Slims American women's opinion poll.* New York: Roper Organization.

Rubin, Z. 1973. *Liking and loving.* New York: Holt, Rinehart and Winston.

Spanier, G. B. 1976. Perceived sex knowledge, exposure to criticism, and premarital sexual behavior: The impact of dating. *Sociological Quarterly* 17:247–261.

Tennov, D. 1979. *Love and limerance.* New York: Stein & Day.

Walster, E., & Walster, G. W. 1978. *A new look at love.* Menlo Park, CA: Addison-Wesley.

Zelnick, M., & Kantner, J. 1980. Sexual activity, contraceptive use and pregnancy among metropolitan-area teenagers: 1971–1979. *Family Planning Perspectives* 12:230–231, 233–237.

PART THREE

TYPICAL STAGES OF FAMILY DEVELOPMENT

Chapter 7

Young Married Couples

MAJOR CONCEPTS

Variations of legal marriage
  Companionate marriage
  Marriage in two steps
  Renewable contracts
  Serial monogamy
  Probationary marriage
Marriage readiness
Developmental tasks of married
    couples
  Husbands' developmental tasks
  Wives' developmental tasks
  Family developmental tasks
  Conflicting and complementary tasks
Marital roles
  Husband/wife interdependencies
  Overlapping marital roles
  Conjugal options
  Flexible husband/wife roles
  Sex-neutral work
  Nontraditional jobs
Marital power
  Equalitarian marriages
  Sex-role transcendence

Role reversal
  Marital reciprocity
Problem solving
  Conflict resolution
  Communicator styles
Sexual intimacy
Family limitation and fertility
  Contraception
  Abortion
  Voluntary sterilization
  Pronatalism
  Antinatalism
Infertility
  Impotence
  Miscarriage
  Artificial insemination
  Surrogate pregnancy
  In vitro fertilization
Preparation for parenthood
  The couvade syndrome
  Pregnancy monitoring
  Genetic counseling
  The lineage bridge

Among couples marrying for the first time, marriage represents the *critical transition* from being single adults to becoming a married pair. For the remarried, the transition is from an earlier conjugal relationship ended by death or divorce to one with a new mate in a new marriage. Typically, a young couple have a year or two, more or less (as in the case of the pregnant bride), in which to establish their marriage before the first baby turns their marriage into a new family unit.

Most young American men and women expect to marry. A recent study of 16,524 seniors in the class of 1980 from 127 high schools found 82 percent of the girls and 74 percent of the boys saying they expected to get married "in the long run," and most of them expected to stay married to the same person (Herzog & Bachman 1982, 206). Fully two-thirds of 192,248 entering freshmen in 368 colleges' fall 1981 class considered raising a family an important objective (Astin, King, & Richardson 1981, 25, 41).

Why marry? A study of 600 eleventh graders of (1) both sexes, (2) white, black, or Hispanic ancestry, and (3) low- or middle-class status in (4) public, Roman Catholic, and private high schools in New York City and suburbs found girls seeing marriage as giving them financial security, emotional support, and prestige. Boys in the same sample anticipated that marriage would provide them with a normal home life, a home of their own, and a feeling of leadership (Tittle 1981). Although percentages of noncouple households (never married, divorced, separated, and widowed) have been rising in recent decades, reliable data and projections find most households in the United States still headed by married couples through to the 1990s (Masnick & Bane 1980, 49).

THE WEDDING AND THE HONEYMOON

Plans for the wedding and the honeymoon dominate many couples' thoughts about marriage. Although these events are important, they are but stepping stones into the real marriage to be built. The marriage may consist of a simple civil or religious ceremony, or it may involve an elaborate wedding with hundreds of guests at a cost of thousands of dollars. In the United States approximately 80 percent of weddings are performed by a religious official. The president of the Association of Bridal Consultants sees weddings as a major industry in the multibillion dollar class, with annual expenditures for such things as catered food and drink,

126

flowers, rings, wedding and bridesmaids' gowns, luggage, and the many etceteras totaling literally billions of dollars every year (Roessing 1982, 8). Modest or elaborate, most wedding costs are borne by the bride and her family, whereas the groom typically pays for the honeymoon. Many couples plan their honeymoons privately, keeping the details secret from friends and some family members.

The honeymoon is designed to give the newly married pair a chance to discover one another intimately and to meld them into a conjugal unit. A virgin may experience *honeymoon cystitis* for a while until her genitals become accustomed to coitus. In his eagerness to prove himself for his bride, an inexperienced bridegroom may ejaculate prematurely or be unable to maintain an erection. Each is becoming fully acquainted with his or her own body as well as the partner's. Each is learning more about the personal habits and idiosyncrasies of the other. Both are becoming accustomed to the joint use of facilities previously used alone. The surprises and disappointments in establishing marital relations may result in periods of mutual avoidance of sustained intimacy, making other honeymoon activities attractive for a while.

Partners who have been sexually intimate before marriage will have already encountered some honeymoon problems, but one or both may have inappropriate habits and responses to modify. Furthermore, they may see a honeymoon as a chance to get away for a while, to enjoy one another in a new setting, and to carry out the expectations of their friends and families.

Upon their return home from the honeymoon the couple work at settling into their first home or apartment, consulting one another about plans, accepting feelings and preferences, resolving their differences, and enjoying their honeymoon in retrospect for some time to come.

DEVELOPMENTAL TASKS OF THE MARRIED COUPLE

The developmental tasks of the newly married couple originate from three sources: (1) physiological maturation impels them to coordinate their adult drives for growing sexual fulfillment, (2) cultural pressures push the pair to settle down and behave as married couples are expected in a given community, and (3) their own personal aspirations guide them to establish their marriage according to the dreams they have fashioned over the years.

The multiple nature of the origins of the developmental tasks at this stage makes for some difficulties. What the culture expects and what the young couple wants do not always coincide. What the realities of the situation are and what the married pair dream of as right for them are rarely identical. The goals of the wife and husband may mesh in many respects but may be a poor fit in others. Being married involves coming to terms with what is expected —by one's culture, by one's mate, by oneself, and as a couple.

Unfinished earlier developmental tasks put a burden on early marriage. A girl still rebelling from her father may carry over her resistance against male control to her mate, much as young men often continue to protect themselves from their mothers' solicitude as they push off their wives' attempts to care for them. Formerly promiscuous individuals may have trouble becoming sexually exclusive after marriage. Those who have not learned to handle money wisely find it hard to become financially responsible after they marry. Marriage does not automatically complete the maturation process; it does test it severely.

Teenage marriage may be an escape from failure in earlier developmental tasks for any of the following reasons: (1) social disadvantages, (2) unsatisfactory family situations, (3) personal inadequacies, (4) limited interest in education, and (5) early sexual involvements. Incomplete present and former developmental tasks and immaturity are twin hazards of early marriage. So it is not surprising that over the years significantly more marriages of teenagers have ended than those of more mature persons (Burchinal 1965; Chilman 1980; Glick & Mills 1974).

Variations of legal marriage have long been proposed as efforts to deal with the realities of marital failure. Several decades ago, Lindsay proposed *companionate marriage* for childless couples who could break up by mutual consent (Lindsay & Wainwright 1927). Mead proposed *marriage in two steps:* the first as an "apprenticeship" and the second, following establishment of a firm relationship, as "marriage for parenthood" (Mead 1963, 1966). Others have suggested *renewable contracts* for marriage, with a trial period of living together (Satir 1970); *marriage as a nonlegal, voluntary association* (Greenwald 1970); *serial monogamy* (Alpenfels 1970); and *probationary marriage* (Toffler 1970). In recent years more young people have been living together until they are ready to marry (Glick & Norton 1977); and most have been delaying marriage until they are well into their twenties (see Tables 2.1 and 2.2).

Readiness for marriage is necessary to undertake its many developmental tasks successfully. The majority of Americans eventually marry, usually when they are well into their twenties. By then they have had more than two decades of personal development, and they are more or less ready for the privileges and responsibilities of marriage. Their friends and families expect them to marry at this time, reflecting the norms and expectations that serve as prods on their behavior (Elder 1972; Neugarten 1968). Family situations, educational success or failure, individual differences, personal experiences, and changing socio-economic conditions (such as in times of war, depression, or runaway inflation) account for wide *variations in the timing of marriage.* A person may be considered ready for marriage when he or she can pass tests of *readiness for marriage* such as those listed in Table 7.1.

Table 7.1   TESTS OF MARITAL READINESS

Marital readiness is shown by:
Being emotionally mature enough to manage one's feelings responsibly.
Being able to get along well with most people.
Being willing and able to become an exclusive sexual partner.
Being ready to establish an intimate sexual relationship.
Having tenderness and affection for the other.
Being sensitive to the other's feelings and development.
Being able to communicate freely one's thoughts, feelings, and wishes.
Being ready to merge personal plans with those of the other.
Having a mature acceptance of one's own limitations.
Being realistic about the other's characteristics.
Having the capacity to deal effectively with economic problems.
Being ready to become a responsible husband or wife.

Source: Freely adapted and expanded from Rhona Rapoport, "Normal Crises, Family Structure and Mental Health," *Family Process* 2 (1963): 68–80.

A NEW HUSBAND'S DEVELOPMENTAL TASKS

A new husband has all the tasks of an adult male of his age and status as well as those associated with his new marital roles. He must develop the attitudes and behavior required of him as a married man, both with his wife and with former friends of both sexes. He is expected to find and hold a job and to carry his share of the couple's financial obligations. He has roles to play in his new home as a man, as a husband, and as a mate. His wife usually wants to tell him about her day and to hear about his. She expects him to tell her that he loves her as often as she needs to hear it. His competence in two-way communication with his wife underlies many of the other tasks he faces, both now and in later stages of his marriage.

A husband is generally expected to be adequate as a provider, sex partner, companion, confidant, decision maker, and accountant. The husband's role performance is enforced by society at large. If a man does not provide the basic essentials for the support of his family, social workers from community agencies step in to investigate. If he squanders his resources in drink, drugs, or gambling, rehabilitative services may be brought to bear. When he does not file an income tax return, the Internal Revenue Service calls him to account. Should his wife become dissatisfied because of his sexual demands, financial mismanagement, or his neglect of her emotional needs, counselors, therapists, or attorneys may be consulted. Conversely, the husband who performs his marital roles well earns the respect of his wife and the admiration of those who know the couple well.

Each new husband develops his marital competencies in his own way. As long as his performance satisfies his wife, he is free to do whatever is comfortable for him. His roles in the neighborhood, in the larger community, and at his place of work are more subject to the norms of these groups.

A NEW WIFE'S DEVELOPMENTAL TASKS

A wife is expected to perform acceptably in her domestic roles and as a sex partner, confidante, companion, social secretary, and family planner. Her husband, neighbors, and others in the community criticize her if she flagrantly neglects her family. She may be called upon to account for failure to perform her wifely roles. When she plays her marital roles well, her husband, her family, and their friends approve of her as a good wife.

The new wife has developmental tasks as an adult woman and wife that parallel those of her husband sexually, financially, maritally, and emotionally. In addition, she is expected in most communities to take the lead in homemaking and in the social life of the new couple, in consultation with her husband. She may or may not be gainfully employed, but, in either case, her home is expected to be presentable and to be organized to meet the needs of the couple in such elementary matters as adequate sleep, privacy, nutrition, clothing, and recreation.

Whether women marry for the first time in their twenties, as most do, or in their forties, fifties, or later, new wives have the developmental tasks of all others of their age group. They also have those individual tasks that are involved in being the spouse of their particular husband at this specific time. These tasks revolve around their work, families of origin, status, and expectations as individuals. Either spouse may be marrying again after a former marriage has been broken by death or divorce. Latent jealousies and unfavorable comparisons with a former spouse are hazards to be avoided. New brides and grooms must also meet the challenge of relating to their in-laws in such a way that they neither avoid them nor invite their intrusion (Duvall 1954).

CONFLICTING AND COMPLEMENTARY DEVELOPMENTAL TASKS

At times the developmental tasks of husband and wife complement each other. At other times the efforts of one conflict with those of the other (Table 7.2). When the two mutually support each other's efforts to achieve their developmental tasks, those tasks are complementary. When the working through of their tasks as husband and wife pull the members of the pair in opposite directions, the tasks are conflicting (Figure 7.1).

Table 7.2 COMPLEMENTARY AND CONFLICTING DEVELOPMENTAL TASKS OF HUSBANDS AND WIVES

Developmental tasks of the young husband	Developmental tasks of the young wife	Complementary and conflicting possibilities
Becoming established in an occupation Getting specialized training Assuming responsibility for getting and holding a job Working toward security and advancement in his work	Making a home and managing the household Getting settled in the home Establishing and maintaining household routines Learning the many skills of homemaking and housework	Complementary: Both are sharing responsibility in homemaking Conflicting: Husband is engrossed in work away from home, while wife tries to elicit his active cooperation in homemaking
Assuming responsibility for the support of the family Earning what he can Planning for the long pull of family support through the years	Becoming a financial helpmate in establishing the home Developing job competence Seeing her work as possibly intermittent	Complementary: Both are economic partners through establishment phase Conflicting: Her work threatens his status as breadwinner
Establishing mutually satisfying relationships with his wife Satisfying his wife sexually Developing competency as a husband	Becoming a satisfactory sex partner Learning her roles as wife Responding effectively and participating in their mutual fulfillment	Complementary: Each has the task of communicating intimately with the other
Becoming established as a married man Sharing leisure time with his wife Developing mutual interests Cultivating joint activities Getting into the young married set	Assuming social and companionship roles as a married woman Planning recreational activities as a couple Accepting and refusing social invitations Entertaining friends, associates, and families	Complementary: Both husband and wife are learning to move in tandem in their social life as a couple

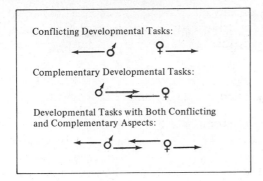

Figure 7.1 Conflicting and complementary developmental tasks.

It takes conscientious effort and a great deal of interpersonal competence on the part of both partners to become aware of one another as distinct individuals with firmly rooted preferences, interests, values, predispositions, and expectations. Differences naturally arise from time to time and must be recognized and evaluated. Minor idiosyncrasies can be modified for the good of the marriage. Other issues are so important that ways must be found for coping with the conflicting forces within the partnership.

Marriage launches the new husband and wife on a new and unfamiliar way of life. Somehow they must develop patterns of daily living that express and satisfy them both. Each day brings decisions to make, problems to solve, and plans to outline for the ongoing development of the marriage they are establishing. Many of these *interdependencies,* which are vital to the continuity of the union, are mutually satisfying. Others are burdensome or confusing for one or both members of the pair.

OVERLAPPING HUSBAND/WIFE ROLES

Marital roles are the behavioral expectations of husbands and wives in a particular society at any given time. Traditionally in America, there were clear distinctions between the roles of husbands and wives. A husband was expected to be the "breadwinner" and the "head of the house," representing his household in the larger community. A wife, until well into the twentieth century, was the "homemaker" in charge of the home and the bearing and rearing of the children. The women's movement has liberated women and given new freedoms to men in recent decades. As women are increasingly able to care for themselves, they are less dependent upon their husbands. As more wives work, their husbands are freed from the burden of their total support. Today men as well as women are more at home in their own households, in whatever way they enjoy being involved.

As styles of femininity change, there is a parallel shift in patterns of masculinity (Komarovsky 1976). Now that a man may be tender and gentle at times—rather than always maintaining "the macho image" of being big, brave, tough, and aggressive—he may be less sure of what is expected of him. A wife, too, has her confusions as she explores new dimensions of life outside as well as within her home. Husbands and wives with a clear sense of their own emerging identity find challenge in the many alternatives open to them.

Conjugal options are greater for both wives and husbands as opportunities for both sexes open up in education, work, and family life. No longer is a girl expected to marry right out of high school, nor a boy before he has found himself. No longer is a wife expected to be "just a housewife" unless that is her preference. No longer is a husband fully responsible for the complete support of his wife and their family unless that is what they want. As wives' conjugal options allow more latitude in developing their talents and interests inside and outside the home, husbands, too, have more freedom to choose their life-styles. More husbands today express their feelings openly without fear of losing face. They can be tender or tough, gentle or vigorous, according to the situation. They can lean on their wives' strength or play the strong, supportive role appropriately. Such freedom is heady stuff, but for the husband and wife who can take it, it has its rewards (Table 7.3).

Effects of increasing marital options are both positive and negative. Men and women have never had more options than they do today. They may select from an assortment of life-styles the one that best suits them. They enjoy new freedom in the expression of love and sex, of gentleness and joy, of real feelings and candid opinions. A wide variety of relationships are available to them, both before and after marriage. They have the benefit of recent shifts of power in the family and community. They may or may not have children; they may bear or adopt and rear as many children, or as few, as they wish and at the times that suit them best. They can stay married for the rest of their lives—or leave when marriage no longer satisfies them with less guilt and sense of failure than ever before. The potential satisfactions of marriage and family life have never been greater for the millions of men and women ready for them.

Yet such great freedom to live as one chooses is a mixed blessing. Confusion and anxiety about what is expected of a man or woman, husband or wife, father or mother abound when marital roles are no longer clearly defined. The societal controls that traditionally limited an

Table 7.3   TREND TOWARD MORE OPEN OPTIONS IN MARRIAGE

From traditional marital roles	Toward more open conjugal options
Husband dominant; wife submissive	Potential marital partnership
Rigid assignment of wives to housework and husbands to provider roles	Wives free to work as pair decide; men more at home with their families
Few wives in prestigious positions and paid less than husbands	Equality of compensation on the basis of merit advocated
Sex-stereotyping restrictions on personal choices	Members of both sexes develop talents and interests with less stigma
Girls encouraged to marry early; boys encouraged to compete for success	Both sexes encouraged in educational, social, and economic fields
Babies come "at the will of God"	Pregnancies and family size planned by responsible parents
Child care the mother's role; child support the father's	Child rearing mutually assumed responsibility of both parents
Romanticism involving young of both sexes, often prematurely	Love developed in lasting relationships fosters maturity
Divorce seen as failure	Marriage dissolved without guilt
Alimony expected and accepted	Alimony questioned as unfair to both
Anger repressed by females; tenderness repressed by males	Increase in understanding and empathy by honest expression of feelings
Discrimination on the basis of gender widely practiced	Sexism decried as deprivation of rights and opportunities of both sexes

individual's opportunities also provided protection from abandonment, exploitation, and anxious feelings of uncertainty. Owing to more flexible marital roles, it is easier for a person of either sex to act impulsively in ways that can be unrewarding personally and harmful to marital and social relationships. On the other hand, now there are more opportunities to develop one's talents, to continue one's education, and to train or retrain for a promising career than have ever before existed for men and women, for husbands and wives.

When divorce is easy, a potentially good marriage can be broken in one impetuous moment—or a potentially tragic marriage can be ended before the couple is destroyed by it. A husband may no longer assume that his wife will accept a subservient role, now that she is free to develop herself and to become more mature and self-supporting on her own. A wife no longer can expect that she has a meal ticket for life when she marries; so she is wise to prepare herself for autonomy and independence both before and after she marries. Questions arising out of today's uncertainty about marital roles are causing distress in marriages. The outcome may well be more divorces but also stronger marriages when married couples handle their many marital options well.

Marriage and family life may benefit from more flexible marital roles (Table 7.4) and increased conjugal options, but it will not be easy. Families are no longer the stable, secure cocoons they once purportedly were. Today's marriages are dynamic, adapting to the realities of life as they find it. They require courage and maturity, but the rewards to the individual, the marriage, and eventually to the family as a whole can outweigh the difficulties.

Each pair approaches their husband-wife-couple developmental tasks with varying degrees of readiness and flexibility. At first this may be done in a spirit of playing at being married. In time the couple begin to feel that theirs is a promising marriage—or one headed

Table 7.4 BENEFITS IN FLEXIBILITY OF HUSBAND-WIFE ROLES

1. Family income is increased with two paychecks.
2. Husband is under less strain with wife's help as provider.
3. Wife is less isolated as husband and children share homemaking.
4. Husband-wife enjoyment is greater as wife's interests expand.
5. Wife's growth as a person increases her satisfaction and fulfillment.
6. Family horizons are broadened as more members become active in community.
7. Husband-wife communication is enhanced by more shared decisions.
8. Children are enriched by increased exposure to life around them.
9. Child-rearing methods are more democratic with both parents involved.
10. Mother's outside interests encourage children's growth.
11. Children are less indulged when given more family responsibilities.
12. There is more family recreation with a higher standard of living.
13. Whole-family activities raise family morale and interaction.
14. There is improved ability to cope with change as marital roles overlap.
15. More acceptable divorce frees miserable mates from poor marriage bonds.
16. Increased remarriage possibilities encourage rebuilt marriages.
17. More education for girls and women develops more latent talent.
18. Fewer wives are entirely dependent on husbands' support and life-style.
19. More autonomy and mature interaction is possible in marriage.
20. There are fewer poor marriages as options increase.
21. Later age at marriage is related to marital success.
22. More husbands are free to train for first and second careers.
23. There are increased opportunities for personal, marital, and family development.
24. Control and power are decentralized on the basis of family member competence.

for failure—depending on how well they accomplish their family developmental tasks as a married couple.

FAMILY DEVELOPMENTAL TASKS OF THE MARRIED COUPLE

A couple must establish their marriage as a functioning unit of society if they are to continue as a married pair. This means that they must accomplish their eight basic family tasks as a married couple. Each couple enters marriage with their particular potentialities and problems. Each pair copes with the tasks of being married and of making the transition from previous roles and statuses with varying degrees of competence and creativity. The couple's success is dependent upon their skill in accomplishing their developmental tasks both as individuals and as a married couple. Their eight family developmental tasks as a married couple (Table 7.5) are elaborated in the sections that follow.

Finding, Furnishing, and Settling into Their First Home

Finding and furnishing a home within their means is a difficult task for young married couples to accomplish on their own. Their budget is more modest now than it will be later in the family life cycle (U.S. Bureau of Labor Statistics 1980). Their expectations of what comes with marriage—built up over the years by romantic myths, personal dreams, and hard-sell advertising—are often unrealistic. Their desire to own a home of their own is strong (Michelson 1977), but as housing costs continue to rise, a young couple may look to their families for financial help. A recent study finds that married couples under the age of 30 with no children receive more help both as renters and as owners from their relatives than those at any other stage of the family life cycle (Kennedy & Stokes 1982).

Furnishing a home for the first time is expensive. One knowledgeable business executive says that furniture sales to newlyweds in the United States came to $3.1 billion, and major appliances accounted for another $920 million in one recent year (Roessing 1982, 8). Friends and family members give bridal showers and wedding gifts as ways of providing young marrieds bed and table linens, kitchen equipment, and other essentials in establishing a home. In times of severe housing shortages, unemployment, and other personal or social uncertainties, couples double up with one set of their parents, or with other young adults, until they can afford a place of their own. More often, they settle into an apartment that will do for a while. If and when something better turns up, they take it.

Settling into their first home is an exciting activity for newlyweds. If they eat off a card table and sit on orange crates at first, they are likely to do it good-naturedly. As they paint

---

Table 7.5 FAMILY DEVELOPMENTAL TASKS OF THE MARRIED COUPLE

1. Finding, furnishing, and settling into their first home as a married pair.
2. Establishing mutually satisfactory ways of supporting themselves.
3. Allocating responsibilities that each partner is willing and able to assume.
4. Building foundations for satisfying marital relationships.
5. Controlling fertility and planning a family.
6. Starting a family.
7. Interacting with relatives on both sides of the family.
8. Maintaining couple motivation and morale.

an old bathroom wall, or redo a rented kitchen they can afford, they know it is for a good cause. Some rare couples are set up in housekeeping by indulgent, affluent parents, but these are exceptions rather than the rule. Previously married mates bring with them not only furnishings from their former homes but also the experience of establishing a household, which may be a real help if it does not threaten the new spouse.

Young adults move more than other age groups in the population as they leave their parental homes, enter the labor force, marry, establish new households, improve their living conditions, or try to live within their incomes. Moving is relatively easy for newlyweds before children come and before they have a full household of goods to take from place to place. Moving is expensive, but if it means getting better housing for less money, with more energy-efficient construction, and closer to work, it may be worth it.

Establishing Mutually Satisfactory Ways of Supporting Themselves

Couples setting up housekeeping for the first time have only a general idea of what it will cost. Housing payments, either for rent or for home ownership costs, take a husky share of each monthly budget. To this is added variable amounts for utilities (gas, electricity, telephone), heating, repairs, replacements, food, clothing, transportation, medical expenses, and the many other regular and occasional costs of being independent consumers (Table 7.6).

Some couples are able to keep food and other costs down, whereas others get carried away when they shop and "blow the budget" on items they can ill afford. They risk spending more than they earn, buying too much on credit and getting into debt. Before they realize how much their regular costs will be for household operation, they are overcommitted. If they look to their relatives for financial assistance beyond what they have already received

Table 7.6 PERSONAL CONSUMPTION EXPENDITURES IN THE UNITED STATES, BY TYPE OF PRODUCT, 1980

Type of product	Personal consumption expenditures (billions of dollars)	Percentage of total
Food (including alcohol)	345.7	20.7
Housing	272.0	16.2
Transportation	243.0	14.5
Household operation	228.9	13.7
Medical care[a]	162.3	9.7
Clothing, accessories, and jewelry	123.5	7.4
Recreation	106.4	6.4
Personal business	89.8	5.4
Private education and research	25.1	1.5
Personal care	23.3	1.4
Religious and welfare activities	23.3	1.4
Tobacco	20.4	1.2
Death expenses	4.8	0.3
Foreign travel and remittances (net)	4.3	0.2
Total	1672.8	100.0

[a] Includes all expenses for health insurance (except loss-of-income type).
Sources: U.S. Department of Commerce, Bureau of Economic Analysis, *Survey of Current Business,* (Washington, D.C.: Government Printing Office, 1981); and Health Insurance Association of America; published in *Source Book of Health Insurance Data 1981–1982* (Washington, D.C.: Health Insurance Association of America, 1982), p. 57.

they risk in-law interference and more "advice" than they can take. So they tend to do what they can to remain independent and support themselves.

The young husband often takes as much overtime as he can get, or he may moonlight on a second job; he learns to be a do-it-yourselfer at home instead of paying others for plumbing, carpentry, painting, and other services householders need from time to time. Some young husbands, such as those training for the professions, have little or no time for such economies. Others go to night school or take correspondence courses to get the additional training that will qualify them for better-paying jobs. The result for many of them is almost chronic fatigue and little time to enjoy their wives and home life.

Wives work to help support themselves and their families. Many women who marry young have few salable skills in the labor market. They often lack both the training and the experience to command good jobs, so they take jobs that pay relatively low wages, with little possibility for advancement. Women at higher educational levels and some job experience are more employable, earn more, and are more likely to continue working until the time that their first child is born (McLaughlin 1982, 419).

In recent years both men and women college students have shifted significantly in their beliefs about a woman's place in the home (see Table 7.7).

The number of women in the U.S. work force grew by 173 percent between 1947 and 1980; the number of men working increased by 43 percent during the same period. By 1980 there were 45.6 million working women, according to a 1983 census report (Bianchi and Spain 1983). These researchers, having pulled together a wide variety of Bureau of the Census studies, find that women of the 1980s (1) are enrolling in college at about the same rate as men; (2) are more likely to finish college than American women of earlier decades; (3) still earn fewer professional and graduate degrees than men; (4) earn only about two-thirds as much as men; and (5) are concentrated in traditionally female jobs, such as nursing, teaching, retail sales, and clerical and office work (Associated Press report 1983). Women's share of major occupational groupings in the United States is overwhelmingly in household employment and clerical work, as shown in Table 7.8.

Recent efforts to close the gap between men's and women's work opportunities are focusing on opening jobs to women that were traditionally considered men's work. A *traditional male job* is defined as one in which women employees hold 25 percent or less of the jobs; a *traditional female job* as one with 55 percent or more women workers; and *sex-neutral work* as one with 25 to 55 percent women workers (Jaffe 1982, 19). Nontraditional jobs for women pay better, often provide on-the-job training, tend to be unionized, and offer more opportunities for advancement and job satisfaction.

A wife interested in "hard-hat" work should have mechanical aptitude; some familiarity with simple tools; physical agility; manual dexterity; a sense of spatial relations; knowl-

**Table 7.7 FEWER COLLEGE FRESHMEN SEE WIVES'
PLACE SOLELY IN THE HOME
(RESPONSES IN PERCENT)**

	1967	1970	1971	1981
Men	61	50	43	35
Women	38	28	23	19

Source: American Council on Education, *Annual Surveys: The American Freshman,* (Los Angeles: University of California, 1967, 1970, 1971, 1981).

Table 7.8 WOMEN'S SHARE OF MAJOR OCCUPATIONAL GROUPINGS

Type of work	Percentage of women workers
Private household workers	96.5
Clerical workers	80.5
Other service workers	59.2
Sales workers	45.4
Professional and technical workers	44.6
Operatives	39.8
Managers and administrators	27.5
Nonfarm laborers	11.5
Transport equipment operatives	8.9
Craft and kindred workers	6.3

Source: U.S. Department of Labor, Bureau of Labor Statistics, *Employment and Earnings, March 1982* (Washington, D.C.: Government Printing Office, 1982).

edge of basic mathematics, science, or computers; and an interest in producing tangible results (Lederer 1979). Of equal importance is her husband's encouragement as she breaks with tradition and goes after a job that interests her.

Decisions about spending the family income are more cooperative and democratic when both work. Husband and wife together make their financial plans, shop together for what they agree they need, read labels, inquire about warranties, and develop awareness of the quality of the goods they buy. Not all of them make and stick to a budget, but they are wiser in their planning than earlier generations were (Hill, Foote, Aldous, Carlson, & Macdonald 1970).

Allocating Responsibilities Each Partner Is Willing and Able to Assume

Traditionally, husband-wife responsibilities were allocated by custom, with the husband earning the living and the wife taking care of the home. Now, when so many wives are employed, the question arises, How should responsibility for housework be divided? Interviews with 720 high school–educated couples in Illinois found 84 percent of both the husbands and wives believing that when the wife works, the husband should do more household work (Ferber 1982, 461). Some wives do receive more help from their husbands when they work (Bahr 1974); but other studies find that a wife's employment does *not* increase the husband's household task performance (Bryson, Bryson, Licht, & Licht 1976; Stafford, Backman, & DiBona et al. 1977). Some husbands do not follow through on their professed belief that they should do more household chores, and their wives are still predominantly responsible for the household (Ferber 1982, 462). Full-time housewives spend 30 or more hours a week doing housework; working wives put in an average of 20 hours a week in household responsibilities, in contrast to husbands who average 10 hours a week. Middletown husbands make household repairs and help pay the bills, but they still "don't wash the dishes very often" (Condran & Bode 1982, 425).

Relative time and talent determine who does what in many marriages. A mathematics major enjoys keeping the household accounts, so her husband has given her his blessing in paying their bills and keeping within their budget. Another husband is a whiz in the kitchen and gets relaxation out of creating his specialities for his wife and their guests. A good gardener of either sex takes over yard work from a spouse without a green thumb. Childhood training and parental modeling shape many of the interests and competencies within a marriage.

Time available at a particular period in their marriage is a factor in how responsibilities are allocated. A man who is temporarily unemployed may take on some of the housework while his wife is away on her job. Another young married man we know cleans up after the evening meal so that his wife can study for her degree. There are men with such exacting schedules that they cannot do much more in their homes, even if they wanted to do so; others can not easily see themselves doing "women's work" under any circumstances (Caplow, Bahr, Chadwick, Hill, & Williamson 1982).

Marital power determines who allocates responsibilities in a marriage to a great extent. Marital power is exercised by the spouse in charge, who tends to control the other and is accepted as having the right to make decisions affecting their lives. Traditionally, the husband wielded the greater power in marriage in most cases. A superior woman may be said to "wear the pants" as she makes the major decisions for her husband and herself. A man who is a "good provider" tends to have high marital power over his wife, who willingly follows his lead. Wives of well-educated husbands in good-paying jobs tend to accept husband dominance (Scanzoni & Scanzoni 1976, 318). Executives accustomed to making decisions at the office continue to make them at home (Aldous 1969).

Equalitarian marriages in which both members of the pair have an equal voice in making decisions and allocating responsibilities are philosophically acceptable to educated married couples, but in actual practice the husbands are found to wield the greater power in family decisions (Centers, Ravan, & Rodrigues 1971). Working-class couples say that the husband should be the dominant partner, but their working wives have a relatively powerful say in household and family decisions (Aldous 1974). A study of 1212 couples in a probability sample in Philadelphia found black more than white couples sharing household tasks. Why? The explanation is that even well-educated black women are not likely to marry economically successful men; so their husbands do more housework than husbands of white women. The higher the wife's status relative to her husband's, the more likely she is to work and the more apt he is to assume responsibilities in the home (Erickson, Yancey, & Erickson 1979).

Switching responsibilities occurs from time to time within equalitarian marriages of equally competent persons. The wife brings home the paycheck while her husband goes back to school, prepares for a better job, writes a book, or stays home as "househusband" for health or other reasons. The success of such *role reversal* depends on the versatility of the pair who now assume nontraditional responsibilities at least for a while.

Sex-role transcendence offers genuine options to both spouses in any situation that arises. Transcendent persons are free to do what seems appropriate to them without regard for masculine-feminine labels. The young husband feels free to sew on a button or to do the laundry while his wife represents them at a community meeting. Such a husband feels secure enough himself to be proud of his wife and confident enough of his masculinity to don an apron upon occasion.

Responsibilities are reciprocal in marriage. Whatever one spouse assumes as his or her responsibilities frees the partner for other tasks. Each partner has rights and responsibilities necessary for the continuation of the marriage. *Reciprocity* is based upon the exchange of services between the spouses. The partners monitor one another's performance by rewarding satisfactory performance ("A delicious dinner, dear" or "Congratulations on the raise you earned") and punishing defaults ("I'm tired of picking up after you all the time" or "Don't come near me until you apologize"). In all of this the couple is establishing acceptable patterns for their marriage that will endure as long as they satisfy the pair.

Building Foundations for Satisfying Marital Relationships

Both husband and wife develop characteristics conducive to high (or low) levels of marital satisfaction long before they marry (see Table 7.9).

There is nothing that can be done to change what has already happened in the past except to understand and to deal with the background characteristics of one another. The current qualities of the marriage itself are strong building blocks for marital satisfaction: the openness with which they express their love for one another, their mutual trust and confidence in each other, the way they make decisions and solve the inevitable problems that surface in their relationship, and the open freedom of their communication emotionally, socially, and sexually.

Problem solving is essential in any relationship. A young romantic couple may feel that their marriage will escape problems—but that is wishful thinking. Any two individuals in a day-by-day association inevitably face problems that must be solved if the relationship is to continue. They are fortunate if they develop effective problem-solving approaches early in their marriage as a rational pattern. Table 7.10 outlines a 10-step procedure for problem solving.

Marital conflict arises out of the differences that make each partner unique. Two people joined in marriage are members of opposite sexes, each with its gender culture. Husband and wife are two quite different persons, each with their own personal histories, experiences, attitudes, and preferences. They come to marriage, the most intimate, emotionally charged, and lasting personal relationship they ever have. So, from time to time they may expect

**Table 7.9 CHARACTERISTICS CONDUCIVE TO HIGH LEVELS OF
MARITAL SATISFACTION**

	Background characteristics
Parents	Happiness of parents' marriage
Childhood	High level of happiness in childhood
Discipline	Mild but firm discipline with only moderate punishment
Sex education	Adequate sex education from encouraging parents
Education	At least through high school
Acquaintance	Substantial time of acquaintance before marriage
	Current characteristics
Affection	Open expression of affection of each for the other
Confidence	Mutual confidence in one another
Equalitarian	Neither dominates the other; decisions are made jointly
Communication	Open, free communication between the partners
Sex	Mutual enjoyment of sexual relations
Social life	Joint participation in outside interests; friends in common
Residence	Relatively stable
Income	Adequate income

Source: Catherine S. Chilman, *Adolescent Sexuality in a Changing American Society: Social and Psychological Perspectives* (Washington, D.C.: U.S. Government Printing Office, 1980), p. 256, with minor modifications of form.

conflicts to arise. They have three options for dealing with conflict: (1) to battle it out in open quarreling, which releases the emotional heat but sheds little light unless it focuses on the issue rather than the partner; (2) to avoid the issue and one another, an approach that keeps arguing minimal but delays resolving the conflict situation; and (3) to initiate conflict resolution that leads to reconciliation.

Conflict resolution by skillful handling of conflict is a goal worth striving toward. It begins with tipping each other off about negative feelings building up within one: "I feel awful today, so tread carefully lest you get hurt." It proceeds with clearly describing feelings directed at the other for any reason: "When you do that, it makes my blood boil." It might include a certain amount of emotional and physical release in sports or hard work, which serves as a safety valve for emotional pressures. It involves getting professional help from a marriage counselor, or a family guidance service, or its local equivalent before running "home to Mother" or calling a divorce lawyer. Resolving conflict as it arises is protection both from long-festering hurts and from a too-hasty dissolution of what may be inherently a good marriage. Developing patterns for conflict resolution derive from the pair's growing empathy, mutual supportiveness, understanding, and genuine communication as a married couple.

Communication systems through which each partner gets across to the other with the understanding, the comfort, the love, the sympathy, the loyalty, and the sense of purpose they

Table 7.10   PROBLEM SOLVING IN 10 STEPS

Steps	Key questions	Purpose
1. Face the problem.	What is the matter? Why do I/we think it is a problem?	To get the problem into words. To uncover the fear involved.
2. Look at the causes.	What has been happening? What has made it a problem now?	To get the buildup of the problem. To get a clear statement of what is bringing it to a head.
3. Set some goals.	What do I want to accomplish for myself? For the other person? What do we/I want the situation to be?	To be sure of desires for self. To be sure that decisions will benefit others as well as self. To set a definite change to work toward.
4. Get more knowledge and understanding.	What knowledge from the biological, psychological, and social sciences is applicable? Have I found all the available material in technical and popular literature? What has been the experience of other people in similar situations?	To increase understanding. To gain insight.
5. Be the other person. (Try to *be* each of the other persons or groups of persons involved in the problem.)	Just how would I, as this other person, think about it? And as this other person, what does he or she feel?	To get the other person's point of view and emotional slant. To allow thinking and feelings of others to be a framework for the next step.

both need are essential if they are to feel truly married. Without such communication one may ache with loneliness even beside one's mate. With a well-developed system of communication, a husband and wife feel united even when they are separated for many months or by many miles.

Communicator styles are the ways in which persons verbally interact to signal how literally meaning should be taken, interpreted, filtered, or understood (Norton 1978, 99). Men tend to be more dominant in cross-sexed conversations, to use fewer pauses, and to be less silent than females (Eakins & Eakins 1978). Practically all interruptions and interjections in mixed-sex dyads were made by males (Zimmerman & West 1975). Females perceive themselves as being more animated and friendly, whereas males see themselves as more precise and dramatic (Montgomery & Norton 1979).

A recent questionnaire study of 40 married couples found happily married pairs using communicator styles such as "friendly," "impression leaving," "precise," and "expressive" within their marriages. Spouses who expressed the most happiness were more relaxed, friendly, open, dramatic, and attentive with one another than less happy couples (Honeycutt, Wilson, & Parker 1982, 403).

Sex as communication is a language all its own. It expresses not only ardor and passion but compassion and tenderness as well. It speaks not only of love but sometimes of anger and hatred, as in cases of marital rape. It is the sweet conclusion of an argument in which each partner tells the other in action, "I'm sorry dear, and, oh, I love you so." Over the years

Table 7.10 *(Continued)*

Steps	Key questions	Purpose
6. Consider what to do.	What could we/I do about it? Will that bring me to my goals? Will it fit the thoughts and feelings of the other person?	To get a list of possible actions. To be sure they lead to the goals. To be sure they will be acceptable to the other person.
7. Make a plan of action.	Just how can this be done? Who will do each part? How will I do it? Who will help me?	To plan how to do it. To develop a one-two-three plan. To select the person to help at each point if needed.
8. Check the plan with the goals.	Will this plan lead me/us to our goals? Does it provide for each goal?	To be sure the plan is really directed at the desired solution. To be sure it covers all the goals set.
9. Plan the follow-up.	What shall I/we watch for to be sure the plan is working?	To encourage watchfulness in using the plan. To encourage abandonment if it seems to be failing.
10. Celebrate success in solving the problem.	Weren't we clever in working this through? Now we can tackle anything, can't we?	To gain strength in coping with problems. To cement the relationship.

sexual relations become eloquently meaningful for the experienced couple. For newlyweds, sex establishes a foundation for getting through to one another in ways for which words are inadequate. All this can occur before the couple may have even given thought to starting a family.

Controlling Fertility and Planning a Family

Children once came as a matter of course. Now, modern contraceptives make possible a conscious choice of parenthood and the timing of the child's arrival. A husband and wife may postpone having children for such reasons as: (1) awaiting their readiness for the responsibilities of parenthood, (2) advancing their careers (including the education and training needed for them), (3) avoiding the tragedy of unwanted children, or (4) helping to curb the world's spiraling population growth, which threatens the quality of life for all mankind (Figure 7.2).

Official estimates of America's growing population, with projections to the year 2025, appear in Table 7.11, p. 144. Series I assumes 2.7 births per woman; Series II, 2.1 births per woman (replacement level); and Series III, 1.7 ultimate completed births per woman. Broadly interpreted, this means that if couples barely replace themselves in the years ahead, by the year 2000 the population will have grown to 262,494,000; and if they have an average of 2.7 children, by the year 2025 the total population will have swollen to 382,011,000.

Recent American trends are for later marriages and delayed first births. Studies find that the later the age at first marriage and the longer the interval between marriage and parenthood, the smaller the number of children (Marini 1981; Wilkie 1981). In the early 1980s single women between ages 18 and 34 expected to have fewer than two children (a 1.8 average per woman) (U.S. Department of Commerce 1981). Actual birthrates have been declining over recent years, with only occasional upturns (National Center for Health Statistics 1982).

Contraception is the use of chemical, hormonal, mechanical, or other means of preventing the union of sperm and ovum. Sixty-three percent of 20- 29-year-old women patients in the nation's family planning clinics were using the pill to avoid contraception in 1980. Less than 21 percent were using an intrauterine device (IUD), a diaphragm, a spermicidal foam or jelly, or other contraceptives (Vital and Health Statistics of the National Center for Health Statistics 1982). The vaginal sponge, once widely used, is again popular. Less reliable methods include coitus interruptus in which the penis is withdrawn from the vagina before the semen is ejaculated; rhythm in which coitus is limited to the woman's "safe" period each month; and douching in which the vagina is flushed out following intercourse. Male use of the condom, in conjunction with diaphragm and a spermicidal jelly, foam, or cream, is a possibility. Each of the current methods of contraception has its limitations. Since there is no ideal contraceptive as yet, a couple is wise to consult their physician or local family planning clinic for methods best suited to them.

Abortion ended one out of every four pregnancies in 1980, double the number of legal abortions on demand in 1973, the first year of legalized abortions in the United States (Alan Guttmacher Institute 1982). Unintended pregnancies are increasing as more women give up the pill, which has caused strokes in susceptible women, and IUDs, some of which have been known to perforate the user's uterus (UPI 1982). Reasons for abortion are: (1) the woman's health is endangered in continuing the pregnancy; (2) the woman was raped and became pregnant; (3) there is a serious defect in the embryo or fetus; (4) a couple cannot afford

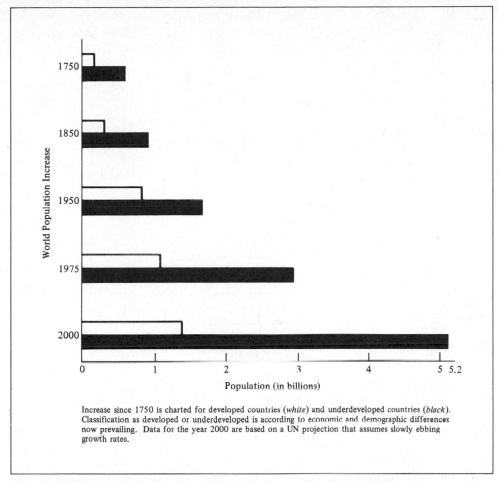

Figure 7.2 World population increase, 1750–2000. *Source:* The Rockefeller Foundation, *RF,* vol. 2, *2,* p. 1, March 1975; "Third World Development: A U.S. Perspective,"
Interdependent, Vol. 7, *5,* 2, July-August 1981.

another baby; (5) an unmarried woman does not want to marry the baby's father; and (6)
a married couple does not want any more children (Ebaugh & Haney 1980).

A study of 225 male and female students at a large southern state university found 59
percent of the men and 73 percent of the women favoring legalized abortion (Finlay 1981).
Policies protecting the rights both of those who favor and of those who oppose abortions are
seen as the only viable solution to the moral and political dilemmas of the abortion controversy (Jaffe, Lindheim, & Lee 1981).

Sterilization is a permanent method of birth control in which the vas deferens of the
man or the Fallopian tubes of the woman are surgically severed to prevent future conception.
In the past decade there has been a threefold increase in the number of vasectomies in the
United States. There are currently some 7 million American men, and about 10.5 percent
of all couples of reproductive age, who have chosen this method (Stokes 1980). In the early
1980s some 13 million men and women in this country depended on voluntary sterilization

**Table 7.11   ESTIMATES AND PROJECTIONS OF TOTAL
U.S. POPULATION, 1970–2025
(NUMBERS IN THOUSANDS)**

Year	Series I	Series II	Series III
Estimates			
1970		204,875	
1974		211,909	
Projections			
1975	213,641	213,450	213,323
1980	225,705	222,769	220,356
1985	241,274	234,068	228,355
1990	257,663	245,075	235,581
1995	272,685	254,495	241,198
2000	287,007	262,494	245,098
2005	303,144	270,377	247,926
2010	322,049	278,754	250,193
2015	342,340	286,960	251,693
2020	362,348	294,046	251,884
2025	382,011	299,713	250,421

Source: U.S. Bureau of the Census, "Projections of the Population of the United States, by Age and Sex, 1975 to 2000, with Extensions of Total Population to 2025 (Advance Report)," *Current Population Reports,* Series P-25, no. 541 (Washington, D.C.: Government Printing Office, February 1975), p. 1.

to avoid unwanted pregnancies. The surgical procedure is a relatively safe and simple one in both sexes (Association for Voluntary Sterilization 1982).

Infertility is an inability to conceive or give birth to a live baby. The wife's infertility may be the result of ovulatory problems—failure to ovulate or extremely irregular ovulation—a blockage of the Fallopian tubes, cervical mucus, or a tendency to abort spontaneously (*miscarriage* in popular parlance). Male infertility usually results from a low sperm count, low sperm motility or other deficiencies, or semen that is too viscous. *Impotence,* defined as the inability to achieve and maintain an erection, is a less common cause of infertility. An infertile person may take fertility hormones, which stimulate female ovulation and male sperm production. The couple may arrange for *artificial insemination,* using either the husband's or an anonymous donor's sperm. Or, rarely, an infertile couple may choose *surrogate pregnancy* in which the husband's sperm inseminates a proxy mother who carries the baby to term for the couple. *In vitro fertilization,* producing "test tube babies," is still largely experimental. The woman's ovum is fertilized by her husband's (or an anonymous donor's) sperm in the laboratory, and the fertilized ovum is implanted in her uterus for prenatal development (Zimmerman 1982). There are personal, marital, medical, and legal complications in some of these newer procedures that merit caution (Blank 1981).

Planning a family may be an academic question for the couple already expecting their first baby at the time of their marriage; for those who are already parents when they marry; and for those who for any reason choose to remain childless. Other options include adopting one or more children to rear as the couple's own and serving as foster parents for children who need parenting.

Starting a Family with the First Pregnancy

Many married couples take it for granted that they will have children; others are not so sure. Recent questionnaire investigations of attitudes toward parenting found college women wanting fewer children and being more accepting of nonparenting decisions in 1979 than in 1972 (Cook, West, & Hamner 1982). Reasons for choosing parenthood or remaining child free are listed in Table 7.12.

The first pregnancy takes a married couple into a family-in-the-making transition. Husband-wife intimacy now enlarges to include the expected baby. One young father says, "We're pregnant at our house." Husbands may identify so closely with their wife's pregnancy that they simultaneously suffer some of her symptoms in what is called the *couvade syndrome* (Colman & Colman 1972; Hott 1976; May 1978). Some couples role-play being parents long

**Table 7.12 TO HAVE OR NOT TO HAVE CHILDREN: REASONS
GIVEN FOR PRONATALISM AND ANTINATALISM**

Pronatalism: Why have children?[a]
1. For love, companionship, stimulation, and fun.
2. To satisfy nurturance needs through love and care for children.
3. To extend the family line: genes, name, traditions.
4. To express adult status, social identity, and maturity.
5. To relive one's own childhood.
6. To accomplish personal and social goals through children.
7. To pressure a partner into marriage and family life.
8. To improve a marriage.
9. To please parents and other relatives.
10. To emulate friends and neighbors.
11. To prove one's ability to reproduce.
12. To justify an unintended pregnancy.
13. For moral and religious reasons.
14. For a sense of achievement and creativity.
15. Ready for parenthood: couple stability, financial security.
16. For security in old age.

Antinatalism: Why no children?[b]
1. To avoid financial costs of childbearing and child rearing.
2. To avoid curtailment of wife's career and fulfillment.
3. To escape decades of hard work and anxiety of child care.
4. To prevent interference with the marital relationship.
5. To prevent infringement upon job requirements and benefits.
6. To preserve wife's self-esteem and creativity in other areas.
7. To choose more challenging and less demanding responsibilities.
8. To safeguard a self-indulging and self-enriching life-style.
9. Infertility: inability to have children easily.
10. To avoid passing on undesirable heritable characteristics.
11. To help control overpopulation.
12. Afraid of childbearing's effect on wife.
13. Don't like children.
14. Have had enough childrearing with younger siblings raised.
15. Alcoholic, drug-addicted, or otherwise unfit for parenthood.

[a] See Hoffman & Manis (1979), and May (1982).
[b] See Limpus (1970), Turchi (1975), and Espenshade (1977).

before their first baby arrives. They develop new ways of caring for one another that prepare them for the tenderness and nurturance their new baby will need (Grossman, Eichler, & Winickoff 1980). Pregnancy has many complex and mixed effects on husbands and wives (see Table 7.13).

As the young couple go through their first pregnancy, there are times when their individual developmental tasks complement each other in shared accomplishments as parents-to-be. Just as naturally, there are times when husband and wife are pulled in opposite directions by their *conflicting developmental tasks,* as suggested in Table 7.14, p. 148. The more the two parents-to-be work together in preparing for their first baby, the greater their chances of success in finding fulfillment in the generative process and in uniting in welcoming their firstborn (Valentine 1982).

Prenatal care begins with the physician's confirmation of the pregnancy and continues at regular intervals throughout the pregnancy. Often the doctor is able to relieve some of the uncomfortable symptoms of pregnancy: for example, nausea and vomiting in the early weeks; and backache, heaviness, and fatigue as the fetus nears term. *Medical monitoring* includes (1) watching the expectant mother for possible problems such as anemia, diabetes, toxemia, obesity, RH incompatibility, and so forth and (2) following the embryo and fetus throughout its growth to make sure development is normal. Doctors usually prescribe proper diet and exercise to protect both mother and baby and proscribe excessive use of harmful substances such as alcohol, drugs, and nicotine. *Genetic counseling* is helpful where the histories of one

Table 7.13 SOME HUSBANDS' AND WIVES' REPORTED REACTIONS TO FIRST PREGNANCY

Phase of pregnancy	Some husbands' reactions	Some wives' reactions
First trimester	Coping with the fact of pregnancy [g,j] Exploring his roles as father [j] Fear of losing wife and/or child [b,c] Self-doubt as a future father [d]	Preoccupation with the embryo [j] Anxiety about the embryo's health [j] Increased introversion [j] Fantasies of embryo's characteristics [j,l] Nausea, vomiting, indigestion [b,k,m] Loss of interest in coitus [a] Less sexual effectiveness [a] Sleepiness and fatigue [a] Increased dependence [b,c]
Second trimester	Increased respect and awe as quickening comes [b,c] Name for the fetus coined [c]	Solemnity, hilarity, and playfulness about fetal movements [c] Talk about and with the fetus, such as, "*We're* going shopping" [c] Increased eroticism [a]
Third trimester	Emotional involvement with the fetus [b] Attendance at parenting classes [b,i] Fear of coitus harming the baby [a] Abstinence difficult [a] Envy and/or pride in wife's creativity [b,c] Worry over approaching birth [b,c,h] Keen awareness of male/female differences [b,c]	Selection of names for the baby [f,l] Specific preparation for the baby [f,l] Identifying self as "Mother" [f,m] Less sexual activity [a]; isolation [b,c] Continence may be advised [a] Sleepiness, backache, abdominal discomfort Heightened sense of femininity [b,c]

or both parental lines suggest the possibility of heritable problems. As the baby nears term, its position in the uterus is ascertained, and plans are made for a safe delivery. Many modern couples take classes in childbearing, learning techniques such as the *Lamaze method* of giving birth, so that they may prepare for their baby's delivery with minimal use of anesthetics that might harm the infant and deprive the mother of the exultation of the birth experience.

Costs of having a baby vary widely: more in urban than in rural areas, more in the North than in the South, slightly more in hospital labor and delivery rooms than in hospital birthing rooms, and more for Caesarean sections than for vaginal births, according to a 1982 survey of hospitals across the United States by the Health Insurance Association of America (1982) (see Table 7.15, p. 149). Specialists' fees are usually more than those of family physicians, and doctors more than midwives. In-hospital costs tend to be greater than those in birthing centers or home deliveries unless complications develop that call for emergency care of the mother, the newborn, or both.

Interacting with Relatives on Both Sides of the Family

A couple's first pregnancy is usually of great interest to their friends and relatives, who make things for the new baby, give showers of infant clothing and equipment, and some-

Table 7.13 *(Continued)*

Phase of pregnancy	Some husbands' reactions	Some wives' reactions
Pregnancy as a whole	Identification with wife's symptoms (couvade)[b,k,m] Increased nurturance and romanticism [d] Increased participation in family life[d] Anxiety about costs[d,h] Concern about lack of baby care skills[d] Concern about wife's aches and pains[h]	Mood swings, intense feelings[l] Periods of depression[j] Pregnancy dreams, fear, anxieties[b] Increased optimism and romanticism[d] Family roles replace marital emphases[b,c] Fears of miscarriage, malformations, and/or death of baby[e] Pride in accomplishment[c]

[a]W. H. Masters and V. E. Johnson, *Human Sexual Response* (Boston: Little, Brown, 1966).

[b]A. D. Colman and L. L. Colman, *Pregnancy: The Psychological Experience* (New York: Herder & Herder, 1972).

[c]M. Deutscher, Unpublished study of dreams and fantasies of first pregnancy, reported in "Pregnancy: The Three Phases," *Time,* December 20, 1971.

[d]H. Feldman, "The Effects of Children on the Family," in *Family Issues of Employed Women in Europe and America,* ed. A. Michel (Leyden, Netherlands: E. J. Brill, 1971).

[e]R. J. Havighurst, *Developmental Tasks and Education* (New York: McKay, 1972).

[f]J. Ballou, *The Psychology of Pregnancy* (Lexington, MA: Lexington Books, 1978).

[g]L. Barnhill, G. Rubenstein, and N. Rocklin, "From Generation to Generation: Fathers-to-Be in Transition." *The Family Coordinator* 28 (1979): 229–236.

[h]D. Entwisle and M. C. Blehar, "Preparation for Childbirth and Parenting," in *Families Today: A Research Sampler in Families and Children,* ed. E. Corfman, vol. 1. (Rockville, MD: National Institute of Mental Health, p. 154), 1979.

[i]R. A. Fein, "Men's Entrance into Parenthood," *Family Coordinator* 25 (1976): 341–350.

[j]F. K. Grossman, L. S. Eichler, and S. S. Winickoff, *Pregnancy, Birth and Parenthood* (San Francisco, CA: Jossey-Bass, 1980).

[k]J. R. Hott, "The Crisis of Expectant Fatherhood," *American Journal of Nursing* 76 (1976):1436–1440.

[l]M. Leifer, "Psychological Changes Accompanying Pregnancy and Motherhood," *Genetic Psychological Monographs* 95 (1977):55–96.

[m]K. A. May, "Active Involvement of Expectant Fathers in Pregnancy: Some Further Considerations," *Journal of Obstetrical, Gynecological and Neonatal Nursing* 7(1978):7–12.

[n]F. T. Melges, "Postpartum Psychiatric Syndromes," *Psychosomatic Medicine* 30(1966):95–108.

**Table 7.14 COMPLEMENTARY AND CONFLICTING DEVELOPMENTAL
                     TASKS DURING PREGNANCY**

Expectant father's developmental tasks	Expectant mother's developmental tasks	Complementary and conflicting possibilities
Accepting the pregnancy Learning what it means to be a father Resolving dependency issues Resolving relationship with his own father Giving his wife his support throughout the pregnancy Planning with his wife for their first child's arrival	Adapting to the pregnancy Becoming emotionally attached to the embryo Resolving dependency issues Resolving relationship with her own mother Learning what it means to be a mother herself Proceeding successfully through the pregnancy	Complementary: both work together in the common task of becoming parents for the first time
Becoming a man in a man's world Finding himself among his male colleagues and fellow workers Taking jeers and taunts of other men good-naturedly as his wife's condition becomes apparent Continuing some activities with "the boys" that do not necessarily include their wives	Becoming a woman in a woman's world Identifying with her women friends and neighbors in feminine ways Participating in baby showers and other "women only" affairs Borrowing and lending, sharing and being shared with in the relationship she develops with "the girls"	Conflicting: the husband is drawn into male circles, whereas his wife is being absorbed in feminine interests and functions
Being responsible as the main support of the family Getting and keeping his job responsibly Carrying a full load as breadwinner for himself and his family	Seeing herself as mother-to-be as well as wife and person Reducing her outside interests as the pregnancy advances Becoming content to be wife and mother primarily, at least for a while	Complementary: both are involved in the common task of nest-building Conflicting: the husband is drawn outward as wife is pulled inward in childbearing

times offer advice that is unacceptable. Parents on both sides of the family see the married couple's first pregnancy as an extension of the family line and of their roles as grandparents. Their enthusiastic interest may make them more intrusive than the young couple finds comfortable. One recent study of married graduate students found that the second most common disagreement couples had was over parents (McRoy & Fisher 1982, 40). Mothers, grandmothers, aunts, and other female relatives have been known to hover around the mother-to-be with advice and old wives' tales that may not be compatible with the regimen the young wife and her doctor are following for her care. One approach to this dilemma is to keep quiet about what she cannot use and accept appreciatively the help she is getting from kinfolks.

Almost half of the married children (49 percent) in a three-generation study received financial help from their relatives (Hill et al. 1970, 67). Some 44 percent were helped by various members of other generations, as shown in Figure 7.3. Help given and received

Table 7.15 AVERAGE COST OF HAVING A BABY, 1982
(IN DOLLARS)

Family's preparation for a baby:	
Maternity wardrobe	235.00
Infant wardrobe and nursery items	184.10
Baby carriage, crib, nursery furnishings	464.80
Feeding equipment	57.50
Bath items	35.10
Miscellaneous	109.70
Total	1086.20
Hospital costs (three days usual):	
Mother's room and board	460.80
Nursery care of the newborn	299.70
Labor room	133.50
Delivery room	240.10
Circumcision setup	22.20
Anesthesia (equipment and supplies)	52.00
Central supplies	93.70
Pharmacy (mother and baby)	59.80
Laboratory (mother and baby)	88.80
Total	1450.60
(Caesarean delivery averages 2511.90)	
Physician's services:	
Attending physician	596.10
Circumcision (some boy babies)	46.00
Physician's fee for usual delivery	642.10
Anesthesiologist's professional fee	150.00
Pediatrician's newborn care	64.00
Total physician's services for hospital delivery	856.10
(Caesarean section averages 1042.40)	
Total average cost of a usual hospital delivery	3392.90

Sources: Health Insurance Association of America, *The Cost of Having a Baby* (Washington, D.C.: Information, Reference and Statistical Services, Public Relations Division, 1982); also see C. S. Edwards, *U.S.D.A. Estimates of the Cost of Raising a Child: A Guide to Their Use and Interpretation,* Miscellaneous Publication no. 1411. (Washington, D.C.: U.S. Department of Agriculture, 1981).

between the generations in a family is impressive both in its extent and in its two-way flow (see Figures 7.3 and 7.4, pp. 150 and 151). Young couples usually receive considerable help from their relatives in getting married and setting up housekeeping. Then, when their first baby is on the way, gifts flow to and through them to their firstborn. Most adults in the Middletown III study say that their relatives are important in their lives and that they keep in touch with their parents regularly (Caplow et al. 1982, 383–384).

Hill et al. (1970, 305) find three-generation linkages developing networks of interdependence that they call *the lineage bridge* in which the middle generation gives more help up and down the generation ladder than it receives. Three-generation visiting and exchanging help are common. Each generation turns to relatives for help from time to time. Family members' assistance makes a difference in providing young married couples not only the material goods that make life comfortable but also the sense of closeness and ongoing interest that give security and stability to the young family-in-the-making.

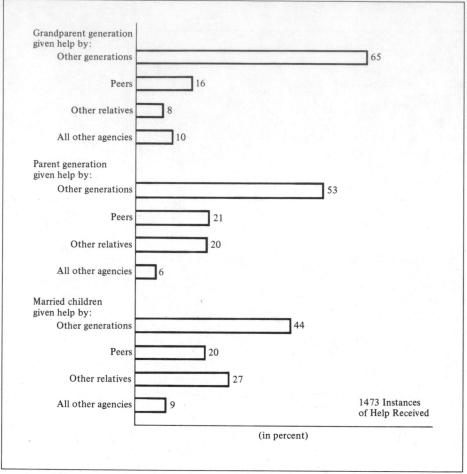

Figure 7.3   Sources of help received by three generations over a year's time by percentages of instances. *Source:* Data from Reuben Hill et al. *Family Development in Three Generations* (Cambridge, MA: Schenkman, 1970, chap. 3).

Maintaining Couple Motivation and Morale

A study of 1056 married mothers of three-generation families found young married couples reporting the highest levels of marital satisfaction and the lowest levels of negative sentiments. Yet these young marrieds often find their relationship unstable, with extremes of feelings and behavior as they work out their accommodations (Gilford & Bengtson 1979, 394–395).

Young couples can be exhilarated by the excitement of getting married, the thrill of furnishing and equipping their first home, and the miracle of discovering that their firstborn is on the way. During the same period of time, they often are frustrated by their ineffectual efforts to accomplish the multitude of developmental tasks as husband, as wife, and as a couple that demand so much more of them both than they find manageable at first. Some

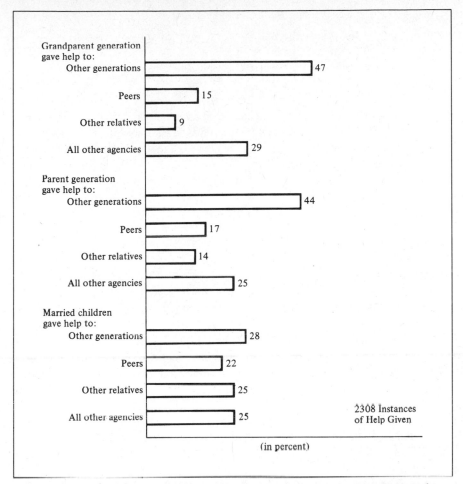

Figure 7.4 Help given by three generations over a year's time by percentages of instances. *Source:* Data from Reuben Hill et al. *Family Development in Three Generations* (Cambridge, MA: Schenkman, 1970, chap. 3).

of their early quarrels arise not so much from annoyance at their spouse but from each one's own embarrassing failures to measure up to what they both expect of themselves. So, it is safe to assume that the early years of marriage are replete with both highs and lows that come with almost roller-coaster-like regularity. Those couples who survive such extremes are learning to maintain the morale from their peak marital experiences long enough to sustain them through their next downturn.

An Eye to Catch

The joy of marriage is an eye to catch
When we go out among our human kind
This secret sharing nothing else can match.
Some unexpected bell is struck . . . I snatch

A surreptitious glance at you to find
The joy of marriage is an eye to catch
When we go out among our human kind!
                              Beth Duvall Russell

Highly motivated couples know enough about what to expect of themselves and of marital interaction not to demand perfection of one another or of their relationship. When the low moments come, they can afford to take the attitude, "This too will pass"; when they ride the crest of a wave, they remember it in energizing ways. Trends in American marriage suggest that even while many marriages are being disrupted, high-quality and high-stability marriages may be increasing—thanks to greater maturity at the time of marriage, better marriage education, increasing visibility of marriage and family therapy, greater acceptance of the many options available, and increasing awareness that individuals can and do influence the outcomes of their marriages (Lewis & Spanier 1982, 64).

SUMMARY

First marriage is a critical transition from single adulthood to married-pair living. Approximately 90 percent of American men and women marry—and for various reasons. Simple or elaborate, the wedding and honeymoon are but stepping stones to the marriage still to be built. Couples face predictable developmental tasks, which they accomplish poorly or well, depending upon their maturity, their readiness for marriage, and their personal characteristics. Husbands' and wives' developmental tasks may be conflicting, complementary, or both. Marital roles range from traditional to liberated, with more conjugal options and flexibility having recognizable benefit to the union.

Family developmental tasks of married couples important to their survival and continuity as a family include: (1) finding, furnishing, and settling into their first residence; (2) establishing mutually satisfactory ways of supporting themselves; (3) allocating responsibilities each partner is willing and able to assume; (4) building foundations for a satisfying marital relationship; (5) controlling fertility and planning a family; (6) starting a family with the first pregnancy; (7) interacting with relatives on both sides of the family; and (8) maintaining couple morale and motivation.

Marital power is exercised by the spouse who makes the decisions affecting the lives of the couple. In equalitarian marriages both members of the pair have a relatively equal voice in their deliberations, although there may be discrepancies in their assumption of household responsibilities. Role reversal, sex-role transcendence, and reciprocity in marriage function well as long as they satisfy the spouses.

Effective problem solving helps avoid marital conflict; conflict resolution protects the pair from both chronic grudges and too-hasty dissolution. Good communication is essential; and communicator styles vary by gender and between individuals. In time, conjugal relations develop many-faceted forms of communication and may result in pregnancy. Contraception, abortion, and sterilization function to limit family size. Infertility may yield to medical intervention or to child-rearing alternatives.

Pronatalism and antinatalism both have their advocates for a dozen or more reasons each. Prenatal care begins with the confirmation of the pregnancy and continues with regular monitoring until the birth of the baby. Husbands' and wives' reactions to pregnancy differ between the individuals and throughout the three trimesters. Relatives express their interest in the new family-in-the-making with gifts and, sometimes, with unwelcome intrusion. Young couples profit by the lineage bridge in which the middle generation gives more help than it receives. Young married couples have both high and low marital satisfaction, alternating with almost roller-coaster regularity. Although many marriages fail, for identifiable reasons marital quality may be increasing in the United States.

REFERENCES

Alan Guttmacher Institute. 1982. *Family planning perspectives.* New York: Alan Guttmacher Institute.

Aldous, J. 1969. Occupational characteristics and males' role performance in the family. *Journal of Marriage and the Family* 31:707–712.

————. 1974. *The developmental approach to family analysis: The conceptual framework.* Vol. 1. Athens: University of Georgia. Mimeographed.

Alpenfels, E. J. 1970. Progressive monogamy: An alternate pattern? In *The family in search of a future,* ed. H. A. Otto, pp. 67–73. New York: Appleton-Century-Crofts.

American Council on Education. 1967, 1970, 1971, 1981. *Annual Surveys: The American Freshman.* Los Angeles: University of California.

Associated Press report. 1983. "Sweeping changes" in role of women. *Sarasota Herald-Tribune.* Sarasota, FL, October 11, p. 1.

Association for Voluntary Sterilization. 1982. Voluntary sterilizations top one million mark in 1980. *AVS News,* January, p. 1.

Astin, A. W., King, M. R., & Richardson, G. T. 1981. *The American freshman: National norms for fall 1981.* Cooperative Institutional Research Program, American Council on Education. Los Angeles: University of California.

Bahr, S. J. 1974. Effects on power and division of labor in the family. In *Working mothers,* ed. L. W. Hoffman & F. I. Nye, pp. 167–185. San Francisco: Jossey-Bass.

Ballou, J. 1978. *The psychology of pregnancy.* Lexington, MA: Lexington Books.

Barnhill, L., Rubenstein, G., & Rocklin, N. 1979. From generation to generation: Fathers-to-be in transition. *Family Coordinator* 28:229–235.

Bianchi, S.M. & Spain, D. 1983. *American women: Three decades of change.* U.S. Bureau of the Census. Washington, D.C.: Government Printing Office.

Blank, R. H. 1981. *The politics of human genetic technology.* Boulder, CO: Westview Press.

Bryson, R. B., Bryson, J. B., Licht, M. H., & Licht, B. G. 1976. The professional pair: Husband/wife psychologists. *American Psychologist* 31:10–16.

Burchinal, L. 1965. Trends and prospects for young marriages in the U.S. *Journal of Marriage and the Family* 27:243–254.

Caplow, T., Bahr, H. M., Chadwick, B. A., Hill, R., & Williamson, M. H. 1982. *Middletown families: Fifty years of change and continuity.* Minneapolis: University of Minnesota Press.

Centers, R., Ravan, B. H., & Rodrigues, A. 1971. Conjugal power structure: A reexamination. *American Sociological Review* 36:264–278.

Chilman, C. S. 1980. *Adolescent sexuality in a changing American society: Social and psychological perspectives.* Washington, D.C.: Government Printing Office, pp. 253–256.

Colman, A. D., & Colman, L. L. 1972. *Pregnancy: The psychological experience.* New York: Herder & Herder.

Condran, J. G., & Bode, J. G. 1982. Rashomon, working wives, and family division of labor: Middletown, 1980. *Journal of Marriage and the Family* 44:421–426.

Cook, A. S., West, J. B., & Hamner, T. J. 1982. Changes in attitudes toward parenting in college women: 1972 and 1979 samples. *Family Relations* 31:109–113.

Deutscher, M. 1971. Unpublished study of dreams and fantasies of first pregnancy, reported in Pregnancy: The three phases. *Time,* December 20.

Duvall, E. M. 1954. *In-laws: Pro and con.* New York: Association Press.

Eakins, R. G., & Eakins, B. W. 1978. *Sex differences in human communication.* Boston: Houghton Mifflin.

Ebaugh, H. R. F., & Haney, C. A. 1980. Shifts in abortion attitudes: 1972–1978. *Journal of Marriage and the Family* 42:491–499.

Edwards, C. S. 1981. *U.S.D.A. estimates of the cost of raising a child: A guide to their use and interpretation.* Miscellaneous Publication no. 1411. Washington, D.C.: U.S. Department of Agriculture.

Elder, G. H. 1972. Role orientations, marital age and life patterns in adulthood. *Merrill-Palmer Quarterly* 18:3–24.

Entwisle, D., & Blehar, M. C. 1979. Preparation for childbirth and parenting. In *Families today: A research sampler in families and children,* ed. E. Corfman. Vol. 1. Rockville, MD: National Institute of Mental Health, p. 154.

Erickson, J. A., Yancey, W. L., & Erickson, E. P. 1979. The division of family roles. *Journal of Marriage and the Family* 41:301–313.

Espenshade, T. 1977. The value and cost of children. *Population Bulletin* 32:1.

Fein, R. A. 1976. Men's entrance into parenthood. *Family Coordinator* 25:341–350.

Feldman, H. 1971. The effects of children on the family. In *Family issues of employed women in Europe and America,* ed. A. Michel. Leyden, Netherlands: E. J. Brill.

Ferber, M. A. 1982. Labor market participation of young married women: Causes and effects. *Journal of Marriage and the Family* 44:457–468.

Finlay, B. A. 1981. Sex differences in correlates of abortion attitudes among college students. *Journal of Marriage and the Family* 43:571–581.

Gilford, R., & Bengtson, V. 1979. Measuring marital satisfaction in three generations: Positive and negative dimensions. *Journal of Marriage and the Family* 41:387–398.

Glick, P., & Mills, K. 1974. Black families: Marriage patterns and living arrangements. Paper presented at the W. E. B. DuBois Conference on American Blacks, Atlanta, Georgia, October 1974.

Glick, P. C., & Norton, A. J. 1977. Marrying, divorcing, and living together in the U.S. today. *Population Bulletin* 32.

Greenwald, H. 1970. Marriage as a non-legal voluntary association. In *The family in search of a future: Alternate models for moderns,* ed. H. A. Otto, pp. 51–56. New York: Appleton-Century-Crofts.

Grossman, F. K., Eichler, L. S., & Winickoff, S. S. 1980. *Pregnancy, birth and parenthood.* San Francisco: Jossey-Bass.

Havighurst, R. J. 1972. *Developmental tasks and education.* New York: McKay.

Health Insurance Association of America. 1982. *The cost of having a baby.* Washington, D.C.: Information, Reference and Statistical Services, Public Relations Division.

Herzog, A. R., & Bachman, J. G. 1982. *Sex role attitudes among high school seniors: Views about work and family roles.* Ann Arbor: Survey Research Center, Institute for Social Research, University of Michigan.

Hill, R., Foote, N., Aldous, J., Carlson, R., & Macdonald, R. 1970. *Family development in three generations.* Cambridge, MA: Schenkman.

Hoffman, L. W., & Manis, J. B. 1979. The value of children in the United States: A new approach to the study of fertility. *Journal of Marriage and the Family* 41:583–596.

Honeycutt, J. M., Wilson, C., & Parker, C. 1982. Effects of sex and degrees of happiness on perceived styles of communicating in and out of the marital relationship. *Journal of Marriage and the Family* 44:395–406.

Hott, J. R. 1976. The crisis of expectant fatherhood. *American Journal of Nursing* 76:1436–1440.

Jaffe, F. S., Lindheim, B. L., & Lee, P. R. 1981. *Abortion politics: Private morality and public policy.* New York: McGraw-Hill.

Jaffe, N. 1982. *Men's jobs for women: Toward occupational equality.* New York: Public Affairs Pamphlets.

Kennedy, L. W., & Stokes, D. W. 1982. Extended family support and the high cost of housing. *Journal of Marriage and the Family* 44:311–318.

Komarovsky, M. 1976. *Dilemmas of masculinity: A study of college youth.* New York: Norton.

Lederer, M. 1979. *Blue collar jobs for women.* New York: Dutton.

Leifer, M. 1977. Psychological changes accompanying pregnancy and motherhood. *Genetic Psychological Monographs* 95:55–96.

Lewis, R. A., & Spanier, G. B. 1982. Marital quality, marital stability, and social exchange. In *Family relationships: Rewards and costs,* ed. F. I. Nye, pp. 49–65. Beverly Hills, CA: Sage.

Limpus, L. 1970. The liberation of women: Sexual repression and the family. In *The uptight society,* ed. H. Gadlin & B. Garskof. Belmont, CA: Brooks/Cole.

Lindsay, B. B., & Wainwright, W. E. 1927. *The companionate marriage.* New York: Boni, Liveright.

McLaughlin, S. D. 1982. Differential patterns of female labor-force participation surrounding the first birth. *Journal of Marriage and the Family* 44:407–420.

McRoy, S., & Fisher, V. L. 1982. Marital adjustment of graduate student couples. *Family Relations* 31:37–41.

Marini, M. M. 1981. Effects of the timing of marriage and first birth on fertility. *Journal of Marriage and the Family* 43:27–46.

Masnick, G., & Bane, M. J. 1980. *The nation's families: 1960–1990.* Boston: Auburn House.

Masters, W. H., & Johnson, V. E. 1966. *Human sexual response.* Boston: Little, Brown.

May, K. A. 1978. Active involvement of expectant fathers in pregnancy: Some further considerations. *Journal of Obstetrical, Gynecological and Neonatal Nursing* 7:7–12.

———. 1982. Factors contributing to first-time fathers' readiness for parenthood: An exploratory study. *Family Relations* 31:353–361.

Mead, M. 1963. Apprenticeship for marriage a startling proposal. *Redbook Magazine,* October, pp. 14, 16.

———. 1966. Marriage in two steps. *Redbook Magazine,* July, pp. 48–49, 84, 86.

Melges, F. T. 1966. Postpartum psychiatric syndromes. *Psychosomatic Medicine* 30:95–108.

Michelson, W. 1977. *Environmental choice, human behavior, and residential satisfaction.* New York: Oxford University Press.

Montgomery, C. B., & Norton, R. 1979. Sex differences in communicator styles. Paper delivered at the International Communication Association Convention, Philadelphia.

National Center for Health Statistics. 1982. *Monthly vital statistics report.* Vol. 31. Hyattsville, MD: National Center for Health Statistics.

Neugarten, B. L., ed. 1968. *Middle age and aging.* Chicago: University of Chicago Press.

Norton, R. 1978. A foundation of a communicator style construct. *Human Communication Research* 4:99–112.

Rapoport, R. 1963. Normal crises, family structure and mental health. *Family Process* 2:68–80.

Rockefeller Foundation, RF. 1975. *Third world development: A U.S. perspective.* Vol. 2, no. 2 (March), p. 1.

Roessing, W. 1982. The romance business is booming again. *Ozark* 11 (June) p. 8.

Satir, V. 1970. Marriage as a human-actualizing contract. In *The family in search of a future: Alternate models for moderns,* ed. H. A. Otto, pp. 57–66. New York: Appleton-Century-Crofts.

Scanzoni, L., & Scanzoni, J. 1976. *Men, women, and change: A sociology of marriage.* New York: McGraw-Hill.

Stafford, R., Backman, E., & DiBona, P. 1977. The division of labor among cohabiting and married couples. *Journal of Marriage and the Family* 39:43–51.

Stokes, B. 1980. *Men and family planning.* Washington, D.C.: Worldwatch Institute.

Tittle, C. K. 1981. *Careers and family: Sex roles and adolescent life plans.* Beverly Hills, CA: Sage.

Toffler, A. 1970. *Future shock.* New York: Random House.

Turchi, B. 1975. *The demand for children: The economics of fertility in the United States.* Cambridge, MA: Ballinger.

United Nations. 1981. *The Interdependent.* Vol. 7, no. 5 (July/August), p. 2.

UPI release. 1982. Legal abortions hit record high in '80: Women spurning pill, IUDs. *Sarasota Herald-Tribune,* February 23, 1982, p. 6-A.

U.S. Bureau of Labor Statistics. 1980. *Three Budgets for an Urban Family of Four Persons,* press releases, and Bulletin No. 1570–5 as published in U.S. Bureau of the Census. *Statistical Abstract of the United States: 1981.* 102d ed. Washington, D.C.: Government Printing Office, p. 473.

————. 1982. *Employment and Earnings, March 1982.* Washington, D.C.: Government Printing Office.

U.S. Bureau of the Census. 1975. Projections of the population of the United States, by age and sex, 1975 to 2000, with extensions of total population to 2025 (advance report). *Current Population Reports,* Series P-25, no. 541. Washington, D.C.: Government Printing Office, February, p. 1.

U.S. Department of Commerce. 1981. *Fertility of American Women: June 1981,* Series P-20, no. 369. Washington, D.C.: Government Printing Office.

U.S. Department of Commerce, Bureau of Economic Analysis. 1981. *Survey of Current Business.* Washington, D.C.: Government Printing Office.

U.S. Department of Labor, Bureau of Labor Statistics. 1982. *Employment and Earnings, March 1982.* Washington, D.C.: Government Printing Office.

Valentine, D. P. 1982. The experience of pregnancy: A developmental process. *Family Relations* 31:243–248.

Vital and Health Statistics of the National Center for Health Statistics. 1982. Contraceptive use patterns, prior source, and pregnancy history of female family planning patients: United States, 1980. Hyattsville, MD.

Wilkie, J. R. 1981. The trend toward delayed marriage. *Journal of Marriage and the Family* 43:-583–591.

Zimmerman, D. H., & West, C. 1975. Sex roles, interruptions and silence in conversation. In *Language and sex,* ed. B. Thorne & N. Henley. Roxley, MA: Newbury House.

Zimmerman, S. L. 1982. Alternatives in human reproduction for involuntary childless couples. *Family Relations* 31:233–241.

Chapter 8

Families with Infants: Transition to Parenthood

MAJOR CONCEPTS

Childbearing
   Natural childbirth
   Preparation for childbirth
   Birth complications
Infant development and care
   Physical-intellectual-social and
      emotional matrix
   Breast-feeding
   Life cycle squeeze
   Bonding
   Sudden infant death syndrome
Human life span development

Watermelon model
Parenting skills
   Repudiating parental handling
   Reproducing parental patterns
   Father-baby interaction
   Parent education
   Alleviating cultural deprivation
   "Ping-Pong" effect
Postpartum depression
Uterine involution
Interdependence

Children come into a marriage through the couple's own childbearing, through adoption, or through children of one of the spouses in a previous relationship. For most couples the transition to parenthood begins with the birth of their first baby and continues until the firstborn is in preschool. It is during this period that husband and wife usually have their first experiences as parents. They enter this stage as a married pair and leave it as established parents of one or more children. This is a fast-moving stage of the family life cycle, starting with the birth itself and proceeding at once to the care of the *neonate,* assuming parental roles and responsibilities, settling down as a family, guiding and stimulating the infant's development and socialization, and undertaking individual and family developmental tasks, most of which are accomplished, to some extent, while the young family goes rapidly on to new demands and challenges.

Stepchildren enter the family as one of their parents remarries and establishes a new home. They may be of any age, usually no longer infants. They bring with them their familiar parent-child relationship and their early personality development with its basic attitudes, habits, and psychological-physical-emotional makeup. They often encounter a parent who is quite new to them, whom they may or may not have known before, whose expectations are unfamiliar, and who may not be comfortable as a stepparent as yet. Father, mother, and child all are members of the newly established family. Each of them now assumes new roles as biological parent, stepparent, or child(ren) as members of the same family. It takes some time, patience, and a lot of loving to settle down as a cohesive family unit. That so many make it is a tribute to their competence in family building.

Adopted children usually become family members after the couple have tried unsuccessfully for an extended period of time to bear their own child. In recent years the number of children available for adoption has declined sharply, largely because contraception and abortion have reduced the number of unwanted children and more unmarried mothers are choosing to keep and rear their own babies. Some American couples adopt orphans of other racial, national, and ethnic groups as did Jan deHartog (1969), who lists objections he and his wife heard when they adopted two Korean girls: (1) you should have adopted a child from your own country, (2) they will never be really yours, and (3) you will never love them as you would your own. Mature adults can and do love their adopted children quite as much as any they might bear. Adoptive parents believe it is nurturing rather than the birth itself that makes a child their own. Although many children are older at the time of their adoption, some are newborn. These infants enter the childbearing stage of the family life cycle with their new parents much as any newborn does.

Bearing a baby begins nine months (more or less) earlier at conception and continues through pregnancy while the embryo and fetus develop in the mother's uterus. The pregnancy is usually filled with the new feelings, roles, responsibilities, and plans of the expectant parents. The months of anticipation culminate in the baby's birth, which unites the new baby, the new mother, and the new father into a new family.

THE BIRTH EXPERIENCE

The process of birth begins with the stretching of the muscles of the *cervix* (the neck of the uterus that hangs into the vagina). As the cervical muscles stretch, the opening enlarges to accommodate the descending newborn; the mother feels this as labor pains. The second stage of *labor* is the bearing down of the muscles of the uterus as it pushes the infant out through *the birth canal* (vagina). The pain is more intense at this stage and may be alleviated either by pain-killing drugs or by the active cooperation of the mother who has learned to control her breathing and to work with each labor pain (contraction of the uterine muscles) in pushing the newborn out. This latter method, often called *natural childbirth,* is safer for the baby and allows the mother to experience the birth of her baby more fully.

The *Lamaze method* of preparing both expectant parents for the birth of their baby is popular now. The father learns to coach the mother's breathing, usually encourages her efforts throughout labor, and often is present at the birth of his baby, as 63 percent of the husbands in one recent study were. Almost all those present at the birth of their babies (95 percent) found it a positive experience (Entwisle & Blehar 1979, 157). Clinicians' studies find the *Lamaze preparation for childbirth* effective in relieving maternal pain and reducing the need for pain medications during childbirth (Greenfield & Tepper 1981, 374).

Complications of childbirth sometimes occur, although not as often as old wives' tales suggest. A difficult birth is one in which either mother or baby or both are under stress. Babies normally are born head first, which is easiest for both mother and child, except in an unusually long, hard labor when there may be some hemorrhaging of the blood vessels of the newborn's head from its prolonged pressure against maternal tissues. *Breach presentations* (buttocks first) occur at times with concomitant maternal pain; breech deliveries require additional obstetrical expertise. In a *dry birth* the bag of waters breaks early, releasing the amniotic fluid that normally moistens the birth canal later in labor. *Anoxia,* failure of the newborn to breathe independently, is a frequent cause of *neonatal death* (National Center for Health Statistics 1981a, 8).

Premature babies (less than 10 percent of all live births) are placed in an incubator where they are given special medical attention until they can survive with usual family care. Babies with *erythroblastosis fetalis* have Rh-positive blood that has stimulated the production of antibodies in an Rh-negative mother. These antibodies cross the placenta and destroy red blood cells in the fetus. Fortunately, this condition can be monitored during pregnancy, and transfusions may reestablish a normal blood supply in the newborn. *Down's syndrome* (a chromosome abnormality causing mental retardation and physical deformities) and other *genetic* and *congenital* problems can be detected during pregnancy by ultrasound or amniocentesis, which allow the physician to determine the fetus's status. Fetal heart monitoring, which may be performed during birth as well as throughout pregnancy, allows physicians to detect distress of the unborn. About 7 percent of babies born with some abnormality and 15 percent of infant deaths are caused by neonatal anomalies. Some newborn problems can be corrected surgically: cleft palate, clubfoot, and congenital heart defects ("blue babies") are notable examples.

Caesarean births are those in which the baby is surgically removed for a variety of reasons: severe fetal distress, absence of strong labor contractions, mother's small pelvic size, and many others. Maternal risks of Caesarean section are two or three times greater than normal deliveries. The number of Caesarean sections performed is increasing: the number rose from 4 percent in 1960 to 20 percent in 1982 (Rosen 1982, 66).

Historically, more women died in childbirth than men in war. Now only 10 mothers die in each 100,000 deliveries. *Perinatal infant mortality* has been cut in half in recent decades: from 35 deaths per 1000 live births in 1960 to some 17 deaths per 1000 live births in the early 1980s, according to the head of the National Institute of Health perinatal research unit (Rosen 1982, 65). Safer childbirth for mothers and babies results from improved procedures during birth, more careful monitoring of pregnancy, better care of neonates (especially premature babies), and fuller cooperation between families and medical personnel throughout pregnancy and birth. Currently, most babies are born in hospitals, with family-centered facilities occasionally available in hospital birthing suites, supervised home deliveries, or special birthing centers.

Traditional medical practices that cause problems for mother and baby are increasingly being questioned: artificial stimulation of labor, routine episiotomy (cutting of the perineum), use of high forceps for delivery, keeping the father away from his wife during labor and birth, and separating the parents from their baby immediately after birth. Increasing numbers of midwives, nurses, doctors, and hospitals are becoming more responsive to parents' wishes, and many now provide family-sensitive delivery care.

Family-affirming births include such elements as: (1) lifting the baby up where the mother and father may see their new baby and hear the cry that draws air into the newborn's lungs for the first time, (2) placing the newborn on its mother's abdomen as soon as possible, (3) describing the baby aloud as the umbilical cord is being tied and cut, (4) giving the freshly bathed and blanketed baby to the mother or the father to hold, and (5) encouraging the mother to nurse her baby by giving them adequate time together, with coaching as needed until breast-feeding is well established.

INFANT CARE

In a simple folk society, infants and young children are cared for cooperatively by any convenient adult. In some American families today, childbearing and child rearing are whole family activities, in which grandmothers and other relatives are active in infant and child care. In most contemporary families, however, infant care is largely the young mother's responsibility with what help her husband provides.

Feeding the newborn need not be an issue, since healthy babies thrive on breast, or bottle, or both. The Committee on Nutrition of the American Academy of Pediatrics strongly recommends breast-feeding for full-term infants. They find that nursing is best established in the baby's first 24 hours. They advise breast-feeding as long as possible, with an occasional bottle of either expressed mother's milk or formula to free the mother's time for her other responsibilities and interests.

Baby foods may be introduced when infants are 4 to 6 months old, when their systems are ready to handle such foods. Dry infant cereals fortified with iron and diluted with milk or formula is the recommended first supplement. Other foods may be introduced later, one at a time. Strained baby foods—either home prepared or commercial—do not need added salt or sugar. Once the child drinks from a cup, fruit juice may be given. By 5 or 6 months infants indicate readiness for food by opening their mouths and leaning forward. When not hungry they lean back and turn their heads away. Pediatricians advise mothers to let their babies decide how much and when to eat (Medical Forum 1982, 3–4).

Usually, keeping baby clean is included in preparation for parenthood classes, where demonstrations and actual practice of diapering and bathing are provided for expectant mothers and fathers. Soft, absorbent diapers of any kind and fold acceptable to the parents and the baby are laundered at home, as they have been for centuries, or by a commercial diaper service or discarded as patented disposable products. The latter are especially convenient when traveling or visiting. Diapering and bathing are good times for parents and babies to enjoy one another, with rubs and pats, gurgles and chats, with plenty of smiling and eye-to-eye contact.

Immunization against preventable diseases begins as early as 2 months with vaccines for diphtheria, tetanus, and whooping cough; vaccinations are repeated at 4 and 6 months, when oral polio vaccine is added. Mumps, measles, and rubella vaccines are usually given at 1 year, after which booster shots (diphtheria, tetanus, and polio) are routinely given (Centers for Disease Control 1981a). Well-baby clinics, county health departments, and private physicians administer the necessary shots when babies are brought in for checkups.

Accidents cause more deaths in infants under 1 year than among preschoolers (1 to 4) or school-agers (5 to 14). Most fatal accidents to infants under 1 year in order of frequency are: motor vehicle, fires and burns, drowning, ingestion of food or objects, falls, and others (National Center for Health Statistics 1981b). Most of these accidents are preventable, so careful parents instruct others who care for the baby on child-safety procedures (see Table 8.1 for childproofing the home).

Childproofing the home with infants serves two important purposes: it safeguards the little child from being needlessly hurt, and it protects the family home from young children's normal exploration, curiosity, and the messiness that is a natural part of the early years.

TRANSITION TO PARENTHOOD—NEGATIVE AND POSITIVE FEELINGS

Although parents may want babies and be glad they have them, they are often dismayed at what the transition to parenthood entails. An early study of 46 couples found 38 (83 percent) of them reporting "extensive or severe crises" in adjusting to their first babies (LeMasters 1957).

More recently, 120 couples expecting their first baby were studied when the wife was in midpregnancy, when the baby was about 6 weeks old, and again when the baby was 8 months old. The most common negative aspects of parenthood these new parents reported were: (1) the physical demands of caring for an infant (fatigue, loss of sleep, extra work, and demands on the mother's time); (2) strains on the husband-wife relationship (less time together as a couple, changes in their sex relationship, and the belief that the child's needs have priority over those of husband and wife); (3) emotional costs of parenthood (the awesome responsibility; uncertainty about their parental competence, anxiety, frustration,

Table 8.1 CHILDPROOFING: THE HOME WITH INFANTS

Item	Danger	Childproofing suggestions
Bathroom fixtures	Falling baby	Provide convenient bathing, changing, and toileting facilities for care of baby and little child.
	Clinging child	Encourage independence as child becomes ready, by low steps by washbowl; low hooks for towel, washcloth, and cup, and so on.
	Training problems	Supply equipment child can manage independently for self.
	Running water	Allow for child's joy in water play by providing time and place for it with supervision.
Locked cupboards	Breaking treasures	Hang key high for door of good dish cabinet, and so on.
	Swallowing poisons	Lock up paints, varnish, cleaning compounds, ammonia, lye, medicines, insecticides, and so on.
	Inflicting wounds	Keep tools, guns, knives, and all other such objects locked away.
Stairs and windows	Falling	Put gates at top and bottom of all stairways; provide child time to learn to go up and down stairs; bar or tightly screen windows.
Electric outlets	Shocking child	Cap low outlets; protect cords and keep to reasonable lengths; fence off with heavy furniture so child cannot introduce finger, tongue, or object into outlet.
Entranceways	Cluttering	Provide shelves for rubbers, mittens, and other small objects; make room for baby buggy, sled, stroller, and so on.
	Soiling	Supply washable mats at outside doors to keep dirt from being tracked in; keep rubbers, boots, and wheeled objects near door.
	Falling	Keep doorway gated or door closed or screen locked when baby begins to get around.
Plants	Poisoning	Get rid of potentially dangerous houseplants; leaves of such houseplants as poinsettias and philodendron are poisonous when eaten.
Furniture	Tipping over on child	Select big-bottomed, heavy, plain pieces (especially lamps and tables).
	Painful bumps	Rounded corners are better than sharp.
	Drawers dumped	Use a safety catch on all drawers (catch pegs at back hold them).
	Breaking treasured items	Pack away breakables or put in inaccessible places; use wall or hanging lamps instead of table and floor lamps wherever possible.
	Soiling upholstery	Choose expendable items or slipcover with washable fabrics or upholster in durable, easily cleaned, figured patterns that can take it (feet, sticky fingers, moist surfaces).

Floors and floor coverings	Chilling in drafts and cold surfaces	Weatherstrip under outside doors in cold weather; supplement heating at floor level; cover with rugs.
	Slipping and falling	Avoid hazardous waxing; discard throw rugs; keep traffic lanes as clear as possible.
	Soiling rugs	Choose colors that do not show dirt, in patterns rather than plain; select washable or reversible rugs; plan to discard after childbearing stage is over.
	Marring floors	Cover with relatively indestructible surface; plan to refinish after heavy-duty phases of family living pass.
Walls	Marking and scratching	Choose washable papers or paints, or spray with washable plastic; convert a sizable section into blackboard (paint or large strips of paper), where child may mark; supply child with washable crayons; plan to redecorate when children are older.
Table tops	Scarring and staining	Cover with formica, linoleum, terrazzo, marble, or other surface not harmed by wetting, soiling, and pounding; use secondhand items at first.
Toys	Littering	Provide low shelves and accessible storage places.
	Ingesting harmful paints	Select things child can suck and chew without harm.
	Sharp edges and corners	Choose toys that will not hurt child in bangs and bumps.
	Swallowing	Frequently monitor the house for small objects a child could swallow or choke on (e.g., a paperclip or a button).
	Breaking	Give child sturdy things not easily broken (frustrating them and you).
	Burning	Provide play space near but not at the stove; keep handles of pans turned in rather than out.
Kitchen		Make burner knobs one of the "no-nos" that baby may not touch.
	Lighting gas	
	Lighting matches	Keep matches on high shelves; establish firm "no-no" policy on them.
	Tripping workers	Fence off child's play area from main traffic lanes in kitchen or provide highchair play during meal preparation.
	Cutting	Hang knives high on wall.
	Hurting baby	Minor cuts, bruises bangs, burns, and the like are taken in stride; major ones are turned over immediately to medical attention (keep doctor's number and other resources on telephone pad).
General	Damaging the house	Keep perspective of child being more important than things; use temporary, expendable things while children are small; plan to redo the place as youngsters near the teen years (they will push for that anyway).

depression, and resentfulness toward both the child and spouse); (4) adult activity restrictions (less interaction with friends, more limited recreation and travel); and (5) financial and career restrictions (loss of mother's job to care for her baby) (Sollie & Miller 1980, 158–164). These same couples told of their babies' bringing them a sense of fulfillment and a new meaning in life and strengthening the husband-wife bond as well as family cohesiveness (Miller & Sollie 1980, 464).

Intensive interviews with another sample of couples when their first babies were 13 to 21 weeks of age found similar negative factors, ranked from worrying about being good parents, losing sleep, worrying about the added responsibility of a child, getting together with friends, and being interrupted by the baby to not being able to get out of the home during the day or the evening. Parental gratifications reported by these couples ranged in rank order from their babies' giving them a purpose for living, making them happy, providing a sense of fulfillment, and feeling closer to the spouse to carrying on the family name and line (Steffensmeier 1982, 323).

These recent studies into the *dynamics of first parenthood* concur that preparation for parenthood is helpful in making the multidimensional transition more easily. Becoming parents is, after all, a normal developmental event in the individual and family life cycle, with stresses that test a family's coping strategies (Miller & Sollie 1980, 464).

INFANT DEVELOPMENT

Babies grow more rapidly during their first months than they ever will again. In fact, development slows from the moment of conception, so that each period of growth is faster than any succeeding it. Human development is sequential, as each new stage of growth derives from what has gone before. Infant development is the foundation for future growth and is, therefore, the most important period of physical, intellectual, social, and emotional development for the individual.

Physical development, outlined in Table 8.2, pp. 166–167, advances most rapidly anteriorly during prenatal life and through infancy. The neonate has a large head and a small abdomen and legs. Within a week after birth, infants normally see, hear, taste, smell, feel, and respond to stimuli. These sensory capacities provide the channels for future intellectual, social, and emotional development.

Intellectual development progresses rapidly from babies' first days, as they wave their arms and legs, cry, suck, turn their heads toward familiar voices, and watch their parents' faces. The more they do these things, the more sure of themselves babies become. Within the first few months babies combine their skills as they look and clutch while they nurse, and turn their heads toward moving objects. Soon they can look for lost things and anticipate attention as a familiar person comes near. By the end of their first year, infants normally work hard to get what they want; they imitate others' actions; they enjoy playing games; and they explore, manipulate, and investigate things within their reach. They learn to sit, to crawl, to pull themselves upright; some begin to walk by their first birthday. Usually, 2-year-olds have begun to talk, to remember where things are, and to test their relationships with others, especially their parents, as they enter a period of *negativism*.

Social and emotional development begins very early as infants interact with their parents and other caretakers. By slowing down films of infant behavior, researchers find that babies interact with their parents from the time they are but a few days old (Belsky 1981;

Lamb 1977). Even during their first hour of life, most newborns are alert and inquisitive; soon thereafter, they wave their arms and legs in synchrony with human speech, they differentiate between their mothers' and other female voices, and they correctly associate their mothers' voices and faces. Infant specialists now believe that increased interaction between mothers and their babies during the first few days and weeks of life has a lasting beneficial effect on maternal behavior and infant development (Restak 1982; Smillie 1982).

Parents encourage their infants' development as they:

1. Care for their babies' physical needs within an atmosphere of warm, continuing relationships;
2. Hold, cuddle, caress, and fondle as they bathe, diaper, and feed their young;
3. Talk with their little children and respond to their efforts to communicate;
4. Play little games with their babies as they show readiness for them;
5. Encourage their infants as they develop new skills and practice familiar ones;
6. Provide a wide variety of stimulating materials, simple equipment, and space for their babies' manipulation and exploration; and
7. Foster warm ongoing relationships between their little children and their parents, grandparents, siblings, caretakers, and friends.

Human development is all of a piece, with physical, intellectual, social, emotional, and personality development all occurring together throughout life, as Aldrich shows in his *watermelon model* of human life span development (Figure 8.1, p. 168). The top half of the figure acknowledges the biological aspects of life, the bottom the psychosocial (note that the word *ekistic* refers to the environmental context). This model suggests that at any given stage of life it takes an entire slice across the many factors that make up a human being to sense what is happening at that time. The lengthwise view of the watermelon model takes the individual's life from conception (C) through rapid development to mature adulthood to gradual contraction as life goes on, culminating with death (D). At each stage throughout the full life span, there are developmental tasks to perform, none more important than those of infancy.

DEVELOPMENTAL TASKS OF INFANCY AND EARLY CHILDHOOD

This first stage of life takes babies from birth to the place where they are becoming somewhat independent of others. By the end of this stage, children normally have acquired some autonomy, they are feeding themselves solid food, they are walking, and they have mastered the first steps in a complex system of communication. Each of these accomplishments represents many hours of practice and real work as little children achieve their developmental tasks (see Table 8.3, p. 169).

DEVELOPMENTAL TASKS OF THE NEW MOTHER OF AN INFANT AND YOUNG CHILD

The first baby arrives in most families while the husband and wife are still establishing their marriage relationship; so there is an inevitable overlapping of the developmental tasks of the young wife with those of the young mother during the first baby's infancy. Concurrently, the young woman carries the unfinished business of being a competent and happy wife with that

Table 8.2 PHYSICAL DEVELOPMENT—NEWBORN TO 2 YEARS

Developmental dimension	Newborn	Infant (0–2 years)
Height	18 to 22 inches	26 to 35 inches
Weight	6 to 8 pounds	Birth weight triples in first year; by 2 years about 30 pounds
Proportions	Head large (one-quarter of total height); chest large; abdomen small; legs short	Face grows rapidly; trunk, legs, and arms lengthen
Bones	Cartilage present in ankles, wrists, soft spots in skull	Soft spots in skull closed at 1 year; leg and arm bones elongated
Muscles	Heart and smooth muscles developed; skeletal muscles uncoordinated; sphincters weak	Coordination improving; sphincters strengthening; back, leg, and arm muscles developing rapidly
Sense organs	Sees, distinguishing light from dark; tastes; smells; and feels with some discrimination	1 week, hears; 3 months, coordinates eyes; all senses developing; equilibrium weak
Posture	Prone (on stomach) or supine (on back)	3 months, raises head and shoulders from prone position; 4 months, sits erect when held by hands; 8 months, sits alone; 9 months, creeps, crawls, stands by chair; 12 months, stands alone, soon walks
Manual skills	Random movements of hands; lashing when angry or crying	4 to 5 months, scoops up block with hand; 8 months, picks up blocks in both hands; 9 months, thumb and finger opposed in pincer grasp of tiny objects; 2 years, prefers one hand to the other
Hair	Varies widely: none to much; often not typical of later hair; is generally lost	Typical color and texture established by second year

Teeth	None usually	Second year, 16 temporary teeth in order: 4 to 15 months, 8 incisors; 12 to 18 months, 4 molars; 18 to 24 months, 4 canines
Digestion	Stomach empties every three to four hours; liquids only	First solids 2 to 6 months; 3 meals a day in first year; eats family foods by second year
Urination	Kidneys functioning; no bladder control; voiding about 20 times daily	Bladder grows slowly; voiding every 2 hours; may be dry by 2 years (varies widely)
Respiration	Some wheezing; low susceptibility to infection; rapid breathing: 34 to 45 inhalations a minute	Regular breathing established; steadies to 25 to 35 inhalations a minute; increased susceptibility to infection
Vocalization	Cries, hiccups, sneezes	Range rapidly increases to grunts, gurgles, babbling, imitating sounds, single words, phrases, short sentences
Heartbeat	130 per minute at rest	Decreases to 125 to 90 per minute by 2 years
Blood pressure	Low: about 40 millimeters	About 80 millimeters

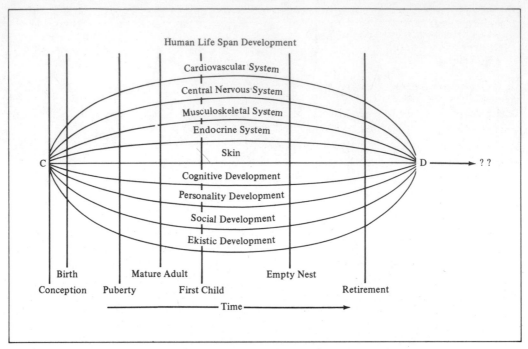

Figure 8.1 Watermelon model of human life span development. *Source:* Reprinted by permission of the publisher, from *Major Transitions in the Human Life Cycle*, edited by Alvin C. Eurich (Lexington, MA: Lexington Books, D.C. Heath & Company, Copyright 1981, D.C. Heath and Company).

of becoming an effective and fulfilled mother. She masters many new skills during the infancy of her firstborn.

Deciding Whether to Nurse Her Baby

One of the first questions a new mother must answer is how she will feed her baby. The hospital staff may or may not encourage her to breast-feed. In some cases newborns are already started on formulas in the nursery before the new mother has made a firm decision. Her husband may discourage her efforts to breast-feed. She may have a job that would make full-time nursing difficult. She may feel uncertain about her ability to nurse her baby successfully. If she decides it is not possible or convenient for her to breast-feed the baby, she learns to prepare, sterilize, refrigerate, and warm a formula for bottle-feedings and to present the bottle while holding the baby closely, as she would in nursing, which gives the infant and the mother an opportunity for cuddling and closeness.

Breast-feeding benefits babies in several ways:

1. Early bonding to their mothers through being held close and fondled while nursing;
2. Higher levels of arousal and alertness;
3. Fewer infections, thanks to immunities in mothers' milk; and
4. Less diarrhea, colic, and diaper rash.

Table 8.3 DEVELOPMENTAL TASKS OF INFANCY AND EARLY CHILDHOOD

1. *Achieving physiological equilibrium following birth:*
   Learning to sleep at appropriate times.
   Maintaining a healthful balance of rest and activity.

2. *Learning to take food satisfactorily:*
   Developing ability to nurse—to suck, swallow, and adjust to nipple comfortably.
   Learning to take solid foods; to enjoy new textures, tastes, and temperatures; to use cup, spoon,
   and dishes competently in ways appropriate to age.

3. *Learning the know-how and the where-when of elimination:*
   Finding satisfaction in early eliminative processes.
   Wanting to adapt to expectations of time and place of functioning as developmental readiness
   and parental pressures indicate.
   Participating cooperatively and effectively (depending on readiness) in the training program.

4. *Learning to manage one's body effectively:*
   Developing coordination (eye-hand, hand-mouth, reach, grasp, handle, manipulate,
   put-and-take).
   Acquiring skills in locomotion through kicking, creeping, walking, and running.
   Gaining assurance and competence in handling himself or herself in a variety of situations.

5. *Learning to adjust to other people:*
   Responding discriminatingly to others' expectations.
   Recognizing parental authority and controls.
   Learning the do's and the don'ts of his or her world.
   Reacting positively to both familiar and strange persons.

6. *Learning to love and be loved:*
   Responding affectionally to others through cuddling, smiling, loving.
   Meeting emotional needs through widening spheres and varieties of contact.
   Beginning to give self spontaneously and trustfully to others.

7. *Developing systems of communication:*
   Learning patterns of recognition and response.
   Establishing nonverbal, preverbal, and verbal communicative systems.
   Acquiring basic concepts (*yes, no, up, down, come, go, hot,* etc.).
   Mastering basic language fundamentals in interaction with others.

8. *Learning to express and control feelings:*
   Managing feelings of fear and anxiety in healthful ways.
   Developing a sense of trust and confidence in his or her world.
   Handling feelings of frustration, disappointment, and anger effectively, in accordance with the
   stage of development.
   Moderating demanding attitudes as time goes on.

9. *Laying foundations for self-awareness:*
   Seeing oneself as a separate entity.
   Exploring rights and privileges of being a person.
   Finding personal fulfillment with and without others.

Breast-feeding benefits mothers through:

1. Speedier uterine contraction from the hormonal stimulation of lactation;
2. Convenience of sterile, warm, ever-ready milk; and
3. The satisfaction of suckling.

Even if she cannot nurse her baby all the time, she can start breast-feeding and supplement either with formula or with milk expressed from her breasts for the times she is not available.

At the close of the childbearing stage, the young mother has, it is hoped, learned to know and to love her baby and to have confidence in herself as a wife, a mother, and a person. These attitudes and values come as she achieves the developmental tasks of this stage of development, outlined in summary form in Table 8.4. This is quite an assignment for the young wife and mother. No wonder so many young women feel overwhelmed during this phase of their lives.

Young families today are usually somewhat removed from the extended family and from the day-to-day supportive relationships it formerly provided. The inexperienced mother is alone with her baby for most of the waking day, and she shares with her mate the child's care around the clock and calendar. In addition to caring for the young baby and providing opportunities for development, the young mother usually does the shopping; prepares food for the family; washes the dishes; cleans the house; washes, irons, and puts away the clothes; assumes responsibility for the family's social life; picks up the ever-present litter that goes with infancy; and pays attention to her marriage as well as working outside the home as many do.

The developmental tasks of the young mother are demanding. She succeeds in them as she gains confidence and acquires competence in her multiple roles. A family-affirming society might provide a variety of services and resources for childbearing families. At the present time, most young mothers do what they can with the help of their husbands and a few close friends or relatives.

DEVELOPMENTAL TASKS OF THE NEW FATHER OF AN INFANT AND YOUNG CHILD

The young father is as responsible for his baby's life as his wife, yet he faces somewhat different developmental tasks arising from his new status as father. The very fact that his wife is more intimately related to the child's birth, feeding, and early care gives rise to some unique developmental tasks. Of course, it is humanly possible, as it is among other species, for the father to escape entirely the experiences of living intimately with his own young offspring. There are men who take little or no responsibility for the bearing and rearing of the child. In earlier times a man left the care of the young child to the women of the household almost entirely. A father began his active role when his youngster could handle himself or herself well enough to go along on hunting and fishing expeditions or on short treks near home. Until then, or at least until the child was "housebroken," father's life was relatively undisturbed by baby.

Nowadays, a man improvises along with his wife as both of them find ways of living with the little newcomer that are mutually pleasant, satisfying, or tolerable. Now, as always,

Table 8.4 DEVELOPMENTAL TASKS OF THE NEW MOTHER OF AN INFANT

1. *Reconciling conflicting conceptions of roles:*
   Clarifying her role as a wife-mother-person.
   Reconciling differences in conceptions of these roles held by herself, her husband, and various relatives, friends, and significant others.
   Developing a sound, workable conception of what she expects of her child.
   Coming to a comfortable understanding of her husband's role as a young father.

2. *Accepting and adjusting to the strains and pressures of young motherhood:*
   Gearing activity to lessened physical vigor in the period of involution and lactation.
   Cooperating in the processes involved in effective infant feeding.
   Balancing the demands of the child, the expectations of the husband, and her commitments as a person with the limits of her abilities.

3. *Learning how to care for her infant with competence and assurance:*
   Assuming responsibility for the care of the child.
   Mastering the skills of feeding, bathing, protecting, and maintaining a healthy, happy baby.
   Learning how to anticipate and to recognize the needs of the baby.
   Becoming increasingly able to enjoy caring for the young child.

4. *Establishing and maintaining healthful routines for the young family:*
   Learning how to choose, prepare, and serve nutritious foods for both adult and infant needs.
   Reorganizing family routines to meet the changing needs of the growing child within the family context.
   Ensuring a sufficiency of rest, relaxation, and sleep for the baby, the young husband, and herself.
   Readjusting time schedules to make way for the necessities and for some purely pleasurable activities within the young family.

5. *Providing full opportunities for the child's development:*
   Enriching the physical situation within the limits of family resources.
   Providing a plentiful variety of experiences in exploring, manipulating, and learning for the infant and small child.
   Protecting the furnishings and equipment in ways that keep to a minimum the physical restrictions imposed on the growing child (child proofing the home).
   Learning to enjoy and to encourage wholeheartedly the child's development and progress.
   Accepting the child as an individual without undue pressure, disappointment, or comparison.

6. *Sharing the responsibilities of parenthood with her husband:*
   Recognizing the importance of the father-child relationship from the beginning, encouraging the participation of the young father in the care of the baby and small child in appropriate ways.
   Bringing the young father into the planning, decision making, and evaluating processes that make him feel that his wishes and values are being respected and appreciated.
   Establishing the habit of thinking of the child as "ours" rather than "mine."

7. *Maintaining a satisfying relationship with her husband:*
   Protecting her husband's values as a person in the midst of the demanding pressures of young parenthood.
   Reestablishing ways of being a couple and preserving the unique values of husband-wife companionship throughout the infancy of the first child.
   Maintaining the joys of being a wife in the sexual, recreational, emotional, intellectual, and spiritual aspects of married living.

8. *Making satisfactory adjustments to the practical realities of life:*
   Assisting her husband in the financial and housing planning for the family.

Table 8.4   *(Continued)*

Adapting happily to the limitations of space and resources of the family.
Enriching the family experience by innovative use of available facilities and resources.
Supplementing the family income when it seems wise or necessary in ways that safeguard the
    well-being of all members of the family.

9. *Keeping alive some sense of personal autonomy through young motherhood:*
Retaining some satisfying contacts with personal interests and stimuli.
Continuing some aspect of personal development that is especially meaningful within the
    realities of the present family situation.
Utilizing the unique experiences of young motherhood to attain the fulfillment inherent within
    it.
Following her child's growth experiences out into new horizons of personal insight and
    growth.

10. *Exploring and developing the satisfying sense of being a family:*
Initiating family recreation in which the whole family may participate with pleasure—picnics,
    trips to zoo and beach, music, automobile trips, and so on.
Participating with other young families in community functions.
Joining with other young wives and mothers in cooperative endeavors.
Providing for whole-family participation in church, neighborhood, and community activities
    suitable to this stage in family development.
Maintaining mutually supportive contacts with parental families.

---

a man is expected to be the primary breadwinner. But here, too, there are puzzling variations
from the older norms. All in all, the young husband-father has quite a surprising number
of developmental tasks to accomplish during the childbearing stage of the family life cycle,
as we see in Table 8.5.

Needless to say, all this is more than the average man bargained for when he fell in
love and got married. As a friend used to say, "Everything is easier to get into than out of."
Parenthood is surely a good example. It is so easy for most people to conceive, and so hard
to deliver; so easy to dream of settling down and having a family, and so hard to meet the
realities of family life.

Few men have been adequately prepared for what to expect when children come. They
only rarely go through schools where boys as well as girls receive an educational program
in preparation for marriage and family life. Traditionally, men have grown up in homes where
little has been expected of them in terms of direct child care. Until the first child appears,
men have usually had very little firsthand experience with a baby. Many men find that their
fingers are all thumbs in those first attempts to change or bathe or dress a baby.

Most difficult of all may be the intimate sharing of his wife with the intrusive little rival
that now claims so much of her attention. The husband has had his wife all to himself during
their courtship and honeymoon days and has learned to take her for granted as his partner
and companion during the establishment phase of marriage. He must now see her time,
energy, and love directed to the demanding baby in ways that may make him feel tense, left
out, and neglected. It is a mature husband, indeed, who soon after becoming a father can
be so centrally involved in the new relationships that he feels a deep sense of security as a
husband and father. One of the hazards to be expected in this stage of the family life cycle
is that the mother may devote herself disproportionately to the new baby and that the young

Table 8.5 DEVELOPMENTAL TASKS OF THE NEW FATHER OF AN INFANT

1. *Reconciling conflicting conceptions of role:*
   Settling on a satisfactory role for himself as father out of the many possible, conflicting conceptions held by himself, his wife, both families, friends, and others of influence.
   Coming to terms with what he expects of his wife, now mother of his child, with the conflicting expectations that each of them has, and with their other significant responsibilities—all of which must be kept in balance.
   Reconciling conflicting theories about childhood and arriving at a realistic set of expectations for his own child.

2. *Making way for the new pressures made upon him as a young father:*
   Accepting a reasonable share of responsibility for the care of the child, compatible with the realities of the situation at home and at work.
   Being willing to accept without undue stress or complaint his wife's increased emotional and physical need of him during the time when she is not yet functioning at peak effectiveness.
   Assuming his share of responsibilities in representing the new family in the community in appropriate ways.

3. *Learning the essentials of baby and child care:*
   Acquiring enough knowledge about and skill in early child care to be able to function effectively in the baby's personal life.
   Practicing the fundamentals required in caring for a tiny baby and small child, both alone and with the mother present.
   Learning enough about early child development to know what to expect and to understand what is relatively normal at a given stage of development.
   Becoming increasingly able to enjoy intimate personal interaction with the baby.

4. *Conforming to the new regimens designed as most healthful for the young family:*
   Adapting his eating habits to conform to the new food intake patterns of mother, baby, and young family as a whole.
   Working out ways of getting enough sleep and rest around the edges of the young child's needs and disturbances.
   Designing new approaches to recreation that will fit in with the needs and limitations now operating in the family.
   Being willing to experiment with any promising possibilities that seem worth trying, rather than insisting that "life go on as usual."

5. *Encouraging the child's full development:*
   Investing in the equipment and resources that will be most helpful and useful.
   Cooperating in childproofing the home for the period of young childhood.
   Planning with his wife for the enriching experiences that will provide opportunities for the child's well-rounded development.
   Accepting the child as an individual and encouraging the child to behave as one, rather than viewing the child as a "chip off the old block" or a vessel for unfulfilled personal ambitions and dreams.

6. *Maintaining a mutually satisfying companionship with his wife:*
   Wooing her back into tender sweetheart and intense lover roles as she recovers from childbirth and the arduousness of the first mothering responsibilities.
   Seeing to it that the husband-wife relationship is neither chronically nor critically submerged beneath new parental responsibilities.
   Taking the initiative, when necessary, in renewing satisfying activities as a couple that may have been suspended during the pregnancy, childbirth, and lying-in periods.

Table 8.5   *(Continued)*

7. *Assuming the major responsibility for earning the family income:*
   Carrying breadwinner responsibilities willingly.
   Augmenting the family income in ways that are appropriate as may become necessary.
   Being willing to accept assistance, as it may be required, from either set of parents, from the
       wife's supplemental earnings, from savings, or from loans or other mortgages on the future,
       at this time of relatively high needs and low income.
   Assisting in financial planning that will keep expenditures within available resources.

8. *Maintaining a satisfying sense of self as a man:*
   Continuing personal interests and pursuits compatible with childbearing responsibilities and
       limitations.
   Finding new levels of fulfillment in the new experiences of fatherhood.
   Growing as a person through the maturing experiences of sharing fully in the development of
       his baby and of enjoying the full bloom of womanhood in his wife.
   Mastering the infantile, jealousy-provoking impulses that might alienate him from his little
       family at the very times when they need each other most.

9. *Representing the family within the wider community:*
   Serving as chief representative of his family in the workaday world.
   Recognizing that he is the one to whom his wife looks for adult stimulus, interest, and
       activities while she is confined with baby care.
   Bringing home the ideas, the people, the projects that will keep the young family in touch with
       the larger community during childbearing days.
   Carrying on the amount of community participation compatible with the pressures at home
       and on the job.

10. *Becoming a* family man *in the fullest sense of the term:*
    Finding satisfactions in whole-family activities
    Cooperating with his wife and baby in the new pursuits that appeal to them.
    Initiating experiences for the whole family that will broaden horizons and enrich their life
        together as a family unit.
    Enjoying the new dimensions of associations with other relatives, now viewed in their new
        roles as aunts, uncles, cousins, and grandparents of the new baby.

father may retreat emotionally to a doghouse of his own making. Until he can share his wife maturely and participate with her in the experiences of parenthood, he may feel like little more than a fifth wheel around the place.

How well the young husband juggles the conflicting loyalties and expectations and manages the multiplicity of roles opening up to him depends in large measure on how ready he is for fatherhood and how successful he is in accomplishing the developmental tasks inherent in the childbearing stage of family life. As he succeeds in achieving his personal developmental tasks, he is able to participate effectively in carrying out the family developmental tasks necessary for the survival, continuation, and growth of the family as a unit.

DEVELOPMENTAL TASKS OF THE CHILDBEARING FAMILY

With the coming of the first baby, the couple now becomes a family of three persons: mother, father, and child. The interrelationships within the family have jumped from one (husband-wife) to three (husband-wife, father-child, and mother-child). Husband and wife are typically in their mid- or late twenties as this stage begins and plus or minus 30 when it ends—2½ years after the baby's birth.

The developmental tasks of the family in the childbearing stage are basically concerned with establishing the young family as a stable unit, reconciling conflicting developmental tasks of the various members, and mutually supporting the developmental needs of mother, father, and baby in ways that strengthen each one and the family as a whole.

With the coming of the first baby, there appear for the first time a new mother (in the sense that this woman has never been a mother before), a new father (who must learn what it means to function as a father), and a new family (that must find its own way of being a family). While the baby is learning what it means to become a human being by growing, developing, and achieving infant developmental tasks, mother is learning how to be a mother; father is practicing what it means to be a father, and the new family is settling itself into family patterns for the first time in its history. This involves the simultaneous working out of the developmental tasks of the baby, the mother, the father, and the family as a whole. The 8 basic developmental tasks of the childbearing family are summarized briefly in Table 8.6, and treated in detail through the rest of the chapter.

Adapting Housing Arrangements for Infants and Little Children

In millions of families around the world, no special provisions are made for the infant and little child. He or she is carried about by the mother or an older sibling, either in someone's arms, in some kind of shawl or sling, or wrapped tightly on a board. The baby sleeps with the parents until he or she is old enough to fend for himself or herself with the other children of the household. There are many homes in the United States where children never know a bed of their own, where everything is "share and share alike" within the home from the babies' first appearance until they are grown and leave for homes of their own.

As the standard of living improves among American families, giving babies a special place of their own and adapting the family housing to the comfort and convenience of little children has become the norm. Families with infants and small children are more likely to move than families at other stages of the life cycle largely because what was suitable for a young married couple now seems inadequate for a family with a baby. Some apartments have no-children restrictions, and some neighborhoods appear unsuitable for rearing young children. This is the time when some couples search for a house with a porch and/or a fenced-in yard where a baby and small child can be outside in safety.

Will and Wilma Waters are a good illustration. They married soon after their courtship

Table 8.6 DEVELOPMENTAL TASKS OF FAMILIES WITH INFANTS AND SMALL CHILDREN

1. Adapting housing arrangements for infants and little children.
2. Meeting the costs of childbearing and child rearing.
3. Sharing responsibilities for the care of the home and children.
4. Developing skills in parenting as new mother and father.
5. Maintaining a good marriage in the midst of little dependents.
6. Planning for future children.
7. Relating to in-laws, who now are grandparents, uncles, aunts, and so on.
8. Maintaining morale, motivation, routines, and rituals.

on a midwestern university campus and settled into a small second-floor apartment near Will's work. As soon as Wilma became pregnant, they became "house hungry" and spent every available hour looking for something suitable. Before their firstborn arrived they were settled into a lovely modern house on a quiet street, with a large porch and fenced yard for baby and a garden. It took all their joint resources (their savings, bonds given to them as wedding presents, a cashed-in trust fund from Will's grandmother, and gifts from both sets of parents) to make the down payment, with a sizable mortgage on the rest. They furnished the house with fine old pieces they bought at auctions and refinished themselves. It was like a dream come true, except that it soon became apparent that the interest on the mortgage was more than they could afford. They tried to sell the house to get back some of their equity, but there were no buyers. Their dream house became a burden too heavy to carry and impossible to sell in today's market. They feel locked in but wonder what they could have done that would have worked out better or what they can do now.

Remodeling an old house is a possibility for a couple with the necessary skills and time. But there may be hidden costs: the foundation may be cracking, the roof in need of major repairs, the plumbing faulty, the wiring wearing, or the lead-based paint peeling. *Lead poisoning* of infants, caused largely by their ingestion of chips of lead paint, can cause irreversible brain damage and other serious problems. Federal monitoring finds that in the first half of 1981, some 20,000 children were under pediatric care for lead toxicity. Most of the known cases are among low-income families and those in large cities (Centers for Disease Control 1981b; National Center for Health Statistics 1982). This hazard is found only in older homes, since lead-based paint is no longer used for residential interiors.

In an uncertain housing market, young couples need to be reminded that having a home of their own may be "dreamy" but that babies can be well cared for in any safe place with loving, responsible parents. As young families accept babies' and young children's immaturity, soiling, and getting into things, they arrange the household so both generations can enjoy it with a minimum of restraint.

Meeting the Costs of Childbearing and Rearing

The first baby usually comes within a year or two of a young couple's marriage, while they are still making payments on their household equipment, furnishings, a car, and possibly debts from their student days. This is the stage of the family life cycle when past, present, and future needs converge and expenses tend to exceed income. With the coming of their first child, the costs of having and rearing children are added.

Costs of having babies vary greatly. Stepchildren come along with their parent at no extra cost at the moment. The costs of adopting a baby may be minimal or excessive, depending on the circumstances and the source of the placement. *Childbearing costs* range from very modest for a baby born at home with a midwife in attendance to several thousands of dollars for complicated hospital births. Caesareans cost up to twice as much as normal deliveries (see Table 7.15, p. 149). Special care for premature babies in hospital nurseries run up the bills. *Neonatal surgery* necessary for survival of babies with birth abnormalities is costly. The attending physician who delivers the baby usually has a flat fee for prenatal care, a normal birth, and routine postnatal care, which, in most cases, was agreed upon the first prenatal visit.

Child-rearing costs vary by region of the country, type of community, level of family living, and age of child (the older, the greater expense). Recent government estimates of family costs in raising a child to age 18 for housing, food, transportation, clothing, medical care, education, and other expenses range from somewhat over $3000 annually during a child's first years to close to $4500 a year for 16- and 17-year-olds, as seen in Figure 8.2.

Projections from the U. S. Department of Agriculture, assuming an 8 percent annual inflation rate through the rest of the twentieth century, estimate costs of raising a child to age 18 in the 1980s and 1990s at $134,414 (Table 8.7). When and if the inflation rate declines, these figures accordingly would be less.

Children born to teenagers are more expensive than those born to women who are at least in their twenties. Studies find a strong association between an early first birth, loss of further education, less work experience, higher fertility, and more limited, unrewarding jobs (Dillard and Pol 1982, 252). Unmarried mothers support themselves and their children without husbands to share the burden. Married or unmarried young mothers apply for government benefits, get help from their relatives, and go to work to support their families. Setting up a household and beginning a family with its economic pressures is seen as the first *life-cycle "squeeze"* families typically experience. A familiar strategy for meeting the situation is young mother's work (Oppenheimer 1982).

Young mothers' work helps ease the financial pressures on families even when there are infants and small children in the home. One national sample of women between 14 and 24 years of age found the higher the mother's educational level, the more likely she was to work

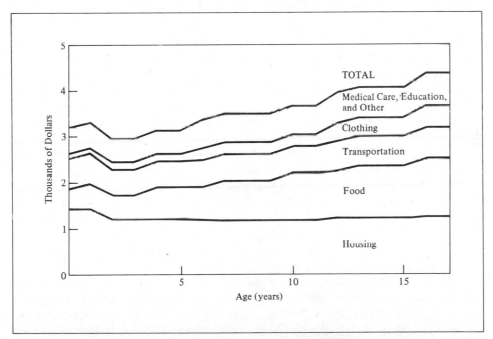

Figure 8.2 Annual cost of raising a child, itemized (rural nonfarm at moderate cost level in the North Central Region). *Source:* Carolyn S. Edwards, *U.S.D.A. Estimates of the Cost of Raising a Child: A Guide to Their Use and Interpretation,* Miscellaneous Publication no. 1411 (Washington, D.C.: U.S. Department of Agriculture, 1981, p. 6).

Table 8.7   COST OF RAISING A CHILD TO THE AGE OF 18, 1960s–1990s (IN DOLLARS)

Child's share of family costs	18-year-old born in:	
	1960s and 1970s	1980s and 1990s
Meals eaten at home	7,918	32,915
Food eaten out of home	848	3,730
Housing costs	10,467	41,121
Clothing costs, birth to 18	3,662	12,129
Medical costs over the years	1,602	6,703
Educational costs to the family	520	2,288
Transportation costs to the family	5,267	20,355
Other family expenses	3,990	15,173
Total	34,274	134,414

Source: U.S. Department of Agriculture, Agricultural Research Service, Washington, D.C., November 1981, as reported in "Child Cost up $100,000 from '60s," *AP* report, November 12, 1981 (allowing for an 8 percent inflation rate annually).

both before and after her first child's coming. Characteristically, these educated mothers stopped working during the month of their first baby's birth; then many returned to work while their babies were still young (McLaughlin 1982, 415). Young mothers whose own mothers have enjoyed working are found to have less stereotyped sex-role expectations and to find more fulfillment in their jobs (Moss & Abramowitz 1982, 363). In another study, mothers who were consistent in their plans not to work until after their babies' first year were compared with mothers who changed their minds and went to work by the end of their infant's first year. Both groups of mothers had some anxiety about being separated from their babies, but they differed in their adaptation to their babies' discontent, beliefs about their babies' attachment, and sense of the importance of a job or career in their lives (Hock, Christman, & Hock 1980, 325).

Caretakers of infants whose mothers are employed are usually found nearby in the form of domestic help, day-care centers, relatives, friends, neighbors, or others. None of these is a perfect solution, especially when the baby gets sick or when the caretaker for any reason is unable to serve. Then the young mother must scurry around for a substitute or stay home from work herself to fill the gap. Even when things go smoothly, it is not always easy. At the end of her working day, a mother sometimes returns from her work to find a petulant baby, a hungry husband, and a household that needs her attention.

Sharing Mother/Father Responsibilities

Traditionally, a mother cared for the children and the home, whereas the husband-father earned the living. This is still the preference of many families (Caplow, Bahr, Chadwick, Hill, & Williamson 1982). In recent years, more young mothers are employed, and more young fathers relate intimately to their babies from birth onward. One study of upperclassmen at the University of Nebraska found these college men expecting to be more nurturing and "recreational" and less active in their provider roles than either their fathers or mothers (Eversoll 1979, 503). Other research into the self-assigned roles of young fathers find that those who have been present at their babies' births tend to feel closer to their infants, to touch and talk with them more actively, and to see themselves as their children's companions and as sensitive to their children's emotional needs (Cordell, Parke, & Sawin 1980; Miller & Bowen 1982, 77).

Father-baby interaction is beneficial for their infants, wives, and families. Young fathers are as responsive to infant cues as are mothers; indeed, fathers are found to be as competent in providing affection, stimulation, and care for newborns as are their wives (Sawin & Parke 1979). There is a special style and quality in fathers' play with their infants that appears to have a strong impact on the social and exploratory competence of their babies (Pedersen 1980). Fathers' involvement with their babies enhances mothers' interest in and affect toward their infants (Sawin & Parke 1979, 509). This increased father-baby-mother interaction augurs well for the future of families (Eversoll 1979, 507). As fathers find fulfillment in assuming family responsibilities as well as their roles as providers, and mothers in their roles in the home and beyond, both parents explore new patterns of carrying their responsibilities as parents and partners.

Ken and Kate demonstrate how this is done. Ken works from late afternoon to midnight five days a week at a local radio station. His wife, Kate, a recent university graduate with a teacher's certificate, found the local community college glad to have her teach morning classes, while Ken stays home with their firstborn son. She comes home eager to share her morning's experiences and to hear what her "men" have been doing while she was away. The three of them have a happy exchange over lunch, naps, and playtime before Ken has to go to work. This leaves mother and baby for their time together at home alone. After "the little guy's" bedtime, Kate grades her students' papers and prepares the next day's materials. Both parents enjoy their lives inside and outside of their home, and the baby thrives with two parents to care for him, interchangeably.

Admittedly, such mutual assumption of home and job responsibilities is not for every couple. The young professional in training or setting up his practice has little time to spare for his family, much as he might enjoy it. The laborer who drives miles to his work and back each day arrives home tired, hungry, and ready for a cool drink and the paper, but even he may find playing with the baby relaxing for a while. Young teenage mothers have too little education and work experience for satisfying jobs, and many do not have husbands to help support them and their babies. Then, too, many men and women opt for traditional male-female divisions of responsibility. In spite of several exceptions, the trend toward interchangeable husband-wife roles is encouraging for family enrichment and stability.

Developing Skills in Parenting

Mothers and fathers learn to be effective parents over many years. They begin as young children themselves as their parents care for them. Later, when they themselves become parents, they tend to (1) *reproduce their parents' patterns* and raise their children as they were brought up or to (2) *repudiate their parents' methods* by developing very different ways of rearing their own children. Peter is a good example of repudiating his father's harsh discipline, as Peter now excessively indulges his sons. He defends his indulgence by saying, "My children will never go through what I had to put up with from my father." The Smiths, both of whom were reared comfortably by wise and loving parents, cannot understand all the fuss their friends and neighbors make of parenting, and they say, "We just do what our parents did with us, and it works out just fine." They illustrate how easy it is to reproduce good parenthood learned in action while young.

Most young parents fall between the extremes of child rearing and continue to perfect their parenting skills over the years: by observing parents of friends and neighbors, by baby-sitting as teenagers, and by participating in child study and parent education groups as they become parents (Steffensmeier 1982).

Impoverished black or white mothers who are *culturally depriving* their babies can be coached to engage their infants in back-and-forth activities with a *Ping-Pong effect* in which the mother elicits, the child responds, the mother replies or corrects, the child responds, the mother reacts, and so forth, from as early as 13 weeks (Gordon & Yahraes 1979, 828). These mothers learn that looking into the baby's face as they change a diaper, that talking and smiling as they feed their children, and that rubbing the little tummy as they bathe the baby seem like simple techniques but are important for children's full development.

> Between 8 months and 24 months or so, one of the most gorgeous experiences you will ever see takes place: children establish a relationship, usually with the mother. They learn thousands of things about what they can and cannot do in their home, what they can and cannot do in interactions with the primary caretaker, about how to read the primary caretaker's different mood states, and an incredible number of other things.
>
> During the first two years a human personality is being formed. The social patterns acquired then, through interactions with the mother and other members of the family, are the ones that will be applied during the next few years to other adults and to children who come into the home. (White & Yahraes 1979, 873) . . . the first three years of life are extraordinarily important to the healthy mental and emotional, as well as physical development of the child. Parents can and should do much to make them productive years, for the child's experiences during that period will determine to a large degree how well he or she will be emotionally and intellectually prepared for school and experiences associated with it. (White & Yahraes 1979, 877)

Parents are expected to give unstintingly to their children over many years with little or no expectation of reciprocation. The parent-child relationship is lopsided: parents provide love, protection, care, goods and services, whereas children return only modest obedience and affection (Caplow et al. 1982, 228). The parents' plight is compounded by their frequent feelings of inadequacy and incompetence. But, somehow, parents learn to live with their unavoidable mistakes and to take their blunders in stride, without piling up feelings of guilt, blame, or recrimination.

Maintaining a Good Marriage in the Midst of Children

Young couples are sometimes so overwhelmed by the miracle of their firstborn's birth, and the responsibilities of infant care, that for a while the marriage relationship no longer has top priority. There is an urgency about a baby's cries for attention that can interrupt a couple's most intimate moments. Young parents—whose first child was 3 to 5 months of age —participating in a recent interview study (Steffensmeier 1982, 323) admitted they were worried about their marital intimacy and stability. Their worries in rank order were:

1. Drifting apart,
2. Sexual relations,

3. Not having enough time together,
4. Spousal understanding,
5. Changes in the marital relationship,
6. Not giving the spouse enough affection and attention, and
7. Talking with spouse.

Another study of couples during the last three months of pregnancy and again six weeks after delivery of their firstborn found that wives' ratings of their marital adjustment decreased significantly after the birth of their first child. Reasons for the decrease suggested by the research team included *postpartum depression* (experienced by many new mothers), feeling tied to home and baby, having less social life, and receiving less positive reinforcement after than before their baby's birth (Waldron & Routh 1981, 787).

Sexual intimacy is usually not advised from the latter weeks of pregnancy until six weeks or so following a baby's birth. By then the young mother's pelvis is back to normal, the postnatal discharge has ceased, *uterine involution* is complete, and she is physically ready for an active sex life again. But it may be a while before intercourse is completely satisfactory. If the woman had an episiotomy, in which the perineum is surgically cut to let the baby through without tearing maternal tissues, her memory of the discomfort in that area may make the reestablishment of sexual relations difficult. The young mother may complain that "the doctor sewed me up too tight" when instead the problem may be the tightening of her muscles as she involuntarily tenses during stimulation of the still-sensitive area. It takes a patient, loving husband and a cooperative wife to mutually find one another with ardor once again.

Husbands who have been active participants in pregnancy, birth, and care of their firstborn are less likely to feel threatened by their wives' preoccupation with parenting roles, since they very probably are sharing them. Nor are they unduly upset by their wives' delay in resuming an active sex life, for sensitive men empathize with what their wives go through in becoming mothers for the first time and often are able to give the tender attention and support women need to give themselves fully to the marital embrace again.

Central in this family developmental task is the setting of priorities between the parent-child and the husband-wife relationship. Until the couple fully realizes that their marriage is the core of their family life, the young mother may be torn by competing loyalties to her husband and baby, with all three family members uneasy about her indecision. The husband's responsibility is to encourage his wife's sweetheart and companion roles, by providing relaxation whenever motherhood becomes too burdensome.

Encouraging findings from a study of 1500 adults over a five-year period suggest that most family transitions are very easily accommodated. New parents may experience a decline in marital satisfaction and yet change but little as individuals. Couples who have a second child within the next five years report their lives are significantly more satisfying (Nock 1981, 711–713). In fact, "All investigators agree that whatever trauma is involved in early parenthood is successfully resolved by most couples within a few years" (Leslie 1979, 485). Indeed, a cross-national interview study of 1569 young wives and a subsample of their husbands found 9 out of 10 of both wives and husbands saying they had a great deal of satisfaction in being married (Hoffman & Manis 1978, 194–195). Such young couples may be said to be accomplishing their developmental task of maintaining a satisfying marriage through their transition to parenthood.

Planning for Future Children

When something tragic happens to their firstborn, a couple may make plans to have another baby soon. Their first child may have been born partly paralyzed, malformed, brain-damaged, or perhaps so defective that it could not live (Pinkerton 1982, 1). It may have been stillborn, or the child may have died within its first few months. There has been a marked decline in *infant mortality* in recent decades, as clearly shown in Table 8.8. "An estimated 45,000 infants died in the United States in 1980. The resulting infant mortality rate of 12.5 deaths per 1,000 births was the lowest annual rate ever recorded in the United States. The 1980 rate decreased nearly 4 percent from the rate of 13.0 for 1979" (National Center for Health Statistics 1981a, 7); in the 1980s it is still declining, having dropped to 11.1 in May 1982 (National Center for Health Statistics 1982, 3). Causes of infant mortality are listed with rates per 100,000 (multiply rates in Table 8.8 by 100) in Table 8.9.

Sudden infant death syndrome (SIDS) kills about 1 in every 500 infants born in the United States. When infants die suddenly for no apparent reason, parents may be reassured that SIDS is neither predictable nor preventable at the present time (Aadalen 1980, 585). Its victims neither suffocate nor suffer. SIDS is not infectious, nor is it hereditary. It is as old as biblical times and occurs all over the world (Pomeroy 1969). Yet it may be so shattering an experience for young parents that they postpone their next baby out of fear of a second disappointment. One or more *spontaneous abortions,* popularly called "miscarriages," may have discouraged the young couple from attempting a further pregnancy. Other personal or family circumstances may make it impossible or unwise to have other children, so the couple take steps to limit their family size.

Planned parenthood may take any of several forms, as reviewed in Chapter 7. Young couples who already have had a child should know that it is possible to conceive again as soon as marital relations are assumed after the birth of their baby. So when the young mother

Table 8.8   DECLINE IN INFANT MORTALITY, IN UNITED STATES, 1950–1980 (RATES PER 1000 LIVE BIRTHS)

	Under 1 year	Under 28 days	28 days to 11 months
1980[a]	12.5	8.4	4.1
1979[a]	13.0	8.7	4.2
1978	13.8	9.5	4.3
1977	14.1	9.9	4.2
1976	15.2	10.9	4.3
1975	16.1	11.6	4.5
1974	16.7	12.3	4.4
1973	17.7	13.0	4.8
1972[b]	18.5	13.6	4.8
1971	19.1	14.2	4.9
1970	20.0	15.1	4.9
1965	24.7	17.7	7.0
1960	26.0	18.7	7.3
1950	29.2	20.5	8.7

[a]Estimate based on a 10 percent sample of deaths; for all other years, based on final data.
[b]Estimate based on a 50 percent sample of infant deaths.
Source: National Center for Health Statistics, "Annual Summary of Births, Deaths, Marriages, and Divorces: United States, 1980," *Monthly Vital Statistics Report* 29 (September 1981): 6, table G.

Table 8.9   U.S. INFANT MORTALITY RATES FOR 10 SELECTED CAUSES OF DEATH, 1980 IN UNITED STATES (RATES PER 100,000 LIVE BIRTHS)

Cause of death	1980[a]
All causes	1251.4
Certain gastrointestinal diseases	8.1
Pneumonia and influenza	28.1
Congenital anomalies	254.3
Disorders relating to short gestation and unspecified low birthweight	107.8
Birth trauma	25.3
Intrauterine hypoxia and birth asphyxia	42.2
Respiratory distress syndrome	139.8
Other conditions originating in the perinatal period	308.2
Sudden infant death syndrome	146.8
All other causes	190.4

[a] Estimates.

Source: National Center for Health Statistics, "Annual Summary of Births, Death, Marriages, and Divorces: United States, 1980," *Monthly Vital Statistics Report* 29 (September 1981): 6, portion of table H.

goes for her six-week checkup after her baby's birth, her physician prescribes the method that best meets her family situation. Even when the married pair is eager for a larger family, they may be advised to space their children for maximum well-being of both the family and the children.

Relating to Relatives

With the coming of the first baby, grandmother comes into her own in many families. She is welcomed as the one who holds things together during the baby's first days at home—the time when the mother is fully absorbed in the baby's care and in regaining her strength. As the young mother is increasingly able to take over full responsibility for her household with the assistance of the baby's father, the grandmother's role recedes in importance. About that time other relatives begin to come by to see the new baby, to call on the new mother, and to bring gifts, advice, and warnings that have to be absorbed and dealt with one way or another.

In-law jealousies and juggling for power not infrequently emerge with the coming of the first baby. One parental family gives more, does more, demands more, or expects more of the new family than does the other. If one or both of the parents are immature or on the defensive, the imbalance of grandparental interest may fan the flames of envy, jealousy, and insecurity to a white heat of passionate resistance.

In an interfaith marriage, the interest of the grandparents in seeing that the new baby is baptized in the church of their faith rather than that of the other mate may become a battle royal. Earlier studies of many cases, in which both sides of the in-law relationship were analyzed, showed that battle tactics may range from covert hints and maneuvers to open aggression and abuse (Duvall 1954). Even if the couple share the same faith, the coming of the first baby may precipitate interference in religious practices, financial plans, household routines, social activities, and the like until the young family is able to establish its autonomy as a family unit.

The childbearing family is now a unit in the larger family circle—with all the problems and promises appertaining thereto. As the young family establishes itself as a comfortably interdependent unit within the larger whole, giving and receiving in ways that are mutually satisfying, it is ready for the years of interlocking family relationships that lie ahead (Hill, Foote, Aldous, Carlson, & Macdonald 1970; Caplow, Bahr, Chadwick, Hill & Williamson 1982).

Maintaining Morale, Motivation, Routines, and Rituals

Faced with the daily round of diapers, feedings, and distractions, a young mother may feel so weighed down by drudgery that she loses her sense of perspective. A young father, burdened with his new responsibilities and the pressures of trying to make ends meet, may be under stress. The parents have invested a great deal of themselves and their resources in equipping a home they can be proud of and along comes Junior with none of the adult values of neatness and cleanliness in his makeup. He, it may well be she, is bent on active exploration of anything that can be reached, crammed into his mouth, pulled apart, pounded to a pulp, sat upon, soiled, or wet. The family soon has its back to the wall in a struggle of values. Which comes first: People or things? Parents or children?

Each generation learns from the other in time. The baby learns that there are certain things that must not be touched and that there are certain values too precious to parents to be ignored. While parents socialize their lusty little human, the baby is changing a new mother and father into a set of experienced parents who take daily issues in stride. The young couple who sees beyond their everyday chores the satisfactions of having their own child to care for find ways to shrug off needless worries with a lighthearted touch. They delight in their youngster's development, emerging skills, and endearing behavior. They are meeting a fivefold challenge of transition to parenthood as they:

1. See beyond the drudgery to the satisfactions of parenthood,
2. Value persons above things,
3. Resolve their conflicting developmental tasks as parents and little children,
4. Establish healthy interdependence as a married couple, and
5. Accept help from others in a spirit of appreciation and growth.

Routines become established as parents find effective ways of doing what has to be done. If each new day in the life of a family with an infant started out with no familiar habits and routines, life would be hectic. Without precedents and established procedures each parent would be faced with a multitude of confusing possibilities. Fortunately, the business of living soon becomes routinized in ways that become familiar patterns of living. Motivation accrues in the step-by-step process in which each procedure trips off the next until the job is done.

Rituals are morale building in that they repeat pleasant experiences of life in expected ways. They are more numerous by far than the celebration of national and religious holidays. In families with infants, rituals provide relaxing interludes that ease parents' nights and days. They give little children reliable, secure expectations of what comes next, and they provide the simple satisfactions that mean so much in family living. Representative routines and rituals at this stage of the family life cycle are suggested in Table 8.10.

Helping one another in and beyond the family circle is morale building. Husband and

Table 8.10 CHILDBEARING FAMILY RITUALS AND ROUTINES

Times and occasions	Rituals, routines, and ceremonies
Morning awakening	Little child climbing into parents' bed Ritualized games and language play
Breakfast	Child eating from special dishes Parents using baby's names for food and functions Routines for cleaning food spills and messes
Naptime	Ritualized procedures by mother and child Special blankets and toys Customary routines
Daily outings	Dressing child for going out Choosing special possessions for the trip Allowing child certain privileges
Father's homecoming	Child watching for father at window or door Mother and child welcoming returning father Father bringing surprises
Baby's bathtime	Special toys and procedures Father-mother-child play Drying, wrapping, cuddling routines
Bedtime for child	Stories, songs, prayers Tuck-in rituals and goodnight kiss "Drink of water" requests for attention Special light and cuddly toy for comfort
Special holidays	Celebrating birthdays and so on Visits to relatives Trips and vacations with baby Photographing baby in holiday settings Sitter routines as parents celebrate as a couple

wife enjoy their increasing interdependence upon one another. They come to appreciate what their relatives and friends do for them and their children. They in turn look out for neighbors, friends, and kinfolks who need their help. A web of interrelationships and interdependence is woven in time in which each person is stronger for the support of the others. The rest of the family life cycle will be easier because of the sturdy foundations built in these early years of marriage and family life or harder because of their lack.

SUMMARY

Transition to parenthood starts with the arrival of children sometimes by adoption, sometimes by parent remarriage, or, most often, by childbearing. Husband and wife may prepare for childbirth and share the experience together. Infant care includes loving interaction while keeping the baby clean, safe from accidents and infectious diseases, and fed. Breast-feeding is recommended for both mother and baby, with supplemental bottles as needed. New mothers and fathers readily express both negative and positive feelings about parenthood. Infant development proceeds rapidly in ways that can be understood and facilitated. Developmental tasks of infants, new mothers, and first-time fathers are many, complex, and the core of this fast-moving stage of the family life cycle.

Stage-sensitive family developmental tasks with infants include: (1) adapting housing arrangements for infants, (2) meeting costs of childbearing and child rearing, (3) sharing responsibilities for the care of the home and children, (4) developing parenting skills, (5) maintaining the marriage in the midst of little ones, (6) planning for future children, (7) relating to in-laws, and (8) maintaining morale and motivation.

Houses are expensive, and remodeling an older place may have hidden costs; so young couples are reminded that in an uncertain housing market a good home for a baby is any safe place with caring parents. Childbearing costs vary greatly, as do the expenses of raising children through the years of their dependency. When young mothers are employed, they need reliable help with baby care and housework. Father-baby interaction is mutually beneficial. Mothers and fathers develop skills in parenting that facilitate their child rearing and enhance their children's development.

Reestablishing a good marriage relationship following the birth of the first baby may pose physical and psychological problems, which are usually resolved in time. Planning for future children may be immediate if something happens to the firstborn. Infant mortality has been declining markedly in recent years, but babies do die in the perinatal period, and others are born with handicaps. Relatives are especially important in the lives of families with infants.

Challenges to new parents are fivefold: (1) seeing beyond the drudgery to the fulfillment of parenthood, (2) valuing persons more than things, (3) resolving the conflicting developmental tasks of family members, (4) establishing sound interdependence, and (5) accepting help from one another and from others, with mature appreciation. Routines and rituals provide familiar procedures that can be anticipated and enjoyed. Webs of interrelationships serve as strong foundations for family living in the years ahead.

REFERENCES

Aadalen, S. 1980. Coping with sudden infant death syndrome: Intervention strategies and a case study. *Family Relations* 29 (October):584–590.

Belsky, J. 1981. Early human experiences: A family perspective. *Developmental Psychology* 17:3–23.

Caplow, T., Bahr, H. M., Chadwick, B. A., Hill, R., & Williamson, M. H. 1982. *Middletown families: Fifty years of change and continuity.* Minneapolis: University of Minnesota Press.

Centers for Disease Control. 1981. *Recommendations of the immunization practices advisory committee.* Atlanta, GA. (a)

———. 1981. Surveillance of childhood lead poisoning—United States. *Morbidity and Mortality Weekly Report* 30:438–439. Washington, D.C.: Government Printing Office. (b)

Cordell, A. S., Parke, R. D., & Sawin, D. B. 1980. Fathers' views on fatherhood with special reference to infancy. *Family Relations* 29:331–338.

deHartog, J. 1969. *The children.* New York: Atheneum.

Dillard, K. D., & Pol, L. G. 1982. The individual economic costs of teenage childbearing. *Family Relations* 31:249–259.

Duvall, E. M. 1954. *In-laws: Pro and con.* New York: Association Press.

Edwards, C. S. 1981. *USDA estimates of the cost of raising a child: A guide to their use and interpretation.* Miscellaneous publication no. 1411. Washington, D.C.: U.S. Department of Agriculture.

Entwisle, D., & Blehar, M. C. 1979. Preparation for childbirth and parenting. In *Families today: A research sampler on families and children.* National Institute of Mental Health Science Monographs. Washington, D.C.: U.S. Department of Health, Education and Welfare.

Eurich, A. C., ed. 1981. *Major transitions in the human life cycle.* Lexington, MA: Heath.

Eversoll, D. 1979. A two generational view of father. *Family Coordinator* 28 (October):503–508.

Gordon, I., & Yahraes, H. 1979. Improving parent skills. In *Families today: A research sampler on families and children.* National Institute of Mental Health Science Monographs. Washington, D.C.: Government Printing Office.

Greenfield, D. S., & Tepper, S. L. 1981. Childbirth preparation at urban clinics. *Journal of the American Medical Women's Association* 36:370–376.

Hill, R., Foote, N., Aldous, J., Carlson, R., & Macdonald, R. 1970. *Family development in three generations.* Cambridge, MA: Schenkman.

Hock, E., Christman, K., & Hock, M. 1980. Career-related decisions of mothers of infants. *Family Relations* 29:325–330.

Hoffman, L. W., & Manis, J. D. 1978. Influences of children on marital interaction and parental satisfactions and dissatisfactions. In *Child influences on marital and family interaction: A life-span perspective,* ed. R. M. Lerner & G. B. Spanier, pp. 165–213. New York: Academic Press.

Lamb, M. E. 1977. A re-examination of the infant's social world. *Human Development* 20:65–85.

LeMasters, E. E. 1957. Parenthood as crisis. *Marriage and Family Living* 19 (November):352–355.

Leslie, G. R. 1979. *The family in social context.* 4th ed. New York: Oxford University Press.

McLaughlin, S. D. 1982. Differential patterns of female labor-force participation surrounding the first birth. *Journal of Marriage and the Family* 44:407–420.

Medical Forum. 1982. New views on feeding babies. *Harvard Medical School Health Letter* 7 (August):3–4.

Miller, B. C., & Bowen, S. L. 1982. Father-to-newborn attachment behavior in relation to prenatal classes and presence at delivery. *Family Relations* 31:71–78.

Miller, B. C., & Sollie, D. L. 1980. Normal stresses during the transition to parenthood. *Family Relations* 29:459–465.

Moss, N. E., & Abramowitz, S. I. 1982. Beyond deficit-filling and developmental stakes: Cross-disciplinary perspective on parental heritage. *Journal of Marriage and the Family* 44:357–366.

National Center for Health Statistics. 1981. Annual summary of births, deaths, marriages, and divorces: United States, 1980. *Monthly Vital Statistics Report* 29 (September):6. (a)

————. 1981. Leading causes of all deaths. In *Accident facts, 1981 edition.* Chicago: National Safety Council, page 8. (b)

————. 1982. Blood lead levels for persons 6 months–74 years of age: United States 1976–1980. *Advancedata* 79 (May):1–5.

Nock, S. L. 1981. Family life-cycle transitions: Longitudinal effects on family members. *Journal of Marriage and the Family* 43:703–714.

Oppenheimer, V. K. 1982. *Work and the family: A study in social demography.* New York: Academic Press.

Pedersen, F. A., ed. 1980. *The father-infant relationship: Observational studies in the family setting.* New York: Praeger.

Pinkerton, W. S., Jr. 1982. Practice of neglecting badly deformed babies stirs troubled debate. *Wall Street Journal,* July 21, 1982, pp. 1, 22.

Pomeroy, M. R. 1969. Sudden death syndrome. *American Journal of Nursing,* September.

Restak, R. M. 1982. Newborn knowledge. *Science:*23–28.

Rosen, M. G. 1982. Childbirth gets safer for mothers and babies. *U.S. News & World Report* 93 (September 13):65–66.

Sawin, D. B., & Parke, R. D. 1979. Fathers' affectionate stimulation and caregiving behaviors with newborn infants. *Family Coordinator* 28 (October):509–513.

Schaper, K. K. 1982. Towards a calm baby and relaxed parents. *Family Relations* 31:409–414.

Smillie, D. 1982. Rethinking Piaget's theory of infancy. *Human Development* 25:282–294.

Sollie, D. L., & Miller, B. C. 1980. The transition to parenthood as a critical time for building family strengths. In *Family strengths: Positive models for family life,* ed. N. Stinnett, B. Chesser, H. DeFrain, & P. Knaub. Lincoln: University of Nebraska Press.

Steffensmeier, R. H. 1982. A role model of transition to parenthood. *Journal of Marriage and the Family* 44:319–334.

U.S. Department of Agriculture. 1981. Child cost up $100,000 from '60s. *AP* release based on report of the Agricultural Research Service, Washington, D.C., November.

Waldron, H., & Routh, D. K. 1981. The effect of the first child on the marital relationship. *Journal of Marriage and the Family* 43:785–788.

White, B. L., & Yahraes, H. 1979. Developing a sense of competence in young children. In *Families today: A research sampler on families and children.* National Institute of Mental Health Science Monographs. Washington, D.C.: Government Printing Office, pp. 865–878.

Chapter 9

Families with Preschool Children

MAJOR CONCEPTS

Normative development of preschool
    children
A social being
Individual differences
Development of special talents
Development of independence
Genetic factors
Congenital factors
Acquired characteristics
Unique individuality
Role sharing
Physical punishment

Positive reinforcement
Self-directing children
Children's aggression
Sibling rivalry
Regressive behavior
Exceptional children
Family planning
Reconstituted families
Family dilemmas
Upward-mobile parents
Family morale

While the first child is between 2½ and 6 years of age, the preschool family typically has a second child and possibly a third, making a total of three to five persons, with the possibility of from 3 to 10 interpersonal relationships. The possible positions in the family are husband-father, wife-mother, son-brother, and daughter-sister—each with its own developmental tasks. While the adults struggle with their child-rearing and personal tasks, the preschool child faces the crisis of initiative (expanding imagination) versus guilt (developing conscience), whereas younger siblings retrace, each in his or her own way, the developmental stages the eldest child has completed.

PRESCHOOL CHILDREN'S DEVELOPMENT

Preschool children develop according to predictable principles of human development (Table 3.3). They are attaining some autonomy, and they have made notable advances in terms of imagination, initiative, and independence. They are toilet trained (most of the time), and they are greatly impressed with a sense of their own bodies. They get about easily and communicate freely with words and symbols. Children of this age have already attained half of their adult height and intelligence (Bloom 1964). They like to know how to do things, such as solving a problem or riding a tricycle. Their own abilities arise from three types of stimuli: (1) physical growth and development—necessary for such skills as hopping, skipping, jumping, and running; (2) availability of a variety of objects such as scissors, crayons, blocks, and toys; and (3) interaction with adults and children—through which they gain social experience (Bijou 1975, 833).

Once past the preoccupation with self that characterizes babyhood, the preschool child begins to emerge as *a social being*—one who can share with others and participate as a member of a family. The pace of physical growth is slowing down, and many body activities are becoming routine. Progress in emotional and intellectual development is increasingly apparent in growing abilities in speech and in greatly expanded acquaintance with the environment. *Normative development* of preschool children, studied extensively through the years, is summarized in Table 9.1.

Preschoolers can choose between two alternatives (orange or tomato juice), describe recent experiences (trip to the zoo), tell how to do things (play a game or hammer a nail); and they have begun to use categories (they can select one color, shape, or type from an assortment of mixed objects). The preschool years are the time in a child's life when a foundation is being laid for the "complex psychological structures that will be built in a child's lifetime. It is this period, more than any other, that makes each child a unique personality" (Bijou 1975, 836).

Table 9.1 NORMATIVE DEVELOPMENT OF THE PRESCHOOL CHILD

Characteristic	2½ to 4 years of age	4 to 6 years of age
Height	33 to 44 inches (range)	38 to 48 inches (range)
Weight	23 to 48 pounds (range)	30 to 56 pounds (range)
Bones	All seven ankle bones begun; bridge of nose forming; fusions occurring in skull; spinal curvature beginning	
Muscles	Steady growth and development; coordination increasing; sphincters maturing and becoming controllable	
Sense organs	Equilibrium improving	Farsighted by 6 years
Locomotion	Walks up and down stairs; runs well; jumps; tiptoes; hops with both feet; rides tricycle	Skips; gallops; hops on one foot; alternates feet in descending stairs; walks straight line
Manual skills	Small muscle skills developing in drawing, building, and so on	
Eye-hand coordination	Uses spoon; pours; puts shoes on; copies circle; draws straight line; catches ball; builds with blocks	Dresses self; cuts with scissors; copies square; designs and letters; throws and catches ball
Teeth	4 molars appear; 20 temporary teeth by 3 years	Loss of baby teeth begins
Digestion	General diet	Appetite slackens; less interest in food
Urination	Sense of bladder fullness developing	Complete control by 6 years usually
Respiration	20 to 30 inhalations per minute	Increased susceptibility to infection
Vocabulary	896 words by 3 years; 1540 words by 4 years; simple sentences; "what" and "where" questions predominate	2072 words by 5 years; 2562 words by 6 years; more complex sentences of six to eight words; "how," "when," and "why" questioning
Thinking	Increasingly flexible through preschool years; concepts first acquired through concrete experience become abstract with experience in grouping objects, dealing with time, space, numbers, and processes; varies widely with intelligence and interaction with others	
Character	Increasing knowledge of rules; growing ability to judge right from wrong, to control self, to internalize standards, and to make explicit demands upon self	
Dominant emotions	Anger, temper tantrums, and negativism	Fears peak; fighting especially among boys; sympathy, empathy in simple forms evident
Social life	Parallel play; imaginary playmates; dramatizations	Social adjustment under way; varies according to playmates available

INDIVIDUAL DIFFERENCES

Each child is unique, growing at an individual pace and becoming unlike any other human being in all respects. Normative listings, like that in Table 9.1, merely indicate the levels of development that most children of a given age have attained in terms of various characteristics. Many facets of a child's development cannot, of course, by included in such gross categories as height, weight, vocabulary, and mental, emotional, or social life. Within any of these broad groupings of characteristics there are tremendous differences (in literally thousands of qualities) and wide variations in patterns of growth and status of development among children of any age. Some children mature rapidly, others slowly. However, most grow at a pace that falls within the ranges indicated in general patterns of child development derived from the study of many children over the years. No individual child is a statistic but a living, growing human being. Although it is best to understand them as individuals, it is sometimes helpful to consider them in relation to other children of about the same age and stage of development.

Physically, children range from broad and stocky to tall and thin, from large- to small-boned, from robust to weak, from obese to underweight. These differences, plotted on the Wetzel grids, can help doctors to evaluate children's progress in their individual growth tracks.

Mentally, children range from slow to quick within the "normal" IQ of 90 to 110, more or less. IQs below this range represent various levels of retardation. Higher scores indicate very bright children, some of whom test out as geniuses. Musical ability, rhythm, creativity, imagination, dramatics, swimming, acrobatics, language, and mathematics interests manifest themselves in some children quite early. This is especially true in families that encourage the *development of special talents* important to one or both parents. Children who go on to high levels of accomplishment are usually the ones with the greatest interest in excelling in areas their parents value highly. These are the youngsters who get individualized instruction over the years, so that their learning is maximized at each step along the way. The critical factors in the development of special talents are *motivation* and *quality of instruction* (Alper 1982, 30).

Emotionally, some children are fearful, anxious, or easily upset, whereas others seem to fear little or nothing. Some children are loving cuddlers, others seemingly less affectionate "by nature." Some children anger easily, lose their tempers, and fight their way through situations, whereas others just as naturally cope more rationally with their problems. Some children tend to be outgoing and friendly, some are shy and retiring, and still others can react either way, depending on how they feel about the situation and the people involved.

Individual differences arise from a complex of sources. Genetic programming is a factor. Some differences (present and to come) are determined by inherited *genetic factors* present in the DNA (deoxyribonucleic acid) and RNA (ribonucleic acid) molecules found in the cells of the body (coloring, body type, and handedness, for example). Other differences among children are *congenital,* arising in the developing embryo or fetus before birth (for instance, due to thalidomide, Rh problems, congenital syphilis, or rubella).

A host of *acquired characteristics* arise after birth. These come about from the way children are nurtured and the way they respond to the signals they receive from others (or from within themselves). There is a tremendous difference (in end results) between the TLC (tender, loving care) children receive from parents who love and rear them in a happy home and the neglect children know at the hands of unloved and unloving parents. At the far end of the spectrum is the "battered baby" syndrome, seen in young children who have been beaten by one or both of their parents. Wide variations are found between children not only in their nutrition and general health but also in their interest in learning, their response to others, and their basic stance toward life.

Children who are mentally alert and emotionally healthy also tend to be physically well developed. Psychological states affect biological processes (and vice versa) in children as well as in adults, according to clinical evidence from psychosomatic medicine. Even within this broad generalization there are many exceptions, depending on the repertoire of responses individuals have for their many life situations. Much depends on the ways in which children accomplish their developmental tasks step by step through their growing years. In no other period of life do individuals face quite the same dramatic complex of roles and developmental tasks as that which confronts preschool children when they begin to see themselves and to be seen by others as no longer babies but as individuals in their own right (see Table 9.2).

The preschool child must achieve enough *independence* to be comfortable without his or her parents in a variety of situations. The child must become reasonably self-sufficient both in the home and in outside settings, in keeping with his or her particular stage of development. The child who has had preliminary practice in crossing streets, managing outside garments, going to the toilet alone, washing his or her own hands, and handling everyday routines, accidents, and minor crises will be ready to enter school feeling self-confident enough to be ready for its challenges. If the child's parents have introduced stories, songs, pictures, conversations, excursions, and creative play materials into the child's life, he or she will be able to enter school as a contributor as well as a recipient. When the preschool child has successfully accomplished the developmental tasks of this stage, he or she is ready to go to school (see Table 9.3, p. 196).

Value of Preschool

Many of a child's developmental tasks are made easier when he or she is exposed to the social interaction, physical environment, and competent direction provided by a good preschool. Preschool enrollment has increased dramatically in recent years (see Table 9.4, p. 196). Experience in a nursery school, kindergarten, Project Head Start, a day-care center, or any of the other programs designed to encourage the young child's development has been shown to have measurable value.

The major objectives of nursery schools for culturally deprived children are embodied in programs (1) that stimulate children to perceive aspects of the world around them and to fix these aspects by their use of language; (2) that develop more extended and accurate speech; (3) that develop a sense of mastery over facets of the immediate environment and an enthusiasm for learning; (4) that develop the ability to make new discoveries, to think, and to reason; and (5) that develop purposeful learning activity and the ability to attend and to concentrate on an activity for longer periods of time (Bloom 1965, 23–24).

DEVELOPMENTAL TASKS OF PARENTS AT THE PRESCHOOL AGE

One fascinating facet of family life is that it is forever changing. No sooner has a fence been built to keep a 2-year-old out of the street than the child is a 3-year-old, capable of under-

Table 9.2 DEVELOPMENTAL TASKS OF PRESCHOOL CHILDREN

1. *Settling into healthy daily routines of rest and activity:*
   Going to bed and getting needed rest without a struggle.
   Taking a nap or rest and learning to relax when tired.
   Enjoying active play in a variety of situations and places.
   Becoming increasingly flexible and able to accept changes.

2. *Mastering good eating habits:*
   Becoming adequate in the use of the customary utensils for eating.
   Accepting new flavors and textures in foods with interest.
   Enjoying food with lessening incidents of spilling, messing, and toying.
   Learning the social as well as the sensual pleasures of eating.

3. *Mastering the basics of toilet training:*
   Growing in ability to indicate needs for elimination.
   Cooperating comfortably in the toilet-training program.
   Finding satisfaction in behaving appropriately as to time, place, and ways of toileting expected
       of boys/girls of his or her age.
   Becoming flexible in ability to use the variety of resources, places, and personnel available.

4. *Developing the physical skills appropriate to stage of motor development:*
   Learning to climb, balance, run, skip, push, pull, throw, and catch in whole-body use of large
       muscle systems.
   Developing manual skills for buttoning, zipping, cutting, drawing, coloring, modeling, and
       manipulating small objects deftly.
   Becoming increasingly independent in a variety of physical situations.

5. *Becoming a participating member of the family:*
   Assuming responsibilities within the family happily and effectively.
   Learning to give and receive affection and gifts freely within the family.
   Identifying with parent of the same sex.
   Developing ability to share parents with another child and with others generally.
   Recognizing the family's ways as compared with ways of friends and neighbors.

6. *Beginning to master impulses and to conform to others' expectations:*
   Outgrowing the impulsive, urgent outbursts of infancy.
   Learning to share, take turns, and enjoy the companionship of other children—and at times to
       play happily alone.
   Developing the sympathetic, cooperative ways with others that ensure being included in
       groups.
   Learning appropriate behavior for various situations (times and places for noise, quiet,
       messing, nudity, etc.).

7. *Developing healthy emotional expressions for a wide variety of experiences:*
   Learning to play out feelings, frustrations, needs, and experiences.
   Learning to postpone and to wait for satisfactions.
   Expressing momentary hostility and making up readily afterward.
   Refining generalized joy or pain into discriminating expressions of pleasure, eagerness,
       tenderness, affection, sympathy, fear, anxiety, remorse, sorrow, and so on.

8. *Learning to communicate effectively with an increasing number of others:*
   Developing the vocabulary and ability to talk about a rapidly growing number of things,
       feelings, experiences, impressions, and curiosities.
   Learning to listen, take in, follow directions, increase attention span, and respond intellectually
       to situations and to others.

Table 9.2   *(Continued)*

Acquiring the social skills needed to get over feelings of shyness, self-consciousness, and awkwardness and to participate with other people comfortably.

9. *Developing the ability to handle potentially dangerous situations:*
   Learning to respect the dangers in fire, traffic, high places, bathing areas, poisons, animals, and many other potential hazards.
   Learning to respond effectively without undue fear in situations calling for caution and safety precautions (crossing streets, greeting strange dogs, responding to a stranger's offer of a ride, etc.).
   Becoming willing to accept help in situations that are beyond the child without undue dependence or too impulsive independence.

10. *Learning to be an autonomous person with initiative and a conscience of his or her own:*
    Becoming increasingly responsible for making decisions in ways appropriate to one's readiness.
    Taking initiative for projecting oneself into situations with innovations, experiments, trials, and original achievements.
    Internalizing the expectations and demands of the family and culture in developing conscience.
    Becoming reasonably self-sufficient in a variety of situations—in accordance with one's own makeup and stage of development.

11. *Laying foundations for understanding the meanings of life:*
    Beginning to understand the origins of life and how the two sexes differ; and to be aware of his or her gender.
    Trying to understand the nature of the physical world—what things are, how they work and why, and what they mean.
    Accepting the religious faith of parents and learning about the nature of God and about the spiritual nature of life.

---

standing why he or she must keep to the sidewalk. The period of teaching the youngster to keep dry is succeeded by one of helping him or her to get used to sharing parents with a new baby.

Parenting Without a Partner

The vast majority of 3- to 5-year-old children live in families: 99.7 percent of white and 98.4 percent of black preschoolers. But some 14 percent of the white and 53 percent of the black children between 3 and 5 years of age were living with only one parent in a recent year (Metropolitan Life Insurance Company 1979, 15). This means that millions of children are growing up in one-parent homes, and the proportion of children living with only one parent, usually the mother, is at an all-time high.

A mother raising a little child alone usually must earn the family income in addition to caring for her home and child(ren). Fully 60 percent of single mothers with children under 6 years of age were working in one recent year; this contrasts with 45 percent of all married mothers in the labor force (Glick 1981, 16). These children are still young, still dependent, and still in need of regular supervision and guidance, even though their mothers must go out to work. A high-salaried woman can employ a competent housekeeper, if she can find one. More often the grandmother or some other woman attempts to replace her in the home. A

Table 9.3 CHARACTERISTICS OF A COMPETENT 6-YEAR-OLD

1. Can get and maintain the attention of adults acceptably.
2. Uses adults as resources in socially acceptable ways.
3. Can express both affection and hostility to adults.
4. Can lead, follow, and compete with peers and express both affection and hostility to them.
5. Expresses pride in something he or she has done or is doing or in something he or she possesses.
6. Occasionally acts out a typical adult activity or in other ways expresses a desire to grow up.
7. Expresses himself or herself verbally in ways that are generally understood.
8. Is able to think things through, to note discrepancies in the environment, and to enjoy intellectual activities.
9. Is gaining in ability to deal with such abstractions as numbers, letters, and rules.
10. Can take another's point of view and see things from another person's perspective.
11. Can make associations between the things he or she sees and hears and his or her own real or imaginary experiences.
12. Is able to plan and carry out activities requiring several steps, with effective use of available resources.
13. Can attend to two things at once, such as being able to concentrate on a task at hand, while being aware of what is going on around him or her.

Source: Burton L. White and Herbert Yahraes, "Developing a Sense of Competence in Young Children," in *Families Today: A Research Sampler on Families and Children,* National Institute of Mental Health Science Monographs (Washington, D.C.: Government Printing Office, 1979), pp. 865–866.

nearby day-care center that can care for her child while she is away from home during the day is a blessing, especially if it provides more than minimal supervision, food, rest, and play materials—all so important at this stage of development.

Even so, when the working mother picks up her little one on the way home from work, she is tired and hungry. Once her preschooler has been fed and tucked into bed, she faces the later hours in an empty house, with no mate to share with her or to give her the solace and support she needs. Fathers raising their children alone face most of the same problems, for much the same reasons. It is no wonder that so many one-parent families and other families with preschoolers rely so heavily on television to occupy the child's time while the adults are busy.

Relying on Television—A Mixed Blessing

The television set is an ever-present, inexpensive, and effective baby-sitter for busy parents and a locus of fascination for preschoolers. But the price may be a heavy one. The National Institute of Mental Health's 94-page study "Television and Behavior: Ten Years of Scientific

Table 9.4 PUBLIC AND PRIVATE NURSERY SCHOOL AND KINDERGARTEN ENROLLMENTS, 1965–1980

	Public		Private	
Year	Nursery school	Kindergarten	Nursery school	Kindergarten
1965	100,000	2,400,000	400,000	600,000
1970	300,000	2,600,000	800,000	500,000
1975	600,000	2,900,000	1,200,000	500,000
1980	600,000	2,700,000	1,400,000	500,000

Source: U.S. Bureau of the Census, *Statistical Abstract of the United States: 1981,* 102d ed. (Washington, D.C.: Government Printing Office, 1981), p. 137.

Progress and Implications for the Eighties" reports consistent associations between heavy television viewing of violent programs and *aggressive behavior* in preschool children. The report states: "Both prime time and weekend children's television are dominated by action, power, and danger. There is an average of five violent acts per hour of prime time and 18 acts per hour on children's weekend programs" (Connell 1982).

Television has a powerful influence on little children. Long before they can read and write, their television viewing has been shaping their attitudes toward themselves and others. Used constructively, television enlarges a child's world and brings him or her face to face with persons, places, ideas, and ideals. There are many ways in which parents can guide their children's television viewing, as we see in Table 9.5.

Programs designed especially for children of preschool age are shown on many channels at times convenient for both parents and their small children. Such programs as "Sesame Street," professionally developed to offer preschoolers the basic knowledge and attitudes they need to develop well, make a valuable contribution to the life of the family with preschool children. That so many preschoolers are interested in them is a tribute both to the youngsters and the programs.

Giving Little Children the Stimulation and Affection They Need

Young children are hungry for new experiences. They enjoy working with new materials, exploring new territories, and having a wide variety of new experiences. Families stimulate their little children's development as they provide a variety of play materials: cardboard cartons to climb into and to serve as trains, planes, boats, tables, and the many other things an imaginative child "sees" in them; blocks of varied sizes and shapes; sandboxes and water play materials; and especially access to the kitchen to help prepare food and clean up afterward. No family member is more eager to help wash and wipe dishes than a resident 3-year-old, especially when he or she has the affirming companionship of a beloved adult.

A preschool child has special needs for being loved, appreciated, and enjoyed for himself or herself. Both parents should try to avoid trying to make their child over to fit some "norm" in their mind's eye. Father and mother may help each other to minimize criticism of their little one and to maximize their encouragement of him or her with appreciative little pats. Their job now is to help their child develop capacities in his or her own way—and at the most comfortable rate. Their primary developmental task is to enjoy the *unique individuality* of each child for what he or she is.

Safeguarding the Marriage Relationship

Having little children ties a couple down. Fully a third of mothers of preschoolers in a cross-national study of 1569 young wives and a subsample of their husbands interviewed by staff of the Institute for Social Research said their youngsters interfered with their freedom to go places. Even more husbands (42.9 percent) than wives (28.2 percent) felt their children prevented them from socializing and going out with friends. Others said their preschool children cut into their time for themselves as adults and curtailed their travel and vacations, their time for their careers, and their opportunities for further education. At the same time, the great majority of mothers and fathers saw their children as a source of deep satisfaction, particularly when they were preschoolers (Hoffman & Manis 1978, 194–194, 205, 209).

Table 9.5 HOW PARENTS CAN GUIDE THEIR CHILDREN'S TELEVISION VIEWING

1. Become aware of what children are watching, rather than consistently using the television set as a baby-sitter.
2. Turn off undesirable programs and interpret the reason for doing so to their child: "Our family does not like such behavior."
3. Prepare a television guide for young children, using pictures of the clock, channel numbers, and television characters for children not old enough to read.
4. Help little children to see television commercials as ways people try to sell things—things that may or may not be chosen by those who do the buying.
5. Tell local television stations and the networks your choices, objections, and preferences.
6. Write sponsors of objectionable programs about what it is you as a parent want and do not want presented to your child(ren).
7. Let the networks know of your concern about the predominance of violence, especially in their programs aimed at children.
8. Encourage adequate financing of the Public Broadcast Corporation to enable it to offer high-quality alternatives to violent programs for children.
9. Limit television viewing time for children to those periods and programs that are most acceptable.
10. Provide a variety of alternatives to television watching for little children, with resources for outdoor and indoor play, with robust and quiet activities, and with suitable equipment and materials.
11. Read to the children for brief intervals from their own books as well as those from the local library (letting the children help in the selection).
12. Watch occasional programs with the children that their questions may be answered as they arise, and so that you as a family can discuss the what and the why of a particular program.

Husbands and wives in families with preschool children have fewer jaunts away from home, and they less often laugh together or join one another in stimulating projects. They seem to have settled into the business of child rearing with fewer negative feelings but have less fun as a married pair than they had earlier in their marriage. They appear to have fallen into the habit of taking for granted their mate's love and companionship, even when they need it most.

The many demands and pressures on each parent tend to leave little time for them to enjoy each other's company and the hobbies or pursuits that may have been initially responsible for drawing them together. The mother may be so concerned with the demands of child care and homemaking that she gives little thought to her need for continuing to develop as a person. The father may be so taken up with his work that he no longer takes time for just enjoying life with his wife.

Yet this is the time when husband and wife must learn to keep their marriage alive and growing. If their relationship is to be enduring and satisfying, it must meet their needs as persons and as a couple. Couples who succeed in this developmental task encourage those individual and joint tastes, interests, and friendships that strengthen their confidence in themselves and in each other.

FAMILY DEVELOPMENTAL TASKS AT THE PRESCHOOL STAGE

While the preschool child is achieving developmental tasks, and the adults are attempting to accomplish theirs as parents and as husband and wife, the family as a whole is also facing the family developmental tasks of the preschool stage (Table 9.6).

Table 9.6 FAMILY DEVELOPMENTAL TASKS AT THE PRESCHOOL STAGE

1. Supplying adequate space, facilities, and equipment for the expanding family.
2. Meeting predictable and unexpected costs of family life with small children.
3. Sharing responsibility for household management and care within the young family.
4. Maintaining mutually satisfying intimate communication in the family.
5. Rearing children already present and planning future family size.
6. Relating to relatives on both sides of the family in creative ways.
7. Tapping resources outside the family in the wider community.
8. Maintaining morale in the face of life's changes and dilemmas.

Supplying Adequate Space, Facilities, and Equipment for the Expanding Family

Throughout the preschool stage a preschooler needs opportunities for large muscle exercise and skill development through climbing, pulling, running, and hauling equipment. This takes him or her out from underfoot and gives parents and younger sibling(s) some relief from such boisterous activity. Readily accessible play facilities, recreation areas, parks, and playgrounds are needed now to provide outlets for family tensions and facilities for the preschooler's development.

Families with preschool children are most likely to move if they can find suitable housing at a price they can afford. Housing costs are by far the most important consideration at the preschool stage of the family life cycle (McAuley & Nutty 1982, 306–308). Inner-city families often feel hemmed in by physical and social barriers, which limit the full expression of their children and make for varied family problems; so a move to a suburb may be considered at this stage of the family life cycle.

A forced-choice interview study of a random sample of 454 residents in a Milwaukee suburb, one-half of whom had children under 6 years of age, found a great majority of the parents generally satisfied with their housing, the quality and cost of their health care, and their recreational facilities. Less than 10 percent of these families expressed dissatisfaction with any aspect of their family environment (Chilman 1980, 339–343). Families with young children in small towns or rural areas have space for preschoolers' play, room for pets, and freedom from the neighborhood pressures so much more prevalent in metropolitan communities. But even in a small apartment on a busy city street, a family can find, at modest cost, ways of providing the space they need in nearby parks, playgrounds, preschool facilities, and community resources.

Meeting Predictable and Unexpected Costs of Family Life with Small Children

The preschool stage is notorious for its unpredictability. The family may be getting along fine, with income matching expenses, when suddenly something happens that throws the whole financial picture out of focus. In early childhood there are a multiplicity of minor illnesses, any one of which can upset the family budget temporarily. As the older child ranges further afield in the neighborhood—to nursery school, kindergarten, play lot, park, and beach—contact is made with many more children. These increased contacts multiply *exposure to infections,* so that childhood diseases are common for the preschooler and quite often for siblings as well. Accidents add the factor of suddenness to the possibility of hospitalization and the high costs of medical care. Unemployment of the breadwinner throws a family into a reassessment of its resources. The response in many a family is the mother's employment.

Mothers work in most families with preschool children. At the 1980 White House Conference on Families, two changes affecting families were highlighted: "dramatic increases of working married women with preschool children" and "growing numbers of female-headed households" (White House Conference on Families 1980, 161). Within one recent decade there was nearly a 50 percent increase in the labor force participation of married women living with their husbands whose children were under 6 years of age: from 30.3 percent in 1970 to 45 percent in 1980. By 1980, 68 percent of the nation's divorced women with children under 6 were working, and 13 percent more were listed as unemployed (U.S. Bureau of the Census 1981, 388). Black mothers of children under 5 are younger, less likely to be married and living with their husbands, and more apt to be disadvantaged both in education and income level (Powers & Salvo 1982, 24).

Part-time employment may be more compatible with motherhood than a full-time job. The combination of full-time employment and the care of young children is more burdensome than many a mother finds comfortable; so if she can find a part-time position, she is apt to take it (Thomson 1980). Sometimes it is possible for a mother to find a job at hours when her husband can be home with their young children. Otherwise, she relies on day-care centers (as 20 percent do), relatives, friends, or private or home-care programs (Sullivan 1981).

Flexible working hours are available in 37 percent of the top 1300 corporations surveyed recently, and a full 73 percent of these large companies favor flexible alternatives to the nine-to-five working day (Klemesrud 1982). Some 17 percent of U.S. companies and 237 government agencies offer flexitime options in which workers can start and finish work at their own discretion (Sullivan 1981, 610–611):

1. Compressing 30 or more hours into a three- or four-day workweek;
2. Working 30 days on and 30 days off;
3. Working six months on and six months off;
4. Participating in job-sharing opportunities;
5. Working at home using telephone lines and home computers; and
6. Having long-distance marriages in two-career families.

Whatever the type of a mother's employment, she still has the responsibility of child care and housework, with what help she can get.

Sharing Responsibility for Child Care and the Household

Daily round-the-clock child care (involving "chasing the children" as they play in the yard and the neighborhood, to supervise properly their play and protect them from danger), attending to the needs of the infant, and doing the housework (marketing, cooking, baking, cleaning, dishwashing, sewing, washing, ironing) are tasks generally assigned the young wife and mother in our society. In former days these many responsibilities were divided among other grown and growing members of the family.

Do fathers of young children really help? Some do and most do not. Men who perceive their role as sole breadwinner are reluctant to acknowledge either that they need help in earning the family income or that they have a responsibility in homemaking (Caplow, Bahr, Chadwick, Hill, & Williamson 1982, 351–352; Lein 1979, 489). Other fathers are actively involved in *role sharing* with their wives, as seen in a study of 31 role-sharing couples who sought practical benefits in sharing their responsibilities (Haas 1980):

1. Four-fifths adopted role sharing so that the wife could work outside the home;
2. Three-fourths wanted to do away with the overload of working mothers' carrying the primary responsibility for housework and child care;
3. One-half adopted role sharing so that the husband would not be more burdened than the wife with the provider role and its concomitant anxiety and stress;
4. One-fourth wanted to avoid economic dependence of the wife; and
5. One-sixth were trying to avoid husband's dependence in cooking, laundry, mending, and so on.

How did their role sharing work out? On the whole, very well. Several couples said that having so much in common caused them to appreciate each other more, gave them opportunities to do things together, and enriched their closeness as a couple. The wives felt they were better mothers because of working and sharing child care with their husbands. They felt less bored, less harassed, and less resentful in shouldering the entire burden of the children. Three out of four felt that the children got to know their father better and that they had more financial security with more income on a permanent basis. Role sharing is not for everyone. It demands wholehearted and enthusiastic willingness of both husband and wife to make a go of it. Husbands generally felt that their wives were too finicky, and wives that their husbands were too sloppy, in doing household chores. Certain strategies helped: cutting down on housework, maintaining a daily schedule so that things would not get out of hand, and setting priorities of what had to be done (Haas 1980).

Preschoolers' work in the family should not be dismissed for two reasons: (1) little children love to feel that they are participating as real members of the family, and (2) they can be a real help not only now but over the years. It is easy for a busy parent to brush aside little ones who crowd close with a "Run along now, can't you see I'm busy?" But by spending a few moments to demonstrate some simple chore, letting the youngster assist, a child can take over such tasks as setting the table, clearing the table after a meal, washing and wiping dishes, filling the dishwasher, dusting, folding clothes, putting toys and clothes away, straightening the family room, and even running the vacuum cleaner as he or she gets bigger. Such chores learned early when motivation is high continue on as part of the family pattern.

A survey of a random sample of 790 Nebraska parents found children's work ubiquitous in their families. Children began having regular chores very early and were assigned more extensive work as they got older. The overwhelming majority of these parents (80.5 percent of those with children under 5), gave developmental reasons for children's work in the family, such as: (1) doing chores develops responsibility and helps children learn. Other less frequent parental responses were: (2) reciprocal obligations ("They live here, don't they?"), (3) extrinsic (parents need help), (4) task learning, and (5) residual (the child has to earn an allowance, or needs something to do). Clearly, most parents assign their children chores as a means of building character (White & Brinkerhoff 1981, 793, 797).

There comes a time when older children start meal preparation in anticipation of their parents' return at the end of the day and find satisfaction in knowing they are competent and appreciated members of the family team. A fringe benefit of working together in the family is the chance it provides for mutual interaction and discussion. Success in achieving this developmental task is not just a matter of how much or how little there is to be done but rather of how decisions are made, how roles are assigned, and how the several family members feel about their responsibilities. If each family member feels pride and pleasure in doing tasks, if each is accountable to the others for common concerns, if each feels needed and appreciated, the family is finding happiness and achieving integration as a working unit.

Maintaining Mutually Satisfying Intimate Communication

Finding the time, privacy, and energy for tender, close relationships as a married couple may be difficult when children are young. Sharing bed or room with a child old enough to be aware of what is going on robs a husband and wife of much-needed privacy. Days and nights of nursing a sick youngster rob even the most loving husband and wife of their ardor for each other. Just getting through the day's work may bring the couple to bed too tired for anything but sleep. Knowing from experience the power of their fertility tends to make the woman wary of her husband's approaches unless she has confidence in their family planning procedures. What once was entered into with joyous abandon now may become a marital duty unless the couple provides for their sex life together amid the welter of other demands.

Wives whose husbands frequently communicate with them are more likely to be satisfied with their marriage. But the man who has had to talk all day on his job may want nothing more when he gets home than a little peace and quiet. This is especially so when he interprets his wife's conversation as belittling, ridiculing, embarrassing, or domineering (Nye 1982, 227–229). When he senses that her attitude affirms both him and their marriage, he is encouraged to tell her what is bothering him.

When each marital partner is available to the other with warmth and openness, they can communicate either with or without words. If the husband is too tired to talk at length when he returns from work, his wife can accept his fatigue with empathy, get food on the table, and await his readiness for conversation with understanding. If she wants to relax at the end of a busy day, he can indulge her need for a quiet hour to herself with any number of little acts of thoughtfulness that help her feel loved and cared for. Then, when they want to get away for a while together, they are ready for the hearty togetherness that shared activities can bring.

Joint recreation gives the young couple a chance to get through to one another in a spirit of fun; and it is positively related to marital stability (Nye 1982, 237–238). Each may encourage the other to relax in mutually enjoyable activities at this stage of their lives when marital communication is so crucial.

Sex questions of preschoolers openly discussed by comfortable parents go a long way in keeping communication open between parents and their young children. This is the age when children are eager to learn about themselves—why they differ from members of the other sex, and from their parents, and what these differences mean for their lives now and later. It is not enough to tell children they will understand when they grow up. They want to know *now.* Parents who find it hard to give simple, honest responses to their children's questions may find help in their local library, child study association, parent education group, or family guidance center. For their sake as well as for their ongoing relationships with their children, few things are more worth the effort. *Sex education* is already under way in the way parents bathe and diaper the baby, avoid or answer the preschooler's questions, teach correct names for body parts and functions, handle sex play, and express their love for one another. Experts advise parents to be free and comfortable about sex without being either aggressive or entirely uninhibited about it (Masters & Johnson 1975, 68). This expanding stage of the family life cycle is so full of new experiences, feelings, and decisions that keeping communication lines open in the family is extremely important.

Rearing Children Already Present and Planning Future Family Size

Child rearing during the preschool stage is one of the family's most urgent developmental tasks. This is the time in children's lives when they are forming basic attitudes toward themselves, their family, and their world. They need sound knowledge and wholesome attitudes as firm foundations for their future development. They identify with their parents, who serve as all-important models of how to live. Problems in child rearing surface daily, taxing parents' ingenuity and forcing them to examine the values they profess to hold. For instance, does physical punishment teach a child that it is all right to hit another person? Or, when a parent is too indulgent with a child, is the child learning to be exploitive of others? The answers to both of these questions may be yes.

Physical punishment as a technique in child rearing has been researched for decades. Years ago, intensive interviews with 379 American mothers on how they were bringing up their children from birth to kindergarten age concluded that *punitiveness* (in contrast to *positive reinforcement*) is ineffectual and that harsh physical punishment is associated with high childhood aggression (Sears, Maccoby, & Levin 1957, 484). In both nursery school and kindergarten children, a positive relationship has been found between physical punishment and children's aggression (Steinmetz 1979, 407–408).

The *social class* of a family influences its child-rearing methods. Blue-collar parents more often than white-collar parents use physical punishment in getting their children to conform and obey. In general, the higher the social class, the greater the parents' emphasis on guiding children toward self-discipline. An in-depth review of research finds that parents reinforce behavior they have found useful. Middle-class parents value self-direction and self-control, so they tend to rear their children to be *self-directing* (Gecas 1979, 369–393; Nye 1982, 251–252).

Minority children who encounter racial and ethnic insults outside their homes need to know that such attacks are more demeaning to those who denigrate them than to those insulted. Such children can be assured that while fighting for a cause of justice is praiseworthy, a person's inner controls are indispensable. This is especially relevant for those cultural groups living in hostile environments (Comer & Poussaint 1975).

Overly indulged children tend to be spoiled brats as youngsters and demanding tyrants as they grow older. Parents who are too permissive with their preschoolers tend to rear children who become impatient as they approach problems. They develop aggressive and demanding ways and find it hard to accept frustrations (Baumrind 1971). The dilemma parents face is avoiding the extremes of harsh punishment, on the one hand, and overindulgence, on the other.

Typically, a new baby enters the family circle while the first child is a preschooler. While the parents make way for the little newcomer, they do what they can to safeguard the security of their firstborn. The older child sometimes lets parents know of a need to be babied, too, in *regressive behavior:* wetting when he or she has long since learned to be dry, wanting to take milk from a bottle when he or she has already learned to drink from a cup, wanting to be cuddled the way the baby is, even trying to put himself or herself in the baby's place —literally in the infant carriage or crib. These are signals a sensitive parent sees as indications that the older child needs closer demonstrable affection than he or she may have been getting.

Wise parents devote some special time to their preschool children when the new baby cannot intrude. It sometimes helps to let the older child know that because he or she is older, he or she occupies a special place in the family no younger one can ever fill. Giving special responsibilities to the elder child may be reassuring at this time. Before the baby ever arrives, the firstborn can be helped to understand that this is to be *his* or *her* baby as well as the parents' and that he or she will be loved as much as ever after the little new one comes. Thus any incipient jealousy and *sibling rivalry* may be reduced somewhat.

Exceptional children present special problems. In one recent year there were nearly 3 million youngsters receiving special help for handicaps such as—in rank order of their numbers—learning disabled, speech impaired, mentally retarded, emotionally disturbed, multihandicapped, orthopedically impaired, hearing impaired, deaf, and visually handicapped (U.S. Bureau of the Census 1981, 141). Families first face the shock of having an exceptional child and then the long process of getting the handicap evaluated, alleviated, or provided the particular training or education that will help the children make maximum use of their abilities.

By the time an American mother is 29, typically, her last child has been born (Table 2.1). Some 12 percent of America's families go on to have more children (U.S. Bureau of the Census 1981, 46). Most Americans barely replace themselves in the population. A mother of 29 has about two more decades in which she could bear another 10 or more children unless plans are laid as to when the desired family size has been reached and how best to limit it. A *reconstituted family* has joined parents from former unions with their children into a new family unit. This reconstituted family may be larger than either of the original units since the parents may conceive offspring in addition to those they have by their former marriages.

Family planning resources are widely available in most communities through private physicians, hospitals, and *planned parenthood* clinics. In most instances, procedures for limiting family size are discussed with one or both parents, and the method of choice is implemented, with possibilities for its future evaluation and alteration as situations change.

Relating to Relatives on Both Sides of the Family

Relatives are a haven for many a family when the breadwinner is laid off from his job. The young family moves in with, or close to, their kinsfolk, where father, and perhaps mother, too, looks for work while relatives look out for the family. This is especially true of blue-collar families. White-collar workers tend to get a job before the family moves, and they are less apt to relocate near their relatives (Nye 1982, 239).

Most Middletown III families receive help from their parents in the form of: gifts, advice on a decision, help with a childbirth or other special occasion, assistance with child care, and financial help. Most of them pay weekly visits to their parents, who live within a radius of 50 miles, and the majority telephone their children's grandparents once a month or more (Caplow et al. 1982, 383). Grown children express affection for their parents throughout their lives; they see more of their closest kin than of their closest friends, and they do more with them (Caplow et al. 1982, 222–223). So, too, with families (one-half of whom had children under 6) in the Milwaukee area, who were found to maintain regular contacts with their parents, with a full 70 percent reporting parental assistance from time to time (Chilman 1980, 343).

Grandparents can do much to ease the pressures on the parents while children are young. A loving relative who is on hand while the new baby is coming and through the illnesses and accidents that occasionally hit the young family cushions these crises in many a home. An aunt and uncle may get valuable experience at the same time that they relieve the young parents of their child-care responsibilities. They may take over for a long evening, for a weekend, or even for a week or two while father and mother slip off to regain their perspective as a couple on a brief vacation, on a business trip, or on a brief visit to old friends.

Problems come up, of course, when the substitute parents do not agree with the child guidance procedures or philosophy that the parents are trying to practice. A grandmother can "spoil" her young charges, so that it may take weeks to rehabilitate them, if she is not aware of the parents' goals for their children. Or a too-rigid program of discipline suddenly imposed by some well-meaning aunt or uncle may boomerang in any number of ways. These things are being openly discussed in many families today. Thus the parents can give an explicit briefing to any child-serving relative on what is the usual practice and why; what the child is and is not customarily allowed to do and why; what routines are followed most conscientiously; and which of these can be allowed to slide when the situation warrants.

Children are remarkably resilient creatures and can take a great deal of inconsistency from the various adults that attend them as long as they feel basically secure. Few children can be severely damaged by occasional lapses or changes of pace. Extremists who insist that grandparents are bad for children fail to see how much a child can learn from being handled differently by different persons; or how much a youngster benefits from the sense of ongoing family relations as he or she begs the grandparents for tales of when his or her mother or father was young. One 9-year-old puts both values neatly when he says solemnly, "I like to go to Grandma's house, because she scolds so soft, and she tells me all about the olden days when Daddy was a little boy just like me."

Tapping Resources Outside the Family

One hazard faced by the family with little children is preoccupation with itself. The young father puts in a full day on his job, then rushes to night school or union meeting to better his chances for advancement, helping out at home as he can. The young mother is tied down with little children so much day after day that she may long for adult companionship and stimulation unless she, too, has a job with its outside contacts. Working mothers have fewer children than do full-time housewives, and 90 percent of employed mothers have regular child-care arrangements and share the responsibility for child rearing with others (Powers & Salvo 1982, 24, 30). Thus we see that a mother's employment taps resources within the larger community both for herself and for her children.

The preschool child leads the family out into wider horizons—going to day-care centers, nursery school, and then kindergarten; bringing home new experiences and friends; and taking parents out to neighborhood projects and community affairs. Now the preschooler is big enough to go to church school, and this youngster often starts the family in church activities that carry through the years. Periodic trips to family physician or pediatrician for preventive shots and checkups, as well as for treatment of the various illnesses and accidents he or she may have, bring both the youngster and the parents into relationships with the health facilities of the community. Trips to the park, the playground, the zoo, and the library sometimes get the whole family out for jaunts into activities and facilities never before explored. Although many of these resources are available to everyone, less-privileged families tend to use them less than do those with more education and incomes.

Some financial resources are available for low-income families, for one-parent households, and for families whose adults are disabled or otherwise unemployed. Local, state, and federal programs are designed to assist in rearing children whose parents are not able for any reason to care for them properly. The family must apply for programs for which it is eligible; this involves knowing where to apply, for what, and how—a task not easily undertaken by parents with little experience with such programs. Second- and third-generation welfare families know their way around bureaucratic rules and regulations as few newly impoverished parents do. Until they learn, they tend to rely on what help their relatives can give them, or they "make do" with what they have.

Maintaining Morale in the Face of Life's Dilemmas

Preschool children bring their parents a great deal of pleasure. A cross-national study of 1569 young wives and a subsample of their husbands, interviewed by the staff of the Institute for Social Research, were asked the question, "What age child provides the most happiness?" Fully two-thirds of the men and women with more than 12 years of education, with preschool children, responded that their greatest happiness was found when children were under 5 years of age. Men more than women (20 percent versus 8.9 percent) found pleasure in school-age children; and from then on but small percentages expected to find happiness in adolescents and young adult children (Hoffman & Manis 1978, 197). When asked what values in life were most important, these respondents said "Having a happy family" in larger percentages than any other value, with "Being close to spouse" ranking second (Hoffman & Manis 1978, 179). With such evidence of satisfaction at this stage of the family life cycle, maintaining morale would seem not to be too difficult—until one considers the problems of wrestling with the inevitable dilemmas at this stage of life.

Dilemmas (Kirkpatrick 1963, 90–95) in the family with preschool children are:

1. Freedom versus order and efficiency,
2. Free expression of personal potentials versus stable goal expectations,
3. Personal self-expression versus child rearing,
4. Work achievement versus love and reproductive functions,
5. Flexible training versus rigid child rearing,
6. High aspiration levels for children versus realistic expectations,
7. Family loyalty versus community loyalty, and
8. Extensive casual association versus restrictive intensive association.

The horns of each dilemma have their values and their cost. For instance, freedom is greatly to be desired, but its price is conflict, confusion, and a certain amount of chaos in the family. Order and efficiency are worthwhile values, but their cost is personal frustration and submission to rules and routines. And so it goes for each of the others of life's dilemmas.

Every family must work out, in ways that make sense to its members and to itself as a unit, those answers to the eternal questions of life that suit them and their situations.

Aspirations and the drive for future security may rob a family of time together that will never come again in just the same way. This is particularly true of the aspiring young father who, driven through his twenties and thirties to establish himself vocationally and to keep his family afloat financially, pushes himself so hard that he has little time for his personal interests or for enjoying his young family as he might. The young wife and mother, in her eagerness to develop herself, and to give her family what her earnings will buy, may sacrifice time with her husband and children by her ambitions to further her education and to keep employed. These tend to be problems of the *upward-mobile* lower- and middle-class adults who want their children to have better lives than they have had.

In the last analysis family morale may be a matter of realistic expectations of oneself and other family members. The perfectionist parent who is never satisfied and the spouse who is hard to please make life miserable for themselves and their loved ones. Developmental tasks are demanding—that is true—but in striving to succeed in them, parents can enjoy their children as they are, and husbands and wives can take pleasure in just being together. In their enjoyment of one another, family morale is ensured, and their many developmental tasks are accomplished more easily.

SUMMARY

Families with preschool children have a firstborn under 6 years of age and possibly a second and third infant. Preschoolers develop according to predictable principles of child development, each in his or her own way. Genetic, congenital, and acquired characteristics account for individual differences in the way preschool children accomplish their developmental tasks. Preschooling helps a child develop toward becoming a competent 6-year-old.

Rearing children without a partner is the experience of 14 percent of white mothers and 53 percent of the black. Fully 60 percent of these lone mothers work, using what supplemental child care they can tap. Television is a mixed blessing; so parents find ways of guiding their children's viewing. The twin developmental tasks of married parents are (1) giving their children the stimulation and affection they need and (2) keeping their marriage alive and growing.

Family developmental tasks at the preschool stage are urgent and remarkably predictable. There are needs for space for the expanding family, and income for its costs. Most mothers of preschool children work full-time or part-time, sometimes with flexible working hours.

Whether or not the mother works, she still has major responsibility for the care of her child(ren) and the household. Some husbands and wives engage in role sharing. Little children feel important as family members when they are encouraged to assume some responsibility for themselves and the family.

Communication is enhanced by joint recreation for the parents and an open response to children's urgent questions. Patterns of child rearing vary by social class and by individual parents, from rigid rules and punishment for their infraction to overindulgence; neither extreme is effectual. Sibling rivalry can be reduced by sensitive parents who prepare their firstborn for an expected baby and give the older child the attention and affection he or she needs.

Unless a couple want many children, they engage in family planning. Relatives are a source of satisfaction, assistance, and differing child-rearing methods. Resources in the community can be tapped for enrichment as well as for basic support when needed.

Preschool children bring their parents pleasure—along with a number of dilemmas. Family members' morale is dependent upon realistic expectations and upon their mutual enjoyment of one another as persons.

REFERENCES

Alper, M. 1982. All our children can learn. *University of Chicago Magazine* 74:30.

Baumrind, D. 1971. Current patterns of prenatal authority. *Developmental Psychology* 4:1–103.

Bijou, S. W. 1975. Development in the preschool years. *American Psychologist* 30:829–837.

Bloom, B. S. 1964. *Stability and change in human characteristics.* New York: Wiley.

———. 1965. Early learning in the home. First B. J. Paley lecture. University of California at Los Angeles, July 15, 1965. Mimeographed.

Caplow, T., Bahr, H. M., Chadwick, B. A., Hill, R., & Williamson, M. H. 1982. *Middletown families: Fifty years of change and continuity.* Minneapolis: University of Minnesota Press.

Chilman, C. S. 1980. Parent satisfactions, concerns, and goals for their children. *Family Relations* 29:339–345.

Comer, J. P., & Poussaint, A. F. 1975. Interview with Richard Flaste, "Childbearing from a black viewpoint," New York *Times* May 30, 1975, p. 36-C.

Connell, C. 1982. U.S. study concludes TV violence influences youth. *AP* release, May 6, 1982.

Gecas, V. 1979. The influence of social class on socialization. In *Contemporary theories about the family,* W. R. Burr, ed. R. Hill, F. I. Nye, & I. L. Reiss, pp. 365–404. Vol. 1. New York: Free Press.

Glick, P. C. 1981. Children from one-parent families: Recent data and projections. Paper presented at the Special Institute on Critical Issues in Education, sponsored by the Charles F. Kettering Foundation and held at the American University in Washington, D.C., June 22, 1982. Manuscript, p. 16.

Haas, L. 1980. Role-sharing couples: A study of egalitarian marriages. *Family Relations* 29:289–296.

Hoffman, L. W., & Manis, J. D. 1978. Influences of children on marital interaction and prenatal satisfaction and dissatisfactions. In *Child influences on marital and family interaction: A life-span perspective,* ed. R. M. Lerner & G. B. Spanier, pp. 165–213. New York: Academic Press.

Kirkpatrick, C. 1963. *The family as process and institution.* 2d ed. New York: Ronald Press.

Klemesrud, J. 1982. Two-career couples: Employers listening. New York *Times,* as reported in *Family Therapy News,* May, pp. 4, 11.

Lein, L. 1979. Male participation in home life: Impact of social supports and breadwinner responsibility on the allocation of tasks. *Family Coordinator* 28:489–495.

McAuley, W. J., & Nutty, C. L. 1982. Residential preferences and moving behavior: A family life-cycle analysis. *Journal of Marriage and the Family* 44:301–309.

Masters, W. H., & Johnson, V. E. 1975. Teaching your children about sex. *Redbook,* September, pp. 68–71.

Metropolitan Life Insurance Company. 1979. Characteristics of children under 14, United States. *Statistical Bulletin* 60:15.

Nye, F. I. 1982. Propositions and hypotheses from the theory. In *Family relationships: Rewards and costs,* ed. F. I. Nye, pp. 205–258. Beverly Hills, CA: Sage.

Powers, M. G., & Salvo, J. J. 1982. Fertility and child care arrangements as mechanisms of status articulation. *Journal of Marriage and the Family* 44:21–34.

Sears, R. R., Maccoby, E. E., & Levin, H. 1957. *Patterns of child rearing.* Evanston, IL: Row, Peterson.

Steinmetz, S. K. 1979. Disciplinary techniques and their relationship to aggressiveness, dependency, and conscience. In *Contemporary theories about the family,* ed. W. R. Burr, R. Hill, F. I. Nye, & I. L. Reiss, pp. 405–438. Vol. 1. New York: Free Press.

Sullivan, J. 1981. Family support systems paychecks can't buy. *Family Relations* 30:607–613.

Thomson, E. 1980. The value of employment to mothers of young children. *Journal of Marriage and the Family* 42:551–566.

U.S. Bureau of the Census. 1981. *Statistical Abstract of the United States: 1981.* 102d ed. Washington, D.C.: Government Printing Office.

White, B. L., & Yahraes, H. 1979. Developing a sense of competence in young children. In *Families today: A research sampler on families and children.* National Institute of Mental Health Science Monographs. Washington, D.C.: U.S. Government Printing Office.

White House Conference on Families. 1980. *Listening to America's families.* The report to the president, Congress, and the nation. Washington D.C.

White, L. K., & Brinkerhoff, D. B. 1981. Children's work in the family: Its significance and meaning. *Journal of Marriage and the Family* 43:789–798.

Chapter 10

Families with Schoolchildren

MAJOR CONCEPTS

Piaget's "concrete operations"
Gender roles
Stage-sensitive developmental tasks
High-stress neighborhoods
Low-stress neighborhoods
Child abuse
Incest
Constant dollars
Dual-career families
Combining work and family roles
  Split shifts
  The "latchkey child"
  Conjugal options
  Task sharing
  Role sharing
"Best friends"
Parental sex education
Negative feelings
Sibling birth order
  Firstborn

Middleborn
Lastborn
Sibling coalitions
Sibling services
Types of parenting
  Authoritarian parents
  Egalitarian parents
  Traditional child rearing
  Developmental child rearing
Control attempts
  Coercion
  Induction
  Love withdrawal
Parental support
One-parent families
Reconstituted family relationships
Mastery learning
Factors in learning ability
Peer pressures
Stages in moral development

210

When the first child goes to school, at about 6 years of age, the family enters a new stage of its life cycle. This stage, which is characterized by the presence of school-age children, continues until the child becomes a teenager at 13. Before the end of this period, it is likely that the family will have seen the birth of younger siblings and that it will have reached its maximum size in number of members and number of interrelationships. Typically, the American family at this stage consists of 4 to 5 persons, who maintain from 6 to 10 interpersonal relationships. The range in age is from infancy (youngest child) through plus or minus 40 (father). The eldest child is a school-ager. The parents' crisis continues to be that of self-absorption versus finding fulfillment in rearing the next generation. The school-age child's developmental crisis is risking a sense of inferiority as he or she develops the capacity of work enjoyment (industry). The family developmental tasks revolve around the major goal of reorganization to make way for the expanding world of school-agers.

These are busy, full years of family living. Children are running in and out of the house; many projects are under way; and the adults are busy keeping the household in running order and following their youngsters out into wider contacts in the larger community. Concurrently, school-agers, younger siblings, parents, and the family as a unit work at their developmental tasks—sometimes in harmony, sometimes in discord, but always with the urgency that accompanies growth.

DEVELOPMENT OF SCHOOL-AGE CHILDREN

Elementary schoolchildren differ considerably within a wide range of normal physical, mental, and social development. They enter school as little children and emerge seven years later in various stages of puberty. Growth in height is steady until the years between 9 and 12, when early developing youngsters, especially girls, grow taller owing to the pubertal growth spurt. Weight increases gradually, and more mature distribution of fat occurs in most children. Appetite varies from poor to ravenous, and digestion is generally good. Bladder control is established, with only infrequent lapses. Bone replaces cartilage in the skeleton, and permanent teeth come in as baby teeth are lost. Muscular strength and skills increase, bringing a sense of mastery to many children. The school years are a vigorous, healthy period for most children.

Intellectually, schoolchildren are involved in what Piaget has called *concrete operations*. Children develop concepts (mental tools making sense of a multitude of particulars) through ordering and classifying objects and ideas. This includes collecting and arranging things, learning to read, playing with words and their meanings, and enjoying riddles, jokes, and jingles. They begin to see order in the universe through their study of mathematics and science, to know where places are through geography, and to understand the sequence of events through history. Everything they learn later in school is largely determined by what has been learned by the end of the third grade, and by the time they reach the eighth grade, they will have completed 75 percent of their development of general learning (Bloom 1964, 110).

Appropriate gender roles are quickly learned in the early grade school years (Baldigo 1975, 38). Children soon find out what they may do as boys, as girls, or as members of either sex. In recent decades increasing flexibility in gender roles within the larger culture makes it possible for members of one sex to engage in activities once assigned only to the other. Occasionally, adults holding more traditional gender-role opinions confuse children by denial of behavior freely allowed elsewhere.

Most fifth graders are found to believe that either sex may become doctors, lawyers, or college professors, but 54 percent of the children studied asign nursing to women only (Hammel 1975). Children of working mothers are found to have more flexible sex roles than children of full-time housewives (Etaugh 1974). In general, older children have less flexible gender roles than do younger children (Baldigo 1975, 38).

Playmates and schoolmates become increasingly important to children throughout the school years. Peers play and work together, share confidences, give or withhold approval, and compete in games, sports, and school activities. Both boys and girls have friends of both sexes, and most of them acknowledge having sweethearts while in elementary school (Lewis 1960; Broderick and Fowler 1961). During the school years children move forward in many areas of their lives, as reflected in the age-specific developmental tasks listed in Table 10.1, p. 214.

Success depends on the opportunities available for development in the home, in the school, and in community life. It depends in large measure on how skilled parents and teachers are in anticipating and recognizing the child's developmental tasks as they come along and in providing growth opportunities at crucial times. But children differ widely, as do parents. And while children are struggling through their growth stages, the parents, too, are hard at work on their developmental tasks.

DEVELOPMENTAL TASKS OF SCHOOLCHILDREN'S PARENTS

Parents know full well that they are needed throughout the bustling years of the school-age period. But, on the whole, this is a less hectic time, since household routines have become established and the children are growing at a less rapid rate than they did as infants or preschoolers. School-age children are generally satisfied with their relationships with their parents and are involved to a considerable degree in family activities.

Encouraging Children's Growth

Encouraging children's growth involves letting them go. As the school years progress, there are longer and longer absences from home. The children are away from home throughout the school hours, which often include the lunch period as well as morning and afternoon sessions. If he or she is getting normally involved in sports, clubs, and friendship groups, the after-school hours are increasingly given to these interests; so the youngster comes home tired and bedraggled just in time for the evening meal. There are frequent requests to spend the evening at someone else's home and occasions when spending the night with a close buddy is terribly important. Soon there are weekend trips with Scouts or other youth groups, and then come the longer periods during summer vacation when children of school age are off to camp or visiting relatives for weeks at a time. All this is good for the child—developing independence, widening social experience, and generally contributing to personality growth.

As children become increasingly involved with friends their own age, their orientation tends increasingly toward their peers. Parents should encourage these associations, because research shows that children who are well-adjusted family members tend to retain family identifications, norms, and values even while associating with others (Bowerman & Kinch 1959). Mothers with emotionally satisfying friendships may find it easier to let their children go. Unfortunately, however, mothers old enough to have school-age children may have fewer close friends than do younger and older wives (Williams 1958).

School-agers often quote other adults as authority figures. A secure parent can take children's "But the teacher says so" as an indication that the youngsters are venturing away from home intellectually as well as physically. They are finding new models, new attitudes, and new viewpoints to explore beyond the immediate family. Parents who can empathize with their children's interests and who can loosen the apron strings at this point have less difficulty untying them in another few years, when the youngsters become teenagers.

Parents who cultivate interests beyond their children probably have less difficulty letting them go than do those who devote their lives to their children. Husbands and wives with school-age children work together on projects more often than do those at either the preschool or the teenage stage of the family life cycle (Feldman, 1961). Now, too, entertaining others in the home and going as a family to company picnics and social affairs with work associates are at an all-time high (Blood & Wolfe 1960, 158–159). Such activities shared with the children (as part of an overall parental stance of involvement in whole-family pursuits) may develop into continuing interests for the married pair as a couple.

Safeguarding the Marriage Relationship

Children are hard on marriage, a large body of accumulating evidence concludes. Perfectly normal, average youngsters adversely affect the quality of marriage, both in the population as a whole and in several large subpopulations that have been studied (Glenn & McLanahan 1982). Data from the National Opinion Research Center indicate that the negative effects of children on marriage are pervasive among husbands and wives of all races, major religious preferences, educational levels, and employment status (Davis 1978). Six national surveys conducted from 1973 through 1978 find that children tend to reduce their parents' happiness as long as they remain at home. How? Children in the family:

1. Interfere with marital companionship;
2. Lessen spontaneity of sexual relations between husband and wife;

Table 10.1   DEVELOPMENTAL TASKS OF SCHOOL-AGE CHILDREN

1. *Learning the basic skills required of schoolchildren:*
   Mastering the fundamentals of reading, writing, calculating, and the scientific, rational approach to solving problems.
   Extending understanding of cause-and-effect relationships.
   Developing concepts essential for everyday living.
   Continuing to develop the ability to reason and to do reflective thinking.

2. *Mastering the physical skills appropriate to their development:*
   Learning the games, the sports, and the various roles in activities pursued by children of their age and sex in the community (ride a bike, swim, skate, play ball, row a boat, climb a tree, etc.).
   Developing abilities needed in personal and family living (bathe and dress themselves, care for their clothing, make beds, cook and serve food, clean up after activities, maintain and repair simple household equipment, etc.).

3. *Developing a practical understanding of the use of money:*
   Finding socially acceptable ways of getting money for what they want to buy.
   Learning how to buy wisely the things they most want with what they have, and to stay within their available resources.
   Learning the value of saving for postponed satisfactions.
   Reconciling differences between their wants and resources and accepting the fact that others may be poorer or richer than they are.
   Acquiring a basic grasp of the nature and function of money in everyday life in the family and in the larger community.

4. *Becoming active, cooperative members of the family:*
   Gaining skill in participating in family discussions and decision making.
   Assuming responsibilities within the household and finding satisfaction in accomplishment and belonging.
   Becoming more mature in giving and receiving affection and gifts—between themselves and their parents, their siblings, and their relatives within the extended family.
   Learning to enjoy the full resources and facilities available within the family and to take the initiative in enriching them as they become able.

5. *Extending their abilities to relate effectively to others, both peers and adults:*
   Making progress in their ability to adjust to others.

   3. Increase potential for jealousy and competition for affection, time and attention; and
   4. Keep unhappy couples from divorcing—at least for a time (Glenn & McLanahan 1982, 69–72).

   Marriage problems of parents with school-age children are more numerous and more severe than at any other time since the pair began having children. Indeed, married couples with school-agers have four times more problems than marriages at the empty nest stage of the family life cycle, as we see in the last column of Table 10.2, p. 216. The largest number of marriage problems while school-age children are in the home concern child rearing, with expression of affection ranking second in frequency (Swensen & Moore 1979). One wonders whether it is conflict over policies and philosophies of raising their children that reduces essential expressions of affection between husbands and wives.

   Marital love expression declines throughout marriage, according to research of five different samples of married couples. This is especially true of couples with stereotyped role expectations whose relationships become matters of habit rather than of vitality over the

Table 10.1 *(Continued)*

Learning to stand up for their rights.

Improving their abilities both to lead and to follow others.

Meeting basic social expectations—learning simple conventions, rules, customs, courtesies, and standards of family and groups.

Learning genuinely cooperative roles with others in many situations.

Making and keeping close friends.

6. *Continuing the learning involved in handling their feelings and impulses:*

Growing in their ability to cope with simple frustrations.

Exploring socially acceptable ways of releasing negative emotions effectively.

Becoming more mature in expressing feelings in ways and at times and places appropriate within the culture.

Gaining skill in sharing their feelings with those who can help (parents, teachers, close friends, scout leaders, etc.).

7. *Coming to terms with his or her own sex role, both now and as it will become:*

Learning what is expected as appropriate behavior for boys, for girls, for men, for women, for married people, for parents, and for other adults.

Clarifying knowledge about the nature of sex and reproduction.

Adjusting to a changing body in the pubertal growth spurt as teen years approach (accepting the new size and form, function and potentials of pubertal growth).

Thinking ahead wholesomely to what it will be like to be grown up as a man or woman.

8. *Continuing to find themselves as worthy persons:*

Identifying with their own age and sex in appropriate ways.

Discovering many ways of becoming acceptable as a person; gaining status.

Growing in self-confidence, self-respect, self-control, and self-realization.

Extending the process of establishing their own individuality.

9. *Developing a conscience with inner moral controls:*

Distinguishing right from wrong in a variety of situations.

Learning that rules are necessary in any social enterprise.

Developing the ego strength for principled moral behavior.

Trying to live according to appropriate social and moral values.

Source: Adapted from R. J. Havighurst, *Developmental Tasks and Education,* 3d ed. (New York: McKay, 1972), 29–30.

years. Couples who transcend *traditional role expectations* develop marital interaction based on the reality of their needs, feelings, wishes, and expectations of one another. These married pairs are more capable of coping with conflict through discussion rather than avoidance, expressing their love spontaneously in a marriage that becomes more vital over the years (Swensen, Eskew, & Kohlhepp 1981).

Safeguarding marriage through the school-age stage is accomplished by putting one's spouse ahead of the children at times, with the realization that marital happiness is important not only for the husband and wife but for their children as well. Besides, the youngsters will leave, whereas the marriage continues on.

FAMILY DEVELOPMENTAL TASKS AT THE SCHOOL-AGE STAGE

To reiterate from Chapter 3, there are basic family tasks that must be accomplished throughout the family life cycle if it is to continue and survive. At each stage within the family career, there are *stage-sensitive developmental tasks* that are especially crucial at that time. Stage-

Table 10.2 FREQUENCY OF MOST SEVERE PROBLEM IN MARRIAGE BY STAGE OF MARRIAGE AND TYPE OF PROBLEM

Stage of marriage	Marriage Problems						Total
	Problem solving	Child rearing	Relatives and in-laws	Personal care	Money management	Expression of affection	
I. Beginning families	15	5	28	6	29	27	110
II. Childbearing families	9	11	3	4	4	13	44
III. Preschool children	7	19	5	3	8	12	54
IV. School-age children	8	19	11	6	4	13	61
V. Teenagers	5	9	2	7	4	13	40
VI. Launching center	1	8	0	2	6	6	23
VII. Empty nest	2	0	4	1	0	8	15
VIII. Retirement	4	0	0	3	0	0	7
IX. Throughout marriage	14	1	8	3	9	16	51
Total	65	72	61	35	64	108	405

Source: Clifford H. Swensen and Charlotte Dickinson Moore, "Marriages that Endure," in *Families Today: A Research Sampler on Families and Children*, vol. 1., National Institute of Mental Health Science Monographs (Washington, D.C.: Government Printing Office, 1979), p. 272.

sensitive family developmental tasks for families with school-age children are presented in Table 10.3 and discussed in the following sections.

Providing Suitable Housing and Health Care

Providing suitable housing is easier for some families than for others. Families with school-age children look for housing they can afford. They prefer energy-efficient and expandable homes near good schools and job security (McAuley & Nutty 1982). Rich or poor, black or white, families share much the same aspirations and problems; they "are more similar than dissimilar regardless of their neighborhoods or residence, race or economic factors" (Hauenstein & Blehar 1979, 385). Hauenstein came to this conclusion from her study of 508 married women in the Detroit area, half black, half white, half housewives, and half employed outside their homes. She divided her population into *high-stress neighborhoods* characterized by crowded, run-down, inadequate dwellings of families having trouble making ends meet; and *low-stress neighborhoods* containing some of the best housing Detroit had to offer, the most stable families, and the safest streets, as we see in Table 10.4. The point here is that no one *wants* to live in a high-crime area where dangers abound for children and adults alike and where families less often own their own homes, are more often unemployed, and have less stable marriages. They live where they do because that is the best they can find for what they can afford to pay—a fact of socioeconomic status.

A family with young children, more than those at later stages of the family life cycle, want to own their own home (Michelson 1977). But spiraling of home ownership costs is seen in mortgage rates that were three times higher in 1982 (15.43 percent) than they were in 1960 (5.10 percent), according to the Federal Home Loan Bank Board. Even the expense of moving an average family is increasing so rapidly that many families now stay put rather than try to improve their housing (Gage 1982). At a time of high housing costs, few young families can afford to buy a home without the help of their kinfolks. Not surprisingly, it is during the early stages of the family life cycle that young families are most likely to receive extended family support (Kennedy & Stokes 1982). Thus we see that providing suitable housing is a formidable task in today's economy, presenting a challenge to families with school-agers and their kin.

Keeping school-agers healthy requires shots to prevent communicable diseases and care for youngsters who are ill or recovering from accidents. Many school systems require proof of children's immunization before admitting them to school each year. A series for

Table 10.3 FAMILY DEVELOPMENTAL TASKS OF FAMILIES WITH SCHOOL-AGE CHILDREN

1. Providing suitable housing and health care for the family.
2. Meeting family costs and making adjustments when the wife/mother works.
3. Allocating and monitoring responsibilities for maintaining the home.
4. Continuing socialization through wider community participation.
5. Encouraging husband-wife, parent-child, and child-child communication.
6. Rearing children with appropriate parenting skills in two-parent, one-parent, or reconstituted family households.
7. Demonstrating interest in children's schooling and in their acquisition of basic skills and knowledge.
8. Recognizing achievement and worth of individual family members and building solid values and morale in the family.

Table 10.4 SOCIOECONOMIC AND INSTABILITY CHARACTERISTICS OF WOMEN IN FOUR CONTRASTING NEIGHBORHOODS

Variable	Black		White	
	High stress	Low stress	High stress	Low stress
Total dwelling units	4118	1910	4410	1811
Socioeconomic variables	%	%	%	%
Median education (years)	9.6	13.2	9.0	11.7
Percentage unemployed	4.0	0.0	0.0	0.0
Home ownership (percentage)	19.0	92.0	40.0	90.0
Professional/managerial (percentage)	9.0	49.0	7.0	19.0
Instability variables				
Adult crime rate per 10,000	89.0	55.9	60.0	9.9
Juvenile crime rate per 10,000	17.2	6.4	13.5	1.3
Percentage in residence five years or more	27.0	51.0	48.0	86.0

Source: Louise S. Hauenstein, and Mary C. Blehar, "Married Women: Work and Family," in *Families Today: A Research Sampler on Families and Children,* vol. 1, National Institute of Mental Health Science Monographs (Washington, D.C.: Government Printing Office, 1979), p. 368.

diphtheria, tetanus, and pertussis (DTP), a series for polio, and single doses for measles, mumps, and rubella (or one combined: MMR) are the usual immunizations required for youngsters from kindergarten through high school. It is a family responsibility to be met by the family's physician or through the County Health Department or clinic. Table 10.5 shows that children lose more days of school from respiratory diseases than all other illnesses. Influenza is the major culprit, with upper-respiratory conditions next in frequency of time lost at school.

Dental health in children and adults is also a family responsibility. Routine fluoride treatment of community water supplies has greatly reduced dental caries in children. However, families are still expected to seek regular checkups, cleaning, and orthodontia (when

Table 10.5 DAYS LOST FROM SCHOOL PER 100 CHILDREN (6 TO 16 YEARS) PER YEAR, OWING TO ACUTE CONDITIONS, BY SEX AND CONDITION GROUP: UNITED STATES, 1980

Condition group	Both sexes	Male	Female
All acute conditions	487.2	432.1	544.4
Infective and parasitic diseases	93.3	82.4	104.7
Respiratory conditions	284.8	251.5	319.5
Upper-respiratory conditions	107.6	88.8	127.1
Influenza	157.4	143.9	171.4
Other respiratory conditions	19.9	18.8	21.0
Digestive system conditions	22.3	[a]	28.0
Injuries	40.1	50.7	29.0
All other acute conditions	46.7	30.8	63.2

[a] Figures do not meet standards of reliability or precision.

Note: Details may not add to totals owing to rounding.

Source: U.S. Department of Health and Human Services, National Center for Health Statistics, *Current Estimates from the Health Interview Survey: United States—1980;* published in *Source Book of Health Insurance Data 1981–1982* (Washington, D.C.: Health Insurance Association of America, 1981–1982) p. 77, table 6.6.

indicated) as well as to brush and floss regularly after eating—often requiring persistent monitoring and modeling on the part of parents.

Accidents are the leading cause of death among American school-agers. Although not as numerous as the number of accidents in the teen years (Chapter 11), they are real nevertheless, as we see in Table 10.6. Note that boys have twice as many fatal accidents as girls and that the highest mortality involves motor vehicles. Progress has been made in reducing accidental death in recent years. "However, accidents remain the major killer of children of school age. In addition to the large number of fatalities, accidents can also cause permanent impairments, disabling injuries, and considerable loss of time from school" (Metropolitan Life Insurance Company, 1981, 12).

Child abuse is a problem few families like to face, but the evidence is that the battered child syndrome can occur at any age, with an estimated 500,000 to 1.5 million abused children annually. Discipline by hitting is normal in some families, and a sizable percentage of parents admit kicking, biting, hitting with fist or object, beating, and threatening or actually using knives or guns. Tens of thousands of children receive not love and support but rage and severe batterings from their parents (Segal 1979, 581). Violence among siblings

Table 10.6 MORTALITY FROM LEADING TYPES OF ACCIDENTS AT AGES 5 TO 14, UNITED STATES, 1977–1978

Type of accident	Average annual death rate per 100,000		
	Ages 5–9	Ages 10–14	Ages 5–14
Boys			
Accidents—all types	21.5	24.8	23.2
Motor vehicle	10.4	11.5	11.0
Pedestrian	5.7	2.7	4.1
Drowning[a]	4.2	4.4	4.3
Fires and flames	2.3	1.1	1.7
Firearm missile	.8	2.0	1.4
Falls	.4	.6	.5
Water transport	.3	.4	.4
All other	3.1	4.8	3.9
Girls			
Accidents—all types	12.1	10.3	11.1
Motor vehicle	6.7	6.0	6.4
Pedestrian	3.1	1.7	2.3
Drowning[a]	1.2	1.1	1.1
Fires and flames	1.9	1.1	1.5
Firearm missile	.3	.3	.3
Falls	.2	.1	.2
Water transport	.2	.1	.1
All other	1.6	1.6	1.5
Accidental deaths as a percentage of all deaths			
Boys	54	56	55
Girls	44	41	42

[a]Exclusive of deaths in water transportation.

Sources: Metropolitan Life Insurance Company, "Fatal Accidents among School-Age Children," *Statistical Bulletin* 62 (1981): 12; basic data: Reports of the Division of Vital Statistics, National Center for Health Statistics.

may be more predictive of later adult violence than abusive parents (Gully, Dengerink, Pepping, & Bergstrom 1981, 337). Adults who themselves were abused as children are more prone to become child abusers themselves. Physical abuse is more common in poor families, but more affluent families may pass off abuse as "accidents." Many families under economic stress take out their frustrations on their children (Sanoff & Thornton 1982, 55–56). Child abuse is often triggered by a youngster's response to discipline by talking back, defying, or ignoring the parent; then the frustrated parent loses control and uses even more harsh methods of discipline, escalating into abuse (Kadushin 1982). Parents Anonymous is a national organization to which tens of thousands of families belong who help one another keep violence in check by meeting regularly and using crisis phone lines for parents needing help.

Incest is a major mental health problem occurring in all social classes and all ethnic and racial groups. Father-daughter incest is the most frequently reported form of sexual abuse in the family. It usually begins when the girl is between 6 and 12 years of age and often continues for many years, proceeding from fondling and masturbation to actual intercourse. Children who are victims of incest are usually afraid to tell anyone about it. The only clues are vague: withdrawal, generalized anxiety, nightmares, or bodily complaints—especially urinary problems or pelvic pain. Help for incest victims and their families can be found in local child protective services, rape crisis centers, or women's centers. The best way to prevent child abuse is through sex education in the home and in the school (Harvard Medical School Health Letter 1981).

Health care costs are escalating, but most families have some form of health insurance to help defray hospital costs and doctor bills. Some 88.3 percent of American employees work for companies with health insurance benefits. Large firms with union contracts are most likely to assume a greater share of the cost (U.S. Department of Health and Human Services, National Center for Health Services Research 1981).

Financing the Family with School-agers

The largest bite in consumer dollars is for food, followed closely by outlays for housing, transportation, and household operation, as we see in Table 10.7, which lists personal consumption expenditures in the United States in 1980. These top four items alone account for about two-thirds (65.1 percent) of all money spent per individual in a family. What money is left goes for medical care, clothing, recreation, and so forth, as indicated by dollar amounts and percentages of total costs.

American family incomes have been increasing in recent years, but the more rapid increase in consumer prices has caused a net decline in real family income, as we see in Figure 10.1, p. 222. In 1980 the median family income was some $1330 *lower* than the 1973 median in *constant dollars*. White families (with median incomes of $21,900) fared better than blacks, whose median family income was $12,670 (U.S. Bureau of the Census 1981, 1). There were 29.3 million persons classified as poor in 1980, an increase of 3.2 million over 1979. During 1979–1980, the poverty rate rose from 11.7 to 13.0 percent, largely because of the 13.5 percent rise in the Consumer Price Index (U.S. Bureau of the Census 1981, 3).

Mothers often work to help finance the family with children. In the early 1980s, 66 percent of married mothers (with husband present) having children 6 to 17 years of age were working; and 78 percent of lone mothers with no husband present and children in the

Table 10.7 U.S. PERSONAL CONSUMPTION EXPENDITURE
BY TYPE OF PRODUCT, 1980

Type of product	Personal consumption expenditures (billions of dollars)	Percentage of total
Food (including alcohol)	345.7	20.7
Housing	272.0	16.2
Transportation	243.0	14.5
Household operation	228.9	13.7
Medical care[a]	162.3	9.7
Clothing, accessories, and jewelry	123.5	7.4
Recreation	106.4	6.4
Personal business	89.8	5.4
Private education and research	25.1	1.5
Personal care	23.3	1.4
Religious and welfare activities	23.3	1.4
Tobacco	20.4	1.2
Death expenses	4.8	0.3
Foreign travel and remittances net	4.3	0.2
Total	1672.8	100.0

[a]Includes all expenses for health insurance (except loss-of-income type).

Source: U.S. Department of Commerce, Bureau of Economic Analysis, *Survey of Current Business,* July 1981; published in *Source Book of Health Insurance Data 1981–1982* (Washington, D.C.: Health Insurance Association of America, 1981–1982), p. 57.

same age range worked (Glick 1981). Most of these mothers work at whatever jobs are available locally that call for the salable skills they have to offer. Their incomes are usually not as great as their husbands, but what they earn helps provide the things their families need and want.

Part-time employment may work well for mothers with children at home when work can be found during the hours when children are in school or when their fathers can be with them. Some businesses encourage two mothers to share one job with hours both find acceptable. Others match teenagers with married women so that both may be employed at hours best for them. *Split shifts* make possible many a mother's working while her husband is at home. The working mother's success depends upon her education and training, her previous work experience, her husband's cooperation, the age of her children, her health, and available backup help from nearby kinfolks and others. Even so, when one of the children is sick, or has an accident, or some other crisis befalls the family, the working mother is usually the one who must make rapid, effective adjustments to the situation.

Dual-career families are those in which both husband and wife have careers in positions that are highly salient personally, that are demanding, with developmental sequence and evolving expertise, and that require a high degree of competence and commitment. When one of these dedicated workers has a career opportunity in another locale, the traditional solution is for the wife to go along with her husband's career and sacrifice hers by staying home, taking a dead-end job, or starting out all over again in the new location. Some men refuse to relocate. Merrill Lynch Relocation Management Inc. estimates that of the 200,000 to 300,000 employees who would be asked to transfer, from one-third to one-half would object (Kilpatrick 1982).

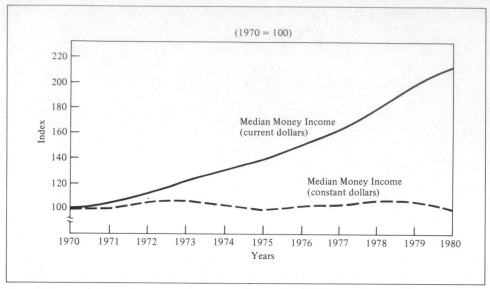

Figure 10.1   Index of median family income in current and constant dollars, 1970–1980.
Source: U.S. Bureau of the Census, "Consumer Income 1981. Money Income and Poverty Status of Families and Persons in the United States: 1980," *Current Population Reports,* Series P-60, no. 127 (Washington, D.C.: Government Printing Office, 1981), p. 2.

Commuting is the path taken by some dual-career couples. One spouse stays home, whereas the other commutes to his or her job during the week, returning to the family for weekends and vacations. The big advantage is professional development, with the side benefits of separation of work from family time. There were no negative influences either in the children's development or in the marriage reported. This course is possible when there is active cooperation and mutual trust between the spouses, open communication in the family, determination to surmount problems, resourcefulness, flexibility, and strong value commitment to both family and career (Farris 1978).

Combining work and family roles calls for keeping the two in balance. Full-time housewives and working wives are found to be about equally satisfied with their lives. Millions of American couples appear to be making the adjustments of simultaneous employment of both husband and wife with positive results in family life (Hill 1978).

Children share their mother's interest when they are involved in her work, visit her place of employment, meet her colleagues, and see what she does. Most youngsters (69 percent in one study) say their mother's coming home from work is what they most look forward to after school (Trimberger & MacLean 1982). When a mother works, her children come home from school to an empty house, unless some provision is made for them in their schools, churches, neighborhood facilities, and families (Wellborn 1981). A child's level of maturity and the extent to which he or she has begun to assume responsibility in the home are major factors in how well *the latch-key child* fares. Children who have worked beside their parents in everyday homemaking tasks feel important when they are trusted to begin preparation for the evening meal, and do their other chores while awaiting their parents' homecoming.

Allocating Responsibilities in Maintaining the Home

Household tasks today take less time than they once did, thanks to modern equipment, electrical appliances, man-made fibers, and quickly prepared foods. The Middletown III studies found less time now than in 1924 spent doing housework, washing and ironing, and sewing and mending (Caplow, Bahr, Chadwick, Hill, & Williamson 1982). It is probably safe to say that today less time is spent in meal preparation and dishwashing than in earlier times when most meals were prepared from scratch and table service was more elaborate in many families. Since more meals are eaten out of the home now than formerly, less food preparation takes place at home. In many a modern-day family, the kitchen is no longer mother's exclusive territory, as father and older children feel more and more at home there preparing their particular specialties.

Children's participation in housework is considerable, depending upon the family, the children's age and sex, and whether or not their mother works. Both boys and girls help with cooking and house cleaning. Twice as many girls as boys wash the dishes, and many more boys than girls help take care of home maintenance, yard work, cars, and pets. Children's help with housework increases with their age: 78 percent of the 6- to 8-year-olds, 93 percent of the 9- to 11-year-olds, and 95 percent of the 12- to 14-year-olds. Both full-time homemakers and full-time working mothers have high levels of children's participation, but oddly, part-time working mothers are found to get less help from their children with the housework (Cogle & Tasker 1982).

Husbands help with housework in some families. A study of 1212 couples in the Philadelphia area found black couples more likely to share housework than white couples (Ericksen, Yancey, & Ericksen 1979, 311). Members of the Working Family Project, a Boston-based group of young social scientists, "made a distinction between role-sharing and task-sharing. *Role-sharing,* [emphasis added] they say, involves the assumption of responsibility for the execution of tasks by both partners. Accordingly, in a role-sharing family the husband considers himself obligated to see that certain things are done, without advice or reminders from his wife. *Task-sharing* is a second mechanism for dividing labor without actually changing underlying assumptions about proper roles of the marital partners. The task-sharing husband 'helps out' his wife as she needs his assistance, either on a short-term or a long-term basis. But the ultimate responsibility for seeing that something gets done remains hers" (Lein & Blehar 1979, 313).

The Wellesley College Center finds that men's total family work averages 96 minutes a day for a total of 11.2 hours per week in contrast to housewives' 53.2 hours a week and working women's 28.1 hours per week (Pleck & Corfman 1979, 397). Husbands of working wives spend more time in their family roles than do husbands of nonworking wives—but not much: 1.8 more hours per week in housework and 2.7 more hours per week in child care. "Though these increments are small, they should not be dismissed. They may indicate that husbands . . . are beginning to compensate for their wives' outside work by increasing their (the husbands') own family work" (Pleck & Corfman 1979, 398).

The actual division of housework in the Middletown 1978 study found little difference between business-class and working-class families. The wife assumed entire responsibility in 45 percent of the families; the wife did more than the husband in 40 percent of the couples; the husband and wife shared the housework equally in 7 percent of the marriages studied; the husband performed more tasks than the wife in 3 percent; and some third person was involved in the remainder of the families studied (Caplow et al. 1982, 368). A further study in the same community found wives twice as likely to be responsible for all household chores except paying the bills; indeed wives are three times more apt to discipline the children than are their husbands. In spite of what the researchers call "glacially slow" changes in sex-role performance, they suggest that as millions of wives remain at work, division of labor in the home will eventually have to change (Condran & Bode 1982, 425). Two other studies see men beginning to increase their work in the family when their wives work (Quin & Staines 1978, 487; Pleck 1979, 481).

Using Duvall's eight-stage family life cycle, Lewis (1972) found wives more active in decision making when children are in the home (see Figure 10.2). He found wives wanting more and husbands wanting fewer decisions in the family; thus more equalitarian marital decision making may well lead to more satisfying family life for both husbands and wives.

Fathers make good parents, especially when they are active family participants. A Cornell University study compared father-absent with father-present children in the same school. Fathers who interacted with their children helped improve their attitudes toward school as well as their relationships with peers, parents, and siblings (Feldman & Feldman 1975). Child development specialists say that a child does not need to be cared for by his mother all the time; he profits from contact with others—especially his father (Smart & Smart 1972, 559–568).

The husband-wife relationship is enhanced as both share in the care of the children and the household. A man is free to relax and enjoy his home when he has a spouse on whom he can rely. The wife-mother is under less strain when her husband joins her as a partner in their family living. Whatever their choice of *conjugal options* a husband and wife are less shackled today by marital roles they find inappropriate. As women have greater opportunities for developing their talents at home and abroad, men too have more freedom to choose the family and work roles they prefer. Husbands as well as wives find challenges in the many roles opening up for them.

Continuing Socialization Through Wider Community Participation

Socialization is the process by which individuals are helped to:

1. Become acceptable members of the group;
2. Develop a sense of themselves as social beings;
3. Interact with other persons in various roles, positions, and statuses;
4. Anticipate the expectations and reactions of other persons; and
5. Prepare for future roles they will be expected to fill.

It is through socialization that individual family members acquire the knowledge and develop the skills, attitudes, and competence that enable them to function in society (in the family, in the community, or in the world at large). Socialization continues throughout life as new roles are played in each new situation or group that the individual enters. Socialization always takes place in interaction with others. Social pressures mold the newcomer so that he or she conforms to the expectations and the customs of the particular culture he or she is entering. Families with school-age children develop many ties with other people beyond the immediate family. Whole family units go on trips. Fully 70 percent of some 356 recrea-

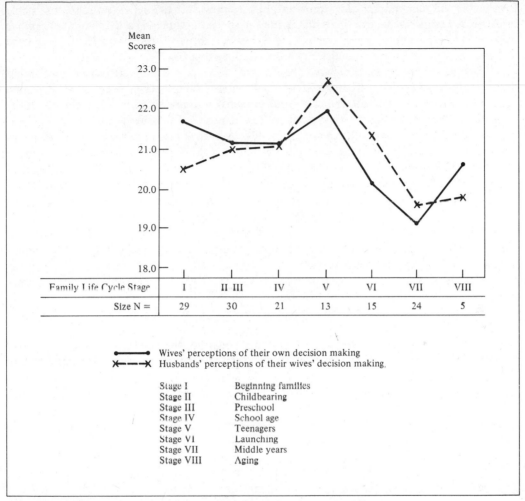

Mean Scores

Family Life Cycle Stage	I	II III	IV	V	VI	VII	VIII
Size N =	29	30	21	13	15	24	5

●——● Wives' perceptions of their own decision making
✕—–✕ Husbands' perceptions of their wives' decision making.

Stage I   Beginning families
Stage II   Childbearing
Stage III   Preschool
Stage IV   School age
Stage V   Teenagers
Stage VI   Launching
Stage VII   Middle years
Stage VIII   Aging

Figure 10.2 Perception of wives' decision making by husbands and wives by stage of the family life cycle. *Source:* Robert A. Lewis, "Satisfaction with Conjugal Power over the Family Life Cycle (paper presented at the National Council on Family Relations, Portland, Oregon, October 31, 1972).

tional activities are engaged in with other family members (Kelly 1975). Families do less arguing and feel less annoyance and tension on vacation than they usually do at home (Rosenblatt & Russell 1975). Once they get away from the stress of their usual roles at home, school, and work, they find interests beyond themselves and their daily routine.

A feeling of closeness to the *relatives of the family* is achieved over the years by letter writing, visiting, participating in holiday observances, vacation sharing, family reunions, gift giving, and services rendered and received—by any means that help the members of the family to maintain contact with each other. The process is furthered by family loyalties that bind the family together, regardless of what any member may do.

A school-age boy or girl is old enough to visit relatives for a week or more—or even for a whole summer vacation—without becoming homesick or too dependent on a hospitable household. Going to the grandparents' home for special holidays is a thrill now, when the children are old enough to appreciate such treats and able to take care of their own needs and interests in new settings with only casual supervision.

Even more important than what the relatives do for the school-age boy or girl is what they are. In even the most homogeneous family, many differences in personality strengths and weaknesses, behavior patterns, and value systems are represented by the members of the extended family group. These variations are fascinating and instructive to all.

Left to themselves, children make friends with all kinds of people. When they are allowed to relate to many different types of children, they learn ways of coping with life situations that will help them now and in the future. "Undesirable friends," from the parents' viewpoint, can be discouraged when (1) the children engage in disturbing or compulsive sex play, (2) the other child tends to violence, or (3) the friends engage in lawless behavior when they are together (Brenton 1975, 21). Otherwise, children from different ethnic, racial, and social class backgrounds expand one another's experience of the real world. Thus the child who is allowed to associate with only "our kind of people" is deprived of a valuable component of education for life in the community.

"Little sweethearts" are important to boys and girls. Understanding that they are a normal part of growing up, that they are usually outgrown in time, and that they can be safely accepted within the family as "best friends" at the moment helps parents to keep the perspective they—and their children—need.

Family involvement in the community is intensified when parents believe that their children will benefit directly from their efforts. Getting pledges for a special neighborhood project, a new school addition, or playground equipment now takes on special meaning. Ridding the community of harmful influences on children now becomes urgent family business.

Schoolchildren take their families with them into the larger community and its activities. Parents are pressured to become active in parent-teacher associations, youth-serving agencies, church programs, and athletic and cultural functions in which their children are taking part. Parents visit schools for special programs, participate in parents' study groups, and become active in community life as soon as their children are in school. These widening involvements help all members of the family to mature as they carry out this developmental task together.

Encouraging Communication in the Family with School-agers

The school-age family is a network of communication channels. There are 36 possible interpersonal relationships in a three-child family, counting parents and grandparents (Figure 2.3). Now most children are full of experiences to relate, questions to ask, and sheer exuberance to express. Each is uniquely at work on his or her developmental tasks within his or her position in the family. Boy or girl, firstborn or younger, each struggles to establish identity as a separate person within the family—one who is and who must be different from his or her siblings (Koch 1960). Longitudinal studies indicate that earlier problems such as destructiveness, temper tantrums, and overactivity decline rapidly throughout the school years (Macfarlane, Allen, & Honzik 1954). However, new challenges surface at this time, notably the beginning of *pubescence* in most grade school children.

Parent-child communication is encouraged when children feel free to take their questions and personal concerns about the onset of puberty in themselves and their peers to their parents. *Effective sex education* in the early years lays the foundation for openly discussing with boys and girls:

1. What is happening as their bodies mature,
2. Differences between the two sexes,
3. Differences among members of the same sex in time of onset and rate of maturation,
4. How to accept and deal comfortably with menstruation in girls and seminal emissions in boys,
5. How to cope with acne and other evidence of increased glandular functioning in both sexes, and
6. What physical maturing means for present and future relationships between the sexes.

This is an area of embarrassment for some parents and children who have not yet learned to articulate their personal problems to those closest to them. Parents who answer their children's questions openly as they arise tend to maintain good communication with their children in other areas, too.

Parental acceptance of real feelings in themselves as well as in their children encourage healthy expression of emotional states such as fear, anxiety, resentment, anger, and jealousy among children and toward parents. Refusing to acknowledge so-called *negative feelings* only send them underground where they fester and close channels of communication better left open. This is especially true of children's bickering, teasing, and quarreling among themselves. A parent who wants to encourage open expression of feelings does not deny a youngster's feelings but tries to keep their expression within acceptable bounds.

Sibling services to one another are often overlooked in a family that focuses too intently on *sibling rivalry* and other evidences of friction among brothers and sisters. Current family theory (Schvaneveldt & Ihinger 1979) sees some advantages in having siblings:

1. Older siblings blaze trails for younger ones,
2. A sibling identifies with another in certain areas,
3. Differentiation from one's siblings assists the development of a sense of oneself,
4. Siblings serve as sounding boards and testing grounds for one another,
5. Siblings exchange goods and services, and
6. Siblings serve as a bridge for one another between their world and that of adults.

Sibling coalitions in hierarchical families where children are rigidly controlled start early as mechanisms for children to band together in what may become lifelong bonds between the siblings (Johnson 1982, 165).

Siblings tend to have particular places in the family according to the order in which they were born, their spacing, and their sex. Birth order studies suggest that *firstborn children* have their parents all to themselves for a while and continue to be unique as the eldest siblings in their families. *Lastborn children* are cherished as youngest by parents who tend to be more lenient with "the baby of the family." *Middleborn children,* having neither the status of the eldest nor that of the youngest, may feel that their parents are more punitive and less supportive of them than of their older and younger siblings. In one study, middleborns were found to have significantly lower self-esteem compared with firstborns or lastborns, possibly because of their lack of uniqueness and of feeling special in their parents' eyes. However, the only boy in a family of girls occupies a unique place in the family that gives him significant self-esteem enhancement (Kidwell 1982, 234). Study of a national sample of 1700 boys find that spacing children about five years apart is best in that it allows parents and children the most one-to-one relaxed and supportive interaction (Kidwell 1981, 329). More research is needed in this area only recently explored.

Family communication is dynamic and multifaceted as the two spouses interact with one another, the parents with their children, and sons and daughters with each other. The marital relationship influences, and in turn is influenced by, the concerns of the two parents for their children. The children's interaction with each other reflects their feeling of acceptance by their parents. So husband-wife, parent-child, and child-child communication is intermeshed within the family. It is not surprising that these networks occasionally become tangled, especially when one or more family members are under undue strain.

School-age youngsters come home from their rigorous day in the classroom and at the playground full of pent-up emotions that could not be fully expressed in front of teachers and classmates. They bring frustrations, disappointments, and *unexpressed hostilities* home, where they very likely take them out on the first available family member. This is both natural and healthy. One of the chief functions of the home is to serve as an emotional reconditioning center for its members. This does not make for peace and quiet. On the contrary, feelings explode all over the place, and the children get into squabbles seemingly without provocation.

When communication systems are open within a family, love can flow through, counteracting the destructive emotions produced by everyday stress and renewing the spirit of every member. Love implies a two-way flow between each person and the next—an exchange that removes hates and angers and restores the warmth of belonging and the joy of living in a family. Like a river that purifies itself so long as it runs free, the stream of human emotions within a family renews and refreshes the human spirit as long as communication systems allow it free passage.

Rearing Children Effectively

Children do things that annoy their parents. A General Mills family survey found parents complaining about their children's eating habits, wasting too much time in television viewing, demanding too many advertised items, and exhibiting bad-tempered behavior. Many children complain that their parents intrude into their eating patterns and their television time; and they resent their parents' unfair punishment (Hill 1982, 316). How parents handle these and many other problems in child rearing influences children's development and the parent-child relationship.

Parental discipline varies greatly from one family to another. *Authoritarian parents* rely on rules, scolding, punishment, and "because I say so" responses to children's protests. *Egalitarian parents* try to be flexible and democratic with their children by encouraging their participation in family decisions, stressing self-control, and giving reasons rather than demanding blind obedience. Authoritarian parents, found more often at the lower socioeconomic levels, are seen as *traditional.* Parents at middle- and upper-class levels are seen as *developmental* because rather than asserting their power as parents, more often they explicitly encourage their children's development (Duvall 1946).

Social class differences in child rearing have been widely studied in recent decades. In general, the lower the family's economic and social status, the greater its deprivation. With deprivation often comes fatalism, with an increase in physical punishment and an emphasis on children's obedience. The higher the social class, the greater is the ability of family members to defer gratification and to foster internal control, achievement motivation, and self-esteem in one another (Gecas 1979, 392–397).

A comprehensive review of 235 published and unpublished studies makes a distinction between parents' *control attempts* and *parental support.* Control attempts include: (1) *coercion* (parental pressure upon a child to do as the parent wishes), which includes punishment, direct or threatened application of force, or deprivation of things or privileges; (2) *induction* (efforts a parent makes to induce a child into voluntary compliance with parental desires), which avoids conflict with the child by giving reasons for desired behavior; and (3) *love withdrawal* (parents' expressed disapproval by implying love will not be restored until the child changes his or her objectionable behavior), which includes ignoring or isolating the child, expressing explicit disappointment, rejection, or coldness to the child in response to what he or she has done that displeases the parent (Rollins & Thomas 1979, 321–322).

Parental support confirms in a child's mind that he or she is basically accepted and approved of as a person. Support involves such parental behaviors as encouraging, helping, cooperating, and expressing approval, love, and physical affection. Research finds that the greater the parental support, the higher the child's cognitive development and the greater the child's conformity and moral behavior. In contrast, the greater the parent's use of coercion, the less the child's moral behavior and the greater his or her behavior problems. The research reviewers conclude, "Parental support is consistently found to have a positive relationship in all aspects of social competence in children" (Rollins & Thomas 1979, 333). Other studies find that mother's use of punishment produces aggressive behavior in children, who also tend to be low in conscience development (Steinmetz 1979, 423). Parents of creative children tend to be secure, competent, and encouraging of their children's freedom and self-respect (Miller & Gerard 1979).

One-parent families, rearing their children without the presence of a mate, rely on other family and community adults for social and emotional support. Contrary to general assumptions, black boys 7 to 12 years of age in low- and middle-income homes in which fathers have been absent four or more years were found to be seeing their fathers frequently and to have other adults in the family and neighborhood available to provide the guidance and attention they need (Earl & Lohmann 1978). The self-esteem of schoolboys who saw their absent-from-home parent once a month or more was significantly higher than the self-esteem of boys having less contact with the absent parent (Lowenstein & Kooperman 1978). It is not easy raising children without a mate; but divorced, widowed, and separated parents appear to be making all-out efforts to do the best they can for their children.

Reconstituted families (one in which one or both parents have previously been married) have special problems in child rearing. Parents who have children from earlier marriages have such challenges as their relationships with their ex-spouse(s), each other as mates, their own biological children, their stepchildren, and their children's grandparents and other relatives. Children in reconstituted families have problems centering in their relationships with their stepparents while maintaining contact with biological parents, grandparents, and relatives (Landau, Egan, & Rhode 1978).

Stepfathers do as well as natural fathers, according to their wives. In fact, mothers who have remarried thought their children got along better with their stepfathers in some instances. Generally, research finds, "Children living with stepparents do just as well, or just as poorly, on all the many behavioral characteristics studied as children living with natural fathers. They are also just as happy, on the average, or just as unhappy. They do as well in school and in their social life. In general, they get along with their stepfathers as well as the other children do with their own fathers" (Bohannan & Yahraes 1979, 349). These researchers conclude, "Fathering is fathering. In the job description there is simply no difference. The stepfathers and the fathers do the same thing" (ibid., 356).

Stepmothers live under the cloud of the Cinderella "wicked stepmother" myth. Children often have difficulty accepting their "new mother" and have been known to openly remind her. "You aren't my real mother!" Such initial rejection requires a great deal of patience and understanding on the part of the stepmother—and her husband as well. In time many a stepmother wins a place for herself with her children by marriage. But it is rarely easy.

Encouraging Children's Education

American families are ambitious for their children. Three out of four parents want their children to fare better and to be more successful than they, the parents, are (Yankelovich 1981, 74). Children's perceptions of their parents' expectations reflect their families' ambitions for them: 75 percent of all children studied felt their parents expect them to do well in school; significantly more minority children (90 percent) and children from low-income families (85 percent) said their parents expected them to do well in school. These same children felt they were expected to be the best in class and to be good in sports in higher percentages than children from more favored backgrounds (Caplow et al. 1982, 391). Education is clearly important in the lives of school-agers' families.

School enrollments declined between 1969 and 1985, largely because of fewer school-age children in the population. There were 5 million fewer elementary school pupils enrolled in 1980 than in 1970, and their numbers are not expected to increase until the late 1980s (U.S. Bureau of the Census 1981, 137). This means that schools close in some communities and make readjustments in others to keep open during population declines of school-age children.

Handicapped children between 5 and 17 years of age, some 2.293 million of them, were not being served in one recent year (U.S. Department of Health and Human Services 1981). However, there has been some increase in special school resources for handicapped children 6 to 12 years of age. Improvement has been particularly noted in resources used by children who are slow learners, those with speech impediments, and those with hearing and visual handicaps (ibid. 204).

Differences in children's learning have been attributed to genetics, to luck, and to various other factors. However, research finds that the two most influential factors in a child's learning ability are school and family environment. Schools using *mastery learning*—in which each child achieves mastery in an area before moving on to the next step—have been especially effective. Through the use of evaluation and feedback, teacher and pupils find out where mistakes are being made, and corrective work is under way in small groups, individual workshops, one-to-one attention, and so on. Mastery learning has the advantage of giving more children a feeling of adequacy with the desire to keep on learning (Alper 1982).

Families influence children's learning ability. Success in school depends on family factors such as:

1. Early encouragement of learning,
2. Achievement rewards at home,
3. Parents' language and speech standards,
4. Guidance and help at home,
5. Family stimulation,
6. Intellectual interests and activities in the home, and
7. Work habits, routines, and regularity in the household (Bloom 1965, 23).

A study of 7119 6- to 11-year-olds found mothers playing a pivotal role in the intellectual development of their children (Mercy & Steelman 1982, 537). The Middletown III survey found an encouraging increase in the time mothers are spending with their children (Caplow et al. 1982, 368).

A summary of the findings of more than a score of studies comparing families whose children do well in school with families whose children generally do poorly (more typical of low-income families) is presented in Table 10.8. Each child must accomplish his or her own learning with what help the family and school provide. If a youngster masters the skills society advocates as desirable, the child learns to read with comprehension, to write with clarity, to compute with accuracy, and to become familiar with his or her world. These are complex tasks that take time to accomplish and that require family encouragement over the years.

Building Morale and Inculcating Values

Families tend to feel good about themselves; 8 out of 10 Americans say their families are one of the most important, if not *the* most important, elements in their lives (White House Conference on Families 1981, 180). Some 90 percent of those in the General Mills survey say their families are in good shape, and fully 80 percent are satisfied with the way "the family works together" (Hill 1982, 314). Most men and women would rather be known for excellence in their family roles than in their work accomplishments (Veroff, Douvan, & Kulka 1981). Nearly half (47.7 percent) of mothers and 36.6 percent of fathers of 5- to 12-year-olds say having a happy family is the most important value in life (Hoffman & Manis 1978, 179–180).

Peer pressures upon schoolchildren force their parents either to yield to the plea "All the other kids are doing it" or to stand firm for "This is the way OUR family does it." Reviewing and testing family values may become heated as children become preadolescents. Then it becomes imperative to interpret moral values in terms of why some things are wrong and others right. This is rarely easy, but few things are more important for a family's integrity or for children's sense of what they and their family stand for in today's complex world.

Kohlberg's research (see Table 10.9, p. 233) traces the sequential *stages of moral development* and finds that this sequence is not affected by cultural or religious orientation. The difference is in the rate at which persons progress toward moral thinking. Children of

**Table 10.8 FAMILY FACTORS CONDUCIVE TO AND
LIMITING OF CHILDREN'S SCHOOL ACHIEVEMENT**

Conducive	Limiting (more typical of low-income families)
1. Infant and child given freedom within consistent limits to explore and experiment	Limited freedom for exploration (partly imposed by crowded and dangerous aspects of environment)
2. Wide range of parent-guided experiences, offering visual, auditory, kinesthetic, and tactile stimulation from early infancy	Constricted lives led by parents; fear and distrust of the unknown
3. Goal-commitment and belief in long-range success potential	Fatalistic, apathetic attitudes
4. Gradual training for and value placed upon independence	Tendency for abrupt transition to independence: parents tend to "lose control" of children at an early age
5. Parents who serve as models of educational-occupational success and continuing development; high-achievement needs in parents	Tendency to educational-occupational failure; reliance on personal versus skill attributes of vocational success
6. Reliance on objective evidence	Magical, rigid thinking
7. Much verbal communication with a flexible, conceptual style and emphasis on both speaking and listening	Little verbal communication, especially of an interactive, conceptual, flexible kind
8. High value placed on academic success	Academic achievement not highly valued
9. Democratic child-rearing attitudes	Authoritarian child-rearing attitudes
10. Collaborative attitudes toward the school system	Fear and distrust of the school system
11. Value placed on abstractions	Pragmatic, concrete values

Source: Catherine S. Chilman, *Growing Up Poor,* Welfare Administration Publication no. 13 (Washington, D.C.: Government Printing Office, 1966), p. 43.

middle-class parents move faster and farther in their moral thinking than do lower-class children, possibly because of the conscientiousness with which middle-class families uphold standards (Kohlberg 1968, 30).

Accomplishing the many developmental tasks, in satisfying ways, of all members of the family with schoolchildren is a challenging job. Its rewards are in the sense of accomplishment that comes from individual and family achievements and in the family solidarity that is particularly meaningful at this stage.

SUMMARY

Children in the United States generally go to school at 6 and become teenagers at 13; in the intervening years both the youngsters and their families are involved in home and community activities as they work on their individual and family developmental tasks.

Marriage problems of school-agers' parents are more numerous and severe than at any time since children came into the home. Couples who transcend traditional role expectations, more than those with stereotyped role expectations of self and mate, cope with their conflicts and express their love more freely.

Table 10.9 SEQUENTIAL DEVELOPMENT OF MORAL THINKING

Moral levels	Moral stages	Moral reasons	Human life valued
Preconventional (Ages 4–10)	1. Unquestioning deference to authority figures; good and bad behavior depend on physical consequences	Obey rules to avoid punishment	Value of human life confused with value of things
	2. Reciprocity, fairness, and equal sharing seen pragmatically	Return favors and conform for rewards	Human life satisfying to self and others
Conventional (Varies widely)	3. Conforming to, maintaining, supporting, and justifying the rules of one's family, group, and nation	Conform to escape disapproval	Value of human life based on love and empathy
	4. Doing one's duty, respecting authority, and maintaining the social order for its own sake	Conform to avoid blame and guilt	Life is sacred
Postconventional (Attained by exceptional adults)	5. Right action defined in terms of rights and standards of whole society; legalistic, official morality of American government	Conform to gain respect of those concerned with community well-being	Life is a universal human right
	6. Self-chosen ethical principles, such as justice, equality of human rights, and respect for individual dignity	Conform to avoid self-condemnation	Belief in the sacredness of human life as a universal respect for the individual

Source: Adapted from Lawrence Kohlberg, "The Child as a Moral Philosopher," *Psychology Today* 2 (September 1968): 25–30. Reprinted from *Psychology Today Magazine,* copyright ® 1968, Ziff-Davis Publishing Company.

Families with schoolchildren like to own their own homes in low-stress neighborhoods if possible, at prices they can afford.

Children must be immunized against communicable diseases and protected from accidents, child abuse, and incest.

Today's family has a higher income that buys less than formerly because of rising prices. Most mothers now work at least part-time. Dual-career families face special problems in relocating when one or both have opportunities for advancement.

Family members do what they can to keep the household running smoothly. Wives carry the major responsibility in routine family tasks, husbands "help" in most families, and children's participation increases with age. Family relationships improve as both parents share in the care and guidance of the children.

School-agers make friends with more kinds of persons than before, necessitating both family guidance and community involvement. Parent-child communication is encouraged when parents deal openly with their youngster's sex education. Parental acceptance of real feelings helps keep communication open. Siblings are both a source of rivalry and of service to each other.

Child rearing ranges from authoritarian reliance on rules to equalitarian efforts to help children develop self-discipline. Parental control includes coercion, induction, and love withdrawal. Parental support involves approval, encouragement, and affection.

One-parent families and reconstituted families have special challenges in both parent-child relationships and guidance. Education is important, with families playing a major role in children's learning. Families and schools can do much to help handicapped children to learn.

Family morale tends to be high. Parents who stress values help their children go through the stages of moral development at a faster rate than do children whose parents place little emphasis on values. Peer pressures during the school years test family consistency and integrity.

REFERENCES

Alper, M. 1982. All our children can learn. *University of Chicago Magazine* 74:2–9, 30.

Baldigo, J. 1975. Parental role reversals: Elementary school children's conceptions and assessments. Paper read at the annual meeting of the American Sociological Association, San Francisco, August 1975.

Blood, R. O., & Wolfe, D. M. 1960. *Husbands and wives: The dynamics of married living.* New York: Free Press.

Bloom, B. S. 1964. *Stability and change in human characteristics.* New York: Wiley.

———. 1965. Early learning in the home. First B. J. Paley lecture. Los Angeles: University of California, July 19, 1965. Mimeographed.

Bohannan, P., & Yahraes, H. 1979. Stepfathers as parents. In *Families today: A research sampler on families and children.* Vol. 1. National Institute of Mental Health Science Monographs. Washington, D.C.: Government Printing Office.

Bowerman, C. E., & Kinch, J. W. 1959. Changes in family and peer orientation of children between the fourth and tenth grades. *Social Forces* 37:206–211.

Brenton, M. 1975. *Playmates: The importance of childhood friendships.* New York: Public Affairs Committee.

Broderick, C. B., & Fowler, S. E. 1961. New patterns of relationships between the sexes among preadolescents. *Marriage and Family Living* 23:27–30.

Caplow, T., Bahr, H. M., Chadwick, B. A., Hill, R., & Williamson, M. H. 1982. *Middletown families: Fifty years of change and continuity.* Minneapolis: University of Minnesota Press.

Chilman, C. S. 1966. *Growing up poor.* Welfare Administration Publication no. 13. Washington, D.C.: Government Printing Office.

Cogle, F. L., & Tasker, G. E. 1982. Children and housework. *Family Relations* 31: 395–399.

Condran, J. G., & Bode, J. G. 1982. Rashomon, working wives, and family division of labor: Middletown, 1980. *Journal of Marriage and the Family* 44:421–426.

Davis, J. A. 1978. *General social surveys 1972–1978: Cumulative codebook.* Chicago: National Opinion Research Center.

Duvall, E. M. 1946. Conceptions of parenthood. *American Journal of Sociology* 52:193–203.

Earl, L., & Lohmann, N. 1978. Absent fathers and black male children. *Social Work* 23: 413–415.

Ericksen, J. A., Yancey, W. L., & Ericksen, E. P. 1979. The division of family roles. *Journal of Marriage and the Family* 41:301–313.

Etaugh, C. 1974. Effects of maternal employment on children: A review of current research. *Merrill-Palmer Quarterly* 20:71–98.

Farris, A. 1978. Commuting. In *Working couples,* ed. R. Rapoport, R. N. Rapoport, & J. M. Bustead. New York: Harper & Row.

Feldman, H. 1961. The development of the husband-wife relationship. Personal communication, used with permission.

Feldman, H., & Feldman, M. 1975. Beyond sex role differentiation. Paper read at International Seminar on Changing Sex Roles in Family and Society, Dubrovnik, Yugoslavia, June 18, 1975.

Gage, R. 1982. 3 reasons that Roots took hold. *U.S. News & World Report,* August 9, 1982, pp. 93–96.

Gecas, V. 1979. The influence of social class on socialization. In *Contemporary theories about the family,* ed. W. R. Burr, R. Hill, F. I. Nye, & I. L. Reiss, pp. 365–404. Vol. 1. New York: Free Press.

Glenn, N. D., & McLanahan, S. 1982. Children and marital happiness: A further specification of the relationship. *Journal of Marriage and the Family* 44:63–72.

Glick, P. C. 1981. Children from one-parent families: Recent data and projections. Paper presented at the Special Institute on Critical Issues in Education, sponsored by the Charles F. Kettering Foundation and held at the American University in Washington, D.C., June 22, 1981.

Gully, K. J., Dengerink, H. A., Pepping, M., & Bergstrom, D. 1981. Research note: Sibling contribution to violent behavior. *Journal of Marriage and the Family* 43:333–337.

Hammel, L. 1975. "When I grow up I'm going to be . . . "—An old game, new ideas. New York *Times,* June 12, 1975, p. 43.

Harvard Medical School Health Letter. 1981. Incest. *Medical Forum* 6:3.

Hauenstein, L. S., & Blehar, M. C. 1979. Married women: Work and family. *Families today: A research sampler on families with children.* Vol. 1. National Institute of Mental Health Science Monographs. Washington, D.C.: Government Printing Office.

Havighurst, R. J. 1972. *Developmental tasks and education.* 3d ed. New York: McKay.

Hill, R. 1978. The family and work: Rivals or partners? *Family Perspective* 12:57–64.

———. 1982. American families during the twentieth century. In *Middletown families: Fifty years of change and continuity,* ed. T. Caplow, H. M. Bahr, B. A. Chadwick, R. Hill, & M. H. Williamson, pp. 271–321. Minneapolis: University of Minnesota Press.

Hoffman, L. W., & Manis, J. D. 1978. Influences of children on marital interaction and parental satisfactions and dissatisfactions. In *Child influences on marital and family interaction,* ed. R. M. Lerner, & G. B. Spanier, pp. 165–213. New York: Academic Press.

Johnson, C. L. 1982. Sibling solidarity: Its origin and functioning in Italian-American families. *Journal of Marriage and the Family* 44:155–167.

Kadushin, A. 1982. Myths about child abuse. *Family Therapy News* 13:7, 10.

Kelly, J. R. 1975. Life styles and leisure choices. *Family Coordinator* 24:185–190.

Kennedy, L. W., & Stokes, D. W. 1982. Extended family support and the high cost of housing. *Journal of Marriage and the Family* 44:311–318.

Kidwell, J. S. 1981. Number of siblings, sibling spacing, sex, and birth order: Their effects on perceived parent-adolescent relationship. *Journal of Marriage and the Family* 1981:315–332.

———. 1982. The neglected birth order: Middleborns. *Journal of Marriage and the Family* 44:225–235.

Kilpatrick, A. C. 1982. Job change in dual-career families: Danger or opportunity? *Family Relations* 31:363–368.

Koch, H. L. 1960. *The relation of certain formal attributes of siblings to attitudes held toward each other and toward their parents.* Monograph of the Society for Research in Child Development, serial no. 78. vol. 25, no. 4.

Kohlberg, L. 1968. The child as a moral philosopher. *Psychology Today* 2 (September):25–30.

Landau, E. D., Egan, M. W., & Rhode, G. 1978. The reconstituted family. *Family Perspective* 12:65–77.

Lein, L., & Blehar, M. C. 1979. Working couples as parents. *Families today: A research sampler on families and children.* Vol. 1. National Institute of Mental Health Science Monographs. Washington, D.C.: Government Printing Office.

Lewis, G. 1960. *Educating children in grades four, five and six.* Washington, D.C.: U.S. Office of Education.

Lewis, R. A. 1972. Satisfaction with conjugal power over the family life cycle. Paper presented at the National Council on Family Relations, Portland, Oregon, October 31, 1972.

Lowenstein, J. S., & Kooperman, E. J. 1978. A comparison of the self-esteem between boys living with single-parent mothers and single-parent fathers. *Journal of Divorce* 2:195–208.

McAuley, W. J., & Nutty, C. I. 1982. Residential preferences and moving behavior: A family life-cycle analysis. *Journal of Marriage and the Family* 44:301–309.

Maccoby, E. E., & Jacklin, C. N. 1975. *The psychology of sex differences.* Stanford, CA: Stanford University Press.

Macfarlane, J. W., Allen, L., & Honzik, M. P. 1954. *A developmental study of the behavior problems of normal children between twenty-one months and fourteen years.* Berkeley: University of California Press.

Mercy, J. A., & Steelman, L. C. 1982. Familial influence on the intellectual development of children. *American Sociological Review* 47:532–542.

Metropolitan Life Insurance Company. 1981. Fatal accidents among school-age children. *Statistical Bulletin* 62:10–12.

Michelson, W. 1977. *Environmental choice: Human behavior, and residential satisfaction.* New York: Oxford University Press.

Miller, B. C., & Gerard, D. 1979. Family influences on the development of creativity in children: An integrative review. *Family Coordinator* 28:295–312.

Pleck, J. H. 1979. Men's family work: Three perspectives and some new data. *Family Coordinator* 28:481–488.

Pleck, J., & Corfman, E. 1979. Married men: Work and family. *Families today: A research sampler on families and children.* Vol. 1. National Institute of Mental Health Science Monographs. Washington, D.C.: Government Printing Office.

Quin, R., & Staines, G. 1978. *The 1977 quality of employment survey.* Ann Arbor, MI: Institute for Social Research.

Rollins, B. C., & Thomas, D. L. 1979. Parental support, power, and control techniques in the socialization of children. In *Contemporary theories about the family,* ed. W. R. Burr, R. Hill, F. I. Nye, & I. L. Reiss, pp. 317–364. Vol. 1. New York: Free Press.

Rosenblatt, P. G., & Russell, M. G. 1975. The social psychology of potential problems in family vacation travel. *Family Coordinator* 24:209–215.

Sanoff, A. P., & Thornton, J. 1982. Our neglected kids. *U.S. News & World Report,* August 9, 1982, pp. 54–58.

Schvaneveldt, J. D., & Ihinger, M. 1979. Sibling relationships in the family. In *Contemporary theories about the family,* ed. W. R. Burr, R. Hill, F. I. Nye, & I. L. Reiss, pp. 453–467. Vol. 1. New York: Free Press.

Segal, J. 1979. Child abuse: A review of research. *Families today: A research sampler on families and children.* Vol. 2. National Institute of Mental Health Science Monographs. Washington, D.C.: Government Printing Office.

Smart, M. S., & Smart, R. C. 1972. *Children development and relationships.* 2d ed. New York: Macmillan.

Smart, M. S., & Smart, R. C., & Smart, L. 1982. *Children development and relationships.* 4th ed. New York: Macmillan.

Steinmetz, S. K. 1979. Disciplinary techniques and their relationship to aggressiveness, dependency, and conscience. In *Contemporary theories about the family,* ed. W. R. Burr, R. Hill, F. I. Nye, & I. L. Reiss, pp. 405–438. Vol. 1. New York: Free Press.

Swensen, C. H., Eskew, R. W., & Kohlhepp, K. A. 1981. Stage of the family life cycle, ego development, and the marriage relationship. *Journal of Marriage and the Family* 43:841–853.

Swensen, C. H., & Moore, C. D. 1979. Marriages that endure. *Families today: A research sampler on families with children.* Vol. 1. National Institute of Mental Health Science Monographs. Washington, D.C.: Government Printing Office.

Trimberger, R., & MacLean, M. J. 1982. Maternal employment: The child's perspective. *Journal of Marriage and the Family* 44:469–475.

U.S. Bureau of the Census. 1981. Consumer income 1981. Money income and poverty status of families and persons in the United States: 1980. *Current Population Reports,* Series P-60, no. 127. Washington, D.C.: Government Printing Office, 1981. (a)

U.S. Bureau of the Census. 1981. *Statistical Abstract of the United States: 1981.* Washington, D.C.: Government Printing Office. (b)

U.S. Department of Commerce, Bureau of Economic Analysis. 1981. *Survey of Current Business,* published in *Source Book of Health Insurance Data 1981–1982.* Washington, D.C.: Health Insurance Association of America.

U.S. Department of Health and Human Services. 1981. *The Report of the Select Panel for the Promotion of Child Health.* Vol. III. *A Statistical Profile.* Washington, D.C.: Public Health Service.

U.S. Department of Health and Human Services, National Center for Health Services Research. 1981. Study: 12.6 Percent of Americans Do Not Carry Health Insurance. *UPI* release, November 9, 1981.

U.S. Department of Health and Human Services, National Center for Health Statistics. 1981–1982. Current estimates from the health interview survey: United States—1980, published in *Source Book of Health Insurance Data 1981–1982.* Washington, D.C.: Health Insurance Association of America, 1981–1982, p. 77, table 6.6.

Veroff, J., Douvan, E., & Kulka, R. 1981. *The inner American: A self-portrait from 1957 to 1976.* New York: Basic Books.

Wellborn, S. 1981. When school kids come home to an empty house. *U.S. News & World Report,* September 14, 1981, pp. 42, 47.

White House Conference on Families. 1981. *Listening to America's families: The report to the president, Congress, and families of the nation.* Washington, D.C.: White House Conference on Families.

Williams, J. H. 1958. Close friendship relations of housewives residing in an urban community. *Social Forces* 36:358–362.

Yankelovich, D. 1981. New rules in American life: Searching for self-fulfillment in a world turned upside down. *Psychology Today* 15:35–91.

Chapter 11

Families with Teenagers

MAJOR CONCEPTS

Puberty
  Early puberty
  Pubescence
Adolescence
  Prolonged adolescence
Identity confusion
Identity formation
Role experimentation
Psychological moratorium
Upward mobility
Downward mobility
Culture of poverty
Ethnic differences
SES (socioeconomic status)
  White-collar families (business-class)

Blue-collar families (working-class)
Communication competence
Generation gap
  Generational stake
Teenage pregnancy
  Unwed motherhood
  Putative fathers
  Abortion politics
  Contraception controversy
  Sex education
Delinquency
  Drug usage
  Drinking and driving
Social development
Moral development

A family enters the teenage stage of the family life cycle when the oldest child becomes 13 and leaves it when the first child departs for marriage, for work, or for other pursuits as a young adult. Typically, the teenage stage lasts six or seven years, but it may be as short as three or four years—if, for instance, the oldest child marries or drops out of school and goes to work at 16. The stage is prolonged when the first child to be launched delays leaving home until later. At the beginning of the teenage stage the father is usually close to, or in, his forties. His wife is typically about two years younger, entering the stage in her late thirties (Figure 2.1). By this time the other children are most likely school-agers.

A family with four sons and daughters is made up of six persons holding a maximum of four positions: husband-father, wife-mother, son-brother, and daughter sister. Each has his or her own developmental tasks as parent, teenager, school-ager, or younger child. Father and mother cope with guiding the next generation and face the possible risk of interpersonal impoverishment. The overall family goal at the teenage stage is that of loosening family ties to allow greater responsibility and freedom, preparatory to releasing young adults at the launching stage.

Boys and girls enter the teen years as children and leave as young adults. It is during the teen years that young people begin to live their own lives as autonomous persons. The major thrust of the second decade of life is maturation.

Pubescence (puberty) is the period of maturing of the sex glands in both males and females. *Adolescence* is the period of psychological, emotional, social, and personal development between puberty and adulthood. Both puberty and adolescence have been intensively studied throughout this century. Erikson (1959, 92) spoke of *identity confusion* in young adolescents whose bodies are flooded with the sex hormones of an adult, sparking new drives and presenting young persons with conflicting choices. He saw *role experimentation* in the *psychological moratorium* of adolescence as allowing a teenager to find a niche for himself or herself in the world (ibid, 111). By the end of adolescence, *identity formation* is well under way, usually continuing on throughout life (ibid, 113).

Earlier puberty has been noted during recent decades. It is not unusual for fourth and fifth grade girls to show signs of early maturation and to be well into adolescence as they reach their teens. Boys also mature earlier than they once did, but generally their puberty is later than girls, as it has always been. Bodily changes that come with physical maturation tend to give the pubescent child an unwarranted sense of being grown up. But the youngster of 13 is still a child psychologically, no matter how physically mature he or she may look (Blos 1971, 970). Girls in their early teens tend to be physically larger and socially more mature than boys of the same age and grade. During the junior high school years the discrepancies in development of the two sexes tend to make them somewhat uncomfortable with each other.

Prolonged adolescence (the extension of the full process of maturing) is characteristic of contemporary youth. At the turn of the century, when most Americans lived on farms, a boy could do a man's work by his midteens. Great-grandfather typically left school at 14 and went to work. This is no longer the case. Today's vocations require levels of education and training usually not attained until the early twenties, or even later in the professions. Thus with puberty coming earlier, and adulthood later, adolescence stretches out "like Route 66 that goes on and on," as one 18-year-old put it.

Research on adolescence, much of it with a longitudinal dimension, is available in impressive quantities. Over a 10-year period the River City longitudinal study pursued the development of all students in the sixth grade (most of them 11 when the study began) until they reached the age of 20 (Havighurst, Bowman, Liddle, Matthews, and Pierce 1962). Thousands of high school seniors have been studied recently in the Institute for Social Research *Monitoring the Future* series (Herzog & Backman 1982, Johnston, Bachman, & O'Malley 1981). Hundreds of thousands of entering college freshmen have been surveyed annually for the past 16 years (Astin, King, & Richardson 1981). The Middletown III studies update research in one midwestern city begun in 1924 (Caplow, Bahr, Chadwick, Hill, and Williamson 1982). Periodic surveys and polls, ongoing studies and reports (such as the interdisciplinary conferences on major transitions in the human life cycle [Eurich, 1981, pt. 2]), and the psychoanalytic contributions to understanding the course of life (Greenspan & Pollock 1980, vol. 2) provide a wealth of objective data for students of adolescence.

DEVELOPMENTAL TASKS OF TEENAGERS

Adolescents' developmental tasks (see Table 11.1, pp. 242–243) were originally formulated from intensive longitudinal studies. Young people themselves have been found able to identify their own developmental tasks (Dales 1955). The ethnic, racial, and social class backgrounds from which adolescents come influence the priorities they place on the several concurrent developmental tasks confronting them and the success they have in achieving them. Lower- and lower-middle-class teenagers striving toward *upward mobility* set tasks for themselves that are more ambitious than those content to continue the patterns of their past. Conversely, middle- and upper-class young people unwilling or unable to live up to the traditions of their families may rebel and become *downwardly mobile* by adopting lower-class behavior and goals.

Teenagers from impoverished backgrounds who drop out of school—as 15 to 20 percent of high school students do before graduation (Golladay 1976, 1977)—find it hard to get jobs when times are bad. Students from poor families and those with the worst grades have the highest dropout rates; and more than 27 percent of the dropouts are either unemployed or are so dissatisfied with their jobs that they are looking for other work, according to a recent two-year study (National Center for Education Statistics 1983).

Underprivileged boys tend to give primary loyalty to their peers; before the teen years have ended, they may become delinquent. Somewhat more than half of all working-class boys and girls are upwardly mobile, succeeding in the developmental tasks that make for success in middle-class life. Inner-city adolescents become more sexually active in the early teens, so that in many cases early pregnancy cuts short girls' education and efforts at upward mobility.

Middle- and upper-class teenagers are under strong family pressure to associate with young people from families like their own, to cultivate a variety of social, cultural, and athletic skills, to get wide social experience, to complete their education, and to establish themselves vocationally before getting married. Middle-class parents tend to be protective of their adolescents, especially their daughters, and to keep their teenagers financially dependent until their education is complete. Upper-class adolescents are often away from home attending school, after which some girls marry, whereas other girls and most sons pursue careers.

Minority young people find the path to fulfillment particularly rigorous. Researchers estimate that 20 percent or more of all teenagers find it extremely difficult to grow into responsible adulthood. These are the youngsters who, for one reason or another, drop out of school with a history of failure, frustration, and maladjustment in school, home, and community (Havighurst 1960, 52–62; National Center for Education Statistics 1983). Five teenagers commit suicide in the United States every day. This is "more than a 200 percent rise since 1955 in youngsters between the ages of 15 and 19" (Frederick 1982). Accidents (in some cases, masked suicides) top all other causes of teenage deaths by a wide margin (U.S. National Center for Health Statistics 1978). Suicides rank number three for males and number four for females as cause of death in the teen years. That some adolescents feel so desperate that they take their own lives is a challenge to all caring adults.

Adolescents need parents and they know it. The teen years are a strain on members of both generations in the family. As teenagers strive to emancipate themselves from their parents, they are often critical to the point of disrespect and defiance. At the same time, teenagers believe that adults generally undervalue them. Studies find, however, that adolescents have a higher opinion of adults than do their parents, that both generations have favorable opinions of teenagers, and that adolescents rate parent-adolescent relationships more favorably than do their mothers and fathers (Hess & Goldblatt 1957, 459–468; Henderson, Connor, & Walters 1961). Parents and high school students are found to exaggerate the power they each have in the family but to agree on their degree of closeness to one another (Jessop 1981).

Attitude-behavior differences between parents and youth have been reported by some researchers (Connell 1972; Payne, Summers, & Stewart 1973; Gallagher 1974; Tedin 1974). Other research found high levels of intergenerational similarity (Aldous & Hill 1965; Hyman 1969; Troll, Neugarten, & Kraines 1969, Hill, Foote, Aldous, Carlson, & Macdonald 1970; Kandel & Lesser 1972; Thomas 1974; Bengtson 1975; Lerner & Knapp 1975; Acock & Bengtson 1977, 1978). Study of 466 family triads made up of mother-father-youth in the same family concludes that the "generation gap" is far more apparent in the minds of children . . . than it is evident in comparisons of actual opinions of the two generations (Acock & Bengtson 1980, 511).

Gradually throughout adolescence, teenagers shift their orientation from family to friends. During this transition, teenagers tend to be parent oriented when making important decisions about questions of right or wrong; they more often follow their peers in matters of taste and dress, movies, television, and music (Brittain 1963; Stinnett & Walters 1967).

Table 11.1 DEVELOPMENTAL TASKS OF TEENAGERS

1. Accepting one's changing body and learning to use it effectively:
Coming to terms with the new size, shape, function, and potential of one's maturing body.
Accepting differences between one's own physique and that of age-mates of the same and other sex as variations that are normal and to be expected.
Understanding what puberal changes mean and wholesomely anticipating maturity as a man or a woman.
Caring for one's body in ways that ensure its health, optimum development, and acceptability by others.
Learning to handle oneself well in a variety of recreational, social, and family situations that require learned physical skills.

2. Achieving a satisfying and socially accepted masculine or feminine role:
Learning what it means to be masculine or feminine in one's culture.
Anticipating realistically what will be involved in becoming a man or a woman.
Setting one's personal course within the sex-role expectations and practices accepted by one's family and community.

3. Developing more mature relationships with one's age-mates:
Becoming an acceptable member of one or more groups of peers.
Making and keeping friends of both sexes.
Getting dates and becoming comfortable in social situations.
Gaining experience in loving and being loved with or without premarital sexual involvements.
Adapting to a wide variety of age-mates in school, neighborhood, and community.
Developing skills in inviting and refusing, solving problems and resolving conflicts, making decisions, and evaluating experiences with one's peers.

4. Achieving emotional independence from parents and other adults:
Outgrowing childish dependence upon one's parents.
Developing more mature affection for parents as persons.
Learning how to be an autonomous person capable of making decisions and managing one's own life.
Working through the impulsive independence of adolescence toward mature interdependence with others (parents, teachers, and leaders especially).

On questions of educational plans and future life goals, parents have a stronger influence than do peers. Furthermore, in critical areas teenagers' interactions with one another tend to reflect their parents' views (Kandel & Lesser 1972).

During the teen years young people gradually come to understand themselves as members of their own generation. They must explore and draw on the resources within and beyond their families for all they require to accomplish the developmental tasks that lead into effective adulthood.

Parents' Dilemmas at the Teen Stage

Modern parents ride the horns of at least six dilemmas throughout the teen years (Duvall 1965):

1. Firm family control versus freedom for the teenager,
2. Responsibility vested in parents versus responsibility shared with teenagers,
3. Emphasis on social activities versus academic success,
4. Mobility versus stability for the family and for the teenager,

Table 11.1   *(Continued)*

5. *Getting an education for present and future roles in life:*
   Acquiring basic knowledge and skills for today's world.
   Clarifying one's sex-role attitudes regarding future work and family roles.
   Considering possible occupations in line with one's interests, abilities, and possibilities.
   Preparing oneself through specialized training and assumption of personal responsibility to
      obtain and hold a position.

6. *Preparing for marriage and family life:*
   Formulating appropriate sex-role attitudes involved in marriage and family living.
   Enjoying the responsibilities as well as the privileges of family membership.
   Developing responsible attitudes toward and understanding of what it means to get married and
      raise a family.
   Learning to distinguish between infatuation and more lasting forms of love.
   Developing mutually satisfying personal relationships through dating, going steady, effective
      courtship, and becoming involved with loved one(s).
   Making decisions about the timing of engagement, marriage, completion of one's education,
      military service, and other multiple demands on youth.

7. *Developing the knowledge, skills, and sensitivities required for civic competence:*
   Gaining ability to communicate competently as a citizen in a democracy.
   Becoming involved in causes outside oneself and becoming a socially responsible person.
   Acquiring problem solving methods for dealing effectively with modern problems.
   Developing concepts of law, government, economics, politics, geography, human nature, and
      social organization relevant to the modern world.

8. *Establishing one's identity as a socially responsible person:*
   Developing a workable philosophy of life.
   Implementing worthy ideals and standards in one's life.
   Assuming social obligations that express one's feeling of relatedness to others and to society at
      large.
   Attaining a mature sense of values and ethical controls.
   Dealing effectively with discouragement and depression and coming to feel good about oneself.

Note: Review Table 3.4 to see how the developmental tasks of adolescence are built upon the achievement of those of
childhood and lead into the developmental tasks of adulthood.

   5. Open communication with outspoken criticism versus respect with peace and quiet,
        and
   6. Focused lives versus uncommitted lives.

Each dilemma involves the challenge of choices to be made and values to be held.

Adolescents' success in achieving their developmental tasks is influenced profoundly by the ways parents perform their developmental tasks at this stage. So we turn now to a discussion of the developmental tasks of teenagers' parents.

DEVELOPMENTAL TASKS OF TEENAGERS' PARENTS

Parents find it hard to guide their teenagers today. The mass media portray values inherent in materialism and hedonism. Self-indulgence, immaturity, overt sexuality, sadism, and violence are exploited as part of the multimillion dollar business of attracting young consumers. Parents tend to value consideration above violence, sexual fidelity above promiscuity, and planning for the future above irresponsible self-indulgence (LeMasters 1969, 176–191).

When he reaches the teenage stage of the family life cycle, the father is carrying many responsibilities. He must perform a series of developmental tasks if he is to come through this period without faltering. He usually is and sees himself as the family's main source of financial support—his wife and older children contributing whatever they can at this expensive stage of family life. This is the time of life when a man needs to bolster his feeling of inadequacy, to broaden his interests, and to keep up to date on current thinking, social attitudes, and changing folkways so that he will not feel that life is passing him by. He does what he can to keep up his personal appearance and to give his wife the attention that keeps their marriage from going stale.

A mother of teenagers often has the task of trusting her adolescent children, of believing in them, and of delighting in their development—instead of feeling bereft when they no longer need her mothering as they did as little children. She may have to remind herself that her own health and grooming are quite as important for family well-being as her looking after her growing children. Now is the time of life when she can encourage her teenagers to become active partners in running the household and in making decisions that affect the family. She takes pride in creating a family atmosphere that is relaxed, comfortable, friendly, and cooperative, one in which "everyone spoils everyone else."

Whether or not she has an outside job, a wise wife thinks of herself as her husband's partner and companion as they guide their children and plan for their future together. She encourages her husband's development as a person and looks to him to support her interests, as well as those they share as a couple. Her response as a marriage partner grows out of her need for her husband's love and out of her sensitivity to his need for her. Parents of teenagers find this stage of life satisfying when they do not expect too much of themselves, or of their children, but are content to enjoy one another and their lives as a family.

FAMILY DEVELOPMENTAL TASKS AT THE TEENAGE STAGE

While mother, father, teenager, and, possibly, younger siblings are working through their individual developmental tasks in the midst of social pressures that often thwart and hinder them, the family as a whole is busy at the essential family developmental tasks of the teenage stage, as shown in Table 11.2 and discussed in the following sections.

Stage-sensitive family developmental tasks of the family with teenagers are of paramount importance to the maturation of the young people and to the continuity and survival of the family as a whole.

Providing for Widely Differing Needs Within the Family

At no other time in the family life cycle do family members feel as intensely about the house and its facilities as they do during the teenage family stage. Now the teenager's need for acceptance in larger social circles makes him (or, more often, her) push for nicer, better, bigger, more modern furnishings and equipment. The house that some years ago was child-proofed and stripped of all breakable elegance now blooms in the styles of the day, since teenagers see the house as a reflection of themselves and of their family.

The dating adolescent girl wants an attractive setting in which she can entertain her boy- and girlfriends. She needs some privacy in these facilities at least part of the time, away from the ever-watchful eyes and ears of siblings, parents, and other family members. The rest of the family needs to be somewhat protected from the noisy activities of teenagers—radios turned up full blast; recorders blaring out the same popular tune over and over again; the

Table 11.2 DEVELOPMENTAL TASKS OF FAMILIES WITH TEENAGERS

1. *Providing for widely differing needs within the family:*
   Furnishing a home base, adequate food, clothing, and health care for teenager(s), their younger siblings, and parents.
2. *Allocating the family's resources according to each member's needs:*
   Financing the ever-changing costs of a teenager's family and dividing the use of space, facilities, and equipment equitably.
3. *Sharing responsibilities in the support, management, and care of the home:*
   Encouraging each family member to participate in homemaking, according to his or her talents, time, and interest.
4. *Facing up to the premarital intercourse and adolescent marriage issue:*
   Discussing openly the facts, feelings, concerns, and consequences of youth's sexual activities as experienced vicariously by peers and contemporaries.
5. *Bridging the communication gaps in a family with teenagers:*
   Encouraging expression of real feelings between parents and teenagers and between husband and wife in comfortable ways.
6. *Dealing with drugs, drinking, destructive driving, and delinquency:*
   Helping teenage sons and daughters understand the potential dangers of illegal behavior while encouraging them in responsible self-discipline.
7. *Coping with outside influences impinging on families with teenagers:*
   Appreciating persons with widely variant life-styles (peers in school, work, and community) with discretion in accepting the deviant behavior.
8. *Maintaining the ethical and moral stance the family holds dear:*
   Encouraging teenagers' development of mature competence, independence, and autonomy within a framework of family loyalty and values.

giggles, the chatter, the shrieks, and the endless telephone conversations that mean so much to teenagers and yet so often fray the nerves of adults. Now, when so much emphasis is placed on popularity and social life, middle-class families do what they can to provide facilities for it.

Some of the pressure on their homes is lessened by teenagers' being out so much. Roughly one out of five Middletown teenagers (24 percent of the boys and 18 percent of the girls) say they spend *every* evening out of their homes (Caplow et al. 1982, 371). Some of these may be working-class young people, where the generation gap is the widest (Caplow et al. 1982, 147–148). Many teenage boys go out for sports, whereas later-maturing boys tend to cultivate a series of hobbies, play in musical groups, or throw themselves into other interests where physical size and social competence are not requisites.

While the teenager is crowding the house with his or her dating, recreational, and work interests, younger siblings are growing up, and their interests and needs must be taken into account. At the same time, father and mother continue to be persons who need and have a right to a little peace and quiet in their lives. The family that tries to meet this multidimensional demand for adequate facilities during the teenage stage has some tall stepping to do. The adaptations and improvements involved more than likely cost money—plenty of it—as we see in the next section.

Stretching the Family's Resources

The teenage family feels pressure for physical expansion and renewal of its facilities. The refrigerator is no longer large enough to stock with the volume and variety of snacks and meals needed now. It would be nice to have another bathroom, car, television set, deep freeze, or rumpus room; or a den (where mother and father could take refuge when the teenagers are entertaining); or some new furnishings to replace "this old stuff" that is suddenly so hideous in adolescent eyes. Meanwhile, the parents begin thinking about the costs of college, social life, and weddings ballooning up ahead.

Father works especially hard now. The overwhelming majority of prospective college students' fathers work full-time: 9 out of 10 work full-time all of the time, and another 7 percent are in full-time employment most of the time (Table 11.3). This is a higher percentage than is found in the general population of employed married men between the ages of 45 and 64, whose work force participation was 84.3 percent in 1980 (U.S. Bureau of the Census 1981, 386).

Prospective freshmen's parents are the principal source of their educational expenses in nearly 7 out of 10 cases, with students' savings from summer jobs and part-time employment helping out (Astin, King, and Richardson 1981, 58–61). It costs less to live at home than in a college dormitory. So, although most entering freshmen prefer to live in a college dormitory or a private home or apartment, as many as 30.3 percent realistically plan to live with parents or relatives (see Table 11.4).

Most teenagers' mothers work at least some of the time, especially when they have young

Table 11.3 FAMILY BACKGROUND OF 192,248 ENTERING COLLEGE FRESHMEN, FALL 1981

	Percentage of students	
	Men	Women
Parents lived together		
All of the time	85.7	84.0
Most of the time	7.1	7.9
Occasionally	3.5	4.0
Never	3.6	4.1
Father worked full-time		
All of the time	91.1	89.5
Most of the time	6.6	7.5
Occasionally	1.3	1.8
Never	1.0	1.2
Mother worked full-time		
All of the time	21.3	22.3
Most of the time	19.6	20.8
Occasionally	22.1	18.1
Never	37.0	38.8
Mother held part-time job		
All of the time	5.1	5.3
Most of the time	11.4	11.8
Occasionally	37.6	34.7
Never	45.9	48.2

Source: Alexander W. Astin, Margo R. King, and Gerald T. Richardson, *The American Freshman: National Norms for Fall 1981,* Cooperative Institutional Research Program (Los Angeles: American Council on Education, University of California, December 1981), pp. 30, 46. Data used with permission.

**Table 11.4 COLLEGE FRESHMEN'S RESIDENTIAL PLANS AND PREFERENCES
(RESPONSES OF ENTERING FRESHMEN IN ALL INSTITUTIONS OF HIGHER
LEARNING SURVEYED, FALL 1981, BY PERCENTAGE OF 192,248 STUDENTS)**

	Residence planned during fall term	Residence preferred during fall term
College dormitory	60.6	45.8
With parents or relatives	30.3	18.5
Other private home or apartment	5.9	24.7
Other campus housing	1.7	4.0
Fraternity or sorority house	0.7	4.9
Other	0.8	2.3
Total	100.0	100.2

Source: Alexander W. Astin, Margo R. King, and Gerald T. Richardson, *The American Freshman: National Norms for Fall 1981,* Cooperative Institutional Research Program (Los Angeles: American Council on Education, University of California, December 1981), p. 61. Data used with permission.

people who hope to go to college. Then more than 4 out of 10 mothers work full-time either all the time or most of the time, and another 1 out of 5 are in full-time employment occasionally (Table 11.3). The chances are that these mothers value education for their sons and daughters and quite probably have educational levels themselves that prepare them for fairly good jobs. High school seniors agree that a wife who works has more of a chance to develop as a person than the full-time homemaker (Herzog & Bachman 1982, 61). Teenagers whose mothers are employed tend more than others to feel that a wife's working does not threaten her marriage. Furthermore, both girls and boys accept their mothers' employment, especially in homes where the fathers participate in household tasks (King, McIntyre, & Axelson 1968, 633–637).

Ethnic differences in women's employment are still a fact of life. An exploratory study of black, white, and Mexican-American working wives found white women more likely to be employed in white-collar jobs (66 percent) than are black (42 percent) or Mexican-American women (47 percent). Twice as many blacks (39 percent) as white women (20 percent) work in service or farm occupations (U.S. Department of Labor 1977). Interviews with married Chicano couples found that when the wife works, housework and child care are shared by both parents. Indeed, these couples tend to be more equalitarian than other Chicano married pairs in which the wife is not employed (Ybarra 1982, 169).

Two earners in husband-wife families will continue, according to projections of the Joint Center for Urban Studies of MIT and Harvard University. The 1980s will see increasing numbers of women working at least part-time, so that they may adjust their work schedules to accommodate their family responsibilities (Masnick & Bane 1980, 73, 76). Wives' earnings are smaller than husbands' generally (Table 11.5), but they are enough oftentimes to lift their families out of poverty and into higher living levels. This will become even more important over the next decade (Masnick & Bane 1980, 81).

Husband/wife families, constituting 62.1 percent of all American households in 1977, had larger mean earnings than any other household type whether or not the wife was working. Husbands and wives whose ages were between 45 and 54 (when teenagers are most likely to be present) have the highest mean incomes of all age groups in the population (U.S. Bureau of the Census 1979, tables 20, 21). Many wives find it impractical to work outside

Table 11.5   TYPES OF HOUSEHOLDS AND EMPLOYMENT WITH MEAN INCOME IN 1977, UNITED STATES

Type of household	Percentage	Mean income
Husband works full-time; wife working also	20.1	$24,726
Husband works full-time; wife not working	20.5	21,824
Male family head works full-time	1.1	19,345
Male primary individual works full-time	4.7	15,206
Female family head works full-time	3.6	13,795
Husband is not working full-time	21.5	13,260
Male family head is not working full-time	1.0	12,787
Female primary individual works full-time	4.0	10,885
Female family head not working full-time	7.2	7,840
Male primary individual not working full-time	5.5	6,690
Female primary individual not working full-time	10.7	5,080

Source: U.S. Bureau of the Census, Consumer Income. *Current Population Reports.* series P-60, no. 118, March 1979, tables 20 and 21.

their homes. But a family now has more choice in the matter with the lessening of restrictions on women's working. That so many families in the teenage stage find economic and emotional pressures eased by mothers' working is a trend worthy of note.

Teenagers' employment is a third source of income in the family at this stage. Single males between 16 and 19 years of age more often are working than not—even in the depressed economy of 1980 when 59.9 percent had jobs. More than half (53.6 percent) of America's single girls between 16 and 19 years of age were working in 1980. In fact, many more teenagers have jobs now than in either 1960 or 1970 (U.S. Bureau of the Census 1981, 386).

In 1977 Middletown adolescent girls were more than four times likely to be earning their own spending money than were an earlier generation of girls their age: 40 percent versus 9 percent in 1924 (Caplow et al. 1982, 139). More Middletown boys get their spending money from their families in 1977 than in 1924, and some 45 percent of them now earn money from part-time jobs as well (Caplow et al. 1982, 371).

Thus the general picture is that while families with teenagers face rising costs for present and future needs, the whole family pitches in to help earn what they can in many cases. However, getting a job is not the only way to help out. Keeping up grades, perfecting skills, fine-tuning talents, serving others, and developing oneself may be more important than giving time to a job, even if a good one can be found. Equitable sharing of what time, money, talents, and facilities the family members have is one way of stretching the family's resources at the teenage stage.

Sharing Responsibilities at the Teenage Stage

Studies show that while most people think they should share responsibilities in the home, in actual practice this is far from the case. Fully half of all 340,374 respondents in the 35 to 54 age range in a national survey of American families said, "A husband should share in the responsibility of cooking and cleaning up." Indeed, many more men than women (64 versus 52 percent) felt men should share such family responsibilities (Report on the American family 1972, 26). But the majority of husbands are not taking a sizable share of household tasks. Respondents said the husband frequently shares in grocery shopping (31 percent), kitchen cleanup (25 percent), housework (17 percent), and cooking (17 percent). Most husbands only help sometimes (What's happening to the American family? 1978, 16).

Some families are more traditional than others. In the Middletown III study 74 percent of the husbands said that housekeeping was primarily a wife's responsibility, and 90 percent of them said their own wives did the housework. "The shared roles were less equally shared than people said they ought to be, and in the usual case, it was the wife who ended up performing most of the roles that were supposed to be shared" (Caplow et al. 1982, 71). Wives in business-class families were more apt to prefer equal sharing of housekeeping chores, but 13 percent of them and 6 percent of working-class wives actually did the housework. "So, who does what in Middletown families?" the writers ask, and they answer: in about 84 percent of families "the husband earns most or all of the family income, and in 90 percent the wife does all or most of the housekeeping" (ibid., 71).

Studies of thousands of graduating high school seniors of classes 1976 through 1980 found a tendency toward believing duties should be shared between marital partners, but the final responsibility is still seen as that of the partner who traditionally assumes that particular duty (Herzog & Bachman 1982, 107). The most traditional of these seniors were young men with strong religious commitments, politically conservative views, and low academic abilities, but the overall finding was that opinions about division of paid work and housework "have undergone some change in the non-traditional direction during the last five years" (ibid., 71).

A 1981 survey of 192,248 new college freshmen, conducted by the Graduate School of Education, University of California at Los Angeles, found significant differences in the responses of these students by race, sex, and type of college attended (see Table 11.6). Thus we see that in terms of women's place being in the home the most traditional of 1981 freshmen men and women are those attending predominantly black colleges, whereas the least traditional are university women (Table 11.6).

How about teenagers? Are they willing to do their fair share of their families'

Table 11.6 1981 FRESHMEN AGREEING "WOMEN'S ACTIVITIES BEST IN HOME" (PERCENTAGE AGREEING STRONGLY OR SOMEWHAT)

	Percentage
All entering freshmen, fall 1981	26.9
Two-year colleges	30.1
All universities	22.0
Predominantly black colleges	41.1
All freshmen women	19.3
Women entering two-year colleges	22.1
Women entering all universities	14.5
Women entering predominantly black colleges	38.8
All freshmen men	35.0
Men entering two-year colleges	38.7
Men entering all universities	29.1
Men entering predominantly black colleges	44.5

Source: Alexander W. Astin, Margo R. King, and Gerald T. Richardson. *The American Freshman: National Norms for Fall 1981,* Cooperative Institutional Research Program (Los Angeles: American Council on Education, University of California, 1981), pp. 24, 40, 56. Data used with permission.

housework? There are few definitive answers, but the Middletown III study found 45 percent of the boys and 46 percent of the girls reporting disagreements with their parents over home duties such as cooking, helping around the house, and so on. Since it is unlikely that today's youth argue for more of the family's chores, we can only conclude that what they object to is their parents' urging them to help with the housework (Caplow et al. 1982, 373).

Projections of the MIT–Harvard University team indicate not so much a reallocation of housework as a reduction of it, which was the pattern between 1965 and 1975. These social scientists recognize that negotiating the sharing of housework may be more difficult than deciding to let it go. However, they conclude that we may be seeing some reallocation of household tasks as more women continue to work (Masnick & Bane 1980, 101). In sum, family members today have three choices as far as housework is concerned: do it, share it, or skip it.

Facing Up to Premarital Intercourse and Teenage Marriage

Adolescents may deal very early with masturbation, homosexual play, petting, and inter-course. An early maturing generation, they cope with powerful drives at a time when sensuality is widespread in the culture. Peer pressures, their own sexual urges, and permissive media images influence many young people to question older taboos and to seek new free-doms of sexual expression. A variety of factors and incidences from more than a dozen pieces of research of teenagers' premarital sexual intercourse are summarized in Table 11.7.

A national probability sample of 15- to 19-year-old young women found that those whose values were similar to their friends had high levels of premarital sexual experience. A majority of the sexually experienced had used contraceptives, but not consistently, so they had higher levels of premarital pregnancy than did girls influenced by their parents (Shah & Zelnik 1981).

The rate of gonorrhea has risen in teenagers in recent years; it has tripled since 1956. The Center for Disease Control estimates upward of 2.6 million cases of gonorrhea annually. The rates for females are rising faster than for men. The highest rates are among 20- to 24-year-olds, followed by rates for 15- to 19-year-olds (Chilman 1980, 145; also see Figure 12.2). Herpes, syphilis, and occasional infestations of genital lice add their dimensions of discomfort and danger to premarital sex with promiscuous aspects. "The acceptance of casual sex seems to be linked to an easy acceptance of sex relationships for young adolescents" (Chilman 1980, 148).

Early marriage is not a good response to early sexual experience. Teenage marriages are vulnerable to disruption, dissolution, and distress, as scores of studies and census reports have found over the years. Recently, there has been a trend away from early marriage as both men and women generally delay first marriage until they are well into their twenties (Figure 2.2). National longitudinal surveys of thousands of young men found that those who married early had lower aspirations than those who waited and that high school boys' marriages appeared to depress both their attainments and their aspirations (Kerckhoff & Parrow 1979, 104).

In summary, "the factors most closely associated with early marriage appear to be (or to have been) the following: being premaritally pregnant; dating; going steady; 'falling in love' at an early age; having premarital intercourse at an early age (for girls); coming from families of lower SES [socioeconomic status]; having domestic interests, a traditional view of the

Table 11.7 SUMMARY OF MAJOR FACTORS APPARENTLY ASSOCIATED WITH ADOLESCENT PREMARITAL INTERCOURSE

Factor	Males	Females
Social situation and culture		
Equal sex-role norms	Probably	Yes
Permissive sex norms of the larger society	Yes	Yes
Racism and poverty	Yes	Yes
Rural-urban migration	Unknown	Yes
Father with less than college education	Unknown	Yes, for blacks
Peer group pressure	Yes	Not clear
Lower social class membership	Yes (probably)	Yes?
Sexually permissive friends	Yes	Yes
Psychological		
Use of drugs and alcohol	Yes	Yes
Low self-esteem	No?	Yes?
Desire for affection	No?	Yes?
Low educational goals and poor educational achievement	Yes	Yes
Attitudes of alienation	No?	Yes?
Deviant attitudes	Yes	Yes
Low religiosity	No	Yes
High social criticism	No?	Yes?
Strained parent-child relationships	Yes	Yes
Going steady, being in love	Yes	Yes
Risk-taking attitudes	Yes?	Yes?
Passivity dependence	No?	Yes?
Aggression, high activity	Yes?	No?
Biological		
Early puberty	Yes	Yes?

Note: Variables followed by a question mark are supported by only one or two small studies; the other variables are supported by a number of investigations.

Source: Catherine S. Chilman. *Adolescent Sexuality in a Changing American Society: Social and Psychological Perspectives* (Washington, D.C.: Government Printing Office. 1980), p. 145.

female sex role, and a low achievement drive (in the case of girls); and coming from either an unusually happy or unusually unhappy family situation" (Chilman 1980, 262).

A review of the effects of teenage marriage concludes that most adolescents have neither the financial resources nor the emotional maturity to find happiness in marriage (Walters & Walters 1980, 196–197). Black girls more than white tend to come from families with single parents, many siblings, marital disruption, and lack of money, education, and jobs—all attributes leading to dropping out of school and getting married. However, fewer black than white girls with similar histories marry in their teens. Among white girls, getting pregnant before marriage leads to marriage, but among black to illegitimate births (Carlson 1979, 349).

Marriage by poor young unwed mothers does not solve their problems; indeed it often compounds them. Fellows who are the *putative fathers* in most cases are the kind of people for whom high school education and steady jobs are difficult. Unless the young couple has had a good relationship for a period of time, their marriage may be fraught with conflict and soon end (Chilman 1980, 245).

Teenage pregnancy is a problem for the girl, her male partner, her family, her baby, and society as a whole. Yet in one study of nonvirgin teenagers, 50 percent of the 13- to 15-year-old girls and 36 percent of the 16- to 19-year-old females did not care if they got pregnant (Sørensen 1973). Interviews with pregnant adolescent girls registered at one prenatal clinic (and with their boyfriends, their mothers, and the young mothers themselves when their babies were 1, 3, and 5 years of age) found that premarital pregnancy was not a ploy to get married since most of the young mothers would marry their baby's father only if and when he became capable of supporting a family (Furstenberg 1976, 155). Indeed, "it hardly matters whether the young mother marries. In time, she may be almost as likely as the unwed mother to bear the major, if not the sole, responsibility for supporting her child" (ibid., 157).

Study of 487 black mothers in southside Chicago over a 15-year period found teenage mothers with more than one child tended to be living alone by the time their children entered first grade and to be alone 10 years later. They were described as getting little help from others in their child rearing. The researchers hypothesize that teenage mothers lack the competence to develop and maintain intimate, loving relationships with other adults; such incompetence may arise from the teenage mother's early child-rearing responsibilities, which abort her own socialization and isolate her from other adults and community resources that might provide much needed support (Kellam, Adams, Brown, Ensminger 1982, 551).

Who are America's unwed mothers? Summarizing research findings over many years brings Chilman to the tentative conclusion that more than other adolescents unmarried mothers have a number of predisposing characteristics (see Table 11.8). Studies of social network influences on adolescent exposure to pregnancy risk find it is the young pair's interpersonal relationship that is related more consistently to pregnancy among teenagers than either their peer or family relationships (Jorgensen, King, & Torrey 1980, 141).

Abortion politics directly affect unmarried mothers by either allowing or restricting access to pregnancy termination services when the girl or woman does not want to have the baby. The issues are hotly debated by both *pro-life* advocates (who contend that life begins at conception and that anything that dislodges the conceptus is murder) and *pro-choice* advocates (who argue that a girl or woman should have a choice about what happens to her own body—that if she does not want to have a baby, she should not be compelled to bear and raise it). Scholars of the question suggest a neutral abortion policy protecting the rights of both those who favor and those who oppose abortion as the only viable solution, since the different positions on the morality of abortion are basically irreconcilable (Jaffe, Lindheim,

Table 11.8   CHARACTERISTICS OF UNWED TEENAGE MOTHERS
(SUMMATION OF MANY STUDIES OVER RECENT YEARS)

1. Coming from low-income homes where the parents have little education and low occupational status.
2. Being highly fecund.
3. Having low educational goals for the self and a poor record of educational achievement.
4. Having little employment experience and little hope for the future as an employee.
5. Having low ego strength, poor self-concepts, and traditional sex-role attitudes.
6. Coming from female-headed households.
7. Being fairly accepting of illegitimacy and being distrustful of marriage.
8. Having partners who have little education and are unemployed.
9. Being a rural-urban migrant and living in the city or on the fringes of a metropolitan area.
10. Lacking access to contraceptive and abortion services.
11. Being black and a member of a poverty-stricken family.

Source: Catherine S. Chilman. *Adolescent Sexuality in a Changing American Society: Social and Psychological Perspectives* (Washington, D.C.: Government Printing Office, 1980), p. 278.

& Lee 1981). In the meantime, unwanted babies arrive in alarming numbers to reluctant young mothers.

Contraception that is safe and relatively effective is generally available to all females of all ages who can afford the services of a physician. *Planned Parenthood Clinics* across the country meet the needs of those girls and women who want to protect themselves from unwanted pregnancy until they are ready to bear children. At this writing, controversy rages over whether parents should be informed when a teenager under 18 is provided prescription contraceptives. Those who favor mandatory parental notification take the position that parents have a right to know when their teenagers are seeking contraceptive help. Those opposed fear that notifying parents will deter many girls from getting effective birth control information when they most need it. In 1982 one 16-year-old girl wrote the Department of Health and Human Services:

> If you pass a regulation which forces agencies . . . to tell parents when a teenager gets a prescription, teenagers will be afraid to get birth control. More of them will get pregnant. Kids who don't talk to their parents won't talk just because you pass a new rule. (Rosoff 1982, 1)

Efforts to remove the government altogether from sex education and family planning leaves only the family to cope with teenage sexuality (Ooms 1981).

For decades *sex education* for children and teenagers has been recognized as the province of the family, with what help the schools, churches, and community resources can provide members of both parent and younger generations. Responsible parents who are comfortable with their own sexuality tend to be effective sex educators of their children through the years. Such families often utilize community resources in teaching their sons and daughters the knowledge, skills, attitudes, and values of responsibile personhood in a sex-oriented society. But, anxious, threatened, insecure, uncaring and inept parents fail to give their children the guidance they need, and they sometimes alienate them when they do try.

Ever since the turn of the century, sex education in the public schools has been argued pro and con. Those opposed to school programs in family life education insist this is a field for families alone and not suitable for the classroom. Those for sex education in the schools maintain that many families cannot or do not carry their responsibility and that under capable, objective leadership, classroom discussions can be helpful. Volumes have been written, hundreds of conferences and workshops have been held on the issue, but it still remains to be resolved.

Articulate famlies are able to discuss openly the facts, feelings, concerns, and consequences of sexual activities as observed in the community. A pregnant girl drops out of school, and the family's teenage daughter asks what will happen now to her classmate and her expected baby. A gang of teenagers harass an effeminate boy in the school yard, and that, too, is discussed in a comfortable family. A neighbor's daughter is sexually assaulted, and family discussion does not dodge the unpleasant episode but suggests possible ways it could be avoided and handled. In a caring family, sons' and daughters' questions are openly answered as they arise, as they have been since the children were small.

Parental models of masculinity, femininity, and marriage in action are the core of what a family's young see and live by or rebel from as they grow up. Some teenagers' sexual escapades are attempts to defy parents and to repudiate their family life-style. Others are bumbling efforts of inexperienced young persons to assert themselves and to find out about life on their own. How parents deal with the inevitable lapses from family norms makes the difference between families who gain strength in their crises and those who come apart at the seams. This requires *communication competence,* which bridges the differences between the generations and enables each member of a family to get through to the others, especially when it becomes most difficult.

Bridging Communication Gaps

Adolescents turn increasingly to their peers with their intimate confidences during the teen years. Parents who understand that young people must identify with their own generation if they are to emerge as full-fledged young adults refrain from prying pressures that alienate them even further from their teenagers. Wise parents guide their adolescents with a loose rein, letting them have their heads, knowing that they will not stray too far if they are not driven away. Being available for companionable chats now and then is better than unleashing a barrage of questions as soon as a teenager sets foot in the door. Adolescents need parents and go to them willingly in families where communication is good.

Two important factors in the parents' ability to communicate with teenagers are their willingness to listen and ongoing acceptance and affection. When parents are attentive to what a teenager is trying to tell them, the teen senses their interest and respect. Runaways are found to report that their parents did not listen (Blood & D'Angelo 1974, 490), and runaway adolescent girls tend to feel unloved at home (Robey, Rosenwald, & Rosenwald 1964). Feelings of alienation predominate when affectional ties are weak (Allen & Sandhu 1967).

Young people have a vested interest in accentuating differences between the generations, whereas parents have a stake in minimizing those differences, a reality that has been called the *generational stake* (Bengston 1971, 89). Youth is more explorative, daring, and up to the minute than is maturity. Young people enjoy the contrast. They want to be out ahead. But it is also important to the adolescent for dad and mom not to get too far behind. In addition to being proud of parents who possess social poise and enjoy cultural activities and events, young people also seem to find it easier to communicate with them.

Nationwide interviews of representative teenagers found a majority (54 percent) of 1087 volunteering that their parents' disciplinary efforts were "just about right." Perceptions of parental strictness are related to teenagers' feelings of how well they get along with their parents. Such feelings of both boys and girls were identical on their overall relationships with their parents, which most evaluated as good. Neither were there significant differences on this item by teenagers' age or family background, whether they came from white-collar or blue-collar families (Gallup 1978).

Improvement in parent-adolescent relationships was found in comparing Middletown adolescents of 1924 and 1977. There was a major positive change in male teenagers' responses to the way their fathers respected their opinions (34 percent in 1924 versus 62 percent in 1977). Both boys and girls said their mothers now more often respect their opinions: boys, 24 percent in 1924 versus 57 percent in 1977; and girls, 22 percent in 1924 in contrast to 72 percent in 1977 (Caplow et al. 1982, 377).

In summary, it appears that there is less of a communication gap between today's parents and teenagers than headline stories would make it seem. As more parents have the advantage of education, talk and work with their teenagers, and make concerted efforts to improve the communication channels within the family, generation gaps may continue to diminish.

Dealing with Drugs, Drinking, and Delinquency

Years of surveying how Americans feel about many aspects of life have continued to find that although major shifts are taking place, the vast majority still hold to traditional norms. Nearly 9 out of 10 (87 percent) still feel that the use of hard drugs is "morally wrong" (Yankelovich 1981, 74). Yet confusion persists among many adults as well as young people about the drug scene.

Teenagers use drugs. One out of five 14- to 15-year-olds smokes pot, and the use of marijuana in this age group more than doubled between 1972 and 1974 (National Institute on Drug Abuse 1975). Millions of teenagers have experimented with illicit drugs, and millions are regular users today. Some 4 million teenagers use marijuana at least once a month, and those between 12 and 17 make over 100,000 drug-related visits to medical facilities every year. The surgeon general reports that persons between 15 and 24 have a higher death rate than 20 years ago as a result of drugs and alcohol and a very high suicide rate (Reagan 1982, 49).

Discouraged teenagers are especially vulnerable to drug abuse. Some 70 percent of drug abusers have been expelled from school, 66 percent have run away from home, 47 percent are unable to finish projects, and 43 percent say "things often seem hopeless" (Table 12.2). Some adolescents use drugs, including alcohol, for psychological reasons—to overcome depression or to modify inner feelings and emotional states (Kohlberg & Gilligan 1971, 1060).

Youth and adults concur that drug usage is dangerous. Most entering freshmen in fall 1981 agreed that marijuana should *not* be legalized (Astin, King, & Richardson 1981, 56). In answer to the question, "How would you feel if you found out your teenager smokes marijuana?", 59 percent of adults between 35 and 54 in one nationwide survey said that would be "very upset" (39 percent), "extremely angry" (10 percent), and "mildly upset" (10 percent). Another 36 percent said they would be "disappointed," and only 2 percent said "it wouldn't bother them" (What's happening to the American family? 1978, 84). A sample of 3988 parent-adolescent pairs found major agreement in both generations that it is all right for parents to make rules about the use of drugs, with 77 percent of the parents and 74 percent of the students agreeing that there were rules about drugs in their families (Jessop 1981, 103).

Teenagers' drug use has been tapering off in recent years. High school seniors' use of cocaine, amphetamines, and methaqualone began to decline for the first time in 1982; and the use of marijuana had been declining since 1979, according to annual nationwide surveys (Cody 1984, 4–13; Johnston, Bachman, & O'Malley 1983). Teenagers are inventing new social controls to limit the dangers of drug abuse, such as self-education about the effects of drugs and the conditions under which the dangers of using drugs can be minimized. Some 35 percent of all students refuse to use drugs on moral grounds. Another 23 percent of all students have been dubbed by the researchers as "conscious non-users." These are young people who represent a new value system that pervades all phases of life: (1) new moral norms in personal and public morality, (2) changing attitudes toward work and money as measures of success, and (3) concern about self-fulfillment and gratification (Yankelovich 1975, 41–42).

Social drinking is so much a part of American society that it is hard for families to suggest abstinence to their teenagers. This is particularly true when parents themselves drink. The five o'clock cocktail hour is an accepted ritual in many families. Spouses welcome each other home with a cold beer or a cocktail. Drinking is assumed in many social circles, taken for granted in the mass media, and promoted actively by billion-dollar commercial interests. It takes an unusual adult to request ginger ale or fruit juice when others are ordering alcoholic drinks. It is much harder for teenagers to resist pressures to drink unless their families have prepared them well for such situations.

Last year some 28 percent of 13,000 teenagers in 450 schools around the country reported that they had been drunk at least four times in the past year and that this had resulted in trouble with their peers or superiors at least twice during the year. Sons and daughters of drinking parents drink more frequently, and boys drink more often and more heavily than girls (National Institute of Alcohol Abuse and Alcoholism 1975). Alcohol continues to be used in high schools on a more widespread basis than drugs, according to a national survey of representative high school and college students made for the Drug Abuse Council (Yankelovich 1975, 39–42; see also Cody 1984, 4–13).

The majority of parents surveyed said they would be angry or upset if they discovered that their teenagers were drinking beer or liquor. Another 40 percent would be disappointed to learn of their teenagers' drinking (What's happening to the American family? 1978, 83). Yet many families are baffled about how best to deal with teenage drinking and do the best they can with or without the cooperation of their own adolescent sons and daughters.

Drinking and driving laws have impressed many teenagers of the folly of being caught DWI (driving while intoxicated). Tougher laws in many states have put severe penalties on drivers under the influence and seem to be effective in reducing the number of drunken drivers on the highways and drinking among teenage drivers, whose accident rates have always been high. Such legislation strengthens the hands of parents who would like to curtail their teenagers' drinking and reduces the cost of automobile insurance on cars driven by teenagers.

Delinquency is anything that gets a minor into trouble with the law. This includes possessing illegal drugs, drinking in public places, being truant from school, running away from home, stealing, destroying property, mugging, committing physical assault and battery, attacking helpless persons, engaging in illicit sexual offenses and participating in gang warfare or terrorism of any kind.

Some adolescents are more vulnerable to delinquency than others. Research finds that most teenagers who violate the law are disadvantaged lower-class youths in open rebellion against society. Young offenders from the middle class are more apt to be emotionally disturbed (Kvaraceus, Miller, Barron, Daniels, McLendon, and Thompson 1959, 54). Acceptance of the fact that the vast majority of teenage boys and girls are respsonsible, law-abiding young people has reduced stereotyping anyone between 12 and 20 as potential trouble-maker or an out-and-out delinquent (ibid., 24–31).

Families walk a narrow line between having enough faith in their young to encourage their full development and safeguarding them from the dangerous episodes that entrap many teenagers. A general maxim is to protect adolescents from life's disasters but not from its bruises. This means letting teenagers take their bumps and learn from them as long as the consequences will not be life shattering. Setting limits beyond which their young are likely to get into serious trouble is a major responsibility of families with teenagers.

Coping with Outside Influences

The mass media regularly present persons whose behavior is based upon materialism, hedonism, and sometimes self-destructiveness. Immaturity, casual sex, sadism, and violence are used in the multimillion-dollar business of selling products. Peers and adults in school, work, and community situations are often not the wholesome influences families want for their children. Families cope by guiding their teens to use caution in adopting deviant behavior while trying to understand and appreciate the persons involved.

Widening horizons are characteristic of families with teenagers. The family ranges farther afield now, both collectively and individually. Teenagers are off to work, off to school, on trips with friends, off for extended visits over the holidays, or out on their own for a while. Father is away on business or looking for something better; mother is working outside the home or volunteering in the community. The family begins to scatter, foreshadowing the individualization process of the launching stage ahead.

Teenagers' social development depends on friendships with members of both sexes in activities that go with dating, courtship, and becoming emotionally involved (review Chapter 5). Little change in white high school students' dating has been noted since 1964, whereas the dating behavior of black teenagers is becoming more like that of their white peers (Dickinson 1975). During the entire second decade of life it is in face-to-face contacts with friends one's own age that decisions are made, skills are developed, attitudes are formed, and values are weighed.

Significant adults (especially admired teachers, counselors, youth leaders, sports heroes, etc.) become models for adolescents stretching beyond parental patterns. Parents may become threatened by outside adults who seem to be closer to their adolescents than they themselves at times. Such parents retreat in defeat; others resist and fight these significant others. By the time children reach their teens, however, they have already been imprinted with their parents' life-style and now test it with other available alternatives.

Maintaining an Ethical and Moral Stance

During their restless searching, teenagers need reliable points of reference. These are the years when parents must defend and firmly adhere to sound principles and standards of conduct. Their own genuine commitment is the most eloquent argument they can offer. A family cannot allow itself to be buffeted about by every social wind that blows and still feel steady and strong within itself. Conversely, a family that does not bend with the pressures of the times breaks under their stresses. With no convictions or values, a family is a tumbleweed without roots or stability. With a philosophy of life that is too rigid and narrow a family risks the alienation of its teenagers and loss of its own integrity as a unit.

Young people significantly more than parents value self-fulfillment; on the other hand, parents much more than students put higher value on hard work and saving money (Yankelovich, Skelly, & White, Inc. 1977, 391). Most parents agree they want to pass on the values of the American creed to their children: 90 percent, "duty before pleasure"; 91 percent, "not as important to win as how the game is played"; 86 percent, "happiness is possible without money"; 84 percent, "prejudice is morally wrong"; and 72 percent, "having sex outside of marriage is morally wrong" (Yankelovich, Skelly, & White, Inc. 1977, 315). Today some teenagers challenge these traditional values; others accept them wholly or in part. A family's task at the teenage stage is to maintain its central values while encouraging its adolescents' autonomy and independence within a framework of family loyalty.

Moral development may undergo a major shift during the teen years. Through childhood, stress is normally placed on accepting the rules of the family, the group, and the country as being valid in their own right. In adolescence, conformity is no longer automatic; rather it is increasingly based on understanding. The social order is examined, justified, and finally preserved and supported. An occasional adolescent may adopt an autonomous moral stance that isolates him or her from family, former companions, and groups with which he or she has been identified (Kohlberg and Gilligan 1971, 1066–1067). Questioning adolescents have always expected to remake the adult world along the lines of their youthful dreams, and every once in a while they have succeeded (Kohlberg & Gilligan 1971, 1081).

Parents and teenagers learn from one another in a fast-changing society. Their value orientations mutually reinforce one another. The anxieties parents have about the hazards confronting youth in the areas of drugs, drinking, sexual activities, and other risk-taking conduct are often muted when family discussions reveal their adolescent child's emerging values. "These new values are not simply a matter of adopting a freer and more casual life style. They symbolize a profound value transformation affecting every phase of life" (Yankelovich 1975, 41).

SUMMARY

The family with teenagers faces the central task of encouraging adolescent autonomy and identity while maintaining equilibrium as a family. Adolescence is under way in the teen years, and adolescents enter young adulthood as they leave their teens. Teenagers face urgent developmental tasks that must be accomplished in order to ensure their happiness as adolescents and their successful emergence into young adulthood. Teenagers' parents have a challenging task in setting limits protecting their young from potential disasters while encouraging their freedom to mature through ever greater responsibility for themselves.

Developmental tasks of families with teenager are: providing for the needs of all family members; allocating family resources equitably; sharing responsibilities in the home; facing up to issues such as premarital sex, early marriage, drug use, drinking, delinquency, and other potential hazards of the teen years; bridging communication gaps; coping with outside influences both good and bad; and maintaining a strong central core of values while growing flexibly with younger members of the family.

Fathers, mothers, and teenagers all work at least some of the time through these years promoting both the family and individual maturation. Shared responsibilities in the home are still more an ideal than a reality, as housework yields to "do it, share it, or skip it" approaches.

Public policies complicate questions such as abortion, contraception, and sex education, with lines drawn pro and con for each issue, which can be argued either way, depending upon one's orientation.

The generation gap is more symbolic and talked about than real, as parent-teen relationships are generally considered to be good by members of both generations. Discouraged and alienated teenagers fall into a variety of traps in contemporary society, but the vast majority of today's adolescents are responsible, law-abiding young people. Moral development undergoes a major shift during the teen years, as families guide their young by example into young adulthood.

REFERENCES

Acock, A. C. & Bengtson, V. L. 1977. Opinions within the family: What parents think and what children think they think. Paper presented at the annual meeting of the Pacific Sociological Association, March 1977.

———. 1978. On the relative influence of mothers and fathers: A covariance analysis of political and religious socialization. *Journal of Marriage and the Family* 40:519–530.

———. 1980. Socialization and attribution processes: Actual versus perceived similarity among parents and youth. *Journal of Marriage and the Family* 42:501–515.

Aldous, J. & Hill, R. 1965. Social cohesion, lineage type, and intergenerational transmission. *Social Forces* 43:471–482.

Allen, D. E., & Sandhu, H. S. 1967. Alienation, hedonism, and life vision of delinquents. *Journal of Criminal Law, Criminology and Police Science* 58:325–329.

Astin, A. W., King, M. R., & Richardson, G. T. 1981. *The American freshman: National norms for fall 1981.* Cooperative Institutional Research Program. Los Angeles: American Council on Education, University of California.

Bengtson, V. L. 1971. Inter-age perceptions and the generation gap. *Gerontologist* 11:85–89, pt. 2.

———. 1975. Generation and family effects in value socialization. *American Sociological Review* 40:358–371.

Benson, L. G. 1955. Family social status and parental authority evaluations among adolescents. *Southwest Social Science Quarterly* 36:46–54.

Bienvenu, M. J. 1969. *Parent-teenager communication.* Public Affairs Pamphlet no. 438. New York: Public Affairs Pamphlets.

Blood, L., & D'Angelo, R. 1974. A progress research report on value issues in conflict between runaways and their parents. *Journal of Marriage and the Family* 36:486–491.

Blos, P. 1971. The child analyst looks at the young adolescent. *Daedalus* 100:961–978.

Bowerman, C. E., & Kinch, J. W. 1959. Changes in family and peer orientation of children between the fourth and tenth grades. *Social Forces* 37:206–211.

Brittain, C. V. 1963. Adolescent choices and parent-peer cross-pressure. *American Sociological Review* 28:385–391.

Butler, R. M. 1956. Mothers' attitudes toward the social development of their adolescents. *Social Casework,* May–June.

Caplow, T., Bahr, H. M., Chadwick, B. A., Hill, R., & Williamson, M. H. 1982. *Middletown families. Fifty years of change and continuity.* Minneapolis: University of Minnesota Press.

Carlson, E. 1979. Family background, school and early marriage. *Journal of Marriage and the Family* 41:341–353.

Chilman, C. S. 1980. *Adolescent sexuality in a changing American society: Social and psychological perspectives.* Washington, D.C.: Government Printing Office.

Cody, B. 1984. Alcohol and other drug abuse among adolescents, *Statistical Bulletin* 65: 4–13.

Connell, R. W. 1972. Political socialization in the American family: The evidence reexamined. *Public Opinion Quarterly* 36:321–333.

Dales, R. J. 1955. A method for measuring developmental tasks: Scales for selected tasks at the beginning of adolescence. *Child Development* 26:111–222.

Dickinson, G. E. 1975. Dating behavior of black and white adolescents before and after desegregation. *Journal of Marriage and Family Counseling* 37:602–608.

Dubbe, M. C. 1957. What young people can't talk over with their parents. *National Parent-Teacher* 52:18–20.

Duvall, E. M. 1965. Family dilemmas with teenagers. *Family Life Coordinator* 14:35–38.

———— 1976. *Parent and teen-ager: Living and loving.* Nashville, TN: Broadman Press.

Erikson, E. H. 1959. *Identity and the life cycle.* New York: International Universities Press.

Eurich, A. C., ed. 1981. *Major transitions in the human life cycle.* Lexington, MA: Heath.

Frederick, C. 1982. U.S. suicide rate climbing. *Family Economist.* Washington, D.C.: American Council of Life Insurance release.

Furstenberg, F. F. 1976. The social consequences of teenage parenthood. *Family Planning Perspectives* 8:148–164.

Gallagher, B. J. 1974. An empirical analysis of attitude differences between three kin-related generations. *Youth and Society* 4:327–349.

Gallup, G. 1978. *Gallup youth survey.* Princeton, N.J.: George Gallup Inc.

Golladay, M. 1976. *The condition of education.* National Center for Education Statistics. Washington, D.C.: Government Printing Office.

————. 1977. *The condition of education.* Vol. 3, part 1. National Center for Education Statistics. Washington, D.C.: Government Printing Office.

Greenspan, S. I., & Pollock, G. H., eds. 1980. *The course of life: Psychoanalytic contributions toward understanding personality development.* Washington, D.C.: Department of Health and Human Services.

Havighurst, R. J. 1960. Adolescence and the postponement of adulthood. *School Review,* Spring: 52–62.

———— 1972. *Developmental tasks and education.* 3d ed. New York: McKay.

Havighurst, R. J., Bowman, P. H., Liddle, G.P., Matthews, C. V., & Pierce, J. V. 1962. *Growing up in River City.* New York: Wiley.

Henderson, P. M., Connor, R., & Walters, J. 1961. Family member perceptions of parent role performance. *Merrill-Palmer Quarterly* 7:31–37.

Herzog, A. R., & Bachman, J. G. 1982. *Sex roles attitudes among high school seniors: Views about work and family roles.* Ann Arbor: Survey Research Center, Institute for Social Research, University of Michigan.

Hess, R. D., & Goldblatt, I. 1957. The status of adolescents in American society: A problem in social identity. *Child Development* 28:459–468.

Hill, M. 1973. *Parents and teenagers.* Public Affairs Pamphlet no. 490. New York: Public Affairs Pamphlets.

Hill, R., Foote, N., Aldous, J., Carlson, R., & Macdonald, R. 1970. *Family development in three generations.* Cambridge, MA: Schenkman.

How is work affecting American families? 1981. *Better Homes and Gardens*, Des Moines, IA: Meredith Corporation.

Hyman, H. 1969. *Political socialization.* Glencoe, IL: Free Press.

Jaffe, F. S., Lindheim, B. L., & Lee, P. R. 1981. *Abortion politics: Private morality and public policy.* New York: McGraw-Hill.

Jessop, D. J. 1981. Family relationships as viewed by parents and adolescents: A specification. *Journal of Marriage and the Family* 43:95–106.

Johnston, L. D., Bachman, J. G., & O'Malley, P. M. 1981. *Monitoring the future: Questionnaire responses from the nation's high school seniors.* Ann Arbor: Institute for Social Research, University of Michigan.

————. 1983. Teenage drug use. *ISR Newsletter.* Ann Arbor: Institute for Social Research, University of Michigan, p. 3.

Jorgensen, S. R., King, S. L., & Torrey, B. A. 1980. Dyadic and social network influences on adolescent exposure to pregnancy risk. *Journal of Marriage and the Family* 42:141–155.

Kandel, D., & Lesser, G. 1972. *Youth in two worlds.* San Francisco: Jossey-Bass.

Kellam, S. G., Adams, R. G., Brown, C. H., & Ensminger, M. E. 1982. The long-term evolution of the family structure of teenage and older mothers. *Journal of Marriage and the Family* 44:-539–554.

Kerckhoff, A. C., & Parrow, A. 1979. The effect of early marriage on the educational attainment of young men. *Journal of Marriage and the Family* 41:97–107.

King, K., McIntyre, J., & Axelson, L. 1968. Adolescents' views of maternal employment as a threat to the marital relationship. *Journal of Marriage and the Family* 30:633–637.

Kohlberg, L., & Gilligan, C. 1971. The adolescent as a philosopher: The discovery of the self in a postconventional world. *Daedalus* 100:1051–1086.

Kvaraceus, W. B., Miller, W. B., Barron, M. L., Daniels, E. M., McLendon, P. A., and Thompson, B. A. 1959. *Delinquent behavior.* Vol. 1. Washington, D.C.: National Education Association.

LeMasters, E. E. 1969. Parents, mass media, and the youth peer group. In *Parents in modern America,* chap. 10. Homewood, IL: Dorsey Press.

Lerner, R. M., & Knapp, J. R. 1975. Actual and perceived intrafamiliar attitudes of late adolescents and their parents. *Journal of Youth and Adolescence* 4:17–36.

Maas, H. S. 1951. Some social class differences in the family systems and group relations of pre- and early adolescents. *Child Development* 22:145–152.

Masnick, G., & Bane, M. J. 1980. *The nation's families: 1960–1990.* Boston: Auburn House.

National Center for Education Statistics. 1983. Two-year study finds many dropouts regret decision to leave school. AP release in *Sarasota Herald-Tribune*, December 5, 1983, p. 6-A.

National Institute of Alcohol Abuse and Alcoholism. 1975. Report in School study calls 28% of teen-agers "problem" drinkers, New York *Times,* November 21, 1975, p. 41.

National Institute on Drug Abuse. 1975. Report in Alcohol and marijuana spreading menace among teen-agers. *U.S. News & World Report* 24:28–30.

Nye, I. 1951. Adolescent-parent adjustment—Socio-economic level as a variable. *American Sociological Review* 16:341–349.

Ooms, T., ed. 1981. *Teenage pregnancy in a family context: Implications for policy.* Philadeldphia: Temple University Press.

Otto, L. B., & Haller, A. O. 1979. Evidence for a social psychological view of the status attainment process: Four studies compared. *Social Forces* 57:887–914.

Payne, S., Summers, D. A., & Stewart, T. 1973. Value differences across three generations. *Sociometry* 36:20–30.

Reagan, N. 1982. How parents can help teenage drug users. *U.S. News & World Report* 92:49–50.

Report on the American family. 1972. *Better Homes and Gardens,* Des Moines, IA: Meredith Corporation.

Robey, A., Rosenwald, S., & Rosenwald, L. 1964. The runaway girl, a reaction to family stress. *American Journal of Orthopsychiatry* 34:762–767.

Rosoff, J. I. 1982. Special report: Mandatory parent notice proposal generates overwhelming response. *Washington Memo.* New York: Planned Parenthood–World Population.

Shah, F., & Zelnik, M. 1981. Parent and peer influence on sexual behavior, contraceptive use, and pregnancy experience of young women. *Journal of Marriage and the Family* 43:339–348.

Sørensen, R. C. 1973. *Adolescent sexuality in contemporary America: Personal values and sexual behavior ages 13–19.* New York: World.

Spenner, K. I., & Featherman, D. L. 1978. Achievement ambitions. In *Annual Review of Sociology,* ed. R. H. Turner, J. Coleman, & R. C. Fox. Palo Alto, CA: Annual Reviews.

Stinnett, N., Farris, J. A., & Walters, J. 1974. Parent-child relationships of male and female high school students. *Journal of Genetic Psychology* 125: 99–106.

Stinnett, N., & Walters, J. 1967. Parent-peer orientation of adolescents from low-income families. *Journal of Home Economics* 59:37–40.

Tedin, K. L. 1974. The influence of parents on the political attitudes of adolescents. *American Political Science Review* 68:1579–1592.

Thomas, L. E. 1974. Generational discontinuity in beliefs: An exploration of the generation gap. *Journal of Social Issues* 30:1–22.

Thurnher, M., Spence, D., & Lowenthal, M. F. 1974. Value confluence and behavioral conflict in intergenerational relations. *Journal of Marriage and the Family* 36:308–319.

Troll, L., Neugarten, B. L., & Kraines, R. J. 1969. Similarities in values and other personality characteristics in college students and their parents. *Merrill-Palmer Quarterly* 15:323–336.

U.S. Bureau of the Census. 1979. Consumer income. *Current Population Reports,* P-60, no. 118. Washington, D.C.: Government Printing Office.

U.S. Bureau of the Census. 1981. *Statistical Abstract of the United States 1981.* Washington, D.C.: Government Printing Office.

U.S. Department of Labor. 1977. *U.S. Working Women: A Databook.* Washington, D.C.: Bureau of Labor Statistics.

U.S. National Center for Health Statistics. 1978. *Vital Statistics of the United States,* vol. 2, *Mortality,* pt. A. Washington, D.C.: Government Printing Office.

Walters, J., & Walters, L. H. 1980. Trends affecting adolescent views of sexuality, employment, marriage, and child rearing. *Family Relations* 29:191–198.

What's happening to the American family? 1978. *Better Homes and Gardens,* Des Moines, IA: Meredith Corporation.

Withrow, J. L., & Trotter, V. Y. 1961. Space for leisure activities of teenagers. *Journal of Home Economics* 53:359–362.

Yankelovich, D. 1975. How students control their drug crisis. *Psychology Today* 9:39–42.

———1981. New rules in American life: Searching for self-fulfillment in a world turned upside down. *Psychology Today* 15:35–91.

Yankelovich, Skelly, and White, Inc. 1977. *General Mills American family report 1976–1977: Raising children in a changing society.* Minneapolis, MN: General Mills.

Ybarra, L. 1982. When wives work: The impact on the Chicano family. *Journal of Marriage and the Family* 44:169–178.

Chapter 12

Families Launching Young Adults

MAJOR CONCEPTS

Nuclear family
Extended family
Empty nest
Release of family members
The "baby boom"
Population profile, bubble in the
Upward mobility
Alienated youth
Identification
Autonomy
Sexual involvement
Fidelity
Love involvement
Premarital sex
Living together
Progressive couple involvement
Permissiveness

Premarital dyadic formation
Promiscuity
Couple identity
Homogamy
Endogamy
Propinquity
Intermarriage
Engagement rituals
Traditional wedding ceremonies
Conventional weddings
"New weddings"
Mature roles
Revitalizing marriage
Unlaunchable young
The elemental triangle
Social heirs
Generational stake

The launching stage of the family life cycle is sharply marked by the young person's departure from home—to begin military service, to attend college or obtain other post–high school training, to marry, or to take a self-supporting job. In each case the young person leaves the parental home, and his or her periodic return visits will not be as the child he or she was before. The stage begins with the first child leaving home as a young adult; it ends with the empty nest, as the last child leaves home for a life of his or her own.

The launching stage may extend over a considerable period of time, as happens occasionally when an unmarried son or daughter stays at home indefinitely as a dependent, or it may be extremely short. No matter how abrupt it may seem, the departure of the young person from home is actually a culmination of a process that has been going on through the years. The processes of launching start during the earlier life cycle stages of the family, as children prepare for the decisions that will shape their futures.

From maximum size at the beginning of the stage, the nuclear family shrinks during the launching years to the original married pair. Before the stage is completed, the husband-father may also be a grandfather, and the wife-mother a grandmother, as the first-married son or daughter has children. Similarly, with the marriage of the first child, the mother becomes a mother-in-law, the father a father-in-law, and their children brothers- and sisters-in-law of the newly recruited family members by marriage.

The launching stage is marked by the simultaneous *release of the family's children* and the *addition of new members* (and their families) by marriage. Positional developmental tasks continue for the parents: as mother, wife, person, and probably mother-in-law and grandmother; as father, husband, person, and possibly father-in-law and grandfather. The children have their developmental tasks as young adults and younger children in the family of orientation and, when they marry, as husbands and wives in the establishment phase of their family of procreation (Chapter 7). The major *family goal* is the reorganization of the family into a continuous unity while releasing matured and maturing young people into lives of their own.

Babies were born in record numbers after World War II (1946–1964), and the period became popularly known as "the baby boom." As these babies grow up, the population swells in successively older age groups in what can be likened to a bubble in the *population profile* that moves steadily upward over the years (see Figure 12.1). This means for young adults (and their families) of the 1980s and 1990s: less college entrance competition, a possible easing of unemployment for young adults (depending on the economy), and a lessening of the youth culture phenomenon that dominated the 1960s and 1970s.

DEVELOPMENTAL TASKS OF YOUNG ADULTS

Throughout the first two decades of life as a child and as a teenager, a person lives within the expectations of age and grade. Now, as a young adult, he or she emerges from the norms of the age-grade system and steps out into a future of his or her own making. From now on success or failure depends largely on the choices he or she makes as a person (see Table 12.1). Face to face with the adult world, the young man or woman is eager to learn—in action. Few formal or theoretical opportunities are available for learning what is involved in the most crucial of life's decisions. Indeed, "early adulthood is the most individualistic period of life, and the loneliest one, in the sense that the individual, or at the most, two individuals, must proceed with a minimum of social attention and assistance to tackle the most important tasks of life" (Havighurst 1972, 83).

Establishing Autonomy as an Individual

Becoming a free and independent person involves more than reducing one's dependence upon one's parents. It involves learning to stand upon one's own feet, to make one's own decisions, to cope with life's problems responsibly, and to become a self-governing person. *Establishing*

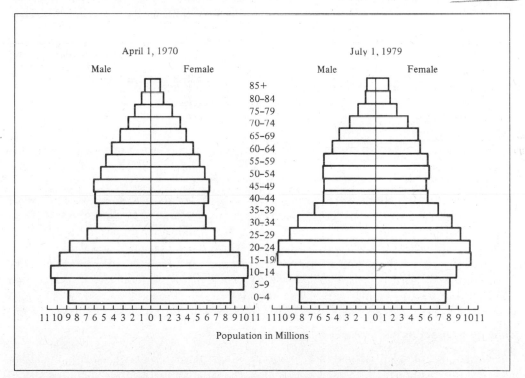

Figure 12.1 Age-sex distribution of the U.S. population (including armed forces overseas), 1970 and 1979. *Source:* Metropolitan Life Insurance Company, "Age-Sex Distribution of United States Population," *Statistical Bulletin* 61 (1980):16.

Table 12.1 DEVELOPMENTAL TASKS
OF A YOUNG ADULT

1. Establishing one's autonomy as an individual.
2. Planning a direction for one's life.
3. Getting an appropriate education.
4. Heading toward a vocation.
5. Appraising love and sexual feelings.
6. Becoming involved in love relationship(s).
7. Selecting a marriage partner.
8. Getting engaged.
9. Being married.

one's autonomy means attaining a sense of who one is and what one is to do with one's life. This is not automatically accomplished by leaving one's parental home for more independent living. It is a process that requires time and reflection and the clarification of one's own sense of self.

Not long ago, a girl was seen as leaving her father's protection for that of her husband, much as a young man left his mother's caretaking for that of his wife. This no longer tends to be the case. Today many young adults of both sexes postpone marriage in order to establish themselves with a sense of personal accomplishment, freedom, and autonomy. Demographer Paul Glick (1975) suggests a number of interrelated factors accounting for the delay in marriage:

1. The larger number of women going to college,
2. An excess of women of marriageable age, resulting in a "marriage squeeze,"
3. The sharp increase in women's employment,
4. The decline in the birthrate,
5. Expanding roles open to women outside the home, and
6. The revival of the women's movement. (ibid., 304)

There is a male counterpart for each of these factors in addition to the widely recognized desire of both males and females to experience life for themselves before settling down into marriage.

Some of today's adults will never marry; others are merely postponing love and marriage commitments until they feel ready for them. There is a ground swell of interest among today's young people to become mature human beings. This surge may be a conscious response to teenage marriages and pregnancies, which are notoriously unstable; a way to minimize the risk of becoming a divorce statistic; or an attempt to develop one's own potentials educationally, occupationally, sexually, socially, and emotionally before undertaking the responsibilities of marriage and family life.

Planning a Direction for One's Life

Some young people plan farther ahead than do others. Research over the years finds that interest in life planning and the ability to plan one's life are a predictable function of social class level—the higher the level, the greater the interest and ability to plan (Brim & Forer 1956). *Upwardly mobile families* tend either to carry their children along with them or to encourage their young people to climb, whereas young people from nonmobile families tend to remain static—85 percent in one study years ago (McGuire 1952, 113).

A greatly admired older adult may serve as a model for the emerging young adult. A young woman identifies with her computer teacher and sees herself as a computer specialist. A young man patterns himself after his father and plans to follow the same profession or enter the same business. Parents usually encourage a child whose plans conform to family tradition, so the young adult's progress is eased along the way.

There tends to be more upward mobility among those whose family relations have been difficult than among those whose early interpersonal relations have been satisfying (Ellis 1952). High levels of aspiration have been found to be related to (1) feelings of not being wanted by parents, (2) favoritism shown by parents for one's sibling(s), and (3) little attachment to parents (Dynes, Clarke, & Dinitz 1956). These findings support psychoanalytic and general social theories that unsatisfactory personal relationships in the family of orientation are significantly related to high levels of aspiration. The hypothesis is that a young person whose family life has been unhappy may struggle to better himself or herself as soon as he or she can cut loose from family ties. In some cases, the high levels of aspiration are fantasies unrelated to what is possible; in others, success results from realistic and highly motivated efforts to improve one's lot in life.

Other young adults may be so discouraged that they make few life plans. These so-called losers may turn to cults or drugs to ease their pain. Psychologically, drug abusers feel *alienated,* left out, lonely, like second-class citizens. An eight-year national longitudinal study of 1600 young men found that drug usage peaked in the college and military years. By the age of 23, 62 percent had tried marijuana (one-third used it weekly); 32 percent, amphetamines; 22 percent, psychodelics; 19 percent, barbituates; and more than 6 percent, heroin (Johnston, O'Malley, & Eveland 1975).

Although many students use drugs upon occasion, few show such symptoms of drug abuse as preoccupation with drugs, exclusive association with other drug users, negative self-esteem, and inability to carry on student life. The research team distinguished between drug abusers and drug users, who are found to closely resemble nonusers (Table 12.2). Only about one-third of 1981 entering freshmen felt that marijuana should be legalized, indicating that favorable attitudes toward drugs are declining among college students (Astin, King, & Richardson 1981, 56).

Getting an Appropriate Education

More young adults in the population (Figure 12.1) means higher college enrollments in the 1980s than in the 1970s. But, during the 1970s the percentage of male students of college age dropped, whereas the numbers and percentages of women students rose significantly from 20.3 percent in 1970 to 25.0 percent in 1980 (End of the youth boom 1981, 67). The question arises: Are there differences in the reasons why today's male and female students go to college? Both men and women college students say they go to college to enhance their earning power. Somewhat more coeds than male students rank learning more about things, getting a general education, and meeting new and interesting people as very important reasons for going to college. Slightly more women than men indicate they are heading toward graduate school (Table 12.3). However, the top six reasons for college attendance by both sexes are the same.

In the fall of 1981, nearly half of entering freshmen women (46.7 percent) and men (48.8

Table 12.2 DRUG ABUSE AMONG THE DISCOURAGED

Student's self-reported behavior	Drug abusers	Drug users	Nonusers
"Unable to finish projects"	47%	26%	26%
"I never found a group where I belong"	34	8	8
"Things often seem hopeless"	43	17	19
"Every time I try to get ahead someone or something stops me"	47	21	18
"Feel angry and frustrated most of the time"	42	24	20
"Often find it hard to get through the day"	36	19	18
Have run away from home	66	37	
Have failed courses	36	16	
Have been expelled	70	41	
Have damaged property on purpose	62	43	
Buy drugs to keep on hand	89	41	
Sell drugs for profit	51	14	

Source: Daniel Yankelovich, "Drug Users Vs. Drug Abusers," *Psychology Today* (October 1975): 41. Reprinted from *Psychology Today Magazine,* copyright © 1975, Ziff-Davis Publishing Company.

percent) came from families with annual incomes between $15,000 and $35,000. Another 27.8 percent of the men and 27.1 percent of the women had families with incomes between $40,000 and $100,000. Significantly larger percentages of women (48.5 percent) than men (37.5 percent) students in predominantly black colleges have families with incomes under $8,000 a year. This finding suggests that in the social and economic climate of the 1980s black women are highly motivated to educate themselves, and more of their low-income parents contribute to their college costs than do those of men in black colleges (Astin, King, & Richardson 1981, 16, 32). About half of all freshmen have some concern about financing their college costs, which they meet in a variety of ways: summer jobs, part-time employment, student loans, grants, scholarships, and savings (ibid., 58–61).

Getting an education appropriate to one's goals is a challenging developmental task for most students today. It is not easy to choose a college suited to one's needs nor to pursue a program leading to the life-style to which one aspires. Even more difficult is deciding when to stick with one's original choices and when to switch to possibly more promising alternatives.

Table 12.3 TOP-RANKING REASONS FOR GOING TO COLLEGE GIVEN AS "VERY IMPORTANT" (ENTERING FRESHMEN MEN AND WOMEN, FALL 1981)

Men's reasons	Percentage	Women's reasons	Percentage
Get a better job	75.7	Learn more about things	77.8
Make more money	70.5	Get a better job	76.8
Learn more about things	68.6	Gain a general education	73.4
Gain a general education	61.0	Make more money	63.6
Meet new, interesting people	46.7	Meet new, interesting people	63.6
Prepare for graduate school	43.4	Prepare for graduate school	47.3

Source: Alexander W. Astin, Margo R. King, and Gerald T. Richardson, *The American Freshman: National Norms for Fall 1981,* Cooperative Institutional Research Program Los Angeles: American Council on Education, University of California, 1981), pp. 18, 34. Data used with permission.

Heading Toward a Vocation

In some cultures a young man is expected to follow in his father's footsteps and carry on the family business. In the United States this pattern seems to be most pervasive in upper-class families where sons are groomed to carry on the family traditions. Young adults today face many more vocational possibilities than were formerly available. In 1870 there were only 338 vocations, in contrast to the tens of thousands by the late twentieth century—in electronics, atomic energy, space science, radar, television, plastics, and the medical, chemical, biological, and behavioral sciences.

More entering freshmen of both sexes see themselves as eventually becoming business executives, computer programmers and analysts, accountants, and actuaries than as pursuing other careers (Table 12.4). Nearly one out of five freshmen men see themselves as future engineers, and another 11 percent feel they are headed toward becoming business executives —the number-one-ranking career choice of freshmen women. More women than men (11.3 and 8.8 percent, respectively) are undecided about their probable future careers (Table 12.4). By the mid-1970s the majority of college women in one study believed their careers were of equal importance to those of their husbands. They expected to work all their lives and to get substantial help from their husbands with household chores when they married (Parelius 1975, 151).

The U.S. Department of Labor predicts better-than-average prospects in those fields where there has been a marked increase of jobs already: secretaries, cashiers, registered nurses, bank clerks, auto mechanics, accountants, and computer operators lead all others by wide margins (Outlook for 105 occupations 1982, 85). There are urgent needs for more satellite engineers and communications specialists. For every genetic scientist five research assistants are needed, and the shortage of computer programers is progressive (Taylor 1981, 70). Meanwhile, many college graduates are being forced into lower-level jobs. Labor experts predict that during the 1980s one in four college graduates will take a job not requiring college education (Greenberger 1982, 29). Some authorities believe America has oversold college as a path to vocational success.

While in the process of deciding what to do with one's life, some young adults sign up for a stint in the military. All four American services recently met or exceeded their recruiting goals. This trend is expected to continue as high rates of civilian unemployment, a prolonged recession, better pay, and renewed prestige of the military make service to one's country especially attractive. The percentage of high school graduates among new recruits rose from 68 percent in 1980 to 81 percent in 1981—with even better prospects for the future now that

Table 12.4 TOP-RANKING PROBABLE OCCUPATIONS OF ENTERING FRESHMEN, 1981

Men	Percentage	Women	Percentage
Engineer	19.5	Business executive	9.4
Business executive	11.2	Nurse	7.3
Computer programmer or analyst	7.5	Computer programmer or analyst	6.4
Accountant or actuary	4.9	Elementary teacher	6.4
Lawyer or judge	4.5	Accountant or actuary	6.1
Undecided	8.8	Undecided	11.3

Source: Alexander W. Astin, Margo R. King, and Gerald T. Richardson. *The American Freshman: National Norms for Fall 1981,* Cooperative Institutional Research Program Los Angeles: American Council on Education, University of California, 1981), pp. 22, 38. Data used with permission.

the army no longer accepts high school dropouts (Dudney 1982, 47). However, less than 2 percent of all freshmen men in 1981 anticipate making a career of military service (Astin, King, & Richardson 1981, 22), suggesting that enlistment is but an interval before heading into a career.

Specific aids in choosing a career are: (1) vocational guidance; (2) testing and counseling programs designed to clarify young adults' interests, aptitudes, and career goals; (3) part-time jobs, summer employment, and apprentice-like opportunities giving brief experience in various types of work without final commitment; and (4) concentrated career programs in which young adults interview and observe established adults in a variety of fields. Business executives advise liberal arts students to focus their career goals and to take business and technical courses to broaden their salable skills (Hacker 1976, 4). Parents who encourage their sons and daughters to investigate and train fully for their career choice greatly facilitate this developmental task.

Appraising Love and Sexual Feelings

Love is usually a requisite for close friendship, lasting intimacy, and marriage. But love feelings are hard to evaluate during the young adult years because they tend to be confused and intertwined with maturing sex drives (Chapter 6). In a culture that allows free access between the sexes and that sees love as a basis for marriage, it is important to understand and to appraise love accurately. By the late teens and early twenties a typical young person has experienced many kinds of love from intense short-lived infatuations to longer-lasting attachments that continue over many years. Differences between infatuation and love are summarized in Table 12.5.

The question of sexual involvement begins in the early teens and continues throughout adulthood. It centers in the way a given person views sexuality. It is closely related to one's self-image (MacCorquodale & DeLamater 1979). It is tied up with one's moral choices that lean toward fidelity or variety. It is central in what marriage means to an individual and to a couple. Being attracted to another person may or may not mean sexual expression of one's feelings. One decides whether or not to get involved sexually. As a person learns to recognize affection in himself or herself and significant others, love becomes valuable in itself and can be expressed in many ways.

Two important things each individual begins to learn within the family of orientation are to love and to wait. Each human being grows through successive stages of emotional maturity from early infancy onward. Learning to wait begins in the first few months of life when a baby so trusts his or her loving parents that the child is willing to wait a bit to be fed and cared for. Learning to wait for satisfaction continues in healthy development based upon trust and affection throughout the years. Learning to love is a lifelong process that goes through many stages and has a wide variety of expressions.

Premarital sex experience has increased over recent decades, and guilt about it has decreased (Bell & Coughey 1980, 355). *Living together* in college provides greater opportunity to interact, it may influence the development of dating relationships, and it appears not to pose a threat to marriage (Risman, Hill, Rubin, & Peplau 1981, 77). On the other hand, a sizable majority of undergraduates are found to be opposed to extramarital sexual involvements while approving nonsexual couple recreation (Weis & Slosnerick 1981). Both positive and negative attitudes toward coeducational living abound, with students generally

Table 12.5 DIFFERENCES BETWEEN INFATUATION AND LOVE

Infatuation	Love
1. Is the term applied to past attachments, often.	1. Is the term used to refer to a current attachment, usually.
2. Focuses frequently on quite unsuitable persons.	2. Object of affection is likely to be a suitable person.
3. Parents often disapprove.	3. Parents tend to approve.
4. Feelings of guilt, insecurity, and frustration are frequent.	4. Is associated with feelings of self-confidence, trust, and security.
5. Tends to be self-centered and restricted.	5. Kindlier feelings toward other people generally are associated.
6. Narrowly focuses on only a few highly visible or fantasied traits.	6. Broadly involves the whole personality.
7. Most frequent among young adolescents and immature persons.	7. Grows through the years with emotional maturity.
8. Simultaneous attachments to two or more at the same time are possible.	8. Loyalty centers in mutual commitment and involvement.
9. Can reoccur soon after a previous affair is over.	9. May slowly develop again after a previous lover has gone.
10. Boredom is frequent when sexual excitement dies down.	10. An ongoing sense of being alive when together precludes boredom.
11. Partners depend on external amusement for fun.	11. Joy is in many common interests and in each other.
12. Little change in the relationship over time.	12. Relationship changes and grows with ongoing association.
13. Shallow sensations come and go.	13. Deepening feelings provide steady warmth as more of life is shared.
14. Problems and barriers are usually disregarded.	14. Problems are tackled and worked out as they arise.
15. Romantic illusions have little regard for reality.	15. Faces reality with faith in growth and improvement.
16. Tends to last only a short time.	16. Tends to last over a long period of time.
17. Little mutual exploration of personality values and aspirations.	17. Shares hopes and dreams, feelings and meanings.
18. May be stereotyped "romance for romance's sake."	18. Tends to be highly individual, unique, and person-centered.
19. Can exploit the other as a person.	19. Has a protective, nurturing, caring concern.
20. A poor basis for marriage.	20. Enough to build a marriage on, perhaps—if other things are right.

Source: Evelyn Millis Duvall and Reuben Hill, *When You Marry,* rev. ed. (New York: Association Press; Boston: Heath, 1967), pp. 40–41. Reprinted with permission.

agreeing only that they be given the right to choose their campus living arrangements (Ferretti 1981).

Both men and women students see the permissive coed as immoral, immature, irresponsible, and insecure in contrast to the more sexually conservative student (Bridgwater 1982). There is little question that promiscuous young adults are more likely to be infected with venereal diseases. Both syphilis and gonorrhea rates are significantly higher for males than females and are highest in the young adult years by a wide margin (Figure 12.2). One further problem with premarital intercourse, even when confined to loving relationships, lies in its disapproval by adults (see Table 6.2) as well as many young people (Table 6.5).

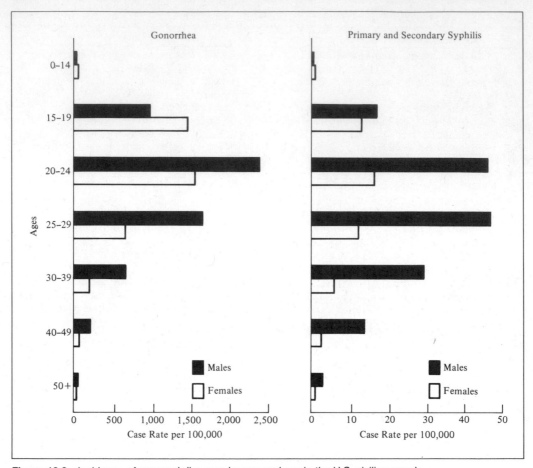

Figure 12.2   Incidence of venereal diseases by age and sex in the U.S. civilian population, 1978. *Source:* Metropolitan Life Insurance Company, *Statistical Bulletin* 61 (1980): 14.

Becoming Involved in Love Relationship(s)

Occasionally one hears of a couple who "fell in love at first sight," married within a few days, and lived happily ever after. Usually the process of becoming a pair is neither that simple nor that fast (see Chapters 5 and 6). Social scientists who have studied the *progressive involvement of couples* are able to trace the process of pair formation through dating and courtship in a series of steps that lead to marriage.

Lewis's (1973a) *premarital dyadic formation* (PDF) framework, which consists of six sequential achievements, was presented in Chapter 5 (see Figure 5.4). It is elaborated below as an illustration of how partners might become increasingly committed to each other.

1. The achievement of perceiving similarities (in each other's sociocultural background, values, interests, and personality);
2. The achievement of pair rapport (as seen in the couple's ease of communication,

positive evaluations of each other, satisfaction with their relationship, and validation of themselves by one another);

3. The achievement of openness between partners through mutual self-disclosure;
4. The achievement of role-taking accuracy (competence in mutual empathy);
5. The achievement of interpersonal role fit (as evidenced by the pair's observed similarity of personalities, role complementarity, and need complementarity); and
6. The achievement of dyadic crystallization (as seen in the pair's progressive involvement, functioning as a dyad, boundary establishment, mutual commitment to one another, and identity as a couple).

Friends and family members push promising pairs together when they invite the two, as a couple, to social events, family meals, and trips; assume that the pair will come together; comment on what a nice pair the two make together; and tell them that they are "made for each other." The positive social reactions of significant others enhance the couple's commitment, their boundary maintenance, dyadic functioning, value consensus, and dating-courtship status. As the pair internalize the social acceptance of their relationship, they are launched into a still-more-permanent union (Lewis 1973b).

Systematic study of communication among casual dating couples, seriously dating pairs, and engaged couples shows that communication develops within the dating relationship, so that marriage-bound pairs are more able to discuss and manage possible conflict than are couples at earlier stages of the courtship process. The researcher suggests not only that couples at later stages of dating have gone through developmental processes successfully but that they have also survived what might be a filtering or selective process (Krain 1975).

Selecting a Marriage Partner

Couples may break up at any stage of their association. Those who continue on into marriage proceed through the dating and courtship process with some mutual feeling that they are right for each other. Folklore has it that opposites attract, but marriage partners tend to be similar to one another in physical, psychological, and social characteristics (see Chapter 5).

Homogamy, the tendency for marriage partners to have similar characteristics, has been found in hundreds of studies of many thousands of couples over several decades of the twentieth century. Racial *endogamy* divides possible marriage partners into pools of one's own racial group and other racial groups, the tendency being for an individual to choose a mate within his or her own race. Religion divides each race into even smaller pools of eligible partners. In the United States the overwhelming tendency is for Jews to marry Jews, Catholics to marry Catholics, and, to a somewhat lesser degree, Protestants to marry Protestants (see Chapter 5). Ethnic origins further limit an individual's marital choice. Social class and education decrease still further the size of the pool of eligibles from which a person is likely to find a marriage partner. In most cases, a person eventually marries someone very similar to him- or herself.

Black women more than white marry men who are less well educated than they and have higher rates of marital instability, possibly associated with their higher incidence of deviation from normative mate selection patterns (Spanier & Glick 1980, 723). Interracial marriages may continue to increase somewhat as opportunities increase for members of minority races to secure an education, earn a good income, and move into social circles where potential mates are found. Interfaith marriages are hard to estimate because the 50 states do not require information about the religious affiliations of applicants for a marriage license. Cavan (1970) hypothetically suggests the probabilities of interfaith marriage by the nature of the in-groups involved. These may be hostile, indifferent, or friendly to each other. They may show a strong preference for marriage within their own group (endogamy), or they may endorse preferential endogamy or relatively permissive endogamy (Table 12.6).

Propinquity (living nearby) is a powerful factor in mate selection. Americans tend to marry their neighbors and associates at school and work. Studies of both rural and urban populations in the several regions of the country show a continuing tendency for marrying couples to come from the same county or from within 20 city blocks of one another (Bossard 1932–33; Davie & Reeves 1938–1939; Kennedy, 1942–1943; McClusky & Zander 1940; Mitchell 1941; Clarke 1952; Catton and Smircich 1964; and Clayton 1975). Mobile as Americans are, when they reach the point in their lives for serious courting and marriage, they tend to choose someone nearby.

Becoming Engaged

Getting engaged may seem like a pleasant "task" for young adults, but it is a many-faceted responsibility that is not easy for many couples. In-depth studies of couples approaching marriage consider three crucial tasks: (1) making oneself ready to take over the role of husband or wife, (2) disengaging oneself from especially close relationships that compete or interfere with commitment to the new marriage, and (3) adapting the patterns of gratification of premarital life to patterns of the newly formed couple relationship. To prepare themselves for marriage there must be a shift from self-orientation to mutuality and the development of a *couple identity* by the end of the engagement period (Rapoport 1964).

Engagement rituals contribute to the success of the engagement period. Many engaged pairs share the rituals of their respective families as a way of giving a sense of belonging to both families and as a way of selecting those common rituals that they both enjoy and want

Table 12.6   PROBABLE INTERMARRIAGE AMONG HOSTILE,
INDIFFERENT, AND FRIENDLY IN-GROUPS

	In-Group A: hostile to other in-groups; strongly endogamous	In-Group B: indifferent to other in-groups; preferential endogamy	In-Group C: friendly to other in-groups; permissive endogamy
In-Group D: hostile to other in-groups; strongly endogamous	No intermarriages	Almost no intermarriages	Few intermarriages
In-Group E: indifferent to other in-groups; preferential endogamy		Many intermarriages	Many intermarriages
In-Group F: friendly to other in-groups; permissive endogamy			Almost no restrictions on intermarriage

Source: Ruth Shonle Cavan, "Concepts and Terminology in Interreligious Marriage," *Journal for the Scientific Study of Religion* 9, no. 4 (Winter 1970): 314. Reprinted with permission.

to continue in their own family-to-be. Having Sunday dinner with his or her family, participating in family celebrations, going on family picnics, and attending church and community functions with one of the families are illustrations of the way rituals in the engagement weave the couple into the established larger family life.

Some engagement rituals are oriented toward the future—anticipating and preparing for the couple's marriage and family life. Ritualized house hunting, Saturday afternoon window-shopping, contributing to the piggy bank for special funds, calling on recently married friends, having a series of premarital conferences, and attending courses for engaged couples are all practices that tend to become future-oriented rituals during the engagement period.

A couple may move directly into marriage from a personal understanding that may have been tested in a period of living together without the formality of an engagement. But by the time they marry, they will have accomplished three important tasks: (1) established themselves as a pair—in their own eyes and in the eyes of both families and their mutual friends; (2) worked through intimate systems of communication that allow for exchange of confidences, an increasing degree of empathy, and the consequent ability to predict each other's responses; and (3) planned specifically for the marriage that lies ahead, both in practical matters (deciding where and on what they will live) and in the realm of values (reaching a consensus on how the common life will be lived).

Being Married

A bride and groom may be married barefoot at the edge of a beach, on a mountain ski slope, under a flowering tree, in a quick civil ceremony in the office of a justice of the peace, or in a *traditional ceremony* in the bride's church with some or all of the trappings of a church wedding: long white bridal gown and veil, bridesmaids and ushers, music, flowers, one or more officiating clergy, and members of both families and their friends present.

Marriage comes at later ages now than it formerly did. The bridegroom of the 1980s is about 25 years old; and his bride is some two years younger (Tables 2.1 and 2.2). These young adults have probably completed their education and had some work experience; some have money of their own for the kind of wedding they prefer. College-educated couples were the innovators who introduced the *new weddings* (Seligson 1973) that break tradition and follow the idiosyncratic ideas of the young pair. The overwhelming majority of weddings in upper-class families have remained rigidly conventional throughout recent decades. Most marriages of people in the Social Register are solemnized in church weddings—only a small percentage in civil ceremonies (Blumberg & Paul 1975). Americans in all social classes spend billions of dollars annually on weddings and the accompanying activities. A working man has been known to spend thousands of hard-earned dollars on an elaborate wedding for his only daughter with the idea that "nothing is too good for our little girl." Other families and their young adults prefer to use the money that might have gone into an expensive wedding for furnishing the couple's first home. One harassed father is said to have offered his daughter a check for $1000 if she and her husband-to-be would elope.

Whatever the type of ceremony and its social accompaniments, the most important factors are the persons involved rather than the things. A wedding that is planned to meet the needs of the situation as well as the preferences of the couple and their families is a multifaceted responsibility involving numerous specific decisions (Duvall & Hill 1960, 171–191). These choices are usually made by the couple and their families, the bride and her parents taking the major responsibility for the social aspects of the affair. The newly married pair now enter the establishment phase of the family life cycle, facing all of the developmental tasks it holds for them—as individuals and as a pair (Chapter 7).

DEVELOPMENTAL TASKS OF FAMILIES LAUNCHING YOUNG ADULTS

As they always have, most families today play active roles—over a considerable period of time—in getting their young people successfully launched into the world. While the first child is busy getting established as an autonomous young adult, there are probably one or more younger children still in the family, each with his or her own developmental tasks to accomplish. So the family's tasks involve not only assisting the young adult to become successfully *autonomous* but also maintaining a home base in which the other members of the family can thrive. Family developmental tasks at the launching-center stage are shown in Table 12.7 and elaborated in the following sections.

Adapting Physical Facilities and Resources for Releasing Young Adults

These are the accordion years of family life. The young adult's room lies empty through the college year, or while he or she is away for service, only to suddenly come alive during a holiday, or a leave, when the young person and his or her friends swoop in for a few days and nights. The family goes along on an even keel for some weeks and then must mobilize itself and all of its resources for a wedding, or a graduation, or both, which in turn will keep the household humming and the house bulging at the seams.

The physical plant is sorely taxed at this stage. The family car used for getting to work, and for shopping, is in constant demand by the young man or woman of the family whose engagements far and wide loom large in importance during the launching stage. Teenage siblings clamor for their share of the use of the car, the telephone, the television set, and the living room until, as one father described it, "This is the stage of life when a man is dispossessed in his own home." A mother comments somewhat ruefully that she does not mind the noise and the expense of young people in the home but that she will be glad to regain the use of her own living room when the courting couples have finally found homes of their

Table 12.7   STAGE-SENSITIVE FAMILY DEVELOPMENTAL TASKS AS LAUNCHING-CENTER FAMILIES

1. Adapting physical facilities and resources for releasing young adults.
2. Meeting launching-center families' costs.
3. Reallocating responsibilities among grown and growing offspring and their parents.
4. Developing increasingly mature roles within the family.
5. Interacting, communicating, and appropriately expressing affection, aggression, disappointment, success, sexuality, and so forth.
6. Releasing and incorporating family members satisfactorily.
7. Establishing patterns for relating to in-laws, relatives, guests, friends, community pressures, and impinging world pressures.
8. Setting attainable goals, rewarding achievement, and encouraging family loyalties within a context of personal freedom.

own. Few families complain when facilities are sorely taxed at this stage of family living, but the fact remains that for many the flexible rearrangement of available resources to meet the variety of functions within families at the launching-center stage is a task indeed.

Meeting the Expenses of a Launching-Center Family

With some exceptions, families at this stage are carrying their peak load of family expenses. These are the years when young adults need financial help to carry them through college or other educational programs, to obtain specialized training and experience, to become established during the "starvation period" of any of the professions, to pay union initiation fees and dues as workers, and to finance the wedding and the new home-in-the-making. Such costs are over and above the already established expenditures budgeted for the family. Many young people today help by earning what they can, as young adults always have, but few are in a position to contribute heavily to the family budget at the very time that they are establishing themselves independently.

Family expenditures are highest when the oldest child is about 19 in families of one, two, or three children. Costs mount during this period and rapidly decline as the children are launched. A professional or business executive is, fortunately, at the height of his or her earning power; but clerical people, salespersons, operatives, and service workers now are earning less than they did before inflation was so great (Oppenheimer 1974, 236). So some supplementation may be necessary to carry the costs of launching-center functions.

The husband may work overtime as a laboring man, get a summer job as a teacher, or try to fit a part-time job in with his regular position. His wife is possibly in the labor force. The young adult and other children in the family may have jobs of some kind on a part-time basis while in school and full-time after their education is completed. These sources of income may not be sufficient to meet such special costs as those involved in an expensive wedding or college tuition and fees.

A United Press International survey predicts that a four-year college education soon will cost more than $50,000 in the most expensive institutions of higher learning (McCormack 1982). With spiraling college costs, many families consider alternatives to college for some young hopefuls, or they look into possibilities at state universities or community colleges where costs are lower. They also explore the various grants, scholarships, and loans available through college-aid offices. Even so, a family may have to float a loan, borrow on life insurance, increase the mortgage on their home, or tighten its belt wherever it can to meet current and prospective costs.

Reallocating Responsibilities Among Grown and Growing Children in the Family

This is the stage in many a family when father and mother can sit back and let their children run the house and their own affairs. Older sons and daughters thrive on accepting real responsibilities when they feel they are on their own. Younger children in a family tend to model themselves after their older brothers and sisters, and often they are more inclined to follow their lead than to obey their parents. The young adult about to be launched often has special prestige among his or her younger siblings, who willingly work under any new shift in family leadership.

Parental flexibility and the growing competence of the family's children in carrying through effectively the tasks of the household and the management of their own lives work together for the successful accomplishment of this task. As young adults begin to take on more real responsibility for their own and the family's welfare, the parents play the complementary roles of letting go and standing by with encouragement, reassurance, and appreciation.

Developing Increasingly Mature Roles Within the Family

Parents often live vicariously through all the terrors and threats of emancipation that beset their young people at the same time that they themselves are living through crises in their own lives. A woman old enough to have young adult children today has a "head of steam" up both physically and emotionally, thanks to better nutrition, medical services, lightened burdens at home, and shifting feminine roles, all unknown to women of an earlier age. She is apt to be vigorous, often feeling better than she has her whole life. She probably has a job of her own, with its problems and rewards. But she may feel somewhat confused as her older children no longer need her mothering. Before she has quite prepared herself for it, her children are no longer children. They now are taking their confidences to others; their expressions of affection are now for strangers. In comparison with their youthful attractiveness, she may feel dowdy and neglected, as indeed she may be. Through the years she might have put her home and children first, even to the point of neglecting her own appearance and sense of self.

This is the time when a young adult can assume a mature role in encouraging his or her mother to (1) retool for work at the level of her potential, (2) take new interest in her appearance (make her a gift of a new hairstyle or a garment she would not buy for herself, for instance), and (3) join with her in a health program of mutually beneficial diet and exercise. Similarly, young people in the family can assume more mature roles in relation to their father, who has his own struggles these days. They can build up his ego, consult him about problems, discuss common interests, and give him the respect he deserves.

The launching stage father is in a critical bind between the pressures and dissatisfactions of his work and his anxiety about his diminishing masculinity—an attribute highly prized by men. His characteristic slowing down in contrast with the youthful vigor of his growing sons and daughters is personally threatening. He may attribute his reduced potency to monogamous monotony. The "dangerous period" arrives when a man feels he must prove his virility—even, if need be, with more youthful partners. This makes him feel guilty and easily upset by his son's girl troubles or his daughter's sexual involvement. The launching time brings the crises of both generations onto a collision course.

Parents grapple with the haunting fear that somehow, someway, they might have done a better job in raising their children, now so nearly grown. The family recognizes that it is being evaluated by how well its children turn out. Yet the problems that attend achieving full adulthood maritally, vocationally, and socially are so many and the solutions so few! Six sequential national surveys find little evidence of parental happiness emanating from their children. As long as children are in the home, they are found to have a negative effect on their parents' psychological well-being (Glenn & McLanahan 1981, 409). More interdependent, mature young adults might reverse this trend.

Revitalizing the marriage may be an urgent part of this developmental task. For years the husband and wife have focused their attention on maintaining their home and attending their children's needs. Now they are wise to turn toward one another for the nurturance, companionship, and support they both may long for, even without realizing it. As the marriage relationship improves, the pair find more satisfaction in one another, their emotional investment in their children undergoes a healthy reappraisal, and they ready themselves for the latter half of their lives together.

Maintaining Communication in the Family

Both happily and unhappily married men and women feel that communication contributes more to happiness in marriage than any other factor. Being in love with each other is ranked second in importance for marital happiness, and their emotional need for each other is rated third. By contrast, such things as possessions and good food are considered least important (Landis 1969).

Being able to get through to one another in the family is especially important during the launching stage. This is the time when the young adult is emerging from the family and working through some of the most important and most complex tasks of his or her life. The young person who can freely bring questions and alternative solutions to his or her parents as sounding boards can get invaluable help from their perspective. At the same time, the parents face the possibility that critical young adults will challenge their way of life. As Russell Baker wryly observes, "Now they are trapped between grandfather's wheezing and the homiletic tedium of two or three young fogies denouncing the shallowness of their goals" (Baker 1967.)

Young adults and their parents often disagree on matters that affect them both. More young than older adults hold liberal attitudes regarding religion, abortion, premarital sex, and smoking marijuana (*NBC National News Poll* 1976). It is not unusual for parents to question their nearly grown sons' and daughters' choice of vocation, intimate associates, and marriage partners, their use of time and money, and many other decisions that young adults feel they have a right to make on their own. When parents have difficulty freeing their young adult children to live their own lives, communication between the generations in the family is especially difficult.

Peer pressures on young people and their parents often pull in opposite directions, further complicating family interaction; so this developmental task is difficult to achieve satisfactorily. It can be successfully accomplished if a solid foundation of good parent-child relationships has been established and if now, at the "proving time," the young adults feel that whatever happens, their family is back of them—with faith in their ability to work things through and the willingness to look at any situation with loving concern.

Releasing and Incorporating Family Members Satisfactorily

Some supposedly emancipated young adults come flying back to the nest. A daughter's marriage fails, unemployment removes a grown son's sole source of support, military service temporarily scars a young man, or some other trauma sends previously launched young adults back to their parents' home, sometimes with their children and all their worldly goods. Successful refilled nests seem to be those with plenty of space and good communication established over the years (Langway, Kirsch, & Hewitt 1980).

Unlaunchable young are still another phenomenon that delays the accomplishment of this family developmental task. Handicapped sons and daughters may linger on in their family of orientation until they can be rehabilitated for independent living, or they may stay on indefinitely. Other seemingly able-bodied young adults stay on in their parents' home, sometimes for years, with no reason given or asked. Allotting space, sharing responsibilities for the household (financial and otherwise), arranging for privacy, and caring for dependents are but surface manifestations of this iceberg in the family home (Foote 1978).

When grown sons and daughters do not leave home on time, or fail to "turn out right," their parents are left with a sense of personal failure and confusion (Nydegger & Mitteness 1979; Wilen 1979). Parents expect that upon the launching of their children they as the parental pair will at last be freed to work on some of their own developmental tasks. Studies of generations in the family conclude that although parents and children mutually shape one another's developmental milieux, there is little knowledge of what each generation expects of the other or of what they take for granted (Hagestad 1981).

Widening the family circle begins with the first marriage of a son or daughter. The extended family now includes both the new family unit being established and—with more or less interaction—the family of the son- or daughter-in-law. The family in its earlier expanding stages took upon itself one child at a time (except in multiple births), and that as a tiny infant. The widening of the family circle at the launching-center stage is dramatically different in two major respects: (1) the addition is multiple, consisting of the entire family of in-laws, and (2) the additional persons are at varying levels of maturity, with a preponderance of adults.

The situation is complicated by the fact that while the young adult of the one family is intimately known within his or her own family, for a while he or she remains an outsider to the young mate's family of orientation. If there is too close a bond between one young adult and his or her parents, it is difficult for the new unit to achieve equilibrium, as we see in the following analysis.

Every married couple belongs to three families. They belong first of all to themselves. They are the "we" of the new family they are founding together. But at the same time they also belong to his family and to hers. If they are to establish a strong family unit of their own, they must inevitably realign their loyalties to the place where "our" family comes before either "yours" or "mine." This is *the elemental triangle of married living.* Unless the cohesive force in the new family unit is stronger than that which ties either of the couple to the parental home, the founding family is threatened (see Figure 12.3).

In Figure 12.3A, you have in-law trouble because my family is too close. It may be because I am still immature and not ready to emancipate myself from my parental home. It may be that one or more members of my family are possessive and find it difficult to let me go. It may be that circumstances within my family require from me more loyalty and attention than I can comfortably give at the time that I am involved in building my own home and marriage. Whatever the reason, if the forces pulling me/us toward loyalties to my home are too strong, the development of our common sense of identity is delayed or weakened.

In Figure 12.3B, your family is too close, and so I have in-law trouble. Because you are bound so tightly to your family, I am pulled away from mine, and we make little progress in establishing ours.

In Figure 12.3C, our family unit comes first in our joint loyalties. We are threatened neither by the ties that bind us to your family nor by the bonds that unite us to mine. We

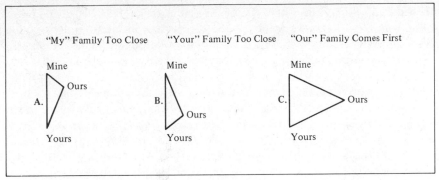

Figure 12.3 The elemental triangle of married living. *Source:* Evelyn Millis Duvall, *In-laws: Pro and Con* (New York: Association Press, 1954), p. 279.

are able to make progress as a new family because the force of our common identification pulls us out and away together into a home of our own. Now we can share in the common heritage of both your family and mine because we are not threatened by the pull from either. We are free to enjoy being members of the entire extended family, without the stress of in-law strains (Duvall 1954, 278–279).

Accomplishing this developmental task paves the way for success in the next, which has to do with coping with the many influences from outside the original family circle.

Establishing Patterns for Dealing with Influences from Outside

At the launching stage the family is bombarded as never before with a wide variety of outsiders in the form of in-laws, relatives, guests, neighbors, friends, community pressures, and impinging world stresses. Young adult sons and daughters have been bringing guests and friends home for years. But now it is different in that any one of them may become a roommate, a sweetheart, or a marriage partner. Now parents have to be on guard lest they say or do something that threatens a significant relationship about which they have known nothing.

Community pressures to conform can put a strain on a family, especially when the push is in opposite directions. Friends of the young pair go along with their sharing the same room when they come to visit, but their parents and their peers are often of a more traditional mind. So what is a family to do? Liberal-conservative stances on all kinds of issues can split a family and strain their relationships until they have learned how to deal with controversy effectively.

Headline issues cause open warfare in some families as a member takes such an intransigent stand that no other position in a widely discussed conflict is possible. One does not have to be an Archie Bunker to be hard to get along with on today's issues. In an age when all kinds of world problems surface daily in the news, a family must be prepared to cope with widely differing opinions and values within its membership.

Encouraging Family Loyalties Within a Context of Freedom

This is a time when a young adult tries out conflicting ways of life to test the family's values and to catch a glimpse of his or her own future. This is the only time in life—when he or she is being launched from home base into a life of his or her own—that the young adult is free to pull loose from old allegiances without basic threats and instabilities. The young man or woman critically reviews life within the family of orientation and makes comments from time to time that may severely challenge the parents and their ways of dealing with him or her.

The two generations even see their differences differently. Members of the younger generation want to establish their own values in line with the changing world around them, so they stress the differences between themselves and their elders. Their parents are concerned with having *social heirs,* so they tend to minimize conflicting value systems that might jeopardize the cohesion of the family (Bengtson & Kuypers 1971). The tendency for the older generation to view parent-child relations more favorably than the younger has been termed the *generational stake.*

However, evidence from a number of substantial studies points to a remarkable congruence of values and attitudes between the young adult and parental generations (No silence please 1969). Less than one-fourth of the most liberal students feel that the differences between their own values and those of their parents are very great. The majority of 18- to 24-year-old men and women in and out of college clearly identify more with their families than with their own generation, according to their own reports (Table 12.8). Sons are found to desire more intimate relationships with their fathers in this than in earlier generations (Zick 1982, 29). Good father-son relationships are marked by "feelings of identification and pride, concern and support" (ibid., 33).

Some young people get into trouble as they sample strange new ways. Queenie, in Noel Coward's *This Happy Breed,* runs off with a married man, is deserted, tries to make a go of running a tea shop in southern France, and finally is brought back home to a reconciliation by a loyal lover who grew up next door. Not all youthful mistakes are as critical. Not all turn out so well in the end. But in some way or other, most young people blunder as they try their wings and attempt to fly off into life on their own. Parents who are patient while these efforts are being made are of far more help than those who stand by clucking their fears as the fledgling leaves the nest. Families who stand by, offering assurance, encouragement, and help as needed, especially in any of life's first (first formal party, first job, first trip away from home, and the rest), give their young people the stable home base that is required for a successful launching.

Table 12.8   YOUNG ADULTS' VALUES AND IDENTIFICATION WITH THEIR FAMILIES AND PEERS (IN PERCENT)

	No college	Practical college[a]	Forerunner college[b]
Differences between parents' and your values:			
Very great	15	11	24
Moderate	41	49	51
Slight	44	40	25
Identification and sense of solidarity with:			
Family	82	78	65
Own generation	60	65	68

[a]Students in practical colleges have definite career plans (business, engineering, etc.).
[b]Students in forerunner colleges have intangible career plans (arts and humanities largely).
Source: Fortune-Yankelovich Survey, "What They Believe," *Fortune,* January 1969, pp. 70–71, 179–181.

Families that succeed in maintaining a secure home base for the younger members of the family during the launching-center stage are those that attempt to accept comfortably the way of life the young adult has chosen. They do not feel too threatened by it. They help younger siblings to see that there are many good ways to live a life and that when their time comes, they, too, will find their way.

SUMMARY

The launching stage of the family life cycle begins with the first child leaving home to go to college, to marry, or to go into military service or some other form of independent living; it ends with the parents in an empty nest as the last child leaves home for a life of his or her own. From maximum size at the beginning of this stage, the nuclear family shrinks to the original husband-wife pair at the end. By then both parents are probably grandparents as one or more of their sons or daughters marries and has children. Recruitment of family members takes place as relatives by marriage become part of the extended family. The major family goal is reorganization of the family into a continuous unity as grown children are released.

Young adults, now a declining part of the population, struggle with at least nine developmental tasks: planning a direction for life, heading toward a vocation, getting an appropriate education, establishing autonomy as an individual, appraising love and sexual feelings, becoming involved in one or more love relationships, selecting a marriage partner, being engaged, and getting married. Each of these developmental tasks of young adulthood has its rewards and its challenges, its successes and its failures, that lead in turn to either satisfaction or disappointment with oneself and with life.

Meanwhile, crucially important family developmental tasks are being tackled to assist maturing young people in becoming autonomous while maintaining a secure home base for other members of the family. Stage-sensitive family developmental tasks as launching-center families are: adapting physical facilities for releasing young adults, meeting launching family costs, reallocating responsibilities among grown and growing offspring and their parents, developing increasingly mature roles within the family, maintaining intrafamily communication, releasing and incorporating family members, establishing patterns for dealing with influences from outside, and encouraging family loyalties within a context of freedom. Conflicts and confrontations between young adults who are struggling to be free and their families who are trying to ensure ongoing continuity and unity are normal and serve as a challenge to both generations.

REFERENCES

Astin, A. W., King, M. R., & Richardson, G. T. 1981. *The American freshman: National norms for fall 1981.* Cooperative Institutional Research Program. Los Angeles: American Council on Education, University of California.

Baker, R. Observer: Youth as a tiresome old windbag. New York *Times,* October 17, 1967, p. 46.

Bell, R. R., & Coughey, K. 1980. Premarital sexual experience among college females, 1958, 1968, and 1978. *Family Relations* 29:353–357.

Bengtson, V. L., & Kuypers, J. A. 1971. Generational differences and the developmental stake. *Aging and Human Development* 2:249–259.

Blumberg, P. M., & Paul, P. W. 1975. Continuities and discontinuities in upper-class marriages. *Journal of Marriage and the Family* 37:63–77.

Bossard, J. H. S. 1932–1933. Residential propinquity as a factor in marriage selection. *American Journal of Sociology* 38:219–224.

Bridgwater, C. A. 1982. Do sexually active women have less character? *Psychology Today* 16:22.

Brim, O. G., & Forer, R. 1956. A note on the relation of values and social structure to life planning. *Sociometry* 19:54–60.

Catton, W. R., & Smircich, R. J. 1964. A comparison of mathematical models for the effect of residential propinquity on mate selection. *American Sociological Review* 29:522–529.

Cavan, R. S. 1970. Concepts and terminology in interreligious marriage. *Journal for the Scientific Study of Religion* 9:314.

Clarke, A. C. 1952. An examination of the operation of residential propinquity as a factor in mate selection. *American Sociological Review* 27:17–22.

Clayton, R. R. 1975. *The family, marriage, and social change.* Boston, MA: Heath.

Davie, M. R., & Reeves, R. J. 1938–1939. Propinquity of residence before marriage. *American Journal of Sociology* 44:510–517.

Dudney, R. S. 1982. All-volunteer force gets new lease on life. *U.S. News & World Report,* May 17, 1982, pp. 47, 50.

Duvall, E. M. 1954. *In-laws: Pro and con.* New York: Association Press.

Duvall, E. M., & Hill, R. 1960. *Being married.* Boston, MA: Heath.

———. 1967. *When you marry.* rev. ed. New York: Association Press; Boston: Heath.

Dynes, R. R., Clarke, A. C., & Dinitz, S. 1956. Levels of occupational aspiration: Some aspects of family experience as a variable. *American Sociological Review* 21:212–215.

Ellis, E. 1952. Social psychological correlates of upward social mobility among unmarried career women. *American Sociological Review* 17:558–563.

End of the youth boom 1981. *U.S. News & World Report,* November 9, 1981, pp. 66–67.

Ferretti, F. 1981. Students report advantages, problems of coed campus living. New York *Times News Service,* March 30, 1981.

Foote, A. C. 1978. The kids who won't leave home. *Atlantic* 241:118–122.

Fortune-Yankelovich Survey. 1969. What they believe. *Fortune,* January 1969, pp. 70–71, 179–181.

Glenn, N. D., & McLanahan, S. 1981. The effects of offspring on the psychological well-being of older adults. *Journal of Marriage and the Family* 43:409–421.

Glick, P. C. 1975. Living arrangements of children and young adults. Paper read at the annual meeting of the Population Association of America, Seattle, Washington, April 17–19, 1975.

Greenberger, R. S. 1982. An oversupply of college graduates forces some into lower-level jobs. *Wall Street Journal,* February 25, 1982, pp. 29, 35.

Hacker, D. W. 1976. Jobs for new grads: The hunting is still tough. *National Observer,* January 3, 1976, p. 4.

Hagestad, G. O. 1981. Parent and child: Generations in the family. In *Human development,* ed. T. Field, chap. 28. New York: Wiley.

Havighurst, R. J. 1972. *Developmental tasks and education.* New York: McKay.

Hollingshead, A. B. 1950. Cultural factors in the selection of marriage mates. *American Sociological Review* 15:619–627.

Johnston, L., O'Malley, P., & Eveland, L. 1975. *Drugs and American youth.* Ann Arbor: Institute of Social Research, University of Michigan.

Kennedy, R. J. R. 1942–1943. Premarital residential propinquity and ethnic endogamy. *American Journal of Sociology* 48:580–584.

Krain, M. 1975. Communication among premarital couples at three stages of dating. *Journal of Marriage and the Family* 37:609–618.

Landis, J. T. 1969. Functional and dysfunctional aspects of stress in happy and unhappy marriages.

Paper read at the annual meeting of the National Council on Family Relations, Washington, D.C., October 22–25, 1969.

Langway, L., Kirsch, J., & Hewitt, B. 1980. Flying back to the nest. *Newsweek,* April 7, 1980, p. 86.

Lewis, R. A. 1973. A longitudinal test of a developmental framework for premarital dyadic formation. *Journal of Marriage and the Family* 35:16–25. (a)

Lewis, R. A. 1973. Social reaction and the formation of dyads: An interactionist approach to mate selection. *Sociometry* 36:409–418. (b)

McClusky, H. Y., & Zander, A. 1940. Residential propinquity and marriage in Branch County, Michigan. *Social Forces* 79–81.

McCormack, P. 1982. Higher education costs stay on upward spiral. *UPI* release, February 15, 1982.

MacCorquodale, P., & Delamater, J. 1979. Self-image and premarital sexuality. *Journal of Marriage and the Family* 41:327–339.

McGuire, C. 1952. Conforming, mobile, and divergent families. *Marriage and Family Living* 14:113.

Metropolitan Life Insurance Company. 1980. Age-sex distribution of United States population. *Statistical Bulletin* 61:14.

Mitchell, D. 1941. Residential propinquity and marriage in Carver and Scott Counties, Minnesota. *Social Forces* 20:256–259.

NBC National News Poll. 1976. Network report, January 4, 1976.

No silence please. 1969. *Center Magazine* 2:83–86.

Nydegger, C. N., & Mitteness, L. 1979. Role development: The case for fatherhood. Paper presented at the annual meeting of the Gerontological Society, Washington, D.C.

Oppenheimer, V. K. 1974. The life-cycle squeeze: The interaction of men's occupational and family life cycles. *Demography* 11:227–245.

Outlook for 105 occupations: Estimates for growth in jobs by 1990. 1982. *U.S. News & World Report,* May 17, 1982, p. 85.

Parelius, A. P. 1975. Emerging sex-role attitudes, expectations, and strains among college women. *Journal of Marriage and the Family* 37:146–153.

Rapoport, R. 1964. The transition from engagement to marriage. *Acta Sociologica* 9.

Risman, B. J., Hill, C. T., Rubin, Z., & Peplau, L. A. 1981. Living together in college: Implications for courtship. *Journal of Marriage and the Family* 43:77–83.

Seligson, M. 1973. *The eternal bliss machine: America's way of wedding.* New York: Morrow.

Spanier, G., & Glick, P. C. 1980. Mate selection differentials between whites and blacks in the United States. *Social Forces* 58:707–725.

Taylor, R. A. 1981. Where hot new careers will open in the '80s. *U.S. News & World Report,* December 7, 1981, pp. 70–71.

Weis, D. L., & Slosnerick, M. 1981. Attitudes toward sexual and nonsexual extramarital involvements among a sample of college students. *Journal of Marriage and the Family* 43:349–358.

What's happening to the American family? 1978. *Better Homes and Gardens*, Des Moines, IA: Meredith Corporation.

Wilen, J. B. 1979. Changing relationships among grandparents, parents, and their young adult children. Paper presented at the annual meeting of the Gerontological Society, Washington, D.C.

Yankelovich, D. 1975. Drug users vs. drug abusers. *Psychology Today* 9:39–42.

Zick, R. 1982. Fathers and sons . . . the search for reunion. *Psychology Today* 16:23–33.

Chapter 13

Middle-aged Parents in an Empty Nest

MAJOR CONCEPTS

The bridging generation
   Care giver of the very old
Kin-keeping roles
Lineage bridge
Middle age, middlescence
   Male climacteric
   Menopause
   Midlife transition
Postparental middle years
Parent-caring roles
Redefinition of roles
Social roles
Husband/wife roles

Traditional, stereotyped roles
Complementary roles,
   complementarity
   Flexible roles
Middle-aged as new pioneers
Need to nurture
   Reciprocal bolstering
The lineage bridge
   Care giver of the very old
   Parent caring
Repudiation of family values
Reaffirmation of life's values

The family life cycle stage of the middle years begins with the departure of the last child from the home and continues to retirement or death of one of the spouses. This may be a period of only a few months, as in the case of the late launching of a son or daughter or the early retirement of the husband. The stage may stop abruptly with the premature death of either husband or wife, or it may be prolonged by continued employment. It may be delayed indefinitely by a dependent child who stays on at home.

The husband and wife are usually in their fifties when they enter the postparental middle years and somewhere near their mid-sixties when the man's retirement takes them into the final stage of the family life cycle. Throughout the middle years the married couple alone constitute the nuclear family, maintaining their husband-wife interaction as the central interpersonal relationship. At this time each occupies several positions with multiple roles in the family: husband, father, father-in-law, and grandfather; wife, mother, mother in law, and grandmother; and son or daughter of aging parents. Husband and wife in the middle years are the *bridging generation,* with both younger and older members of the family looking to them for strength and support from time to time.

The departure of grown children from the home to establish their independence is a turning point for the family. It could be considered a crisis in the sense that each member, and the family as a whole, enters a period in which new patterns must be established and former habits abandoned as inappropriate. However, Neugarten (1970, 87) observes that when the empty nest stage comes at the expected time, it represents not so much a crisis as a matter of timing and adjustment—to a normal aspect of the sequence and rhythm of the life cycle.

In these latter decades of the twentieth century, the middle-aged couple stage typically lasts longer than any previous stage in the family life cycle. Up to the turn of the century, the likelihood was that a woman would be widowed before her last child left home or that a mother would have died before seeing the first of her children married. Now a married couple typically have 12 to 15 years together between the launching of their last child and the death of the first spouse (Table 13.1; see also Figure 2.1 and Tables 2.1 and 2.2).

Statistically speaking, middle-aged parents are new in this century. As seen in the 1890 column of Table 13.1, in the last decade of the nineteenth century the typical husband and wife did not survive the marriage of their last child. Today more adults live out their life span;

Table 13.1   AGES OF HUSBAND AND WIFE AT CRITICAL STAGES IN THE FAMILY LIFE CYCLE, UNITED STATES, 1890–1980s

Stage of the family life cycle	1890	1940	1950	1980s[a]
Median age of husband at:				
First marriage	26.1	24.3	22.8	25+
Birth of last child	36.0	29.9	28.8	31+
Marriage of last child	59.4	52.8	50.3	55+
Death of one spouse (husband)	57.4	63.6	64.1	69+
Death of other spouse (wife)	66.4	69.7	71.6	78+
Median age of wife at:				
First marriage	22.0	21.5	20.1	23+
Birth of last child	31.9	27.1	26.1	29+
Marriage of last child	55.3	50.0	47.6	53+
Death of one spouse (husband)	53.3	60.9	61.4	67+
Death of other spouse (wife)	67.7	73.5	77.2	78+

[a] Projections.

Source: Paul C. Glick, "The Life Cycle of the Family," *Marriage and Family Living* 17 (February 1955): 4; and current unpublished census data projections for the 1980s by Paul C. Glick, personal communication, 1982.

and since they have fewer children, they spend more years as middle-aged and older adults in an empty nest.

The fastest-growing segments of the population of the United States between now and the year 2000 will be among men and women 35 years of age and older (Table 13.2). By the year 2025, 24 percent of all Americans will be middle-aged (Kranczer 1984, 17). This means that as middle-aged and older people become more numerous, the empty nest stage of the family life cycle will increasingly be seen as normal and expected by more and more families (Norton 1983, 268).

Recent U.S. Departments of Commerce and Labor reports indicate that Americans between 45 and 64 are at the peak of their earning power, family oriented, and politically active. They vote in significantly larger percentages than do citizens of younger ages; fewer live below the poverty level; and few are inclined to move from place to place (Latest findings on middle age Americans 1981, p. 41; Middle age the best of times?, 1982, 67–68).

Multidisciplinary study of the middle years of the human life span is relatively recent

Table 13.2   U.S. POPULATION GROWTH BY AGE GROUPS, 1980–2000 (IN THOUSANDS)

Population by age groups	1980	2000	Percentage change
All ages	227,729	266,497	+17.0
Children and teenagers	71,965	78,134	+ 8.6
Young adults (20 to 34)	59,035	52,915	− 10.4
Younger middle-aged (35 to 49)	37,864	62,119	+64.1
Older middle-aged (50 to 64)	33,549	40,884	+21.9
65 and over	25,316	32,445	+28.2

Source: U.S. Bureau of the Census, unpublished data, provided by Dr. Paul Glick, who says, "All the above figures were published in 1977, well before the 1980 Census was taken, but they agree so closely with the 226 million or so shown by the 1980 census count that they are still being provided to users of the Bureau data, pending a time-consuming adjustment to the 1980 census figures," personal communication, 1982. Official projections show even larger proportions of the population will be middle-aged during the first half of the twenty-first century (U.S. Bureau of the Census 1983).

(Eurich 1982; Greenspan & Pollock 1981). Robert Havighurst sees the dominant concern of the years between 50 and 60 to be that of creating a new life-style, whereas the decade between 60 and 70 is usually devoted to deciding whether to *disengage* and how (Havighurst n.d., 28, 31–36). "The change which comes in the fifties makes the future seem to be a short period of time, in which there may not be time to do everything one wants to do" (ibid., 32).

DEVELOPMENTAL TASKS OF THE POSTPARENTAL WOMAN

The developmental tasks of the pre-middle-aged wife and mother required that top priority and most of her time and attention went to the bearing and rearing of her children. When the last child leaves home, her central mothering tasks become obsolete, and she must undertake new roles for the years ahead. Up to this point she has invested a great deal of emotional energy in her children. Now that they are no longer at home, her first tendency may be to follow them with her continuing maternal concern in ways that delay their full autonomy as young adults. Her first task, then, is to set her children free at the same time that she frees herself from her emotional need to be needed by her children. The formerly dependent mother-child relationship must be converted into one of mature interdependence in which mother and grown children mutually support and encourage one another without intruding into one anothers' lives.

This task is easier for the mother who has been releasing her children to make their own decisions all through the years. It is harder for the mother who clings and refuses to let her children go, now that they have become adults. In either case a mother can encourage her children to become autonomous by seeking other outlets for her need to provide nurturance. She may throw herself into other projects, into her career, and/or into community service and concern for children and youth generally. Freed of a consuming need to be needed by her own children, she can accept young adult sons and daughters, their husbands, wives, and children as dear friends whose independence is respected and promoted.

Maintaining Health and a Sense of Well-being

Menopause takes place sometime between a woman's late forties and early fifties. Biologically, menopause signals the close of the reproductive cycle, the cessation of menses, and the slowing down of ovarian functioning. The latter upsets the endocrine balance and brings on one or more of the familiar signs of the woman's "change of life": hot and cold flashes, sweating, excitability, and other symptoms. How well a middle-aged woman weathers her menopause depends on her success in adapting to its inevitable physical changes and those that are to come—changes in skin, hair, eyes, energy level, and body tone, and weight gain. *Middle age* was once defined as "that time of life when one stops growing everywhere except in the middle."

Many women find that the middle years have their own charm. With a healthful regimen of weight control, regular exercise, a well-balanced diet high in proteins, fresh fruits and vegetables, adequate rest, and whatever else her doctor prescribes to keep her fit, she feels as good now as she ever did. Now she has time to do the things she has always enjoyed and to develop new interests that keep her vitally alive.

Going back to school is a route many midlife women take to develop talents, to continue education interrupted many years earlier, to sharpen skills for a better job, or to enrich their sense of well-being. "Midlife Women in the 1980s," prepared for the Select Committee on Aging, U.S. House of Representatives, reports:

> An important new trend is that older women are being welcomed back on campuses. There has been a dramatic change in the age of the college population, with well over ten percent of all college students who are now 35 or older, but the spectacular increase in this age group has occurred among women rather than men. Most of these women are furthering career-related goals, but as lifelong education becomes a widely accepted way of improving the general quality of life, it will probably be women more than men whose lives will be affected, at least in the near future.
>
> Continuing education programs have mushroomed and they offer special benefits for those women who have interrupted their education to marry and rear children. These programs generally include one or more of the following features: part-time enrollment, flexible course schedules, short-term courses, counseling services, financial aid for part-time study, removal of age restrictions, curriculum geared to adult experience, credit by examination, refresher courses, child care facilities, and job placement assistance. Other education reforms important to women are variously designated by such terms as "external degrees," "the open university," and "universities without walls." (Neugarten & Brown-Rezanka 1978, 6)

Now more women are college graduates, and higher proportions are earning advanced degrees. Middle age has the possibility of new beginnings for many contemporary women (Rubin 1979). The Wellesley study of women between 35 and 55 found more than half reporting a greater feeling of self-worth than they had felt before; and 88 percent felt satisfied with their lives (Baruch & Barnett 1982). "Middle-aged women have already been reporting that they feel and act younger than their mothers did at the same age—that they are not only healthier and more vigorous, but more youthful in outlook and in expectations of life. There is every reason to expect this trend to accelerate" (Neugarten & Brown-Rezanka 1978, 18).

Enjoying Career and Creative Accomplishment

The more education a woman has, the more likely she is to be working. Less than 40 percent of women high school dropouts, in contrast to 65 percent of women who had four or more years of college, were employed in 1976. "The greatest growth of women workers in recent years has taken place among well-educated wives from families whose incomes are moderate but insufficient to maintain the desired pattern of consumption. Before World War II married women workers came almost exclusively from low-income families, but it is now about as likely for a middle-class wife to be employed as for a working-class wife" (Neugarten & Brown-Rezanka 1978, 11–12).

More than half of America's middle-aged women are employed. Some have been working for many years; others are newcomers to the work force at the empty nest stage of family life. Postparental wives help their husbands to build up the financial resources depleted during childbearing and rearing. Also rewarding is the sense of being productive and of making progress in line with their mature wisdom and talents. Other satisfactions can be found in being of service, in being creative, and in being recognized as competent on the job. Success in her work depends on how well the middle-aged woman allots the time and energy she gives to her job, to homemaking, and to other responsibilities.

Stanford University's 50-year study of 700 gifted women, initiated by Lewis Terman in the 1920s, shows that career women are more satisfied with their lives than women who have been full-time housewives. Of these talented women 79 percent of those who followed careers and not quite 20 percent of the homemakers were highly satisfied (Stanford University 1975).

In many places extension programs of universities and community colleges and adult education programs help mature women to upgrade their skills, if and when they reenter the labor force.

Creative activity in the arts, music, literature, sports, writing, and volunteer work gives many women a sense of accomplishment that is not contingent on monetary reward. Bev Menninger, wife of psychiatrist Roy Menninger, president of the famous Menninger Foundation, speaks as a full-time wife of a busy professional man. She believes that the advantages of being the wife of a dynamic, ambitious husband (comfortable standard of living, freedom from financial worries, and the option to stay home and rear the children) far outweigh the disadvantage of always being at the edge of her husband's spotlight. She tells of finding moments in a spotlight of her own through the discovery and development of her artistic talents: "My painting has been a source of tremendous joy and satisfaction to me. It has led me into a new world, with new friends, new experiences and new excitements that are my very own" (Menninger 1982, 132). Other wives find deep satisfaction in working side by side with their husbands as one or both of them run for public office, cooperate in a business or profession, or give themselves to community service. The answer is not to work or not to work as a postparental wife but to take part in life around her in creative ways.

Relating to Aging Parents

Both middle-aged parents may have aging parents. In most American families the wife assumes the responsibility for older relatives, her husband contributing whatever help he is inclined to give. Theoretically, this is a family developmental task that both members of the middle-aged couple jointly assume. In actuality, it is the wife who is generally expected to look after aging relatives as one of her social roles as wife. It is she who is more active in maintaining kinship ties (Troll & Bengtson 1979, 153) and who specializes in kin keeping (Caplow, Bahr, Chadwick, Hill, & Williamson 1982, 210). It is the wife more than the husband who keeps in touch by telephone, letter, and visiting. It is she who remembers birthdays and other special occasions. It is she who serves as a buffer between the demands of the older and the younger generations in the family. It is she who, in consultation with other kinfolk, helps both sets of aging parents find satisfactory supports for their failing powers.

The various social classes have different ways of viewing this task and of accomplishing it. In upper-class families the elders live well by themselves; they take an interest in, but are not dependent on, their grown sons and daughters. In middle-class families unresolved parent-child conflicts may surface and cause problems when the older and middle generations are thrown too close together. In lower-class families three generations often live together, the grandparents keeping house and looking after the children while the middle-aged support them all (Havighurst 1972, 105).

The time comes in all families when failing health and eventually death overtake the aging members of the family. It is usually the middle-aged daughter or daughter-in-law who steps in to give supportive care during critical and chronic illnesses and at the time of bereavement and adjustment to widowhood. These critical tasks take precedence over others in the expectations of most middle-aged women and their families.

Keeping Social Life Satisfying

The postparental wife is free at last to use her leisure time as she herself chooses. While she was rearing children, her social life was bounded on one side by her children's commitments (school, PTA, Little League, recitals, etc.), and on the other side by the expectations and demands connected with her own or her husband's work. Now that both children and job-related social activities are less demanding, a woman has the time and the resources with which to pursue her own interests.

She accomplishes this developmental task as she pursues interests and skills that bring her special satisfaction, recognition, and a sense of fulfillment. She may throw herself entirely into some all-absorbing project, or she may balance active and passive, collective and solitary, service-motivated and self-indulgent pursuits. Many a middle-aged woman makes an art of friendship, keeping in touch with old friends, cultivating new ones among the refreshing personalities she meets, exchanging social invitations with people she enjoys, and becoming an increasingly friendly person who values her friends and enjoys being with them. Middle- and upper-class women make up the women's clubs that abound in American life. As long as a woman keeps vitally alive and involved in something she finds rewarding, she is doing well.

Assuming Civic and Community Responsibilities

Middle-aged women are often sought after as leaders in the community. In many cases civic involvement fills the vacuum left by their recently departed grown sons and daughters. At this stage of life a woman may take on responsibilities in the church, in social service organizations, or in political groups for which she had little time before.

Civic involvement varies according to social class. Middle-class and upper-class women are generally more concerned with a wide variety of local, state, national, and world affairs. Working-class women tend to have less interest in the social and civic life of the community except as it affects their husbands' work or their children's lives (Havighurst 1972, 99). With the spread of education, the upgrading of television programming, and the general increase of interest in social problems, more and more women of various social class levels may be expected to play active roles as citizens.

Sooner or later every wife and mother faces her developmental tasks in her own way with the coming of her middle years. She is successful if she finds happiness and satisfaction at this stage of life. National surveys report that postparental women experience greater happiness and enjoyment of life than do women of similar age with one or more children still at home (Glenn 1975). For instance, when University of Michigan research teams asked, "Taken all together, how would you say things are these days—would you say that you are very happy, pretty happy, or not too happy?" more postparental than parental wives said they were "very happy" (Glenn 1975).

For the first time in her life a woman is now free to live on her own terms. For the first 20 or more years she did what her parents wanted her to do; for the next 20 years or so she did what her husband and children asked her to do. Now she and her husband are free to do what they want to do—if they can achieve the developmental tasks of this stage of life.

DEVELOPMENTAL TASKS OF THE MIDDLE-AGED HUSBAND

A husband and father in the middle years finds some of his developmental tasks easier than the parallel tasks his wife has. It is probably easier for him than it is for her to encourage the autonomy of their children because the children have been her main responsibility through the years of their growing up. Even so, a longitudinal study of families over the family life cycle finds 22 percent of postparental fathers unhappy about their last child's leaving home (Lewis, Freneau, & Roberts 1979, 514). If he is unhappy in his marriage, or discouraged about his work, losing a favorite child can be difficult.

Keeping Up His Health and Appearance

Between the ages of 45 and 64, a man is more likely to die of heart disease or cancer or to have a stroke than ever before in his life (see Table 13.4, page 297). So he may worry about his health and what will happen as he goes through his midlife crisis.

There is no male menopause per se since menopause is the cessation of menses. The middle-aged and older man, however, does experience a gradual diminution of gonadal functioning. A New York University Medical Center endocrinologist reports that about one-third (30 to 35 percent) of men experience a *male climacteric* between the ages of 58 and 68. This is a physiological condition that responds well to hormone therapy (Kupperman 1975, 61). More usual in the middle-aged male are emotional and cultural anxiety about growing older. The man worries about his weight, his thinning hair, his waning virility. In the "frenzied fifties" he undergoes strains and frustrations that express themselves in ulcers and other illnesses, real or fantasied. He may nurse a continuing discontent with himself and undertake an unending search for self-esteem. That is enough to give him a chronic feeling of fatigue, even when he is in fact not working that hard.

Yale's 10-year study of middle-aged men found that 80 percent of their sample of 40- to 65-year-old American males went through crises of one kind or another in their *midlife transition*. The majority of them had to face up to the fact that they probably would never realize their earlier dreams; even some who had found their success less than satisfying. It is during this period of a man's life when he must redefine his roles and find new sources of vitality for the years that lie ahead (Levinson, Darrow, Klein, Levinson, & McKee 1977).

The middle-aged man who keeps up his appearance, upgrades his wardrobe, and pays attention to his grooming improves his self-image and feels better for it. Many a 50-year-old man exercises regularly, has periodic medical and dental checkups, and eats a well-balanced diet. Quite possibly his wife encourages these healthful practices and looks out for his well-being. As she expresses her pride in the way he looks and feels, he responds to her admiration and maintains an active interest in her and in their marriage. The middle years can be good ones when a man finds that he can enjoy maturity for all it has to offer.

Pursuing His Job Interests

Many a midlife man finds his work boring and frustrating (Hess & Markson 1980; Zube 1982, 149). He may have to face the fact that he has gone as far as he will ever go and come to terms with reality without regret, recrimination, or discouragement. His satisfaction in his work is intensified when he feels needed and useful, when is able to help younger men take over without feeling personally threatened, and as he lets established routines and experience replace his earlier drive.

The blue-collar working man often finds his job monotonous after 20 or 30 years of the same operation. He may go after an advancement with some encouragement from his superiors. His chances of employment elsewhere are not great in a time of general unemployment and company reluctance to hire middle-aged and older men. A working man may give more of his time to his union and find some satisfaction in working with his fellow members to improve their situation.

As the middle-aged man anticipates his retirement, he is no longer so stressed with job anxieties and may focus increasingly on making life comfortable for himself and his wife. Early retirement for many men may actually be an understandable escape from the stresses and strains too long endured on the job.

Redefining His Roles in Marriage

The middle years find a man turning toward his wife for intimacy and nurturance with a central family focus (Kerckhoff 1966; Neugarten & Gutmann 1968; Lowenthal, Thurner, & Chiriboga 1975). These are the years when a husband shows a tendency toward mellowness and self-satisfaction as he sheds some of his former roles and moves toward interpersonal commitment. He tends to enjoy family activities more now and may feel contentment with his life (Lowenthal, Thurner, & Chiriboga 1975). Husbands even more than wives turn toward their spouses for emotional support and intimacy, perhaps because they do not have as many intimate relationships as do women (Bultena 1976; Lowenthal & Robinson 1976; Keith 1979). Middle-aged husbands say they feel tender toward their wives; and four out of five of them are found to hold positive evaluations of their spouses (Lowenthal, Thurner, & Chiriboga 1975).

Most husbands and wives agree on *traditional husband/wife roles* in which he earns the living and makes home repairs while she does the housekeeping (Caplow et al. 1982, 69) with which he may or may not help out from time to time. As long as husband and wife agree on playing traditional roles, they may be expected to feel relatively comfortable in the division of labor in their marriage. Similarly, couples who mutually agree on more *flexibility in their husband/wife roles* may be redefining their functioning in the home in ways that work for them.

Cultivating Satisfying Leisure-Time Activities

The middle-aged man probably has more leisure now than he has ever had. A shorter workweek, less pressure to get ahead, and seniority built up over the years allow a man time for pleasure where he finds it. Now he has the resources to do some of the things he has always wanted to do. He may master some art or skill sufficiently well to gain recognition and a heightened sense of pride in his workmanship. He probably spends less time engaging in team sports and gets more pleasure from activities that he can carry on through the years—golf, tennis, fishing, boating, swimming, gardening, camping, and travel.

A man is wise to balance active with sedentary leisure interests; to enjoy both solitary and social hours; to spend more time with his wife—doing together with her the things they both enjoy; and in general to use his leisure in ways that refresh and renew his own outlook on life.

Carrying Community and Political Responsibility

Middle-aged people carry the greater share of the obligations of citizenship. They have the greatest influence and tend to be sought after as leaders in a community's civic life (Havighurst 1972, 98). Many a man enjoys keeping abreast of what is happening locally and on the wider scene. He sees much that should be done in government and may throw his own hat in the ring or back some other person for a political office. He is at the age when his counsel is sought, so he may enjoy serving as a volunteer or as a board member in any of the many agencies that see to the needs of the community.

The man who is willing to keep alert and active during his middle years can reap the harvest of good living that he has sown in earlier years. He can relax now and enjoy the fruits of his labors in the sense that "you can't take it with you." Now he can discover the richness of mature marriage, the satisfaction of fellowship with grown children, the warmth of friendships that have lasted over the years, the excitement of adventure and novel experience, and the rewards of productivity. None of these dividends "come due" in the middle years without some investment of himself. They are all satisfactions that grow out of successfully achieving the developmental tasks of this stage of life. When a man does a good job with these tasks, he finds that happiness is a by-product of his efforts. As long as there is life, there can be growth, and the middle years are no exception.

FAMILY DEVELOPMENTAL TASKS IN THE MIDDLE YEARS

The empty nest stage of the family life cycle has a full complement of family developmental tasks that are necessary for family continuity, survival, and growth. These basic family developmental tasks run through the full family life cycle (Chapter 2) with each stage having its own specific stage-sensitive family developmental tasks that must be accomplished to ensure the happiness of the family in this and later stages (Chapter 3). Stage-sensitive family developmental tasks of the middle-aged couple in an empty nest are listed in Table 13.3 and discussed in the following sections.

Providing for Comfortable, Healthful Well-being

Most couples are home owners by the time they have launched their children. Three out of four middle-aged couples own their own homes, acquired while they were raising their children. Now that the children have grown and gone, the chances are good that the middle-aged couple will stay on in their home for a number of reasons: (1) they feel that this

Table 13.3 FAMILY DEVELOPMENTAL TASKS OF THE MIDDLE-AGED COUPLE

1. Providing for comfortable, healthful well-being in a home appropriate for the later years of marriage.
2. Allocating resources (time, money, facilities, etc.) for present and future needs of the husband, wife, and their loved ones.
3. Determining who does what in the support, management, and care of the household, with mutually agreed upon patterns of husband/wife complementarity.
4. Encouraging both husband's and wife's development of increasingly mature roles in the family and beyond.
5. Ensuring husband/wife interaction, communication, and expression of real feelings (love, sex, anger, disappointment, success, etc.) necessary for marital satisfaction.
6. Enlarging the family circle through incorporation of sons- and daughters-in-law, their relatives, and children, with appropriate kin-keeping care for members of the extended family.
7. Participating in life beyond the home in satisfying ways and establishing mutually agreed upon policies for entertaining other people, ideas, philosophies, sports, art forms, and so on within the home.
8. Affirming life's central values, meeting personal and family crises, setting reasonable goals, and developing family loyalties in ways that maintain morale and encourage achievement.

is home for them; (2) they are near their work; (3) they have familiar neighbors, friends, and ways of life established over the years; (4) their grown children return home for family celebrations and enjoy having a familiar home base; and (5) the middle-aged couple provide continuity by maintaining the home site, keepsakes, traditions, memories, and customs that contribute much to family stability and enjoyment.

Some 27 percent of the population do move during their middle years (Middle age the best of times? 1982, 67). There is some evidence that married persons with no children in this age group tend to consider most important in their new residence: (1) housing costs, (2) convenience to medical facilities, and (3) peace and quiet (McAuley & Nutty 1982, 306). As the middle-aged couple move, they need to look not only for present convenience but also for their comfort in the years ahead. Their task is to arrange for a home that reflects their interests, so that it becomes for both of them a satisfying place in which to live. Remodeling their home after their children leave can be a pleasant project for the middle-aged couple. Now the place is theirs alone, and it can be refurbished around their special interests rather than in terms of what the children need. If they anticipate an aging family member to be in their household, that, too, can be part of their planning.

Occasionally, a long-married working couple, freed from child rearing, may elect to live apart for a time in order to further their careers (Gross 1980, 574). Dr. H. is a case in point. By the time he and his wife had launched their last child, the physician—grown weary of his heavy practice—left for a year of advanced study in a medical school across the country. His professional wife stayed on at home where she reduced her work load to half-time so she could take a long-delayed program of study of her own. By year's end they were happily reunited, both stronger for their year apart. Whether the midlife couple remodel their present home or move to a new place, their plans express their needs, interests, and values now and for the forseeable future.

With the increase in average life expectancy, the majority of midlife women can look forward to living well into their eighties and a sizable proportion on into their nineties (Neugarten & Brown-Rezanka 1978, 2). On the average, middle-aged men have two or more decades ahead of them, some more than others. The greatest threat to the life of a middle-aged woman is cancer, followed by heart disease as the number two killer of women between 45 and 64 years of age (Table 13.4). For middle-aged men, heart disease ranks first, with cancer second, according to the national death rates (Table 13.4). These hazards usually include long periods of invalidism, unemployment, and a fresh awareness of the importance of good health habits. Let one of the couple's friends die of a heart attack, and they are motivated as never before to protect their health by taking such measures as: (1) getting regular daily exercise, (2) reducing or altogether halting their use of tobacco and alcohol, (3) having regular physical checkups, (4) regulating their diet to maintain optimum weight and height, (5) avoiding unnecessary stress, strain, and tension, and (6) getting health and hospitalization insurance to protect them from overly burdensome medical costs.

Health and hospitalization insurance helps pay spiraling medical costs that nationally will reach $462 billion in 1985 and $821 billion by 1990, according to projections made by the Health Care Financing Administration. This means $1946 per person in 1985, almost double the 1980 figure of $1067. By 1990 per capita expenditures will exceed $3300 a year, according to official government projections (Health Insurance Association of America, 1981–1982, 42, 51). By the end of 1980 more than 186 million Americans were covered by hospital expense insurance, and 154 million persons had major medical coverage through

Table 13.4 MAJOR CAUSES OF DEATH AMONG AMERICAN MEN AND WOMEN
(AVERAGE ANNUAL DEATH RATE PER 100,000)

	All ages	Under 1 year	15–24 years	25–34 years	35–64 years	45–54 years	55–64 years
Men							
Accidents	65.6	42.1	100.5	74.3	61.6	60.4	68.7
Homicide	14.5	5.0	20.4	27.7	23.1	16.5	11.2
Suicide	19.0	—	20.0	25.5	21.9	23.4	27.5
Cancer	203.5	3.8	7.7	14.0	45.1	152.2	522.0
Heart disease	375.3	28.4	3.2	11.6	73.3	298.0	791.3
Stroke	65.4	5.8	1.2	2.6	10.2	28.6	85.3
Women							
Accidents	28.3	36.6	28.0	18.1	17.5	20.0	26.5
Homicide	4.1	5.1	5.9	6.4	5.4	3.7	2.7
Cancer	161.4	4.4	4.9	14.3	53.9	177.1	365.7
Suicide	6.3	—	4.7	8.1	10.1	11.2	5.7
Heart disease	295.5	24.1	2.1	5.0	21.4	85.2	275.7
Stroke	51.0	5.1	1.1	2.7	9.4	26.2	64.1
Men							
Motor vehicle accidents		7.5	70.5	45.3	31.3	26.7	27.0
All other accidents		34.6	30.1	29.0	30.4	33.6	41.7
Women							
Motor vehicle accidents		9.0	22.1	12.1	9.8	9.7	11.4
All other accidents		27.6	5.9	6.1	7.7	10.3	15.1

Source: U.S. National Center for Health Statistics, *Vital Statistics of the United States,* vol. 2, *Mortality* pt. A, 1978. Washington, D.C.: Government Printing Office.

insurance company policies, Blue Cross, Blue Shield, HMO (Health Maintenance Organization), and other independent plans (ibid., 8–9). The staff of each state's insurance commissioner's office can help a couple find the right insurance plan to fit their purpose and budget.

Allocating Resources for Present and Future Needs

In the middle years the husband's income is at its peak, and with his wife working also, their joint income is even greater (Table 13.5). According to Flain and Fullerton (1978, 25–35), 9 out of 10 men under 65 in husband/wife families and 60 percent of all married women without children will be working by 1990; a projection already realized in the early 1980s (U.S. Bureau of the Census 1982–1983).

After age 65, if the husband is no longer working full-time and his wife is not employed, their mean family income drops to less than half ($10,880) that of their midlife working years, according to the same official government source used in Table 13.5. Typically, the middle-aged couple have lower costs after their children leave home; costs are also lower than they will be later as their health fails in the later years. They probably have fewer debts now than at any time since they married. Their home is furnished, the car and the last baby are paid for, and their scrimping days are over for a while before retirement and the costs of old age are upon them.

Financial planning for their later years is highly motivated during a couple's empty nest stage. Few parents want to be dependent on their grown children for support during their declining years. They realize that Social Security will not keep them on anything more than a subsistence level, so they put more emphasis on building up their reserves than they ever have before.

Recognizing that a woman is more apt to be widowed than a man, the middle-aged couple have the task of preparing the wife to fend for herself if and when it becomes necessary. She probably works at least part-time not only to augment the present family income but also to build up her own Social Security benefits. The longer she has worked, the more she looks forward to retiring when the time comes (Johnson & Price-Bonham 1980, 383). Few husbands complain of their wife's neglect because of her work, and more husbands (38 percent) than wives (26 percent) say they are happier at home than at work (How is work

Table 13.5   **MEAN INCOME OF FAMILIES OF HUSBANDS WORKING FULL-TIME, WITH AND WITHOUT EMPLOYED WIFE'S INCOME, BY AGE GROUPS (IN DOLLARS)**

Age	Husband full-time, wife employed[a]	Husband full-time, wife not employed[b]
Total	24,726	21,982
18–24	16,340	12,345
25–34	21,646	18,148
35–44	25,625	22,885
45–54	28,338	25,547
55–64	26,523	23,734

[a]N = 1,532,076.
[b]N = 1,491,311.

Source: U.S. Bureau of the Census, Consumer Income. *Current Population Reports,* Series P-60, no. 118, March 1979, tables 20 and 21.

affecting American families? 1981, 27–28). This family developmental task is achieved in midlife as the couple enjoy their partnership that may involve team earning, shared planning, joint spending, and saving for the future.

Developing Patterns of Complementarity

Once the middle-aged couple is alone in their home, determining who does what in the support, management, and care of the household is theirs to decide. The Middletown III family role survey found 81 percent of the husbands and 76 percent of the wives agreeing that the husband should provide the family income. Both partners are in accord that it is up to the wife to keep house: 74 percent of the husbands and 80 percent of the wives surveyed (Caplow et al. 1982, 351). Almost 9 out of 10 of these midwestern American couples rate themselves average or above average in their housekeeping competence (88 percent) and being supportive of one another (91 percent), suggesting that they appear satisfied with rather traditional husband/wife roles (ibid., 355). Other Americans seem to reject *stereotyped roles* of husband as breadwinner and wife as homemaker. A nationwide poll of 302,602 men and women (What's happening to the American family? 1978, 4) found greater freedom in 1977 than in 1972 for each spouse to be an equal partner in marriage. Nearly half of the men (48 percent) and 60 percent of the women said they would *not* disapprove if the wife were the main breadwinner and the husband had the responsibility of homemaking (ibid., 88). Interestingly, the Middletown III survey found that while 74 percent of the husbands and 80 percent of the wives say the wife *should* do the housekeeping, in fact 9 of 10 wives actually do the housekeeping, as reported by both husbands and wives (Caplow et al. 1982, 351). Such findings suggest that during a period when *stereotyped husband/wife roles* are being challenged, attitudes about what should be done outpace actual behavior.

Complementary roles have been defined as

> interlocking systems in which each unit shapes and directs the other units in the system. This effect is reciprocal; changes in one role cannot be made without corresponding changes in other roles which are involved in it. For example, changes in the role of wife will be accompanied by changes in the role of husband; changes in the role of employer will involve changes in the role of employee. Changes in the role of mother will involve changes in the role of the father and in the role of the child. (Hartley & Hartley 1952, 495–496)

Deutscher (1954) describes six different patterns of complementarity in the Kansas City middle-class panel of middle-aged adults that he interviewed:

1. *Reciprocal bolstering*—through appreciation, consideration, and standing by with encouragement through crises;
2. *Mutual activities*—participation in recreational pursuits that both enjoy together;
3. *Relaxing together*—as "joint idlers in a restful paradise of peace and quiet";
4. *Joint participation* in husband's occupation—in which the wife becomes absorbed in helping her husband in his work;
5. *Constructive projects*—in which both members of the couple join forces to fix things up, in one project after another; and

6. *Separate interests*—as the husband remains absorbed in his work, and the wife goes on with whatever special interests she has or can find.

The self- and other role images of both men and women appear to change as they grow older in two distinctly different patterns. Men, oriented primarily outside the family in their young adulthood, show a gradual decline in affective expressiveness and a withdrawal from emotional investments as they age. In contrast, as women move through the middle years, they become more self-confident, emotionally more expressive, more expansive, and in some ways even dominant over their husbands.

One student of the roles played by middle-aged husbands and wives finds a direct relationship between the complementarity of their roles during the postparental years and their satisfaction with the period. Three-fourths of the husbands and wives interviewed evaluated the postparental phase of the family life cycle as better than or as good as the preceding stages, and only three individuals reported the postparental stage as worse than earlier periods of the marriage (Deutscher 1959, 44).

Undertaking Appropriate Social Roles

A *social role* is a pattern of learned behavior appropriate to a given social status. A social role is developed by an individual as a response to what is expected of him or her by others —modified by his or her own perceptions, values, and aspirations.

A man or woman in modern society is expected to fill such social roles as (1) parent, (2) spouse, (3) child of aging parent, (4) homemaker (male or female), (5) worker, (6) user of leisure time, (7) church member, (8) club or association member, (9) citizen, and (10) friend. The quality of a person's life is judged, generally, by the way he or she fills these roles.

Specialists in human development are able to score performance of adults on the developmental tasks of middle age. They find that the higher the social class, the higher the performance score on developmental tasks for both men and women in all social roles. Women tend to do better than men in such roles as parent and church member; but men received higher performance scores than women as club and association members and as citizens, generally for all social class levels (Havighurst & Orr 1956, 32).

The lower-class man or woman views the years between 40 and 60 as a decline in which he or she is "slowing down," a "has-been." The middle-class man sees the middle years as the period of his greatest productivity and major rewards, the "prime of life." The upper-status woman feels the loss of her children from the home but also a sense of mellowness and serenity. It is a time when "you enjoy life—you're comfortable with yourself and the world—you're no longer adjusting as you were before" (Neugarten & Peterson 1957, 500).

Leisure activities (enjoying weekend recreation together, working together around the house and yard, attending plays and musical events) contribute to marital satisfaction in the middle years (Deutscher 1959, 110). Leisure activities are especially critical in determining marital satisfaction before children come and again after they are launched—"when the marital relationship is reestablishing itself and a new dyadic adjustment becomes necessary" (Orthner 1975, 101).

Ensuring Marital Interaction and Satisfaction

An important task of the middle years is finding each other as husband and wife again. Not since their honeymoon days has the couple been without children and free of the responsibilities of child rearing. From a distance one would expect such a state of affairs to be welcomed by both the man and the woman. Yet for many couples it is a real task to be worked on if they are to reach the point where life together once more has meaning, purpose, and richness.

Studies find that the marriage relationship is important for life satisfaction. Postparental couples tend to turn to one another and to recultivate their relationship once their children are no longer dependent on them in the home (Petranek 1970). A good marriage is of increasing significance for life satisfaction as the years pass (Peterson 1968). Whether couples have more or less marital satisfaction in their middle years than formerly is a question research has sought to answer. Table 13.6 lists representative studies pointing both to improved and to worsened satisfaction in postparental couples. The majority of findings, however, suggest that marital relations are better in the postparental stage than when children are still living at home.

Contradictory findings on marital satisfaction in the middle years (Table 13.6) may be the result of differences in research design and method, in the populations studied, or in other factors in the studies themselves. Or, it could be that the differences represent the success or failure couples have in accomplishing their developmental task of building a satisfying union over the years. Success is seen in "the abiding desire of each mate to maintain a relationship in which each feels accepted, valued, recognized, and loved as an attractive, stimulating, and dependable companion" (Anderson 1974, 467–469). At a time when the wife becomes more independent and achievement oriented, her husband may be less enthusiastic about his work, and the reversal of their roles is new and confusing to them both (Cohen 1979, 468).

According to a popular myth, a man's "dangerous years" come at this stage. Is this fact or fantasy? True for some, not at all true for others, depending upon many factors, chief of which are the man's sexual orientation, whether he values fidelity or variety, and the success of his marriage in meeting his ego, emotional, personal, and sexual needs. Another myth is seen in a thick book entitled *Sex after Sixty* that circulates in schools and colleges. It holds nothing but blank pages, implying there is no sex in the later years. This amuses the young, but it is far from fact, as shown in Table 13.7, p. 303.

The man who must be the strong, silent he-man finds communication with his wife difficult, and "resolution of his mid-life crisis may be impossible" (Cohen 1979, 469). A critical review of the literature suggests that the empty nest stage can be one of renewed marital satisfaction and that part of the midlife man's crisis is his need to reopen full communication with his wife (ibid., 468).

When each partner understands what the other is going through (the wife's menopause, new outside commitments; the husband's anxiety about his aging appearance and functioning), they are more likely to support one another than to become alienated and disillusioned about their marriage. Meeting each other's needs emotionally as well as sexually draws the mates together as a couple. Now especially, the middle-aged man and woman each need the reassurance, the appreciation, and the encouragement that helps them feel accepted and truly close to each other. Failure in this task brings the aching loneliness so frequent in later years.

Table 13.6   MARITAL SATISFACTION IN THE MIDDLE YEARS—WORSE OR BETTER? (SUMMARY OF REPRESENTATIVE STUDIES OVER THE YEARS)

	Research
Worse:	
Less in the middle than early years	Bossard & Boll 1955
	Blood & Wolfe 1960
	Gurin, Veroff, & Feld 1960
	Pineo 1961
	Feldman 1965
Time of disenchantment	Pineo 1961
Period of disengagement	Cumming, Dean, Newell, & McCaffrey 1960
Mate choice may not have been wise	Cuber & Harroff 1965
Love expression less in middle years than before	Swenson, Eskew, & Kohlhepp 1981
Marriage taken for granted now	Gilford & Bengtson 1979
Better:	
Marital satisfaction increase to early high levels	Rollins & Feldman 1970
Higher satisfaction in marital relation than any other area of life	Hayes & Stinnett 1971 (Figure 13.1)
Fewer marital problems now than before	Swenson, Eskew, & Kohlhepp 1981
Higher marital adjustment now than before children were launched	Saunders 1969
Companionship now most rewarding	Hayes & Stinnett 1971
Mutual understanding keeps pair from drifting apart	Dizard 1968
Communication and empathy contribute to good marital adjustment	Johnson 1968
	Saunders 1969
	Lowenthal & Chiriboga 1972
Highest marital satisfaction except newly married stage on two of three measures	Rollins & Cannon 1974
Highest marital companionship except newly weds; next-to-highest marital satisfaction	Miller 1976
Satisfaction higher in postparental marriages than marriages with children still living at home	Glenn & McLanahan 1982
Highest marital satisfaction except newly wed stage in two of three samples	Spanier, Lewis, & Cole 1975

Success in their intimate interaction brings immediate contentment and paves the way for smooth going throughout the rest of their lives together.

Enlarging the Family Circle

Periods of unemployment, retooling between jobs, illness, and other needs of one generation for help from another can bring previously launched adults back into their parents' home for a time. One grandfather in his fifties asks, "What's all this talk about the empty nest?

Table 13.7 SEXUAL SATISFACTION OF WIVES AND HUSBANDS IN THE MIDDLE YEARS (REPRESENTATIVE STUDIES IN THE UNITED STATES)

	Research
Wives' sexual satisfaction:	
Satisfaction is related to communication.	Levin & Levin 1975
Satisfaction is tied to marital happiness.	Levin & Levin 1975
Two-thirds say their sex lives are good, regardless of how long they have been married.	Levin & Levin 1975
Between ages 43 and 53, wives develop renewed interest in sexual relationships.	Neugarten 1970
Married women have as high or a higher rate of orgasm in their forties and fifties as in their twenties.	Kinsey, Pomeroy, Martin, & Gebhard 1953
Happy, well-adjusted wives go through the middle years with little or no interruption in frequency or enjoyment of sex with their husbands.	Masters & Johnson 1968
Husbands' sexual satisfaction:	
Active marital relations well into their seventies and eighties are not unusual.	Masters & Johnson 1968
Decline in sexual adequacy is related to boredom, job preoccupation, mental or physical fatigue, overindulgence of food and/or alcohol, infirmities in self or spouse, and fear of poor sexual performance.	Masters & Johnson 1966
Anxiety about declining virility may lead some to look for variety; one out of four have had extramarital affairs.	Johnson 1968
Poor marital adjustment is significantly related to husbands' extramarital involvements.	Johnson 1968

The old nest here is bursting at the seams with five wonderful grandchildren and two sons-in-law extra—all besides the two daughters who used to roost with us."

The lineage bridge allows members of each generation to get across to the others as help is given and received. In times of trouble it is relatives who step in to help. In one year of a three-generation family study, a vast network of interaction between generations was reported with 3781 specific instances of help given and received in illness, financial binds, child-care, household problems, and emotional distress (Hill, Foote, Aldous, Carlson, and Macdonald 1970, Chapter 3).

Couples in the early stages of the family life cycle are most likely to get help from their middle-aged parents in financing costly outlays—for a car, a baby, or a home. Research finds that young parents who are eager for a home of their own (Michelson 1977) turn to their parents for help in meeting the rising costs of housing. This is not so much a function of economic status as of life cycle stage and housing tenure (Kennedy & Stokes 1982, 317). The Middletown kinship survey found 80 percent of the women reporting gifts from their parents. More than half (52 percent) acknowledge help on special occasions such as childbirth and sickness, and 44 percent said their parents gave them financial assistance. Families help members of the older generation, too: more than half (54 percent) take their parents to the doctor or care for them when they are sick; 3 out of 4 help their parents care for their home or yard; and 9 out of 10 give their parents gifts of one kind or another (Caplow et al. 1982, 383).

Care giver of the very old is a new role that has emerged for the midlife woman. Brody sees the empty nest being filled with grandparents. The myth that accuses families of abandoning their elderly folks is not borne out in fact. Half the institutionalized old have no living children, and those who do have families only reluctantly send their frail elders to a nursing home—and then only after severe personal, social, and economic stress in caring for them themselves (Brody 1978).

Ethel Shanas (1980) calls today's middle-aged couples the *new pioneers* as they care for and support their elderly parents, just when they had looked forward to freedom from major family responsibilities after their children were launched: "The generation in the middle tell us, 'I've raised my family. I want to spend time with my husband or wife. I want to enjoy my grandchildren. I never expected that when I was a grandparent, I'd have to look after my parents' " (ibid., 14). *Parent caring* has become a major source of stress in family life (Lieberman 1978).

Most men and women consider relatives important and keep in touch regularly with them with visits, telephone calls, and letters. The overwhelming majority keep in touch simply because they enjoy their relatives; somewhat fewer because they feel an obligation to do so, because they need help, or because they are needed by their parents or grown children (Caplow et al. 1982, 383–384). One study of visits by out-of-town relatives concludes: "The potentials for such support, sympathy, and sharing may well be part of the glue that keeps families cohesive" (Rosenblatt, Johnson, & Anderson 1981, 409).

Participating in Community Life

More middle-aged Americans vote than citizens of other ages: 68 percent of 45- to 54-year-olds and 71 percent of 55- to 64-years-olds, in contrast to 59 percent of all those voting. There is time and interest in political affairs now as postparental men and women get more involved beyond their homes (Latest findings on middle-age Americans 1981, 41).

Freed of regular supervision of his own children, a middle-aged man may become a Big Brother, volunteer at the local Boys' Club, teach a Sunday school class, or help raise money for a new community swimming pool. The mother who has had her fill of PTA and scouting with her own children can fill the gap of their leaving home with any of the many kinds of community service to others. This is filling *"the need to nurture* [emphasis added] and to act as model, guide, or mentor to the young" (Neugarten 1979, 890). Serving on boards of community organizations, banks, and businesses reaches a peak among middle-class postparental men and women. Working-class men find satisfying roles in their unions, women in their churches, and middle-aged people of all social classes in neighborhood improvement and political activities.

Involvement in varied social and political interests can breed dissension in a family unless tolerance has become a pattern for the pair. Mrs. M. grins as she sets out cold cuts and beer for her husband's local cronies. She is amused at the way they spend their time, and she can not consider "the boys" as friends of hers. But she has learned to go along with her husband's activities, much as he backs her "good works," as he calls them, with good grace. They have learned to disagree without being disagreeable about whom they entertain (individually or collectively), what television programs they see, and how they spend their time and other resources.

Social participation is associated with life satisfaction among both men and women (Rose 1955; Hayes & Stinnett 1971). Successful participation in community life in the middle years depends upon the foundations laid for it in the earlier years of their marriage. As the family has projects and purposes beyond its own immediate interests through the years, it prepares for wider participation and accomplishment in the middle and later years.

Affirming Life's Central Values

"Middlescents go through a deep and sometimes agonizing reappraisal of values they may have taken for granted" (Fabry 1977, 80). They look back on the years since they became adults and realize they have about the same amount of time left. Middle age is a watershed period, with years past leading up to the present and the years ahead to be faced with more freedom than was available in the earlier years.

Repudiation of family values by adult sons and daughters can trip off midlife reappraisal of a couple's life-style. Some adult children reaffirm their parents' patterns as they conform to them; others repudiate them as they espouse markedly different ways. Urbane Carolyn Lewis speaks for many when she writes, "My two sons live lives starkly different from my own. They make their homes in small rural places, and theirs are lives of voluntary simplicity" (Lewis 1982, 11). The president of a prestigious university has a son who lives with a cult in India. The superintendent of Sunday school has a daughter who is living with a successful lawyer without benefit of marriage. Another couple spent weeks of time and thousands of dollars trying to keep their drug-addicted son out of jail, as did the John Hinckleys whose son shot the president of the United States. Why? What happened? These are but two of the questions that haunt a midlife parent.

Values reflect each person's unique life-style, so they vary widely (Bengtson 1975). The middle-aged live in the middle of things as a link in the continuing story of life (Janeway 1971, 174). Mature adults both influence and are influenced by the young, reciprocally. Some midlife parents, noting that their young find life more fulfilling, human, and pleasurable, may adopt their hang-loose attire and nontraditional behavior (Bengtson, Furlong, & Laufer 1974, 25). Others remain work oriented and, significantly more than young adults, believe that hard work and self-sacrifice lead to success. They say they like their jobs, and they are proud of the work they do (Report on the American family 1972, 116–123).

Talking about the values one lives by is seldom necessary. Most men and women reveal their value systems eloquently through their actions—by the stand they take on current issues; in the way they are willing to be counted in a controversy; by what they do about what they believe to be right and just and good and true.

Middle-aged couples express their values in the way they go about their developmental tasks at this stage of their lives: as they maintain their home; as they plan their resources for the present and the years ahead; as they carry their household responsibilities together; as they draw closer together as a couple; as they maintain mutually satisfying relationships with their kinfolk; and as they participate in the larger community. Thus they find themselves as persons, as a couple, as family members, as workers, as citizens, and as all the other roles society expects of them and that their personal aspirations define for them.

The married get significantly greater satisfaction from life than do single, separated, divorced, or widowed men and women (Neugarten, Havighurst, & Tobin 1961). These findings suggest that marriage contributes to satisfaction with life and that many married people succeed in their developmental tasks on through their middle years.

In the reaffirmation of life's values, a couple can still make progress toward developing unity and integrity in their middle years. Nothing can bring greater satisfaction than finding that—viewed from a mature vantage point—life all adds up and that together the two know who they are and where they are headed in the business of living.

SUMMARY

The empty nest stage of the family life cycle lasts from the time the last child leaves home until the retirement or the death of one of the spouses. Statistically, middle-aged parents are new in this century now that both parents typically live beyond the launching of their children. Midlife people are the fastest growing segment of the population; they are at the peak of their earning power; and they are family oriented and politically active and move less than other age groups, in general.

Developmental tasks of the postparental woman include freeing her children for full autonomy, taking her menopause in stride while keeping mentally and physically vigorous, finding satisfaction in creative accomplishment through work and other interests, looking out for aging parents, and being involved in social, civic, and community life. Meanwhile, the middle-aged husband works at keeping up his health and personal appearance, coping with possible boredom and frustration in his work, becoming more flexible in his marital roles, and dividing his time between leisure, community, and political activities.

There are eight stage-sensitive family developmental tasks in the empty nest stage of the family life cycle: (1) adapting their home for the present and later years of marriage, (2) allocating their resources for present and future needs, (3) determining patterns of husband/wife complementarity, (4) encouraging each other's development of increasingly mature roles, (5) rekindling a sense of closeness in their marriage, (6) providing kin-keeping care for members of the extended family, (7) participating in life beyond their home, and (8) reappraising their values in motivating ways. Success in their developmental tasks brings greater satisfaction to the married than is found among the single, separated, divorced, or widowed.

REFERENCES

Anderson, W. J. 1974. *Challenges for successful family living.* Minneapolis, MN: T. S. Denison.

Baruch, G., & Barnett, R. 1982. *Lifeprints: New patterns of love and work for today's women.* New York: McGraw-Hill.

Bengtson, V. L. 1975. Generation and family effects in value socialization. *Marriage and Family Living* 22: 66–68.

Bengtson, V. L., Furlong, M. J., & Laufer, R. S. 1974. Time, aging, and the continuity of social structure: Themes and issues in generational analysis. *Journal of Social Issues* 30:1–30.

Blood, R. O., & Wolfe, D. M. 1960. *Husbands and wives: The dynamics of married living.* New York: Free Press.

Bossard, J. H. S., & Boll, E. S. 1955. Marital unhappiness in the life cycle. *Marriage and Family Living* 17:10–14.

Brody, E. 1978. The aging of the family. *Annals of Political and Social Science* 438:13–27.

Bultena, G. 1976. Sex differences in intimate friendships of old age. *Journal of Marriage and the Family* 38:739–747.

Caplow, T., Bahr, H. M., Chadwick, B. A., Hill, R., & Williamson, M. H. 1982. *Middletown families: Fifty years of change and continuity.* Minneapolis, MN: University of Minnesota Press.

Cohen, J. F. 1979. Males roles in mid-life. *Family Coordinator* 28:465–471.

Cuber, J. F., & Harroff, P. B. 1965. *The significant Americans: A study of sexual behavior among the affluent.* New York: Appleton-Century-Crofts.

Cumming, E., Dean, L. R., Newell, D., & McCaffrey, I. 1960. Disengagement—A tentative theory of aging. *Sociometry* 23:34–35.

Deutscher, I. 1954. Husband-wife relations in middle-age: An analysis of sequential roles among the urban middle classes. Unpublished manuscript, Department of Sociology, University of Missouri, pp. 122–130.

———. 1959. Married life in the middle years. *Community Studies.* Kansas City, MO.

———. 1964. The quality of postparental life: Definitions of the situation. *Journal of Marriage and the Family* 26:52–59.

Dizard, J. 1968. *Social change and the family.* Chicago: University of Chicago, Family Study Center.

Eurich, A. C., ed. 1982. *Major transitions in the human life cycle.* Lexington, MA: Heath.

Fabry, J. 1977. The crises of mid-life. *PHP,* September 1977, pp. 78–83.

Feldman, H. 1965. *Development of the husband-wife relationship.* Ithaca, N.Y.: Cornell University.

Flain, P., & Fullerton, H. 1978. Labor force projections to 1990: Three possible paths. *Monthly Labor Review* 101:25–35.

Gilford, R., & Bengtson, V. 1979. Measuring marital satisfaction in three generations: Positive and negative dimensions. *Journal of Marriage and the Family* 41: 387–398.

Glenn, N. D. 1975. Psychological well-being in the postparental stage: Some evidence from national surveys. *Journal of Marriage and the Family* 37:105–110.

Glenn, N. D., & McLanahan, S. 1982. Children and marital happiness: A further specification of the relationship. *Journal of Marriage and the Family* 44:63–72.

Glick, P. C. 1955. The life cycle of the family. *Marriage and Family Living* 17 (February): 1, 4.

Greenspan, S. I., & Pollock, G. H., eds. 1981. *The course of life: Psychoanalytic contributions toward understanding personality development.* Vol. 3. *Adulthood and the aging process.* Washington, D.C.: Department of Health and Human Services.

Gross, H. E. E. 1980. Dual-career couples who live apart: Two types. *Journal of Marriage and the Family* 42:567–576.

Gurin, G., Veroff, J., & Feld, S. 1960. *Americans view their mental health: A nationwide interview study.* New York: Basic Books.

Hartley, E. L., & Hartley, R. R. 1952. *Fundamentals of social psychology.* New York: Knopf.

Havighurst, R. J. n.d. *Dominant concerns in the life cycle.* Sonderdruck aus: Festschrift fur Charlotte Buhler gegenwartsprobleme dser entwick-lungspsychologie. verlag fur psychologie. Göttingen.

———. 1972. *Developmental tasks and education.* 3d ed. New York: McKay.

Havighurst, R. J., & Orr, B. 1956. *Adult education and adult needs: A report.* Chicago: Center for the Study of Liberal Education for Adults.

Hayes, M. P., & Stinnett, N. 1971. Life satisfaction of middle-aged husbands and wives. *Journal of Home Economics* 63: 669–674.

Health Insurance Association of America. 1982. *Source book of health insurance data* 1981–1982. Washington, D.C.: Health Insurance Association of America.

Hess, B. B., & Markson, E. 1980. *Aging and old age.* New York: Macmillan.

Hill, R., Foote, N., Aldous, J., Carlson, R., & Macdonald, R. 1970. *Family development in three generations.* Cambridge, MA: Schenkman.

How is work affecting American families? 1981. *Better Homes and Gardens,* Des Moines, IA: Meredith Corporation.

Janeway, E. 1971. In praise of middle age. *McCall's,* October 1971, p. 112.

Johnson, C. K., & Price-Bonham, S. 1980. Women and retirement: A study and implications. *Family Relations* 29:380–385.

Johnson, R. E. 1968. *Marital patterns during the middle years.* Ph.D. dissertation, University of Minnesota.

Keith, P. M. 1979. Life changes and perceptions of life and death among older men and women. *Journal of Gerontology* 34:870–878.

Kennedy, L. W., & Stokes, D. W. 1982. Extended family support and the high cost of housing. *Journal of Marriage and the Family* 44:311–318.

Kerckhoff, D. 1966. Family patterns and morale in retirement. In *Social aspects of aging,* ed. I. Simpson & J. C. McKinney. Durham, N.C.: Duke University Press.

Kinsey, A. C., Pomeroy, W. B., Martin, C. E., and Gebhard, P. H. 1953. *Sexual behavior in the human female.* Philadelphia: Saunders.

Kranczer, S. 1984. United States population outlook. *Statistical Bulletin* 65 (January–March): pp. 16–17.

Kupperman, H. S. 1975. The so-called 'male menopause.' *Modern Maturity*, August 1975, pp. 61–62.

Latest findings on middle-age Americans. 1981. *U.S. News & World Report*, August 3, 1981, pp. 41.

Levin, R. J., & Levin, A. 1975. Sexual pleasure: The surprising preferences of 100,000 women. *Redbook,* September 1975, pp. 51–58.

Levinson, D., Darrow, C., Klein, E., Levinson, M., & McKee, B. 1977. Periods in adult development of men: Ages 18 to 45. In *Counseling adults,* ed. N. Schlossberg & A. Entine. Monterey, CA: Brooks/Cole.

———. 1978. *The seasons of a man's life.* New York: Knopf.

Lewis, C. 1982. My unprodigal sons. *Newsweek,* May 10, 1982, p. 11.

Lewis, R. A., Freneau, P. J., & Roberts, C. L. 1979. Fathers and the postparental transition. *Family Coordinator* 28:514–520.

Lieberman, G. I. 1978. Children of the elderly as natural helpers: Some demographic considerations. *American Journal of Community Psychology* 6:489–498.

Lowenthal, M. F., & Chiriboga, D. 1972. Transition to the empty nest: Crisis, challenge, or relief? *Archives of General Psychiatry* 26:8–14.

Lowenthal, M. F., & Robinson, B. 1976. Social networks and isolation. In *Handbook of aging and the social sciences,* ed. R. Binstock & E. Shanas. New York: Van Nostrand.

Lowenthal, M. F., Thurner, M., & Chiriboga, D. 1975. *Four stages of life.* San Francisco: Jossey-Bass.

McAuley, W. J., & Nutty, C. L. 1982. Residential preferences and moving behavior: A family life-cycle analysis. *Journal of Marriage and the Family* 44:301–309.

Masnick, G., Bane, M. J. 1980. *The nation's families: 1960–1990.* Boston: Auburn House.

Masters, W. H., & Johnson, V. E. 1966. *Human sexual response.* Boston: Little, Brown.

———. 1968. Human sexual response: The aging female and the aging male. In *Middle age and aging,* ed. B. L. Neugarten, pp. 271–275. Chicago: University of Chicago Press.

Menninger, B. 1982. The woman behind the man. *Ladies' Home Journal,* July 1982, p. 92.

Michelson, W. 1977. *Environmental choice: Human behavior, and residential satisfaction.* New York: Oxford University Press.

Middle age the best of times? 1982. *U.S. News & World Report,* October 25, 1982, pp. 67–68.

Miller, B. C. 1976. A multivariate developmental model of marital satisfaction. *Journal of Marriage and the Family* 38:643–657.

Neugarten, B. L. 1970. Dynamics of transition of middle age to old age: Adaptation and the life cycle. *Journal of Geriatric Psychiatry* 4:71–87.

——— 1979. Time, age, and the life cycle. *American Journal of Psychiatry* 136:887–894.

Neugarten, B. L., & Brown-Rezanka, L. 1978. Midlife women in the 1980s. Paper prepared for the Select Committee on Aging, U.S. House of Representatives, September 1978.

Neugarten, B. L., & Gutmann, D. L. 1968. Age-sex roles and personality in middle age: A thematic apperception study. *Psychological Monographs* 72:32–33.

Neugarten, B. L., Havighurst, R. J., & Tobin, S. S. 1961. The measurement of life satisfaction. *Journal of Gerontology* 16:134–143.

Neugarten, B. L., & Peterson, W. A. 1957. A study of the American age-grade system. *Proceedings of the Fourth Congress of the International Association of Gerontology.* Vol. 3, Sociological Division. Merano, Italy, pp. 497–502.

Norton, A. J. 1983. Family life cycle: 1980. *Journal of Marriage and the Family* 45: 267–275.

Orthner, D. K. 1975. Leisure activity patterns and marital satisfaction over the marital career. *Journal of Marriage and the Family* 37:91–102.

Peterson, J. A. 1968. *Married love in the middle years.* New York: Association Press.

Petranek, C. F. 1970. *Postparental spouses' perception of their dyadic interaction as related to their life satisfaction.* Tallahassee: Department of Sociology, Florida State University.

Pineo, P. C. 1961. Disenchantment in the later years of marriage. *Marriage and Family Living* 23:3–11.

Report on the American family, 1972. *Better Homes and Gardens,* Des Moines, IA: Meredith Corporation.

Rollins, B. C., & Feldman, H. 1970. Marital satisfaction over the family life cycle. *Journal of Marriage and the Family* 32:24.

Rollins, B. C., & Cannon, K. L. 1974. Marital satisfaction over the family life cycle: A reevaluation. *Journal of Marriage and the Family* 36:271–282.

Rose, A. M. 1955. Factors associated with the life satisfaction of middle-class, middle-aged persons. *Marriage and Family Living* 17:15–19.

Rosenblatt, P. C., Johnson, P. A., & Anderson, R. M. 1981. When out-of-town relatives visit. *Family Relations* 30:403–409.

Rubin, L. 1979. *Women of a certain age.* New York: Harper & Row.

Saunders, L. E. 1969. Social class and postparental perspective. Ph.D. dissertation, University of Minnesota.

Shanas, E. 1980. Older people and their families: The new pioneers. *Journal of Marriage and the Family* 42:9–15.

Spanier, G. B., Lewis, R. A., & Cole, C. L. 1975. Marital adjustment over the family life cycle: The issue of curvilinearity. *Journal of Marriage and the Family* 37:263–275.

Stanford University. 1975. Study shows career women happiest. *UPI* release, November 1975.

Swensen, C. H., Eskew, R. W., & Kohlhepp, K. A. 1981. Stage of the family life cycle, ego development, and the marriage relationship. *Journal of Marriage and the Family* 43:841–853.

Troll, L. & Bengtson, V. 1979. Generations in the family. In *Contemporary theories about the family,* ed. W. R. Burr, R. Hill, F. I. Nye, & I. L. Reiss, pp. 127–161. Vol. 1. New York: Free Press.

U.S. Bureau of the Census. 1979. Consumer income. *Current Population Reports,* Series P-60, no. 118, March 1979, tables 20, 21.

U.S. Bureau of the Census. 1982. Unpublished data provided by Paul C. Glick, personal communication.

U.S. Bureau of the Census. 1982–1983. *Statistical Abstract of the United States*, 103d ed., p. 382, table 636.

U.S. Bureau of the Census. 1983. Population of the United States, 1970–2050. *Current Population Reports*, Series P-25, nos. 917 and 922.

U.S. National Center for Health Statistics. 1978. *Vital Statistics of the United States,* Vol. 2, Mortality Pt. A. Washington, D.C.: Government Printing Office.

What's happening to the American family? 1978. *Better Homes and Gardens,* Des Moines, IA: Meredith Corporation.

White, N. J. 1982. Now it's terrific to be over 40. *Ladies Home Journal,* June 1982, pp. 88.

Zube, M. 1982. Changing behavior and outlook of aging men and women: Implications for marriage in the middle and later years. *Family Relations* 31:147–156.

Chapter 14

The Aging Couple

MAJOR CONCEPTS

Longevity
  Increasing longevity
The elderly
  Frail elders
  The insults of aging
  The vigorous aging
  The young-old
Retirement
  Voluntary retirement
  Mandatory retirement
  Flexible retirement policies
Housing alternatives
  Equity conversion
  Shared housing: group homes
  Granny flats: accessory apartments
  Displacement protection

Congregate housing
Cooperative housing
Tax credits for families of the aged
Retirement centers
Nursing homes: nursing home care
Income curtailment and supplements
Government programs for the aging
  Social security
  Medicare
  Medicaid
Health maintenance in the later years
Community involvement of the aging
Lifetime learning, institutes of
  Elderhostels
  Emeritus programs

Having seen the family through the first seven stages, the original pair now face the final stage of their family life cycle and their own waning years.

"Every man desires to live long, but no man would be old," wrote a seventeenth-century satirist. This is as true today as when it was first written. Aging is a lifelong process, but in the later decades its ravages are unmistakable. The body gradually loses its elasticity, its strength, its endurance, and its ability to throw off diseases. The senses dim: sight, hearing, and taste loss is apparent. The skin wrinkles, the hair thins and loses its color, the joints stiffen and become painful, muscles weaken, bones become brittle, and the body refuses to do what a person has always expected of it. Heart, lungs, and kidneys function at half the efficiency they did in their peak years. As though this were not enough, older people complain that they do not remember as they once did, and some fear they may be losing their minds. Even so, growing old is not so bad when one considers the alternative.

The search for longevity is as old as history. Some live longer than others. Why? One can understand some young dying in accidents or from the onslaught of a deadly disease, but why do some normally well individuals live so much longer than others? No one knows for sure, but a number of theories are being researched. One hypothesis is that the answer lies in the genes. "If you would live long, choose long-lived parents" suggests that longevity runs in families, as indeed it does, but the answer is not as simple as that. Another theory is that the cells of the body are programmed to divide just so many times, and after that the clock of life runs down. A third attempt to explain longevity is that individuals who have taken care of their bodies over the years outlive those who have abused them in some way.

There is no inherent reason why the human life span cannot be extended to beyond 100 years of age. Robert Butler, former director of the National Institute on Aging, says, "Most gerontologists feel the natural or inherent genetic limit for human beings is about 110 years" (Butler 1981). The Committee for an Extended Lifespan has been investigating more than 100 centenarians in an attempt to discover why they have lived so long. They were found to be moderate in everything, busy people, hard workers, and self-protective in refusing to let life's problems distress them (McGarry 1982).

AGING IN AMERICA

More Americans are living longer now. Life expectancy has dramatically increased since the turn of the century. Then a male child at birth could expect to live to 46 years of age, a female to 48; now life expectancy for both sexes is 73 (Butler 1981), and many individuals live longer than that. The number and percentage of older people in the population will continue to rise until well into the twenty-first century. The number of the nation's elderly will double by the year 2020 (Table 14.1). Death rates of the over-65 population, especially women, have fallen considerably over the past 40 years. Indeed, the over-65 population grew twice as fast as the nation's total population between 1960 and 1980. The fastest-growing segment of the aged are the 85-and-over group, up 165 percent in the past 22 years. Longevity, however, is not the only cause of the current growth of the over-65 population; the prime cause is the steady increase in the nation's birth rate, especially through the post-World War II baby boom. The millions of infants born in the 1950s will be in their seventies by the 2020s, thus accounting for the exceptionally large proportion of the elderly in the population (U.S. Bureau of the Census 1983). Old age has become so commonplace that families must come to terms with their aging family members.

Frail Elders

Life becomes burdensome for many frail old people. Their critical and chronic illnesses have drained their physical strength, their joy of living, and their financial resources. One vivid illustration of the costs of illness among the aged is seen in the spiraling growth of Medicare payments in recent years, estimated to reach $150 billion by 1990, as shown in Figure 14.1. Since Medicare pays only part of the costs of treating older persons, their own expenses for health care escalate at an equally rapid rate.

The very old outlive their friends and families. They, and many others in failing health, are lonely, alone, and dependent on the resources of the community. The elderly often resent the *insults of aging* as they lose their strength, their eyesight, their hearing, their former sources of satisfaction, and the desire for life itself. The feeble old fill nursing homes and come to the attention of the public and members of the helping professions.

Social workers, physicians, psychiatrists, and other professionals who work with the aging see those whose needs are greatest. They emphasize the needs of the weak and helpless elderly for adequate food, living arrangements, health care, financial assistance, and supportive services of all kinds. Research findings show that some 40 percent of all Americans over 65 must limit their activities for health reasons (Neugarten 1975a, 7).

Table 14.1 UNITED STATES' FAST GROWING OVER-65 POPULATION

Year	Population over 65	Proportion of total population over 65
1980	25.5 million	1 in every 9
2000	32.5 "	1 in every 8
2020	51.4 "	1 in every 6
2030	64.3 "	1 in every 5

Source: U.S. Bureau of the Census. 1983. *America in transition: An aging society.* Washington, D.C.: Government Printing Office, September 29, 1983.

People over 65 are more susceptible to mental illness than any other age group. Psychiatric research finds that the incidence of suicide increases with age, especially among elderly white men, probably because of the loss of status, the desire to protect their widows' financial security, and the wish to escape physical dependence and suffering (Butler 1975, 893). Studies of the aging process find that the decline of intellectual abilities is precipitated by specific diseases rather than by senescence. The psychiatric disorders commonly found among the elderly are similar to those that affect the young (Butler 1975, 899).

Individual differences are especially great among the aging because people become more and more themselves as they grow older. Some are miserable; others are enjoying the best years of their lives. Some continue working into the seventies or longer; others retire in anticipation of "living it up" after a lifetime of hard work. Some older people are rigid and ineffectual in coping with change; others enjoy the continuing challenges of life. Some are depressed and self-pitying; others are optimistic and outgoing. The future may bring with it attitudes of greater tolerance and social permissiveness. Acceptance of a wider variety of

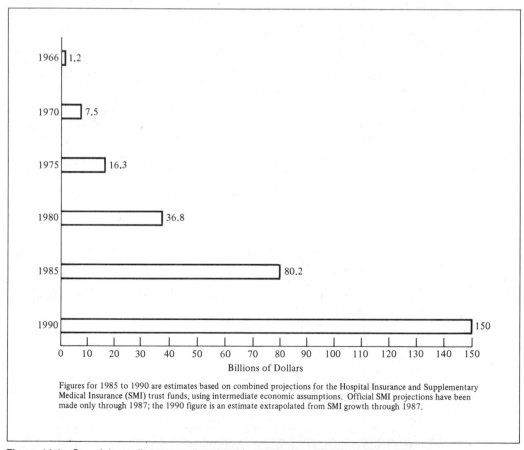

Figures for 1985 to 1990 are estimates based on combined projections for the Hospital Insurance and Supplementary Medical Insurance (SMI) trust funds, using intermediate economic assumptions. Official SMI projections have been made only through 1987; the 1990 figure is an estimate extrapolated from SMI growth through 1987.

Figure 14.1 Growth in medicare spending as evidenced by federal outlays, 1966–1990. *Source:* Health Care Financing Administration in Pamela Fessler for the Congressional Quarterly, "Health Costs Increase for the Over-65 Group, Sarasota *Herald-Tribune*, December 26, 1981, p. 4-C.

life-styles would encourage people to be themselves—to develop and to seek fulfillment according to individual preferences. "We may come to diminish the importance of chronological age as a major distinguishing feature between individuals, and instead of speaking of social roles for the aged, come to speak of the social roles of individuals who happen to be young, middle-aged or old, but more important, who happen to have different tastes, different goals, and different ways of enhancing the quality of their lives" (Neugarten 1970, 23).

The Vigorous Elderly

Stereotypes about aging have it that the old are feeble, dependent, petulant, and impoverished —well, some of them are. But recognition of the great diversity among retirees is growing. Many remain active, vigorous, and blessed with good health for years after they have retired. Since more people are living longer, more of the population is between 55 and 75. Among these are the *young-old* who are comfortably well-off, in the prime of life, increasingly well educated, politically active, and freer from family and work responsibilities than they, or their age group, have been in any era (Neugarten 1975b, 22–23). This is a new phenomenon in the history of humanity—the first generation of self-fulfilled, able people ready to serve their world with their time and talents.

Studies of a group of people during their young adulthood and then some 40 years later show a conspicuous continuity in personal characteristics. These older people are adaptive, resourceful, and diverse in life-style and personality (Maas & Kuypers 1974). Biography is replete with vivid examples of creativity lasting well into the later decades. Agatha Christie wrote mysteries until her death in her eighties. At 76 Bernard Baruch became the U.S. representative on the Atomic Energy Commission of the United States and formulated the Baruch Proposals for international control of nuclear energy. Konrad Adenauer was chancellor of West Germany from age 73 to age 87. Julia Ward Howe, author of "The Battle Hymn of the Republic," wrote her familiar "At Sunset" when she was 91. Charles Kettering was director of General Motors until he was 71. Helen Keller, deaf and blind from early childhood, was traveling all over the world at 77 when she said, "Joy in adventure, travel, and love of service to my fellowmen was stronger than physical handicaps" (Keller 1956, 2).

Age is not measured by chronological age alone. Out of a group of typical old people, half of those between 65 and 69 answered the question "How old do you feel?" by replying "middle-aged" or even "young." Only those past 80 answered invariably that they felt "old" or "aged" (Havighurst & Albrecht 1953, 9). In contrast, when undergraduates were asked "How young or old do you feel?" a surprising number said they felt old (Sarason, Sarason, & Cowden 1975, 586; see also Maynard 1973). Either optimism or excessive anxiety about one's present and future condition can occur at any age. There are at least three patterns of aging. These may be observed in (1) creative and autonomous people such as Toscanini, whose essential aliveness of spirit keeps the body alive; (2) adjusted people, such as the professional man who prides himself on being "well-preserved"; and (3) anomic people, who die soon after retirement or upon being widowed, in a metaphorical suttee; "such people live like cards, propped up by other cards" (Reisman 1954, 383).

Vigorous older people remain intellectually alert. They enjoy learning and flock to programs where they are exposed to fresh experience in new areas of knowledge. Psychologists today find that the intelligence of the elderly remains as great as it ever was. They learn in a different way than the young, but they learn with a basis in knowledge and experience.

It may take them longer to sort things out to make way for the new material, but this is real learning, and they know it. As long as a person is physically vigorous, intellectually alert, and mentally well, he or she will continue to be very much alive.

THE AGING COUPLE STAGE OF THE FAMILY LIFE CYCLE

The final stage of the family life cycle begins with the man's retirement, goes through the loss of the first spouse, and ends with the death of the second. Because women live longer than men and usually are younger than their husbands, they are more often widowed (Chapter 17).

The aging family stage begins with two positions, husband and wife, and ends with one, the surviving spouse. Beginning with one interpersonal relationship, the nuclear family ends with none. The aging couple continue to be "family" to their grown children, grandchildren, and great-grandchildren. Together the pair face the family developmental tasks of the final stage of the family life cycle. The challenge of senescence is the preservation of ego integrity —without which despair may mark the final years. The final goal of this period is successful aging through continued activity and comfortable disengagement.

Retirement Adjustments and Plans

Almost everyone who is employed retires in time, some earlier than others. When a spouse retires, the couple face major adjustments in their life-style, the ways they spend their time individually and together, their financial planning for the present and the future, and other facets of their lives, as detailed by an expert in the subject who lists 10 questions facing a couple on or before their retirement:

1. Move to a new locality, or stay within a familiar circle of friends?
2. Continue in a variation of the old job, or go on to something new?
3. Live in a house, an apartment, or a retirees' community?
4. Find a climate conducive to maximum health?
5. Explore all available medical resources?
6. Compare cultural resources?
7. Devise a realistic budget for present and future needs?
8. Seek opportunities for satisfying volunteer activities?
9. Consider possible dependent others in future planning?
10. Locate where family ties may be maintained—neither too far nor too close? (Felix 1975)

A study by the Section on Mental Health of the Aging, of the National Institute of Mental Health, identifies four patterns of retirement: (1) maintenance—a common pattern in which the retiree tries, after retirement, to satisfy the same needs in the same way as before, making extraordinary efforts to continue working in one form or another; (2) withdrawal— an equally common pattern in which retirement is seen as a time to relax and to give up many former interests without adopting new ones; (3) changed activities—in which the individual attempts to satisfy the same needs by engaging in a different set of activities; and (4) efforts to satisfy a new and different set of needs after retirement than he or she did before. These are the people who see retirement as a chance to do things they have always wanted to do (Sheldon, McEwan, & Ryser 1975).

Some people retire because they and their spouses want to spend their remaining years in activities they have not had time for while working. Others retire because the organization they work for has set ages at which their employees must step down and let younger workers take their jobs. *Mandatory retirement* is unfortunate for many able older workers whose sense of self depends on being needed. Many feel satisfaction in doing what they do well and making a contribution befitting their competence. In recent years there has been discussion about *flexible retirement policies* that allow able workers of any age to continue working as long as their performance and their preference for work allows. There has been a countertrend to retire early, even before the sixty-fifth birthday.

In recent decades smaller percentages of American men over 65 are still in the labor force, as shown in Table 14.2. In 1960 nearly one-third of men over 65 were still working (33.1 percent); 20 years later less than one out of five were still employed (19.1 percent).

The trend has been similar for women workers over the years, although smaller percentages of them have been employed. In 1960 some 10.8 percent of women over 65 years of age were working. Then over the following 20 years the proportion of women over 65 still working dropped gradually to 8.1 percent in 1980 (U.S. Bureau of the Census 1981). When both members of the pair, or only one, retire, the couple faces the adjustment of retirement as one of the developmental tasks of this stage of their marriage.

DEVELOPMENTAL TASKS OF THE AGING COUPLE

Family development continues through the final stage of the family life cycle in the interaction of the original pair and their interaction with other members of their family. By this time their children are established adults with concerns for the well-being of their parents; very possibly they are participants in the plans being laid by and for the aging couple. An aging pair's developmental tasks are intertwined now that they face the rest of life together. Both seek mutually satisfactory answers to such questions as where they will live, and on what, and how they will relate to one another and to the other important people in their lives. Both husband and wife now face the common task of developing a life-style that will be meaningful to both. Each must adjust to his or her declining health and strength and to that of the other member of the pair.

In time one spouse dies and leaves the other widowed; or, in some cases, the original marriage ends in divorce. But most older couples continue on for as long as they both live, carrying out during this final stage of the family life cycle their joint family developmental tasks. Family developmental tasks of the aging couple are listed in Table 14.3 and discussed in the following sections.

Table 14.2 MEN OVER 65 IN THE LABOR FORCE, UNITED STATES, 1960–1980

Percentage working						
1960	1965	1970	1975	1978	1979	1980
33.1	27.9	26.8	21.7	20.5	20.0	19.1

Source: U.S. Bureau of the Census, Department of Commerce, *Statistical Abstract of the United States* 1981, p. 394. Washington, D.C.: Government Printing Office.

**Table 14.3   FAMILY DEVELOPMENTAL TASKS
OF THE AGING COUPLE**

1. Making satisfying living arrangements as aging progresses.
2. Adjusting to retirement income.
3. Establishing comfortable routines.
4. Safeguarding physical and mental health.
5. Maintaining love, sex, and marital relations.
6. Remaining in touch with other family members.
7. Keeping active and involved.
8. Finding meaning in life.

Making Satisfying Living Arrangements

After retirement an aging couple may live where they please. They usually want to live independently as long as possible, in a place where they have privacy, safety, a sense of mastery over their environment, psychological stimulation, convenience, quiet, and congenial neighbors, at a price they can afford. Early in the retirement years their options include: (1) remaining in their own home, (2) moving into an apartment or mobile home, (3) establishing themselves in a retirement community; and/or (4) settling in a warmer climate. As health fails, it may become necessary to consider nursing homes, extended care facilities, or living with grown children.

In earlier times, aging parents took it for granted that they would live out their lives with their families, where they helped with the household, cared for growing children, and worked on the farm. In some parts of the nation this is still a common practice. Across northern Indiana and in parts of Pennsylvania one often sees a small house built for aging parents close to the larger farmhouse. In a declining number of instances, an old couple live in the same house with one of their adult children's families. Today this is generally not the option of choice for either generation, who value their privacy and independence as long as possible. But these values can be safeguarded by the establishment of intrafamily policies designed for harmonious three-generation living, such as:

1. Develop together a clear understanding of financial, household, and other responsibilities so that each one may know just what is expected of him or her.
2. Be reasonable in your expectations of one another. No one is perfect. Everyone makes mistakes from time to time. Perfectionists are hard to live with at any age in any family.
3. Make some provision for protecting the personal property of each member of the family. It may be little more than a closet or a bureau of his or her own, but everyone welcomes some place for personal things that will be respected as his or hers alone.
4. Respect each person's need for privacy. It is not only the great who need their "islands of solitude," as Adlai Stevenson suggested. The eldery, the adolescent, and all the rest of us from time to time desire undisturbed privacy. We have the right to open our own mail, answer our own phone calls, and make our own friends with some sense of privacy.
5. Encourage all members of the household to develop their own talents and to pursue their own interests.
6. Jointly plan for whole-family activities so that each may have a share in deciding what is to be done and what part he or she will play in the affair.

7. As disagreements arise, and they will from time to time, take the time to hear the other(s) out. Listen well enough to grasp what the situation means to those who differ. Respond to their feelings as well as to the "sense" of the situation.

8. Unify the larger family unit, sharing the household's hospitality by celebrations and rituals that bring the family closer together in its own most meaningful ways.

9. Take a positive attitude toward joint living arrangements by being appreciative of the benefits derived from sharing the household, instead of merely bemoaning the sacrifices involved.

10. Gain some perspective by realizing that through the ages families have lived more often together than in the little separate family units more popular today. (Duvall 1954, 323–324)

Group homes take the place of living with one's family, in some instances. Such congregate homes, housing 9 or 10 older people who share expenses and the housework, are proving to be an answer for older people who want to be independent but need help with everyday chores and the costs of living. Such group homes can be set up in large older houses anywhere. Like a family, the residents provide companionship and security as some of their members become ill or temporarily incapacitated (Streib & Hilker 1980). This is but one of the housing alternatives for older persons today, as outlined by the White House Conference on Aging in 1981 (see Table 14.4).

Retirement centers attract increasing numbers of more affluent older persons. Such centers offer privacy in one's own villa or apartment within the security of an establishment providing full maintenance of building and grounds, meal service when desired, health care, recreation, and comfortable living within a pleasant setting with congenial neighbors. These residential units usually have their own kitchens where food can be prepared and served independent of the central dining room. The residents have round-the-clock medical facilities available, with nurses and other professional staff seeing to their well-being. The aging couple buy a lifetime use of their apartment or villa and pay a monthly maintenance fee that covers

Table 14.4 HOUSING ALTERNATIVES FOR THE ELDERLY

Equity conversion
　Enabling older home owners to convert their home equity into income while remaining in their
　　own homes.
Shared housing
　Utilizing sizable residences for older persons under flexible zoning regulations.
Granny flats or accessory apartments
　Adapting local dwelling units for housing needs of the elderly.
Displacement protection
　Protecting the elderly from displacement due to demolition of mobile home parks, rental
　　housing, and conversion of rental units to condominiums and cooperatives.
Congregate housing for the impaired
　Tailoring construction and rehabilitation to meet specific needs of the functionally impaired.
Cooperative housing
　Encouraging and supporting privately owned and financed cooperatives for the elderly.
Tax credits for families
　Caring for older family members residing with them, with IRS regulations conforming to those
　　for Child Care Tax Credit.

Source: Selected data from White House Conference on Aging, "Housing Alternatives," Report of Committee 8, *Summary Reports of the Committee Chairmen,* December 3, 1981, pp. 50–51.

insurance, mortgage, taxes, and staff services. Upon the death of the couple, their unit reverts to the corporation to be resold to new residents.

The move to a retirement home is usually seen as the last move a couple will make in their independent living; so it is not undertaken lightly. When the decision is finally made, the aging parents dispose of many of their former possessions for which there will not be room in their unit. The older person(s) then must become accustomed to living in a community of their peers, often far removed from their family and former friends. Newcomers' groups and resident associations in some retirement centers help newer residents learn the regulations and discover the opportunities in their new locale (Levy-Reiner 1981).

Nursing home care involves the institutionalization of the person who is no longer able to be independent. In a nursing home the patient foregoes much of his or her former freedom, privacy, and personal dignity. By the time he or she needs nursing home care, incontinence is often chronic, and round-the-clock nursing is imperative. This greatly increases the cost of the patient's care and subjects him or her to the strict regulations necessary in an institution. Many nursing home patients would not need to be there if they could get the care they need in their own homes. Many housebound and bedfast old people are being cared for at home. Two-thirds of the men are being cared for by their wives. Frail older women are more apt to be taken care of by their children, according to a recent nationwide probability sample of the noninstitutional elderly over 65 years of age (Shanas 1979; see also Maddox & Dellinger 1978).

Whatever the situation, whatever the decisions that have to be made, the developmental tasks of the aging man and his wife must be accomplished as a team. Together they make their home where it suits them best, for as long as it meets their needs. As they accomplish this task successfully, they are content in their surroundings and happy in their physical setting. When they fail to work out the fundamental responsibilities of finding a satisfactory and satisfying home for their later years, they face the unhappiness that so often accompanies failure in any of the developmental tasks at any stage of the life cycle.

Adjusting to Retirement Income

In the United States it is generally assumed that one will retire at or near age 65. This is true particularly of those employed in industry and in some professions, such as teaching, where policies for retirement may be fixed. In general, fewer are employed now after age 65 than was true in earlier decades (see Table 14.2).

On the other hand, there is nothing mandatory about retirement for others. Many self-employed people continue to work on through their later years. The doctor, lawyer, writer, farmer, artist, carpenter, or businessperson who is not retired under company policy often continues to work long after retirement age, thus postponing the problems of retirement for the individual and his or her family.

Sharp curtailment of family income is one of the immediate retirement adjustments an aging couple must make. Gone is the regular income, and in its stead may be a pension at but a fraction of the former paycheck. Inflation takes a big bite out of every dollar whether it is spent or saved. Retirees are boxed in by reduced earnings and eroding buying power brought on by rising costs and inflation. The financial pinch felt by many aging family members is significantly greater than that affecting middle-aged parents or their married children, as seen in the responses of the members of all three generations studied by Reuben Hill (see Table 14.5).

Meeting the high costs of living in the later years is possible with careful planning before retirement, as well as after, in ways such as these:

1. The older couple voluntarily assume a reduced standard of living,
2. They plan on working longer before they retire,
3. They make wise investments of what money they have,
4. They defer taxes in an individual retirement account (IRA),
5. They consider the Keogh plan sheltering money for the self-employed, and
6. They participate in a pension plan, with its interest tax deferred.

A review of research of older families in the decade of the 1970s concludes that during the next 10 years the most fruitful studies will be in the areas of the effects of bureaucracy, pension provisions, service programs for the elderly, and changes in medical care provisions (Streib & Beck 1980). These areas already command the attention of national, state, and local leaders concerned with protecting the older citizen within budgetary constraints.

Government help for the elderly is widely discussed in these days of national budget deficits and increased numbers of older people in the population. At the 1980 White House Conference on Families, recommendations in order of priority listed by the delegates were as shown in Table 14.6.

Social Security is a trio of trust funds. One covers pension for retirees and their survivors; the second pays disability benefits; and the third makes Medicare payments. The Social Security system is financed by taxes withheld from payrolls of workers. In recent decades the proportion of workers supporting those receiving Social Security has steadily declined; in 1950 for every person receiving benefits, 16 workers paid Social Security taxes; in 1960 for every person receiving benefits, 5 workers paid Social Security taxes; in the 1980s only 3 workers pay Social Security taxes for each individual receiving benefits (Hildreth 1981).

Medicare is a federally sponsored hospital and medical insurance program for people 65 and older. It provides basic protection against the costs of inpatient hospital care, posthospital extended care, and posthospital health care; and supplemental protection against costs

Table 14.5 ADEQUACY OF FAMILY INCOME IN THREE GENERATIONS (IN PERCENT)

	Grandparents	Parents	Married children
Do without many needed things	28.0	4.7	1.2
Have the things we need but none of the extras	23.5	5.9	4.8
Have the things we need and a few of the extras	30.5	61.0	76.0
Have the things we need and any extras we want	3.5	14.2	16.8
Have the things we need and any extras we want, and still have money left over to invest	14.5	14.2	1.2
Total	100.0	100.0	100.0
Number of families	85	85	83

Source: Reuben Hill, "Decision Making and the Family Life Cycle," in *Social Structure and the Family: Generational Relations,* ed. Ethel Shanas and Gordon F. Streib (Englewood Cliffs, N.J.: Prentice-Hall, 1965), p. 123.

Table 14.6 RECOMMENDATIONS FOR THE AGING
(RANKED BY PERCENTAGES OF "YES" VOTES IN ALL THREE CONFERENCES)

Recommendation	Percentage
Tax policies to encourage home care of aging and handicapped persons.	92.0
Greater assistance to families with a handicapped member—tax credits, financial help, and so on.	91.0
Encourage independence and home care for aging persons—tax incentives, housing programs, and so on.	88.0
Reform of Social Security—eliminate bias toward families, marriage, and homemakers.	84.9

Source: Top-ranking recommendations from the White House Conference on Families, *Listening to America's Families,* October 1980, p. 24.

of physicians' services, medical services, and supplies, home health care services, outpatient hospital services and therapy, and other services. All this costs the government many billions of dollars every year (see Figure 14.1). Even so, Medicare pays only about 44 percent of the hospital and medical costs of those who are insured (Fessler 1981).

Medicaid, an assistance program jointly financed by federal, state, and local taxes, pays medical bills for eligible needy and low-income persons: the aged, the blind, the disabled and members of families with dependent children. Medicaid differs from state to state, since each state designs its own Medicaid program within federal guidelines. Medicaid pays for these services across the board: inpatient hospital care, outpatient hospital services, laboratory and X-ray services, skilled nursing home service, and physicians' services; in many states, Medicaid also pays services such as dental care, prescribed drugs, home health care, eyeglasses, clinic services, and other diagnostic screening and preventive and rehabilitation services.

Health care costs in the United States are growing faster than the rate of inflation, and the elderly account for an increasingly large share of this big slice of the federal budget. As the government cuts back on its share of health care, aged parents must pay amounts beyond their means for their essential medical and hospital bills.

Upon reaching age 65 (or somewhat before), Americans must apply for Social Security and Medicare, neither of which come automatically. As retirement approaches it is wise for the couple to review their assets and to shift at least some of their holdings into high-income stocks and bonds that will give them an assured income. Profits can be taken after retirement when their income tax bracket is lower. This is the time to clear up long-term debts and to avoid installment buying, speculation, and other high-risk ventures. Retirees are wise to establish a comfortable cushion fund, to live within a realistic budget, and to consider putting some of their assets into an annuity and/or a trust fund to ensure an adequate income for their remaining years, insofar as possible.

Postponing retirement makes sense for many able older workers and their families. Each year of employment after 65 increases the amount of retirement benefits. Working men and women are better off than the retired of the same age and occupational level, both economically and psychologically. Students of the problem lean toward a general recommendation of more *flexible retirement ages,* with more opportunities for creative activity for the man or woman who wants to continue active production.

Establishing Comfortable Routines

One of the most baffling tasks facing the aging couple involves adjusting to being at home together all day—a potential source of friction. Always before, except for brief periods of illness or layoffs, the husband has been away at work during the working day, leaving the home and its care in the hands of the wife. Now that both of the pair are at home all day, every day, the man may "rattle around like a pebble in a pail," as one older man puts it, with nothing to do except get in his wife's way and feel that he is a nuisance around the place.

The problem is quite different for the wife. She, in one sense, "retired" some years ago when the last child was launched and by now has made her adjustment to life. In another sense she never really "retires" as long as there are meals to prepare, beds to make, and household routines to see to. In her later years she tapers off in the amount of heavy physical work she undertakes. She may get some additional equipment to carry some of the load that is now too burdensome for her failing strength. She may hire some of the heavy work done on a regular or seasonal basis, but fundamentally her job as housekeeper and homemaker continues.

In many families today, patterns of working jointly as homemakers have been established through the years, so that now, in the postretirement period, the two continue on in the double harness to which they have become accustomed. Responsibilities are assumed on the basis of interest, ability, and strength, the husband routinely assuming some chores, the wife others, and both tackling together the jobs that they prefer doing as a team. When illness strikes, or when one of the partners is out of the home for a time, the other can take over, because he or she is already familiar with the processes involved. Decisions are jointly made; and authority is assumed by the couple as a unit. Each is accountable to the other and to the realities of the situation in the family that has already laid a foundation for joint homemaking responsibilities throughout the various stages of the family life cycle (Schafer & Keith 1981).

Protecting Physical and Mental Health

The process of aging brings with it a variety of human needs that husband and wife can help each other meet—as individuals and as a couple. Physical vitality declines. Eyes, ears, and teeth perhaps need mechanical assistance in the form of glasses, hearing aids, and dentures. In time the couple finds that they do not get around as much, as far, or as easily as they once did. All of these things are normal and to be expected in the later years.

Illnesses and accidents are more costly and critical, and ailments are more apt to be chronic in old age. Since women tend to live longer than men, on the average, it is usually the wife who nurses her husband through the illnesses that beset him in the later years. At first she may consider his condition to be temporary. In time comes the realization that the husband cannot recover and that the disease will cause death, after a long period of disability. The wife's acceptance of the chronic nature of her husband's illness is made easier by the fact that many of the illnesses of the aging begin with mild disabilities and progress very slowly toward complete helplessness; so she adjusts slowly, taking each change as it comes. One by one she takes over responsibilities new to her. She may have to make decisions with which she has had little practice or previous experience, such as taking charge of the finances of the household. She may have to provide physical care for a disabled patient, keep the house reasonably neat and clean, and function in what traditionally is the woman's sphere of the home.

Traditionally oriented men who have never learned to be at home in the house are apt to be uncomfortably awkward when the burden of homemaking falls on them. Men who define their roles as males more flexibly, who have always been at ease with the intimate, everyday routines of family living, find these tasks much easier and far more comfortable.

Husbands and wives who have maintained healthful routines through the years fare better in their nurturance of each other as an aging pair than those who have neglected their common health in the earlier stages of life together as a married couple. A good example is nutrition, so closely related to the well-being of the older person. The family that has existed for 30 or 40 or more years on a meat-and-potato-and-gravy diet may find it difficult to switch to the high-protein and fresh fruit and vegetables regimes recommended for the aging.

Malnutrition can be a problem when an old couple settle for tea and toast instead of the nourishing food their bodies need. Increasingly, today's family members turn to natural foods and the balanced diets that are good for them. Such a change of habits can result in improved appearance, increased vitality, and better self-image. Sleep comes naturally after a day of healthful exercise, without having to resort to drugs or drink to fight off insomnia (Roglieri 1980).

Drugs and alcohol are problems for many an older person. Drugs prescribed to relieve the pain of arthritis or to treat anemia, diabetes, high blood pressure, and other afflictions of an aging body are taken without question. But topped with self-administered over-the-counter medications, these can be more than an old body can take. Even more serious is alcoholism in the aging. It may be the continuation of a lifelong habit, or it may begin when physical disabilities, loneliness, depression, or inertia "drive a person to drink." Blood alcohol in old people remains high longer than in young adults, so they get drunk more quickly. The family can watch for signs of alcoholism in their aging parents: blackouts, loss of control, falling, preoccupation with drinking, and being on the defensive about it. Recognizing such signs and helping the individual cope more effectively with his or her physical, psychological, social, and economic pressures can help prevent alcohol abuse in older as well as in younger family members (Buys & Saltman 1982).

Preventive regimens, such as a healthful balance of rest and activity; regular medical, dental, and eye checkups; sensible acceptance of whatever aids and supplements may be prescribed; a variety of absorbing interests; the avoidance of extreme stress; and good mental hygiene go a long way toward ensuring both husband and wife of maximum well-being during their later years together.

Maintaining Love, Sex, and Marriage Relationships

Studies of the aging agree that married people are happier and live longer than do those who are single, widowed, or divorced. In a good marriage each partner receives the love and attention of someone who is needed and cherished. Both are able to relax and to feel settled when things are going well and to support one another mutually when life's problems come. Their marriage solves most of the needs for love and companionship of the aging pair.

Some 408 older husbands and wives connected with senior centers say that companionship and the ability to express their true feelings are the most rewarding aspects of the present phase of their marriage, which they see as the happiest period of their lives together. They list respect, sharing common interests, and love as most important for success in marriage. The morale of these older people is positively related to their happiness in marriage and to the feeling that their marriage is becoming better as time goes on (Stinnett, Carter, & Montgomery 1972).

Many older adults have been conditioned to believe that sexual capacity declines with age, that sexual activity is bad for their health, and that the continuing presence of sexual desire is abnormal. Sex research finds that although there is a slowing down of sexual capacity in both males and females in the later years, the pleasure in sexual activity continues and may actually increase (Lobsenz 1975). Ill-health can diminish the sex drive, but decreased sexual activity stems more from social prohibitions and emotional problems than from the process of aging itself (Young 1975).

Studies of 700 older people (Martin 1974) conducted at the National Gerontology Research Center show that sexual performance persists at least into the seventies and eighties and that sexual activity is highly beneficial to health. Furthermore, many elderly couples perfect the art of lovemaking, so that they reach new levels of satisfaction. Education and high socioeconomic levels are associated with positive interest in sex at advanced ages (Feigenbaum, Lowenthal, & Trier 1966).

In a study of 799 predominantly white, educated, middle-class couples classified according to Duvall's eight stages of the family life cycle, retired couples were found to be happier in their marriages than they had ever been. Some 9 out of 10 of the husbands (94 percent) and wives (88 percent) said that their marriages were going well most or all of the time. Few husbands (6 percent) and wives (10 percent) said that they had negative feelings about their marital relationship more often than once or twice a month. Positive daily companionship with each other was reported by one out of three husbands and wives. The overwhelming majority of the husbands (66 percent) and wives (82 percent) found the present stage of the family life cycle "very satisfying" (Rollins & Feldman 1970).

On Golden Pond, successful Broadway and film portrayal of an elderly married couple during their last season in their summer cottage, was vivid in presenting the mutual need of one another that develops in many long-married couples. In one scene, Norman Thayer, just turning 80, becomes confused and tells his wife, "So I came running back here, to you, to see your pretty face" (Thompson 1979). Studies of long-term marriages find "a special inner quality" in some aging couples. The more successful older marriages maintain the capacity to grow and to change, to transcend traditional roles without distress, and to like themselves as well as one another (Collins 1981).

Less tangible but quite as important is the emotional buildup that each spouse gives the other through their everyday life together. The embittered couple is bent on belittling and tearing each other down by assaults on ego and self. More productive is the support given to one another by husbands and wives who have built up patterns of mutual encouragement and appreciation on which they can lean as other faculties fail. A heartwarming way of doing this was chosen by a man who, on his fifty-fifth wedding anniversary, inserted the following advertisement in his local paper:

To my sweetheart, Sophie Hensel, I wish to thank you publicly for your love and devotion and for fifty-five years of wedded happiness made possible by your unmatched qualities as wife, mother, mother-in-law, grandmother, and great-grand-mother. We all revere you. Your husband, Henry Hensel. (*AP* release 1953)

Maintaining Contact with the Family

Four out of five older Americans are members of families, and most of them are glad of it. A two-way, three-generational flow of emotional and financial support between older parents and their grown children's families is common. The poor generally look to their relatives for assistance, and the more affluent get and give help in gifts and legacies made especially attractive under recent gift tax and inheritance legislation. The process of disengagement involves reentry into the family; as the aging selectively retire from many active and time-consuming community roles, they characteristically enjoy more family interaction on through the later years.

People who marry within their own group usually experience less conflict with their own parents than do those whose marriages have been less homogamous. Some family members love and revere their aging relatives and welcome a chance to serve them even in a culture that fosters individualism and the independence of family members. To other families, older parents are a burden that is assumed only reluctantly and as a last resort.

The problem is especially acute when the elderly person is blind, crippled, bedridden, or so senile that he or she needs protective supervision. If the family must provide the constant supervision that such care entails, it can become a severe mental and physical strain unless a companion or nurse is employed to share the load. In cases where institutionalization is indicated, the family must not only carefully select the most suitable resource and prepare the senile person for it but must also cope effectively with the feelings of guilt and implied rejection that "putting a loved one away" has meant in our culture.

Most grandparents find significance in their grandparenting roles. Maintaining close and meaningful contact with married children and grandchildren can be a rewarding task of the later years. Now that more aging couples live long enough to see their children and their grandchildren married, they often welcome their great-grandchildren and their great-great-grandchildren as well. Watching the flow of family life through three or more generations gives an older pair a long view of family continuity. Relating to members of several younger generations has satisfactions unknown to harrassed young parents. At a time when one's contemporaries are slipping away, it is heartening to watch one's grandchildren and great-grandchildren in robust interaction. Gratifying, too, is seeing one's children grow up to be competent adults rearing attractive children and grandchildren of their own. This may be one reason why older family members tend to evaluate the quality of intergenerational ties more positively than do members of younger generations (Hagestad & Speicher 1981).

Keeping Active and Involved

"Use it or lose it" is true not only of talents and organ systems but of one's life itself. Aging parents who look and act young for their age are those who have kept involved in full and meaningful living. They remain active in things they enjoy doing. They stay as long as possible in the mainstream of life in their families and communities. They keep up with what is happening in the world, and they enjoy new experiences and the opportunities of learning new things.

Institutes of Lifetime Learning have grown rapidly over the years. In these programs retired persons volunteer their years of knowledge and experience to lecture, lead discussions, participate in study groups, and conduct seminars with other alert and eager senior citizens who enjoy learning for learning's sake. *Elderhostels* are available on many campuses for older students who work, study, live, and play side by side with regular students for short periods of time at modest costs. *Emeritus programs* of study are becoming widely available for older persons who want to learn new subjects or refresh old areas of knowledge with or without college credit. The U.S. Bureau of the Census predicts that by the end of the decade there will be as many older students as younger ones enrolled in the nation's college classes ("Grownups on Campus" 1981).

Gerontologists see development as continuous throughout life. Changes are multiple and multidirectional. Some are incremental over the span of life, like the ability to generalize from experience. Development is obvious in infancy and childhood; it occurs in old age, too. "Human behavior is malleable. Infants learn, old people learn. We all learn best when we are motivated to learn. We all seek ways of exercising our competencies as long as we live" (Neugarten 1982). It is in this spirit that the Bill of Rights for Older Americans was drafted at a recent White House Conference of Aging (see Table 14.7). Success in the developmental tasks of keeping active and involved lies in the ability to remain curious and concerned and to retain patience in the presence and faith in the future. Those who find the aging years good are "self-educable, self-sufficient, and aware of all that is taking place about them. They smile and stand straight. They listen and they give of themselves to others of every vintage" (Perara 1974, 33).

Finding Meanings in Life

It is well known that old people reminisce about their earlier life experiences. Reminiscing is not a sign of senile maladjustment but of a search for the central meanings of life. This is essentially healthful because it (1) provides material for a life review, (2) makes it easier to adjust sensibly to difficult situations, and (3) contributes to a perspective in which life makes sense.

Late in life many earlier activities are no longer possible, but religious faith and practice have no age limits. However, many people drop out of church in the later years for reasons of failing health, reduced income, and feelings of being unappreciated or of being pushed out by younger generations. Life-history interviews with over 600 men ranging in social status from New York's skid row and urban lower classes to the upper-middle class found wide-

---

Table 14.7 BILL OF RIGHTS FOR OLDER AMERICANS

1. The right to be heard.
2. The right to economic well-being.
3. The right to function in the mainstream of American life to their fullest potential.
4. The right to freedom from discrimination because of age, race, sex, creed, or marital status.
5. The right to freedom of choice in housing, working, volunteering, health care, and social life-style.

Source: White House Conference on Aging, *Summary Reports of the Committee Chairmen,* December 3, 1981, pp. 10–11.

spread religious disaffiliation at all socioeconomic levels. With advancing age, church attendance becomes less important to rich and poor alike. An exception is found in skid row men, who, having dropped out of society, maintain ties with few organizations—save for the churches that have been established to serve them (Bahr 1970).

A Duke University study of people ranging in age from 60 to 94, conducted over a 20-year period, concluded that the elderly do not become preoccupied with religion or religious activities. In fact, there is a general shift from more church attendance in childhood to less in old age. However, positive religious attitudes remain despite a decline in religious activities. Religion was found to be an important factor in promoting a feeling of usefulness, happiness, and personal adjustment ("Study Refutes Ideas about the Elderly" 1976, 39).

Many older people today want to live more, not just longer. They value a sense of dignity and worth as persons. An official government publication says in part, "To most older Americans, a high degree of independence is almost as valuable as life itself. It is the touchstone of self-respect and dignity. It is the measure they use to decide their importance to others. And, it is their source of strength for helping those around them" (*The Older American* 1963, 7).

As one grows older, although the sight is dimmed, one perceives more acutely the glint of dew on the iris, the glory of a storm, the sweet peace of the woods at dusk—as one did as a child.

> The real bond between the generations is the
> insights they share, the appreciation they have
> in common, the moments of inner experience in
> which they meet. . . .
> Old men need a vision, not only recreation.
> Old men need a dream, not only a memory.
> It takes three things to attain a sense of
> significant being: God, A Soul, And a Moment.
> And the three are always here.
> Just to be is a blessing. Just to live is holy.
>
> (Heschel 1961, 15–16)

SUMMARY

The aging face their own later years, some with vigor and some with rapidly declining health. The elderly are among the fastest growing segments of the population now that American men and women live longer than did earlier generations. All face the adjustments of retirement as the man and sometimes his wife are no longer employed. Together they work on the individual developmental tasks of the later years. Each aging couple in their own way must accomplish the family developmental tasks of this final stage of the family life cycle: (1) making satisfying living arrangements as aging progresses; (2) adjusting to retirement income; (3) establishing comfortable routines; (4) safeguarding physical and mental health; (5) maintaining love, sex, and marital relations; (6) remaining in touch with other family members; (7) keeping active and involved; and (8) finding meanings in life.

Recent White House Conferences on the Family and on Aging have focused attention on the elderly in our society and drafted recommendations pertinent to the problems of this stage of the family life cycle.

REFERENCES

A.A.R.P. 1982. *News Bulletin* 23 (May): 1–2.

Bahr, H. M. 1970. Aging and religious disaffiliation. *Social Forces* 49: 59–71.

Butler, R. N. 1975. Psychiatry and the elderly: An overview. *American Journal of Psychiatry* 132: 893–900.

———. 1981. Interview: Latest on extending the human life span. *U.S. News & World Report,* August 24, 1981, pp. 35–36.

Buys, D., & Saltman, J. 1982. *The unseen alcoholics—the elderly.* Public Affairs Pamphlet No. 602. New York: Public Affairs Committee.

Collins, G. 1981. Quality of long-term marriages focus of study. New York *Times News Service,* January 17, 1981.

Duvall, E. M. 1954. *In-laws: Pro and con.* New York: Association Press.

Feigenbaum, E. Lowenthal, M. F., & Trier, M. L. 1966. Sexual attitudes in the elderly. Paper read at the Gerontological Society, New York.

Felix, R. H. 1975. *Ready for retirement?* Austin: University of Texas.

Fessler, P. 1981. Health costs increase for the over-65 group. *Congressional Quarterly.* Reprinted in *Sarasota Herald-Tribune,* December 26, 1981, p. 4-C.

Grownups on campus. 1981. *Newsweek,* December 21, 1981, pp. 72–73.

Hagestad, G. O., & Speicher, J. L. 1981. Grandparents and family influence: Views of three generations. Paper read at the annual meeting of the Society for Research in Child Development, Boston.

Havighurst, R. J., & Albrecht, R. 1953. *Older people.* New York: Longmans, Green.

Heschel, A. J. 1961. The older person and the family in the perspective of Jewish tradition. Paper read at the White House Conference on Aging, January 9, 1961, pp. 15–16.

Hildreth, J. M. 1981. The battle to save Social Security. *U.S. News & World Report,* July 20, 1981, pp. 41–44.

Hill, R. 1965. Decision making and the family life cycle. In E. Shanas & G. F. Streib, p. 123. *Social structure and the family: Generational relations.* Englewood Cliffs, N.J.: Prentice-Hall.

Keller, H. 1956. My luminous universe. *Guideposts,* June 1956, p. 2.

Levy-Reinger, S. 1981. Physicians help elderly draw upon strengths. *Menninger Perspective* 12: 9–10.

Lobsenz, N. M. 1975. *Sex after sixty-five.* Public Affairs Pamphlet No. 519. New York: Public Affairs Committee.

Maas, H. S., & Kuypers, J. A. 1974. *From thirty to seventy* (a forty-year longitudinal study of adult life styles and personality). San Francisco: Jossey-Bass.

McGarry, T. W. 1982. Committee finds key to extended lifespan. Sarasota *Herald-Tribune* (UPI release), March 14, 1982, p. 5-C.

Maddox, G. L., & Dellinger, D. C. 1978. Assessment of functional status in a program evaluation and resource allocation model. *Annals of the American Academy of Political and Social Science* 438:59–70.

Martin, C. E. 1974. Aging and society study. Reported by Jack Gourlay in Sarasota *Herald-Tribune,* March 1, 1974, p. 10-A.

Maynard, J. 1973. *Growing old in the sixties.* Garden City, N.Y.: Doubleday.

Neugarten, B. L. 1970. The old and the young in modern societies. *American Behavioral Scientist* 14:13–24.

————. 1975. The future and the young old. *Gerontologist* 15:4–9. (a)

————. 1975. The young-old. *University of Chicago Magazine* 68: 22–23. (b)

————. 1982. Understanding psychological man: A state-of-the-science report. *Psychology Today* 16:54–55.

Perara, G. A. 1974. Finding golden threads among the silver. New York *Times,* March 6, 1974, p. 33.

Reisman, D. 1954. Some clinical and cultural aspects of aging. *American Journal of Sociology* 59: 379–383.

Roglieri, J. L. 1980. *Odds on your life: How to make informed decisions about the health factors you control.* New York: Seaview Books.

Rollins, B. C., & Feldman, H. 1970. Marital satisfaction over the family life cycle. *Journal of Marriage and the Family* 32:20–28.

Sarason, S. B., Sarason, E. K., & Cowden, P. 1975. Aging and the nature of work. *American Psychologist* 30:584–592.

Schafer, R. B., & Keith, P. M. 1981. Equity in marital roles across the family life cycle. *Journal of Marriage and the Family* 43: 359–367.

Shanas, E. 1979. National survey of the elderly. *Report to Administration on Aging.* Washington, D.C.: Department of Health and Human Services.

Sheldon, A., McEwan, P. J. M., & Ryser, C. P. 1975. *Retirement patterns and predictions.* Washington, D.C.: Government Printing Office.

Stinnett, N., Carter, M., & Montgomery, J. E. 1972. Older persons' perceptions of their marriages. *Journal of Marriage and the Family* 34: 665–670.

Streib, G. F., & Beck, R. W. 1980. Older families: A decade review. *Journal of Marriage and the Family* 42: 937–956.

Streib, G. F., & Hilker, M. A. 1980. The cooperative family: An alternative life style for the elderly. *Alternative Lifestyle* 3: 167–184.

Study refutes ideas about the elderly. 1976. *AD* 5 (February):39.

The Older American. 1963. Washington, D.C.: Government Printing Office.

Thompson, E. 1979. *On Golden Pond.* New York: Dramatists Play Service, act 1, sc. 3.

U.S. Bureau of the Census. 1981. *Statistical Abstract of the United States.* 102nd ed. Washington, D.C.: Government Printing Office, p. 381.

U.S. Bureau of the Census, 1983. *America in Transition: An Aging Society.* Washington, D.C.: Government Printing Office, September 29, 1983.

White House Conference on Aging. 1981. Housing alternatives. Report of Committee 8. *Summary report of the committee chairmen,* December 3, 1981, pp. 10–11, 50–55.

White House Conference on Families. 1980. *Listening to America's families,* October 1980, p. 24.

Young, P. 1975. For a zestier life . . . Rx sex over sixty. *National Observer,* February 1, 1975, p. 1.

PART FOUR

VARIATIONS, STRESSES, AND ENDING RELATIONSHIPS

Chapter 15

Divorce, Remarriage, and Single- and Co-Parenthood

MAJOR CONCEPTS

Marital dissolution
  Annulment
  Desertion
  Separation
  Divorce
Divorce rates and ratios
  Marriage-divorce ratio
  Crude divorce rate
  Refined divorce rate
  Age-specific divorce rate
  Standardized divorce rate
  Divorce rates by states
  Trends in incidence of divorce
Divorce-proneness
  "Causes" and "reasons"
Process of alienation
Divorce laws
  Grounds for divorce
  No-fault divorce
  Alimony
  Property settlements
Divorce in the lineage bridge
Divorce recovery

Developmental tasks of recovery
Remarriage
  Remarriage rates
  Predictable transitions
  Developmental tasks of remarriage
Single parenthood
  Task overload
Co-parenthood
  Custody of children
Combined families
  Blended families
  Merged families
  Rebuilt families
  Reconstituted families
Children of divorce
Stepchildren
  Stepsiblings
Stepparenthood
  Stepgrandparenthood
  Adoption of stepchildren
Societal adhesive family bonds
Familial cohesive forces

When a marriage breaks up, urgent tasks confront everyone in the family—husband, wife, children, and kinfolk. The couple sever their marriage contract and all of their intertwined habits of living together. They must adjust to living apart and to financing two households. They must go about healing the wounds of their broken marriage, helping their children to adjust to disrupted family patterns and their relatives to accept their changed status. Their social life must be adapted to the new situation, which is awkward because it calls for neither congratulations nor condolences. Mixed feelings of failure, defensiveness, guilt, regret, recrimination, and relief are expressed or repressed. Relatives are informed—but not in the happy mood of the original wedding announcements. Some take sides with one or the other of the partners. There is often speculation about who the injured party is and why the union broke up.

Society expresses its concern for the preservation of family life in laws regulating the establishment and the termination of marriage. Legal regulation of marriage attempts to (1) promote public morality, (2) protect family stability, (3) ensure support obligations, and (4) assign child support and responsibility (Weitzman 1974, 1243).

MARITAL DISSOLUTION

A marriage may be terminated in any of five ways: naturally by the death of one or both of the partners (Chapter 17) or legally by annulment, desertion, separation, or divorce. *Annulment* is the legal erasure of a marriage for reasons of force, fraud, bigamy, insanity, falsified age at marriage, or any gross misrepresentation by either party that voids the contract. Annulment means in effect that there never has been a marriage, so that both parties return to their previous status. Fewer than 5 percent of all legal terminations of marriage are annulments, and these occur mainly in religious groups in which divorce is not permitted, notably the Roman Catholic church.

Desertion occurs when either the husband or the wife abandons the spouse and leaves the home. Estimates of the number of mates that run away each year range up to 1 million. Some runaways never return; others stay away only until they get over being "fed up" with conditions at home. Men have traditionally outnumbered women in deserting their families. A New York agency specializing in locating missing persons describes the typical runaway husband as being 44 to 51 years old, college educated, a salesman or middle-level executive, amiable, and outgoing and having a liberal expense account.

Since 1974, however, missing persons firms have been asked to find more runaway wives than deserting husbands (Ogg 1975, 3). Typically, the woman who deserts her family is well educated and about 35 years old; she married at 18 or 19 and had her first two children during the first two years of marriage. Now, after 15 years or so of marriage, her husband and children no longer seem to need her, and she feels unappreciated and useless. Desertion is a form of escape. Some people take drugs; others drink or have nervous breakdowns; a few commit suicide; more simply run away (Hampton 1975, 1, 12).

Desertion in most families comes when the burdens of child rearing are heaviest, especially in low-income families. Children may be a precipitating factor in desertion, especially when public support is more readily available for mothers rearing children alone.

Separation differs from desertion in that the couple has agreed to separate, and each spouse knows where the other is. Separation provides the time some couples need either to become reconciled or to proceed with a formal divorce. The legally separated couple live apart, do not have sexual access to each other, continue to be responsible for the care and support of their children, and are not free to marry anyone else. A separation may be officially recorded, but more frequently it is an informal agreement in which the pair live apart

DIVORCE IN THE UNITED STATES

The prevalence of divorce is widely discussed in both popular and professional literature. There is general agreement that there is more divorce now than formerly, but widespread confusion exists as to how great the increase is. This uncertainty arises in part from the different ways of measuring the incidence of divorce.

Divorce, Ratios, Rates, and Numbers

The *divorce-marriage ratio* is a popular way of referring to the prevalence of divorce in a community, in a state, or in the nation at large. It is a simple ratio of the number of divorces filed per number of recorded marriages in any given year. This is misleading in that it draws from two different populations and does not include the many couples who remain married throughout the year in question and are thus not counted among the married in the ratio.

The *crude divorce rate* is the number of divorces per 1000 population. This is a general indicator of the prevalence of divorce. It is crude in that the general population includes many children and others who are not married and who therefore do not risk divorce.

The *refined divorce rate* is the number of divorces per 1000 married persons. This measure confines itself to the already married and is superior to the crude divorce rate because it excludes those in the population for whom divorce is not applicable. The major problem with the refined divorce rate is that it is insensitive to variations in the age composition of the married population (England & Kunz 1975, 41). Thus a retirement community having an aging population would have a lower refined divorce rate than an area of young marrieds, among whom divorce is more prevalent.

The *age-specific divorce rate* is the number of divorces per 1000 married women in each age group from 14 to 85 plus by five-year intervals. Since more divorces occur among younger than among older people, this method compares populations with different age distributions without the distortion of the age factor. The problem with age-specific divorce rates is that they do not give a single summary figure for comparison purposes.

A *standardized divorce rate* starts with the age-specific divorce rate of a given population. The expected number of divorces in each age category is added, the total is divided by the population size, and the result is multiplied by 1000. This makes possible the construction of a single summary statistic for each population unit for comparison purposes, based on age-specific divorce rates and age distribution. However, in reaching a summary figure, some valuable detail information is lost (England & Kunz 1975, 42–43).

The *number of divorces* granted in any given years is still another measure of the prevalence of divorce in the United States. The sheer number of divorces in a given year does not take into account the size of the population or the number of married persons in that time period.

Divorce rates by states is a measure used to show the wide variation in incidence of divorce between 2 or more of the 50 states. Such comparisons only imply (1) the relative ease or difficulty of obtaining a divorce in the several states and (2) the number of nonresidents who get divorced in states where divorces are quickly obtained.

Trends in divorce rates have been upward through this century, as shown in Figure 15.1. Note the decline in the 1930s during the depression, the high rates during World War II in the mid-1940s, and the steady rise in recent years to a peak in 1979, followed by a slight decline in 1980 (National Center for Health Statistics, 1983, 3). Census projections of these trends suggest that some 38 percent of the women who were between 25 and 29 years of age in 1975 may divorce and that of the three-fourths who later remarry some 44 percent may again get divorced (Norton & Glick 1979).

The Increase in Divorce—Why?

There are many complex and interrelated factors behind the increase in divorce, as Table 15.1, p. 338, suggests. As long as these factors persist, divorce may be expected to be a part of the American scene.

The Divorce-Prone

Who are the divorce-prone? Those who marry in their teens are twice as likely to divorce as those who marry in their twenties (Mott & Moore 1979; Norton & Glick 1979). Premarital pregnancy with its lack of responsible planning, inadequate preparation for marriage, hurried courtship, and inherent economic problems is correlated with divorce (Furstenberg 1976). Children of divorced parents more often divorce in time, possibly because divorce openly recognizes parental dysfunction rather than ignoring its existence (Greenberg & Nay 1982, 344) or possibly because the personality problems of the parents produce similar patterns in their children (Pope & Mueller 1976). These researchers found that daughters of divorce are more likely to marry at younger ages, to become premaritally pregnant, and to marry men with low-status occupations (Mueller & Pope 1977).

Causes of divorce such as drinking, cruelty, financial problems, and extramarital affairs may have existed for years before they are cited when one or both members of the pair want to get out of the marriage (Rasmussen & Ferraro 1979).

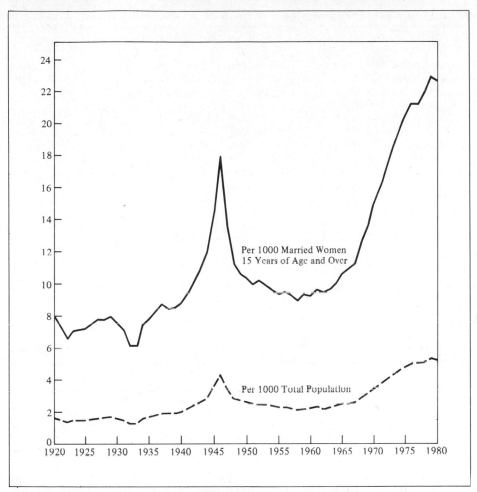

Figure 15.1 Divorce rates in the United States, 1920–1980. *Source:* National Center for Health Statistics, "Advance Report of Final Divorce Statistics, 1980." *Monthly Vital Statistics Report* 32 (June 27, 1983):1, supp.

Reasons for divorce given by husbands and wives often differ. Wives significantly more often complain of physical and verbal abuse, financial problems, drinking, neglect of home and children, and lack of love, whereas husbands' complaints run more to in-law problems and sexual incompatibility (Levinger 1966; Weiss 1975; Kitson & Sussman 1982, 91). Or, a person may be completely bewildered when divorce abruptly ends what seemed to be a good marriage. When Ann Landers, after 36 years of marriage and 20 years of writing her popular personal advice column, announced her own divorce, she wrote of the strange irony of her broken home as she asked, "How did it happen that something so good for so long didn't last forever? The lady with all the answers does not know the answer to this one" (Landers 1975).

Table 15.1　FACTORS BEHIND THE INCREASE IN DIVORCE

1. The rise of individualism emphasizes the right of the individual to personal fulfillment with less obligation "to do one's duty."
2. Increased education and employment of women make for their independence.
3. Higher family incomes help finance divorce and separate households.
4. Social disruption such as the Vietnam War, inflation, crime, urban unrest, and so on contribute to marital instability.
5. Secularization of life dilutes the influence of religion in stabilizing marriage and family life.
6. Churches' relaxation of their stand against divorce makes it a viable option for their members.
7. General acceptance of divorce provides a way out of marital stress.
8. Increased equality of the sexes makes living alone more acceptable for both men and women.
9. Marriage and divorce counseling assist incompatible couples to dissolve intolerable marriages.
10. Legal reforms make divorce easier in many states.

Sources: Paul C. Glick, "Some Recent Changes in American Families," *Current Population Reports: Special Studies,* Series P-23, no. 52 (Washington, D.C.: Government Printing Office, 1975); Paul C. Glick and Arthur Norton, "Marrying, Divorcing, and Living Together in the United States Today," *Population Bulletin,* vol. 32, updated reprint (Washington, D.C.: Population Reference Bureau, 1979); and G. C. Kitson and H. J. Raschke, "Divorce Research: What We Know; What We Need to Know," *Journal of Divorce* 4 (1981): 1–37.

ATTITUDES TOWARD DIVORCE

Attitudes toward divorce have become generally more accepting as the numbers of divorced persons in the population have increased. Studies of a city in Indiana over many years found divorce increasing from 1890 to a peak in 1920, reaching its highest peak after World War II, and then in the 1970s finding a level between the two postwar highs. But, contrary to popular opinion, it has not risen dramatically since the 1920s, and currently it is not rising at all (Caplow, Bahr, Chadwick, & Hill 1982, 51). Even when there is no runaway divorce problem in the community, people tend to say that almost "everyone" is getting or thinking of a divorce (ibid., 49). As people become familiar with divorce in their own families, or those of their friends, their attitudes toward it are affected. Middletown both condemns and facilitates divorce. Most Middletowners are satisfied with their own marriages and are thoroughly committed to marriage as the way to live. They applaud divorce as the way out of destructive relationships and have anxiety about couples who use divorce to escape minor problems that might be corrected (ibid., 133).

Of some 302,602 men and women responding to a nationwide poll, 84 percent agreed that couples who simply cannot get along should divorce; and 75 percent saw divorce as acceptable even when children are involved (What's happening to the American family? 1978, 41). (See Table 15.2.) Entering college freshmen are somewhat more conservative, with 44 percent of 192,248 of them agreeing that divorce laws should be liberalized (Astin, King, and Richardson 1981, 56). There is widespread recognition that when divorce is too easy, many otherwise good marriages are broken by impulse, anger, or ill-advised haste.

THE PROCESS OF ALIENATION

Within a conflict-torn marriage alienation proceeds to the point where it cannot easily be turned around. Each additional crisis or conflict redefines the relationship in a way that precipitates it toward even greater alienation. Destructive quarrels, characteristic of marriages that end in divorce, alternate with intervals of peace during which there may be efforts to

Table 15.2 RESPONSES OF 302,602 AMERICAN MEN AND WOMEN TO THE QUESTION: "DO YOU THINK IT'S RIGHT OR WRONG FOR A COUPLE WHO SIMPLY CAN'T GET ALONG TO GET A DIVORCE?" (IN PERCENT)

	Total	Age of respondent			Education of respondent			Who filled out the questionnaire		
		Under 35	35–54	55 and over	High school graduate or less	Attended college, graduated	Graduate work	Man of the house	Woman of the house	Both
When children are involved										
Right	75	80	74	61	73	76	77	66	76	71
Wrong	22	19	23	34	24	22	20	31	21	26
Did not answer	3	1	3	5	3	2	3	3	3	3
When no children are involved										
Right	84	86	83	82	82	85	88	85	85	82
Wrong	12	12	12	9	12	12	10	13	11	15
Did not answer	4	2	5	9	6	3	2	2	4	3

Source: A Report from the Editors of *Better Homes and Gardens, What's Happening to the American Family?* (Des Moines, IA: Meredith Corporation, 1978), p. 38. © Meredith Corporation 1978.

continue to live together. Then the conflict resumes around another sore point and continues until separation is more bearable than continuing to live together. The process of alienation proceeds through a series of crises that bring the couple to the final break (Table 15.3).

DIVORCE LAWS

Each of the 50 states enacts and enforces its own divorce laws. As a result there are wide variations among the different states in the relative ease or difficulty of obtaining a divorce. States with the most permissive divorce laws have the most divorces, as might be expected (Stetson & Wright 1975). In states with tough divorce laws a disenchanted spouse who is able to finance an expensive lawyer or a trip to Nevada or Mexico can get a divorce—but such a solution is beyond the reach of a less affluent pair.

Grounds and Reasons for Divorce

Each state has its own grounds for divorce, and these vary widely. Across the country there are some 45 legal grounds for divorce, "cruelty" accounting for most of the divorces granted. Desertion for varying lengths of time, nonsupport, adultery, habitual drunkenness, drug addiction, impotence, conviction of a crime, insanity, and other grounds are recognized in some states but not in others. At one time New York State recognized only adultery as grounds for divorce. The grounds were extended in 1966, and New York's divorce rate trebled within two years (Clayton 1975, 499). Generally, the easier it is to get a divorce in a given state, the higher its incidence.

No-Fault Divorce

The traditional adversarial system of proving in the courts the innocence of the injured party led to abuses, collusion, and inequities. Conflicting couples did what they could to dissolve their marriages, whether or not grounds for divorce were allowed in their state. Divorce legislation reforms attempt to make possible the termination of a marriage that is no longer viable without prevarication, collusion, and undue cost to the courts or to the families

Table 15.3 THE PROCESS OF ALIENATION LEADING TO DIVORCE

Steps	Progressive alienation from destructive quarreling to divorce
1	Mutually destructive quarreling weakens the marriage.
2	Affection is withheld and loving responses decline.
3	Possibility of divorcing is mentioned and considered.
4	Others discover the couple's marital trouble.
5	The married pair admit failure to themselves and others.
6	Moving to separate bedrooms accentuates the break.
7	Husband and wife break up housekeeping and establish separate households.
8	Efforts at reconciliation are unsuccessful.
9	Divorce action is undertaken.

Source: Adapted from Evelyn Millis Duvall and Reuben Hill, *When You Marry,* rev. ed. (Boston, MA.: D.C. Heath, 1953), pp. 285–288; and based on formulations of Willard Waller, *The Old Love and the New: Divorce and Readjustment* (New York: Liveright, 1930), pp. 131–132.

involved. *No-fault divorce* allows the estranged couple to terminate an intolerable marriage without being required to prove that one of the partners is at fault.

There has been a significant increase in the proportion of husbands petitioning for divorce in California since the enactment of its no-fault divorce law, which reduced men's fear that their wives would contest the divorce or file countercharges that would lead to long, drawn-out court battles (Dixon & Weitzman 1982). An earlier study found male-initiated divorce actions more often resulting in final decrees rather than in reconciliations, especially under no-fault divorce laws (Gunter 1977).

Legal scholars who are studying the question believe that no-fault divorce reforms are not as far-reaching as their advocates would like. In several states in which the no-fault feature was added to other grounds for divorce, one spouse may still blame the other and then agree to a more favorable property or support settlement under the no-fault legislation. "Under a 'true' no-fault divorce law, a couple may terminate its marriage without any expectation of punitive consequences resulting from the action" (Glick 1975, 9).

ALIMONY AND PROPERTY SETTLEMENTS

The financial arrangements surrounding divorce are rarely easy, especially for families already having money problems. The Family Service Association of America finds that hard times produce "an across the board increase in anxiety and irritability" in both husbands and wives. Financial problems are more pronounced among middle-class couples who have not previously felt such pressures; among the poor and the underemployed the money struggle is an old story (Stevens 1975, 17). When families already under financial strain go through divorce, their money problems are compounded. A cross section sample of the entire United States population found income dropping precipitously after marital dissolution, and income reduction "appears to persist as long as households remain headed by female single parents" (Weiss 1984, 126).

Alimony is derived from a Latin word meaning "sustenance." The idea behind it is that the husband as head of the family is responsible for the support of his wife and children no matter how able they are to support themselves independently. Alimony is granted by court order; and if it is not paid, the offending ex-spouse is guilty of contempt of court. Usually, the husband pays the alimony designated by the court on the basis of his income, the duration of the marriage, and other factors in the case. Occasionally, a well-to-do woman is held responsible for her husband's support through alimony payments to him after their divorce. Either spouse may petition to change the alimony arrangements as their financial conditions change. In most cases alimony stops when the ex-spouse receiving it remarries (Bohannan 1970, 483). Alimony is hard to collect and rarely sufficient to meet expenses without some supplementation. Some see alimony as "severance pay" for the wife who has worked for years as an unpaid domestic. Others view alimony as rehabilitative in that it enables the ex-wife to gain the salable skills she needs to become self-supporting (Ogg 1975, 11). Alimony is actually awarded in less than 10 percent of divorce cases (Weitzman 1974, 1186).

Property settlements are made at the time of divorce to divide the material assets (and liabilities) built up during the marriage between the two spouses. *Marital property* includes those assets that belong jointly to husband and wife, which are divided between the two when they divorce. *Separate property* belongs solely to one of the partners, and, therefore, it is not divided unless the court decides that it is in fact jointly held (Warner 1974, 87). Occasionally a man holds in his name alone all of the accumulated assets of his career. His wife, who assisted in the growth of her husband's business, career, property, and income, may find that her contribution to the partnership is unrecognized upon dissolution of the marriage (Weitzman 1974, 1192). It can happen the other way around, too. For tax and liability purposes, a man may have put most of his assets in his wife's name, only to find at the time of their divorce that she has full title to the wealth he has accumulated.

In most divorce settlements, the wife receives from one-third to one-half of the property, depending on how diligent her lawyer is, how indulgent the court is, and how much she has contributed to the couple's assets. Several new divorce laws aim at giving a wife who has worked to help her husband earn a professional degree her fair share of his increased earning power: (1) *reimbursement* provides that the exact amount contributed toward a spouse's professional license be paid back at the time of the divorce (ignoring its appreciated current value); (2) *present value* awards to the spouse who aids the other to earn a professional degree current value as established by the court, as in the case of equity in the house or the car; and (3) *share of future earnings* awards to the spouse who worked to pay for the other's professional education a share of all future earnings to be determined annually (O'Brien 1982, 46). Such laws are not universal, but they do suggest a trend toward trying to award divorcing partners each their fair share of the couple's marital assets.

DIVORCE IN THE LINEAGE BRIDGE

Middle-aged parents of married children serve as a bridge across which members of the older and younger generations get through to one another with mutual concern and support (Hill 1970). When middle-aged parents divorce, reverberations are felt by their aging parents, their adult sons and daughters, and other close kinfolk who serve as supports in various ways.

An exploratory study of the impact of divorce in middle age finds a number of differences between divorcing husbands and wives and in the ways in which they relate to older and younger generations. Wives saw the dissolution of their marriages as a long, painful process; for men it was more often a sudden event. Many more middle-aged mothers (two-thirds) than fathers (one-fourth) discussed their marital problems with their grown children. Her grown children tend to be the "linchpin" of a mature woman's support system; but only 5 percent of the men mentioned a grown son or daughter as most helpful through his divorce process. Men felt more negative reactions to their divorce among their adult children; women sensed more often their children's relief (Hagestad, Smyer, & Stierman 1982).

There is an enduring quality in parent-child bonds. Even past the age of 50, divorcing adults are concerned about their parents' approval and support; and aging parents still worry about their middle-aged sons' and daughters' well-being. The eldest generation in the family appears to provide a sense of "backing" simply by being there. But it is more to grown children than to parents that middle-aged women turn for support in their divorce trauma. Aging parents seem to facilitate the family resources in siblings and others during critical times, especially for their middle-aged divorcing daughters (Hagestad, Smyer, & Stierman 1982).

DIVORCE RECOVERY

Getting over a divorce is like learning to walk on one leg after the other has been cut off. Divorce is the amputation of a marriage. No matter how necessary it is, it hurts; and there is a period of recovery before the formerly married can go it alone again without difficulty. At first one feels crippled, helpless, and/or free of a former part of oneself. It takes time to get one's bearings as a lone man or woman after having shared one's life with another even in a marriage marked by conflict. The process of divorce recovery may be seen as involving the accomplishment of several developmental tasks (see Table 15.4).

The absence of societal norms for divorced persons makes their transition difficult, especially since no one is quite sure as to what is expected of the formerly married in a wide variety of situations (Kitson & Raschke 1981, 19). Postdivorce adjustment appears to be easier for men who have not been totally dependent emotionally and socially upon their wives (White & Asher 1976). Divorced men may have more symptoms of disturbance than women, possibly because men generally have fewer social supports (Gove 1973). Women, on the other hand, undergo more economic, situational, and subjective stress because of inequalities in employment patterns and the responsibility they usually carry with custody of their children (Brown & Fox 1978, 119). Divorcees more than widows are socially restricted, exploited, conscious of being stigmatized, and given less support by others (Kitson, Lopata, Holmes, & Meyering 1980).

Summarizing research on factors making for divorce adjustment, Kitson and Raschke (1981, 25–27) report that higher social participation, greater dating activity, equalitarian gender-role attitudes, tolerance for change, open-mindedness, independence, and self-esteem have been found related to less distress and more successful postdivorce adjustments. Counseling throughout the painful process of divorcing and recovery can be helpful, particularly when its emphases are concern for the well-being of all family members and when the approach is one of mediation (Haynes 1981; Irving 1981). Recovery from divorce may be relatively easy when there are prospects of remarriage on the horizon.

REMARRIAGE

Most divorced persons eventually remarry. Only 1 out of 7 divorced men and women remarry within the first year after divorce; 4 out of 10 divorced men and somewhat fewer divorced women remarry within three years after their divorce; and eventually 5 out of 6 divorced men and 3 out of 4 divorced women remarry. A woman with several children has less chance of remarrying than a divorced mother with one or two children, but most remarry in spite of the number of their dependents. Only one out of five divorced persons never remarries (Hunt & Hunt 1977a).

Table 15.4 DEVELOPMENTAL TASKS OF DIVORCE RECOVERY

1. Severing the lingering attachment to the former spouse that deters the establishment of a secure sense of self and independence.[a]
2. Developing a new identity for oneself separate from one's former marital status, with the ability to function fully in daily life.[b]
3. Handling the legal problems of the divorce with as few corrosive feelings as possible.
4. Becoming financially independent and self-sufficient now that two households divide the resources formerly used by one.
5. Interpreting the divorce to other members of the family who have a right to be concerned.
6. Establishing oneself in the community of former friends, colleagues, and associates of both members of the divorced pair.

[a] See Hynes 1979; and Brown, Felton, Whiteman, & Manela 1982.
[b] See Kitson & Raschke 1981.

The majority of remarried persons report they are satisfied with their current marriages, which have restored love, sex, home, and friends and added new interests and sharing with a new mate. The lifetime chance that a second marriage will end in divorce is only slightly higher than that of a first marriage (Hunt & Hunt 1977b, 114).

With high rates of divorce and remarriage, along with growing numbers of middle-aged and older persons in the population, May-December marriages are expected to increase. Furthermore, the rising status of women gives them greater flexibility in choosing a mate, even to the point of marrying a younger man. Further research would be helpful in detailing both the problems and the benefits of age-discrepant marriages (Berardo, Vera, & Berardo 1983).

Spanier and Furstenberg (1982, 719) found in their study of 180 divorced men and women that divorced persons, remarried or not, generally have a greater sense of well-being over time and that individuals with the greatest sense of well-being are most likely those who remarried three or four years after their divorces; in fact, when second marriages are successful, the persons usually fare better than if they had remained divorced.

Predictable transitions in the remarriage developmental sequence include: (1) the first married family; (2) the marital separation, divorce, and establishment of two separate households; and (3) the plans for and establishment of the remarriage. As in all critical transitions, these involve the disruption of the former equilibrium, the transition period itself, and the reestablishment of a new equilibrium (Whiteside 1982, 59). Remarriage involves the accomplishment of several developmental tasks (see Table 15.5).

Individuals accomplish these developmental tasks with varying degrees of success and failure. Remarriage is at best challenging, especially when there are children involved. But in spite of all the difficulties, most couples say they would make the same choice again (Landau, Egan, & Rhode 1978, 77).

SINGLE PARENTHOOD, CO-PARENTHOOD, AND CHILDREN OF DIVORCE

Single parents raise their children alone without the presence, support, or responsibility of a spouse or the children's other parent (Sager, Walker, Brown, Crohn, & Rodstein 1981, 4). When or if the other parent expresses an interest in, or helps support, the child(ren), he or

---

Table 15.5 DEVELOPMENTAL TASKS OF REMARRIAGE

1. Emotional remarriage—the slow process of reestablishing bonds of trust and commitment with the new partner.
2. Psychic remarriage—changing conjugal identity from individual to couple and seeing oneself as a marital partner again.
3. Community remarriage—realigning relationships within the community and reentry into the social life of couples.
4. Parental remarriage—becoming a stepparent and sharing the rights and responsibilities of parenthood.
5. Economic remarriage—establishing a new household as a unit of production and consumption.
6. Legal remarriage—solving the problems involved in alimony, child support, property allocation, and responsibilities to former and present marriage.

Source: Adopted freely from A. Goetting, "The Six Stations of Remarriage: Developmental Tasks of Remarriage after Divorce," *Family Relations* 31 (1982), 213–222.

she becomes a *co-parent* (Goldsmith 1980, 15). When a divorced parent remarries, the spouse becomes a *stepparent.*

The 1980 U.S. Bureau of the Census *Current Population Survey* reported that 18 percent of America's children under 18 years of age were living with their mothers only and 2 percent were living with their fathers only. The proportion of children living with a divorced parent reaches a peak when children are 10 to 13 years of age and is lowest when children are under 3, reflecting the tendency of couples with serious marital problems to wait until their children are of school age before divorcing (Glick 1981). Booth and White (1980) found preschoolers' parents more than twice as likely as either nonparents or parents of older children to have considered divorce; but the probability of divorce among couples with preschoolers is only half that of couples with no children or with older children (Cherlin 1977). The number and spacing of children as well as the presence of handicaps may heighten tensions between parents and possibly lead to divorce (Kanoy & Miller 1980, 313).

The proportion of mother-headed families in which mothers have at least completed high school rose from 45 percent in 1970 to 60 percent in 1979. Most of these lone mothers with children 6 to 17 years old were working (78 percent). The mother-child family lacks the male breadwinner, so the typical three-person mother–two children family has far less than three-fourths as much income ($7,035 versus $20,400) as the typical four-person mother–father–two children family (Glick 1981). The rising divorce rate has led to a sharp jump in the number of single-parent families headed by women, which tend to have much lower incomes than two-parent families (U.S. Bureau of the Census 1982). The average women's earnings are only 57 percent of what their male counterparts make, so they have less to support themselves and their children than do their former husbands (Jencks 1982). Reliable projections indicate that female-headed households will continue to increase in numbers and proportions to 29 percent of the total households in the United States by 1990 (Masnick & Bane 1980, 50).

There are great differences in the structure and composition of households headed by single parents, as shown by the numerous classifications in Table 15.6. The column headed "example" vividly illustrates the support various relatives provide in raising children in single-parent headed households. An interview study found divorced mothers maintaining high levels of contact with their relatives (Spicer & Hampe 1975, 118). Low-income single-parent mothers are found to be less distressed with the social support of friends and family, public agencies, and organizations (Hynes 1979).

Children of divorce are its most helpless victims and feel its impact deeply. Major findings of recent studies, a number of which were supported by the National Institute of Mental Health, show that for most children the first year after divorce causes the most intense disruptions, more so in boys than in girls. Two years after their parents' divorce, many boys still exhibit high levels of dependency, excessive physical aggression, or withdrawal behavior; the consequences for girls seem less dramatic. Children of homes broken by divorce grow up faster than other children. Young children and adolescents assume genuine responsibility in the single-parent household, are consulted in important decisions about the family, and become confidants of their parents, says Teresa Levitin (1982, 1), health scientist administrator of the National Institutes of Health.

Grown children of divorced parents are not likely to forego marriage because of their experience with divorce in their families of orientation. Most 18-year-olds agree that it is

Table 15.6 TYPOLOGY OF SINGLE-PARENT–HEADED HOUSEHOLDS

Type	Example
Modified nuclear (only head and children in the home)[a]	
1. Natural parent[b] Own children—all related to the head by blood, marriage, or adoption	Divorced, separated, widowed, or never-married parent raising his or her own children.
2. Surrogate parent Other children—all children other than the head's own	Lone adult raising his or her grandchildren, younger siblings, nieces, nephews, cousins, or foster children.
3. Natural-surrogate parent Own *and* other children	Divorced, separated, widowed, or never-married parent raising his or her own children *and* grandchildren, younger siblings, nieces, nephews, cousins, or foster children.
Modified extended (head, children, and additional adults in the home)[a] Natural parent—own children	
4. Own adult children—all adults related to the head by blood, marriage, or adoption	Divorced, separated, widowed, or never-married parent sharing his or her home with only own children *and* adult children.
5. Other adults—all adults other than the head's own adult children	Divorced, separated, widowed, or never-married parent sharing his or her home with own children *and* other adults, such as siblings, parents, nieces, nephews, cousins, and/or friends of either sex.
6. Multiadults—own adult children *and* other adults	Divorced, separated, widowed, or never-married parent sharing his or her home with own children *and* adult children *and* other adults, such as siblings, parents, nieces, nephews, cousins, and/or friends of either sex; spouses of adult children and/or other relatives.
Surrogate parent—other children	
7. Own adult children—all adults related to the head by blood, marriage, or adoption	Adult head sharing his or her home with grandchildren, younger siblings, nieces, nephews, cousins, or foster children *and* adult children.
8. Other adults—all adults other than the head's own adult children	Adult head sharing his or her home with grandchildren, younger siblings, nieces, nephews, cousins, or foster children *and* other adults, such as siblings, parents, nieces, nephews, cousins, and/or friends of either sex.

better for a person to marry than to go through life being single, according to the Institute for Social Research 1980 Study of American Families (Thornton & Freedman 1982, 8).

Single mothers with the helpful backing of friends and family are found to be less punitive and restrictive with their children than are those with few such supports (Colletta 1979). Research finds that single-parent mothers, their children, and others working with them develop confidence in time in the mothers' ability to be competent heads of their families; and that most single-parent families, when not plagued by poverty, are quite as successful as two-parent families (Cashion 1982, 83).

Table 15.6 *(Continued)*

Type	Example
9. Multiadults—own adult children *and* other adults	Adult head sharing his or her home with grandchildren, younger siblings, nieces, nephews, cousins, or foster children *and* adult children *and* other adults, such as siblings, parents, nieces, nephews, cousins, and/or friends of either sex; spouses of adult children and/or other relatives.
Natural-surrogate parent—own *and* other children	
10. Own adult children—all adults related to the head by blood, marriage, or adoption	Divorced, separated, widowed, or never-married parent sharing his or her home with own children *and* grandchildren, siblings, nieces, cousins, or foster children *and* adult children.
11. Other adults—all adults other than the head's own adult children	Divorced, separated, widowed, or never-married parent sharing his or her home with own children *and* grandchildren, siblings, nieces, nephews, cousins, or foster children *and* other adults, such as siblings, parents, nieces, nephews, cousins, and/or friends of either sex.
12. Multiadults—own adult children and other adults	Divorced, separated, widowed, or never-married parent sharing his or her home with own children *and* grandchildren, siblings, nieces, nephews, cousins, or foster children *and* other adults, such as siblings, parents, nieces, nephews, cousins, and/or friends of either sex; spouses of adult children and/or other relatives.

[a] Children are all persons less than 18 years of age regardless of their relationship to the head. Adults are all persons 18 or more years of age.

[b] All of the children are the head's own children; this is considered as the traditional nuclear single-parent household.

Source: Isabelle S. Payton, "Single-Parent Households: An Alternative Approach." *Family Economics Review,* winter 1982, p. 12.

Custody and Co-Parenting

At the time of the divorce, *custody of the child(dren)* is awarded one or both of the parents, who thereafter maintain separate households. When both parents assume some responsibility for and interest in their child(ren), they are considered to be co-parents. Interviews with divorced fathers and mothers selected from court records found that when noncustodial fathers remained involved with their child(ren), both parents continued to share the responsibilities, concerns, and joys of child rearing in spite of their being ex-spouses (Goldsmith 1980, 15).

A study of Parents Without Partners found 4 out of 5 of their postdivorce problems in:

1. Former spouse contacts,
2. Parent-child interaction,
3. Interpersonal relationships,

4. Loneliness,

5. Practical problems of everyday living, and

6. Financial problems (Berman & Turk 1981, 183).

Research comparing white, middle-class children and their parents from homes in which custody had been granted to the mother with the same number of children and parents from intact families found change and stress (1) in such practical areas as economic and occupational problems and those connected with running the household single-handedly; (2) in emotional distress and shifts in self-concept and identity; and (3) in interpersonal problems in social life, intimate relationships, and interactions with the former spouse and child(ren). Mothers complained of *task overload* from assuming alone the responsibilities formerly carried by both spouses. Divorced mothers and their children were less likely to eat dinner together or to play together. Divorced mothers were also less likely to read aloud to their children when putting them to bed, and their children had more erratic bedtimes. The researchers found the households of divorced mothers and fathers more disorganized than those of the nondivorced (Hetherington, Cox, & Cox 1982, 224).

Recent studies find that parenting becomes more difficult after divorce. Divorced parents communicated less well with their children, were less affectionate with them, and were less consistent in their discipline than were still-married parents. Mothers tended to give more commands and to be more restrictive, which the children either ignored or resisted. Divorced fathers began by being indulgent and then over a two-year period became increasingly restrictive, although never as restrictive as still-married fathers were (Hetherington, Cox, & Cox, 1982, 252).

In-depth interviews with custodial mothers and fathers found fathers reporting better child behavior toward them than did mothers. Children of custodial fathers expressed more appreciation and gave their fathers more parenting satisfaction than divorced mothers reported (Ambert 1982). Divorced mothers and their children tend to give each other a hard time, with children's negative behavior (whining, nagging, making demands) peaking about one year after the divorce and improving somewhat a year later (Hetherington, Cox, & Cox 1982, 258). Most divorced parents and children adapted to their new family situation within two years (ibid., 285). Ahrons (1980), who views divorce as a crisis in family transition, suggests that the maintenance of good parenting requires both parents to redefine their roles from spousal to co-parental. She suggests that the continuation of meaningful attachment bonds between parents and children reduces major stresses in divorced families.

STEPCHILDREN AND STEPPARENTING

His children, her children, and their children may all be part of the *combined families* (also called *blended families,* or *merged families,* or *rebuilt families,* or *reconstituted families*) of the formerly married. Brothers and sisters, half-brothers, half-sisters, "own" children, and stepchildren all may share the home of remarried parents. Some of the stepchildren may be only occasionally present, according to the visiting privileges of the parent and the age of the child. This gives an accordion-like quality to combined families and makes for difficulties in allocating personal space for each of the children (Berman 1982, 8–9).

Nationally, most children live with both their parents; a rising percentage live with their mothers or with stepparents (see Table 15.7).

Table 15.7 LIVING ARRANGEMENTS OF CHILDREN UNDER 18 YEARS OF AGE, UNITED STATES, 1960–1990 (IN PERCENT)

Living arrangement	1960	1970	1978	1990[a]
Total number (thousands)	64,310	69,523	63,206	64,776
Living with two parents	87.5	83.1	77.7	71
With two natural parents				
Both married once	73.3	68.7	63.1	56
One or both remarried	5.7	5.0	4.4	4
With one natural parent and one stepparent	8.6	9.4	10.2	11
Living with one parent	9.1	13.4	18.6	25
With mother only	7.9	11.5	17.0	23
Divorced	1.9	3.5	6.9	10
Married, husband absent	3.7	4.5	5.6	7
Separated	2.3	3.4	4.7	6
Widowed	2.0	2.4	2.0	2
Never married	0.3	1.1	2.6	4
With father only	1.1	1.9	1.6	2
Divorced	0.2	0.3	0.7	1
Married, wife absent	0.5	1.0	0.5	1
Separated	0.2	0.2	0.3	1
Widowed	0.4	0.4	0.3	0
Never married	0.0	0.2	0.1	0
Living with neither parent	3.4	3.5	4.2	5
With other relatives only	2.4	2.3	3.0	4
With nonrelatives only	1.0	1.2	1.2	1
With foster parents	0.8	0.8	0.8	1
In institution	0.2	0.4	0.4	0
Total	100.0	100.0	100.0	100

[a]Projected.

Source: Figures for 1960 and 1970 are primarily from various reports of the U.S. Bureau of the Census; those for 1978 are primarily from unpublished Current Population Survey data; those for 1990 are projections by Paul C. Glick, "Children with Divorced Parents in Demographic Perspective," *Journal of Social Issues* 35 (1979): 4.

Stepsiblings compete for space, privacy, and the affection and attention of the adults in the household. From childhood onward, stepsiblings may engage in sexual games or in fights that arise out of their attraction for one another without the controls of well-established incest taboos (Berman 1982, 23). Shifting coalitions between long-established sibling relationships and new ones in the family may be a problem for a while (Kleinman, Rosenberg, & Whiteside 1979, 81).

Grandparents of children of divorce, along with other relatives of noncustodial parents, may feel estranged from their grandchildren at the same time that the youngsters are deprived of ongoing contact with members of the extended family on the noncustodial side. Studies find that the quality of kin relationships across the generations—which upon divorce tends to lessen considerably—depends upon the mediation of the middle generation (Hagestad 1981, 26).

Stepfamilies' money problems are stressful in many combined families. Financial obligations to former spouse and children limit what a father can do for his present family. The family's life-style may be dependent upon child-care payments from an absent father, which may or may not be received regularly. Sources of income and how it is to be apportioned have to be decided. Some households establish joint accounts into which all monies flow. Others maintain separate accounts, with each of the partners responsible for his or her own children and share of the common household (Berman 1982, 16–18).

Adopting a stepchild provides a common surname for all members of the combined family, ensures the right of children to inherit from the stepparent, gives the stepparent the right to make decisions for stepchildren in medical emergencies, and awards the stepparent custody if anything happens to the biological parent. On the other hand, a child may prefer to keep his or her own surname as a way of feeling related to the natural parent and having a sense of family roots (Berman 1982, 25).

Stepparenting is rarely easy, especially at first. Stepchildren have at least three parent figures and sometimes more, which makes for divided authority and the "You are not my father" type of rebellion characteristic of older children. The "mean old stepmother" of fairy tales reflects not only the difficulty of mothering another woman's child but also the resistance of the youngster(s) to a woman who occupies the mother's place through marriage to the child(ren)'s father (Berman 1982, 3). Adolescents have long been known to have more trouble accepting a new stepparent than do very young or grown-up children (Bernard 1956, 216). Stepparents negatively affect the adjustment of children to their natural parents; and stepmothers have more difficult roles than stepfathers, especially when there are adolescents in the combined family (Bowerman & Irish 1973, 500). By and large, stepchildren fare about as well in combined families of divorced parents as do children in unbroken homes, any of whom can have positive, negative, or mixed family experiences, depending upon a wide array of factors (Wilson, Zurcher, McAdams, & Curtis 1975, 535).

Patterns of authority already established in the child's original family will quite likely differ in some respects from the stepparent's discipline, bringing possible rebellion and/or indifference on the part of the stepchild at times (Hunt & Hunt 1977a, 112). The good news is that stepparents often enjoy their stepchildren, and many become deeply attached to them and accept them as an integral part of the family (ibid., 112).

HOW SERIOUS IS AMERICA'S DIVORCE PROBLEM?

No one questions the seriousness of divorce to the persons involved. But what the rising divorce rate is doing to American families is a perennial question for which there is no single answer. Amitai Etzioni asks why our society does little about the progressive crumbling of the American family (Phillips 1976). Many others claim that the increasing incidence of divorce so threatens families that few will survive. Many concerned people feel that divorce is a sign of general disintegration of the family that so threatens the stability of society that future generations will be endangered.

Another view is that divorce is a realistic way of freeing spouses and their children from unacceptable family situations. This point of view recognizes that modern families are changing in many respects: fewer marriages and at later ages, greater sexual freedom and experience, more flexible egalitarian roles for men and women both before and within marriage, fewer children, higher educational levels for all family members, generally, and more opportunities for fulfilling relationships than have previously been possible.

It may be because Americans care so much for their families that they are willing to undergo long and painful divorce experiences in a search for fulfillment within marriage and family life. Twentieth-century efforts to strengthen families and to improve the lot of their members include more humane and equitable divorce legislation, family counseling and reconciliation services, comprehensive family courts, cooling-off periods to discourage impetuous divorce action, preparation for marriage and family living programs, and counseling (premarital, marital, divorce, and family).

Now that more adults remain single, perhaps more of those ready for the responsibilities and privileges of marriage will undertake it. Now that the age at first marriage is rising, perhaps immaturity will become less of a hazard. Now that more married couples are planning their families, in time fewer unwanted children will burden uneasy marriages. Now that divorce is becoming an acceptable way of dissolving conflict-ridden marriages, fewer unhappy families become a possibility. Indeed, such selective factors might eventually strengthen American families.

Traditionally, families were held together with the *adhesive bonds* of conventions, laws, and economic necessity. In modern times the *cohesive forces* inherent in families themselves (love, companionship, enjoyment of one another as growing persons, caring for one another, showing appreciation and respect, and getting through to one another with thoughts, feelings, preferences, and a sense of the ongoing nature of family life) may have a chance to supply the inner strength and flexibility that marriage needs to flourish in the contemporary world.

SUMMARY

Divorce is one of the four legal ways of dissolving a marriage. The incidence of divorce is monitored by numbers, rates, ratios, and trends over the years. The incidence of divorce in the United States has been rising since 1921 with a number of interrelated factors. Some persons are more prone to divorce than others. "Causes" and "reasons" for divorce differ by gender of divorcing partners, who often are confused as to why their marriage failed.

As divorce has increased, attitudes toward it have become more accepting. Americans are committed to marriage but see divorce as an unfortunately necessary way out of destructive unions. The process of alienation from destructive quarrels to divorce, first outlined more than 50 years ago, is still helpful in tracing a couple's step-by-step breakup.

Since each state enacts and enforces its own divorce laws, there is wide variation in ease of obtaining a divorce and grounds for which it may be granted. Alimony—originally seen as the wife's "severance pay" or as a means to aid her rehabilitation as a self-supporting person—may now be granted to either party or neither. Spousal help in increasing earning power may be legally recognized via reimbursement, present value, or share of future earnings in divorce settlements.

Divorce in the middle generation affects elder and younger family members as well. Divorce recovery entails the accomplishment of developmental tasks in the transition to new roles and status. Remarriage is a probability for about four-fifths of divorced men and women, most of whom become more satisfied with their new marriages than with their old ones.

Children of divorce are raised by single parents, by co-parents, or by stepparents. Research finds problems in postdivorce parenting, which are usually solved within two years following divorce. Stepchildren grow up in combined families. Stepsiblings compete for privacy, space, and adult attention. Stepgrandparents may be estranged from grandchildren on the noncustodial side of the divorced family. Stepparenting is often more difficult than parenting one's own children, but it can be rewarding in time.

Divorce is seen as the deterioration of marriage or as a necessary escape from a nonviable relationship. Recent trends in marriage and societal changes may ultimately strengthen marriage. In contemporary families, inherent cohesive forces keep family members together by preference for one another rather than by intense social pressures or feelings of obligation.

REFERENCES

Ahrons, C. R. 1980. Divorce: A crisis of family transition and change. *Family Relations* 29:533–540.

Ambert, A. 1982. Differences in children's behavior toward custodial mothers and custodial fathers. *Journal of Marriage and the Family* 44:73–86.

Astin, A. W., King, M. R., & Richardson, G. T. 1981. *The American freshman: National norms for fall 1981.* Los Angeles: University of California.

Berardo, F. M., Vera, H., & Berardo, D. H. 1983. Age-discrepant marriages. *Medical Aspects of Human Sexuality* 17:57–76.

Berman, C. 1982. *Stepfamilies—a growing reality.* New York: Public Affairs Committee.

Berman, W. H., & Turk, D. C. 1981. Adaptation to divorce: Problems and coping strategies. *Journal of Marriage and the Family* 43:179–189.

Bernard, J. 1956. *Remarriage: A study of marriage.* New York: Dryden Press.

Bohannan P., ed. 1970. *Divorce and after.* Garden City, N.Y.: Doubleday.

Booth, A., & White, L. 1980. Thinking about divorce. *Journal of Marriage and the Family* 42:605–616.

Bowerman, C. E., & Irish, D. P. 1973. Some relationships of stepchildren to their parents. In *Love-marriage-family: A developmental approach,* ed. M. E. Lasswell & T. E. Lasswell. Glenview, IL: Scott, Foresman.

Brown, P., Felton, B. J., Whiteman, V., & Manela, R. 1982. Attachment in adults: The special case of recently separated marital partners. *Journal of Divorce.* Vol. 5.

Brown, P., & Fox, H. 1978. Sex differences in divorce. In *Gender and psychopathology: Sex differences in disordered behavior,* ed. E. Gomberg & V. Franks. New York: Bruner-Mazel.

Caplow, T., Bahr, H. M., Chadwick, B. A., & Hill, R. 1982. *Middletown families: Fifty years of change and continuity.* Minneapolis: University of Minnesota Press.

Cashion, B. G. 1982. Female-headed families: Effects on children and clinical implications. *Journal of Marital and Family Therapy* 8:77–85.

Cherlin, A. 1977. The effect of children on marital dissolution. *Demography* 14:265–272.

Clayton, R. R. 1975. *The family, marriage and social change.* Lexington, MA: Heath.

Colletta, N. D. 1979. Support systems after divorce: Incidence and impact. *Journal of Marriage and the Family* 41:837–846.

Dixon, R. B., & Weitzman, L. F. 1982. When husbands file for divorce. *Journal of Marriage and the Family* 44:103–115.

Duvall, E. M., & Hill, R. 1953. *When you marry.* rev. ed. Lexington, MA: Heath.

England, J. L., & Kunz, P. R. 1975. The application of age-specific rates to divorce. *Journal of Marriage and the Family* 37:40–46.

Furstenberg, F. F., Jr. 1976. Premarital pregnancy and marital instability. *Journal of Social Issues* 32:67–86.

Glick, P. C. 1975. Some recent changes in American families. *Current Population Reports: Special Studies.* Series P-23, no. 52. Washington, D.C.: Government Printing Office.

———. 1979. Children with divorced parents in demographic perspective. *Journal of Social Issues* 35:4.

———. 1981. Children from one-parent families: Recent data and projections. Paper presented at the

Special Institute on Critical Issues in Education, sponsored by the Charles F. Kettering Foundation and held at the American University, Washington, D.C., June 20, 1981.

Glick, P. C., & Norton, A. J. 1979. Marrying, divorcing, and living together in the United States today. *Population Bulletin,* vol. 32, updated reprint. Washington, D.C.: Population Reference Bureau.

Goetting, A. 1982. The six stations of remarriage: Developmental tasks of remarriage after divorce. *Family Relations* 31:213–222.

Goldsmith, J. 1980. Relationships between former spouses: Descriptive findings. *Journal of Divorce* 2:1–20.

Gove, W. R. 1973. Sex, marital status, and mortality. *American Journal of Sociology* 79:45–67.

Greenberg, E. F., & Nay, W. R. 1982. The intergenerational transmission of marital instability reconsidered. *Journal of Marriage and the Family* 44:335–347.

Gunter, B. G. 1977. Notes on divorce filing as role behavior. *Journal of Marriage and the Family* 39:95–98.

Hagestad, G. O. 1981. Problems and promises in the social psychology of intergenerational relations. In *Stability and change in the family,* ed. R. Fogel, New York: Academic Press.

Hagestad, G. O., Smyer, M. A., & Stierman, K. L. 1982. Parent-child relations in adulthood: The impact of divorce in middle age. In *Parenthood as an adult experience,* ed. R. Cohen, S. Weissman, & B. Cohler. New York: Guilford Press.

Hampton, H. 1975. When the millstone gets too heavy . . . they cut and run. *National Observer,* September 6, 1975, p. 1.

Haynes, J. M. 1981. *Divorce mediation: A practical guide for therapists and counselors.* New York: Springer.

Hetherington, E. M., Cox, M., & Cox, R. 1982. Effects of divorce on parents and children. In *Nontraditional families: Parenting and child development,* ed. M. E. Lamb. Hillsdale, N.J.: Lawrence Erlbaum.

Hill, R. 1970. Interdependence among the generations. In *Family development in three generations,* ed. R. Hill, et al., Cambridge, MA: Schenckman, chap. 3.

Hunt, M., & Hunt, B. 1977. After divorce who gets married again—and when? *Redbook Magazine,* October 1977, p. 106 (a)

———. 1977. *The divorce experience.* New York: McGraw-Hill. (b)

Hynes, W. J. 1979. Single parent mothers and distress: Relationships between selected social and psychological factors and distress in low-income single parent mothers. Ph.D. dissertation, Catholic University of America.

Irving, H. H. 1981. *Divorce mediation: A rational alternative to the adversarial system.* New York: Universe Books.

Jencks, C. 1982. Divorced mothers, unite! *Psychology Today* 16:73–75.

Kanoy, K., & Miller, B. C. 1980. Children's impact on the parental decision to divorce. *Family Relations* 29:309–315.

Kitson, G. C., Lopata, H. Z., Holmes, W. M., & Meyering, S. M. 1980. Divorcees and widows: Similarities and differences. *American Journal of Orthopsychiatry* 50:291–301.

Kitson, G. C., & Raschke, H. J. 1981. Divorce research: What we know; what we need to know. *Journal of Divorce* 4:1–37.

Kitson, G. C., & Sussman, M. B. 1982. Marital complaints, demographic characteristics, and symptoms of mental distress in divorce. *Journal of Marriage and the Family* 44:87–101.

Kleinman, J., Rosenberg, E., & Whiteside, M. 1979. Common developmental tasks in forming reconstituted families. *Journal of Marital and Family Therapy* 5:79–86.

Landau, E. D., Egan, M. W., & Rhode, G. 1978. The reconstituted family. *Family Perspective* 12:65–77.

Landers, A. 1975. A sad and personal message. Syndicated column, July 2, 1975.

Levinger, G. 1966. Sources of marital dissatisfaction among applicants for divorce. *American Journal of Orthopsychiatry* 36: 803–807.

Levitin, T. 1982. Divorce's most scarred victims: The children. *Family Economist.* Washington, D.C.: American Council on Life Insurance, June 30, 1982, p. 1.

Masnick, G., & Bane, M. J. 1980. *The nation's families: 1960–1990.* Boston, MA: Auburn House.

Mott, F. L., & Moore, S. F. 1979. The causes of marital disruption among young American women: An interdisciplinary perspective. *Journal of Marriage and the Family* 41:355–365.

Mueller, C. W., & Pope, H. 1977. Marital instability: A study of its transmission between generations. *Journal of Marriage and the Family* 39:83–93.

National Center for Health Statistics. 1983. Advance report of final divorce statistics, 1980. *Monthly Vital Statistics Report* 32 (June 17, 1983).

Norton, A. J., and Glick, P. C. 1979. Marital instability in America: Past, present, and future. In *Divorce and separation: context, causes, and consequences,* ed. G. Levinger & O. C. Moles. New York: Basic Books.

O'Brien, L. 1982. My fair share: Divorce law update. *Ladies' Home Journal,* November 1982, p. 46.

Ogg, E. 1975. *Divorce.* New York: Public Affairs Committee.

Payton, I. S. 1982. Single-parent households: An alternative approach. *Family Economics Review,* Winter 1982, p. 12.

Phillips, K. P. 1976. Politicians awake! Family is ideal political issue. Philadelphia *Evening Bulletin,* February 9, 1976.

Pope, H., & Mueller, C. W. 1976. The intergenerational transmission of marital instability: Comparisons by age and sex. *Journal of Social Issues* 32:49–66.

Rasmussen, P. K., & Ferraro, K. J. 1979. The divorce process. *Alternative Lifestyles* 2:443–460.

Sager, C. J., Walker, E. Brown, H. S., Crohn, H. M., & Rodstein, E. 1981. Improving functioning of the remarried family system. *Journal of Marital and Family Therapy* 7:3–13.

Spanier, G. B., & Furstenberg, F. F. 1982. Remarriage after divorce: A longitudinal analysis of well-being. *Journal of Marriage and the Family* 44:709–720.

Spicer, J. W., & Hampe, G. D. 1975. Kinship interaction after divorce. *Journal of Marriage and the Family* 37:113–119.

Stetson, D. M., & Wright, G. C., Jr. 1975. The effects of law on divorce in American states. *Journal of Marriage and the Family* 37:537–547.

Stevens, W. K. 1975. If recession comes in the door, love may fly out the window. New York *Times,* July 28, 1975, p. 17.

Thornton, A., & Freedman, D. 1982. Marriage vs. single life: Has the rising divorce rate caused Americans to become more wary of marriage? *ISR Newsletter.* Ann Arbor, Michigan: University of Michigan Institute for Social Research. August 1982.

U.S. Bureau of the Census. 1982. *Changing Family Composition and Income Differentials.* Washington, D.C.: Government Printing Office.

Waller, W. 1930. *The old love and the new: Divorce and readjustment.* New York: Liveright.

Wallerstein, J. S., & Kelly, J. B. 1980. *Surviving the breakup: How children and parents cope with divorce.* New York: Basic Books.

Warner, J. R. 1974. Arriving at a property settlement. *Marriage and Divorce* 1:86–91.

Weiss, R. S. 1975. *Marital separation.* New York: Basic Books.

———. 1984. The impact of marital dissolution on income and consumption in single-parent households. *Journal of Marriage and the Family* 46:115–127.

Weitzman, L. J. 1974. Legal regulation of marriage: Tradition and change. *California Law Review* 62:1169–1288.

What's happening to the American family? 1978. *Better Homes and Garden,* Des Moines, IA: Meredith Corporation.

White, S. W., & Asher, S. J. 1976. Separation and divorce: A study of the male perspective. Unpublished manuscript, University of Colorado.

Whiteside, M. F. 1982. Remarriage: A family developmental process. *Journal of Marital and Family Therapy* 8:59–68.

Wilson, K. L., Zurcher, L. A., McAdams, D. C., & Curtis, R. L. 1975. Stepfathers and stepchildren: An exploratory analysis from two national surveys. *Journal of Marriage and the Family* 37:-526–536.

Chapter 16

Racial, Ethnic, and Social Class Variations

MAJOR CONCEPTS

Residential concentration
Americanization
  Melting pot
Sense of cultural identity
Ethnicity
  Ethnic succession
Intermarrriage
  Interracial marriage
  Outmarriage
Rural-urban migration
Native American families
  Bicultural families
  Traditional families
  Transitional families
  Marginal families
Asian-American families
  Extended family continuity
Families of Spanish origin
  Hispanics
  Migrant farm families
  Spanish identity
  Tribal allegiance
Culture shock

Matrilocal families
Patrilocal families
Multiple households
Extended family continuity
Assimilation
American black families
  Equal opportunities
  Fair employment practices
  Occupational inequalities
  Racial pride
Kin support
Feminization of poverty
Social class
  Socioeconomic status
  Culture of affluence
  Culture of poverty
  Vicious cycle of poverty
  "New poor"
  Psychological costs of
    unemployment
Downward social mobility
Upward social mobility
Destination class

There is no such thing as *the* American family. Families are of many types and kinds in this country. People from all over the world have come to live in the United States in wave after wave of migration over hundreds of years. They brought with them their own histories, traditions, and cultures, still evident to a greater or lesser extent in their families today.

Concentration in areas where others of the same background have settled is found among all racial, ethnic, and national groupings. Scandanavian families located in the rural Midwest; the Irish, in Boston and New York; and Jewish families, in urban areas near others of their national origin. Blacks brought into the cotton growing South migrated to the North to concentrate in Harlem, Chicago, and Detroit as soon as they had a chance. Asian Americans established themselves in Hawaii and along the coast of California where they still are found in large numbers. This human tendency to move near relatives, friends, and others who speak the same language and share a common culture has made for group solidarity and perpetuation of ethnic, racial, and national identity over the years.

Americanization efforts have helped newcomers acquire the language and the skills they need to get and hold jobs and to become assimilated into the mainstream of society. But America has never completely become a *melting pot* of homogeneity. Many families and cultural groups remain happily distinguishable entities with pride in their history and sense of identity.

Their *sense of cultural identity* has strengthened families of many foreign-born American citizens and contributed a rich diversity to the nation as a whole. Racial and ethnic solidarity has helped many minority families in their struggle for equality in recent years. Most minority families have been disadvantaged economically, educationally, culturally, and politically. Their inherent sense of self-worth has powered action programs that fight for civil rights and racial justice, make "war on poverty," do battle for fair employment practices, and struggle for equal opportunities in education, with the help of sensitive citizens in the mainstream of American life.

The walls of segregation have been crumbling since the mid-1960s with more frequent interracial, interethnic, and multinational contacts in schools, neighborhoods, and places of work. The number of whites favoring "strict segregation" declined from one-quarter to one-tenth of those interviewed between 1964 and 1974. Those who felt that blacks have the

357

right to move into any neighborhood they can afford increased from 65 to 87 percent in that decade (Institute for Social Research 1975).

A position paper on family diversity prepared for the White House Conference on Families notes:

> There is some evidence . . . that American society is becoming more respectful toward ethnic/racial differences in culture and languages; e.g. the proliferation of courses in black history or, in the Southwest, of Spanish language/culture course options. Despite such positive changes, however, there is still an invidious tendency to oversimplify family types: *the* American family, *the* black family, *the* Chicano family. These over-simplifications distort the great variation which exists within categories, and therefore makes planning and programming less effective." (Hutchison 1980)

ETHNICITY AND FAMILY VARIATIONS

Ethnicity is the sumtotal of those qualities of an ethnic group who see themselves as alike by virtue of their common ancestry, language, and ways of life and are so perceived by others (Shibutani & Kwan 1965). Ethnicity shapes family traditions, determines many family patterns and beliefs, is carried on through generations, and influences a family's identification of self and others. McGoldrick (1982, 23) sees ethnicity filling deep psychological needs while it patterns how a family thinks, feels, behaves, and eats; how family members earn a living; how the family celebrates the important moments of family life; and how the individuals in the family feel about illness, life, and death.

Different ethnic groups define *family* in various ways. For instance, white, Anglo-Saxon Protestants (WASPS) emphasize the intact nuclear family of mother, father, and children. Blacks see families in terms of networks of relatives and significant others. To Italians and Spanish Americans, a family is a tightly knit three or four generational unity that may include godparents and old friends. Chinese families include in their definition of *family* all their ancestors and descendants (McGoldrick 1982, 23). American Indians look to their tribal groups as others do "family."

Family transitions are variously celebrated according to ethnic traditions. The Irish see death as most important and place great emphasis on the wake. Italians emphasize the wedding, and Jews the Bar Mitzvah. Some groups celebrate by drinking, some by dancing and eating; and many family gatherings are marked by anecdotes, recollections, and tales of family members' exploits, triumphs, and tragedies.

Occupations tend to run in families of common ethnic background. Traditionally, both Chinese and Greek Americans went into the restaurant business; Asians and Scandanavians, into farming; Germans, into scientific pursuits; Jews, into business, banking, and medicine (especially psychiatry); the English, into law; and the Irish, into politics and police work (McGoldrick 1982, 24).

Ethnicity influences what families see as problems and how they go about solving them. Native Americans tend to be concerned about their tribal independence; Jewish families worry that their children will not succeed; Greeks see as problematic any insult to their pride; and Spanish Americans express more than the usual concern about their children's disrespect.

Intermarriage between persons of different ethnic backgrounds has helped each group become familiar with the other's family traditions. Italian American Eileen prepares lasagna for her family's Christmas Eve as her mother and grandmother did before her. Her English American husband wants plum pudding for Christmas dinner and Yorkshire pudding with his roast beef as is traditional in his family. Their teenage son prefers pizza for his birthday party instead of the ice cream and cake that his parents consider appropriate. As long as traditions are flexible enough to allow for individual preferences, they can be a source of deep satisfaction and enrichment to the family and the nation as a whole.

Ethnic succession is an historic pattern of one group replacing another in neighborhoods, jobs, leadership, schools, and other institutions. As poor ethnic newcomers replace older residents, housing is transferred down the social scale and neighborhoods change as the more established groups move to better communities (Sowell 1981, 277–280).

Migration from farm to city life cuts across all racial and ethnic groups. Farm families tend to be self-supporting, hard working, and independent. They know their neighbors and come to aid one another in times of trouble, to help with seasonal work, and to participate in community affairs. When farm families move into big cities, as they have in large numbers, they lose much of their sense of belonging to a community of like-minded folk. They work for wages and salaries rather than for themselves. They cluster with others of similar economic level in housing quite unlike that to which they have been accustomed. Their children attend big city schools where neither they nor their families are known, as they have been in rural schools. Their clothes, speech, and lack of familiarity with city life put them at a disadvantage with other children on the playground and in the classroom. Family support systems no longer operate on a friendly neighborhood basis but through government agencies and large organizations with strange personnel and procedures. An excellent example of difficulties families have in adapting to urban life is witnessed by the cultural dilemmas of American Indians as they come off the reservation and into the cities, as many have in recent years.

NATIVE AMERICAN FAMILIES

Native Americans do not think of themselves as "Indians." In fact, "The word *Indian* means little to an Indian. . . . The first thing you ask another Indian is, 'What tribe are you?' And you think of yourself as Blackfeet, or Sioux, and so on. . . . Indian people feel they belong first to their tribe. Very few white people have come to understand what that means. It's not like belonging to a country, or a sorority, or a church. It is all of that and more, a difficult concept to grasp" (Miller & Moore 1979, 448). Within the past two or three decades, Native Americans have joined other ethnic American groups in rising consciousness, growing pride, and self-awareness. Their more extensive use of *Native American* stands for a proud heritage as well as a correction of Columbus's mistake in believing he had reached the shores of India (Miller & Moore 1979, 443).

Native Americans, unlike most other Americans, have no ancestral homeland. Their former hunting grounds are cities and highways and shopping malls owned and occupied by others. Except for the reservations—on which half of them still live—there are no geographical areas they can call home. Most of them live in isolated areas with little contact with other people. Native American families are widely dispersed across the length and breadth of North America. Their society is basically tribal rather than familial, as are other groups. They are more adamantly against assimilation into the mainstream of society than any other minority in the United States (Price 1976; Staples & Mirande 1980, 898).

Native Americans are alike in their tribal allegiance but widely variant otherwise. They are organized into 280 tribes, speaking more than 252 languages (Wax 1971). Their families range from polygamy to monogamy, matrilineality to patrilineality (McAdoo 1978), and matrilocal (Navajos) to patrilocal (Sioux) family types (Miller & Moore 1979, 449).

Culture shock of Native Americans leaving the reservation for jobs in the city is three dimensional: (1) rural to urban; (2) Indian-other; and (3) Indian-Indian (in which members of one tribe cannot talk with or understand members of other tribes they encounter in pow-wows, at gatherings, or in everyday life in the city). Studies find more different tribal tongues in Oklahoma and California alone than in all the languages of Europe (Miller & Moore 1979, 444).

Dorothy Miller (Miller & Moore 1979), a grandmother and Phi Beta Kappa of Indian heritage, designed and led a five-year (1972–1977), three-wave study of how Native American families adapt to city living. Using trained interviewers of the same tribal origin and gender as their respondents, the research team first conducted a field study of 120 Native American families as a "snowball sample" of some 30,000 American Indians representing over 100 tribes in the San Francisco Bay area.

Navajos are the largest of the tribes, estimated as high as 100,000. They have lived in isolated areas of the Southwest until recently when a constant stream of young couples migrated to the cities for the money to be earned there, returning to the reservation when the routine and loneliness of urban living became too great. Most Navajos still speak their own language, retain their own culture more than other tribes, and continue to be strongly matrilocal. Navajo women carry tremendous responsibility for family, school, work, and emotional problems with such ability that they are considered "bearers of the tribe" (Miller & Moore 1979, 450).

The *Sioux* have been located in nine reservations in the Dakotas, northern Nebraska, and parts of Minnesota. Now the 50,000 descendants of this formerly powerful tribe are scattered among reservations, cities of the Northern Plains, and areas of the West Coast. Dispersed as they are, their language is spoken by only some of their people. Their *patrilocal family* style and warrior society backgrounds decimated their male leadership and led to the disintegration of their social and family structures. The Sioux male, faced with unemployment and the inability to support himself and his family, faces a more serious blow to his self-concept than do his counterparts in tribes not so bound to male dominance (Miller & Moore 1979, 451). Abnormally high divorce rates and broken homes left grandmothers as keepers of the children, with the result that descendants of the Great Plains buffalo hunters have suffered the effects of cultural disaster, suppression, and forced change (Fuchs & Havighurst 1972).

The *California tribes* have been decimated, too—first, by the Spanish whose missions used Native Californians as virtual slaves and, later, by the Anglo settlers, ranchers, and miners. An estimated 18,000 (80 percent) decline in population resulted from sickness and conquest between 1850 and 1880. "Like most Native Americans who have lived in or near 'white' towns, they still feel like outsiders. Many have low expectations of themselves, mirroring the prevailing opinion of their neighbors. Most know that education is the path their children should follow, but they are loath to have these children forget or forsake their own way" (Miller & Moore 1979, 452).

A classification of the original 120 Native American families allocated each into one of four major bicultural types as follows:

1. *Bicultural families* still use their native language and practice many of their tribal beliefs while "making it" in the city. Their children know something of both worlds and attend public schools but are sent back to the reservation for the summer. They value education, have at least a high school diploma, earn their own living, and have a decent standard of living. These 28 families (almost one-fourth of the sample) were seen as making the best social and psychological adjustment to the city (Miller & Moore 1979, 479).

2. *Traditional families,* 22 percent of the study sample, know and use their native tongue, practice Indian ways, and are close to other Indian families who also live much as they did on the reservation. In three-fourths of these families the mothers are at home and unemployed. Fully 92 percent are married to Indians. Some 40 percent of their children do not like school, possibly because education is not important to their mothers. Most of the husbands are in job training or are employed in blue-collar jobs. They may be impoverished financially, but they have a close supportive family life (Miller & Moore 1979, 480).

3. *Transitional families,* one-third of the 120, are moving toward the adoption of white ways, letting go their Indian language and values. Two-thirds of the mothers are emloyed outside their homes as clerks, domestics, or secretaries. Over half of these families have no father, and one-fourth of the fathers are non-Indian. As many as 60 percent came to the city on their own with no help from the Bureau of Indian Affairs. These are the families most likely to become assimilated into the city life, to move into the lower class, and to attempt to "become white" (Miller & Moore 1979, 481).

4. *Marginal families* (16 percent) seem maladjusted to both the Indian and the white ways. Nearly half are on welfare, and one-third have no father at home. One out of four of their children no longer attend school; only 11 percent of the mothers feel children's education is important. These are the families who suffer most from the impact of urbanization (Miller & Moore 1979, 482).

By 1979, 40 percent of the original sample of Native American families had returned to the reservation "in neither triumph nor disaster." Some one-third of these came back better educated, more sophisticated, and ready to take their place in leadership among their people (Miller & Moore 1979, 482).

Native American families generally have high fertility rates, out-of-wedlock births, strong roles for women, female-headed households, and high rates of unemployment, and many are on welfare (Unger 1977; U.S. Department of Health, Education, and Welfare 1980; Staples & Mirande 1980, 898). Extended families and *multiple households* share many family functions (Redhorse 1979; Staples & Mirande 1980, 898). Native American children are trained for independence at significantly earlier ages than are either white or black urban children. On the reservation they belong to the tribe and are cared for by any convenient adult. As their families move to the cities and their mothers work, responsible child care is sometimes lacking (Miller & Moore 1979, 464). Summarizing her revealing research, Miller says:

Most people, when they look at the Native American in the city, talk about the alcoholism, the poverty, and so on. That's one perspective, but that doesn't tell the story, which is really much more—how the family maintain themselves, keeping a psychological richness that you just feel when you're with the people in their homes. So much of the cultural life is still there, there in the way the water is for the fish. It's part of them and it *is* their life. (Miller & Moore 1979, 483)

ASIAN-AMERICAN FAMILIES

The Chinese came to the United States, especially to the West Coast, in large numbers as they fled from famine and wars at home in the middle of the nineteenth century. Here they found jobs created by the Civil War and the construction of the Union Pacific Railroad. In 1852 some 18,000 Chinese arrived in San Francisco, which at that time had fewer than 37,000 inhabitants (Andrews 1962, 177). In all, more than one-half million (540,000) Chinese immigrated to the United States between 1820 and 1979 (U.S. Bureau of the Census 1981, 87). Chinese American families have settled in "Chinatowns" in San Francisco, Chicago, New York, and other cities across the continent, where they have made a place for themselves in American life in manufacturing, banking, importing, exporting, the professions, and family-operated restaurants. Chinese American children are brought up to respect their elders, to desire an education, and to become worthy citizens like their parents.

Japanese Americans represent 1.1 percent of the population of the United States. As many as 411,000 Japanese immigrated here between 1820 and 1979 (U.S. Bureau of the Census 1981, 87), most of them following World War II and the closing of relocation camps set up for Japanese in the United States following the attack on Pearl Harbor. It was during that time that Japanese Americans born and educated in the United States were known as *Nisei,* whereas those born in Japan were called *Kibei,* terms rarely in use today, as Japanese Americans have become honored citizens in the mainstream of American life. Japanese Americans continue to make significant contributions in architecture, the arts and sciences, the professions, technology, and their stable family life.

Asians have migrated into the United States in ever-increasing numbers in recent decades (Figure 16.1). Throughout 1971 to 1979 inclusive some 1,352,100 Asians arrived here, three times the number of the previous decade, which was nearly triple that of the 1951–1960 period (U.S. Bureau of the Census 1981, 87). In the decade of the 1970s, 34.1 percent of all immigrants into the United States came from countries of Asia, notably the Phillipines, Korea, India, and Vietnam, in descending percentiles. Between 1978 and 1980, the number of Asian births in the United States rose by 30 percent, 4 times the increase of whites (8 percent), or blacks (7 percent) (National Center for Health Statistics 1984, 1). However, Asians make up less than 1 percent of the U.S. population and fewer than 10 percent of all our minorities.

Asian Americans are not highly visible as "problems" in American society because of their conforming, hard-working, cohesive family groups, which are so similar to middle-class Anglo families (Sue & Kitano 1973). Indeed, they fit better into American middle-class culture than do other minorities and often do better in educational achievement, family income, and marital stability than do many white Americans (U.S. Department of Health,

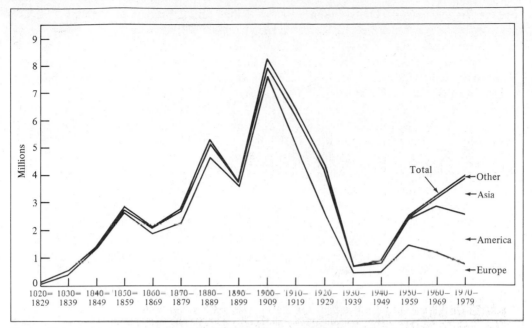

Figure 16.1 Immigrants by continent, 1820–1979. *Source:* U.S. Bureau of the Census, *Statistical Abstract of the United States 1981*, 102d ed. (Washington, D.C.: Government Printing Office, 1981), p. 85.

Education, and Welfare 1980). For example, out-of-wedlock childbearing is significantly less frequent among Asians than among either white or black women in the United States (National Center for Health Statistics 1984, 3).

Most Asian American families settled in Hawaii and the western mainland of the United States until in recent years federal and state governments appealed to communities across the continent to help resettle thousands of "boat people" stranded in Southeast Asia. The state of Iowa, for instance, successfully relocated thousands of families in small towns and cities where citizen committees helped newly arrived former residents of Vietnam, Laos, and Cambodia find homes, food, clothing, schooling for their children, adult education in English, and job skills so that these Asian American families might become independent residents of America's Midwest.

In comparison with other minority groups, Asian American families have more conservative sexual values, fewer illegitimate babies, and more traditional attitudes toward the roles of women (Monahan 1977; Braun & Chao 1978; Leonetti 1978). Young American-born Asians have tended to take on American values and traditions (Kuroda, Suzuki, & Hayashi 1978; Staples & Mirande 1980, 897). Adoption of American values has proved a mixed blessing in accentuating generational differences in language, customs, and values, which threaten *extended family continuity* and cohesiveness.

One study of families from India and Pakistan who settled in a city in western Canada found older family members viewing with horror adolescent dating and romantic love, which they saw as contributing to youthful rebellion, premarital sex, weak family ties, and lack of respect for their elders. The young people saw dating and courtship as acceptable ways of growing up in Western society and accused their parents and other elders of being repressive and not understanding them (Wakil, Siddique, and Wakil 1981, 939).

Another illustration is seen in the high rates of intermarriage of young Asians with non-Asians. Marriage records show Chinese, Japanese, and Korean women, more than men, marrying outside their racial group, with third-generation Japanese *outmarrying* at higher rates than first-generation Japanese (Kitano, Yeung, Chai, and Hatanaka 1984). Most third-generation Japanese American young women marry non-Japanese men, largely because of their dissatisfaction with the traditional Japanese male's sex-role attitudes (Braun & Chao 1978). However, research by Johnson (1977) reveals an increase in kinship contact among third-generation Japanese American families. Even while they are undergoing high mobility and assimilation, they get together with their kinfold frequently and share extensive help, services, and emotional support within the extended family (ibid., 361).

Family life is important to traditional Asians even at the expense of the individual. Child rearing and socialization have resulted in patterns of self-control and achievement of societal goals that ease the assimilation of Asian American families into the mainstream of life in the United States (Staples & Mirande 1980, 897).

AMERICAN FAMILIES OF SPANISH ORIGIN

In recent decades there has been a steady influx of Hispanic immigrants into the United States from Mexico, Central and South American countries, and the islands of the Caribbean, notably Puerto Rico and Cuba (Figure 16.1). Between 1820 and 1979 less than one in five immigrants (18.8 percent) into the United States were from Central and South America. Between 1961 and 1970 the percentage of Hispanic immigrants rose to 51.7 percent of all newcomers, and this high level was approached in the decade ending 1979 with 44.9 percent of all immigrants arriving from the Western Hemisphere (U.S. Bureau of the Census 1981, 87).

Spanish Americans, our fastest-growing minority, tend to hold to their heritage and continue to speak Spanish, which has become the largest second language spoken in the United States. Spanish Americans have a high fertility rate (99.2) compared with blacks' 81.3 and whites' 68.5 per 1000 women aged 18 to 44 (More babies 1982, 49). Out of a total population of about 6 million in 1980, persons of Spanish origin have completed fewer years of school than either blacks or whites in the United States (U.S. Bureau of the Census 1981, 142).

Mexican Americans (colloquially *Chicanos*) outnumber all other American families of Spanish origin, with a total of 2 million immigrating legally from Mexico over the years. *Wetbacks* is a derogatory term for those who cross the Rio Grande in uncounted numbers and make their way into the fields of the Southwest looking for jobs. Mexican Americans outnumber immigrants from Cuba and the West Indies by more than two to one (U.S. Bureau of the Census 1981, 87).

Most Spanish American families have two, three, or four persons, with 30 percent of them consisting of five or more persons. At the time of this writing, persons of Spanish origin make up 4.8 percent of married couple families and nearly 8 percent of families headed by women in the United States (see the last line of Table 16.1). Hispanic couples with three or more minor children tend to live in nonmetropolitan areas of the United States, but female householders of Spanish origin tend to live in metropolitan areas, regardless of the size of their families (U.S. Bureau of the Census 1982c, 16).

Since 1970, research and writing about Mexican American families has greatly increased. Until 1970, descriptions of the life of families from Mexico tended to be perjorative and based upon unfounded generalizations (Montiel 1970, 62). Since then both research and writing about Hispanic American families has greatly increased in volume (Padilla, Olmedo, & Perez 1978) and become more positive in its depictions (Staples & Mirande 1980, 893–896). For instance, studies of migrant farm families in California found clear evidence of egalitarian decision making rather than hypothesized male dominance in Mexican American families (Hawkes & Taylor 1975; Ybarra 1977). Likewise, research of Mexican Americans in Kansas City failed to find evidence of *machismo,* but rather found equalitarianism the most common pattern in Chicano families (Cromwell & Cromwell 1978). Mexican fathers are seen playing with their children as companions (Burrows 1980); and Chicano parents more than either Anglos or blacks were found to be supportive in their relationships with their children (Bartz & Levine 1978, 715).

Sena-Rivera, a Mexican American sociologist who has been studying families as they migrate from Mexico to Texas and thence to the Midwest, reports that (1) their families are larger in the second than the first generation, thanks to better health care; (2) that one-half of their marriages are to non-Mexicans, who are then drawn into Mexican ways; (3) that the large "familia" is highly valued and does not diminish even with the third generation; and (4) that respect for elders is integral in Mexican American family socialization (Sena-Rivera & Moore 1979, 124).

There has been a marked tendency among Mexican Americans to hold to their identity, cherish their heritage, and resist melting pot Americanization (Malloy 1976, 1, 12). Retaining a Spanish identity is easier in big Hispanic communities such as Los Angeles, Miami, New York, and the Southwest, where Spanish newspapers, radio, television, and businesses prevail. Spanish restaurants have spread across the continent as millions of Americans have acquired a taste for chili, tacos, tortillas, hot peppers, and other Mexican foods.

Parents born and raised in Puerto Rico tend to have a modified patriarchal family form in the United States, whereas the child generation, born and raised in this country, is transitionally egalitarian. Significant differences were found between parent and child generations in levels of *assimilation;* and the higher the wife's socioeconomic achievements, the less the husband's power in decision making (Cooney, Rogler, Hurrell, & Ortiz 1982).

Table 16.1 WHITE, BLACK, OTHER RACES, AND HOUSEHOLDS OF SPANISH ORIGIN BY PERCENTAGE OF THE POPULATION, 1981

	All households	Family households				Nonfamily households
		Total	Married-couple family	Male house-holder	Female house-holder	
White	87.3	87.4	91.0	81.9	69.0	86.9
Black	10.7	10.5	6.9	15.1	29.0	11.5
Other race	2.0	2.1	2.1	3.0	2.0	1.7
Spanish origin	4.7	5.4	4.8	8.5	7.8	3.0

Source: U.S. Bureau of the Census, *Household and Family Characteristics: March 1981, Current Population Reports,* Series P-20, no. 371 (Washington, D.C.: Government Printing Office, 1982), p. 4.

Divorce rates for persons of Spanish origin in the United States are less than half those of blacks and 10 percent higher than whites: 110 for Hispanics, 233 for blacks, and 100 for white divorced persons per 1000 married persons in 1981 (U.S. Bureau of the Census 1982d, 3).

Median incomes of all married-couple families in the United States were less for those of Spanish origin ($11,969) than for black families ($13,280) or white families ($16,554) in 1977 (U.S. Bureau of the Census 1978, 35). Poor as they are, many Hispanic families have escaped the abject poverty of their former homes in Latin America, where an estimated 50 million persons are destitute. Even though the percentages of the poor in South and Central America have dropped in recent years, because of the great population growth throughout Latin America, the absolute numbers of the very poor have remained virtually unchanged. "It is clear that the fruits of spectacular economic growth are not reaching all parts of the population" concludes a recent review of poverty in Latin America (Novak 1982, 75). Latin American countries, like many others in the developing world, have a small percentage of very wealthy families at the top, many extremely impoverished persons at the bottom, and a relatively small middle class compared with the United States. Upon migrating to the United States, those able and willing to work have a chance to better themselves and, in time, become productive middle- or working-class citizens.

AMERICAN BLACK FAMILIES

In 1977 millions of American families of all races sat enthralled before the televised dramatization of Alex Haley's *Roots,* which told the story of generations of his family history back to their origins in Africa. For eight consecutive evenings, 130 million Americans gave up their other evening activities to watch the unfolding of Haley's black American heritage. Then millions went forth to buy the 688-page book on which the television series was based. Why such an amazing reception? One possible explanation is that there was a readiness to better understand and appreciate the intertwining of black and white roots in American life. It is not a happy history for members of either race, but the time had come when families of both races could take its full impact and suffer together the agony of their past.

Texas Congresswoman Barbara Jordan explains the phenomenon:

Everything converged—the right time, the right story and the right form. The country, I feel, was ready for it. At some other time I don't feel it would have had that kind of widespread acceptance and attention—specifically in the '60s. Then it might have spawned resentments and apprehensions the country couldn't have taken. But with things quiet, and with race relations moving along at a rate that's acceptable to most Americans, we were ready to take in the full story of who we are and how we got that way (Morrow 1977, 71).

Efforts locally and nationally both in the private and governmental sectors have focused in recent decades on *equal opportunities* in voting, education, housing, and the right to work for Americans of all ethnic and racial groups. *Fair employment practices* aim at giving members of both sexes of all ages and racial and ethnic backgrounds jobs commensurate with their abilities. Marked progress has been made in improving the lot of minority Americans in many areas. But problems persist, owing in part to the large and growing numbers of blacks in the population.

Table 16.2 NUMBERS OF BLACK AND OTHER HOUSEHOLDS IN THE UNITED STATES, 1981 (IN THOUSANDS)

Race and Spanish origin	All households	Family households				Nonfamily households
		Total	Married-couple families	Male householder	Female householder	
White	71,872	52,710	44,860	1,584	6,266	19,162
Black	8,847	6,317	3,392	291	2,634	2,530
Other race	1,649	1,282	1,042	58	182	367
Spanish origin	3,906	3,235	2,365	164	706	671

Source: U.S. Bureau of the Census, *Household and Family Characteristics: March 1981, Current Population Reports,* Series P-20, no. 371 (Washington, D.C.: Govenrment Printing Office, 1982), p. 3.

In 1981 black households outnumbered all other minority households in the United States (Table 16.2). A UPI release dated November 2, 1982, projected that the nation's black population would rise from 11.9 percent in 1981 to 13.4 percent in the year 2000 and to 16.8 percent by 2050. This expected rise in the proportion of blacks in the population is based upon declining birthrates of whites and rising birthrates of blacks, as well as declining death rates of blacks as health care at all ages improves. The greatest differences in fertility rates between blacks and whites are in the large numbers and percentages of out-of-wedlock babies born to black girls. More than half of all black births now are illegitimate, and most of them take place when the mother is very young (see Table 16.3).

Black teenage girls become sexually active at earlier ages and in larger numbers than do white teenagers (Zelnik & Kantner 1980). Teenage marriages have declined over recent years—but far more rapidly among young black than white women, according to census reports from 1969 to 1979. Increases in sexual activity, decline in marriage rates, ineffective contraceptive usage, and desire for something of one's own result in high levels of out-of-wedlock births (Alan Guttmacher Institute 1981, 49). Research comparing 150 white adolescents and 150 black adolescents found boys more than girls of both races placing high value on having children. Black adolescents of both sexes believed more strongly than whites that

Table 16.3 ILLEGITIMACY AMONG BLACKS AND WHITES IN THE UNITED STATES (ILLEGITIMATE FIRST BIRTHS IN 39 STATES AND THE DISTRICT OF COLUMBIA, 1979)

Age of mother	All races		Whites		Blacks	
	Number	Percentage	Number	Percentage	Number	Percentage
Under 15	6,357	89.0	2,350	73.8	3,897	98.4
15–19	258,872	47.3	184,102	32.1	68,036	88.1
20–24	345,057	16.7	292,979	10.4	44,016	57.9
25–29	203,314	5.8	182,194	3.7	14,758	31.7
30–34	55,432	5.6	49,149	3.9	3,811	28.3
35–39	8,449	8.9	7,172	6.8	815	28.8
40–44	1,011	11.0	849	8.8	98	31.6
45–49	25	16.0	21	9.5	1	—

Source: Unpublished data from the National Center for Health Statistics, provided by Paul C. Glick, personal communication, December 1981; see also U.S. Bureau of the Census, *Statistical Abstract of the United States: 1982–1983*, 103d ed. (Washington, D.C.: Government Printing Office 1982), p. 6.

having children is conducive to marital success, personal security, and approval from others. Black 15- to 17-year-olds also expressed strong beliefs that couples should have as many children as they wish (Thompson 1980, 133).

Illegitimacy is significantly greater among blacks of all ages than among whites, as Table 16.3 clearly shows. Note especially in the right-hand column the almost universal tendency of black girls under 15 years of age to bear babies nonmaritally. Virtually all black mothers keep their babies rather than place them for adoption. These children are usually raised by their young mothers with the help of their grandmothers and other relatives (Zelnik & Kantner 1978).

More than half of all black children under the age of 18 lived in one-parent families in 1981, double the percentage in 1970 (Table 16.4). Comparing black and white children's families, we find that only 8 percent of all America's children living in two-parent families in 1980 were black, whereas 35 percent of all children in one-parent families were black (Glick 1981). Single black mothers often move in with their parents (Anderson-Khleif 1979; Bane & Weiss 1980). Older black women have more young relatives living with them than do older white women (Williams 1980). Other studies have found elderly black females forming two- or three-generation households by including young children or single parents and their children in their homes (Payton 1982, 11).

In the lower-working-class neighborhoods studied, *child rearing* by black parents, compared with white or Chicano parents, was found to stress early autonomy, strictness, and disallowance of wasted time and to evidence an atmosphere both highly supportive and controlling (Bartz & Levine 1978, 709). Child-rearing practices generally tend to be similar for both black and white parents, as do levels of children's self-esteem (Staples & Mirande 1980, 892). The Middletown III study found some significant differences in religious beliefs between black and white adolescents, with blacks tending more toward fundamentalist Christianity and being less likely to view the United States as the best country in the world; otherwise, the social values of Middletown's black and white students were practically indistinguishable (Caplow, Bahr, Chadwick, Hill, & Williamson 1982, 15).

Kin support is a prominent factor in black family life at all economic levels. Among the poor, it is literally life sustaining. Among black middle-class urban and suburban families

Table 16.4   BLACK CHILDREN LIVING IN ONE-PARENT FAMILIES, UNITED STATES, 1970–1981 (NUMBERS IN THOUSANDS)

Black families with own children under 18	1981		Change from 1970 to 1981	
	Number	Percentage	Number	Percentage
Total families	3917	100.0	933	31.3
Two-parent families	1938	49.5	−61	−3.1
One-parent families	1979	50.5	994	100.9
Maintained by mother	1862	47.5	950	104.2
Never married	641	16.4	475	286.1
Spouse absent	591	15.1	137	30.2
Separated	548	14.0	166	43.5
Divorced	465	11.9	314	207.9
Widowed	164	4.2	23	16.3
Maintained by father	117	3.0	44	Less than 75,000

Source: U.S. Bureau of the Census, *Household and Family Characteristics: March 1981, Current Population Reports,* Series P-20, no. 371 (Washington, D.C.: Government Printing Office, 1982), p. 7.

the tradition of reliance on family rather than on outside agencies prevails. *Upward mobility* among 178 black families in one recent study was found to have been a pattern for three generations. The grandparents had been born in poverty, the parents had moved into stable working-class status, and the parents of the school-age children had risen to the middle class as a direct result of their own efforts. These black families valued education and were aware of racism's impact on themselves and their children, but they were high achievers and made the grade with the supportive help of their families (McAdoo 1982, 486).

Black family incomes are about half those of all other races combined, as they have been for some years. Black families whose incomes have increased significantly are those whose wives work (Table 16.5). Many more black wives work full-time and year-round than those of other races in the United States. Black wives' earnings make up a full one-third of their families' incomes as compared with one-fourth of all other races' family incomes. However, the overall poverty rate is three times as high for black families as for all families in the United States, largely because so many more black families are maintained by women (Glick 1981, 122). See the last column of Table 16.5.

Larger proportions of black than other husbands are in the armed forces, or institutionalized, and so do not live with their families. Because so many black families are poor, the husband's presence, in some instances, is not reported so that their chances of getting welfare benefits will be increased (Glick 1981, 124). Black men who are with their families are more

Table 16.5 MEDIAN FAMILY INCOME BY TYPE OF FAMILY AND RACE IN ONE RECENT DECADE, UNITED STATES

Year and race	All families	Married-couple families		Male householder, no wife present	Female householder, no husband present
		Wife in paid labor force	Wife not in paid labor force		
Percent					
All races					
1980	100.0	40.7	41.8	2.9	14.6
1970	100.0	34.1	52.6	2.4	10.9
Black					
1980	100.0	32.8	22.7	4.3	40.2
1970	100.0	36.3	31.8	3.7	28.3
Black as percentage of all races					
1979	54.1	82.9	65.3	74.0	69.5
1969	53.1	65.6	52.8	62.3	57.9
Median family income					
All races					
1979	21,521	24,973	17,791	16,888	9,933
1969[a]	18,677	23,025	17,580	16,513	9,547
Black					
1979	11,648	20,704	11,616	12,497	6,907
1969[a]	9,916	15,099	9,277	10,287	5,523

[a] In 1979 dollars.

Source: Paul C. Glick, "A Demographic Picture of Black Families," in *Black Families,* ed. H. P. McAdoo (Beverly Hills, CA: Sage, 1981), p. 121, with basic data from U.S. Bureau of the Census, 1970, 1980, and unpublished Current Population Survey data.

often unemployed than are other men, or their own wives, whose low-level jobs are available in most communities.

Inequalities in occupational attainment are greater in some places than in others, but levels of racial occupational inequality are great in all cities (Fossett & Swicegood 1982, 687). Some years ago, Sorensen (1975) plotted the curves of occupational prestige for whites and blacks by number of years in the labor force. Although the prestige of workers of both races rose over the years, blacks' occupational prestige remained significantly lower (ibid., 463).

Black teenagers have been underemployed for many years. The 1960s saw riots of disillusioned black youths unable to find work, and fears still surface about the possibility of another "long, hot summer" when thousands of young blacks are unemployed and largely unemployable. Instilled with racial pride, many of these able-bodied young blacks refuse to take such dead-end jobs as domestics, janitors, and kitchen helpers (Bacon 1977, 25). Many lack the education or the salable skills that would qualify them for the kind of work they seek.

Black educational achievement in terms of years of school completed has made significant advances in recent years. In 1960 black median education was completion of the eighth grade; by 1980 median school years completed by blacks approximated those of whites (12.0 versus 12.5), with a high school education model (U.S. Bureau of the Census 1981, 142).

However, figures recently released by the College Board show that blacks score an average of 100 points below whites in the Scholastic Aptitude Test (SAT). Of high school seniors who took the SAT in 1981, blacks scored an average of 332 on the verbal part of the test and 362 on the mathematics, compared with 442 and 483, respectively, for whites, out of a possible score of 800 on each part. It is possible that one reason for the low black scores was that while more blacks took the test than any other group except whites, a lower percentage of blacks were in college preparatory programs. School officials are quoted as saying that many minority students do not feel pressured to get a good SAT score, that low-scoring black students sign up for fewer core courses, and that those they do take are less rigorous than those taken by whites (The racial gap in SAT scores 1982, 110). This is along the line of a Stanford University study some years ago that found minority students with unrealistic images of their own achievement. Their teachers give them unwarranted encouragement and unrealistic grades in efforts to motivate them to stay in school. But such a system of carrots with no sticks only serves to blind poor students to their inadequacies. "They do not know their work is poor. They do not know how much work they should do to improve" (Dornbusch, Massey, & Scott 1975).

A bright side of black educational aspirations is seen in the considerably higher percentages of freshmen in predominantly black colleges giving as their primary reasons for going to college "to gain a general education," "to learn more about things," and "to get a better job" than students of other institutions of higher learning (Astin, King, & Richardson 1981, 50). These goals are particularly noteworthy in light of their low family income—45 percent of their parents had incomes of less than $6000 a year—and the fact that more than one-half (58.8 percent) of the students' families were currently supporting four, five, six, or more dependents (ibid., 48).

Black marital status differs markedly from that of other races. More black men and women in their early twenties are unmarried, more are separated or divorced, and fewer are still in intact marriages (see Table 16.6). Black marriages are found to be more equalitarian on the more innovative and behavioral measures of husband-wife roles than white couples.

This same research of black and white married couples in five midwestern states evaluated black wives more positively in task performance than whites, and blacks more instrumental and expressive than whites (Scanzoni 1975, 143). Black couples in North Carolina were found to be as happy in wife-dominant as in egalitarian roles; but husband-led marriages were associated with the highest levels of marital quality (Gray-Little 1982, 642–643). Many point out that while black women are strong because of the adverse forces they face, they are not overbearing matriarchs (Staples & Mirande 1980, 891).

The divorce ratio for black persons is higher than for either whites or those of Spanish origin. The ratio for black women is particularly high—3 divorced for every 10 married with husband present (U.S. Bureau of the Census 1982d, 4). In 1980 there were 15 percent as many black divorced men as black married men and 26 percent as many black divorced women as black married women. Education appears to be a key factor in black women's dissolution of their marriages. Black women who did not finish college have the greatest likelihood of divorce, and those who have some graduate school education also have high divorce rates. The more income women earn, the less likely they are to remain married because (1) their work interferes with their married life, or (2) they earn more than their husbands (Glick 1981, 117), or (3) their economic independence makes freedom of choice possible. The Census Bureau finds rising divorce rates partially responsible for increasing poverty. The increasing number of divorces accounts for the fact that blacks fell further behind whites in income during the past decade (Divorces blamed for poverty 1982).

Black child support is awarded to fewer than one in three (29 percent) black mothers who have sole custody of their children, and fewer than that actually receive child support payments. In fact, very few (7 percent) divorced black women are awarded alimony, and only 7 out of every 10 get any of it (Glick 1981, 123).

Blacks remarry less than whites, possibly because of black men's lower incomes (Glick 1981, 118). Redivorce follows remarriage of black women more than other women in the 35- to 44-year-old range. Black women with no children are more likely to divorce than are black

Table 16.6 MARITAL STATUS OF BLACK AND ALL RACES BY SEX, UNITED STATES, 1980

Marital status, age, and race	Percentage	
	Men	Women
Percentage never married		
20 to 24 years old		
All races	69	50
Black	79	69
Percentage separated or divorced		
25 to 34 years old		
All races	9	14
Black	13	28
Percentage in intact marriages		
35 to 44 years old		
All races	81	84
Black	61	49

Source: U.S. Bureau of the Census, unpublished Current Population Survey data in Paul C. Glick, "A Demographic Picture of Black Families," in *Black Families,* ed. H. P. McAdoo (Beverly Hills, CA: Sage, 1981), p. 115.

mothers of the same age, reflecting childless women's greater ease in being self-supporting (Glick 1981, 118).

Differences between black and other families in America are great, but the gaps are diminishing in several respects: (1) the rate of increase in the percentage of black children in one-parent families has been less rapid since 1970, so the gap between blacks and others in this respect is narrowing; (2) there has been a rapid rise in the level of black mothers' education; (3) a less rapid increase has been evidenced in the proportion of households maintained by unmarried blacks than others; and (4) a more rapid increase has been apparent in the median income of black than other families. This may mean that "black families have managed to sustain their families under pressures that now are being shared by a growing number of nonblack families" (McAdoo 1978).

The relative influence of race and social class on black family problems is a matter of debate among social scientists. Many continue to see racial discrimination as the prime factor in the inequalities blacks endure in housing, education, and employment. Other scholars, such as William Wilson of the University of Chicago (Wilson 1980), argue that the black poor are being held back by class rather than by race. Wilson points to the narrowing gap between whites and blacks in professional and managerial jobs and to the growing gaps between the haves and the have-nots in the black community. Bernard Anderson, head of the Rockefeller Foundation, speaks of the *feminization of poverty* in referring to the fact that families headed by women are at the bottom of the economic ladder and that most female-headed families are black. He agrees with Wilson that blacks with reasonably good education and salable skills can and do get jobs and that it is the very poor blacks, the underclass, who are the challenge (Collins 1982).

SOCIAL CLASS VARIATIONS

Americans differ greatly in affluence, prestige, power, and status (Gecas 1979, 365). Families who have social access to one another belong to the same social class; those whom they consider above them in social position occupy a higher social class; and those whom they look down upon are of a lower social class. Decades ago, W. Lloyd Warner and his associates delineated six social classes in the United States: upper-upper (old established families), lower-upper (newly rich families), upper-middle (civic leaders in the community), lower-middle (good respectable families), upper-lower (honest working men and women), and lower-lower (families at the bottom of the social ladder (Warner 1953, chap. 3).

Caplow et al. (1982) in replicating research of a midwestern city in the 1930s found that families at the lower end of the socioeconomic scale were becoming more like others as they became accustomed to electricity, television, and participation in sports and church and community life. These scholars describe Middletown families of the early 1980s in terms of "working-class" and "business-class," and even these distinctions were often blurred, as more business-class families had working wives who did all their own work; and working-class families traveled in Europe for pleasure and sent their children to college (ibid., v).

A position paper for the 1980 White House Conference on Families said in part:

There is extensive similarity between families at a given economic level despite other differences (for instance, race or ethnic status). While not ignoring other differences, families which are in the "culture of poverty" and are black, white, Cuban, Vietnamese, rural, urban, young, old, Protestant or Catholic have much in common. At the other end of the spectrum one might find a "culture of affluence." The obvious implications of economic sufficiency do not need mention; the less obvious do. Economic "success" or at least stability influences self-esteem, the quality of family relationships, aspirations and motivations in children and virtually every area of family life. Economic status, and therefore, patterns of interaction, tend to be tri-generational; that is, expectations and styles of relationships may resist change because they have been carried from the grandparental to the parental to the present generation relatively intact. (Hutchison 1980, 3)

The Culture of Affluence

The men who "have it made" came out of the right wombs, went to the right schools, belong to the right clubs, and shoot a good game of golf. These are the leaders of the social register world, the newly rich, and the professionals of status in the community. Mafia people may be rich, but they do not rate even middle-class status (Coleman 1981). Fathers' occupational status has been found to be the strongest single background characteristic related to sons' occupational success. Those from advantaged families go farther in school, and amount of education is the best readily observable predictor of job status and income, according to research by the Institute for Social Research (Jencks, Bartlett, Crouse, Jackson, Mueser, & Schwartz 1979).

Children's development is more influenced by their families' socioeconomic status than by any other factor. Boys from families high on the social class ladder are more likely to have the intellectual abilities important for success in our society. They tend to have more positive performance, aspirations, and self-concepts than boys from homes lower in social class (Bachman 1970, 3). Social psychiatrist Robert Coles (1978) who over many years studied 85 privileged children of well-to-do families across the country found them accustomed to comfort, used to privacy, and feeling entitled to their place in the world. These upper-class boys and girls put strong emphasis on "the self"—its display, its possibilities, its cultivation, and its development. They were taught by experts: tennis and swimming and skiing and golf by private coaches and dancing and music and art by expensive teachers. They knew languages and foreign travel. They understood when to defer and when to speak up; they knew how to be attractive and charming; and they had a sustained self-assurance and faith that life works out for the best. Other children of the very rich know emotional deprivation: they are brought up with all the "things" they want but lack closeness with their parents, who are too busy to spend time with them; so these "poor little rich kids" grow up feeling unloved, with poor self-concepts.

Affluent families have ready access to anything they want. Their wealth cushions them from many of the crises that shake families without their material resources: unemployment, illness, accidents, and community unrest. Their children are sent to the best schools, and members of their families belong to all "the right" clubs. Their marriages are traditional, as they have been over several generations in the family.

The upper class has remained remarkably intact and but slightly affected by social change. In spite of the civil rights momentum that has swept across the country, affluent families' schools, neighborhoods, clubs, and the Social Register remain "the most racially segregated turf in America" (Blumberg & Paul 1975, 75).

The Culture of Poverty

At the other end of the socioeconomic status system, rejects from the various racial, ethnic, and national groups vie with one another for sleeping spots in public places: doorways, park benches, and flophouses. These are the alcoholics, chronic drug users, and malcontents who have dropped out of mainline America and who survive without family, friends, or community supports on the whole. In desperate straits, a hungry man can get food from a soup kitchen, the Salvation Army, or a skidrow mission. But food stamps, welfare, and other official aids to the poor are rarely tapped. Lacking residence, these derelicts are largely uncounted in official figures.

Families of the lower-lower class are usually female headed and nonwhite and may be on welfare rolls for generations. These impoverished families live in neglected buildings in the least desirable neighborhoods and get along on food stamps, free or reduced-price school lunches, subsidized housing, Medicaid, and direct cash benefits (U.S. Bureau of the Census 1982a). In 1981 there were 32 million residents of the United States classified as poor by agencies of the federal government. Numbers of families below the poverty level fluctuate from year to year as economic conditions in the nation change (U.S. Bureau of the Census 1982e).

The vicious cycle of poverty persists as the poor get sick more often than others, stay sick longer, and remain unemployed or unemployable in many instances. These poverty-stricken families tend to be pessimistic, disillusioned, and devoid of hope. In the early years of the twentieth century, the European immigrants who swarmed into our big city slums lived in crowded run-down buildings, with little to live on but their aspirations for a better life. Their aspirations for their children lifted many of the second generation out of poverty and into middle-class status. Unlike their aspiring predecessors, today's slum dwellers feel hopeless, helpless, and isolated from society. Generation after generation rely on welfare in what is truly a culture of poverty that resists efforts to reduce its crushing dependence.

"Poverty in America, as officially measured, went from 25.4 million persons below poverty level in 1970 to 31.8 millions in 1981. With seeming incongruity, that rise took place during the very period when federal programs to combat poverty were greatly expanded" says the director of the U.S. Bureau of the Census (Chapman 1982). Why this increase in numbers of the poor in this richest of nations? There is no simple answer but rather a number of contributing factors.

Single-parent families, more than half of them poor (U.S. Bureau of the Census 1982b, 2), increased by 69 percent during the decade of the 1970s; 1 out of 5 of all families with children are poor; and 9 out of 10 of America's single-parent families are maintained by women. This increase in female-headed families has resulted from recent surges in divorce, separation, and out-of-wedlock births. Chapman (1982) continues, "The single-parent family is the newly significant factor in the nation's high poverty figures and in growing social spending. It is not that such families are poorer today (they are not), but that there are so many more of them swelling the ranks of the poor" (ibid., editorial page). A study of 3690 women between the ages of 30 and 44 inclusive in 5 waves of data from the National Longitudinal Surveys found marital instability increasing the need for welfare, Aid to Families with Dependent Children (AFDC), and food stamps (Draper 1981, 293).

Nonwhite families are three times more likely to have incomes under $5000 a year than are white families (17.9 percent versus 5.4 percent). At the other end of the income spectrum,

16.6 percent of white families—in contrast to 7.2 percent of black families and those of other races—have incomes over $35,000 a year (U.S. Bureau of the Census 1981, 435). More nonwhites are unemployed, and those who have jobs work at lower rates than whites.

Unemployment results in part from production cutbacks during periods of economic slumps. Many workers find themselves living on their benefits from unemployment as long as they last and then dependent on whatever other members of the family can earn. Rising unemployment during the early 1980s (Figure 16.2) increased the numbers of working men's families among the new poor. These families were doing all right until the industrial slowdown laid off their wage earner, sometimes indefinitely. When a husband and father loses his job, his wife and older children get what work they can, at usually considerably less pay than he earned when he was working. Then, a family accustomed to a comfortable standard of living finds itself with greatly reduced income at the time of rising prices. Even so, wives' wages keep many a family afloat when times are bad (Hymowitz 1982, 25).

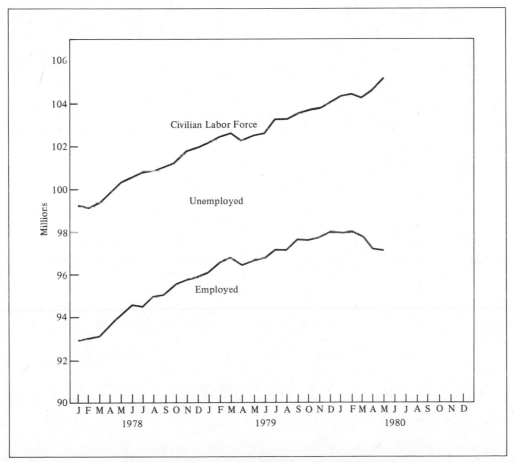

Figure 16.2 Civilian labor force, the employed, and the unemployed, 1978–1980.
Source: Current population survey, published in *Monthly Labor Review*, August 1980, p. 4.

Psychological costs of unemployment are great in many a working man's family. Hard-working men who have been proud of their ability to care for their families begin to feel guilty when they become dependent upon their wives' earnings. This role reversal in the family makes both members of the pair uncomfortable to the point of hostility. Wives, understandably, resent having to work hard all day only to come home to find their unemployed husbands depressed, dependent, and sometimes drunk. Husbands' anger at such humiliation can explode into family violence. A recent study of 1553 couples found that when a wife's work is better than her husband's, life-threatening acts occur six times more often than when their jobs are compatible (Hornung, McCullough, & Sugimoto 1981, 690). Some unemployed family men reveal their stress in physical or psychological symptoms: "One man's ulcer and another man's anomie may be different but equivalent ways of responding to the same problem" (Ferman & Blehar 1979, 417).

Poor families have more children than do those with higher incomes. There is a straight-line relationship between a family's income and the number of its children. In 1981 families with incomes under $5,000 a year had nearly twice as many babies as those with incomes over $25,000 (Table 16.7).

Families with the lowest birthdates have incomes over $25,000 a year. "The rich get richer and the poor get children" is a popular ditty based upon fact.

Downward social mobility occurs when some member of a family slips from his or her social class to a lower socioeconomic level. The downward-mobile person loses the status of his or her origin through alcoholism, drug addiction, crime, marriage to a member of a much lower class, irresponsible childbearing, marital disruption, running away from home, rebelling from the family's educational and cultural heritage, or other down-spiraling life experience. The family may or may not cast wayward ones out, but the community usually recognizes the decline in their social status by limiting their social access and occupational opportunities.

Upward-mobile families tend to have fewer children than more static families in the same socioeconomic status. Studies find that fertility is more sensitive to behavior of *destination class* than to class of origin; so early upward mobility affects the onset and pacing of children, which in turn strongly affects completed family size (Stevens 1981, 583). These are the families who tend to value education, to encourage their children to continue their schooling, and to be achievers.

Johnson and Watt (1983) have constructed a continuum from poor families who struggle for survival, at one end of the scale, to more affluent families whose drive is overachievement, at the other. As family therapists, Johnson and Watt find family dysfunc-

Table 16.7   BIRTHS PER 1000 WOMEN AGED 18 TO 44,
BY FAMILY INCOME, 1981

Annual family income (dollars)	Births per 1000 women
Less than 5,000	95.5
5,000 to 14,999	80.4
15,000 to 24,999	76.9
More than 25,000	52.4

Source: Basic data from the U.S. Department of Commerce and the U.S. Department of Health and Human Services, published in "More Babies . . . But No Baby Boom," *U.S. News & World Report,* November 29, 1982, p. 49.

tion at both ends of the continuum because many of the same factors that create dysfunction exist in both the culture of poverty and that of overachievement in our society.

Better-educated families are usually more optimistic, less cynical, more sociable, more inclined to be work oriented, and less addicted to television than others, according to recent Harvard studies of achievement variables and class cultures (Davis 1982, 584). Although Davis's research fails to find support for an occupational return on educational achievement, U.S. Bureau of the Census data show a direct relationship between income and education (see Table 16.8).

Locksley (1982, 438) suggests that what is usually considered the working-class culture of routinized, tedious work may instead be "high school culture" as a consequence of more limited education. Her research has found that college-educated individuals more readily admit to having had problems in their marriages and to have felt inadequate as spouses and as parents but that more rate their marriage as very happy and affectionate than do couples with less than ninth-grade education. Her explanation is that education facilitates both verbalization and conflict resolution, which enhance marital quality and companionship (ibid., 437).

Middle-class families predominate in the United States, both in numbers and in influence. They are more at home with schools, courts, hospitals, and political and community life than are families in the lower strata. Middle-class families are less vulnerable to economic disasters. They are subject to loss of health, loss of spouse, and loss of jobs, as are persons in all other social classes, but since they have greater resources within themselves and in the larger society to tap when problems arise, they weather them better (Gecas 1979, 391). Enhanced by higher levels of education and training, middle-class families make up the bulk of the professions and successful members of the business and scientific sectors of the economy. Their children tend to do well and to follow the relatively comfortable family patterns in which they are raised.

Every human being is born into a world that person never made, regardless of the ethnic or social class label he or she bears. It is not personal merit but simply good fortune to be born into a group whose values and skills make life easier. But easy or difficult, the history of America is a story of similar patterns and profound differences, of pain and of pride and achievement—the drama of the human spirit in many guises (Sowell 1981, 274–296).

Table 16.8 MEDIAN MONEY INCOME BY SEX AND EDUCATION, UNITED STATES, 1980 (IN DOLLARS)

Education	Male	Female
Less than eight years	$7,035	$3,643
Eight years	8,960	4,177
One to three years of high school	9,924	4,242
Four years of high school	14,583	6,080
One to three years of college	15,674	6,985
Four years of college	22,173	10,119
Five or more years of college	26,927	15,108

Source: U.S. Bureau of the Census, *Statistical Abstract of the United States: 1982–1983,* 103d ed. (Washington, D.C.: Government Printing Office, 1983), p. 146.

SUMMARY

American families vary widely by racial, ethnic, and social class status. Ethnicity shapes family traditions and patterns how a family lives. Rural-urban differences in family life cut across all racial and ethnic groups. Native American families are tribally oriented and differ greatly from tribe to tribe. Asian American families conform well to the mainstream of life in the United States. American families of Spanish origin tend to continue to speak Spanish and to hold to their Latin ways. American black families tend to be headed by women who often support their children and grandchildren. Black family incomes are low but improve as wives work. Gaps between black families and others in the society are narrowing as blacks improve their status.

Social class variations are found among all racial and ethnic groups, ranging from the culture of affluence to the culture of poverty. Massive unemployment in adverse economic conditions brings about widespread marital and family readjustment. Downward mobility occurs for many reasons; upward mobility usually comes through educational and occupational achievement. Middle-class families are the burden bearers of American society in professional, business, and social spheres.

REFERENCES

Alan Guttmacher Institute. 1981. *Teenage pregnancy: The problem that hasn't gone away.* New York: Alan Guttmacher Institute.

Anderson-Khleif, S. 1979. Strategies, problems, and policy issues for single parent housing. Prepared for the U.S. Department of Housing and Urban Development, in cooperation with the Joint Center for Urban Studies of MIT and Harvard University.

Andrews, W., ed. 1962. *Concise dictionary of American history.* New York: Scribner.

Astin, A. W., King, M. R., & Richardson, G. T. 1981. *The American freshman: National norms for fall 1981.* Los Angeles: Cooperative Institutional Research Program, University of California.

Bachman, J. 1970. *Youth in transition, Vol. II: The impact of family background and intelligence on tenth-grade boys.* Ann Arbor, MI: Institute for Social Research.

Bacon, D. 1977. Young blacks out of work: Time bomb for U.S. *U.S. News & World Report,* December 5, 1977, pp. 22–25.

Bane, M. J., & Weiss, R. S. 1980. Alone together—the world of single-parent families. *American Demographics* 2:11–15, 48.

Bartz, K., & Levine, E. 1978. Childrearing by black parents: A description and comparison to Anglo and Chicano parents. *Journal of Marriage and the Family* 40:709–719.

Blumberg, P. M., & Paul, P. W. 1975. Continuities and discontinuities in upper-class marriages. *Journal of Marriage and the Family* 37:63–77.

Braun, J., & Chao, H. 1978. Attitudes toward women: A comparison of Asian-born Chinese and American Caucasians. *Psychology of Women Quarterly* 2:195–201.

Burrows, P. 1980. Mexican parental roles: Differences between mother's and father's behavior to children. Paper presented to the annual meeting of the Society for Cross-Cultural Research, Philadelphia, February, 1980.

Caplow, T., Bahr, H. M., Chadwick, B. A., Hill, R., & Williamson, M. H. 1982. *Middletown families: Fifty years of change and continuity.* Minneapolis: University of Minnesota Press.

Chapman, B. 1982. Seduced and abandoned: America's new poor. *Wall Street Journal,* October 5, 1982, editorial page.

Coleman, R. P., ed. 1981. *Social standing in America.* New York: Basic Books.

Coles, R. 1978. *Children of crisis: Privileged ones.* New York: Atlantic-Little, Brown.

Collins, G. 1982. Some blacks blaming own class divisions. Sarasota *Herald-Tribune,* December 5, 1982, p. 10-C.

Cooney, R. S., Rogler, L. H., Hurrell, R., & Ortiz, V. 1982. Decision making in intergenerational Puerto Rican families. *Journal of Marriage and the Family* 44:621–631.

Cromwell, V., & Cromwell, R. 1978. Perceived dominance in decision making and conflict resolution among black and Chicano couples. *Journal of Marriage and the Family* 40:749–759.

Davis, J. A. 1982. Achievement variables and class cultures: Family, schooling, job, and forty-nine dependent variables in the cumulative GSS. *American Sociological Review* 47:569–586.

Divorces blamed for poverty. 1982. Sarasota *Herald-Tribune,* September 24, 1982, p. 6A.

Dornbusch, S. M., Massey, G. C., & Scott, M. V. 1975. *Racism without racists: Institutional racism in urban schools.* Palo Alto, CA: Stanford Center for Research and Development in Teaching.

Draper, T. W. 1981. On the relationship between welfare and marital stability: A research note. *Journal of Marriage and the Family* 43:293–299.

Ferman, L. A., & Blehar, M. C. 1979. Family adjustment to unemployment. In *Families today: A research sampler on families and children.* Vol. 1. National Institute of Mental Health Science Monographs. Washington, D.C.: Government Printing Office.

Fossett, M., & Swicegood, G. 1982. Rediscovering city differences in racial occupational inequality. *American Sociological Review* 47:681–689.

Fuchs, E., & Havighurst, R. J. 1972. *To live on this earth: American Indian education.* Garden City, N.Y.: Doubleday.

Gecas, V. 1979. The influence of social class on socialization. In *Contemporary theories about the family,* ed. W. R. Burr, R. Hill, F. I. Nye, & I. L. Reiss, pp. 365–404. Vol. 1. New York: Free Press.

Glick, P. C. 1981. A demographic picture of black families. In *Black families,* ed. H. P. McAdoo, pp. 106–126. Beverly Hills, CA: Sage.

Gray-Little, B. 1982. Marital quality and power processes among black couples. *Journal of Marriage and the Family* 44:633–646.

Hawkes, G., & Taylor, M. 1975. Power structure in Mexican and Mexican American farm labor families. *Journal of Marriage and the Family* 37:807–811.

Hornung, C. A., McCullough, B. C., & Sugimoto, T. 1981. Status relationships in marriage: Risk factors in spouse abuse. *Journal of Marriage and the Family* 43:675–692.

Hutchison, I. W. 1980. Family diversity. Position paper prepared for the White House Conference on Families, Washington, D.C.

Hymowitz, C. 1982. Wives of jobless men support some families—but at heavy cost. *Wall Street Journal,* December 8, 1982.

Institute for Social Research. 1975. Cross-racial contact increases in seventies: Attitude gap narrows for blacks and whites. *ISR Newsletter,* Autumn 1975, pp. 4–7.

Jencks, C., Bartlett, S., Crouse, J., Jackson, G., Mueser, P., & Schwartz, J. 1979. *Who gets ahead?: The determinants of economic success in America.* New York: Basic Books.

Johnson, C. L. 1977. Interdependence, reciprocity and indebtedness: An analysis of Japanese American kinship relations. *Journal of Marriage and the Family* 39:351–364.

Johnson, J., & Watt, W. 1983. The survival to overachievement continuum: A new construct for clinical use. *Family Therapy* 10:77–90.

Kitano, H. H. L., Yeung, W., Chai, L., & Hatanaka, H. 1984. Asian-American interracial marriage. *Journal of Marriage and the Family* 46:179–190.

Kuroda, Y., Suzuki, T., & Hayashi, C. 1978. A cross-national analysis of the Japanese character among Japanese-Americans in Honolulu. *Ethnicity* 5:45–59.

Leonetti, D. L. 1978. The bicultural pattern of Japanese-American fertility. *Sociol Biology* 25:38–51.

Locksley, A. 1982. Social class and marital attitudes and behavior. *Journal of Marriage and the Family* 44:427–440.

McAdoo, H. P. 1978. Factors related to stability in upwardly mobile black families. *Journal of Marriage and the Family* 40:761–776.

———. 1982. Stress absorbing systems in black families. *Family Relations* 31:479–488.

McGoldrick, M. 1982. Ethnicity and family therapy. *Family Therapy Networker* 6:22–26.

Malloy, M. T. 1976. "We want no melting pot." Hispanics, the largest and fastest growing minority, hold on to their heritage. *National Observer,* August 7, 1976.

Miller, D. L., & Moore, C. D. 1979. The native American family: The urban way. In *Families today: A research sampler on families and children.* Vol. 1. National Institute of Mental Health Science Monographs. Washington, D.C.: Government Printing Office.

Monahan, T. 1977. Illegitimacy by race and mixtures of race. *International Journal of Sociology of the Family* 7:45–54.

Montiel, M. 1970. The social science myth of the Mexican American family. *El Grito: A Journal of Contemporary Mexican American Thought* 3:56–63.

More babies . . . but no baby boom. *U.S. News & World Report,* November 29, 1982, p. 49. Basic data from U.S. Departments of Commerce, and Health and Human Services.

Morrow, L. 1977. Why "Roots" hit home. *Time,* February 14, 1977, pp. 69–77.

National Center for Health Statistics. 1984. Characteristics of Asian Births: United States, 1980. *Monthly Statistics Report* 32: no. 10 supplement, February 10, 1984. Hyattsville, MD: Public Health Service.

Novak, M. 1982. Why Latin America is poor. *Atlantic Monthly* 249:66–75.

Padilla, A. M., Olmedo, S., & Perez, R. 1978. Hispanic mental health bibliography. Spanish Speaking Mental Health Research Center, University of California, Los Angeles, Monograph no. 6.

Payton, I. S. 1982. Single-parent households: An alternate approach. *Family Economic Review,* Winter 1982, p. 11.

Price, J. 1976. North American Indian families. In *Ethnic families in America,* ed. C. Mindel & R. Habenstein, pp. 248–270. New York: Elsevier.

Racial gap in SAT scores. 1982. *Newsweek,* October 18, 1982, p. 110.

Rawlings, S. 1978. Perspectives on American husbands and wives. U.S. Bureau of the Census, *Current Population Reports.* Series P-23, no. 77.

Redhorse, J. G. 1979. American Indian elders: Needs and aspirations in institutional and home health care. Unpublished manuscript, Arizona State University.

Scanzoni, J. 1975. Sex roles, economic factors, and marital solidarity in black and white marriages. *Journal of Marriage and the Family* 37:130–144.

Sena-Rivera, J., & Moore, C. D. 1979. La familia Chicano. In *Families today: A research sampler on families and children.* Vol. 1. National Institute of Mental Health Science Monographs. Washington, D.C.: Government Printing Office.

Shibutani, T., & Kwan, K. M. 1965. *Ethnic stratification.* New York: Macmillan.

Sorensen, A. B. 1975. The structure of intragenerational mobility. *American Sociological Review* 40:463.

Sowell, T. 1981. *Ethnic America.* New York: Basic Books.

Staples, R., and Mirande, A. 1980. Racial and cultural variations among American families: A decennial review of the literature on minority families. *Journal of Marriage and the Family* 42:887–903.

Stevens, G. 1981. Social mobility and fertility: Two effects in one. *American Sociological Review* 46:583.

Sue, S., & Kitano, H. 1973. Asian American stereotypes. *Journal of Social Issues* 29:83–98.

Thompson, K. S. 1980. A comparison of black and white adolescents' beliefs about having children. *Journal of Marriage and the Family* 42:133–139.

Unger, S. 1977. *The destruction of American Indian families.* New York: Association of American Indian Affairs.

U.S. Bureau of the Census. 1978. Persons of Spanish Origin in the United States: March 1977. *Current Population Reports.* Series P-20, no. 329. Washington, D.C.: Government Printing Office.

————. 1981. *Statistical Abstract of the United States: 1981.* 102d ed. Washington, D.C.: Government Printing Office.

————. 1982. Characteristics of Households Receiving Selected Noncash Benefits: 1981. *Current Population Reports.* Series P-60, no. 135. Washington, D.C.: Government Printing Office. (a)

————. 1982. Characteristics of the Population Below the Poverty Level: 1980. *Current Population Reports.* Series P-60, no. 133. Washington, D.C.: Government Printing Office. (b)

————. 1982. Household and Family Characteristics: March 1981. *Current Population Reports.* Series P-20, no. 371. Washington, D.C.: Government Printing Office. (c)

————. 1982. Marital Status and Living Arrangements: March 1981. *Current Population Reports.* Series P-20, no. 372. Washington, D.C.: Government Printing Office. (d)

————. 1982. *Money Income and Poverty Status of Families and Persons in the United States, 1981.* Washington, D.C.: Government Printing Office. (e)

————. 1983. *Statistical Abstract of the United States: 1982–1983.* 103d ed. Washington, D.C.: Government Printing Office.

U.S. Department of Health, Education, and Welfare. 1980. *Health Status of Minorities and Low-Income Groups.* Washington, D.C.: Government Printing Office.

Wakil, S. P., Siddique, C. M., & Wakil, F. A. 1981. Between two cultures: A study in socialization of children of migrants. *Journal of Marriage and the Family* 43:929–940.

Warner, W. L. 1953. *American life: Dream and reality.* Chicago: University of Chicago Press, chap. 3.

Wax, M. L. 1971. *Indian Americans: Unity and diversity.* Englewood Cliffs, N.J.: Prentice-Hall.

Williams, B. S. 1980. Characteristics of the black elderly—1980. *Statistical reports on older Americans.* Washington, D.C.: U.S. Department of Health and Human Services, Office of Human Development Services.

Wilson, W. 1980. *The declining significance of race.* Chicago: University of Chicago Press.

Ybarra, L. 1977. Conjugal roles relationships in the Chicano family. Ph.D. dissertation, University of California.

Zelnik M., & Kantner, J. F. 1978. First pregnancies to women aged 15–19. *Family Planning Perspectives* 10:11.

————. 1980. Sexual activity, contraceptive use and pregnancy among metropolitan-area teenagers: 1971–1979. *Family Planning Perspectives* 12:230.

Chapter 17

Death in the Family Context

MAJOR CONCEPTS

Premature death
  Stillborn
  Prematurity
  Sudden infant death syndrome
  Accidental death
Death's inevitability
  The ageds' final transition
  Universality of death in the family
Awareness of dying
Death education
Hospice
Suicide
Death with dignity
  Euthanasia (negative and active)

The right to die
  Mercy killing
  Quality/quantity of life
  The living will
Funeral service
Memorial service
Human remains
  Burial
  Cremation
  Donation to science
Widowhood
  Remarriage
Bereavement

Not all deaths take place within a family context. Mrs. L at 94 has outlived all other members of her family. Blind and unaware of her surroundings for years, she leaves no one to mourn her passing, except the nursing home staff who have been caring for her. The unknown soldier buried with military honors dies outside the context of his family, if indeed he had one. The runaway teenage orphan killed in a big city drug scene dies outside the family context. The newborn found wrapped in brown paper outside a college dormitory, discarded as an embarrassment to its mother, never knew a family. There are other instances that one can think of, but these are not typical of death in this country. Our concern here is with what death of a family member does to the surviving members and to the family as a whole.

Death is a family affair in most instances. When a family member dies, relatives, friends, and neighbors rally around, attend the funeral if at all possible, and attempt to comfort those most personally involved. Every family faces death sooner or later—each in its own time, each in its own way.

TOO YOUNG TO DIE!

When life is snuffed out at an early age, one hears such phrases as "too young to die," "whole life still ahead," "before he/she had a chance." An infant may die even before it is born. *Stillborn* is the word used for the delivery of a baby who never breathes. Death may have occurred in utero sometime before delivery, or it may have resulted from an accident in the birth process. Unexplained stillbirth accounts for 7 percent of perinatal deaths, which rank third in the United States as cause of death (Duhring, 1974).

Society takes little notice of the stillborn. There may or may not be a memorial or funeral service, or other public recognition of the family's loss. Yet the grief of the mother, father, grandparents, and other members of the family may be intense. Their loss is very real to them, and their emotions may include sorrow, helplessness, depression, guilt, blame, bitterness, and anger with a deep pain that lasts for a long while. Well-intentioned friends may try to console the grieving family with words they do not want to hear: "You are still young enough to have another baby," "You now have a little angel in Heaven," or "Just be thankful the mother came through all right."

Professional recommendations for helping a family through the tragedy of losing a stillborn child include the following:

1. Encourage contact with the stillborn. It is not unusual to hear mothers, years later, wishing they might have seen or touched the baby before he or she was taken away.
2. Provide a simple funeral or memorial service with close family and friends with or without the body of the stillborn present.
3. Arrange for the grieving parents to meet with others who have suffered similar losses, for mutual support and talking out their feelings.
4. Make sure the other children in the family receive special attention, with emphasis on listening to their questions, feelings, and needs for reassurance (Klaus & Kennell 1976; Case 1978; Kirkley-Best, Kellener, Gould, & Donnelly 1982).

Prematurity (delivery of a live baby after less than nine months in the uterus) is the principal cause of death during the first year of life. This is one reason for postponing pregnancy until the mother is old enough to have a full-term baby, and also for prenatal care throughout her pregnancy.

Sudden infant death syndrome (SIDS), popularly known as "crib death," is a leading cause of death in infants after the first week of life. In these cases the baby dies suddenly in sleep for reasons that are not yet understood. The mystery of what may have caused the baby's death adds a factor of speculation and, often, of undeserved blame, guilt, or accusation on the part of one or both of the shocked parents (National Center for Health Statistics 1983, 10).

Accidents are the leading cause of death in little boys between 1 and 4 years of age (43 percent) as well as 39.7 percent of girls of the same age (National Center for Health Statistics 1978). Families of preschool children are sometimes stricken by the sudden death of one of their youngsters in a highway accident, drowning, fire, accidental poisoning, a fatal fall, or another of the catastrophic events that can take the life of a child. Accidental death triggers blame, guilt, and remorse in the ones thought to be responsible, as well as grief over the premature snuffing out of a life.

Thousands of families know the agony of having a child who is terminally ill. Leukemia, the form of cancer most prevalent in children, each year afflicts thousands of boys and girls under 15. Child psychologists advise parents to watch their fatally ill child for cues that will alert them to the child's readiness to discuss his or her fears and fantasies. For instance, when a terminally ill youngster draws a picture filled with dark shadows and holes, a perceptive adult can say, "That's a scary picture: shall we talk about it?" This tells the child that it is all right to talk about fear of dying, if and when he or she is ready.

What children think about death depends on the individual child, on his or her family, and on the child's psychological development. Under the age of 2, a child has no conception of death and reflects only the parents' reaction. Between 2 and 4, a child sees death as separation, most often temporary. Between 4 and 6, preschoolers have seen or heard of animals being killed in traffic, and think of death as punishment or mutilation. In the early school years, most children think of death as permanent and fear it as inevitable.

Teenagers more often die as the result of accidents than of any other cause of death (Figure 17.1). More teenage boys and young men are killed in accidents than young girls and young women; but as Figure 17.1 clearly shows, accidents cause more deaths of both sexes

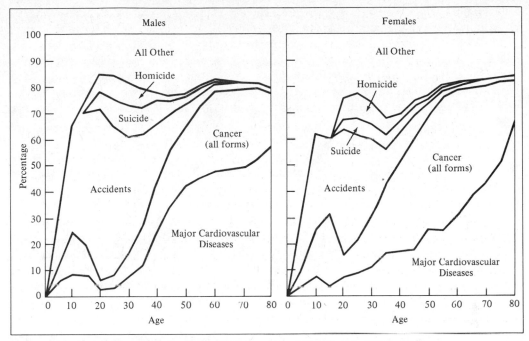

Figure 17.1 Percentage of deaths from selected causes, 1980. *Source:* Metropolitan Life Insurance Company, *Statistical Bulletin* 62 (October-December 1981).16.

in the United States throughout the second and third decades of life than any other kind of fatal incident. In the most recent year for which reliable figures are available, 45.9 percent of the young women and 58.0 percent of the young men who died between the ages of 15 and 24 were killed in accidents. This is five times greater than any other cause of death at these ages (National Center for Health Statistics 1978, 2). As highway safety measures are more widely practiced, as laws requiring reduced driving speeds are enforced, and as programs designed to cut down driving while intoxicated become more effective, the loss of young lives in highway accidents may be reduced.

Death of young men in war has been a reality for the human race over many centuries, including our own. Only as peacekeeping efforts succeed will families be freed from the loss of their able-bodied young people on the field of battle. Until the twentieth century more women died in childbirth than men in war, as one notes in a stroll through any old cemetery in this country. Now, with improved nutrition and medical attention through prenatal, delivery, and postnatal care, maternal death is becoming increasingly rare. Accidents, homicides, and suicides, in that order, lead all other causes of death among young adult men under 35 years of age. Many more young women between 25 and 34 years of age die as a result of accidents (22.8 percent) and cancer (18.0 percent) than of any other cause of death (National Center for Health Statistics 1978, 2).

Most of the 30,000 adults who responded to a *Psychology Today* questionnaire about death said that they first became aware of death when they were between the ages of 3 and 10. Their first personal involvement was the death of grandparents or great-grandparents (43 percent) or of animals (18 percent). Only 3 out of 10 recalled open discussion of death in their families when they were growing up (Table 17.1). Nearly half of these respondents, predominantly young adults, recalled a "heaven-or-hell" concept of death when they were children (48 percent). As children, equal percentages (10 percent) conceived of death as sleep and as mysterious and unknowable. As young adults, more than four times as many (43 percent) believe in life after death than believed as children (9 percent); and a majority (55 percent) strongly wish for life after death. More than two out of three (68 percent) would prefer their own death to be sudden, nonviolent, quiet, and dignified (Shneidman 1971, 74).

DEATH—THE FINAL TRANSITION

All living things die in time, and there are no exceptions. Most persons realize that they are mortal and, as such, will pass away when their time comes. There is general recognition that the aged are headed toward their final transition, as life ebbs away.

Not only are there more older men and women now, but their numbers will be increasing as will their percentage of the population throughout the rest of this century (Table 17.2). Furthermore, the number of persons over 75 years of age has been increasing and will steadily do so at least until well into the twenty-first century. Cardiovascular diseases and cancer of all forms may be expected to claim increasing numbers of persons of both sexes (Figure 17.1), partly because more men and women are living to the later years when such causes of death lead all others.

In the family context, this means that more grandparents, great-grandparents, and even great-great-grandparents will face the infirmities of old age that require both family and community concern and care. As their time comes to die, both the aged and their families must come to terms with death as the final stage of life.

Awareness of Dying

Young adults magnify the "crisis of dying," but the aged tend to take it in stride. In one study of dying elderly patients, only 3 out of 80 found it difficult to discuss death. In spite of their recognition that death was imminent, there was no storminess, no disruptiveness—"It was as if they were dealing with a developmental task they were coping with adequately. . . . It is the rare case for an individual to have lived into the seventh or eighth decade of life without having come to grips with his own death and without having developed some personal

Table 17.1   DISCUSSION OF DEATH IN THE FAMILY
         (30,000 ADULTS RECALL THEIR CHILDHOOD EXPERIENCE)

My family's discussion of death when I was a child	Percentage of replies
Never recall any discussion	33%
Discussed death openly	30
Talked about death with some discomfort	20
Only when necessary, then excluded children	15
As though it were a taboo subject	2
	100%

Source: Edwin S. Shneidman, "You and Death," *Psychology Today* 5, no. 1 (June 1971): 44.
Reprinted from *Psychology Today Magazine,* copyright © 1971, Ziff-Davis Publishing Company.

Table 17.2 POPULATION AT AGES 65 AND OVER, BY SEX AND AGE, UNITED STATES, 1960–2000

Sex and age	Population in thousands					Percentage Change			
	1960	1970	1980	1990	2000	1960–1970	1970–1980	1980–1990	1990–2000
Men									
65 and over	7,503	8,366	10,153	12,020	13,777	11.5	21.4	18.4	14.6
65–69	2,931	3,124	3,815	4,408	4,080	6.6	22.1	15.5	–7.4
70–74	2,185	2,316	2,841	3,257	3,471	6.0	22.7	14.6	6.6
75 and over	2,387	2,926	3,497	4,355	5,226	22.6	19.5	24.5	20.0
Women									
65 and over	9,057	11,605	15,164	18,371	19,752	28.1	30.7	21.1	7.5
65–69	3,327	3,872	4,732	5,423	4,921	16.4	22.2	14.6	–9.3
70–74	2,554	3,130	3,970	4,534	4,713	22.6	26.8	14.2	3.9
75 and over	3,176	4,603	6,462	8,314	10,118	44.9	40.4	28.7	21.7

Source: Paul C. Glick, unpublished data based upon U.S. Bureau of the Census, 1970 Census of the Population, Vol. I, B-I, *General Population Characteristics*. United States Summary, Table 3; and unpublished data consistent with Series II projections in "Projections of the Population of the United States: 1977 to 2050." *Current Population Reports*, Series P-25, no. 704 (Washington, D.C.: Government Printing Office, July 1977), personal communication to author, used with permission, November 1981.

philosophical system—although possibly a primitive one—for accounting for and dealing with it" (Lieberman 1973, 13). Most people sense that there is a time for living and a time for dying, and the process appears to be easier for those who feel that the timing is appropriate.

Many dying patients do not need to be told that their death is expected. They know it anyway—intuitively and by the change in the people around them. They see it in their loved ones' tears and in the too-brave smiles of those who cannot hide their true feelings. They sense it in the lowered voices of those who attend them and in their doctors' less frequent calls when there is no hope of recovery. Elizabeth Kübler-Ross (1970, 1976) a psychiatrist who has worked with dying patients since 1965, has observed a sequence of five reactions to the knowledge of impending death (Table 17.3).

When the end comes, the majority of the dying have reached a stage in which they are able to accept death without despair or fear—and with a sense of having come full circle in life. When the illness has lasted for a long time and has been marked by great pain and suffering, death may be a welcome relief and release for the patient and the family. Kübler-Ross (1976) described her own mother's death, which came after four years of total paralysis, as a blessing.

The Dying Person's Family

Family and friends tend to avoid mentioning even to each other the imminent death of loved ones, except in somber whispers and veiled allusions to their "passing away." The tendency is to put up a bright, brave front with dying persons and to deny that life is about to end. When those whose life is ebbing away try to talk with family members about death, many relatives are quick to change the subject.

As soon as patients become critically ill, they are sent to a hospital where medical personnel take over and where family visits are limited. Many terminally ill older persons are in the care, however expert, of strangers; and the inevitable tubes and machines intensify the impression of strangeness. They may hear their case discussed as though they were not there. When patients worry about what the hospital care is costing, they get little reassurance from either the medical attendants or nearest of kin, who try to spare their dying such worries on the deathbed.

The aging wife whose husband is desperately ill may be so frightened that she is unable to give him the support he needs. If she has always depended on him, her security is threatened and she wonders how she can carry on without him. The elderly husband whose

**Table 17.3   FIVE STAGES IN DYING PATIENTS' REACTION
              TO IMPENDING DEATH**

Stage	Emotional meaning
1. Denial and isolation	"No, not me."
2. Anger, rage, envy, resentment	"Why me?" "Why not someone else?"
3. Bargaining with death for time	"Just one more, then I'll be ready."
4. Preparatory grief and depression	"Losing everything and everyone."
5. Acceptance	"I'm ready now."

Source: Data from Elizabeth Kübler-Ross, *On Death and Dying* (New York: Macmillan, 1970); PBS interview, January 8, 1976, and other appearances.

wife is about to die may have an even greater sense of loss in that he, who has always been waited on, is now expected to do the thoughtful, personal things for which he is unprepared. He may resent this reversal of roles. "Why did she have to get sick on me?" one such man asked (Kübler-Ross 1970, 158). The couple may have fought like cat and dog over the years, but—faced with final separation—the survivor is torn with anguished regret: "Why wasn't I nicer to him/her while there was yet time?"

Those who are about to be left often blame themselves for their loved one's condition: "If only I'd insisted . . . " "If only I hadn't let him . . . " "If only I'd looked after her better." Members of the family may try to assuage their guilt by spending all the time permitted at the dying person's bedside, rather than allowing the individual some time to be alone with his or her thoughts—and themselves the necessary intervals of rest to keep up their strength for the difficult days ahead.

The dying person's problems come to an end, but those of the family members left behind are just beginning. They are about to face a series of difficult decisions and tasks: disposing of the body, carrying out of the wishes of the deceased, closing ranks in the family circle, financing the terminal illness and death, and handling their own feelings. For the first few days the family is busy alerting relatives and friends, getting obituary material together, and going through the funeral or memorial service. Then comes the time for tangled emotions to surface—numbness, emptiness, grief for the loved one and for the loss in their own lives. Grown children and grandchildren cannot be expected to react to the death in the same way as one who for many years has shared the life of the person who has died. Yet, they can encourage the widowed to weep and to work through the feelings that should be ventilated at this time (Kübler-Ross 1970, 178–179).

Experiencing the death of a beloved person is never easy: it can be a shattering experience, or it can be one that, after a time, leads one to new levels of awareness of the quality of life itself. One particularly sensitive man shares some of the intensely personal experiences he had upon the death of his father and the reaction of his children to the loss of their grandfather:

> One by one they [the children] came to me to say goodnight and to share some of their thoughts and concerns of the day [of the funeral], their inability to understand some of their own reactions and feelings. And I listened and heard them in a way that I had never known before. In some ways their loss was indeed greater than mine. And I mourned more for them than for myself. In my relationship with my children, that night has become a watershed. I think of it often. How glad I was that the children had come with us. They had gained, I later learned from them, a bit of their past and who they were in relationship to it, even in this brief and seemingly disturbing experience. Their roots of self had sunk a bit deeper. (Gaylin 1975, 253)

Death education and counseling, as a part of ongoing family life education, do much to help individuals and families cope with the experience of dying. Death is universal and comes to tens of thousands of families each year. Yet few adults remember having discussed death as children in their families of orientation.

High school and college courses using examples from literature and drama are helping students and future teachers to gain insights into death as a family experience and to form wholesome attitudes toward dying (Somerville 1971). Adults attend seminars on death and dying in many communities. Nursing and medical personnel are learning how to ease the psychological suffering of dying patients in their care (Kübler-Ross 1975; Weisman 1972). Those responsible for counseling families of dying persons aim at helping family members to achieve three goals: (1) accepting death and their feelings about it, (2) mourning their loss, and (3) facing the stress of functioning as a family in new and different ways (Krieger & Bascue 1975, 354).

Hospice Care

Hospice is the medieval word for a place of shelter for travelers on difficult journeys. Today it means programs designed to relieve the physical and emotional suffering of the terminally ill and their families. Under medical direction, trained staff and volunteers assist with (1) pastoral care, (2) therapy (physical, occupational, and speech), (3) social work services, (4) nursing, (5) companionship, and (6) recreation for patient and family. Specialized consultants in psychiatry, oncology, radiology, financial problems, and legal assistance are available as needed.

Hospices may be places where the terminally ill are cared for; or more often in this country they are programs designed to help the dying patient and his or her family deal with the many problems of the final days. The goals of hospice are:

1. To keep the patient at home as long as possible,
2. To educate health professionals and lay people,
3. To supplement existing services,
4. To support the family as the unit of care,
5. To help the patient live as fully as possible, and
6. To keep costs down (Markel & Sinon 1978, 10).

Some hospice programs provide professional services during the period of mourning for the surviving family members. The expression of grief and the experience of bereavement are highly individual emotional experiences. Yet the members of the family must come to terms with the death in the family and let life go on around the memory of the lost one. The family's support system helps it handle the difficult decisions as they arise. Ideally, family members come to accept their loss philosophically and to see death as the inevitable final stage of life.

SUICIDE—THE PREVENTABLE DEATH

Suicide is a tragedy for the individual and the family. It leaves hurt, disgrace, remorse, and bitterness in its wake in many cases. Because of the stigma attached to suicide, family members often feel shame in addition to their grief. They feel that somehow they must be responsible for not having prevented one of their own from reaching such a point of desolation. They find it difficult, if not impossible, to collect insurance on the life of the suicide victim. In nearly all religious traditions, they have been taught that the taking of one's life is wrong. As human beings they have been reared to see suicide as a crime, immoral, and taboo. Yet thousands of Americans commit suicide each year. Counting only recorded suicides—and excluding many questionable "accidents"—there were 27,294 suicides among

Americans of all ages in one recent year. Of these, 20,188 were males and 7,106 were females (National Center for Health Statistics 1978, 2). In recent years suicide has risen to third place as the cause of death among teenagers and young adults for a multitude of reasons including family problems, failure in school, love and friendship disappointments, loneliness, drugs, and alcoholism.

People commit suicide for any number of personal reasons: to get attention, express aggression, to escape pain, or to avoid expected suffering; or because of loneliness, hopelessness, disappointment, or the loss of some significant person. Nearly everyone loses a loved one or is disappointed by someone close to him or her at one time or another. Most people struggle through their pain and problems; others "just can't take any more." Experts classify the motives for suicide in four main categories (see Table 17.4).

The high rate of suicide among the elderly is attributed to their isolation, loss of close relatives and friends, poor physical health, dwindling financial resources, and lack of involvement in the life around them (Bock 1972, 71–79). When healthy young adults were asked, "Has there ever been a time in your life when you wanted to die?" 60 percent replied in the affirmative, mostly because of emotional upsets (37 percent) or to escape an intolerable social or interpersonal situation (18 percent) (Shneidman, 1971, 79).

Suicide prevention centers operate in many communities, maintaining round-the-clock telephone contact with individuals who are threatening to kill themselves. These efforts are expanding, developing into outreach programs in which lonely, discouraged people are visited, their needs explored, and their contact with the community reestablished when possible. Professionals are being trained (1) to recognize the warning signs of a suicide crisis, (2) to distinguish between a genuine threat or one meant merely to gain attention or to manipulate, (3) to assess the seriousness of a suicidal person's "plan of attack," (4) to evaluate the degree of risk inherent in a suicidal crisis, and (5) to respond adequately to a suicidal episode (Miller 1981; *Menninger Perspective* 1983).

In a conference devoted to suicide as an acceptable alternative for the terminally ill, lawyers, clergymen, health care professionals, and social workers overwhelmingly expressed their opinion that an adult of sound mind should not be legally punished for attempting suicide as a release from terminal illness (Neale 1981, 6). When a world-renowned religious leader—who was a former president of Union Theological Seminary—and his wife ended their own lives by suicide, Norman Cousins devoted a full-page editorial to "The Right to Die," in which he concluded, "Death is not the greatest loss in life. The greatest loss is what

Table 17.4   PERSONAL "REASONS" FOR COMMITTING SUICIDE

Category	Illustrations and examples
Impulse	In the heat of anger, frustration, or disappointment a jilted lover walks into traffic or takes sleeping pills.
Depression	"Why go on living?" "Life has no meaning anymore; no one needs me."
Serious illness	Constant pain, long suffering, and high costs of terminal illness make suicide seem like an escape for the invalid and the family.
Communication attempt	A woman begs her husband to be faithful; a man asks his wife to come back to him in suicide attempts.

Source: From *Dealing with the Crisis of Suicide,* by Calvin J. Frederick and Louise Lague, Public Affairs Pamphlet No. 406A. Copyright 1972, 1978 by the Public Affairs Committee, Inc. Used with permission.

dies inside us while we live. The unbearable tragedy is to live without dignity or sensitivity" (Cousins 1975, 4).

DEATH WITH DIGNITY

"Isn't there some way to end her suffering?" The family had watched their beloved mother endure pain month after month. She faced the amputation of a gangrenous leg. The suffering woman had said good-bye to her family when she was fully conscious. Now her groans and whimpers were her wordless testimony of her readiness to die.

Modern medicine has greatly increased man's power over life and death. Blood transfusions, drugs, intravenous feeding, mechanical respirators, heart stimulants, dialysis, organ transplants, and many other heroic measures can prolong life long after a patient is no longer capable of fully human responses. An individual's greatest fear may not be of death but of long, lingering, painful dying. The family stands helplessly by unless some measures are taken to provide the death with dignity that most would prefer (Russell 1975).

Physicians are not deaf to those begging to die, but their training has been to preserve life as long as they possibly can. One physician questions traditional practice with the position, "At the end of life, the point is what the patient wants, not what the doctor wants. Most patients, I am sure, would gladly trade three days of being unconscious in an oxygen tent for one day of consciousness in which to say goodbye" (Barnard 1973, 62). Doctors increasingly are respecting their patients' desire that no "heroic measures" be used to prolong life beyond the point where it has no meaning (Mannes 1974). A woman in her eighties writes:

Hold not My Life

When Death shall draw my number from the Ebon bowl
And there can be no question of His sure approach,
I trust no doctor's skilled hands will hold me back
With modern methods and techniques at his command.
I do not wish intake of food except by nature's way;
Prolong not an already finished life to suffer on awhile.
But pray keep me from agonizing pain or mental aberration
And help me pass into whatever Realm may lie beyond.

Evelyn M. Shafer, 1975, with permission

Euthanasia, a term derived from the Greek words for "a good death" is being widely discussed. *Active enthanasia* is an action taken to end mercifully the life of one who is enduring suffering or meaningless existence. It is illegal under present law in most countries. *Negative euthanasia* is allowing a hopelessly ill patient to die without the use of extraordinary measures to prolong life. There is confusion about the legal status of this approach at the present writing. Legislatures are considering bills to make death with dignity legal in various states (Van Gieson 1974); and the United Nations has had a proposal under study ever since the International Conference on Human Rights in 1968.

Theologians generally affirm a patient's right to life and death. A pronouncement by Pope Pius XII in 1957 advised (1) that it is in accord with the Gospel to use narcotics to relieve suffering in terminal cases, even if by so doing life will be shortened, and (2) that it is not always necessary to use extraordinary means to prolong life. Years ago a professor of Christian ethics said decisively, "Death control, like birth control, is a matter of human dignity. Without it persons become puppets" (Fletcher 1964, 83). A poll of randomly selected clergymen and lawyers found that the great majority of both ministers and attorneys approve of negative euthanasia (Table 17.5).

A number of arguments against death with dignity have been advanced. A governor of Oregon in 1972 (McCall) refuted these as follows: (1) "It's suicide." The motive for the action and the purpose served justify the action. (2) "The hospitals and the doctors will be subject to lawsuits." This is a legalism that can be dealt with. (3) "A doctor declining to use heroic measures violates the Hippocratic oath." The progress of medical science has outstripped both the laws that control it and the moral and ethical concepts upon which it was founded. (4) "God has appointed the time for man to die." If that is so, then it is as immoral to prolong life as it is to shorten it (McCall 1972, 6). There is general agreement that adequate controls will have to be established to prevent political and personal abuse of the practice of euthanasia, either negative or positive. Kübler-Ross (1976), when asked her views on euthanasia, responded that neither *euthanasia* nor *mercy killing* are appropriate terms for what she advocates—allowing a person to die a natural death without prolonging the process in a way that exacts heavy tolls, both emotional and financial.

In recent years public sentiment has been building for the right to die when one's time comes. One widely publicized case was that of Karen Ann Quinlan, who was kept alive by support machines long after she went into a coma in 1976. The case was widely debated, with the predominant sentiment being that she should have been allowed to die. *Whose Life Is It Anyway?*, a successful London stage play with a long run on Broadway, heightened American interest in the right to die movement. In the play a young sculptor, paralyzed from the neck down when his spinal cord was severed in a car crash, demands that he be released from the hospital so that he can die. His doctors, dedicated to preserving life, refuse to release him and question his competence to decide his own fate. Whereupon the patient hires a lawyer, and a judicial hearing provides the climax amid the many vignettes of hospital life that swirl around his bed (Crist 1981, 56). A Miami physician told the White House Conference on Aging, "The prolongation of life, through modern medical miracles, is more inhu-

Table 17.5 MOST CLERGYMEN AND LAWYERS APPROVE NEGATIVE EUTHANASIA (IN PERCENT)

Item	Clergymen (N = 100)			Lawyers (N = 104)			Total (N = 204)	
	Yes	No	?	Yes	No	?	Yes	No
1. Negative euthanasia for member/client	89	8	3	91	7	2	90	7
2. Negative euthanasia for spouse	86	11	3	76	20	4	81	16
3. Positive euthanasia for member/client	30	62	8	50	47	3	40	54
4. Positive euthanasia for spouse	27	64	9	37	59	4	32	62
5. Pain medication	93	4	3	93	1	6	93	2
6. Autopsy/transplant	98	0	2	99	1	0	99	1
7. Have been involved in such decisions	69	28	3	26	69	5	47	49
8. Religion important in such matters	96	1	3	22	70	8	58	36

Source: Caroline E. Preston and John Horton, "Attitudes Among Clergy and Lawyers Toward Euthanasia," *Journal of Pastoral Care* 26 (1972): 111. Used with permission.

mane than the peaceful natural end of such a life. . . . When my time comes, give me death"
(Sackett 1971).

The Living Will is a document that affirms an individual's wish not to have the dying
process prolonged. Since 1967 more than 5 million copies of the document have been
distributed, upon request, to individuals and churches, hospitals, schools, memorial societies,
retirement communities, and organizations for the elderly. The Living Will[1] is a short
testament addressed to one's family, physician, clergyman, and lawyer that says in part, "If
there is no reasonable expectation of my recovery from mental or physical disability, I request
that I be allowed to die and not be kept alive by artificial means or heroic measures." Such
a document has no legal standing, but few can ignore it in good conscience.

LIFE TO THE FULLEST WHILE IT LASTS

Some terminally ill patients do not want to die one day sooner than they must. One middle-
aged mother with four sons was told by her doctors that she would not live to see Christmas.
She filled out that year in medical treatment rejoicing in every day she could spend with her
family. She kept as active as she could in her community and church work while undergoing
treatment at home. Refusing hospitalization that would remove her from her family, she
cooperated happily with all other phases of her therapy. She lived from one milestone to the
next: her husband's new job near her cancer clinic, their move to the new home, the youngest
son's merit badges, his brother's track meets, her eldest son's marriage, the arrival of her first
grandchild, then her second son's graduation, and so on through the years. Seven years later
she was still in charge of her life at home. She was determined to live every new day to the
full as long as she lived, and she did—long after her doctors thought possible.

Norman Cousins's story is in the same direction. Stricken with an illness medical
authorities thought "hopeless," he set out to prove them wrong. He argued that if negative
emotions could make one sick, positive feelings might bring back health. He set himself on
the road to recovery with laughter and faith in his capacity to heal himself while cooperating
fully with his physicians. Now not only is he well—he is also teaching his philosophy and
methods in a prestigious medical school. His research is with other terminally ill patients who
have "miraculously" recovered. He says, "Obviously, we can't expect that every disease will
be reversed. But we can get the most out of whatever is possible. We can give it our best shot.
Not until then do predictions mean anything" (Cousins 1982, 12).

Whatever the death and the way in which it was met, the time comes when the family
faces the challenge of the last rites for the member who has died.

FORMAL FUNERAL OR INFORMAL MEMORIAL SERVICE

Now, when death is being more freely discussed than formerly, many couples have already
decided what kind of last rites they want for themselves and their loved ones. Some families
prefer the traditional funeral, with their religious leader officiating. The deceased is dressed
for viewing by friends and family and laid to rest according to the practices of their faith
and their own wishes. Other families elect a simpler memorial service, with no casket present

[1]Anyone may obtain a copy of The Living Will from Concern for Dying, 250 West 57th St. New York, NY
10017.

—only a gathering of close friends, neighbors, and family members. They may prepare their own service or ask their spiritual leader to conduct it for them. There may or may not be music, prayers for the deceased and those that remain, and memories shared about the one they mourn. In some instances, memorials of various kinds are established to perpetuate the memory of an individual whom death has taken. Whatever the type of last rites, there are many things to be decided immediately after a death in the family. The funeral director or cremation service representative is notified. The hospital releases the body to the mortuary as soon as the doctor has signed the death certificate.

Moderating Funeral Costs

Until recently, the costs of dying could be catastrophic to many an American family (Mitford 1963). An elaborate funeral could cost many thousands of dollars, depending upon the price of the casket, funeral director's charges, rental of limousines for the mourners, music, flowers, vault, cemetery plot, and all of the other miscellaneous costs. In recent years there has been a tendency to arrange for more simple funerals or memorial services, often costing but a few hundred dollars. The goal is to preserve the family's resources for the living rather than lavish them on the dead.

An interesting study of funeral costs found significant differences between deaths that were expected and those that were unexpected. The expenses involved in a long, lingering illness often deplete a family's resources; so when death finally claims the patient, the poor family must economize on the funeral. Middle- and upper-class families tend to spend about the same amount whether or not the death has been expected. In cases of unexpected death, more families of all economic levels—in one survey—spent in excess of $800 for the funeral, in 1970 dollars (see Table 17.6).

Memorial societies offer their members simple, dignified, and economical care and disposal of the dead, with or without a memorial service. Such a service usually takes place after the body has been cremated or interred, to emphasize the spiritual rather than the physical aspects of death and to celebrate the life of the person who has departed.

Increasing numbers of families are choosing cremation in place of burial of human remains. Arrangements are made with a local cremation facility either in advance or at the time the body is released; or the funeral director may arrange for cremation at the request of the family. The ashes are scattered or preserved at the discretion of the family. In some places the *Neptune Society* may be available for their low-cost, reverent service at sea, wherein the body is slipped beneath the waves with suitable ceremony.

Donation of human remains to science eliminates embalming, casket, burial plot, vault, and funeral. A nearby medical school, or designated facility for receiving human remains,

Table 17.6 FUNERAL COSTS BY SOCIAL STATUS AND MODE OF DEATH;
FAMILIES SPENDING MORE THAN $800 (PERCENTAGES)

Mode of death	Lower-class	Working-class	Middle-class	Upper-class	Total
Expected	12.5	38.8	56.1	55.5	45.5
Unexpected	25.0	61.7	56.0	57.1	54.3

Source: Vanderlyn R. Pine and Derek L. Phillips, "The Cost of Dying: A Sociological Analysis of Funeral Expenditures," in *Confrontations of Death,* ed. Francis G. Scott and Ruth M. Brewer (Eugene: Oregon Center for Gerontology, 1971), p. 135. Used with permission.

is called as soon as the death certificate is signed, and the body is released directly from the sickroom. Laws in all 50 states now make it possible for a person to will his or her body or any part of it for transplantation, teaching, or research. Some 99 out of 100 lawyers and clergy support a client's decision to donate his or her body for autopsy or for transplantation of organs. In many communities morticians have forms their future clients may sign, indicating their wish to have their remains donated to nearby medical facilities for scientific purposes. Laymen generally favor the donation of corneas, kidneys and other organs—no longer needed by the deceased—for transplantation into living patients.

Financial resources available upon the death of a family member include the following: (1) life insurance is carried by most families to defray funeral costs and the expenses of the bereaved for a while thereafter; (2) Social Security provides a lump-sum death benefit for recipients of Social Security; and (3) veteran's widows are paid an allowance toward burial expenses of honorably discharged men. In each case the agency must be notified immediately upon the death of the family member so that funds may be released without delay. As more Americans freely discuss death in the family, and plan both for their own demise and for the security of those they leave behind, more reasonable funeral costs may become the norm.

WIDOWHOOD

The death of a spouse is a crisis that is difficult for the surviving partner, that strains a family's resources, and that requires new ways of performing family tasks. Widowhood necessitates a reorganization of family roles appropriate for the new status. An American widow is often uncertain as to how long to mourn, how to make friends aware of her readiness to resume normal social activities, how to manage her or his affairs as a lone person, and, eventually, whether to remarry. When death dissolves a marriage of many decades, ways of living have become so intertwined that it is hard to rebuild one's life without the lost mate. "I find myself going into the other room to ask him which dress to wear; even though I know in my mind that he is gone, I still feel him near," says one older widow after several weeks of mourning.

Women over 65 years of age are much more likely to be widowed than married, and they outnumber men of their age in increasing numbers. About 40 to 50 years ago the American population consisted of approximately equal numbers of men and women over 65 years of age and older. By the year 2000 the ratio will be only 65 men for every 100 women beyond age 65.

Lopata's (1970) study of widowhood finds widows sharing the characteristics of other minority groups in that they are (1) female in a male-dominated society; (2) old in a society that venerates youth; (3) lonely in a country that prefers to ignore such unhappy emotions; (4) without mates in a social network of couples; and (5) poor and uneducated in a wealthy, sophisticated land. In addition, 1.5 million are members of ethnic or racial minorities who already face discrimination (ibid., 92). Lower-class widows have few relatives or longtime friends to help them. Two-thirds of the Chicago widows Lopata studied said that their in-laws did not even help them with their husband's funeral arrangements; and less than one in four had been visited by their in-laws since the funeral. Twice as many black as white widows were accustomed to making their own decisions before they were widowed (Lopata 1970).

Widowed men and women have lower morale than do married persons of both sexes. The widowed tend to be less affluent and to have less active social lives than do the married. More than married men, widowers smoke, drink, and eat too much and rarely get enough exercise. Some men who have lost their wives complain of matchmaking friends and neighbors; others welcome such overtures as a chance to spruce up and go out as they used to do when their wives were still with them. The widowed die earlier than the married, and while living they are more susceptible to suicide, social isolation, and mental illness.

Death Traps and Widows' Rackets

The recently bereaved are vulnerable to exploitation by con men who slip into town, register under assumed names, and set about to bilk widows mentioned in the obituary columns of the local paper. Sylvia Porter (1975) tells of hearse chasers indicted for mailing—COD—bibles priced at many times their worth; of small loan company operators claiming payment and interest on purportedly unpaid loans made to the deceased; and even of persons posing as insurance representatives carrying policies on the deceased, which, having lapsed, required the final premium of $30 or $40 for the face amount of the policy (the widow pays the supposedly lapsed premium and never sees it, her insurance money, or the man again).

Unscrupulous investment counselors, speculators, and seemingly trustworthy "friends" look for windfalls in the legacies of untold numbers of widows each year. Widows as well as widowers are advised to avoid hasty decisions about their money until they have recovered from their first grief and until they have had a chance to check on any "offer too good to miss." A hardheaded member of the family, a lawyer, or some other person in whom the widow and her husband have had confidence may be worth his or her weight in gold in checking into some of the details a widow may overlook in her bereavement. The good news is that coping competence of widows is improving, according to Jacob Siegel, senior statistician for the Census Bureau's Population Division, who predicts, "The world of 2000 will have a population of fairly sophisticated, educated elderly women, many of whom have had outside work and have held managerial and professional positions" (Siegel 1976, 12-A).

Remarriage is likely for the young widower and somewhat less so for the widow, especially if she has children (Chapter 15). A study of remarriage in old age found that widowers tend to remarry in about three years, and widows in seven years, if at all. Over half had known their new spouse a long while before they were widowed, many for most of their lives. The new partner often resembled the first wife or husband, and remarriage was more likely when the first marriage had been good. Three out of four remarriages were rated successful, an outcome that was most likely when: (1) the wife was younger (by less than 14 years); (2) the new couple engaged in many courtship activities; (3) there was a mutuality of interests; (4) the couple was motivated by love or companionship rather than by material goals; (5) both were able to find great satisfaction in life; (6) relations with the respective families (especially with their children) were good; (7) their children approved the marriage; and (8) they had sufficient income (McKain 1969).

When a widow or widower is able to relate well to others, she or he may be helped by the kind of group discussion that takes place at widows' consultation centers, guidance services, and the like. Talking with others and being willing to consider all the aspects of one's situation are two mature coping devices that are useful for successful recovery from widowhood.

Surviving widowhood is a major developmental task for members of both sexes. Those who are most successful have autonomy as persons, enjoy continuing personal interests, have a backing of economic security, possess a comforting philosophy of life, maintain concern for others, and are blessed with meaningful relationships that have lasted over the years.

GRIEF AND BEREAVEMENT

The individual dies, but humanity continues. Death in the family brings heartbreak, but in the larger context death is inevitable and necessary. Without death there can be no new life, for each generation gives up its place to those who are to follow.

Few of us are comfortable with grief, yet grief is the normal reaction to severe personal loss. The bereaved is at first numb and unbelieving, then despairing, angry, guilty and restless as he or she seeks release from distress. Grief is most intense and longest lasting when death comes unexpectedly, with no time to prepare oneself for it. Studies in several countries find that while a long illness prepares survivors for the loss of a loved one, sudden death leaves the widowed still struggling with grief two to four years after their loss. When the grieving person does not recover from the loss, he or she may go into a depression, indicated by such signs as (1) feelings of hopelessness, (2) inability to concentrate, (3) change in physical activities, (4) loss of self-esteem, (5) withdrawal from others, (6) threats of suicide, (7) oversensitivity, (8) misdirected anger, (9) guilt, and (10) extreme dependence upon others (National Association for Mental Health 1975).

The immediate effects and the secondary reactions to bereavement range from total failure to readjust to conspicuous success in the tasks of coping with one's bereavement (Table 17.7). Death opens the human heart to the meaning of life itself. When a family loses a beloved member with whom life has been shared for years, memories of past experiences crowd in upon those that remain. They celebrate life of the departed, renewing their sense of identity as a family and as individuals. "Death is inextriably woven into all that makes life rich, noble, and triumphant. To conceal it is to cheat one's self of what might give meaning to life. Indeed, one cannot accept life without knowing that it must end. Death is not the scissors that cuts the thread of our lives. It is rather one of the threads that is woven into the design of existence" (Elliott 1971, 15).

Religious people are taught to believe that the human spirit lives on, on another plane of being. Many who do not consider themselves particularly devout join in the belief that there is something that lives on long after the physical body is gone. When Elizabeth Kübler-Ross (1976) was asked if she believed that there is life after death, she replied without a moment's hesitation, "Sure there is, without the shadow of a doubt." She went on to tell of her intensive research and clinical work with dying patients over the years. Not infrequently an individual who had been officially pronounced dead came back to life and reported having been aware of floating up out of the physical body and of having been met by some loved person "on the other side."

Most Americans are hopefully optimistic about death. Responses from a representative cross section of 1467 people found that 58 percent view death with hope of optimism, that 24 percent are pessimistic, and that the remaining 18 percent are vague about their beliefs concerning death. Religious faith was related to optimism about death in most instances (National Opinion Research Center 1976). Meanwhile, scientists explore ways of delaying death by slowing the "clock of aging," the genetically based program that determines each individual's rate of aging and dying (Rosenfeld 1976).

The mystery of what happens after death has intrigued humanity through the centuries.

Table 17.7 INDIVIDUAL EFFECTS OF BEREAVEMENT

A. Total failure to readjust
   1. Suicide
   2. Early death
   3. Insanity
   4. Moral disintegration
   5. Obsession

B. Partial failure
   1. Eccentricities
   2. Physical illness or prostration
   3. Aboulia, purposelessness
   4. Isolation
   5. Embitterment, misanthropy, cynicism
   6. Reversion to or recurrence of grief
   7. Self-blame or personal hates
   8. Fears
   9. Loneliness

C. Partial success
   1. Resignation, "God's will," and so on
   2. Stoicism
   3. Stereotyped formulas of immortality, misery escaped, and the like
   4. Sentimental memorials
   5. Effective repression of memories
   6. Intensification of affections
   7. Extension of affections
   8. Deliberate absorption in distractions or duties
   9. New or fantasied love objects

D. Conspicuous success
   1. New love object
   2. Thoroughgoing religious rationalization
   3. Spontaneous forgetting, relaxation of tensions
   4. Devotion to lifework
   5. Identification with role of deceased
   6. Creation of constructive memorials
   7. Transmutation of the experience into a productive reintegration of the personality

Source: Thomas D. Eliot, "The Bereaved Family," *Annals of the American Academy of Political and Social Science,* March 1932, p. 4.

It has been expressed in some of the world's great art, music, and literature. "Secluded behind her father's hemlock hedges, she found the 'polar privacy' she needed to probe the meaning of life and death. Death is the high voltage current that charges her most powerful poetry," writes Nardi Campion (1973) of Emily Dickinson, whose writing she uses to illustrate her point:

> Because I could not stop for Death
> He kindly stopped for me
> The carriage held but just
> Ourselves—
> And immortality.
>
> Emily Dickinson

Death's mystery is no greater than the miracle of birth and of life itself in its myriad forms, its continuing development, and its many expressions of creativity, not the least of which is found in the heart of family living. In the end there are two great mysteries—death and life itself.

SUMMARY

Death comes to all families in time. When children and young people die, there is anguish in the snuffing out of life before its time, especially since so many deaths of the young come about through needless accidents. The old must die, but how they die is a highly individual matter for them and for their families. Community supports for the terminally ill and their families are several: death education at various ages and levels, hospice programs, suicide prevention centers, "death with dignity," and "right to die" approaches. Some terminally ill patients radiantly achieve a quality of living as long as they can. Whatever the approach to dying, the time comes when a family faces the last rites for its members, which may take the form of a formal funeral—at great or moderate cost—or a simple memorial service appropriate to the religious, emotional, and financial life of the family. Memorial societies, dignified burial at sea through such programs as the Neptune Society, donation of human remains to science, and other current practices moderate funeral costs. At the death of a family member financial resources are available to many families.

Widowhood is usually a painful process for the bereaved marital partner. The pain is intensified by falling into one of the death traps or widows' rackets in which the newly widowed are exploited by the unscrupulous. Remarriage is a possibility in time for widowed men more than women.

Grief and bereavement vary widely from total failure to readjust to one's loss to conspicuous success in carrying on after the death of one's partner. Death is still a mystery —but less shattering now that it is more widely discussed, accepted, and planned for within the community and family context.

REFERENCES

Barnard, C. N. 1973. A good death. *Family Health* 4: 41.

Bock, E. W. 1972. Aging and suicide: The significance of marital, kinship and alternative relations. *Family Coordinator* 21:71–79.

Campion, N. R. 1973. A delayed obituary. *New York Times,* May 22, 1973, p. 39.

Case, R. 1978. When birth is also a funeral. *Journal of Pastoral Care* 31: 6–21.

Cousins, N. C. 1975. The right to die. *Saturday Review,* June 1975, p. 4.

———. 1982. Maximizing the possible. *Saturday Review,* May 1982, p. 12.

Crist, J. 1981. A triumph for mortality chic. *Saturday Review,* November 1981, p. 56.

Duhring, J. L. 1974. High risk fetus. *Hospital Medicine* 10: 81–89.

Eliot, T. D. 1932. The bereaved family. *Annals of the Academy of Political and Social Science,* March 1932, p. 4.

Elliott, G. L. 1971. *To come full circle toward an understanding of death.* New York: Union Seminary Book Store.

Fletcher, J. F. 1964. Anti-dysthanasia: the problem of prolonging death. *Journal of Pastoral Care* 18:77–83.

Frederick, C. J., & Lague, L. 1972. *Dealing with the crisis of suicide.* Public Affairs Pamphlet No. 406A. New York: Public Affairs Committee.

Gaylin, N. L. 1975. On the quality of life and death. *Family Coordinator* 24:247–255.

Kirkley-Best, E., Kellener, K. R., Gould, S. & Donnelly, W. 1982. On stillbirth: An open letter to the clergy. *Journal of Pastoral Care* 36:17–20.

Klaus, M. H., & Kennell, J. H. 1976. *Maternal-Infant Bonding.* St. Louis MO: C. N. Mosby.

Krieger, G. W., & Bascue, L. O. 1975. Terminal illness: Counseling with a family perspective. *Family Coordinator* 24:351–355.

Kübler-Ross, E. 1970. *On Death and Dying.* New York: Macmillan.

––––––. 1975. *Death: The final stage of growth.* Englewood Cliffs, N.J.: Prentice-Hall.

––––––. 1976. *Death and dying.* Interview on Public Broadcasting System, January 8, 1976.

Lieberman, M. A. 1973. New insights into crisis of aging. *University of Chicago Magazine* 66: 11–14.

Lopata, H. Z. 1970. *Widowhood in an American city.* Cambridge, MA: Schenkman.

––––––. 1973. Living through widowhood. *Psychology Today* 7:86–92.

McCall, T. 1972. The argument for "death with dignity." *AARP News Bulletin,* September 1972, p. 6.

McKain, W. C. 1969. *Retirement marriages.* Agricultural Experiment Station Monograph 3. Storrs: University of Connecticut.

––––––. 1972. A new look at older marriages. *Family Coordinator* 21:61–69.

Mannes, M. 1974. *Last rights. A case for the good death.* New York. Morrow.

Markel, W. M., & Sinon, V. B. 1978. *The hospice concept.* New York: American Cancer Society.

Menninger Perspective. 1983. When death seems the only solution. 14:24–25.

Metropolitan Life Insurance Company. 1981. *Statistical Bulletin* 62:16.

Miller, M., ed. 1981. *Suicide prevention and intervention by nurses.* New York: Springer.

Mitford, J. 1963. *The American way of death.* New York: Simon & Schuster.

National Association for Mental Health. 1975. Depression danger signals. *U.S. News & World Report,* December 1, 1975, p. 67.

National Center for Health Statistics. 1978. *Vital Statistics of the United States.* Vol. 2. Mortality, Part A. Washington, D.C.: Government Printing Office.

––––––. 1983. *Monthly Vital Statistics Report.* Vol. 32, no. 8 (November 21, 1983). Hyattsville, MD: Public Health Service.

National Opinion Research Center. 1976. Majority of Americans "optimistic" about death. Sarasota *Herald-Tribune,* June 12, 1976, p. 5-B.

Neale, R. E. 1981. Suicide: Is it an acceptable alternative for the terminally ill? *Concern for Dying* 7:6.

Pine, V. R., & Phillips, D. L. 1971. The cost of dying: A sociological analysis of funeral expenditures. In *Confrontations of death,* Ed. F. G. Scott & R. M. Brewer. Eugene: Oregon Center for Gerontology.

Porter, S. 1975. *Sylvia Porter's money book.* New York: Doubleday.

Preston, C. E., & Horton, J. 1972. Attitudes among clergy and lawyers toward euthanasia. *Journal of Pastoral Care* 26:108–115.

Rosenfeld, A. 1976. Are we programmed to die? *Saturday Review,* October 2, 1976, pp. 10–17.

Russell, O. R. 1975. Freedom to choose death. *PHP* 6:17–19.

Sabon, M. B. 1981. Recollections of death: A medical investigation. New York: Harper & Row.

Sackett, W. W. 1971. Death with dignity. Address presented at the White House Conference on Aging, Washington, D.C., November 29, 1971.

Shafer, E. 1975. *Hold not my life.* Personal communication with permission.

Shneidman, E. S. 1971. You and death. *Psychology Today* 5:43.

Siegel, J. S. 1976. Over-65 population continues to grow rapidly. U.S. Bureau of the Census release. Sarasota *Herald-Tribune,* June 1, 1976, p. 12-A.

Somerville, R. M. 1971. Death education as part of family life education: Using imaginative literature for insights into family crises. *Family Coordinator* 20:209–224.

Vanderlyn, R. P. & Phillips, D. L. 1971. The cost of dying: A sociological analysis of funeral expenditures. In *Confrontations of death.* Ed. F. G. Scott & R. M. Brewer. Eugene: Oregon Center for Gerontology.

Van Gieson, J. 1974. Doctor wages two fights. Sarasota *Herald-Tribune,* January 13, 1974, p. 7-B.

Weisman, A. D. 1972. *On death and denying: A psychiatric study of terminality.* New York: Behavioral Publications.

Glossary[1]

abortion The ending or termination of pregnancy. Pregnancies are sometimes aborted spontaneously *(miscarriage),* but in general use abortion now means that pregnancy termination was induced.

abstinence To abstain from or to not participate; in the case of sexual relations, not being sexually active.

adaptability Ability of a person to modify his roles, attitudes, and behavior.

adaptation Process of adjusting to new and different conditions.

adolescence The period of a young person's life between puberty and young adulthood.

affect Emotional feeling, tone; emotion.

affluence Wealthy; a state of plenty; comfortable living.

agape A kind or type of love characterized by selfless giving, sacrificing, and nondemanding affection for another; sometimes called *spiritual love.*

age and sex grades (categories, sets) Ways of classifying the members of a society by age and sex.

alienation Being estranged and cut off from others.

alimony Money paid by one ex-spouse to the other based on the premise that one has been the provider of financial resources in the marriage. Alimony is awarded by court order in only a small percentage of divorces, usually to support a divorced wife.

ambivalence Simultaneous presence of opposite feelings (e.g., love and hate) toward the same person, thing, or possibility.

androgyny Having the characteristics of both sexes (biological and/or psychological).

[1]Selected and adapted from sources representing various disciplines, including: U.S. Bureau of the Census; *A Psychiatric Glossary* (Washington, D.C.: American Psychiatric Association, 1969); Harold T. Christensen, ed., *Handbook of Marriage and the Family* (Chicago: Rand McNally, 1964); F. Ivan Nye and Felix M. Berardo, eds., *Emerging Conceptual Frameworks in Family Analysis* (New York: Macmillan, 1966); American Home Economics Association, "Report of a National Project," in *Concepts and Generalizations* (Washington, D.C.: American Home Economics Association, 1967); and a number of sources of terms in child, adolescent, and adult human development. Omitted are many terms and concepts dealt with in detail in the various chapters of this text, as well as those to be found in any standard dictionary that provides general rather than technical definitions.

annulment   Legally rescinding a marriage and returning the husband and wife to the same legal status they had before they married.

assortative mating   The tendency for marital partners to be sorted or selected rather than chosen randomly. Marital partners have much greater than chance similarities *(homogamy)*.

autonomy   Ability of a person to be self-governing.

basic needs   Those things felt to be essential for the individual, family, or society.

bereavement   The normal process of grieving over the loss of a loved one, usually including disbelief, despair, anger, guilt, and depression.

birth cohorts   Group of persons who were born in a specified calendar period.

birth order   Sequence of children borne alive by the mother (first, second, etc.).

bonding   The formation of attachment bonds between parent and infant; thought to begin with first seeing, touching, holding, and interacting with the infant; also refers to unique relationship of intimate adults, as in marriage.

career   Set of role clusters in sequence; a position in the family consisting of role clusters in sequence over time. See *positional career*.

chauvinism   Boastful devotion to one's own sex, race, or country.

cohabitation   Living intimately with a member of the opposite sex to whom one is not married.

commitment   Intent to follow a given course of action; unreserved devotion to a person or a cause.

communication   Network for transmitting information, ideas, and feelings between members of a group; exchange of meaningful symbols (words and gestures).

companionship   Association of two or more persons based on common interests and mutual acceptance.

compatibility   Condition of getting along well together.

complementarity   Meeting one another's needs in an intimate relationship.

compulsion   Insistent, repetitive, irrational urge to perform an act or ritual.

condonation   Action that erases the grounds for divorce in most states.

conflict   Opposing interests, ideas, drives, or impulses within an individual or between two or more persons.

conjugal family   Family unit in which the husband-wife relationship is given preponderant importance.

conjugal roles   Behavioral expectations of husbands and wives.

consanguineal family   Family unit in which blood relatives take precedence over marriage partners.

consumption   Use of economic resources by the ultimate consumer.

contraception   Preventing conception from occurring through the use of contraceptive devices, including those that block the passage of sperm (condom, diaphragm), prevent ovulation (the pill or oral contraceptive), attack or kill the sperm (spermicidal jelly, foam, or suppository), and so on.

copes   Behaves in a purposeful, problem-solving manner.

courtship system   The structural arrangement in a culture by which young people of opposite sexes enter into marriage; ranges from being free-choice or participant run, to arranged or controlled by parents and elders.

coverture   Legal rights of and status of a wife.

creativity   Ability to invent or improvise new roles or alternative lines of action in problematic situations.

crisis   Any decisive change that creates a condition for which habitual patterns of behavior are inadequate.

critical period   A period of time during which development *must* occur in a timely and normal order for further development to proceed.

cultural conflict   Inconsistencies arising out of incompatible elements in a culture or between cultures.

cultural inconsistency   Discrepancy or contradiction existing between various aspects of a culture.

cultural lag   Discrepancy in a culture resulting from some aspects changing more slowly than others.

cultural patterns   Standardized behavioral forms, practices, rules, and sentiments in a society.

cultural variation   Cross-cultural or historical differences in institutional behavioral patterns in societies corresponding to the different cultures and values represented in the society.

culture   Way of life; the patterned behaviors, knowledge, and attitudes that members of a society learn and teach to their children.

culture of poverty   Distinguishing folkways of the very poor.

customs   Standardized ways of doing, knowing, thinking, and feeling that are valued in a given group at a given time.

cycle of poverty   Poverty extending from generation to generation.

dating   An important element in the American courtship system; socialization experiences common during adolescence and young adulthood that are temporary, shared by two or more persons of opposite sexes, and often event or activity oriented; dates can be very casual or highly formalized, exclusively dyadic or group centered, oriented to having a good time or finding a marital partner.

definition of the situation   Interpreting, making judgments, and representing the elements in a situation to oneself and others.

deprivation   Inadequate standard of living; lacking essential or needed care and attention.

desertion   An ambiguous or uncertain marital status that results when one partner unexpectedly leaves the other; until the marriage is legally terminated, spouses who have been deserted have no legal recourse for meeting financial and other needs.

development   Process leading toward fulfillment and realization of potential of an individual, family, or group over time.

developmental task   Growth responsibility that arises at or about a certain time in the life of an individual, successful accomplishment of which leads to success in later tasks.

differential change   Condition in which one mate outgrows the other, emotionally, intellectually, or socially.

disenchantment   Decline in satisfaction and adjustment.

disengagement   Decline in the number and quality of relationships between a person and other individuals, groups, and associations.

disorganization   Loss of common objectives and functioning roles and tasks.

dissolution   Dissolving of marriage by death, divorce, or separation.

divorce   The legal termination of marriage.

double standard   The sexual standard that is more accepting of or permissive toward the sexual behavior of males than females; the predominant standard in the United States, which is rapidly declining.

dyadic relation   Interaction between two partners.

dysfunction   Negative consequences of an activity; impaired functioning.

economic stratification   Levels in society ordered by differences in income and wealth.

efficiency   Effective use of resources to obtain goals.

Electra complex   Girl's attachment to her father, accompanied by aggressive feelings toward her mother.

empathy   Subtle interpersonal sensitivity enabling a person to step into another's experience and to think and feel as he or she does.

empty nest   That stage of the family life cycle when all children have left home; also referred to as the *postparental period.*

endogamy   The tendency to marry within one's own group (race, religion, social class, etc.); as opposed to *exogamy,* marrying outside one's group.

erogenous zones   Areas of the body susceptible to sexual stimulation.

eros   The type of love that is erotic or physical; referring to sexual attraction and desire.

ethnic   Of human groups sharing a common culture (language, customs, etc.).

euthanasia   The ethically, legally, and medically controversial practices of allowing a person to die without the use of extraordinary medical measures to prolong life *(death with dignity* or *negative euthanasia);* also, ending the life of a person who is terminally ill and suffering constantly until certain death *(mercy killing* or *active euthanasia).*

evaluation   Appraising actions, decisions, and results in relation to goals.

expressed culture   That part of the cultural content that operates on the surface, with activities and words taken at their face value.

expressive feelings   Emotions that reveal personal feeling states.

extended family   A family that includes relatives in addition to the nuclear family of parent and children. A family can be extended vertically to include three or more generations, or laterally to include kin of the same generations (cousins, aunts, uncles, married siblings, etc.).

family   Two or more persons related by marriage, blood, birth, or adoption. Structurally a family is a set of positions each of which is composed of roles, which in turn are composed of norms; dynamically a family is a system of role complexes played sequentially to form a set of related careers.

family developmental tasks   Growth responsibilities that arise at certain stages in the life of a family, achievement of which leads to success with later tasks; sequential functional prerequisites.

family functions   What a family does to meet the needs of its members, to survive, and to make a contribution to the larger society.

family integration   Bonds of unity including affection, common interests, and economic interdependence within a family.

family life cycle   Sequence of characteristic stages beginning with family formation and continuing through the life of the family to its dissolution.

family life education   Systematic study or guidance in the development of knowledge, skills, attitudes, and values conducive to effective functioning as a family member of any age or status.

family life-style   Unique patterning of an individual family seen in its goals and in the way it goes about achieving them.

family of orientation   Family into which one is born and from which one gets most basic socialization.

family planning   Deliberately deciding about having children and taking appropriate steps to control and space their births.

family of procreation   Family one establishes through marriage and reproduction.

family ritual   Established procedure in a family, involving patterned behavior that is valued for itself.

family structure   Regular, routinized characteristics of the family as a whole, observable in style, pattern of interaction, and power hierarchy, and established as properties of the group.

family subculture   Complex of family habits, attitudes, and relationships that aid family members in selecting, interpreting, and evaluating the various cultural patterns to which they are exposed.

family types   Classification of families by descent, location of residence, authority, and life-style.

family values   What a family appreciates and considers desirable and of worth.

femininity   The quality of being feminine as defined with a given society.

feminism   The belief that women should have equal rights with men; the movement to secure economic, political, and social rights for women equal to those of men; popularly known as *Women's Liberation* or *Women's Lib.*

fidelity   Faithful devotion to one's vows; loyalty to one's spouse; exclusiveness in sexual behavior of monogamous mates.

firm discipline   Child-rearing that allows freedom within limits, allowing the child to know clearly what is expected of him without undue harshness.

fixation   Intense attachment to an object; arrest of psychosexual maturation.

functional prerequisites   Conditions necessary for the survival and continuation of a family group, or society; social imperatives.

gay   Popular term used in describing homosexual behavior or individuals.

gender identity   The personal or psychological conception of oneself as being male or female.

gender roles   Behavioral expectations specific to members of either sex.

generational stake   The fact that young people, especially adolescents, have an interest or stake in accentuating differences between the generations, whereas parents and those of the older generation have a stake in minimizing such differences.

generation spiral   Continuous overlapping of family life cycles in one generation after another in a family.

generative   Pertaining to the production of offspring; procreative.

genetic   Determined by heredity.

genital   Pertaining to the reproductive organs.

goals   The ends toward which an individual, family, group, or society directs its efforts in the pursuit of values.

group marriage   Three or more individuals pair-bonded (having sexual access) to one another.

growth   Change in amount, degree, or function of bodily structure, personality feature, or a group as a whole (like a family), over time.

growth and development   Increasing amount or complexity, or both, of and in living things.

habit   Acquired disposition to act in a certain way when in a given situation.

health   Positive realization of physical and emotional potentialities.

heredity   Characteristics and potentialities attributable to the genes.

hermaphrodite   A person who is not clearly a biological male *or* female; someone who has ambiguous or discordant biological sex characteristics such as incomplete or missing genitals, or the anatomy of one sex but genetic characteristics of the other sex.

home management   Making decisions and utilizing resources to attain goals in the family.

homogamy   Denotes partner similarities; tendency of courting and married couples to resemble each other; choosing a marriage partner who is like oneself in many respects.

hospice   A medieval term for a place of shelter for travelers; contemporary hospices are facilities and programs for the terminally ill and their families to help them live as fully as possible with family care supported by professional services.

household   All persons living in the same residence.

human development   Sum total of processes of change in a person from conception through old age.

hypergamy   When women marry above their own social class (the husband's social class is higher than the wife's).

idealization   Consciously or unconsciously overestimating an admired attribute of another person; a mental mechanism.

ideal mate   Preconceived combination of characteristics embodied in one's image of the kind of person he or she would like to marry.

identification   Unconscious endeavor to pattern oneself after another; defense mechanism playing a major role in personality development.

identity confusion   Uncertainty as to what one wants to do with his or her life.

identity crisis   Loss of the sense of continuity within oneself and inability to accept or adopt the role expected of one.

incest   Sexual relationships between close relatives; in the United States, usually defined as sexual relations between immediate family members. Father-daughter incest appears to be most common, but it also occurs between siblings and mother and son.

individual   Sum total of qualities that make each person unique among all others.

insight   Self-understanding; a person's awareness of the origins, nature, and dynamics of his or her attitude and behavior.

instinct   A natural, inborn drive, such as self-preservation.

institution   Reasonably enduring complex pattern of behavior by which social control is exerted and through which social needs can be met.

integration   Effective incorporation of new experience, knowledge, and emotional capacities into the personality or into a relationship, for example, marital integration is the unity between husband and wife that brings mutual satisfaction.

intelligence Capacity to learn and to use appropriately what one has learned.

interaction Mutual stimulation and response between persons, or between individuals and groups, or between families and other institutions in the society.

interpersonal competence Skills contributing to effective social interaction.

interpersonal relationship System of interaction between two or more persons.

intimacy Quality of a personal relationship that satisfies desires for love, affection, understanding, appreciation, sex, and security.

judgment Capacity to evaluate a number of alternatives in a given situation.

kinship Relationships within the larger family to which all the members belong: Kinship may be traced through the father's line (patrilineal), through the moter's line (matrilineal), or through both family lines (bilineal) in *lineage tracing*.

latch key children Children who regularly return to their apartment or home before any adults do; children who must take care of themselves for an extended part of each day.

libido Psychic drive or energy stemming from the life instinct, or the sexual drive, broadly defined.

limerance The sudden overwhelming attraction and attachment to and preoccupation with another person.

lineage bridge Middle-generation parents who provide support to generations preceding and following them: The bridging generation supports both their aging parents and their young adult children as they become established in families of their own.

love Strong attachment, affection, or devotion to a person or object; active concern for the life and growth of the beloved.

machismo Accentuated or exaggerated masculinity.

macho Popular term for extreme emphasis on being and acting masculine.

manifest function Recognized and intended consequences of an activity (in contrast to *latent* function, which is unrecognized and unintended).

marital adjustment Relation between husband and wife on the major issues of their marriage.

marital dissolution The ending of marriage, which occurs most commonly through death or divorce but also through annulment, desertion, or separation.

marital roles Behavioral expectations of husbands and wives.

marital status Condition of being single, married, widowed, or divorced.

marriage Socially sanctioned union of husband and wife with the expectation that they will assume the responsibilities and play the roles of married partners.

marriageability Readiness for marriage based on such factors as adaptability, interpersonal competence, preparation for marital roles, and maturity.

marriage cohorts A group of persons first married in a specified calendar period.

masculinity The quality of being masculine as defined in a given society.

mate selection Process of choosing and being chosen by one's future marriage partner.

mating gradient The result of hypergamy and age norms in courtship. Because women are more likely than men to marry up or above their own social class *(hypergamy)*, upper-class women and lower-class men have reduced marital choices and are more likely to remain single.

maturation Coming to full growth and development.

median A value that divides a distribution into two equal parts (the midpoint).

mental health Having relatively good personal integration so that one can love, work, and play with satisfaction; emotional health and well-being.

mental hygiene Prevention and early treatment of mental disorders.

midlife crisis or transition Common experiences related to the social and physical changes of the middle years, including acceptance that one might not realize some dreams, that health and vigor will decline, and that roles and purposes in life may need to be redefined.

minimum standard of living Material resources in the least amounts consistent with health and decency.

mobility Moving; changing status (upward or downward).

modeling Process by which an individiual incorporates into his behavior the perceived behavior of another with whom he identifies intentionally or unintentionally.

natural childbirth Childbirth for which the mother actively prepares and in which she actively participates by consciously regulating her breathing and muscular contractions through the labor and delivery.

no fault divorce Relatively new form of divorce law that allows spouses to terminate their marriage without assigning blame or proving one of them is at fault.

norm A patterned or commonly held behavior expectation; a learned response held in common by members of a group; that is, ways in which a family member is expected to play one of her roles.

normality Usual, healthy, conforming to expected standards.

nuclear family Husband, wife, and their immediate children.

nurturance Ministering to the vital processes and emotional needs of another person.

obsession Persistent, unwanted impulse or idea that cannot be eliminated by reasoning.

Oedipus complex Attachment of the child for the parent of the opposite sex, accompanied by aggressive and envious feelings toward the parent of the same sex.

orgasm Sexual climax that relieves physical and emotional tension.

parsimony Saving rather than spending money on consumable items; the *law of parsimony* is choosing the simplest of several interpretations of a phenomenon.

permissiveness with affection The premarital sexual standard in which sexual relationships are considered acceptable as long as unmarried partners have strong affection for each other; sometimes called *person-centered permissiveness.*

Permissiveness without affection The premarital sexual standard in which sexual relations are considered acceptable before marriage whether or not affection is present; sometimes called *body-centered permissiveness.*

personality The whole person, embodying all of his physiological, psychological, and social characteristics; distinctive, individual qualities of a person seen collectively; composite of inborn capacities molded and expressed through cultural conditioning.

personification Images a person holds of herself or of another person.

philos The type of love characterized by deep and enduring friendship; sometimes called *brotherly love.*

pleasure principle Tendency to seek gratification independent of all other considerations; striving for pleasure.

position Location in a social structure that is associated with a set of social norms; socially recognized category; the location of a family member in the family structure, that is, husband-father, wife-mother, son-brother, daughter-sister.

positional career Longitudinal history of an individual family position composed of an ever-changing cluster of roles.

power Actions that control, initiate, change, or modify the behavior of others.

premarital sexual standards Social expectations about the sexual behavior of persons who are not married. Frequently identified standards include abstinence, the double standard, permissiveness with affection, and permissiveness without affection.

primary group Face-to-face relationships involving a high degree of intimacy and communication. For example, the family is a primary group.

property settlement The legal division of material belongings, property, and assets that have been acquired during marriage.

propinquity Physical closeness or proximity. Marital partners tend to be from proximate geographic areas.

puberal   Pertaining to puberty, the period of rapid development in which boys begin to mature into men, and girls begin to mature toward womanhood.

readiness   Physical, emotional, and intellectual capacity to learn a particular thing at a particular time.

reconstituted families   Family groups formed by the remarriage of adults who head single-parent families.

recreation   Activities voluntarily engaged in during leisure, primarily motivated by the pleasure they bring or the satisfaction inherent in them.

recrimination   Action that nullifies the ground for divorce in most states. Both partners have committed acts that would be grounds for divorce, thus nullifying the original suit.

residence rules   A society's regulations for the residence of newly married couples: the husband leaves his parental home to live with his bride's family (matrilocal); the bride leaves her parental home to live with or near her husband's family (patrilocal); the young couple live with or near either of the parental homes (bilocal); the newly married couple establish their own independent home (neolocal).

resources   Means available for meeting needs, implementing wishes, and attaining desired goals.

role   Part of a social position consisting of a more or less integrated or related set of social norms, which is distinguishable from other sets of norms forming the same position; for example, father plays many roles: breadwinner, companion, disciplinarian, and so on; generally institutionalized social expectations, obligations, and rights imposed on an individual and arising from the status accorded to him or her (status roles).

role behavior   Actual behavior of the occupant of a position with reference to a particular role, for example, how father performs in the role of breadwinner.

role cluster   Set of roles being played by an occupant of a position at any one time; concurrent roles of a family member.

role complex   Two or more sets of role clusters.

role differentiation   Differences between individuals that affect the role distribution in a family or other group.

role making   Creation and modification of existing roles.

role playing   Acting out assigned roles; living up to obligations because of one's commitments.

role reversal   Swapping roles; for example, the wife works and the husband cares for the children.

role sequence   Series of roles an occupant of a position plays throughout the life cycle; longitudinal expression of roles.

role taking   Modification of one's behavior in anticipation of the responses of others; imagining how one looks from another person's viewpoint.

romantic love complex   The social and cultural complex of mass media, advertising, entertainment, literature, and cultural values that forcefully convey the ideas and images of romantic love.

sanctions   Institutionalized ways of constraining individuals or groups to conform to accepted norms; role behavior having reward or punishment implications.

secondary sex characteristics   Sex-related physical characteristics (facial and body hair, breast enlargement, etc.) that are not primary (present at birth) but which emerge during pubertal development.

self   Way one describes his relationships with others; consciously recognized pattern of perceptions pertaining to an individual; composite of the individual's thoughts, feelings, values, and perceptions of his roles.

self-concept   Who a person thinks she or he is; how an individual perceives herself or himself.

self-consciousness   Ability to call out in ourselves a set of definite responses that belong to the others of the groups; awareness of inner reality; uneasiness in social situations.

self love   Strong affection and positive regard for one's self.

sensitive period   A period of time during which development *should* happen or is best to happen for optimum ease of further development.

sentiments   Complex combination of feelings and opinions as a basis for action or judgment.

separation   A marital status in which spouses are still legally married but are not living together; may be an informal agreement or legal separation imposed by a court before divorce is granted.

sequential roles   Series of roles an occupant of a position (e.g., family member) plays over time.

serial monogamy   Marriage to only one spouse at a time but to one spouse after another following dissolution of the previous marriage through death or divorce.

sex   Being male or female. Biological sex is determined at conception. It includes genetic (chromosomal), hormonal, and anatomical dimensions (see *gender roles* and *gender identity*).

sex education   Guiding individuals of any age or status to achieve a wholesome awareness of what it means to be a male or female person, of the process of individual development, and of the responsible use of sexuality for personal fulfillment and social well-being; the knowledge, skills, attitudes, and values that have to do with healthy, effective relationships with persons of the same and opposite sex.

sexism   Prejudicial restriction of personal roles by gender.

sexuality   Recognition of what it means to be a sexual being with the capacity for interacting with members of the same and opposite sex.

sex role transcendence   Flexible expression of differences in persons regardless of their sex.

sibling rivalry   Competition between brothers and sisters for their parent's love, attention, and favors.

significant others   Persons of special importance in the life of an individual.

singlehood   Remaining unmarried.

situation content   attitudes, ideas, words, and gestures thought of as culture.

social act   Any behavior in which the appropriate object is another person; a social act involves at least two individuals, each of whom takes the other into account in the processes of satisfying impulses and achieving goals.

social context   Complex of interpersonal relationships that help to shape the personality for life.

social control   Ways in which a society or group maintains its integrity, through folkways, mores, customs, sanctions, for example, either coercive or persuasive.

social functions   Ways in which individuals and groups serve society's purposes and serve given ends.

social imperatives   Functional pre-requisites; the things that must be done in any society if it is to continue.

social interest   Concern for the welfare of a group.

socialization   Process by which the individual is taught the ways of a given culture, the cultural expectations related to one's age, sex, and other roles, and the means by which one seeks to conform to those expectations.

socialized person   One who has learned to participate effectively in social groups.

social patterns   Attitudes, values, and behavior ascribed by a society to its members through various roles and statuses.

social process   Operation of the social life; the multitude of actions and interactions of human beings, acting as individuals or in groups.

social relations   Ties by which persons and groups are bound to one another in the activities of social life.

social relationship   Interaction occurring between two or more partners in a relationship.

social status   Place in a particular system occupied by a given individual at a given time.

social structure   Division of society into social groups, based on conventionally standardized social relations between individuals; social organization.

society   Set of individuals organized in a given way of life; an aggregate of social relations; a social system that survives its original members, replaces them through biological reproduction, and is relatively self-sufficient.

solidarity   Mutual affection, value consensus, and interdependence of roles, as in a family.

stages of family life cycle   Qualitatively different and relatively distinct phases in the family life cycle.

The Duvall stages are demarcated by age and school placement of the oldest child and employment status of the breadwinner(s).

standard   Measure of quality and/or quantity that reflects reconciliation of resources with demands.

standard of living   An ideal or desired norm of consumption, usually defined in terms of quantity and quality of goods and services.

status   Social position defined by society; the position a person or a group (family) maintains in society because of the way he (or they) are evaluated.

sterilization   A medical procedure that results in a person being unable to reproduce. In males the usual procedure (vasectomy) is to cut and tie the tubes that transport sperm; in females the procedure is to cut and tie or otherwise close the fallopian tubes.

stimulus   Any action or agent that causes or changes an activity in an organism or group.

styles of loving   The major types or patterns of love experience in relationships, including best friends, game playing, logical, possessive, romantic, and unselfish.

sudden infant death syndrome (SIDS)   A pattern of unexpected infant death that occurs during sleep for no apparent reason; a leading cause of death in infants older than one week. Causes of SIDS are still not understood.

swinging   Married couples swapping partners with one or more couples.

symptom   Specific manifestation of an unhealthy physical or mental state.

syndrome   Combination of symptoms that constitutes a recognizable condition.

task behavior   Interaction directed towards the completion of group or individual tasks.

thinking   Internalized manipulation of symbols by which solutions are found.

two-way communication   Process of understanding each other's thoughts and feelings as well as the implications involved in such thoughts and feelings.

utility   The want-satisfying power of goods; that is, time, place, form, or possession utility.

value   The power of one good to command other goods (or money) in exchange; that which is cherished, appreciated, and sought after.

volition   The process of selecting among alternatives symbolically present in the experiences of the individual.

vulnerability   Being unprotected from or open to criticism, hurt, or rejection from a partner; a result of self-disclosure.

wheel theory of love   An explanation of the process of love development beginning with establishing rapport, leading to self-revelation or disclosure, becoming mutually dependent on each other, to the fulfillment of basic personality needs, to increased rapport and so on around like a wheel. The process also works in reverse to describe declining love.

X and Y chromosomes   the genetic elements that determine biological sex when conception occurs. Each parent contributes one sex chromosome, either X or Y. The XX combination is female, XY is male.

Index of Names

Index of Subjects